CIVILIZATION AND REVOLUTIONS

- -

CRITICAL TOPICS FROM WORLD HISTORY

Custom Textbook Developed by

The Montclair Kimberley Academy's History Department

for Grades 9 and 10

Chapters taken from:

A History of Western Society, **Ninth Edition**
By John P. McKay, Bennett D. Hill, John Buckler, Clare Haru Crowston, and Merry E. Wiesner-Hanks

A History of World Societies, **Eighth Edition**
By John P. McKay, Bennett D. Hill, John Buckler, Patricia Buckley Ebrey, Roger B. Beck, Clare Haru Crowston, and Merry E. Wiesner-Hanks

BEDFORD / ST. MARTIN'S
Boston · New York

Chapters 18, 21, 22, 26, 27, and 31 taken from:

A History of Western Society, Ninth Edition
By John P. McKay, Bennett D. Hill, John Buckler, Clare Haru Crowston, and Merry E. Wiesner-Hanks
Copyright © 2008 by Bedford/St. Martin's

Chapters 1–6, 10, 19, 28, 30, and 32 taken from:

A History of World Societies, Eighth Edition
By John P. McKay, Bennett D. Hill, John Buckler, Patricia Buckley Ebrey, Roger B. Beck, Clare Haru Crowston, and Merry E. Wiesner-Hanks
Copyright © 2009 by Bedford/St. Martin's

Manufactured in the United States of America.

4   3   2
f   e   d   c

For information, write: Bedford/St. Martin's, 75 Arlington Street, Boston, MA 02116 (617-399-4000)

ISBN-10: 0-312-68887-3
ISBN-13: 978-0-312-68887-5

Contents

Civilization and Revolutions allowed for the selection of chapters to align chronologically with the 9th and 10th grade curriculum at The Montclair Kimberley Academy. As a result, not all chapters and pages are numbered sequentially in this textbook.

Chapter 32

LATIN AMERICA, ASIA, AND AFRICA IN THE CONTEMPORARY WORLD   976

Chapter 31

REVOLUTION, REBUIDLING, AND NEW CHALLENGES: 1985 TO THE PRESENT   1018

Peace Panel, Standard of Ur. This scene depicts the royal family on the upper band, and various conquered peoples bringing the king tribute on the lower bands. *(Courtesy of the Trustees of the British Museum)*

1 EARLY CIVILIZATION IN AFROEURASIA, TO 450 B.C.E.

Chapter Preview

Mesopotamian Civilization from Sumer to Babylon (ca. 3000–1595 B.C.E.)

• How did the Sumerians lay the foundations of a flourishing civilization in the hard land of Mesopotamia?

Egypt, the Land of the Pharaohs (3100–1200 B.C.E.)

• How did geography enable the Egyptians easily to form a cohesive, prosperous society?

The Rise of the Hittites (ca. 1650–ca. 1200 B.C.E.)

• How did the Hittites affect the life of the ancient Near East?

The Children of Israel (ca. 950–538 B.C.E.)

• How did the Hebrews form a small kingdom after the fall of larger neighboring empires?

Assyria, the Military Monarchy (859–612 B.C.E.)

• What enabled the Assyrians to conquer their neighbors, and how did they doom themselves by their cruelty?

The Empire of the Persian Kings (ca. 1000–464 B.C.E.)

• How did Iranian nomads create the Persian Empire that ultimately embraced all of these earlier peoples?

Human beings began the long road from their origins to the contemporary world in numerous places and under various circumstances. Although conditions were sometimes similar in all of them, their paths were unique. None fits into a tidy pattern. This chapter begins with the events that shaped the history of one of those places, the ancient **Near East,** or what is today often called the Middle East. Chapter 2 traces the origins of civilization in India, and Chapter 3 in China.

The ancient Near East includes parts of northeastern Africa, western Asia, and Mesopotamia, modern Iraq. It thus forms part of the larger Eurasia, the area from modern England in the west to Japan in the east. Within a small part of Eurasia, ancient Mesopotamian people invented writing, which allowed them to preserve knowledge of their achievements. They recorded their past and spread their learning, lore, and literature to posterity. Their innovations and those of the Egyptians laid the foundations of civilization in the region.

MESOPOTAMIAN CIVILIZATION FROM SUMER TO BABYLON (CA. 3000–1595 B.C.E.)

How did the Sumerians lay the foundations of a flourishing civilization in the hard land of Mesopotamia?

A good place from which to see the long path from nomadic hunters to urban folk is Mesopotamia, the Greek name for the land between the Euphrates and Tigris Rivers. Settled life in this region began only between 7000 and 3000 B.C.E., an era known as the Neolithic period. The term *Neolithic*, which means "neio stone age," comes from the new stone tools that people used to create a life of farming and animal husbandry. By ca. 3000 B.C.E. they had invented the wheel. Sustained agriculture resulted in a more stable life. Larger populations made possible the division of labor. These developments led to the evolution of towns and a new way of life (see Map 1.1). The growth and

● **Stonehenge** Seen in regal isolation, Stonehenge sits among the stars and in April 1997 along the path of the comet Hale-Bopp. Long before Druids existed, a Neolithic society laboriously built this circle to mark the passing of the seasons. (*Jim Burgess*)

Near East *The region between the eastern coast of the Mediterranean Sea and the Tigris and Euphrates Rivers.*

Neolithic period *The period between 7000 and 3000 B.C.E. that serves as the dividing line between anthropology and history. The term itself refers to the new stone tools that came into use at this time.*

diversity of the population created the need for the earliest governments that transcended families. Towns functioned and prospered through a recognized central authority governed by laws. Stable, strong populations organized themselves for peace and war, with the result that towns became the most successful feature of the **Neolithic period**.

The Invention of Writing and Intellectual Advances (ca. 3000–2331 B.C.E.)

By ca. 3000 B.C.E. the Sumerians, whose origins are mysterious, had established a number of towns in the southernmost part of Mesopotamia, which became known as Sumer. Towns grew into cities, and one of the Sumerian's many advances was the invention of writing. This momentous innovation helped unify Sumerian society by making communications much easier and opening Sumerian society to a broader world.

The Sumerians started by drawing pictures of objects, pictographs, from which they developed the style of writing known as cuneiform. The name comes from the Latin term for "wedge-shaped" used to describe the strokes making up the signs. The next step was to simplify the system. Instead of drawing pictures, the scribe made *ideograms:* conventionalized signs that were generally understood to represent ideas. The sign for star could also be used to indicate heaven, sky, or even god. (See line A in Figure 1.1.) The real breakthrough came when the scribe learned to use signs to represent sounds. For instance, the scribe drew two parallel wavy lines to indicate the word *a* or "water" (line E). Besides water, the word *a* in Sumerian also meant "in." The word *in* expresses a relationship that is very difficult to represent pictorially. Instead of trying to invent a sign to mean "in," some clever scribe used the sign for water because the two

● FIGURE 1.1 **Sumerian Writing** *(Source: Excerpted from S. N. Kramer, The Sumerians, University of Chicago Press, Chicago, 1963, pp. 302–306. Reprinted by permission of the publisher.)*

	MEANING	PICTOGRAPH	IDEOGRAM	PHONETIC SIGN
A	Star			
B	Woman			
C	Mountain			
D	Slave woman			
E	Water In			

words sounded alike. This phonetic use of signs made possible the combining of signs to convey abstract ideas.

The Sumerian system of writing was so complicated that only professional scribes mastered it after many years of study. By 2500 B.C.E. scribal schools flourished throughout Sumer. Most students came from wealthy families and were male. Each school had a master, a teacher, and monitors. Discipline was strict, and students were caned for sloppy work and misbehavior. One graduate of a scribal school had few fond memories of the joy of learning:

My headmaster read my tablet, said:
"There is something missing," caned me.
. . . .
The fellow in charge of silence said:
"Why did you talk without permission," caned me.
The fellow in charge of the assembly said:
"Why did you stand at ease without permission," caned me.[1]

Although Sumerian education was primarily intended to produce scribes for administrative work, schools were also centers of culture and scholarship.

Sumerian Thought and Religion

The building of cities, palaces, temples, and canals demanded practical knowledge of geometry and trigonometry. The Sumerians and later Mesopotamians made significant advances in mathematics using a numerical system based on units of sixty, ten, and six. They also developed the concept of place value—that the value of a number depends on where it stands in relation to other numbers.

Sumerian medicine was a combination of magic, prescriptions, and surgery. Sumerians believed that demons and evil spirits caused sickness and that magic spells and prescriptions could drive them out. Over time some prescriptions worked, and in this slow but empirical fashion medical understanding grew.

The Sumerians originated many religious beliefs, and their successors added to them. The Mesopotamians were polytheists—that is, they believed that many gods run the world. They did not, however, consider all gods and goddesses equal. Some deities had very important jobs taking care of music, victory, law, and sex, while others had lesser tasks, overseeing leatherworking and basketweaving. Mesopotamian gods were powerful and immortal and could make themselves invisible. Otherwise, they were very human: they celebrated with food and drink and they raised families. They enjoyed their own "Garden of Eden," a green and fertile paradise. They could be irritable, vindictive, and irresponsible. Nor were the motives of the gods always clear. In times of affliction one could only pray and offer sacrifices to appease them. Encouraged and directed by the traditional priesthood, which was dedicated to understanding the ways of the gods, the people erected shrines in the center of each city around which they built their houses. The best way to honor the gods was to make the shrine as grand and as impressive as possible, for gods who had a splendid temple might think twice about sending floods to destroy the city.

Chronology

ca. 7000–3000 B.C.E.	Neolithic period
ca. 3000–2331 B.C.E.	Sumerian and Akkadian domination
ca. 3000 B.C.E.	Invention of cuneiform writing
ca. 3100–2180 B.C.E.	Rise of Egypt
1792–ca. 717 B.C.E.	Babylonian rule in Mesopotamia
ca. 1790 B.C.E.	*Epic of Gilgamesh* and Hammurabi's law code
ca. 1650–ca. 1200 B.C.E.	Hittite rule in Anatolia
ca. 1570–1075 B.C.E.	New Kingdom in Egypt
1367–1350 B.C.E.	Reign of Akhenaten in Egypt
1100–653 B.C.E.	Third Intermediate Period in Egypt
ca. 1000–587 B.C.E.	Development of Hebrew kingdom
ca. 950–500 B.C.E.	Beginning of Hebrew Bible
ca. 800–612 B.C.E.	Period of Assyrian Empire
550–464 B.C.E.	Creation of Persian Empire
ca. 600–500 B.C.E.	Spread of Zoroastrianism

The Sumerians had many myths to account for the creation of the universe. According to one (echoed in Genesis, the first book of the Hebrew Bible), only the primeval sea existed at first. The sea produced heaven and earth, which were united. Heaven and earth gave birth to Enlil, who separated them and made possible the creation of the other gods. Myths are the earliest known attempts to answer the question "How did it all begin?"

In addition to myths, the Sumerians produced the first epic poem, the *Epic of Gilgamesh*. An epic poem is a narration of the achievements, the labors, and sometimes the failures of heroes that embodies a people's or a nation's conception of its own past. The Sumerian epic recounts the wanderings of Gilgamesh, the semihistorical king of Uruk, and his search for eternal life. He learns that life after death is so dreary that he returns to Uruk, where he ends his life. The *Epic of Gilgamesh* shows the Sumerians grappling with such enduring questions as life and death, people and deity, and immortality. (See the feature "Listening to the Past: A Quest for Immortality on pages 26–27.)

> **Primary Source:**
> **The Epic of Gilgamesh**
> *Find out how Gilgamesh's friend Enkidu propels him on a quest for immortality, and whether that quest is successful.*

Sumerian Society

Sumerian society was a complex arrangement of freedom and dependence, and its members were divided into four categories: nobles, clients, commoners, and slaves. **Nobles** consisted of the king and his family, the chief priests, and high palace officials. The king generally rose to power as a war leader, elected by the citizenry, who established a regular army, trained it, and led it into battle. The might of the king and the

> **nobles** *The top level of Sumerian society: the king and his family, the chief priests, and high palace officials.*

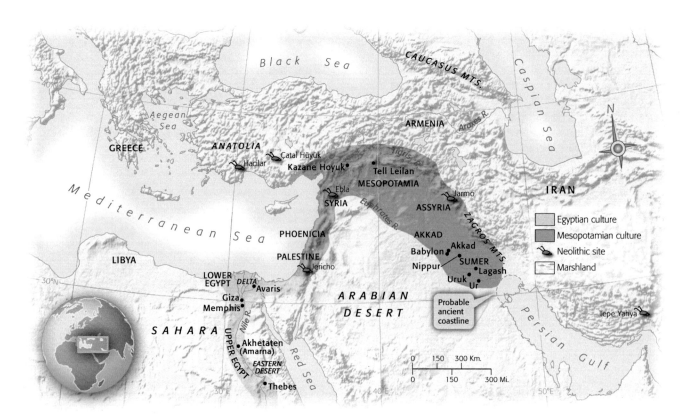

MAP 1.1 **Spread of Cultures in the Ancient Near East** This map illustrates the spread of the Mesopotamian and Egyptian cultures through a semicircular stretch of land often called the Fertile Crescent. From this area, knowledge and use of agriculture spread throughout western Asia.

frequency of warfare quickly made him the supreme figure in the city, and kingship soon became hereditary. The symbol of royal status was the palace, which rivaled the temple in its grandeur.

The king and the lesser nobility held extensive tracts of land that were, like the estates of the temple, worked by clients and slaves. Slaves were prisoners of war, convicts, and debtors. While they were subject to any treatment their owners might mete out, they could engage in trade, make profits, and even buy their freedom. **Clients** were free people who were dependent on the nobility. In return for their labor, they received small plots of land to work for themselves. Although this arrangement assured the clients of a livelihood, the land they worked remained the possession of the nobility or the temple. Commoners were free and could own land in their own right. Male commoners had a voice in the political affairs of the city and full protection under the law. Each of these social categories included both men and women, but Sumerian society also made clear distinctions based on gender. Sumerian society was *patriarchal,* that is, most power was held by older adult men.

● **Ziggurat**   The ziggurat is a stepped tower that dominated the landscape of the Sumerian city. Surrounded by a walled enclosure, it stood as a monument to the gods. Monumental stairs led to the top, where sacrifices were offered for the welfare of the community. *(Charles & Josette Lenars/Corbis)*

clients   *Free men and women who were dependent on the nobility; in return for their labor, they received small plots of land to work for themselves.*

The Triumph of Babylon and the Spread of Mesopotamian Civilization (2331–ca. 1595 B.C.E.)

Although the Sumerians established the basic social, economic, and intellectual patterns of Mesopotamia, the Semites played a large part in spreading Sumerian culture far beyond the boundaries of Mesopotamia. Semites are people related by the Semitic language spoken by Jews, Arabs, Phoenicians, Assyrians, and others. In 2331 B.C.E. the Semitic chieftain Sargon conquered Sumer and created a new empire. The symbol of his triumph was a new capital, the city of Akkad. Sargon led his armies to the Mediterranean Sea, spreading Mesopotamian culture throughout the Fertile Crescent (see Map 1.1). Though extensive, Sargon's empire soon fell to the Babylonians, who united Mesopotamia politically and culturally.

Hammurabi (r. 1792–1750 B.C.E.), king of the Amorites, another Semitic people, won control of the region and established his capital at Babylon. He accomplished three things: he made his kingdom secure, unified Mesopotamia, and joined together the Sumerian idea of urban kingship and the Semitic concept of tribal chieftain. He succeeded culturally in making Marduk, the god of Babylon, the sovereign of all other Mesopotamian deities. Hammurabi's most memorable achievement was the code that

Primary Source:
The State Regulates Health Care: Hammurabi's Code and Surgeons
Consider the various rewards and punishments for surgeons who either succeed or fail at their jobs in 1800 B.C.E.

established the law of the land. Hammurabi claimed that divine authority stood behind the laws that promoted the welfare of the people. The code differentiates people in terms of laws and punishments according to social status and gender.

Because of farming's fundamental importance, Hammurabi's code dealt extensively with agriculture. It governed the duties and rights of tenant farmers, who were expected carefully to cultivate the land. They were also responsible for keeping canals and ditches in good repair. Negligence in either case could ruin or damage crops. Tenants who were negligent either bore the cost of losses or were sold into slavery.

Hammurabi gave careful attention to marriage and the family. The fathers of the prospective bride and groom legally arranged the marriage, with the bride receiving from her father a dowry that remained hers for the rest of her life. The groom's father gave a bridal gift to the bride's father. The wife was expected to be rigorously faithful, primarily to ensure the legitimacy of the children. Only then could they legally inherit their father's property. In cases of adultery, the guilty wife was put to death. But an accused wife could clear herself before the city council. If the investigation found her innocent, she could take her dowry and leave her husband.

The husband technically had absolute power over his household. He could sell his wife and children into slavery for debt and disinherit his son, although the law made it very difficult for him to go to these extremes. Evidence other than the law code indicates that family life was not so grim. Countless wills and testaments show that husbands habitually left their estates to their wives, who in turn willed the property to their children. Though supposedly banned from commercial pursuits, many women engaged in business without hindrance. Though marriage was primarily an arrangement between families, a few poems speak of romantic love.

● **Law Code of Hammurabi**
Hammurabi ordered his code to be inscribed on a stone pillar and set up in public. At the top of the pillar Hammurabi is depicted receiving the scepter of authority from the god Shamash. *(Hirmer Verlag München)*

EGYPT, THE LAND OF THE PHARAOHS (3100–1200 B.C.E.)

How did geography enable the Egyptians easily to form a cohesive, prosperous society?

The Greek historian and traveler Herodotus in the fifth century B.C.E. called Egypt the "gift of the Nile." No other single geographical factor had such a fundamental and profound impact on the shaping of Egyptian life, society, and history as the Nile (see Map 1.2). The Egyptians praised the Nile primarily as a creative and comforting force:

Hail to thee, O Nile, that issues from the earth and comes to keep Egypt alive! . . .
He that waters the meadows which Ra created,
He that makes to drink the desert . . .
He who makes barley and brings emmer [wheat] into being . . .
He who brings grass into being for the cattle . . .
He who makes every beloved tree to grow . . .
O Nile, verdant art thou, who makest man and cattle to live.[2]

Primary Source:

The Hymn to the Nile
Discover the degree to which the Nile River is viewed as godlike, and the perceived power it has over the survival of the people of Egypt.

To the Egyptians, the Nile was the source of life.

Egypt was also nearly self-sufficient. Besides the fertility of its soil, Egypt possessed enormous quantities of stone, which served as the raw material of architecture and sculpture. Abundant clay was available for pottery, as was gold for jewelry and ornaments. The raw materials that Egypt lacked were close at hand. The Egyptians obtained copper from Sinai and timber from Lebanon. They had little cause to look to the outside world for their necessities, a fact that helps to explain the insular quality of Egyptian life.

The God-King of Egypt

Geographical unity quickly gave rise to political unification of the country under the authority of a king whom the Egyptians called **"pharaoh."** The precise details of this process have been lost. The Egyptians themselves told of a great king, Menes, who united Upper and Lower Egypt into a single kingdom around 3100 B.C.E. Thereafter, they divided their history into dynasties, or families, of kings. For modern historical purposes, however, it is useful to divide Egyptian history into periods (see page 10). The political unification of Egypt ushered in the period known as the Old Kingdom (2660–2180 B.C.E.), an era remarkable for prosperity, artistic flowering, and the evolution of religious beliefs.

In religion, the Egyptians developed complex, often contradictory, ideas of their gods. They were polytheistic in that they worshiped many gods, some mightier than others. Their beliefs were rooted in the environment and human ecology. The most powerful of the gods were Amon, a primeval sky-god, and Ra, the sun-god. Amon created the entire cosmos by his thoughts. He brought life to the land and its people, and he sustained both. The Egyptians cherished Amon because he championed fairness and honesty, especially for the common people. The Egyptians considered Ra the creator of life. He commanded the sky, earth, and the underworld. Ra was associated with the falcon-god Horus, the "lord of the sky," who served as the symbol of divine kingship. Horus united Egypt and bestowed divinity on the pharaoh. The obvious similarities between Amon and Ra eventually led the Egyptians to combine them into one god, **Amon-Ra.** Yet the Egyptians never fashioned a formal theology to resolve the differences. Instead, they worshiped these gods as different aspects of the same celestial phenomena.

The Egyptians likewise developed views of an afterlife that reflected the world around them. The dry air of Egypt preserves much that would decay in other climates. The dependable rhythm of the seasons also shaped the fate of the dead. According to the Egyptians, Osiris, a fertility god associated with the Nile, died each year, and each year his wife, Isis, brought him back to life. Osiris eventually became king of the dead, and he weighed human beings' hearts to determine whether they had lived justly enough to deserve everlasting life. Osiris's care of the dead was shared

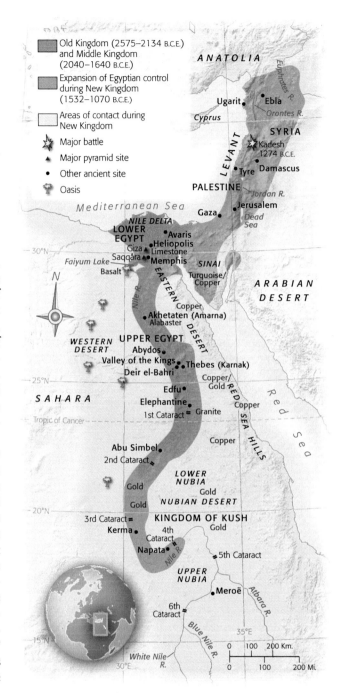

MAP 1.2   Ancient Egypt Geography and natural resources provided Egypt with centuries of peace and abundance.

pharaoh *The leader of religious and political life in the Old Kingdom, he commanded the wealth, the resources, and the people of Egypt.*

Amon-Ra *An Egyptian god, consisting of Amon, a primeval sky-god, and Ra, the sun-god.*

Periods of Egyptian History

PERIOD	DATES	SIGNIFICANT EVENTS
Archaic	3100–2660 B.C.E.	Unification of Egypt
Old Kingdom	2660–2180 B.C.E.	Construction of the pyramids
First Intermediate	2180–2080 B.C.E.	Political chaos
Middle Kingdom	2080–1640 B.C.E.	Recovery and political stability
Second Intermediate	1640–1570 B.C.E.	Hyksos "invasion"
New Kingdom	1570–1075 B.C.E.	Creation of an Egyptian empire Akhenaten's religious policy
Third Intermediate	1100–653 B.C.E.	Political fragmentation

Primary Source:

The Egyptian Book of the Dead's Declaration of Innocence
Read the number of potential sins that would likely tarnish a journeying spirit and prevent entrance into the realm of the blessed.

Book of the Dead *An Egyptian book that preserved their ideas about death and the afterlife; it explains that after death, the soul leaves the body to become part of the divine.*

pyramid *The burial place of a pharaoh; a massive tomb that contained all things needed for the afterlife. It also symbolized the king's power and his connection with the sun-god.*

by Anubis, the jackal-headed god who annually helped Isis resuscitate Osiris. Anubis was the god of mummification, essential to Egyptian funerary rites. The Egyptians preserved these ideas in the *Book of the Dead,* which explained that after death the soul and the body became part of the divine. They entered gladly through the gate of heaven where they remained in the presence of Aton (a sun-god) and the stars. Thus for the Egyptians life did not end with death.

The focal point of religious and political life in the Old Kingdom was the pharaoh, who commanded the wealth, resources, and people of all Egypt. The Egyptians considered him to be Horus in human form. In Egyptian religion Horus was the son of Isis and Osiris, which meant that the pharaoh, a living god on earth, became one with Osiris after death. The pharaoh was the power that achieved the integration between gods and human beings, a pledge that the gods of Egypt (strikingly unlike those of Mesopotamia) cared for their people.

The king's surroundings had to be worthy of a god. Only a magnificent palace was suitable for his home. In fact, the very word *pharaoh* means "great house." Just as the pharaoh occupied a great house in life, so he reposed in a great **pyramid** after death. The massive tomb contained everything the pharaoh needed in his afterlife. The walls of the burial chamber were inscribed with religious texts and spells relating to the king's journeys after death. The pyramid also symbolized the king's power and his connection with the sun-god. To this day the great pyramids at Giza near Cairo bear silent but magnificent testimony to the god-kings of Egypt.

The Pharaoh's People

Because the common folk stood at the bottom of the social and economic scale, they were always at the mercy of grasping officials. Taxes might amount to 20 percent of the harvest, and tax collection could be brutal.

The regularity of the climate meant that the agricultural year was routine and dependable, so farmers seldom suffered from foul weather and damaged crops. Farmers sowed wheat and nurtured a large variety of trees, vegetables, and vines. They tended cattle and poultry, and when time permitted they hunted and fished in the marshlands of the Nile.

Egyptian society seems to have been a curious mixture of freedom and constraint. Slavery did not become widespread until the New Kingdom (1570–1075 B.C.E.). There was neither a caste system nor a color bar, and humble people could rise to the highest positions if they possessed talent. On the other hand, most ordinary folk were probably little more than serfs who could not easily leave the land of their own free will. Peasants were also subject to forced labor, including work on the pyramids and canals. Young men were drafted into the pharaoh's army, which served both as a fighting force and as a labor corps.

To ancient Egyptians the pharaoh embodied justice and order—harmony among people, nature, and the divine. If the pharaoh was weak or allowed anyone to challenge his unique position, he opened the way to chaos. Twice in Egyptian history the pharaoh failed to maintain rigid centralization. During those two eras, known as the First and Second Intermediate Periods, Egypt was exposed to civil war and invasion. Yet the monarchy survived, and in each period a strong pharaoh arose to crush the rebels or expel the invaders and restore order.

Primary Source:
Advice to Ambitious Young Egyptians
This interesting piece of propaganda serves to convince potential scribes that the job of scribe is the best of all possible occupations.

The Hyksos in Egypt (1640–1570 B.C.E.)

While Egyptian civilization flourished behind its bulwark of sand and sea, momentous changes were taking place around it that would leave their mark even on rich, insular Egypt. These changes involved vast and remarkable movements, especially of peoples who spoke Semitic tongues.

The original home of the Semites was perhaps the Arabian peninsula. Some tribes moved into northern Mesopotamia, others into Syria and Palestine, and still others into Egypt. Shortly after 1800 B.C.E., people whom the Egyptians called **Hyksos,** which means "rulers of the uplands," began to settle in the Nile Delta. The movements of the Hyksos were part of a larger pattern of migration of peoples during this period. Such nomads normally settled in and accommodated themselves with the native cultures. The process was mutual, for each group had something to give and to learn from the other.

Hyksos *Called "rulers of the uplands" by the Egyptians, these people began to settle in the Nile Delta shortly after 1800 B.C.E.*

● **Pyramids of Giza**   Giza was the burial place of the pharaohs of the Old Kingdom and of their aristocracy, whose smaller rectangular tombs surround the two foremost pyramids. The small pyramid probably belonged to a pharaoh's wife. *(Jose Fuste Raga/Corbis)*

● **Egyptian Harvest Scene** This cheerful wall painting depicts two aspects of the harvest. Workers at the top right pick bunches of ripe grapes for winemaking. Their colleagues in the center stamp the grapes, and the large pottery jars store the wine. *(Louvre/Réunion des Musées Nationaux/Art Resource, NY)*

Bronze Age *The period in which the production and use of bronze implements became basic to society; bronze made farming more efficient and revolutionized warfare.*

So too in Egypt, where bands of Hyksos entered the delta looking for good land. Their success led them to settle and to establish a capital city at Avaris in the northeastern Nile Delta. They probably exercised direct control no farther south. The Hyksos brought with them the method of making bronze and casting it into tools and weapons that became standard in Egypt. They thereby brought Egypt fully into the **Bronze Age** culture of the Mediterranean world. Bronze tools made farming more efficient than ever before because they were sharper and more durable than the copper tools they replaced. The Hyksos's use of bronze armor and weapons as well as horse-drawn chariots and the composite bow revolutionized Egyptian warfare. Yet the newcomers also absorbed Egyptian culture. The Hyksos came to worship Egyptian gods and modeled their monarchy on the pharaonic system.

The New Kingdom: Revival and Empire (1570–1075 B.C.E.)

The pharaohs of the Eighteenth Dynasty arose to challenge the Hyksos. These pharaohs pushed the Hyksos out of the delta, subdued Nubia in the south, and conquered Palestine and parts of Syria in the northeast. Egyptian warrior-pharaohs thereby inaugurated the New Kingdom—a period characterized by enormous wealth and conscious imperialism. They created the first Egyptian empire, which they celebrated with monuments on a scale unparalleled since the pyramids of the Old Kingdom. Also during this period, probably for the first time, widespread slavery became a feature of Egyptian life. The pharaoh's armies returned home leading hordes of slaves who constituted a new labor force for imperial building projects.

monotheism *The belief in one god; when applied to Egypt, it means that only Aton among the traditional Egyptian deities was god.*

One pharaoh of this period, Akhenaten (r. 1367–1350 B.C.E.), was more concerned with religion than with conquest. Nefertiti, his wife and queen, encouraged his religious bent (see the feature "Individuals in Society: Nefertiti, the 'Perfect Woman'"). They worshiped the sun-god Aton as universal, the only god, whereas the Egyptian people were polytheistic—they believed in many gods. Akhenaten considered all these and other deities frauds and so suppressed their worship. Although the precise nature of Akhenaten's religious beliefs remain debatable, most historians agree that the royal pair were monotheists: they believed in only one god. Yet this **monotheism,** imposed from above and enforced by intolerance, failed to find a place among the people. Akhenaten's religion died with him.

Nefertiti, the "Perfect Woman"

Nefertiti, queen of Egypt.
(Bildarchiv Preussischer Kulturbesitz/
Art Resource, NY)

Egyptians understood the pharaoh to be the living embodiment of the god Horus, the source of law and morality, and the mediator between gods and humans. His connection with the divine stretched to members of his family, so that his siblings and children were also viewed as in some ways divine. Because of this, a pharaoh often took his sister or half-sister as one of his wives. This concentrated divine blood set the pharaonic family apart from other Egyptians (who did not marry close relatives) and allowed the pharaohs to imitate the gods, who in Egyptian mythology often married their siblings. A pharaoh chose one of his wives to be the "Great Royal Wife," or principal queen. Often this was a relative, though sometimes it was one of the foreign princesses who married pharaohs to establish political alliances.

The familial connection with the divine allowed a handful of women to rule in their own right in Egypt's long history. We know the names of four female pharaohs, of whom the most famous was Hatshepsut (r. 1479–1458 B.C.). She was the sister and wife of Thutmose II and, after he died, served as regent for her young stepson Thutmose III, who was actually the son of another woman. Hatshepsut sent trading expeditions and sponsored artists and architects, ushering in a period of artistic creativity and economic prosperity. She built one of the world's great buildings, an elaborate terraced temple at Deir el Bahri, which eventually served as her tomb. Hatshepsut's status as a powerful female ruler was difficult for Egyptians to conceptualize, and she is often depicted in male dress or with a false beard, thus looking more like the male rulers who were the norm. After her death, Thutmose III tried to destroy all evidence that she had ever ruled, smashing statues and scratching her name off inscriptions, perhaps because of personal animosity and perhaps because he wanted to erase the fact that a woman had once been pharaoh. Only within the last decades have historians and archaeologists begun to (literally) piece together her story.

Though female pharaohs were very rare, many royal women had power through their position as "Great Royal Wives." The most famous of these was Nefertiti, the wife of Akhenaten. Her name means "the perfect (or beautiful) woman has come," and inscriptions also give her many other titles. Nefertiti used her position to spread the new religion of the sun-god Aton.

Together she and Akhenaten built a new palace at Akhetaten, the present Amarna, away from the old centers of power. There they developed the cult of Aton to the exclusion of the traditional deities. Nearly the only literary survival of their religious belief is the "Hymn to Aton," which declares Aton to be the only god. It describes Nefertiti as "the great royal consort whom he! Akhenaten! Loves, the mistress of the Two Lands! Upper and Lower Egypt!"

Nefertiti is often shown the same size as her husband, and in some inscriptions she is performing religious rituals that would normally have been done only by the pharaoh. The exact details of her power are hard to determine, however. An older theory held that her husband removed her from power, though there is also speculation that she may have ruled secretly in her own right after his death. Her tomb has long since disappeared, though in 2003 an enormous controversy developed over her possible remains. There is no controversy that the bust shown above, now in a Berlin museum, represents Nefertiti, nor that it has become an icon of female beauty since it was first discovered in the early twentieth century.

Questions for Analysis

1. Why might it have been difficult for Egyptians to accept a female ruler?

2. What opportunities do hereditary monarchies such as that of ancient Egypt provide for women? How does this fit with gender hierarchies in which men are understood as superior?

THE RISE OF THE HITTITES (CA. 1650–CA. 1200 B.C.E.)

How did the Hittites affect the life of the ancient Near East?

Indo-European *Refers to a large family of languages that includes English, most of the languages of modern Europe, Greek, Latin, Persian, and Sanskrit, the sacred tongue of ancient India.*

Around 1650 B.C.E. the Hittites, who had long been settled in Anatolia (modern Turkey), became a major power in that region and began to expand east and south (see Map 1.3). The Hittites were an Indo-European people. The term **Indo-European** refers to a large family of languages that includes English, most of the languages of modern Europe, Greek, Latin, Persian, and Sanskrit, the sacred tongue of ancient India. The Hittite king Hattusilis I built a hill citadel at Hattusas, the modern Boghazköy, from which he led his people against neighboring kingdoms. His grandson and successor, Mursilis I (r. ca. 1595 B.C.E.), extended the Hittite conquests as far as Babylon. Upon his return home, the victorious Mursilis was assassinated by members of his own family, which opened the door to foreign invasion. Only when the Hittites were united behind a strong king were they a power to be reckoned with. Unshaken, the Hittites produced an energetic line of kings who built a powerful empire. Their major technological contribution was the introduction of iron into war and agriculture in the form of weapons and tools.

Around 1300 B.C.E. the Hittites stopped the Egyptian army of Rameses II (r. ca. 1290–1224 B.C.E.) at the Battle of Kadesh in Syria. Having fought each other to a standstill, the Hittites and Egyptians first made peace and then an alliance. The two greatest powers of the Near East thus tried to make war between them impossible.

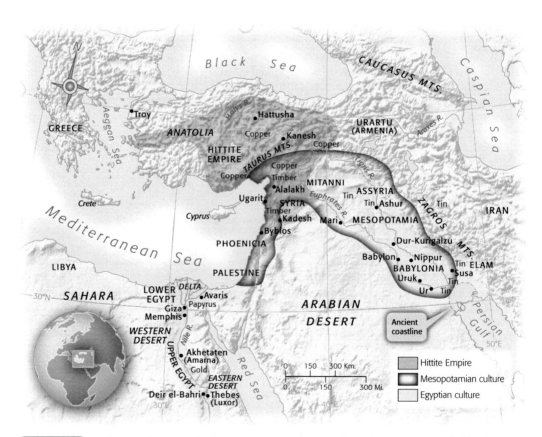

MAP 1.3 **Balance of Power in the Near East** This map shows the regions controlled by the Hittites and Egyptians at the height of their power. The Hittites conquered part of Mesopotamia during their expansion eastward.

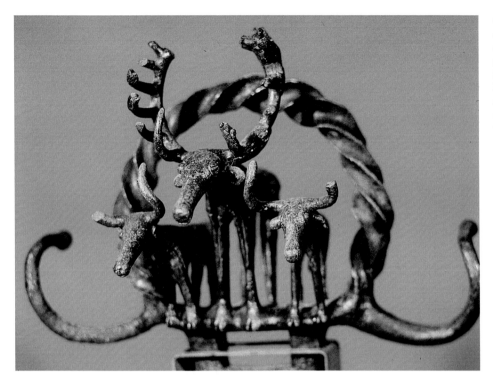

● **Hittite Solar Disk** This cult standard represents Hittite concepts of fertility and prosperity. The circle surrounding the animals is the sun, beneath which stands a stag flanked by two bulls. Stylized bull's horns spread from the base of the disk. The symbol is also one of might and protection from outside harm. *(Museum of Anatolian Civilizations, Ankara)*

The Hittites and Egyptians next included the Babylonians in their diplomacy. They all made alliance for offensive and defensive protection, and swore to uphold one another's authority. These contacts facilitated the exchange of ideas throughout western Asia. The Hittites also passed much knowledge from the east to the newly arrived Greeks in Europe. Like the Hittite kings, Rameses II used the peace after the Battle of Kadesh to promote prosperity and concentrate the income from the natural wealth and the foreign trade of Egypt on internal affairs. In many ways, he was the last great pharaoh of Egypt.

This peaceful situation lasted until the late thirteenth century B.C.E., when both the Hittite and Egyptian empires fell to invaders. The most famous of these marauders, the **Sea Peoples,** remain one of the puzzles of ancient history. The Sea Peoples were a collection of peoples who went their own individual ways after their attacks on the Hittites and Egyptians. They dealt both the Hittites and the Egyptians hard blows, making the Hittites vulnerable to overland invasion from the north and driving the Egyptians back to the Nile Delta. The Hittites fell under these attacks, but the battered Egyptians managed to retreat to the delta and hold on.

Sea Peoples *Invaders who destroyed the Egyptian empire in the late thirteenth century; they are otherwise unidentifiable because they went their own ways after their attacks on Egypt.*

A Shattered Egypt and a Rising Phoenicia

The invasions of the Sea Peoples brought the great days of Egyptian power to an end. The long wars against invaders weakened and impoverished Egypt, causing political upheaval and economic chaos. Egypt suffered a four-hundred-year period of political fragmentation, a new dark age known to Egyptian specialists as the Third Intermediate Period (ca. 1100–653 B.C.E.).

In southern Egypt, meanwhile, the pharaoh's decline opened the way for the energetic Nubians to extend their authority northward throughout the Nile Valley. Since the imperial days of the Eighteenth Dynasty, the Nubians, too, had adopted many features of Egyptian culture. Now they embraced Egyptian culture wholesale.

The reunification of Egypt occurred late and unexpectedly. With Egypt disorganized, an independent African state, the kingdom of Kush, grew up in the region of

● FIGURE 1.2 **Origins of the Alphabet** List of hieroglyphic, Ugaritic, Phoenician, Greek, and Roman sign forms. *(Source: A. B. Knapp, The History and Culture of Ancient Western Asia and Egypt. © 1988 Wadsworth, a part of Cengage Learning, Inc. Reproduced by permission, www.cengage.com/permissions)*

HIEROGLYPHIC	REPRESENTS	UGARITIC	PHOENICIAN	GREEK	ROMAN
	Throw stick	T	⌐	Γ	G
	Man with raised arms	E	⅃	E	E
	Basket with handle	▷	↓	K	K
	Water	⊢T	M	M	M
	Snake	⊷	↘	N	N
	Eye	◁	O	O	O
	Mouth	⊨	?	Π	P
	Head	⊞	9	P	R
	Pool with lotus flowers	◁T↗	W	Σ	S
	House	⊞	9	B	B
	Ox-head	⊶	K	A	A

modern Sudan with its capital at Nepata. Like the Libyans, the Kushites worshiped Egyptian gods and used Egyptian hieroglyphs. In the eighth century B.C.E., their king Piankhy swept through the entire Nile Valley from Nepata in the south to the delta in the north. United once again, Egypt enjoyed a brief period of peace during which the Egyptians continued to assimilate their conquerors. Nonetheless, reunification of Egypt did not lead to a new empire.

Yet Egypt's legacy to its African neighbors remained rich. By trading and exploring southward along the coast of the Red Sea, the Egyptians introduced their goods and ideas as far south as the land of Punt, probably a region on the Somali coast. Egypt was the primary civilizing force in Nubia, which became another version of the pharaoh's realm, complete with royal pyramids and Egyptian deities. Egyptian religion penetrated as far south as Ethiopia.

Among the sturdy peoples who rose to prominence were the Phoenicians, a Semitic-speaking people who had long inhabited several cities along the coast of modern Lebanon. Phoenicians took to the sea to become outstanding explorers and merchants. They played a predominant role in international trade, in which they exported their manufactured goods. Their most valued products were purple and blue textiles, from which originated their Greek name, Phoenicians, meaning **"Purple People."** They also worked metals, which they shipped processed or as ore. They imported rare goods and materials from Persia in the east and from their neighbors to the south. Their exported wares went to Egypt, as far as North Africa and Spain, and even into the Atlantic. The variety and quality of their exports generally made them welcome visitors. Although their goal was trade, not colonization, they nevertheless founded Carthage in 813 B.C.E., a city that would one day struggle with Rome for domination of the western Mediterranean. Their voyages naturally brought them into contact with the Greeks, to whom they introduced the older cultures of the Near East. Indeed, their enduring significance lay in their spreading the experiences of the Near East throughout the western Mediterranean.

Phoenician culture was urban, based on the prosperous commercial centers of Tyre, Sidon, and Byblos. The Phoenicians' overwhelming cultural legacy was the develop-

Purple People *The Greek name for the Phoenicians, a culture that inhabited the eastern coast of the Mediterranean Sea, so called because of the remarkable purple dye they produced from certain sea snails.*

ment of an alphabet (see Figure 1.2). Unlike other literate peoples, they used one letter to designate one sound, a system that vastly simplified writing and reading. The Greeks modified this alphabet and then used it to write their own language. We still use it today.

THE CHILDREN OF ISRAEL (CA. 950–538 B.C.E.)

How did the Hebrews form a small kingdom after the fall of larger neighboring empires?

The fall of the Hittite Empire and Egypt's collapse allowed the rise of numerous small states. South of Phoenicia arose a small kingdom, the land of the ancient Jews or Hebrews. It is difficult to say precisely who the Hebrews were because virtually the only source for much of their history is the Hebrew Bible, a religious document that contains many myths and legends as well as historical material. Like the earlier Hyksos, they probably migrated into the Nile Delta seeking good land. There, according to the Bible, the Egyptians enslaved them. The Hebrews followed their leader Moses out of Egypt, and in the thirteenth century B.C.E. they settled in Palestine. There they encountered the Philistines; the Amorites, relatives of Hammurabi's Babylonians; and the Semitic-speaking Canaanites. Despite numerous wars, contact between the Hebrews and their new neighbors was not always hostile. They freely mingled with the Canaanites, and some went so far as to worship Baal, an ancient Semitic fertility-god represented as a golden calf. Only later did the Hebrews consider Yahweh the only god. Despite the anger expressed in the Bible over Hebrew worship of **Baal,** there is nothing surprising about the phenomenon. Once again, newcomers adapted themselves to the culture of an older, well-established people.

The greatest danger to the Hebrews came from the Philistines, whose superior technology and military organization at first made them invincible. The Hebrew leader Saul (ca. 1000 B.C.E.), while keeping the Philistines at bay, established a monarchy over the twelve Hebrew tribes. David of Bethlehem continued Saul's work and captured the city of Jerusalem, which he enlarged and made the religious center of the realm. His work is consolidating the monarchy and enlarging the kingdom paved the way for his son Solomon (ca. 965–925 B.C.E.). Solomon created a nation by dividing it into twelve territorial districts cutting across the old tribal borders. He also launched a building program that included cities, palaces, fortresses, and roads. The most symbolic of these projects was the Temple of Jerusalem, which became the home of the Ark of the Covenant, the chest that contained the holiest of Hebrew religious articles. The temple in Jerusalem was intended to be the religious heart of the kingdom and the symbol of Hebrew unity.

At Solomon's death his kingdom broke into political halves. The northern part became Israel, with its capital at Samaria. The southern half was Judah, and Jerusalem remained its center. With political division went religious rift: Israel established rival sanctuaries for gods other than Yahweh. Although the Assyrians later wiped out the northern kingdom of Israel, Judah survived numerous calamities until the Babylonians crushed it in 587 B.C.E. The survivors were sent into exile in Babylonia, a period commonly known as the **Babylonian Captivity.** In 538 B.C.E. the Persian king Cyrus the Great permitted some forty thousand exiles to

Baal *An ancient Semitic fertility god represented as a golden calf.*

Babylonian Captivity *The period of Jewish history between 586 and 537 B.C.E. during which the political and spiritual leaders of the kingdom of Judah were deported to Babylon following the defeat of Judah by Nebuchadnezzer.*

● **The Golden Calf** According to the Bible, Moses descended from Mount Sinai, where he had received the Ten Commandments, to find the Hebrews worshiping a golden calf, which was against Yahweh's laws. In July 1990 an American archaeological team found this model of a gilded calf inside a pot. The figurine, which dates to about 1550 B.C.E., is strong evidence for the existence of the cult represented by the calf in Palestine. *(Courtesy of the Leon Levy Expedition to Ashkelon. Photo: Carl Andrews)*

Primary Source:

Moses Descends Mount Sinai with the Ten Commandments

Find out why the God of the Hebrew Bible issued the Ten Commandments, and what he promised Moses's people in return for keeping—or violating—them.

return to Jerusalem. During and especially after the Babylonian Captivity, the exiles redefined their beliefs and practices, thereby establishing what they believed was the law of Yahweh. Those who lived by these precepts came to be called Jews.

Daily Life in Israel

Marriage and the nuclear family were fundamentally important in Jewish life; celibacy was frowned upon and almost all major Jewish thinkers and priests were married. With parents making all the arrangements, boys and girls were often married while little more than children. They were expected to begin their own families at once. Sons were especially desired because they maintained the family bloodline, while keeping ancestral property in the family. A firstborn son became the head of the household at his father's death. Daughters were less highly valued because they would eventually leave the family after marriage. Unlike other cultures, Jews forbade infanticide because Yahweh prohibited it.

Mothers oversaw the early education of the children, but as boys grew older, their fathers gave them more of their education. The most important task for observant Jews was studying religious texts, an activity limited to men until the twentieth century. Women were obliged to provide for men's physical needs while they were studying, so Jewish women were often more active economically than their contemporaries of other religions.

The Hebrews were originally nomadic, but they adopted settled agriculture in Palestine. The development of urban life among Jews created new economic opportunities, especially in crafts and trade. Jewish merchants began to participate in maritime and caravan trade, and in the process entered the mainstream of Near Eastern life. Yet they always faithfully retained their unique religion and culture.

MAP 1.4 **The Assyrian and Persian Empires** The Assyrian Empire at its height (ca. 650 B.C.E.) included almost all of the old centers of power in the ancient Near East. By 513 B.C.E., however, the Persian Empire not only included more of that area but also extended as far east as western India. With the rise of the Medes and Persians, the balance of power in the Near East shifted east of Mesopotamia for the first time.

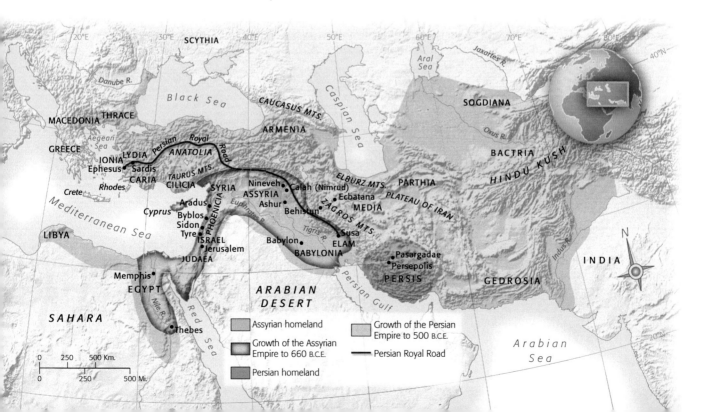

ASSYRIA, THE MILITARY MONARCHY (859–612 B.C.E.)

What enabled the Assyrians to conquer their neighbors, and how did they doom themselves by their cruelty?

● **Siege of a City**   Art here serves to glorify horror. The Assyrian king Tiglath-pileser III launches an assault on a fortified city. The impaled bodies shown at center demonstrate the cruelty of Assyrian warfare. Also noticeable are the various weapons and means of attack used against the city. *(Courtesy of the Trustees of the British Museum)*

Small kingdoms like those of the Phoenicians and the Jews could exist only in the absence of a major power. The beginning of the ninth century B.C.E. saw the rise of such a power in Assyria. The Assyrians dominated northern Mesopotamia with their chief capital at Nineveh on the Tigris River. The Assyrians were a Semitic people heavily influenced by the Babylonian culture to the south. They were also one of the most warlike people in history, and for over two hundred years they fought to dominate the Near East. The Assyrian kings Tiglath-pileser III (r. 774–727 B.C.E.) and Sargon II (r. 721–705 B.C.E.) conquered Syria, Palestine, and the two Jewish kingdoms, and in ca. 717 B.C.E. Sargon defeated the Egyptians before turning against Babylon. By almost constant warfare the two kings carved out an empire that stretched from east and north of the Tigris River to central Egypt (see Map 1.4).

Although atrocity and terrorism struck unspeakable fear into Assyria's subjects, Assyria's success was also due to sophisticated, farsighted, and effective military organization. Assyrian military genius was remarkable for the development of a wide variety of siege machinery and techniques, including excavations to undermine city walls and battering rams to knock down walls and gates. Never before in the Near East had anyone applied such technical knowledge to warfare. The Assyrians even invented the concept of a corps of engineers who bridged rivers with pontoons or provided soldiers with inflatable skins for swimming. The Assyrians also knew how to coordinate their efforts both in open battle and in siege warfare.

Not only did the Assyrians know how to win battles, but they also knew how to use their victories. As early as the reign of Tiglath-pileser III, the Assyrian kings began to organize their conquered territories into an empire. The lands closest to Assyria became provinces governed by Assyrian officials. Kingdoms beyond the provinces were not annexed but became dependent states that followed Assyria's lead. The Assyrian king chose their rulers either by regulating the succession of native kings or by supporting native kings who appealed to him. Against more distant states the Assyrian

Primary Source:
An Assyrian Emperor's Résumé
Read the inscription left behind by Ashur-Nasir-Pal, in which he promotes himself as an especially effective—and brutal—military leader.

kings waged frequent war in order to conquer them outright or make the dependent states secure.

In the seventh century B.C.E. Assyrian power seemed firmly established. Yet the downfall of Assyria was swift and complete. Babylon finally won its independence in 626 B.C.E. and joined forces with a new people, the Medes, an Indo-European-speaking folk from Iran. Together the Babylonians and the Medes destroyed the Assyrian Empire in 612 B.C.E., paving the way for the rise of the Persians. The Hebrew prophet Nahum spoke for many when he asked: "Nineveh is laid waste: who will bemoan her?"[3] Their cities destroyed and their power shattered, the Assyrians disappeared from history, remembered only as a cruel people of the Bible. Two hundred years later, when the Greek adventurer and historian Xenophon passed by the ruins of Nineveh, he marveled at the extent of the former city but knew nothing of the Assyrians. The glory of their empire was forgotten.

• • • • • • • • • • • • • • • • • •

THE EMPIRE OF THE PERSIAN KINGS (CA. 1000–464 B.C.E.)

How did Iranian nomads create the Persian Empire that ultimately embraced all of these earlier peoples?

The Iranians were Indo-Europeans from central Europe and southern Russia. They migrated into the land to which they have given their name, the area between the Caspian Sea and the Persian Gulf. They then fell under the spell of the more sophisticated cultures of their Mesopotamian neighbors. The Persians, the most important of the Iranian peoples, went on to create one of the greatest empires of the ancient Near East. Though as conquerors they willingly used force to accomplish their ends, they normally preferred to depend on diplomacy to rule. They usually respected their sub-

● **Persian Saddle-Cloth**   This elaborately painted piece of leather, dating from the fourth or third centuries B.C.E., served a ceremonial rather than a practical function. *(© The State Hermitage Museum, St. Petersburg)*

jects and allowed them to practice their native customs and religions. Thus the Persians gave the Near East both political unity and cultural diversity.

Persia, modern Iran, is a stark land of towering mountains and flaming deserts, with a broad central plateau in the heart of the country (see Map 1.4). Between the Tigris-Euphrates Valley in the west and the Indus Valley in the east rises an immense plateau surrounded on all sides by lofty mountains that cut off the interior from the sea.

Iran's geographical position and topography explain its traditional role as the highway between western and eastern Asia. Throughout history wild nomadic peoples migrating from the broad steppes of Russia and Central Asia have streamed into Iran. Confronting the uncrossable salt deserts, most have turned either westward or eastward, moving on until they reached the advanced and wealthy urban centers of Mesopotamia and India. When cities emerged along the natural lines of east-west communication, Iran became the area where nomads met urban dwellers, a meeting ground of unique significance for the civilizations of both east and west.

The Coming of the Medes and Persians

The Iranians entered this land around 1000 B.C.E. as nomads who migrated with their flocks and herds. Like their kinsmen the Aryans, who moved into India, they were also horse breeders, and the horse gave them a decisive military advantage over the prehistoric peoples of Iran. The Iranians rode into battle in horse-drawn chariots or on horseback and easily swept the natives before them. Yet, because the influx of Iranians went on for centuries, there continued to be constant cultural interchange between conquering newcomers and conquered natives.

Gradually two groups of Iranians began coalescing into larger units. The Persians had settled in Persia, the modern region of Fars, in southern Iran. Their kinsmen the Medes occupied Media in the north, with their capital at Ecbatana, the modern Hamadan. Even though distracted by grave pressures from their neighbors, the Medes united under one king around 710 B.C.E. and extended their control over the Persians in the south. In 612 B.C.E. the Medes joined the Babylonians in overthrowing the Assyrian Empire. With the rise of the Medes, the balance of power in western Asia shifted for the first time east of Mesopotamia.

The Creation of the Persian Empire (550–464 B.C.E.)

In 550 B.C.E. Cyrus the Great (r. 559–530 B.C.E.), king of the Persians and one of the most remarkable statesmen of antiquity, conquered the Medes. His conquest resulted not in slavery and slaughter but in the union of the Iranian peoples. Having united Iran, Cyrus set out to achieve two goals. First, he wanted to win control of the west and thus of the terminal ports of the great trade routes that crossed Iran and Anatolia (modern western Turkey). Second, he strove to secure eastern Iran from the pressure of nomadic invaders. In a series of major campaigns Cyrus achieved both goals. He swept into Anatolia, easily overthrowing the young kingdom of Lydia. His generals subdued the Greek cities along the coast of Anatolia, thus gaining him flourishing ports on the Mediterranean. From Lydia Cyrus, marching to the far eastern corners of Iran, conquered

● **Funeral Pyre of Croesus** This scene, an excellent example of the precision and charm of ancient Greek vase painting, depicts the Lydian king Croesus on his funeral pyre. He pours a libation to the gods while his slave lights the fire. Herodotus has a happier ending, when he says that Cyrus the Great set fire to the pyre, but that Apollo sent rain to put it out. *(Louvre/ Réunion de Musées Nationaux/Art Resource, NY)*

● **The Impact of Zoroastrianism** The Persian kings embraced Zoroastrianism as the religion of the realm. This rock carving at Behistun records the bond. King Darius I is seen trampling on one rebel with others behind him. Above is the sign of Ahuramazda, the god of truth and guardian of the Persian king. *(Robert Harding World Imagery)*

the regions of Parthia and Bactria. The Babylonians welcomed him as a liberator when his soldiers moved into their kingdom.

With these victories Cyrus demonstrated to the world his benevolence as well as his military might. He spared the life of Croesus, the conquered king of Lydia, to serve him as friend and adviser. He allowed the Greeks to live according to their customs, thus making possible the spread of Greek culture farther east. Cyrus's humanity likewise extended to the Jews, whom he found enslaved in Babylonia. He restored their sacred objects to them and returned them to Jerusalem, where he helped them rebuild their temple.

The Religion of Zoroaster

Around 600 B.C.E. Zoroaster, a religious thinker and preacher, introduced new spiritual concepts to the Iranian people. He taught that life is a constant battleground for the two opposing forces of good and evil. The Iranian god **Ahuramazda** embodied good and truth but was opposed by Ahriman, a hateful spirit who stood for evil and lies. Ahuramazda and Ahriman were locked together in a cosmic battle for the human race, a battle that stretched over thousands of years.

Zoroaster emphasized the individual's responsibility to choose between good and evil. He taught that people possessed the free will to decide between Ahuramazda and Ahriman and that they must rely on their own conscience to guide them through life. Their decisions were crucial, Zoroaster warned, for there would come a time of reckoning. The victorious Ahuramazda, like the Egyptian god Osiris, would preside over a last judgment to determine each person's eternal fate.

Zoroaster's teachings converted Darius, who did not, however, impose it on others. Under the protection of the Persian kings, **Zoroastrianism** won converts throughout Iran. It survived the fall of the Persian Empire to influence Judaism, Christianity, and early Islam. Good behavior in the world, even though unrecognized at the time, would receive ample reward in the hereafter. Evil, no matter how powerful in life,

Ahuramazda *The chief Iranian god, who was the creator and benefactor of all living creatures; unlike Yahweh, he was not a lone god.*

Zoroastrianism *The religion based on the teachings of Zoroaster, who emphasized the individual's responsibility to choose between good and evil. Though Zoroaster's teachings often met with opposition, the Persian ruler Darius was a convert.*

would be punished after death. In some form or another, Zoroastrian concepts still pervade many modern religions.

The Span of the Persian Empire

Cyrus's successors rounded out the Persian conquest of the ancient Near East. In 525 B.C.E. his son Cambyses (r. 530–522 B.C.E.) subdued Egypt. Darius (r. 521–486 B.C.E.) and his son Xerxes (r. 486–464 B.C.E.) unsuccessfully invaded Greece, but Darius in about 513 B.C.E. conquered western India. He created the Persian satrapy of Hindush, which included the valley of the Indus River. Thus, within thirty-seven years (550–513 B.C.E.) the Persians transformed themselves from a subject people to the rulers of an empire that included Asia Minor, Mesopotamia, Iran, and western India. They had created a vast empire encompassing all of the oldest and most honored kingdoms and peoples of these regions (see Map 1.4).

The Persians also knew how to preserve the peace they had won on the battlefield. Unlike the Assyrians, they did not resort to royal terrorism to maintain order. The Persians instead built an efficient administrative system to govern the empire based in their capital city of Persepolis near modern Schiras, Iran. From Persepolis they sent directions to the provinces and received reports back from their officials. To do so they built and maintained a sophisticated system of roads linking the empire. The main highway, the famous **Royal Road,** spanned some 1,677 miles (see Map 1.4). Other roads branched out to link all parts of the empire from the coast of Asia Minor to the valley of the Indus River. These highways meant that the king was usually in close touch with officials and subjects. The roads simplified the defense of the empire by making it easier to move Persian armies. The system also allowed the easy flow of trade. In all, these roads enabled the Persian kings to translate the concepts of right, justice, and good government into a practical reality.

Royal Road   *The main highway created by the Persians; it spanned 1,677 miles from western Turkey to Iran.*

● **The Royal Palace at Persepolis**   King Darius began and King Xerxes finished building a grand palace worthy of the glory of the Persian Empire. Pictured here is the monumental audience hall, where the king dealt with ministers of state and foreign envoys. *(George Holton/Photo Researchers)*

Chapter Summary

Key Terms

Near East
Neolithic period
nobles
clients
pharaoh
Amon-Ra
Book of the Dead
pyramid
Hyksos
Bronze Age
monotheism
Indo-European
Sea Peoples
Purple People
Baal
Babylonian Captivity
Ahuramazda
Zoroastrianism
Royal Road

To assess your mastery of this chapter, go to
bedfordstmartins.com/mckayworld

• How did the Sumerians lay the foundations of a flourishing civilization in the hard land of Mesopotamia?

During the Neolithic period peoples used their new stone tools to create lives centered on towns. In Mesopotamia the Sumerians established the basic social, economic, and intellectual patterns that defined civilized life. These developments brought order and prosperity and led to the unification of Mesopotamia by Hammurabi and the Babylonians. They in turn nurtured and encouraged the spread of this rich life beyond Mesopotamia.

• How did geography enable the Egyptians easily to form a cohesive, prosperous society?

In Egypt, meanwhile, other peoples turned the fertile Nile Valley into the home of a rich, sophisticated society that lived harmoniously under the rule of kings, the pharaohs. This era saw the building of the pyramids, political stability, and long years of prosperity. During a period of internal weakness the Hyksos, a nomadic people, introduced Bronze Age technology into Egypt when they settled in the Nile Delta. Egyptian pharaohs, however, rallied to drive out the Hyksos and establish the rich period of the New Kingdom. A complex polytheistic mythology underlay Egyptian culture, and the pharaoh Akhenaten failed in his attempt to introduce Aton as the only true god.

• How did the Hittites affect the life of the ancient Near East?

From the northern fringes of this sphere came the Hittites, an Indo-European people who introduced iron tools and weapons. After establishing their own empire, they promoted a general alliance with the Egyptians and Babylonians that led to an era of peace.

• How did the Hebrews form a small kingdom after the fall of larger neighboring empires?

In the thirteenth century B.C.E. hostile invaders, the Sea Peoples, disrupted this stable world, which also allowed lesser native folk to become prominent. The Nubians of Africa adopted and preserved the old Egyptian civilization. The Phoenicians built small trading kingdoms that linked the Near East to the broader Mediterranean world. The Hebrews benefited from the absence of major powers to create a minor kingdom. They developed religious beliefs and a code of life that still flourish today.

• What enabled the Assyrians to conquer their neighbors, and how did they doom themselves by their cruelty?

In this world rose the Assyrians, another Semitic people who had lived on its periphery. Through effective military techniques and brutal aggression, they conquered the entire region, until a coalition of peoples utterly destroyed them.

• How did Iranian nomads create the Persian Empire that ultimately embraced all of these earlier peoples?

The Persians, one of the peoples instrumental in overthrowing the Assyrians, were also Indo-Europeans—Iranians from the north. They too created an empire, one that stretched from the eastern Mediterranean to western India. They introduced law, justice, and toleration into their imperial rule. They encouraged political unity and cultural diversity. Through their religion Zoroastrianism they fostered the concept of life as a battleground between good and evil.

Suggested Reading

Brosius, M. *The Persians: An Introduction.* 2006. Covers all of Persian history.

Edwards, D. N. *The Nubian Past.* 2004. Examines the history of Nubia and Sudan.

Hawass, Z. *Silent Images: Women in Pharaonic Egypt.* 2000. Blends texts and pictures to depict the history of Egyptian women.

Herzfeld, E. *Iran in the Ancient Near East.* 1987. Puts Persian history in a broad context.

Kuhrt, A. *The Ancient Near East,* 2 vols. 1995. Covers the region from the earliest times to Alexander's conquest.

Leick, G. *The Babylonians.* 2002. Introduces all aspects of Babylonian life and culture.

Marokoe, G. *The Phoenicians.* 2000. Presents these seafarers at home and abroad in the Mediterranean.

Oren, E. D. *The Hyksos.* 1997. Concentrates on the archaeological evidence for the Hyksos.

Rice, M. *Egypt's Early Making: The Origins of Ancient Egypt.* 2004. Treats the earliest periods of Egyptian history.

Visicato, C. *The Power of Writing.* 2000. Studies the practical importance of early Mesopotamian scribes.

Notes

1. Quoted in S. N. Kramer, *The Sumerians* (Chicago: University of Chicago Press, 1963), p. 238.
2. J.B. Pritchard, ed., *Ancient Near Eastern Texts,* 3d ed., p. 372. Copyright © 1969 by Princeton University Press. Reprinted by permission of Princeton University Press.
3. Nahum 3:7.

Listening to the PAST

A Quest for Immortality

The human desire to escape the grip of death, to achieve immortality, is one of the oldest wishes of all peoples. The Sumerian *Epic of Gilgamesh* is the earliest recorded treatment of this topic. The oldest elements of the epic go back at least to the third millennium B.C.E. According to tradition, Gilgamesh was a king of Uruk whom the Sumerians, Babylonians, and Assyrians considered a hero-king and a god. In the story Gilgamesh and his friend Enkidu set out to attain immortality and join the ranks of the gods. They attempt to do so by performing wondrous feats against fearsome agents of the gods, who are determined to thwart them.

During their quest Enkidu dies. Gilgamesh, more determined than ever to become immortal, begins seeking anyone who might tell him how to do so. His journey involves the effort not only to escape from death but also to reach an understanding of the meaning of life.

The passage begins with Enkidu speaking of a dream that foretells his own death.

Listen, my friend [Gilgamesh], this is the dream I dreamed last night. The heavens roared, and earth rumbled back an answer; between them I stood before an awful being, the sombre-faced man-bird; he had directed on me his purpose. His was a vampire face, his foot was a lion's foot, his hand was an eagle's talon. He fell on me and his claws were in my hair, he held me fast and I smothered; then he transformed me so that my arms became wings covered with feathers. He turned his stare towards me, and he led me away to the palace of Irkalla, the Queen of Darkness [the goddess of the underworld; in other words, an agent of death], to the house from which none who enters ever returns, down the road from which there is no coming back.

At this point Enkidu dies, whereupon Gilgamesh sets off on his quest for the secret of immortality. During his travels he meets with Siduri, the wise and good-natured goddess of wine, who gives him the following advice.

Gilgamesh, where are you hurrying to? You will never find that life for which you are looking. When the gods created man they allotted to him death, but

life they retained in their own keeping. As for you, Gilgamesh, fill your belly with good things; day and night, night and day, dance and be merry, feast and rejoice. Let your clothes be fresh, bathe yourself in water, cherish the little child that holds your hand, and make your wife happy in your embrace; for this too is the lot of man.

Ignoring Siduri's advice, Gilgamesh continues his journey, until he finds Utnapishtim. Meeting Utnapishtim is especially important because, like Gilgamesh, he was once a mortal, but the gods so favored him that they put him in an eternal paradise. Gilgamesh puts to Utnapishtim the question that is the reason for his quest.

Oh, father Utnapishtim, you who have entered the assembly of the gods, I wish to question you concerning the living and the dead, how shall I find the life for which I am searching?

Utnapishtim said, "There is no permanence. Do we build a house to stand forever, do we seal a contract to hold for all time? Do brothers divide an inheritance to keep forever, does the flood-time of rivers endure? . . . What is there between the master and the servant when both have fulfilled their doom? When the Anunnaki [the gods of the underworld], the judges, come together, and Mammetun [the goddess of fate] the mother of destinies, together they decree the fates of men. Life and death they allot but the day of death they do not disclose.

Then Gilgamesh said to Utnapishtim the Faraway, "I look at you now, Utnapishtim, and your appearance is no different from mine; there is nothing strange in your features. I thought I should find you like a hero prepared for battle, but you lie here taking your ease on your back. Tell me truly, how was it that you came to enter the company of the gods and to possess everlasting life?" Utnapishtim said to Gilgamesh, "I shall reveal to you a mystery, I shall tell you a secret of the gods."

Utnapishtim then tells Gilgamesh of a time when the great god Enlil had become angered with the Sumerians and encouraged the other gods to wipe out humanity. The god

Gilgamesh, from decorative panel of a lyre unearthed at Ur. *(The University Museum, University of Pennsylvania, neg. T4-108)*

Ea, however, warned Utnapishtim about the gods' decision to send a great flood to destroy the Sumerians. He commanded Utnapishtim to build a boat big enough to hold his family, various artisans, and all animals in order to survive the flood that was to come. Although Enlil was infuriated by the Sumerians' survival, Ea rebuked him. Then Enlil relented and blessed Utnapishtim with eternal paradise. After telling the story, Utnapishtim foretells Gilgamesh's fate.

Utnapishtim said, ". . . The destiny was fulfilled which the father of the gods, Enlil of the mountain, had decreed for Gilgamesh: In nether-earth the darkness will show him a light: of mankind, all that are known, none will leave a monument for generations to compare with his. The heroes, the wise men, like the new moon have their waxing and waning. Men will say, Who has ever ruled with might and power like his? As in the dark month, the month of shadows, so without him there is no light. O Gilgamesh, this was the meaning of your dream [of immortality]. You were given the kingship, such was your destiny, everlasting life was not your destiny. Because of this do not be sad at heart, do not be grieved or oppressed; he [Enlil] has given you power to bind and to loose, to be the darkness and the light of mankind. He has given unexampled supremacy over the people, victory in battle from which no fugitive returns, in forays and assaults from which there is no going back. But do not abuse this power, deal justly with your servants in the palace, deal justly before the face of the Sun."

Questions for Analysis

1. What does the *Epic of Gilgamesh* reveal about Sumerian attitudes toward the gods and human beings?

2. At the end of his quest, did Gilgamesh achieve immortality? If so, what was the nature of that immortality?

3. What does the epic tell us about Sumerian views of the nature of human life? Where do human beings fit into the cosmic world?

Source: The Epic of Gilgamesh, translated by N. K. Sanders. Penguin Classics 1960, Second revised edition, 1972, pp. 91–119. Copyright © N. K. Sanders, 1960, 1964, 1972. Reproduced by permission of Penguin Books Ltd.

The North Gate at Sanchi, Madhya Pradesh. One of four ornately carved gates guarding this Buddhist memorial shrine, second century B.C.E. *(Jean-Louis Nou/akg-images)*

2

THE FOUNDATION OF INDIAN SOCIETY, TO 300 C.E.

During the centuries when the peoples of ancient Mesopotamia and Egypt were developing urban civilizations, people in India were wrestling with the same challenges—making the land yield food, building cities and urban cultures, grappling with the political administration of large tracts of land, and asking basic questions about human life and the cosmos.

Like the civilizations of the Near East, the earliest Indian civilization centered on a great river, the Indus. From about 2800 to 1800 B.C.E., this Indus Valley, or Harappan, culture thrived, and numerous cities were built over a huge area. A very different Indian society emerged after the decline of this civilization. It was dominated by the Aryans, warriors who spoke an early version of Sanskrit. The Indian caste system and the Hindu religion, key features of Indian society into modern times, had their origins in early Aryan society. The earliest Indian literature consists of the epics and religious texts of these Aryan tribes.

By the middle of the first millennium B.C.E., the Aryans had set up numerous small kingdoms throughout north India. This was the great age of Indian religious creativity, when Buddhism and Jainism were founded and the early Brahmanic religion of the Aryans developed into Hinduism. Alexander the Great invaded north India in 326 B.C.E., and after his army withdrew, the first major Indian empire was created by the Mauryan dynasty (ca. 322–ca. 185 B.C.E.), which unified most of north India. This dynasty reached its peak under the great king Ashoka (r. ca. 269–232 B.C.E.), who actively promoted Buddhism both within his realm and beyond it. Not long afterward, however, the empire broke up, and for several centuries India was politically divided.

Although India never had a single language and only periodically had a centralized government, cultural elements dating back to the ancient period—the core ideas of Brahmanism, the caste system, and the early epics—gave India cultural identity. These cultural elements spread through trade and other contact, even when the subcontinent was divided into hostile kingdoms.

THE LAND AND ITS FIRST SETTLERS (CA. 3000–1500 B.C.E.)

What does archaeology tell us about the earliest civilization in India?

The subcontinent of India, a landmass as large as western Europe, juts southward into the warm waters of the Indian Ocean. Today this region is divided into the separate countries of Pakistan, Nepal, India, Bangladesh, and Sri Lanka, but these divisions are recent, and for premodern times the entire subcontinent will be called India here.

In India, as elsewhere, the possibilities for both agriculture and communication have always been strongly shaped by geography (see Map 2.1). Some regions are among the wettest on earth; others are arid deserts and scrubland. Most areas in India are warm all year, with temperatures over 100°F common. Average temperatures range from 79°F in the north to 85°F in the south. Monsoon rains sweep northward from the Indian Ocean each summer. The lower reaches of the Himalaya Mountains in the northeast are covered by dense forests, sustained by heavy rainfall. Immediately to the south are the fertile valleys of the Indus and Ganges Rivers. These lowland plains, which stretch all the way across the subcontinent, over time were tamed for agriculture, and India's great empires were centered there. To their west are the great deserts of Rajasthan and southeastern Pakistan, historically important in part because their flat terrain enabled invaders to sweep into India from the northwest. South of the great river valleys rise the jungle-clad Vindhya Mountains and the dry, hilly Deccan Plateau. In this part of India, only along the coasts do the hills give way to narrow plains where crop agriculture flourished. India's long coastlines and predictable winds fostered maritime trade with other countries bordering the Indian Ocean.

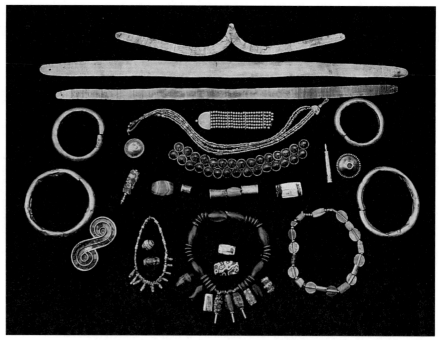

● **Harappan Artifacts** Small objects like seals and jewelry found at Harappan sites provide glimpses of early Indian religious imagination and daily life. The molded tablet shown on the left depicts a female deity battling two tigers. She stands above an elephant. The jewelry found at these sites, such as those pieces shown on the right, makes much use of gold and precious stones. *(J. M. Kenoyer/Courtesy Department of Archaeology and Museums, Government of Pakistan)*

Neolithic settlement of the Indian subcontinent occurred somewhat later than in the Middle East, but agriculture was well established by about 7000 B.C.E. Wheat and barley were the early crops, probably having spread in their domesticated form from the Middle East. Farmers also domesticated cattle, sheep, and goats and learned to make pottery.

The story of the first civilization in India is one of the most dramatic in the ancient world. From the Bible, Europeans knew about ancient Egypt and Ur, but no one knew about the ancient cities of the Indus Valley until 1921, when archaeologists found astonishing evidence of a thriving and sophisticated Bronze Age urban culture dating to about 2500 B.C.E. at Mohenjo-daro in what is now Pakistan.

This civilization is known today as the Indus Valley or the **Harappan** civilization, from the modern names of the river and a major city, respectively. Archaeologists have discovered some three hundred Harappan cities and many more towns and villages in both Pakistan and India, making it possible to see both the vast regional extent of the Harappan civilization and its evolution over a period of nearly a millennium. It was a literate civilization, like those of Egypt and Mesopotamia, but no one has been able to decipher the more than four hundred symbols inscribed on stone seals and copper tablets. Its most flourishing period was 2500 to 2000 B.C.E.

The Indus civilization extended over nearly five hundred thousand square miles in the Indus Valley, making it more than twice as large as the territories of the ancient Egyptian and Sumerian civilizations. Yet Harappan civilization was marked by a striking uniformity. Throughout the region, for instance, even in small villages, bricks were made to standard proportions of 4:2:1. Figurines of pregnant women have been found throughout the area, suggesting common religious ideas and practices.

Like Mesopotamian cities, Harappan cities were centers for crafts and trade surrounded by extensive farmland. Fine ceramics were made on the potter's wheel and decorated with geometric designs. Cotton was used to make cloth (the earliest anywhere) and was so abundant that goods were wrapped in it for shipment. Trade was extensive. As early as the reign of Sargon of Akkad in the third millennium B.C.E., trade between India and Mesopotamia carried goods and ideas between the two cultures, probably by way of the Persian Gulf. The port of Lothal had a stone dock seven hundred feet long, next to which were massive granaries and bead-making factories. Hundreds of seals were found there, some of Persian Gulf origin, indicating that Lothal was a major port of exit and entry.

Both Mohenjo-daro, in southern Pakistan, and Harappa, some four hundred miles to the north, were huge, more than three miles in circumference, and housed populations estimated at thirty-five thousand to forty thousand. They were both defended by great citadels that towered forty to fifty feet above the surrounding plain. Both cities had obviously been planned and built before being settled; they were not the

Chronology

2500–2000 B.C.E.	Height of Harappan civilization
ca. 1500–500 B.C.E.	Aryan civilization
1500–500 B.C.E.	*Rigveda*
ca. 1000 B.C.E.	Introduction of iron
750–500 B.C.E.	*Upanishads*
fl. ca. 520 B.C.E.	Vardhamana Mahavira, founder of Jainism
ca. 513 B.C.E.	Darius conquers Indus Valley
fl. ca. 500 B.C.E.	Siddhartha Gautama, the Buddha
ca. 400 B.C.E.–200 C.E.	Brahmanic religion evolves into Hinduism
326 B.C.E.	Alexander the Great enters Indus Valley
ca. 322–185 B.C.E.	Mauryan Empire
ca. 300 B.C.E.	Jain religion splits into two sects
ca. 269–232 B.C.E.	Reign of Ashoka
ca. 200 B.C.E.–200 C.E.	Classical period of Tamil culture
fl. ca. 100 C.E.	Nagarjuna, theorist of Mahayana Buddhism
ca. 200 C.E.	Code of Manu

Harappan *The first Indian civilization; it is also known as the Indus Valley civilization.*

outcomes of villages that grew and sprawled haphazardly. Streets were straight and varied from nine to thirty-four feet in width. The houses were substantial, many two stories tall, some perhaps three. The focal point of a house was a central courtyard onto which the rooms opened, much like many houses today in both rural and urban India.

Perhaps the most surprising aspect of the elaborate planning of these cities is their complex system of drainage, well preserved at Mohenjo-daro. Each house had a bathroom with a drain connected to brick-lined sewers located under the major streets. Openings allowed the refuse to be collected, probably to be used as fertilizer on nearby fields. No other ancient city had such an advanced sanitation system.

Both cities also contained numerous large structures, which excavators think were public buildings. One of the most important was the large ventilated storehouse for the community's grain. Mohenjo-daro also had a marketplace or place of assembly, a palace, and a huge pool some thirty-nine feet long by twenty-three feet wide and eight feet deep. Like the later Roman baths, it had spacious dressing rooms for the bathers. Because the Great Bath at Mohenjo-daro resembles the ritual purification pools of later India, some scholars have speculated that power was in the hands of a priest-king and that the Great Bath played a role in the religious rituals of the city.

The prosperity of the Indus civilization depended on constant and intensive cultivation of the rich river valley. Although rainfall seems to have been greater then than in recent times, the Indus, like the Nile, flowed through a relatively dry region made fertile by annual floods and irrigation. And as in Egypt, agriculture was aided by a long, hot growing season and near constant sunshine.

Because the written language of the Harappan people has not been deciphered, their political, intellectual, and religious life is largely unknown. There clearly was a political structure with the authority to organize city planning and facilitate trade, but we do not even know whether there were hereditary kings. There are clear connections between Harappan and Sumerian civilization, but just as clear differences. For instance, the Harappan script, like the Sumerian, was incised on clay tablets and seals, but it has no connection to Sumerian cuneiform, and the artistic style of the Harappan seals also is distinct. There are many signs of continuity with later Indian civilization, ranging from the sorts of pottery ovens used to some of the images of gods. Some scholars think that the people of Harappa were the ancestors of the Dravidian-speaking peoples of modern south India. Analysis of skeletons, however, indicates that the population of the Indus Valley in ancient times was very similar to the modern population of the same region.

The decline of Harappan civilization, which began soon after 2000 B.C.E., cannot be attributed to the arrival of powerful invaders, as was once thought. Rather the decline was internally generated. The port of Lothal was abandoned by about 1900 B.C.E., and other major centers came to house only a fraction of their earlier populations. Scholars have offered many explanations for the mystery of the abandonment of these cities. Perhaps an earthquake led to a shift in the

● **Mohenjo-daro** Mohenjo-daro was a planned city built of fired mud brick. Its streets were straight, and covered drain-pipes were installed to carry away waste. From sites like this, we know that the early Indian political elite had the power and technical expertise to organize large, coordinated building projects. *(Josephine Powell)*

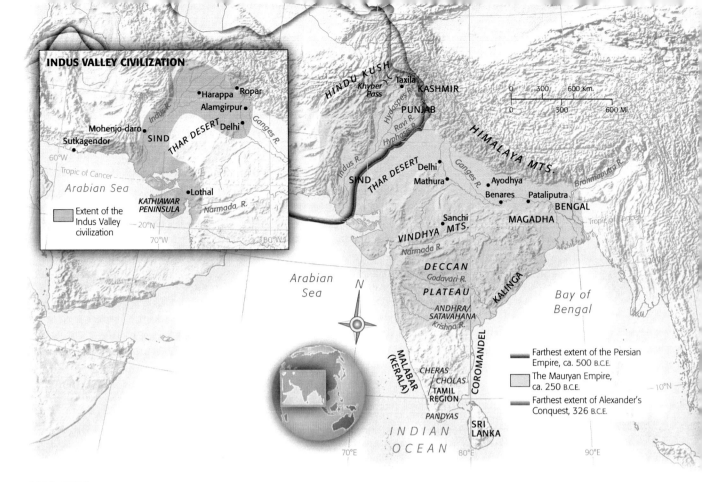

MAP 2.1 **India from ca. 2500 B.C.E. to 300 C.E.** The earliest civilization in India developed in the Indus River valley in the west of the subcontinent. The Ganges River valley was the heart of the later Mauryan Empire. Although India is protected from the cold by mountains in the north, mountain passes in the northwest allowed both migration and invasion.

course of the river, or perhaps rainfall and snowmelt decreased and the rivers dried up. Perhaps the long-term practice of irrigation led to the buildup of salts and alkalines in the soil until they reached levels toxic to plants. Perhaps long-distance commerce collapsed, leading to an economic depression. Perhaps the population fell prey to diseases, such as malaria, that led people to flee the cities. Even though the Harappan people apparently lived on after scattering to villages, they were not able to retain key features of the high culture of the Indus civilization. For the next thousand years, India had no large cities, no kiln-fired bricks, and no written language.

THE ARYANS AND THE VEDIC AGE (CA. 1500–500 B.C.E.)

What kind of society and culture did the Indo-European Aryans create?

After the decline of the Indus Valley civilization, a people who called themselves **Aryans** became dominant in north India. They were speakers of an early form of Sanskrit, which was an Indo-European language closely related to ancient Persian and more distantly related to Latin, Greek, Celtic, and their modern descendants, such as English. The Sanskrit *nava,* "ship," is related to the English word *naval; deva,* "god," to *divine; raja,* "ruler," to *regal;* and so on. The word *Aryan* itself comes from *Arya,* "noble" or "pure" in Sanskrit, and has the same root as *Iran* and *Ireland.*

Until relatively recently, the dominant theory was that the Aryans came into India from outside, perhaps as part of the same movements of people that led to the Hittites

Aryans *The dominant people in North India after the decline of the Indus Valley civilization; they spoke an early form of Sanskrit.*

• **Bronze Sword** A striking example of the quality of Aryan arms is this bronze sword, with its rib in the middle of the blade for strength. Superior weapons gave the Aryans military advantage. *(Courtesy of the Trustees of the British Museum)*

Rigveda *The earliest collection of hymns, ritual texts, and philosophical treatises, it is the central source of information on early Aryans.*

raja *From an ancient Indo-European word meaning "to rule," and related to the modern English "royal," raja refers to an Aryan tribal chieftain who led his people into battle and governed them during peacetime.*

Primary Source:
The *Rigveda*
Read how Indra, "the thunder-wielder," slew Vritra, "firstborn of dragons," and how Purusha created the universe through an act of ritual sacrifice.

occupying parts of Anatolia, the Achaeans entering Greece, and the Kassites conquering Sumer—all in the period from about 1900 to 1750 B.C.E. Some scholars, however, have proposed that the Indo-European languages spread to this area much earlier; to them it seems possible that the Harappan people were speakers of an early Indo-European language. If that was the case, the Aryans would be one of the groups descended from this early population.

Modern politics complicates analysis of the appearance of the Aryans and their role in India's history. It was Europeans in the eighteenth and nineteenth centuries who developed the concept of Indo-European languages, and they did so in an age both highly conscious of race and in the habit of identifying races with languages. The racist potential of the concept was fully exploited by the Nazis, with their glorification of the Aryans as a superior race. But even in less politicized contexts, the notion of a group of people who entered India from outside and made themselves its rulers is troubling to many. Does it mean that the non-Aryans are the true Indians? Or, to the contrary, does it add legitimacy to those who in later times conquered India from outside? Does it justify or undermine the caste system? One of the difficulties faced by scholars who wish to take a dispassionate view of these issues is that the evidence for the earlier Harappan culture is entirely archaeological and the evidence for the Aryans is almost entirely based on linguistic analysis of modern languages and orally transmitted texts of uncertain date.

The central source for the early Aryans is the **Rigveda,** the earliest of the Vedas, a collection of hymns, ritual texts, and philosophical treatises composed between 1500 and 500 B.C.E. in Sanskrit. Like Homer's epics in Greece, these texts were transmitted orally and are in verse. The *Rigveda* portrays the Aryans as warrior tribes who glorified military skill and heroism; loved to drink, hunt, race, and dance; and counted their wealth in cattle. The Aryans did not sweep across India in a quick campaign, nor were they a disciplined army led by one conqueror. Rather they were a collection of tribes who frequently fought with each other and only over the course of several centuries came to dominate north India.

Those the Aryans fought often lived in fortified towns and put up a strong defense against them. The key to the Aryans' success probably lay in their superior military technology: they had fast two-wheeled chariots, horses, and bronze swords and spears. Their epics, however, present the struggle in religious terms: their chiefs were godlike heroes, and their opponents irreligious savages who did not perform the proper sacrifices. In time, however, the Aryans clearly absorbed much from those they conquered.

At the head of each Aryan tribe was a chief, or **raja,** who led his followers in battle and ruled them in peacetime. The warriors in the tribe elected the chief for his military skills. Next in importance to the chief was the priest. In time, priests evolved into a distinct class possessing precise knowledge of the complex rituals and of the invocations and formulas that accompanied them, rather like the priest classes in ancient Egypt, Mesopotamia, and Persia. The warrior nobility rode into battle in chariots and perhaps on horseback; they met at assemblies to reach decisions and advise the raja. The common tribesmen tended herds and in time worked the land. To the conquered non-Aryans fell the drudgery of menial tasks. It is difficult to define precisely their social status. Though probably not slaves, they were certainly subordinate to the Aryans and worked for them in return for protection.

Over the course of several centuries, the Aryans pushed farther east into the valley of the Ganges River, at that time a land of thick jungle populated by aboriginal forest peoples. The tremendous challenge of clearing the jungle was made somewhat easier by the introduction of iron around 1000 B.C.E. Iron made it possible to produce strong axes and knives relatively cheaply.

The Aryans did not gain dominance over the entire Indian subcontinent. South of the Vindhya range, people speaking Dravidian languages maintained their control. In the great Aryan epics the *Ramayana* and *Mahabharata,* the people of the south and Sri

Lanka are spoken of as dark-skinned savages and demons who resisted the Aryans' conquests. Still, in time these epics became part of the common cultural heritage of all of India.

Early Indian Society (1000–500 B.C.E.)

As Aryan rulers came to dominate large settled populations, the style of political organization changed from tribal chieftainship to territorial kingship. In other words, the ruler controlled an area whose people might change, not a nomadic tribe that moved as a group. Moreover, kings no longer needed to be elected by the tribe; it was enough to be invested by priests and to perform the splendid royal ceremonies they designed. The priests, or **Brahmans,** supported the growth of royal power in return for royal confirmation of their own power and status. The Brahmans also served as advisers to the kings. In the face of this royal-priestly alliance, the old tribal assemblies of warriors withered away. By the time Persian armies reached the Indus around 513 B.C.E., there were sixteen major kingdoms in north India.

Early Aryan society had distinguished among the warrior elite, the priests, ordinary tribesmen, and conquered subjects. These distinctions gradually evolved into the **caste system.** Society was conceived in terms of four hierarchical strata whose members do not eat with or marry each other. These strata (called **varna**) are *Brahman* (priests), *Kshatriya* (warriors and officials), *Vaishya* (merchants and artisans), and *Shudra* (peasants and laborers). The lowest level probably evolved out of the efforts of the numerically outnumbered Aryans to maintain their dominance over their subjects and not be absorbed by them. The three upper varnas probably accounted for no more than 30 percent of the population. Social and religious attitudes entered into these distinctions as well. Aryans considered the work of artisans impure. They left all such work to the local people, who were probably superior to them in these arts anyway. Trade, by contrast, was not viewed as demeaning. Brahmanic texts of the period refer to trade as equal in value to farming, serving the king, or serving as a priest.

Those without places in this tidy social division—that is, those who entered it later than the others or who had lost their caste status through violations of ritual—were **outcastes.** That simply meant that they belonged to no caste. In time, some of these people became "untouchables," because they were "impure." They were scorned because they earned their living by performing such "polluting" jobs as slaughtering animals and dressing skins.

Slavery was a feature of early social life in India, as it was in Egypt, Mesopotamia, and elsewhere in antiquity. Those captured in battle often became slaves, but captives could also be ransomed by their families. Later, slavery was less connected with warfare and became more of an economic and social institution. As in ancient Mesopotamia, a free man might sell himself and his family into slavery because he could not pay his debts. And, as in Hammurabi's Mesopotamia, he could, if clever, hard-working, or fortunate, buy his and his family's way out of slavery. At birth, slave children automatically became the slaves of their parents' masters. Indian slaves could be bought, used as collateral, or given away.

Women's lives in early India varied according to their social status, much as men's did. Like most nomadic tribes, the Aryans were patrilineal and patriarchal (tracing descent through males and placing power over family members in the senior men of the family). Thus women in Aryan society probably had more subordinate roles than did women among local Dravidian groups, many of whom were matrilineal. But even in Aryan society, women were treated somewhat more favorably than in later Indian society. They were not yet given in child-marriage, and widows had the right to remarry. In the epics such as the *Ramayana,* women are often portrayed as forceful personalities, able to achieve their goals both by feminine ploys of cajoling men and by more direct action. (See the feature "Listening to the Past: Rama and Sita" on pages 50–51.)

Brahmans *Priests of the Aryans. They supported the growth of royal power in return for royal confirmation of their own religious rights, power, and status.*

caste system *The Indian system of dividing society into hereditary groups that limited interaction with each other, especially marriage to each other.*

varna *The four strata into which Indian society was divided under the caste system.*

outcastes *People not belonging to a caste; they were often scorned and sometimes deemed "untouchables."*

Brahmanism

The gods of the Aryans shared some features with the gods of other early Indo-European societies such as the Persians and Greeks. Some of them were great brawling figures, such as Agni, the god of fire; Indra, wielder of the thunderbolt and god of war, who each year slew a dragon to release the monsoon rains; and Rudra, the divine archer who spread disaster and disease by firing his arrows at people. Varuna, the god of order in the universe, was a hard god, quick to punish those who sinned and thus upset the balance of nature. Ushas, the goddess of dawn, was a gentle deity who welcomed the birds, gave delight to human beings, and warded off evil spirits.

The core of the Aryans' religion was its focus on sacrifice. By giving valued things to the gods, people strengthened them and established relationships with them. Gradually, under the priestly monopoly of the Brahmans, correct sacrifice and proper ritual became so important that most Brahmans believed that a properly performed ritual would force a god to grant a worshiper's wish.

The *Upanishads,* composed between 750 and 500 B.C.E., record speculations about the mystical meaning of sacrificial rites and about cosmological questions of man's relationship to the universe. They document a gradual shift from the mythical worldview of the early Vedic age to a deeply philosophical one. Associated with this shift was a movement toward *asceticism*—severe self-discipline and self-denial. In search of wisdom, some men retreated to the forests. These ascetics concluded that disciplined meditation on the ritual sacrifice could produce the same results as the physical ritual itself. Thus they reinterpreted ritual sacrifices as symbolic gestures with mystical meanings.

samsara *The transmigration of souls by a continual process of rebirth.*

karma *The tally of good and bad deeds that determines the status of an individual's next life.*

Ancient Indian cosmology focused not on a creator who made the universe out of nothing, but rather on endlessly repeating cycles. Key ideas were **samsara,** the transmigration of souls by a continual process of rebirth, and **karma,** the tally of good and bad deeds that determined the status of an individual's next life. Good deeds led to better future lives, evil deeds to worse future lives—even to reincarnation as an animal. Thus gradually arose the concept of a wheel of life that included human beings, animals, and even gods. Reward and punishment worked automatically; there was no all-knowing god who judged people and could be petitioned to forgive a sin, and each individual was responsible for his or her own destiny in a just and impartial world.

To most people, especially those on the low end of the economic and social scale, these ideas were attractive. By living righteously and doing good deeds, people could improve their lot in the next life. Yet there was another side to these ideas: the wheel of life could be seen as a treadmill, giving rise to a yearning for release from the relentless cycle of birth and death. One solution offered in the *Upanishads* was **moksha,** or release from the wheel of life. Brahmanic mystics claimed that life in the world was actually an illusion and that the only way to escape the wheel of life was to realize that ultimate reality was unchanging.

moksha *Release from the wheel of life.*

brahman *The unchanging, ultimate reality, according to the Upanishads.*

This unchanging, ultimate reality was called **brahman.** The multitude of things in the world is fleeting; the only true reality is brahman. Even the individual soul or self is ultimately the same substance as the universal brahman, in the same way that each spark is in substance the same as a large fire. Equating the individual self with the ultimate reality suggested that the apparent duality in the world is in some sense unreal. At the same time it conveyed that all people had in themselves an eternal truth that corresponded to an identical but greater all-encompassing reality.

The *Upanishads* gave the Brahmans a high status to which the poor and lowly could aspire in a future life. Consequently, the Brahmans greeted the concepts presented in these works and those who taught them with tolerance and understanding and made a place for them in traditional religious practice. The rulers of Indian society also encouraged the new trends, since the doctrines of samsara and karma encouraged the poor and oppressed to labor peacefully and dutifully. In other words, although the new doctrines were intellectually revolutionary, in social and political terms they supported the existing power structure.

INDIA'S GREAT RELIGIONS

What ideas and practices were taught by the founders of Jainism, Buddhism, and Hinduism?

By the sixth and fifth centuries B.C.E., cities had reappeared in India, and merchants and trade were thriving. Bricks were again baked in kilns and used to build ramparts around cities. One particular kingdom, Magadha, had become much more powerful than any of the other states in the Ganges plain, defeating its enemies by using war elephants and catapults for hurling stones. Written language had by this point reappeared.

This was a period of intellectual ferment throughout Eurasia—the period of the early Greek philosophers, the Hebrew prophets, Zoroaster in Persia, and Confucius and the early Daoists in China. In India it led to numerous sects that rejected various elements of Brahmanic teachings. (See the feature "Individuals in Society: Gosala.") The two most important in world-historical terms were Jainism and Buddhism. Their founders were contemporaries living in east India in minor states of the Ganges plain. Hinduism emerged in response to these new religions but at the same time was the most direct descendant of the old Brahmanic religion.

Jainism

The key figure of Jainism, Vardhamana Mahavira (fl. ca. 520 B.C.E.), was the son of the chief of a petty state. Like many ascetics of the period, he left home to become a wandering holy man. For twelve years, from ages thirty to forty-two, he traveled through the Ganges Valley until he found enlightenment and became a "completed soul." Mahavira taught his doctrines for about thirty years, founding a disciplined order of monks and gaining the support of many lay followers, male and female.

Mahavira accepted the doctrines of karma and rebirth but developed these ideas in new directions. He argued that human beings, animals, plants, and even inanimate objects all have living souls enmeshed in matter, accumulated through the workings of karma. Even a rock has a soul locked inside it, enchained by matter but capable of suffering if someone kicks it. The souls conceived by the Jains have finite dimensions. They float or sink depending on the amount of matter with which they are enmeshed. The ascetic, who willingly undertakes suffering, can dissipate some of the accumulated karma and make progress toward liberation. If a soul at last escapes from all the matter weighing it down, it becomes lighter than ordinary objects and floats to the top of the universe, where it remains forever in inactive bliss.

Mahavira's followers pursued such liberation by living ascetic lives and avoiding evil thoughts and actions. The Jains considered all life sacred and tried to live without

● **Jain Ascetic** The most extreme of Jain ascetics not only endured the elements without the help of clothes but were also generally indifferent to bodily comfort. The Jain saint depicted in this eighth-century cave temple has maintained his yogic posture for so long that vines have grown up around him. *(Courtesy, Robert Fisher)*

destroying other life. Some early Jains went to the extreme of starving themselves to death, since it is impossible to eat without destroying at least plants, but most took the less extreme step of distinguishing between different levels of life. The most sacred life forms were human beings, followed by animals, plants, and inanimate objects. A Jain who wished to avoid violence to life became a vegetarian and took pains not to kill any creature, even tiny insects in the air and soil. Farming was impossible for Jains, who tended instead to take up trade. Among the most conservative, priests practiced nudity, for clinging to clothes, even a loincloth, was a form of attachment. Lay Jains could pursue Jain teachings by practicing nonviolence and not eating meat. The Jains' radical nonviolence was motivated by a desire to escape the karmic consequences of causing harm to a life. In other words, violence had to be avoided above all because it harms the person who commits it.

For the first century after Mahavira's death, the Jains were a comparatively small and unimportant sect. Jainism began to flourish under the Mauryan dynasty (ca. 322–185 B.C.E.; see pages 44–46), and Jain tradition claims the Mauryan Empire's founder, Chandragupta, as a major patron. About 300 B.C.E. the Jain scriptures were recorded, and the religion split into two sects, one maintaining the tradition of total nudity, the other choosing to wear white robes on the grounds that clothes were an insignificant external sign, unrelated to true liberation. Over the next few centuries, Jain monks were particularly important in spreading northern culture into the Deccan and Tamil regions of south India.

Although Jainism never took hold as widely as Hinduism and Buddhism, it has been an influential strand in Indian thought and has several million adherents in India today. Fasting and nonviolence as spiritual practices in India owe much to Jain teachings. Mahatma Gandhi was influenced by these ideas through his mother, and Dr. Martin Luther King, Jr., was influenced by Gandhi.

Siddhartha Gautama and Buddhism

Siddhartha Gautama (fl. ca. 500 B.C.E.), also called Shakyamuni ("sage of the Shakya tribe"), is best known as the Buddha ("enlightened one"). He was a contemporary of Mahavira and came from the same social class (that is, warrior, not Brahman). He was born the son of a chief of one of the tribes in the Himalayan foothills in what is now Nepal. At age twenty-nine, unsatisfied with his life of comfort and troubled by the suffering he saw around him, he left home to become a wandering ascetic. He traveled south to the kingdom of Magadha, where he studied with yoga masters but later took up extreme asceticism. According to tradition, while meditating under a bo tree at Bodh Gaya, he reached enlightenment—that is, he gained perfect insight into the processes of the universe. After several weeks of meditation, he preached his first sermon, urging a "middle way" between asceticism and worldly life. For the next forty-five years, the Buddha traveled through the Ganges Valley, propounding his ideas, refuting his adversaries, and attracting followers. To reach as wide an audience as possible, the Buddha preached in the local language, Magadhi, rather than in Sanskrit, which was already becoming a priestly language. Probably because he refused to recognize the divine authority of the Vedas and dismissed sacrifices, he attracted followers mostly from among merchants, artisans, and farmers, rather than Brahmans.

In his first sermon, the Buddha outlined his main message, summed up in the **Four Noble Truths** and the **Eightfold Path.** The truths are as follows: (1) pain and suffering, frustration and anxiety, are ugly but inescapable parts of human life; (2) suffering and anxiety are caused by human desires and attachments; (3) people can understand these weaknesses and triumph over them; and (4) this triumph is made possible by following a simple code of conduct, the Eightfold Path. The basic insight of Buddhism is thus psychological. The deepest human longings can never be satisfied, and even those things that seem to give pleasure cause anxiety because we are afraid of losing them. Attachment to people and things causes sorrow at their loss.

Primary Source: Setting in Motion the Wheel of Law *Siddhartha's first sermon contains the core teaching of Buddhism: to escape, by following the Middle Path, the suffering caused by desire.*

Four Noble Truths *The Buddha's message that pain and suffering are inescapable parts of life; suffering and anxiety are caused by human desires and attachments; people can understand and triumph over these weaknesses; and the triumph is made possible by following a simple code of conduct.*

Eightfold Path *The code of conduct, set forth by the Buddha in his first sermon, which began with "right conduct" and eventually reached "right contemplation."*

Gosala

Texts that survive from early India are rich in religious and philosophical speculation and in tales of gods and heroes but not in history of the sort written by the early Chinese and Greeks. Because Indian writers and thinkers of antiquity had little interest in recording the actions of rulers or accounting for the rise and decline of different states, few people's lives are known in any detail.

Religious literature, however, does sometimes include details of the lives of followers and adversaries. The life of Gosala, for instance, is known primarily from early Buddhist and Jain scriptures. He was a contemporary of both Mahavira, the founder of the Jains, and Gautama, the Buddha, and both of them saw him as one of their most pernicious rivals.

According to the Jain account, Gosala was born in the north Indian kingdom of Magadha, the son of a professional mendicant. The name Gosala, which means "cowshed," alluded to the fact that he was born in a cowshed where his parents had taken refuge during the rainy season. The Buddhist account adds that he became a naked wandering ascetic when he fled from his enraged master after breaking an oil jar. As a mendicant, he soon fell in with Mahavira, who had recently commenced his life as an ascetic. After accompanying Mahavira on his travels for at least six years, Gosala came to feel that he was spiritually more advanced than his master and left to undertake the practice of austerities on his own. After he gained magical powers, he challenged his master and gathered his own disciples.

Both Jain and Buddhist sources agree that Gosala taught a form of fatalism that they saw as dangerously wrong. A Buddhist source says that he taught that people are good or bad not because of their own efforts but because of fate. "Just as a ball of string, when it is cast forth, will spread out just as far and no farther than it can unwind, so both fools and wise alike, wandering in transmigration exactly for the allotted term, shall then, and only then, make an end of pain."* Some people reach perfection, but not by their own efforts; rather they are individuals who through the course of numerous rebirths over hundreds of thousands of years have rid themselves of bad karma.

The Jains claimed that Gosala lived with a potter woman, violating the celibacy expected of ascetics and moreover teaching that sexual relations were not sinful. The followers of Gosala, a Buddhist source stated, wore no clothing and were very particular about the food they accepted, refusing food specially prepared

The Jain founder in seated meditation.
(Philadelphia Museum of Art: Acquired from the National Museum, New Delhi, India [by exchange] with funds contributed by Mr. and Mrs. Roland L. Taylor [1969-30-1])

for them, food in a cooking pan, and food from couples or women with children. Like other ascetics, Gosala's followers owned no property, carrying the principle further than the Jains, who allowed the possession of a food bowl. They made a bowl from the palms of their hands, giving them the name "hand lickers."

Jain sources report that after sixteen years of separation, Mahavira happened to come to the town where Gosala lived. When Gosala heard that Mahavira spoke contemptuously of him, he and his followers went to Mahavira's lodgings, and the two sides came to blows. Soon thereafter Gosala became unhinged, gave up all ascetic restraint and, after six months of singing, dancing, drinking, and other riotous living, died, though not before telling his disciples, the Jains report, that Mahavira was right. Doubt is cast on this version of his end by the fact that for centuries to come, Gosala's followers, called the Ajivikas, were an important sect in several parts of India. Ashoka honored them among other sects and dedicated some caves to them.

Questions for Analysis

1. How would Gosala's own followers have described his life? What sorts of distortions are likely in a life known primarily from the writings of rivals?

2. How would the early Indian economy have been affected by the presence of ascetic mendicants?

*A.F.R. Hoernle, "Ajivikas," in *Encyclopedia of Religion and Ethics,* vol. 1, ed. James Hastings (Edinburgh: T. & T. Clark, 1908), p. 262.

● **Gandharan Frieze** This carved stone (ca. 200 C.E.) portrays scenes from the life of the Buddha. The Buddha is seated below the Bodhi tree, where he was first enlightened. The soldiers and animals surrounding him are trying to distract him. Note the camel, elephant, horse, and monkey. *(Freer Gallery of Art, Smithsonian Institution, Washington, D.C., Purchase, F1949.9b)*

The Buddha offered an optimistic message, however, because all people can set out on the Eightfold Path toward liberation. All they have to do is take steps such as recognizing the universality of suffering, deciding to free themselves from it, and choosing "right conduct," "right speech," "right livelihood," and "right endeavor." For instance, they should abstain from taking life. The seventh step is "right awareness," constant contemplation of one's deeds and words, giving full thought to their importance and whether they lead to enlightenment. "Right contemplation," the last step, entails deep meditation on the impermanence of everything in the world. Those who achieve liberation are freed from the cycle of birth and death and enter the state called **nirvana,** a kind of blissful nothingness and freedom from reincarnation.

Although he accepted the Indian idea of reincarnation, the Buddha denied the integrity of the individual self or soul. He saw human beings as a collection of parts, physical and mental. As long as the parts remain combined, that combination can be called "I." When that combination changes, as at death, the various parts remain in existence, ready to become the building blocks of different combinations. According to Buddhist teaching, life is passed from person to person as a flame is passed from candle to candle.

nirvana *A state of blissful nothingness and freedom from reincarnation.*

Buddhism differed from Brahmanism and later Hinduism in that it ignored the caste system. Everyone, noble and peasant, educated and ignorant, male and female, could follow the Eightfold Path. Moreover, the Buddha was extraordinarily undogmatic. Convinced that each person must achieve enlightenment on his or her own, he emphasized that the path was important only because it led the traveler to enlightenment, not for its own sake. He compared it to a raft, essential to cross a river but useless once the traveler reached the far shore. There was no harm in honoring local gods or observing traditional ceremonies, as long as one remembered the goal of enlightenment and did not let sacrifices become snares or attachments.

Like Mahavira, the Buddha formed a circle of disciples, primarily men but including some women as well. He continually reminded them that each person must reach ultimate fulfillment by individual effort, but he also recognized the value of a group of people striving together for the same goal.

The Buddha's followers transmitted his teachings orally until they were written down in the second or first century B.C.E. These scriptures are called **sutras.** The form of monasticism that developed among the Buddhists was less strict than that of the Jains. Buddhist monks moved about for eight months of the year (except the rainy season), consuming only one meal a day obtained by begging, but they could bathe and wear clothes. Within a few centuries, Buddhist monks began to overlook the rule that they should travel. They set up permanent monasteries, generally on land donated by kings or other patrons. Orders of nuns also appeared, giving women the opportunity to seek truth in ways men had traditionally used. The main ritual that monks and nuns performed in their monastic establishments was the communal recitation of

sutras *The written teachings of the Buddha, first transcribed in the second or first century B.C.E.*

the sutras. Lay Buddhists could aid the spread of the Buddhist teachings by providing food for monks and support for their monasteries, and they could pursue their own spiritual progress by adopting practices such as abstaining from meat and alcohol.

Because there was no ecclesiastical authority like that developed by early Christian communities, early Buddhist communities developed several divergent traditions and came to stress different sutras. One of the most important of these, associated with the monk-philosopher Nagarjuna (fl. ca. 100 C.E.), is called **Mahayana,** or "Great Vehicle," because it is a more inclusive form of the religion. It drew on a set of discourses allegedly given by the Buddha and kept hidden by his followers for centuries. One branch of Mahayana taught that reality is empty (that is, nothing exists independently, of itself). Another branch held that ultimate reality is consciousness, that everything is produced by the mind.

Mahayana *The "Great Vehicle," a tradition of Buddhism that aspires to be more inclusive.*

Just as important as the metaphysical literature of Mahayana Buddhism was its devotional side, influenced by the religions then prevalent in Central Asia. The Buddha became deified and placed at the head of an expanding pantheon of other Buddhas and **bodhisattvas.** Bodhisattvas were Buddhas-to-be who had stayed in the world after enlightenment to help others on the path to salvation. These Buddhas and bodhisattvas became objects of veneration, especially the Buddha Amitabha and the bodhisattva Avalokitesvara. With the growth of Mahayana, Buddhism attracted more and more laypeople.

bodhisattvas *Buddhas-to-be who stayed in the world after enlightenment to help others on the path to salvation.*

Buddhism remained an important religion in India until about 1200 C.E. By that time, it had spread widely through East, Central, and Southeast Asia. After 1200 Buddhism declined in India, and the number of Buddhists in India today is small. In Sri Lanka and Nepal, however, Buddhism never lost its hold, and today it is also a major religion in Southeast Asia, Tibet, China, Korea, and Japan.

Hinduism

Both Buddhism and Jainism were direct challenges to the old Brahmanic religion. Both rejected animal sacrifice, which by then was a central element in Brahmanic power. Even more important, both religions tacitly rejected the caste system, accepting people of any caste into their ranks. In response to this challenge, over the next several centuries (ca. 400 B.C.E.–200 C.E.) the Brahmanic religion evolved in a more devotional direction, today commonly called Hinduism. In Hinduism Brahmans retained their high social status, but it became possible for individual worshipers to have more direct contact with the gods, showing their devotion to them without the aid of priests as intermediaries.

The bedrock of Hinduism is the belief that the Vedas are sacred revelations and that a specific caste system is implicitly prescribed in them. Hinduism is a guide to life, the goal of which is to reach union with brahman, the ground of all being. There are four steps in this search, progressing from study of the Vedas in youth to complete asceticism in old age. In their

● **Shiva**   One of the three most important Vedic gods, Shiva represented both destruction and procreation. Here Shiva, mounted on a bull and carrying a spear, attacks the demon Andhaka. Shiva is seen as a fierce and bloodthirsty warrior. *(C. M. Dixon/Ancient Art & Architecture Collection)*

dharma *The moral law that Hindus observe in their quest for brahman.*

quest for brahman, people are to observe **dharma,** the moral law. Dharma stipulates the legitimate pursuits of Hindus: material gain, as long as it is honestly and honorably achieved; pleasure and love, for the perpetuation of the family; and moksha, release from the wheel of life and unity with brahman. Because it recognizes the need for material gain and pleasure, Hinduism allows a joyful embracing of life.

Hinduism assumes that there are innumerable legitimate ways of worshiping the supreme principle of life. Consequently, it readily incorporates new sects, doctrines, beliefs, rites, and deities. After the third century B.C.E., Hinduism began to emphasize the roles and personalities of thousands of powerful gods. Brahma, the creator; Shiva, the cosmic dancer who both creates and destroys; and Vishnu, the preserver and sustainer of creation, are three main male deities. Female deities included Lakshmi, goddess of wealth, and Saraswati, goddess of learning and music. People could reach brahman by devotion to personal gods, usually represented by images. A worshiper's devotion to one god did not entail denial of other deities; ultimately all were manifestations of the divine force that pervades the universe.

A central ethical text of Hinduism is the *Bhagavad Gita,* a part of the world's longest ancient epic, the *Mahabharata.* The *Bhagavad Gita* offers guidance on the most serious problem facing a Hindu—how to live in the world and yet honor dharma and thus achieve release. The heart of the *Bhagavad Gita* is the spiritual conflict confronting Arjuna, a human hero about to ride into battle against his kinsmen. As he surveys the battlefield, struggling with the grim notion of killing his relatives, Arjuna voices his doubts to his charioteer, none other than the god Krishna. When at last Arjuna refuses to spill his family's blood, Krishna instructs him on the true meaning of Hinduism:

You grieve for those beyond grief,
and you speak words of insight;
but learned men do not grieve
for the dead or the living.

Never have I not existed,
nor you, nor these kings;
and never in the future
shall we cease to exist.

Just as the embodied self
enters childhood, youth, and old age,
so does it enter another body;
this does not confound a steadfast man.

Contacts with matter make us feel
heat and cold, pleasure and pain.
Arjuna, you must learn to endure
fleeting things—they come and go!

When these cannot torment a man,
when suffering and joy are equal
for him and he has courage,
he is fit for immortality.

Nothing of nonbeing comes to be,
nor does being cease to exist;
the boundary between these two
is seen by men who see reality.

Indestructible is the presence
that pervades all this;
no one can destroy
this unchanging reality.

Our bodies are known to end,
but the embodied self is enduring,
indestructible, and immeasurable;
therefore, Arjuna, fight the battle!

He who thinks this self a killer
and he who thinks it killed,
both fail to understand;
it does not kill, nor is it killed.

It is not born,
it does not die;
having been,
it will never not be;
unborn, enduring,
constant, and primordial,
it is not killed
when the body is killed.[1]

Krishna then clarifies the relationship between human reality and the eternal spirit. He explains compassionately to Arjuna the duty to act—to live in the world and carry out his duties as a warrior. Indeed, the *Bhagavad Gita* emphasizes the necessity of action, which is essential for the welfare of the world. Arjuna makes it the warrior's duty to wage war in compliance with his dharma. Only those who live within the divine law without complaint will be released from rebirth. One person's dharma may be different from another's, but both individuals must follow their own dharmas.

Besides providing a religion of enormous emotional appeal, Hinduism also inspired the preservation, in Sanskrit and the major regional languages of India, of literary masterpieces. Among these are the *Puranas,* which are stories of the gods and great warrior clans, and the *Mahabharata* and *Ramayana,* which are verse epics of India's early kings. Hinduism also validated the caste system, adding to the stability of everyday village life, since people all knew where they stood in society.

INDIA AND THE WEST (CA. 513–298 B.C.E.)

How did India respond to the expansion of the Persian and Greek empires?

In the late sixth century B.C.E., west India was swept up in events that were changing the face of the ancient Middle East. During this period the Persians were creating an empire that stretched from the west coast of Anatolia to the Indus River (see pages 20–22). India became involved in these events when the Persian emperor Darius conquered the Indus Valley and Kashmir about 513 B.C.E.

Persian control did not reach eastward beyond the Punjab. Even so, it fostered increased contact between India and the Middle East and led to the introduction of new ideas, techniques, and materials into India. From Persian administrators Indians learned more about how to rule large tracts of land and huge numbers of people. They also learned the technique of minting silver coins, and they adopted the Persian monetary standard to facilitate trade with other parts of the empire. Even states in the Ganges Valley, which were never part of the Persian Empire, adopted the use of coinage.

Another result of contact with Persia was introduction of the Aramaic script, used to write the official language of the Persian Empire. To keep records and publish proclamations just as the Persians did, Indians in northwest India adapted the Aramaic script for writing several local languages (elsewhere, Indians developed the Brahmi script, the ancestor of the script used for modern Hindi). In time the sacred texts of the Buddhists and the Jains, as well as the epics and other literary works, all came to be recorded.

The Persian Empire in turn succumbed to Alexander the Great, and in 326 B.C.E. Alexander led his Macedonian and Greek troops through the Khyber Pass into the Indus Valley (see page 89). The India that Alexander encountered was composed of many rival states. He defeated some of these states in the northwest and heard reports of others. Porus, king of west Punjab, fought Alexander with a battalion of two thousand war elephants. After being defeated, he agreed to become a subordinate king under Alexander.

Alexander had heard of the sophistication of Indian philosophers and summoned some to instruct him or debate with him. The Greeks were impressed with Taxila, a major center of trade in the Punjab (see Map 2.1), and described it as "a city great and prosperous, the biggest of those between the Indus River and the Hydaspes [the modern Jhelum River]—a region not inferior to Egypt in size, with especially good pastures and rich in fine fruits."[2] From Taxila, Alexander followed the Indus River south, hoping to find the end of the world. His men, however, mutinied and refused to continue. When Alexander turned back, he left his general Seleucus in charge of his easternmost region.

• • • • • • • • • • • • • • •

THE MAURYAN EMPIRE
(CA. 322–185 B.C.E.)

What were the consequences of the unification of much of India by Chandragupta and Ashoka?

The one to benefit most from Alexander's invasion was Chandragupta, the ruler of a growing state in the Ganges Valley. He took advantage of the crisis caused by Alexander's invasion to expand his territories, and by 322 B.C.E. he had made himself sole master of north India. In 304 B.C.E. he defeated the forces of Seleucus.

With stunning effectiveness, Chandragupta applied the lessons learned from Persian rule. He adopted the Persian practice of dividing the area into provinces. Each province was assigned a governor, usually drawn from Chandragupta's own family. He established a complex bureaucracy to see to the operation of the state and a bureaucratic taxation system that financed public services through taxes on agriculture. He also built a regular army, complete with departments for everything from naval matters to the collection of supplies.

From his capital at Pataliputra in the Ganges Valley (now Patna in Bihar), Chandragupta sent agents to the provinces to oversee the workings of government and to keep him informed of conditions in his realm. For the first time in Indian history, one man governed most of the subcontinent, exercising control through delegated power. In designing his bureaucratic system, Chandragupta enjoyed the able assistance of his great minister Kautilya, who wrote a treatise on how a king should seize, hold, and manipulate power, rather like the Legalist treatises produced in China later that century (see pages 70–71). Kautilya urged the king to use propaganda to gain support—for instance, to disguise secret agents to look like gods so that people would be awed when they saw him in their company. The king was also alerted to the fact that all his immediate neighbors were his enemies but the princes directly beyond them were his natural friends. When a neighboring prince was in trouble, that was the perfect time to attack him. Interstate relations were likened to the law of the fish: the large swallow the small.

Megasthenes, a Greek ambassador sent by Seleucus to Chandragupta's court, left a lively description of life there. He described the city as square and surrounded by wooden walls, twenty-two miles on each side, with 570 towers and 64 gates. It had a university, a library, and magnificent palaces, temples, gardens, and parks. The king personally presided over court sessions where legal cases were heard and petitions received. The king claimed for the state all mines and forests, and there were large state farms, granaries, shipyards, and spinning and weaving factories. Even prostitution was controlled by the state.

Megasthenes described Chandragupta as afraid of treachery and attempts at assassination:

Attendance on the king's person is the duty of women, who indeed are bought from their fathers. Outside the gates of the palace stand the bodyguards and the rest of the soldiers. . . . Nor does the king sleep during the day, and at night he is forced at various hours to change his bed because of those plotting against him. Of his non-military departures from the palace one is to the courts, in which he passes the day hearing cases to the end, even if the hour arrives for attendance on his person. . . . When he leaves to hunt, he is thickly surrounded by a circle of women, and on the outside by spear-carrying bodyguards. The road is fenced off with ropes, and to anyone who passes within the ropes as far as the women death is the penalty.[3]

Those measures apparently worked, as Chandragupta lived a long life. According to Jain tradition, Chandragupta became a Jain ascetic and died a peaceful death in 298 B.C.E. Although he personally adopted a nonviolent philosophy, he left behind a kingdom with the military might to maintain order and defend India from invasion.

The Reign of Ashoka (ca. 269–232 B.C.E.)

The years after Chandragupta's death were an epoch of political greatness, thanks largely to his grandson Ashoka, one of India's most remarkable figures. The era of Ashoka was enormously important in the religious history of the world, because Ashoka embraced Buddhism and promoted its spread beyond India.

As a young prince, Ashoka served as governor of two prosperous provinces where Buddhism flourished. At the death of his father about 274 B.C.E., Ashoka rebelled against his older brother, who had succeeded to the throne, and after four years of fighting won his bid for the throne. Crowned king, Ashoka ruled intelligently and energetically. He was equally serious about his pleasures, especially those of the banquet hall and harem.

In the ninth year of his reign, 261 B.C.E., Ashoka conquered Kalinga, on the east coast of India. In a grim and savage campaign, Ashoka reduced Kalinga by wholesale slaughter. As Ashoka himself admitted, "One hundred and fifty thousand were forcibly abducted from their homes, 100,000 were killed in battle, and many more died later on."[4] Instead of exulting like a conqueror, however, Ashoka was consumed with remorse and revulsion at the horror of war. He embraced Buddhism and used the machinery of his empire to spread Buddhist teachings throughout India. He supported the doctrine of not hurting humans or animals, then spreading among religious people of all sects. He banned animal sacrifices, and in place of hunting expeditions, he took pilgrimages. Two years after his conversion, he undertook a 256-day pilgrimage to all the holy sites of Buddhism, and on his return he sent missionaries to all known countries. Buddhist tradition also credits him with erecting eighty-four thousand stupas (Buddhist reliquary mounds) throughout India, among which the ashes or other bodily remains of the Buddha were distributed, beginning the association of Buddhism with monumental art and architecture.

Ashoka's remarkable crisis of conscience, like the later conversion to Christianity of the Roman emperor Constantine (see pages 126–127), affected the way he ruled. He emphasized compassion, nonviolence, and adherence to dharma. He appointed officials to oversee the moral welfare of the realm and required local officials to govern humanely. He may have perceived dharma as a kind of civic virtue, a universal ethical model capable of uniting the diverse peoples of his extensive empire. Ashoka erected stone pillars, on the Persian model, with inscriptions to inform the people of his policies. He also had long inscriptions carved into large rock surfaces near trade routes. In one inscription he spoke to his people like a father:

Whatever good I have done has indeed been accomplished for the progress and welfare of the world. By these shall grow virtues namely: proper support of mother and father, regard for preceptors and elders, proper treatment of Brahmans and ascetics, of the poor and the destitute, slaves and servants.[5]

These inscriptions are the earliest fully dated Indian texts. (Until the script in which they were written was deciphered in 1837, nothing was known of Ashoka's achievements.) The pillars on which they are inscribed are also the first examples of Indian art to survive since the end of the Indus civilization.

Ashoka felt the need to protect his new religion and to keep it pure. He warned Buddhist monks that he would not tolerate *schism*—divisions based on differences of opinion about doctrine or ritual. According to Buddhist tradition, a great council of Buddhist monks was held at Pataliputra, where the earliest canon of Buddhist texts was codified. At the same time, Ashoka honored India's other religions, even building

● **Ashokan Pillar** The best preserved of the pillars that King Ashoka erected in about 240 B.C.E. is this one in the Bihar region, near Nepal. The solid shaft of polished sandstone rises 32 feet in the air. It weighs about 50 tons, making its erection a remarkable feat of engineering. Like other Ashokan pillars, it is inscribed with accounts of Ashoka's political achievements and instructions to his subjects on proper behavior. These pillars are the earliest extant examples of Indian writing and a major historical source for the Mauryan period. *(Borromeo/ Art Resource, NY)*

shrines for Hindu and Jain worshipers. In one edict he banned rowdy popular fairs, allowing only religious gatherings.

Despite his devotion to Buddhism, Ashoka never neglected his duties as emperor. He tightened the central government of the empire and kept a close check on local officials. He also built roads and rest spots to improve communication within the realm. Ashoka himself described this work: "On the highways Banyan trees have been planted so that they may afford shade to men and animals; mango-groves have been planted; watering-places have been established for the benefit of animals and men."[6] These measures also facilitated the march of armies and the armed enforcement of Ashoka's authority.

Ashoka's inscriptions indirectly tell us much about the Mauryan Empire. He directly administered the central part of the empire, focusing on Magadha. Beyond it were four large provinces, under princes who served as viceroys, each with its own sets of smaller districts and officials. The interior of south India was described as inhabited by undefeated forest tribes. Farther south, along the coasts, were peoples that Ashoka maintained friendly relations with but did not rule, such as the Cholas and Pandyas. Relations with Sri Lanka were especially close under Ashoka, and the king sent a branch of the tree under which the Buddha gained enlightenment to the Sri Lankan king. According to Buddhist legend, Ashoka's son Mahinda traveled to Sri Lanka to convert the people there.

Ashoka ruled for thirty-seven years. After he died in about 232 B.C.E., the Mauryan dynasty went into decline, and India broke up into smaller units, much like those in existence before Alexander's invasion. Even though Chandragupta had instituted bureaucratic methods of centralized political control and Ashoka had vigorously pursued the political and cultural integration of the empire, the institutions they created were not entrenched enough to survive periods with weaker kings.

• • • • • • • • • • • • • • • • • • •

SMALL STATES AND TRADING NETWORKS (200 B.C.E.–300 C.E.)

How was India shaped by political disunity and contacts with other cultures?

After the Mauryan dynasty collapsed in 185 B.C.E., and for much of subsequent Indian history, political unity would be the exception rather than the rule. By this time, however, key elements of Indian culture—the caste system; the religious traditions of Hinduism, Buddhism, and Jainism; and the great epics and legends—had given India a cultural unity strong enough to endure even without political unity.

In the years after the fall of the Mauryan dynasty, a series of foreign powers dominated the Indus Valley and adjoining regions. The first were hybrid Indo-Greek states ruled by the inheritors of Alexander's defunct empire stationed in what is now Afghanistan. The city of Taxila became a major center of trade, culture, and education, fusing elements of Greek and Indian culture.

The great, slow movement of nomadic peoples out of East Asia that brought the Scythians to the Middle East brought the Shakas to northwest India. They controlled the region from about 94 to 20 B.C.E., when they were displaced by a new nomadic invader, the Kushans, who ruled the region of today's Afghanistan, Pakistan, and west India as far south as Gujarat. Their king Kanishka (r. ca. 78–ca. 103 C.E.) is known from Buddhist sources. The famous silk trade from China to Rome (see pages 140–141) passed through his territory.

During the Kushan period, Greek culture had a considerable impact on Indian art. Indo-Greek artists and sculptors working in India adorned Buddhist shrines, modeling the earliest representation of the Buddha on Hellenistic statues of Apollo.

Another contribution from the Indo-Greek states was coins cast with images of the king, which came to be widely adopted by Indian rulers, aiding commerce and adding evidence to the historical record. Cultural exchange also went in the other direction. Old Indian animal folktales were translated into Syriac and Greek and from that source eventually made their way to Europe. South India in this period was also the center of active seaborne trade, with networks reaching all the way to Rome. Indian sailing technology was highly advanced, and much of this trade was in the hands of Indian merchants. Roman traders based in Egypt followed the routes already used by Arab traders, sailing with the monsoon from the Red Sea to the west coast of India in about two weeks, returning about six months later when the direction of the winds reversed. In the first century C.E. a Greek merchant involved in this trade reported that the traders sold coins, topaz, coral, crude glass, copper, tin, and lead and bought pearls, ivory, silk (probably originally from China), jewels of many sorts (probably many from Southeast Asia), and above all cinnamon and pepper. More Roman gold coins of the first and second centuries C.E. have been found near the southern tip of India than in any other area. The local rulers had slits made across the image of the Roman emperor to show that his sovereignty was not recognized, but they had no objection to the coins' circulating. (By contrast, the Kushan rulers in the north had Roman coins melted down to use to make coins with their own images on them.)

Even after the fall of Rome, many of the traders on the southwest coast of India remained. These diasporic communities of Christians and Jews lived in the coastal cities into modern times. When Vasco da Gama, the Portuguese explorer, reached Calicut in 1498, he found a local Jewish merchant who was able to interpret for him.

During these centuries there were significant advances in science, mathematics, and philosophy. This was also the period when Indian law was codified. The **Code of Manu,** which lays down family, caste, and commercial law, was compiled in the second or third century C.E.

Regional cultures tend to flourish when there is no dominant unifying state. In south India the third century B.C.E. to the third century C.E. is considered the classical period of Tamil culture, when many great works of literature were written under the patronage of the regional kings. Some of the poems take a hard look at war:

● **Kushan Gold Coin**
Kanishka I had coins made depicting a standing Buddha with his right hand raised in a gesture of renunciation. The reverse side shows the king performing a sacrifice, the legend reading "Kanishka the Kushan, king of kings." *(Courtesy of the Trustees of the British Museum)*

Code of Manu *The codification of Indian law from the second or third century C.E.; it lays down family, caste, and commercial law.*

Harvest of War

*Great king
you shield your men from ruin,
so your victories, your greatness
are bywords.*

*Loose chariot wheels
lie about the battleground
with the long white tusks
of bull-elephants.*

*Flocks of male eagles
eat carrion
with their mates.*

*Headless bodies
dance about
before they fall
to the ground.*

*Blood glows,
like the sky before nightfall,
in the red center
of the battlefield.*

*Demons dance there.
And your kingdom
is an unfailing harvest
of victorious wars.*[7]

Primary Source:
The Laws of Manu
See how the principle of dharma justifies the traditional roles of men and women, and of priests, warriors, merchants, and servants in Hindu society.

Chapter Summary

Key Terms

Harappan
Aryans
Rigveda
raja
Brahmans
caste system
varna
outcastes
samsara
karma
moksha
brahman
Four Noble Truths
Eightfold Path
nirvana
sutras
Mahayana
bodhisattvas
dharma
Code of Manu

To assess your mastery of this chapter, go to
bedfordstmartins.com/mckayworld

• *What does archaeology tell us about the earliest civilization in India?*

From archaeology, we know that the Harappan civilization emerged in the Indus River valley in the third millennium B.C.E. The large cities that have been excavated were made of kiln-dried brick and were carefully planned, with straight streets and sewers. Although many intriguing artifacts have been excavated, many questions remain about this civilization, and its script has not been deciphered. Scholars can only speculate why Harappan cities were largely abandoned by 1800 B.C.E.

• *What kind of society and culture did the Indo-European Aryans create?*

From originally oral texts like the *Rigveda*, we know much about the values and social practices of the Aryans, speakers of an early form of Sanskrit (which is an Indo-European language). In the period 1500–500 B.C.E. Aryan warrior tribes fought using chariots and bronze swords and spears, gradually expanding into the Ganges River valley. The first stages of the Indian caste system date to this period, when warriors and priests were ranked above merchants, artisans, and farmers. Key religious ideas that date to this period are the notions of karma and rebirth and the importance of sacrifice.

• *What ideas and practices were taught by the founders of Jainism, Buddhism, and Hinduism?*

Beginning around 500 B.C.E. three of India's major religions emerged. Mahavira was the founder of the Jain religion. He taught his followers to live ascetic lives, avoid doing harm to any living thing, and renounce evil thoughts and actions. The founder of Buddhism, Siddhartha Gautama or the Buddha, similarly taught his followers a path to liberation that involved avoiding violence and freeing themselves from desires. The Buddha, however, did not think extreme asceticism was the best path and put more emphasis on mental detachment. In response to the popularity of Jainism and Buddhism, both of which rejected animal sacrifice and ignored the caste system, the traditional Brahmanic religion evolved in a devotional direction that has been called Hinduism. Hindu traditions validated sacrifice and caste but stressed the individual's relationship to the gods he or she worshiped.

• *How did India respond to the expansion of the Persian and Greek empires?*

In the sixth century B.C.E. the Persian empire expanded into the Indus River valley, and in the fourth century Alexander the Great's troops took the same region. From contact with the Persians and Greeks, new political techniques, ideas, and art styles entered the Indian repertoire.

• *What were the consequences of the unification of much of India by Chandragupta and Ashoka?*

Shortly after the arrival of the Greeks, much of north India was politically unified by the Mauryan Empire. Its greatest ruler was Ashoka, who converted to Buddhism and promoted its spread outside India. The inscriptions he had carved on stones and erected many places in his empire provide some of the best-dated sources on early Indian history.

• How was India shaped by political disunity and contacts with other cultures?

After the decline of the Mauryan empire, India was politically fragmented. Indian cultural identity remained strong, however, because of shared religious ideas and shared literature, including the great early epics. Trade and other contact with the outside world brought new elements into Indian civilization. And just as India came to absorb some Persian bureaucratic techniques and Greek artistic styles, other regions borrowed crops, textiles, inventions, and religious ideas from India.

Suggested Reading

Basham, A. L. *The Wonder That Was India,* 3d rev. ed. 1968. Classic, appreciative account of early Indian civilization by a scholar deeply immersed in Indian literature.

Embree, Ainslee, ed. *Sources of Indian Tradition,* 2d ed. 1988. An excellent introduction to Indian religion, philosophy, and intellectual history through translations of major sources.

Koller, John M. *The Indian Way,* 2d ed. 2004. An accessible introduction to the variety of Indian religions and philosophies.

Kulke, Hermann, and Dietmar Rothermund. *A History of India,* 3d ed. 1998. A good, balanced introduction to Indian history.

Lopez, Donald S., Jr. *The Story of the Buddha: A Concise Guide to Its History and Teachings.* 2001. Puts emphasis on Buddhist practice, drawing examples from many different countries and time periods.

Miller, Barbara, trans. *The Bhagavad-Gita: Krishna's Counsel in Time of War.* 1986. One of several excellent translations of India's classical literature.

Possehl, Gregory L. *The Indus Civilization.* 2002. Recent overview of Harappan civilization.

Renfew, Colin. *Archaeology and Language: The Puzzle of Indo-European Origins.* 1987. Analyzes the question of the origins of the Aryans in depth.

Scharff, Harmut. *The State in Indian Tradition.* 1989. A scholarly analysis of the period from the Aryans to the Muslims.

Thapar, Romilia. *Early India to 1300.* A freshly revised overview by a leading Indian historian.

Notes

1. Excerpt from Barbara Stoler Miller, trans., *The Bhagavad-gita: Krishna's Counsel in Time of War* (New York: Columbia University Press, 1986), pp. 31–32. Translation copyright © 1986 by Barbara Stoler Miller. Used by permission of Bantam Books, a division of Random House, Inc.
2. Arrian, *Anabasis* 5.8.2; Plutarch, *Alexander* 59.1. Translated by John Buckler.
3. *Strabo,* 15.1.55. Translated by John Buckler.
4. Quoted in H. Kulke and D. Rothermund, *A History of India,* 3d ed. (London: Routledge, 1998), p. 62.
5. Quoted in B. G. Gokhale, *Asoka Maurya* (New York: Twayne Publishers, 1966), p. 169.
6. Quoted ibid., pp. 168–169.
7. A. K. Ramanujan, ed. and trans., *Poems of Love and War: From the Eight Anthologies and the Ten Long Poems of Classical Tamil* (New York: Columbia University Press, 1985), p. 115. Copyright 1985 by Columbia University Press. Reproduced with permission of Columbia University Press in the format Textbook via Copyright Clearance Center.

Rama and Sita

The Ramayana, an epic poem of about fifty thousand verses, is attributed to the third-century B.C.E. poet Valmiki. Its main character, Rama, the oldest son of a king, is an incarnation of the great god Vishnu. As a young man, he wins the princess Sita as his wife when he alone among her suitors proves strong enough to bend a huge bow. Rama and Sita love each other deeply, but court intrigue disturbs their happy life. After the king announces that he will retire and consecrate Rama as his heir, the king's beautiful junior wife, wishing to advance her own son, reminds the king that he has promised her a favor of her choice. She then asks to have him appoint her son heir and to have Rama sent into the wilderness for fourteen years. The king is forced to consent, and Rama obeys his father.

The passage below gives the conversations between Rama and Sita after Rama learns he must leave. In subsequent parts of the very long epic, the lovers undergo many other tribulations, including Sita's abduction by the lord of the demons, the ten-headed Ravana, and her eventual recovery by Rama with the aid of monkeys.

The Ramayana *eventually appeared in numerous versions in all the major languages of India. Hearing it recited was said to bring religious merit. Sita, passionate in her devotion to her husband, has remained the favorite Indian heroine. Rama, Sita, and the monkey Hanuman are cult figures in Hinduism, with temples devoted to their worship.*

"For fourteen years I must live in Dandaka, while my father will appoint Bharata prince regent. I have come to see you before I leave for the desolate forest. You are never to boast of me in the presence of Bharata. Men in power cannot bear to hear others praised, and so you must never boast of my virtues in front of Bharata. . . . When I have gone to the forest where sages make their home, my precious, blameless wife, you must earnestly undertake vows and fasts. You must rise early and worship the gods according to custom and then pay homage to my father Dasaratha, lord of men. And my aged mother Kausalya, who is tormented by misery, deserves your respect as well, for she has subordinated all to righteousness. The rest

of my mothers, too, must always receive your homage. . . . My beloved, I am going to the great forest, and you must stay here. You must do as I tell you, my lovely, and not give offense to anyone."

So Rama spoke, and Sita, who always spoke kindly to her husband and deserved kindness from him, grew angry just because she loved him, and said, "My lord, a man's father, his mother, brother, son, or daughter-in-law all experience the effects of their own past deeds and suffer an individual fate. But a wife, and she alone, bull among men, must share her husband's fate. Therefore I, too, have been ordered to live in the forest. It is not her father or mother, not her son or friends or herself, but her husband, and he alone, who gives a woman permanent refuge in this world and after death. If you must leave this very day for the trackless forest, Rama, I will go in front of you, softening the thorns and sharp *kusa* grass. Cast out your anger and resentment, like so much water left after drinking one's fill. Do not be reluctant to take me, my mighty husband. There is no evil in me. The shadow of a husband's feet in any circumstances surpasses the finest mansions, an aerial chariot, or even flying through the sky. . . . O Rama, bestower of honor, you have the power to protect any other person in the forest. Why then not me? . . .

"If I were to be offered a place to live in heaven itself, Rama, tiger among men, I would refuse it if you were not there. I will go to the trackless forest teeming with deer, monkeys, and elephants, and live there as in my father's house, clinging to your feet alone, in strict self-discipline. I love no one else; my heart is so attached to you that were we to be parted I am resolved to die. Take me, oh please grant my request. I shall not be a burden to you." . . .

When Sita finished speaking, the righteous prince, who knew what was right and cherished it, attempted to dissuade her. . . .

"Sita, give up this notion of living in the forest. The name 'forest' is given only to wild regions where hardships abound. . . . There are lions that live in mountain caves; their roars are redoubled by mountain torrents and are a painful thing to hear—the forest is

Rama and Sita in the forest, from a set of miniature paintings done in about 1600. *(National Museum, New Delhi)*

a place of pain. At night worn with fatigue, one must sleep upon the ground on a bed of leaves, broken off of themselves—the forest is a place of utter pain. And one has to fast, Sita, to the limit of one's endurance, wear clothes of barkcloth and bear the burden of matted hair. . . . There are many creeping creatures, of every size and shape, my lovely, ranging aggressively over the ground. . . . Moths, scorpions, worms, gnats, and flies continually harass one, my frail Sita—the forest is wholly a place of pain. . . ."

Sita was overcome with sorrow when she heard what Rama said. With tears trickling down her face, she answered him in a faint voice. . . . "If from feelings of love I follow you, my pure-hearted husband, I shall have no sin to answer for, because my husband is my deity. My union with you is sacred and shall last even beyond death. . . . If you refuse to take me to the forest despite the sorrow that I feel, I shall have no recourse but to end my life by poison, fire, or water."

Though she pleaded with him in this and every other way to be allowed to go, great-armed Rama would not consent to taking her to the desolate forest. And when he told her as much, Sita fell to brooding, and drenched the ground, it seemed, with the hot tears that fell from her eyes. . . . She was nearly insensible with sorrow when Rama took her in his arms and comforted her. . . . "Without knowing your true feelings, my lovely, I could not consent to your living in the wilderness, though I am perfectly capable of protecting you. Since you are determined to live with me in the forest, Sita, I could no sooner abandon you than a self-respecting man his reputation. . . . My father keeps to the path of righteousness and truth, and I wish to act just as he instructs me. That is the eternal way of righteousness. Follow me, my timid one, be my companion in righteousness. Go now and bestow precious objects on the brahmans, give food to the mendicants and all who ask for it. Hurry, there is no time to waste."

Finding that her husband had acquiesced in her going, the lady was elated and set out at once to make the donations.

Questions for Analysis

1. What can you infer about early Indian family life and social relations from this story?

2. What do Sita's words and actions indicate about women's roles in Indian society of the time?

3. What do you think accounts for the continuing popularity of the story of Rama throughout Indian history?

Source: The Ramayana of Valmiki: An Epic of India, vol. 2: *Ayodhyakanda,* trans. Sheldon I. Pollock, ed. Robert P. Goldman (Princeton, N.J.: Princeton University Press, 1986), pp. 134–142, modified slightly. Copyright © 1986 by Princeton University Press. Reprinted by permission of Princeton University Press.

Bronze Vessel (twelfth century B.C.E.). About 10 inches
tall, this bronze is covered with symmetrical animal imagery,
including stylized *taotie* masks. *(The Metropolitan Museum of Art.
Purchase, Arthur M. Sackler Gift, 1974 [1974.268.2ab]. Photograph © 1979
The Metropolitan Museum of Art)*

3 CHINA'S CLASSICAL AGE, TO 256 B.C.E.

The early development of China's civilization occurred with little contact with the other early civilizations of Eurasia. The reason for China's relative isolation was geographic: communication with West and South Asia was very difficult, impeded by high mountains and vast deserts. Thus, in comparison to India and the ancient Middle East, there was less cross-fertilization through trade and other contact with other comparably advanced civilizations. Moreover, there were no cultural breaks comparable to the rise of the Aryans in India or the Assyrians in Mesopotamia; there were no new peoples bringing new languages.

The impact of early China's relative isolation is found in many distinctive or unique features of its culture. Perhaps the most important is its writing system. Unlike the other major societies of Eurasia, China retained a logographic writing system with a separate symbol for each word. This writing system shaped not only Chinese literature and thought but also key social and political processes, such as the nature of the ruling class and the way Chinese interacted with non-Chinese.

Chinese history is commonly discussed in terms of a succession of dynasties. The Shang Dynasty (ca. 1500–ca. 1050 B.C.E.) was the first to have writing, metalworking, cities, and chariots. The Shang kings played priestly roles, serving as intermediaries with both their royal ancestors and the high god Di. The Shang were overthrown by one of their vassal states, which founded the Zhou Dynasty (ca. 1050–256 B.C.E.). The Zhou rulers set up a decentralized feudal governmental structure. After several centuries, this structure evolved into a multistate system. As warfare between the states intensified from the sixth century B.C.E. on, social and cultural change also quickened. Aristocratic privileges declined, and China entered one of its most creative periods, when the philosophies of Confucianism, Daoism, and Legalism were developed.

THE EMERGENCE OF CIVILIZATION IN CHINA

When, where, and how did writing, bronze technology, and other elements of civilization develop in China?

The term *China,* like the term *India,* does not refer to the same geographical entity at all points in history. The historical China, also called China proper, was smaller than present-day China, not larger like the historical India. The contemporary People's Republic of China includes Tibet, Inner Mongolia, Turkestan, Manchuria, and other territories that in premodern times were not inhabited by Chinese or ruled directly by Chinese states (see Map 3.1).

China proper, about a thousand miles north to south and east to west, occupies much of the temperate zone of East Asia. The northern part, drained by the Huang (Yellow) River, is colder, flatter, and more arid than the south. Rainfall in many areas is less than twenty inches a year, making the land well suited to crops like wheat and millet. The dominant soil is **loess**—fine wind-driven earth that is fertile and easy to work even with primitive tools. Because so much of the loess ends up as silt in the Huang River, the riverbed rises and easily floods unless diked. Drought is another perennial problem for farmers in the north. The Yangzi River is the dominant feature of the warmer, wetter, and more lush south, a region well suited to rice cultivation and double cropping. The Yangzi and its many tributaries are navigable, so boats were traditionally the preferred means of transportation in the south.

Mountains, deserts, and grasslands separated China proper from other early civilizations. Between China and India lay Tibet, with its vast mountain ranges and high plateaus. North of Tibet are great expanses of desert where nothing grows except in rare oases, and north of the desert stretch grasslands from the Ukraine to eastern Siberia. Chinese civilization did not spread into any of these Inner Asian regions, above all because they were not suited to crop agriculture. Inner Asia, where raising animals is a more productive use of land than planting crops, became the heartland of China's traditional enemies, such as the Xiongnu and Mongols.

The Neolithic Age

From about 10,000 B.C.E. agriculture was practiced in China, apparently originating independently of somewhat earlier developments in Egypt and Mesopotamia, but perhaps influenced by developments in Southeast Asia, where rice was also cultivated very early. By 5000 B.C.E. there were Neolithic village settlements in several regions of China. The primary Neolithic crops were drought-resistant millet, grown in the loess soils of the north, and rice, grown in the wetlands of the lower reaches of the Yangzi River, where it was supplemented by fish. In both areas pigs, dogs, and cattle were domesticated, and by 3000 B.C.E. sheep had become important in the north and water buffalo in the south.

Over the course of the fifth to third millennia B.C.E., many distinct regional Neolithic cultures emerged. For instance, in the northwest during the fourth and third millennia B.C.E., people made fine red pottery vessels decorated in black pigment with bold designs, including spirals, sawtooth lines, and zoomorphic stick figures. At the same time in the east, pottery was rarely painted but was made into distinctive shapes, including three-legged, deep-bodied tripods. Jade ornaments, blades, and ritual objects, sometimes of extraordinary craftsmanship, have been found in several eastern sites but are rare in western ones.

loess *Soil deposited by wind. It is fertile and easy to work.*

● **Neolithic Jade Plaque** This small plaque (2.5 inches by 3.25 inches), dating from about 2000 B.C.E., is similar to others of the Liangzhu area near modern Shanghai. It is incised to depict a human figure who merges into a monster mask. The lower part could be interpreted as his arms and legs but at the same time resembles a monster mask with bulging eyes, prominent nostrils, and a large mouth. *(Zheijiang Provincial Institute of Archaeology/Cultural Relics Publishing House)*

Over time Neolithic cultures came to share more by way of material culture and social and cultural practices. Many practices related to treatment of the dead spread out of their original area, including use of coffins, ramped chambers, large numbers of grave goods, and divination based on interpreting cracks in cattle bones. Fortified walls, made of rammed earth, came to be built around settlements in many areas, suggesting not only increased contact but also increased conflict.

The Shang Dynasty (ca. 1500–ca. 1050 B.C.E.)

After 2000 B.C.E. a Bronze Age civilization appeared in north China with the traits found in Bronze Age civilizations elsewhere, such as writing, metalworking, domestication of the horse, class stratification, and cult centers. These findings can be linked to the Shang Dynasty, long known from early texts.

Shang civilization was not as densely urban as Mesopotamia, but Shang kings ruled from large settlements. The best excavated is **Anyang,** from which the Shang kings ruled for more than two centuries. At the center of Anyang were large palaces, temples, and altars. These buildings were constructed on rammed-earth foundations (a feature of Chinese building practice that would last for centuries). Outside the central core were industrial areas where bronzeworkers, potters, stone carvers, and other artisans lived and worked. Many homes were built partly below ground level, probably as a way to conserve heat. Beyond these urban settlements were farming areas and large forests. Deer, bears, tigers, wild boars, elephants, and rhinoceros were still plentiful in north China in this era.

The divinatory texts found in the royal tombs at Anyang show that Shang kings were military chieftains. The king regularly sent out armies of three thousand to five thousand men on campaigns, and when not at war they would go on hunts lasting for months. They fought rebellious vassals and foreign tribes, but the situation constantly changed as vassals became enemies and enemies accepted offers of alliance. War booty was an important source of the king's revenue, especially the war captives who could be made into slaves. Captives not needed as slaves might end up as sacrificial victims—or perhaps the demands of the gods and ancestors for sacrifices were a motive for going to war.

Bronze-tipped spears and halberds were widely used by Shang warriors. Bronze was also used for the fittings of the chariots that came into use around 1200 B.C.E., probably as a result of diffusion across Asia. The chariot provided commanders with a mobile station from which they could supervise their troops; it also gave archers and soldiers armed with long halberds increased mobility.

Shang power did not rest solely on military supremacy. The Shang king was also the high priest, the one best qualified to offer sacrifices to the royal ancestors and the high god Di. Royal ancestors were viewed as able to intervene with Di, send curses, produce dreams, assist the king in battle, and so on. The king divined his ancestors' wishes by interpreting the cracks made in heated cattle bones or tortoise shells prepared for him by professional diviners.

Chronology

ca. 1500–ca. 1050 B.C.E.	Shang Dynasty
ca. 1200 B.C.E.	Evidence of writing found in royal tombs
ca. 1050–256 B.C.E.	Zhou Dynasty
ca. 900	*Book of Songs, Book of Changes, Book of Documents*
771 B.C.E.	Zhou capital moved to Luoyang
551–479 B.C.E.	Confucius
ca. 500 B.C.E.	Iron technology in wide use
500–200 B.C.E.	Golden age of Chinese philosophy
453–403 B.C.E.	Sun Wu, *The Art of War*
ca. 450 B.C.E.	Mozi
ca. 370–ca. 300 B.C.E.	Mencius
369–286 B.C.E.	Zhuangzi
ca. 350 B.C.E.	Infantry armed with crossbows
ca. 310–ca. 215 B.C.E.	Xunzi
ca. 300–200 B.C.E.	*Laozi* written
ca. 280?–233 B.C.E.	Han Feizi of Legalist school

Anyang *One of the Shang Dynasty capitals.*

● **Royal Tomb at Anyang**
Eleven large tombs and more than a thousand small graves have been excavated at the royal burial ground at Anyang. This grave, about 60 feet deep and 300 feet long, would have taken thousands of laborers many months to complete. But even more wealth was expended to fill it with bronze, stone, pottery, jade, and textile grave goods. Human victims were also placed in it. (*Academia Sinica, Institute of History and Philology, Taiwan*)

Shang palaces were undoubtedly splendid but were constructed of perishable material like wood, and nothing of them remains today, unlike the stone buildings and monuments so characteristic of the ancient West. What has survived are the lavish underground tombs built for Shang kings and their consorts. They were filled with bronze vessels and weapons, jade and ivory ornaments, and often people, some of whom were sacrificed and others who chose to follow their lord in death. Human sacrifice did not occur only at funerals. Inscribed bones report sacrifices of war captives in the dozens and hundreds.

Shang society was marked by sharp status distinctions. The Shang royal family and aristocracy lived in large houses built on huge platforms of rammed earth. The king and other noble families had family and clan names transmitted along patrilineal lines, from father to son. Kingship similarly passed along patrilines, from elder to younger brother and father to son, but never to or through sisters or daughters. The kings and the aristocracy owned slaves, many of whom had been captured in war. In the urban centers there were substantial numbers of craftsmen who worked in stone, bone, and bronze.

Shang farmers were essentially serfs of the aristocrats. Their life was not that different from that of their Neolithic ancestors, and they worked the fields with similar stone tools. They usually lived in small, compact villages surrounded by fields. Some new crops became common in Shang times, most notably wheat, which had spread from West Asia.

● **Jade Figure** Among the valuables placed in royal Shang tombs were many jade objects, such as this figure, 2¾ inches tall. Since Neolithic times, jade has had the place in China occupied by gold in many other cultures: it is valued for its beauty, rarity, and endurance. This figure was one of seven hundred jade pieces in the tomb of Lady Hao. (*Institute of Archaeology, Beijing/DNP Archives*)

Writing The survival of divination texts inscribed on bones from Shang tombs demonstrates that writing was already a major element in Chinese culture by 1200 B.C.E. Writing must have been developed earlier, but the early stages cannot be traced, probably because writing was done on wood, bamboo, silk, or other perishable materials.

Once writing was invented, it had profound effects on China's culture and government. A written language made possible a bureaucracy capable of keeping records and conducting correspondence with commanders and governors far from the palace. Hence literacy became the ally of royal rule, facilitating communication with and effective control over the realm. Literacy also preserved the learning, lore, and experience of early Chinese society and facilitated the development of abstract thought.

Like ancient Egyptian and Sumerian, the Chinese script was **logographic:** each word was represented by a single symbol. In the Chinese case, some of these symbols were pictures, but for the names of abstract concepts other methods were adopted. Sometimes the symbol for a different word was borrowed because the two words were pronounced alike. Sometimes two different symbols were combined; for instance, to represent different types of trees, the symbol for *tree* could be combined with another symbol borrowed for its pronunciation (see Figure 3.1).

logographic *A language in which each word is represented by a single symbol, such as the Chinese script.*

In western Eurasia logographic scripts were eventually modified or replaced by phonetic scripts, but that never happened in China (although, because of changes in the spoken language, today many words are represented by two or three characters rather than a single one). Because China retained its logographic writing system, many years were required to gain full mastery of reading and writing, which added to the prestige of education.

Why did China retain a logographic writing system even after encounters with phonetic ones? Although phonetic systems have many real advantages, especially with

MAP 3.1 **China Under the Shang and Zhou Dynasties** Chinese civilization developed in the temperate regions drained by the Huang (Yellow) and Yangzi Rivers. The early Zhou government controlled larger areas than the Shang did, but the independent states of the Warring States Period were more aggressive about pushing out their frontiers, greatly extending the geographical boundaries of Chinese civilization.

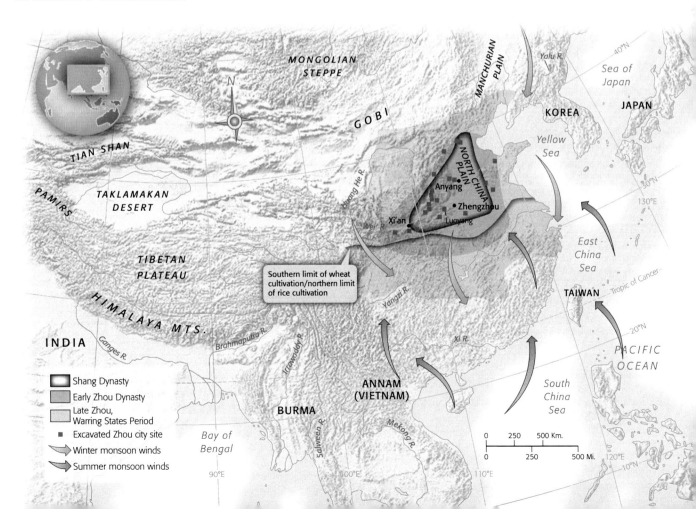

WORD	ox	goat, sheep	tree	moon	earth	water	to show, declare	then (men and bowl)	heaven	to pray
SHANG SYMBOL										
MODERN CHARACTER	牛	羊	木	月	土	水	示	就	天	祝

● FIGURE 3.1 **The Origins of Chinese Writing** The modern Chinese writing system (bottom row) evolved from the script employed by diviners in the Shang period (upper row). *(Source: Adapted from Patricia Buckley Ebrey,* The Cambridge Illustrated History of China *[Cambridge: Cambridge University Press, 1996], p. 26. Reprinted by permission of Cambridge University Press.)*

respect to ease of learning to read, there are some costs to dropping a logographic system. Those who learned to read Chinese could communicate with a wider range of people than those who read scripts based on speech. Since characters did not change when the pronunciation changed, educated Chinese could read texts written centuries earlier without the need for them to be translated. Moreover, as the Chinese language developed regional variants, readers of Chinese could read books and letters by contemporaries whose oral language they could not comprehend. Thus the Chinese script played a large role in holding China together and fostering a sense of connection with the past. In addition, many of China's neighbors (Japan, Korea, and Vietnam, in particular) adopted the Chinese script, allowing communication through writing between people whose languages were totally unrelated. In this regard, the Chinese language was like Arabic numerals, which have the same meaning however they are pronounced.

Bronzes As in Egypt, Mesopotamia, and India, the development of more complex forms of social organization in Shang China coincided with the mastery of metalworking, specifically bronze. Bronze, in Shang times, was used more for ritual than for war. Most surviving Shang bronze objects are vessels such as cups, goblets, steamers, and cauldrons that would have originally been used during sacrificial ceremonies. They were beautifully formed in a great variety of shapes and sizes. Complex designs were achieved through mold casting and prefabrication of parts. For instance, legs, handles, and other protruding members were cast first, before the body was cast onto them.

The decoration on Shang bronzes seems to say something interesting about Shang culture, but scholars do not agree about what it says. In the art of ancient Egypt, Assyria, and Babylonia, representations of agriculture (domesticated plants and animals) and of social hierarchy (kings, priests, scribes, and slaves) are very common, matching our understandings of the social, political, and economic development of those societies. In Shang China, by contrast, images of wild animals predominate. Some animal images readily suggest possible meanings. Jade cicadas were sometimes found in the mouths of the dead, and images of cicadas on bronzes are easy to interpret as images evocative of rebirth in the realm of ancestral spirits, as cicadas spend years underground before emerging. Birds, similarly, suggest to many the idea of messengers that can communicate with other realms,

Table 3.1 Pronouncing Chinese Words

LETTER	PHONETIC EQUIVALENT IN CHINESE
Phonetic equivalents for the vowels and especially perplexing consonants are given here.	
a	ah
e	uh
i	ee; except after *z*, *c*, and *ch*, when the sound is closer to *i* in *it*
u	oo; as in English *food*
c	ts (*ch*, however, is like English *ch*)
q	ch
z	dz
zh	j
x	sh

especially realms in the sky. More problematic is the most common image, the stylized animal face called the **taotie.** To some it is a monster—a fearsome image that would scare away evil forces. Others imagine a dragon—an animal whose vast powers had more positive associations. Some hypothesize that it reflects masks used in rituals. Others associate it with animal sacrifices, totemism, or shamanism. Still others see these images as hardly more than designs. Without new evidence, scholars can only speculate.

Bronze technology spread beyond Shang territories into areas the Shang would have considered enemy lands. In 1986, in the western province of Sichuan, discovery was made of a bronze-producing culture contemporaneous with the late Shang but very different from it. This culture did not practice human sacrifice, but two sacrificial pits contained the burned remains of elephant tusks and a wide range of gold, bronze, jade, and stone objects. Among them were a life-size statue and many life-size bronze heads, all with angular facial features and enormous eyes. No human sacrifices were found, leading some scholars to speculate that the masks were used to top wood or clay statues buried in place of humans in a sacrificial ceremony. Archaeologists are continuing to excavate in this region, and new discoveries may provide fuller understanding of the religion of the people who lived there.

● **Inscribed Pan** This bronze vessel, dating to before 900 B.C.E., was one of 103 vessels discovered in 1975 by farmers clearing a field. The inscription tells the story of the first six Zhou kings and of the family of scribes who served them. It was cast by Scribe Qiang. *(Zhou Yuan Administrative Office of Cultural Relics, Fufeng, Shaanxi Province)*

taotie *A common image in Chinese bronzes; it is a stylized animal face.*

THE EARLY ZHOU DYNASTY (CA. 1050–500 B.C.E.)

How was China governed in the period looked back on as its golden age?

The Shang campaigned constantly against enemies. To the west were the fierce Qiang, considered barbarian tribesmen by the Shang and perhaps speaking an early form of Tibetan. Between the Shang capital and the Qiang was a frontier state called Zhou, which seems to have both inherited cultural traditions from the Neolithic cultures of the northwest and absorbed most of the material culture of the Shang. In about 1050 B.C.E., the Zhou rose against the Shang and defeated them in battle.

> **Primary Source:**
> **The Book of Documents**
> *Discover how rulers gain or lose the right to rule, an authority known as the* Mandate of Heaven.

Zhou Politics

The early Zhou period is the first one for which transmitted texts exist in some abundance. The **Book of Documents** describes the Zhou conquest of the Shang as the victory of just and noble warriors over decadent courtiers who were led by a dissolute, sadistic king. At the same time, these documents show that the Zhou recognized the Shang as occupying the center of the world, were eager to succeed to that role themselves, and saw history as a major way to legitimate power. The three early Zhou rulers who are given the most praise are King Wen (the "cultured" or "literate" king), who expanded the Zhou domain; his son King Wu (the "martial" king), who conquered the Shang; and Wu's brother, the Duke of Zhou, who consolidated the conquest and served as loyal regent for Wu's heir.

Book of Documents *One of the earliest of the "Confucian" classics, containing documents, speeches, and historical accounts.*

Like the Shang kings, the Zhou kings sacrificed to their ancestors, but they also sacrificed to Heaven. The *Book of Documents* assumes a close relationship between Heaven and the king, who was called the Son of Heaven. Heaven gives the king a mandate to rule only as long as he rules in the interests of the people. Thus it was because the last king of the Shang had been decadent and cruel that Heaven took the mandate away from him and entrusted it to the virtuous Zhou kings. Because this theory of the **Mandate of Heaven** does not seem to have had any place in Shang cosmology, it may have been elaborated by the early Zhou rulers as a kind of propaganda to win over the conquered subjects of the Shang. Whatever its origins, it remained a central feature of Chinese political ideology from the early Zhou period on.

Rather than attempt to rule all their territories directly, the early Zhou rulers set up a decentralized feudal system. They sent out relatives and trusted subordinates with troops to establish walled garrisons in the conquered territories. Such a vassal was generally able to pass his position on to a son, so that in time the domains became hereditary fiefs. By 800 B.C.E. there were about two hundred lords with domains large and small. Each lord appointed officers to serve him in ritual, administrative, or military capacities. These posts and their associated titles tended to become hereditary as well.

The decentralized rule of the early Zhou period had from the beginning carried within it the danger that the regional lords would become so powerful that they would no longer obey the commands of the king. As generations passed and ties of loyalty and kinship grew more distant, this indeed happened. In 771 B.C.E. the Zhou king was killed by an alliance of Rong tribesmen and Zhou vassals. One of his sons was put on the throne, and then for safety's sake the capital was moved east out of the Wei River valley to modern Luoyang, just south of the Huang River in the heart of the central plains (see Map 3.1).

The revived Zhou Dynasty never fully regained control over its vassals, and China entered a prolonged period without a strong central authority. For a couple of centuries a code of chivalrous or sportsmanlike conduct still regulated warfare between the states: one state would not attack another while it was in mourning for its ruler; during battles one side would not attack before the other side had time to line up; ruling houses were not wiped out, so that successors could continue to sacrifice to their ancestors; and so on. Thereafter, however, such niceties were abandoned, and China entered a period of nearly constant conflict.

Mandate of Heaven *The theory that Heaven gives the king a mandate to rule only as long as he rules in the interests of the people.*

Zhou Society

During the Zhou Dynasty, Chinese society underwent radical changes. Early Zhou rule was highly aristocratic. Inherited ranks placed people in a hierarchy ranging downward from the king to the rulers of states with titles like duke and marquis, the hereditary great officials of the states, the lower ranks of the aristocracy (men who could serve in either military or civil capacities, known as **shi**), and finally to the ordinary people (farmers, craftsmen, and traders). Patrilineal family ties were very important in this society, and at the upper reaches, at least, sacrifices to ancestors were one of the key rituals used to forge social ties.

Glimpses of what life was like at various social levels in the early Zhou Dynasty can be found in the *Book of Songs,* which contains the earliest Chinese poetry. Some of the songs are hymns used in court religious ceremonies, such as offerings to ancestors. Others clearly had their origins in folk songs. Some of these folk songs depict farmers at work clearing fields, plowing and planting, gathering mulberry leaves for silkworms, and spinning and weaving. Farming life involved not merely the cultivation of crops like millet, hemp (for cloth), beans, and vegetables, but also hunting small animals and collecting grasses and rushes to make rope and baskets.

Many of the folk songs are love songs that depict a more informal pattern of courtship than prevailed in later China. One stanza reads:

shi *The lower ranks of Chinese aristocracy; these men could serve in either military or civil capacities.*

Book of Songs *The earliest collection of Chinese poetry; it provides glimpses of what life was like in the early Zhou Dynasty.*

Please, Zhongzi,
Do not leap over our wall,
Do not break our mulberry trees.
It's not that I begrudge the mulberries,
But I fear my brothers.
You I would embrace,
But my brothers' words—those I dread.[1]

There were also songs of complaint, such as this one in which the ancestors are rebuked for failing to aid their descendants:

The drought has become so severe
That it cannot be stopped.
Glowing and burning,
We have no place.
The great mandate is about at an end.
Nothing to look forward to or back upon.
The host of dukes and past rulers
Does not help us.
As for father and mother and the ancestors,
How can they bear to treat us so?[2]

Other songs in this collection are court odes that reveal attitudes of the aristocrats. One such ode expresses a deep distrust of women's involvement in politics:

Clever men build cities,
Clever women topple them.
Beautiful, these clever women may be
But they are owls and kites.
Women have long tongues
That lead to ruin.
Disorder does not come down from heaven;
It is produced by women.[3]

● **Bronze Relief of Hunters**   Hunting provided an important source of food in the Zhou period, and hunters were often depicted on inlaid bronzes of the period. *(The Avery Brundage Collection/Laurie Platt Winfrey, Inc.)*

Part of the reason for distrust of women in politics was the practice of concubinage. Rulers regularly demonstrated their power and wealth by accumulating large numbers of concubines and thus would have children by several women. In theory, succession went to the eldest son of the wife, then to younger sons by her, and only in their absence to sons of concubines; but in actual practice, the ruler of a state or the head of a powerful ministerial family could select a son of a concubine to be his heir if he wished. This led to much scheming for favor among the various sons and their mothers and the common perception that women were incapable of taking a disinterested view of the larger good.

● ● ● ● ● ● ● ● ● ● ● ● ● ● ●

THE WARRING STATES PERIOD (500–221 B.C.E.)

What were the consequences of the breakup of Zhou unity and the rise of independent states?

Warring States Period *The period of Chinese history between 403 and 221 B.C.E. when states fought each other and one after another was destroyed until only one remained.*

crossbow *A powerful, mechanical bow developed during the Warring States Period.*

Social and economic change quickened after 500 B.C.E. Cities began appearing all over north China. Thick earthen walls were built around the palaces and ancestral temples of the ruler and other aristocrats, and often an outer wall was added to protect the artisans, merchants, and farmers who lived outside the inner wall. Accounts of sieges launched against these walled citadels, with scenes of the scaling of walls and the storming of gates, are central to descriptions of military confrontations in this period.

The old aristocratic social structure of the Zhou was being undermined by advances in military technology. Large, well-drilled infantry armies became a potent military force in the **Warring States Period,** able to withstand and defeat chariot-led forces. By 300 B.C.E. states were sending out armies of a couple hundred thousand drafted foot soldiers, usually accompanied by horsemen. Adding to the effectiveness of armies of drafted foot soldiers was the development of the **crossbow** around 350 B.C.E. The trigger of a crossbow was an intricate bronze mechanism that allowed a foot soldier to shoot farther than could a horseman carrying a light bow. One text of the period reports that a skilled soldier with a powerful crossbow and a sharp sword was the match of a hundred ordinary men. To defend against crossbows, soldiers began wearing armor and helmets. Most of the armor was made of leader strips tied with cords. Helmets were sometimes made of iron.

The introduction of cavalry in this period also reduced the need for a chariot-riding aristocracy. Shooting bows and arrows from horseback was first perfected by non-Chinese peoples to the north of China proper, who at that time were making the transition to a nomadic pastoral economy. The northern state of Jin, to defend itself from the attacks of these horsemen, developed its own cavalry armies. Once it started using cavalry against other Chinese states, they too had to master the new technology. From this time on, acquiring and pasturing horses was a key component of military preparedness.

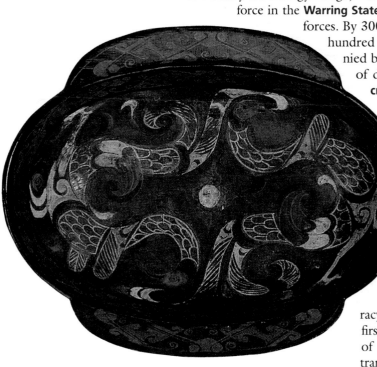

● **Lacquer Cup** This 6-inch-long lacquer cup, decorated with images of two intertwined birds, was one of many lacquered eating vessels found in a third-century B.C.E. tomb. Lacquer is made from the sap of a tree native to China. It is remarkably light, strong, smooth, and waterproof. Lacquered dishes, cups, boxes, musical instruments, and sculptures became highly sought-after luxury items. *(Jingzhou Prefecture Museum/© Cultural Relics Publishing House)*

● **Bells of the Marquis of Zeng** Music played a central role in court life in ancient China. The tomb of a minor ruler who died about 400 B.C.E. contained 124 musical instruments, including drums, flutes, mouth organs, pan pipes, zithers, a set of 32 chime stones, and this 64-piece bell set. The bells bear inscriptions that name the two tones each bell could make, depending on where it was struck. Five men, using poles and mallets and standing on either side of the set of bells, would have played the bells by hitting them from outside. (© *Cultural Relics Publishing House*)

Because these developments made commoners and craftsmen central to military success, rulers tried to find ways to increase their populations. To increase agricultural output, they brought new land into cultivation, drained marshes, and dug irrigation channels. Rulers began surveying their land and taxing farmers. They wanted to undermine the power of lords over their subjects in order to get direct access to the peasants' labor power. Serfdom thus gradually declined. Registering populations led to the extension of family names to commoners at an earlier date than anywhere else in the world.

To encourage trade, rulers began casting coins. The development of iron technology in the early Zhou Dynasty also promoted economic expansion. By the fifth century B.C.E. iron was being widely used for both farm tools and weapons. By the third century B.C.E. the largest smelters employed two hundred or more workmen. A new powerful group also emerged in society—the rich who had acquired their wealth through trade or industry rather than inheritance or political favor. Late Zhou texts frequently mention cross-regional trade in objects such as furs, copper, dyes, hemp, salt, and horses.

Social mobility increased in this period. Rulers more often sent out their own officials rather than delegate authority to hereditary lesser lords. This trend toward centralized bureaucratic control created opportunities for social advancement for the shi on the lower end of the old aristocracy. Competition among such men guaranteed rulers a ready supply of able and willing subordinates, and competition among rulers for talent meant that ambitious men could be selective in deciding where to offer their services. (See the feature "Individuals in Society: Guan Zhong.")

The development of infantry armies also created the need for a new type of general, and rulers became less willing to let men lead troops merely because of aristocratic birth. Treatises on the art of war described the ideal general as a master of maneuver, illusion, and deception. In *The Art of War,* Master Sun argued that heroism is a useless virtue that leads to needless deaths. But discipline is essential, and he insisted that the entire army had to be trained to follow the orders of its commanders without questioning them.

States on the periphery that had been considered barbarian or semibarbarian during the early Zhou were gradually brought into the cultural sphere of the Central States, as the core region of China was called. For instance, the southern state of Chu expanded rapidly in the Yangzi Valley, defeating and absorbing fifty or more small states as it extended its reach north to the heartland of Zhou and east to absorb the old states of Wu and Yue. By the late Zhou period, Chu was on the forefront of cultural innovation and produced the greatest literary masterpiece of the era, the *Songs of Chu,* a collection of fantastical poems full of images of elusive deities and shamans who can fly through the spirit world.

By the third century B.C.E. there were only seven important states remaining. These states were much more centralized than their early Zhou predecessors. The kings of these states had eliminated indirect control through vassals and in its place dispatched royal officials to remote cities, controlling them from a distance through the transmission of documents and dismissing them at will.

CONFUCIUS AND HIS FOLLOWERS

What ideas did Confucius teach, and how were they a response to his times?

The Warring States Period was the era when the "Hundred Schools of Thought" contended. During the same period in which Indian sages and mystics were developing religious speculation about karma, souls, and eons of time, Chinese thinkers were arguing about the ideal forms of social and political organization and man's connections to nature.

Confucius (traditional dates: 551–479 B.C.E.) was one of the first men of ideas. As a young man, Confucius served in the court of his home state of Lu without gaining much influence. After leaving Lu, he set out with a small band of students and wandered through neighboring states in search of a ruler who would take his advice.

Confucius's ideas are known to us primarily through the sayings recorded by his disciples in the *Analects*. The thrust of his thought was ethical rather than theoretical or metaphysical. He talked repeatedly of an ideal age in the early Zhou Dynasty when everyone was devoted to fulfilling his or her role: superiors looked after those dependent on them; inferiors devoted themselves to the service of their superiors; parents and children, husbands and wives, all wholeheartedly embraced what was expected of them.

Confucius considered the family the basic unit of society. He extolled **filial piety**, which to him meant more than just reverent obedience of children to their parents:

The Master said, "You can be of service to your father and mother by remonstrating with them tactfully. If you perceive that they do not wish to follow your advice, then continue to be reverent toward them without offending or disobeying them; work hard and do not murmur against them."[4]

The relationship between father and son was one of the five cardinal relationships stressed by Confucius. The others were between ruler and subject, husband and wife, elder and younger brother, and friend and friend. Mutual obligations of a hierarchical sort underlay the first four of these relationships: the senior leads and protects; the junior supports and obeys. The exception was the relationship between friends, which was conceived in terms of mutual obligations between equals.

A man of moderation, Confucius was an earnest advocate of gentlemanly conduct. He redefined the term *gentleman* (*junzi*) to mean a man of moral cultivation rather than a man of noble birth. He repeatedly urged his followers to aspire to be gentlemen rather than petty men intent on personal gain. The gentleman, he said, "feels bad when his capabilities fall short of the task. He does not feel bad when people fail to recognize him."[5] Confucius did not advocate social equality, but his teachings minimized the importance of class distinctions and opened the way for intelligent and talented people to rise in the social scale. The Confucian gentleman found his calling in service to the ruler. Loyal advisers should encourage their rulers to govern through ritual, virtue, and concern for the welfare of their subjects, and much of the *Analects* concerns the way to govern well.

To Confucius the ultimate virtue was humanity (**ren**). A person of humanity cares about others and acts accordingly:

Zhonggong asked about humanity. The Master said, "When you go out, treat everyone as if you were welcoming a great guest. Employ people as though you were conducting a great

filial piety *Reverent attitude of children to their parents; it was extolled by Confucius.*

ren *The ultimate Confucian virtue; it is translated as perfect goodness, benevolence, humanity, human-heartedness, and nobility.*

Guan Zhong

The inlaid decoration on bronze vessels of the Warring States Period often shows people engaged in warfare, hunting, preparing food, performing rituals, and making music. (From E. Consten, Das alte China)

By the time of Confucius, the success of states was often credited more to the lord's astute advisers than to the lord himself. To Confucius, the most praiseworthy political adviser was Guan Zhong (ca. 720–645 B.C.E.), the genius behind the rise of the state of Qi, in eastern China.

The earliest historical sources to recount Guan Zhong's accomplishments are the "commentaries" compiled in the Warring States Period to elaborate on the dry chronicle known as the *Spring and Autumn Annals.* The *Zuo Commentary,* for instance, tells us that in the year 660 B.C.E. Guan Zhong advised Duke Huan to aid the small state of Xing, then under attack by the non-Chinese Rong tribes: "The Rong and the Di are wolves who cannot be satiated. The Xia (Chinese) states are kin who should not be abandoned." In 652 B.C.E., it tells us, Guan Zhong urged the duke to maintain the respect of the other states by refusing the offer of the son of a recently defeated state's ruler to ally himself with Qi if Qi would help him depose his father. Because the duke regularly listened to Guan Zhong's sound advice, Qi brought the other states under its sway, and the duke came to be recognized as the first *hegemon,* or leader of the alliance of states.

Guan Zhong was also credited with strengthening the duke's internal administration. He encouraged the employment of officials on the basis of their moral character and ability rather than their birth. He introduced a system of drafting commoners for military service. In the history of China written by Sima Qian in about 100 B.C.E., Guan Zhong is also given credit for enriching Qi by promoting trade, issuing coins, and standardizing merchants' scales. He was credited with the statement "When the granaries are full, the people will understand ritual and moderation. When they have enough food and clothing, they will understand honor and disgrace."

Sima Qian's biography of Guan Zhong emphasizes his early poverty and the key role played by a friend, Bao Shuya, who recognized his worth. As young men, both Bao and Guan Zhong served brothers of the duke of Qi. When this duke was killed and a messy succession struggle followed, Bao's patron won out and became the next duke, while Guan Zhong's patron had to flee and in the end was killed. Bao, however, recommended Guan Zhong to the new duke, Duke Huan, and Guan Zhong took up a post under him.

In the *Analects,* one of Confucius's disciples thought that Guan Zhong's lack of loyalty to his first lord made him a man unworthy of respect: "When Duke Huan killed his brother Jiu, Guan Zhong was unable to die with Jiu but rather became prime minister to Duke Huan." Confucius disagreed: "Guan Zhong became prime minister to Duke Huan and made him hegemon among the lords, uniting and reforming all under Heaven. The people, down to the present, continued to receive benefits from this. Were it not for Guan Zhong our hair would hang unbound and we would fold our robes on the left [that is, live as barbarians]."*

A book of the teachings associated with Guan Zhong, the *Guanzi,* was in circulation by the late Warring States Period. Although it is today not thought to reflect the teachings of the historical Guan Zhong, the fact that later statecraft thinkers would borrow his name is an indication of his fame as a great statesman.

Questions for Analysis

1. How did the form of government promoted by Guan Zhong differ from the early Zhou political system?

2. What can one infer about Chinese notions of loyalty from the story of Guan Zhong and his friend Bao Shuya?

3. Did Guan Zhong and Confucius share similar understandings of the differences between Chinese and barbarians?

Analects, 14.18. Translated by Patricia Ebrey.

● **Serving Parents with Filial Piety** This illustration of a passage in the *Classic of Filial Piety* shows how commoners should serve their parents: by working hard at productive jobs such as farming and tending to their parents' daily needs. The married son and daughter-in-law bring food or drink to offer the older couple as their own children look on, thus learning how they should treat their own parents after they become aged themselves. *(National Palace Museum, Taipei, Taiwan)*

sacrifice. Do not do unto others what you would not have them do unto you. Then neither in your country nor in your family will there be complaints against you."[6]

Confucius encouraged the men who came to study with him to master the poetry, rituals, and historical traditions that we know today as Confucian classics. Many passages in the *Analects* reveal Confucius's confidence in the power of study:

The Master said, "I am not someone who was born wise. I am someone who loves the ancients and tries to learn from them."

The Master said, "I once spent a whole day without eating and a whole night without sleeping in order to think. It was of no use. It is better to study."[7]

The eventual success of Confucian ideas owes much to Confucius's followers in the three centuries following his death. The most important of them were Mencius (ca. 370–ca. 300 B.C.E.) and Xunzi (ca. 310–ca. 215 B.C.E.).

Mencius, like Confucius, traveled around offering advice to rulers of various states. (See the feature "Listening to the Past: The Book of Mencius" on pages 74–75.) Over and over he tried to convert them to the view that the ruler able to win over the people through benevolent government would succeed in unifying "all under Heaven." Mencius proposed concrete political and financial measures for easing tax burdens and otherwise improving the people's lot. Men willing to serve an unworthy ruler earned his contempt, especially when they worked hard to fill the ruler's coffers or expand his territory. With his disciples and fellow philosophers, Mencius also discussed other issues in moral philosophy, arguing strongly, for instance, that human nature is fundamentally good, as everyone is born with the capacity to recognize what is right and act on it.

Xunzi, a half century later, took the opposite view of human nature, arguing that people are born selfish and that it is only through education and ritual that they learn to put moral principle above their own interest. Much of what is desirable is not in-born but must be taught:

When a son yields to his father, or a younger brother yields to his elder brother, or when a son takes on the work for his father or a younger brother for his elder brother, their actions go against their natures and run counter to their feelings. And yet these are the way of the filial son and the principles of ritual and morality.[8]

Neither Confucius nor Mencius had had much actual political or administrative experience, but Xunzi had worked for many years in the court of his home state. Not surprisingly, he showed more consideration than either Confucius or Mencius for the difficulties a ruler might face in trying to rule through ritual and virtue. Xunzi was also a more rigorous thinker than his predecessors and developed the philosophical foundations of many ideas merely outlined by Confucius or Mencius. Confucius, for instance, had declined to discuss gods, portents, and anomalies and had spoken of sacrificing as if the spirits were present. Xunzi went farther and explicitly argued that Heaven does not intervene in human affairs. Praying to Heaven or to gods, he asserted, does not induce them to act. "Why does it rain after a prayer for rain? In my opinion, for no reason. It is the same as raining when you had not prayed."[9]

Even though he did not think praying could bring rain or other benefits from Heaven, Xunzi did not propose abandoning traditional rituals. In contrast to Daoists and Mohists (discussed below), who saw rituals as unnatural or extravagant, Xunzi saw them as an efficient way to attain order in society. Rulers and educated men should continue traditional ritual practices such as complex funeral protocols because the rites themselves have positive effects on performers and observers. Not only do they let people express feelings and satisfy desires in an orderly way, but because they specify graduated ways to perform the rites according to social rank, ritual traditions sustain the social hierarchy. Xunzi compared and contrasted ritual and music: music shapes people's emotions and creates feelings of solidarity, while ritual shapes people's sense of duty and creates social differentiation.

The Confucian vision of personal ethics and public service found a small but ardent following in the Warring States Period. In later centuries, rulers came to see men educated in Confucian virtues as ideal advisers and officials. Neither revolutionaries nor toadies, Confucian scholar-officials opposed bad government and upheld the best ideals of statecraft. Confucian political ideals shaped Chinese society into the twentieth century.

The Confucian vision also provided the moral basis for the Chinese family into modern times. Repaying parents and ancestors came to be seen as a sacred duty. Because people owe their very existence to their parents, they should reciprocate by respecting them, making efforts to please them, honoring their memories, and placing the interests of the family line above personal preferences. Since this family line is a patrilineal line from father to son to grandson, placing great importance on it has had the effect of devaluing women.

DAOISM, LEGALISM, AND OTHER SCHOOLS OF THOUGHT

What did those who opposed Confucianism argue?

During the Warring States Period, rulers took advantage of the destruction of states to recruit newly unemployed men to serve as their advisers and court assistants. Lively debate often resulted as these strategists proposed policies and defended their ideas against challengers. Followers took to recording their teachers' ideas, and the circulation of these "books" (rolls of silk, or strips of wood or bamboo tied together) served further to stimulate debate.

Many of these schools of thought directly opposed the ideas of Confucius and his followers. Mozi proposed that every idea should be tested on the basis of utility: does it benefit the people and the state? He objected to Confucian emphasis on ritual because it interrupts work and is wasteful. Mozi did not approve of Confucian emphasis on treating only one's family with special concern, saying that the principle should be concern for everyone equally. The Daoists and Legalists opposed other Confucian principles.

the Way   *The Dao, the whole natural order.*

Daoism

Confucius and his followers believed in moral effort and statecraft. They thought men of virtue should devote themselves to making the government work to the benefit of the people. Those who came to be labeled Daoists disagreed. They thought striving to make things better generally makes them worse. Daoists defended private life and wanted the rulers to leave the people alone. They sought to go beyond everyday concerns and to let their minds wander freely. Rather than making human beings and human actions the center of concern, they focused on the larger scheme of things, the whole natural order identified as **the Way,** or Dao.

Early Daoist teachings are known from two surviving books, the *Laozi* and the *Zhuangzi*, both dating to the third century B.C.E. Laozi, the putative author of the *Laozi*, may not be a historical figure, but the text ascribed to him has been of enduring importance. A recurrent theme in this brief, aphoristic text is the mystical superiority of yielding over assertion and silence over words: "The Way that can be discussed is not the constant Way."[10] The highest good is like water: "Water benefits all creatures but does not compete. It occupies the places people disdain and thus comes near to the Way."[11]

Because purposeful action is counterproductive, the ruler should let people return to a natural state of ignorance and contentment:

Do not honor the worthy,
And the people will not compete.
Do not value rare treasures,
And the people will not steal.
Do not display what others want,
And the people will not have their hearts confused.
A sage governs this way:
He empties people's minds and fills their bellies.
He weakens their wills and strengthens their bones.
Keep the people always without knowledge and without desires,
For then the clever will not dare act.
Engage in no action and order will prevail.[12]

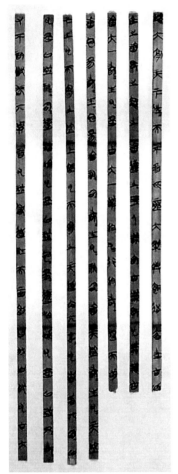

● **Inscribed Bamboo Slips**
In 1993 Chinese archaeologists discovered a late-fourth-century B.C.E. tomb in Hubei province that contained 804 bamboo slips, bearing some 12,000 Chinese characters. Scholars have been able to reconstruct more than a dozen books from them, some of which match transmitted texts fairly closely, but others are books previously unknown. *(Courtesy, Jingmen City Museum, Hubei)*

In the philosophy of the *Laozi*, the people would be better off if they knew less, gave up tools, renounced writing, stopped envying their neighbors, and lost their desire to travel or engage in war.

Zhuangzi (369–286 B.C.E.), the author of the book of the same name, was a historical figure who shared many of the central ideas of the *Laozi*. He was proud of his disinterest in politics. In one of his many anecdotes, he reported that the king of Chu once sent an envoy to invite him to take over the government of his realm. In response Zhuangzi asked the envoy whether a tortoise that had been held as sacred for three thousand years would prefer to be dead with its bones venerated or alive with its tail dragging in the mud. When the envoy agreed that life was preferable, Zhuangzi told the envoy to leave. He preferred to drag his tail in the mud.

The *Zhuangzi* is filled with parables, flights of fancy, and fictional encounters between historical figures, including Confucius and his disciples. A more serious strain of Zhuangzi's thought concerned death. He questioned whether we can be sure life is better than death. People fear what they do not know, the same way a captive girl will be terrified when she learns she is to become the king's concubine. Perhaps people will discover that death has as many delights as life in the palace.

When a friend expressed shock that Zhuangzi was not weeping at his wife's death but rather singing, Zhuangzi explained:

When she first died, how could I have escaped feeling the loss? Then I looked back to the beginning before she had life. Not only before she had life, but before she had form. Not only before she had form, but before she had vital energy. In this confused amorphous realm, something changed and vital energy appeared; when the vital energy was changed, form appeared; with changes in form, life began. Now there is another change bringing death. This is like the progression of the four seasons of spring and fall, win-

● **Embroidered Silk** From ancient times, silk was one of China's most famous products. Women traditionally did most of the work involved in making silk, from feeding mulberry leaves to the silkworms, to reeling and twisting the fibers, to weaving and embroidering. The embroidered silk depicted here is from a robe found in a fourth-century B.C.E. tomb in central China. The flowing, curvilinear design incorporates dragons, phoenixes, and tigers. *(Jingzhou Museum)*

ter and summer. Here she was lying down to sleep in a huge room and I followed her, sobbing and wailing. When I realized my actions showed I hadn't understood destiny, I stopped.[13]

Zhuangzi was similarly iconoclastic in his political ideas. In one parable a wheelwright insolently tells a duke that books are useless since all they contain are the dregs of men long dead. The duke, insulted, threatens to execute him if he cannot give an adequate explanation of his remark. The wheelwright replies:

I see things in terms of my own work. When I chisel at a wheel, if I go slow, the chisel slides and does not stay put; if I hurry, it jams and doesn't move properly. When it is neither too slow nor too fast, I can feel it in my hand and respond to it from my heart. My mouth cannot describe it in words, but there is something there. I cannot teach it to my son, and my son cannot learn it from me. So I have gone on for seventy years, growing old chiseling wheels. The men of old died in possession of what they could not transmit. So it follows that what you are reading are their dregs.[14]

To put this another way, truly skilled craftsmen respond to situations spontaneously; they do not analyze or reason or even keep in mind the rules they have mastered. This strain of Daoist thought denies the validity of verbal reasoning and the sorts of knowledge conveyed through words.

Daoism can be seen as a response to Confucianism, a rejection of many of its basic premises. Nevertheless, over the course of Chinese history, many people felt the pull of both Confucian and Daoist ideas and studied the writings of both schools. Even Confucian scholars who had devoted much of their lives to public service might find that the teachings of the *Laozi* or *Zhuangzi* helped to put their frustrations in perspective. Whereas Confucianism often seems sternly masculine, Daoism is more accepting of feminine principles and even celebrates passivity and yielding. Those drawn to the arts were also often drawn to Daoism, with its validation of spontaneity and freedom. Rulers, too, were drawn to the Daoist notion of the ruler who can have great power simply by being himself without instituting anything.

Legalism

Legalists *Political theorists who emphasized the need for rigorous laws and laid the basis for China's later bureaucratic government.*

As one small state after another was conquered, the number of surviving states dwindled. Rulers fearful that their states might be next were ready to listen to political theorists who claimed expertise in the accumulation of power. These theorists, labeled **Legalists** because of their emphasis on the need for rigorous laws, argued that strong government depended not on the moral qualities of the ruler and his officials, as Confucians claimed, but on establishing effective laws and procedures. Legalism, though eventually discredited, laid the basis for China's later bureaucratic government.

In the fourth century B.C.E. the state of Qin, under the leadership of its chief minister, Lord Shang (d. 338 B.C.E.), adopted many Legalist policies. It abolished the aristocracy. Social distinctions were to be based on military ranks determined by the objective criterion of the number of enemy heads cut off in battle. In place of the old fiefs, Qin divided the country into counties and appointed officials to govern them according to the laws decreed at court. To increase the population, migrants were recruited from other states with offers of land and houses. To encourage farmers to work hard and improve their land, they were allowed to buy and sell it. Ordinary farmers were thus freed from serf-like obligations to the local nobility, but direct control by the state could be even more onerous. Taxes and labor service obligations were heavy. Travel required a permit, and vagrants could be forced into penal labor service. All families were grouped into mutual responsibility groups of five and ten families; whenever anyone in the group committed a crime, all the others were equally liable unless they reported it.

In the century after Lord Shang, Legalism found its greatest exponent in Han Feizi (ca. 280?–233 B.C.E.). Han Feizi had studied with the Confucian master Xunzi but had little interest in Confucian values of goodness or ritual. In his writings he warned rulers of the political pitfalls awaiting them. They had to be careful where they placed their trust, for "when the ruler trusts someone, he falls under that person's control."[15] This is true even of wives and concubines, who think of the interests of their sons. Given subordinates' propensities to pursue their own selfish interests, the ruler should keep them ignorant of his intentions and control them by manipulating competition among them. Warmth, affection, or candor should have no place in his relationships with others.

Han Feizi saw the Confucian notion that government could be based on virtue as naive:

Think of parents' relations to their children. They congratulate each other when a son is born, but complain to each other when a daughter is born. Why do parents have these divergent responses when both are equally their offspring? It is because they calculate their long-term advantage. Since even parents deal with their children in this calculating way, what can one expect where there is no parent-child bond? When present-day scholars counsel rulers, they all tell them to rid themselves of thoughts of profit and follow the path of mutual love. This is expecting rulers to go further than parents.[16]

If rulers would make the laws and prohibitions clear and the rewards and punishments automatic, then the officials and common people would be easy to govern. Uniform laws get people to do things they would not otherwise be inclined to do, such as work hard and fight wars, essential to the goal of establishing hegemony over all the other states.

The laws of the Legalists were designed as much to constrain officials as to regulate the common people. The third-century B.C.E. tomb of a Qin official has yielded statutes detailing the rules for keeping accounts, supervising subordinates, managing penal labor, conducting investigations, and many other responsibilities of officials. Infractions were generally punishable through the imposition of fines.

Legalism saw no value in intellectual debate or private opinion. Divergent views of right and wrong lead to weakness and disorder. The ruler should not allow others to undermine his laws by questioning them. In Legalism, there were no laws above or independent of the wishes of the rulers, no laws that might set limits on rulers' actions in the way that natural or divine laws did in Greek thought. Indeed, a ruler's right to exercise the law as he saw fit was demonstrated in the violent deaths of the two leading Legalist thinkers: Lord Shang was drawn and quartered by chariots in 338 B.C.E., and Han Feizi was imprisoned and forced to drink poison in 233 B.C.E.

Rulers of several states adopted some Legalist ideas, but only the state of Qin systematically followed them. The extraordinary but brief success Qin had with these policies is discussed in Chapter 6.

Yin and Yang

Cosmological speculation formed another important strain of early Chinese thought. The concepts of **yin and yang** are found in early form in the divination manual the *Book of Changes,* but late Zhou theorists developed much more elaborate theories based on them. Yin is the feminine, dark, receptive, yielding, negative, and weak; yang is the masculine, bright, assertive, creative, positive, and strong. Yin and yang are complementary poles rather than distinct entities or opposing forces. The movement of yin and yang accounts for the transition from day to night and from summer to winter. These models based on observation of nature were extended to explain not only phenomena we might classify as natural, such as illness, storms, and earthquakes, but also social phenomena, such as the rise and fall of states and conflict in families. In all these realms, unwanted things happen when the balance between yin and yang gets disturbed.

In recent decades archaeologists have further complicated our understanding of early Chinese thought by unearthing records of the popular religion of the time—astrological manuals, handbooks of lucky and unlucky days, medical prescriptions, exercises, and ghost stories. The tomb of an official who died in 316 B.C.E. has records of divinations showing that illness was seen as the result of unsatisfied spirits or malevolent demons, best dealt with through exorcisms or offering sacrifices to the astral god Taiyi (Grand One).

yin and yang *A concept of complementary poles, one of which represents the feminine, dark, and receptive, and the other the masculine, bright, and assertive.*

● **Dagger Depicting Taiyi** Recent archaeological excavations of manuscripts from the Warring States Period have given us a much clearer understanding of religious beliefs and practices in early China. The deity Taiyi ("Grand One"), depicted on this late-fourth-century B.C.E. drawing of a dagger, was the god of the pole star. Sacrifices were made to Taiyi to avert evil or gain his protection in battle. *(From Michael Loewe and Edward Shaughnessy, eds.,* Cambridge History of Ancient China *[New York: Cambridge University Press, 1999]. Reprinted with permission of Cambridge University Press)*

Chapter Summary

Key Terms

loess
Anyang
logographic
taotie
Book of Documents
Mandate of Heaven
shi
Book of Songs
Warring States Period
crossbow
filial piety
ren
the Way
Legalists
yin and yang

To assess your mastery of this chapter, go to
bedfordstmartins.com/mckayworld

• When, where, and how did writing, bronze technology, and other elements of civilization develop in China?

After a long Neolithic period, China entered the Bronze Age with the Shang Dynasty. In Shang times, the kings served also as priests, and great wealth was invested in extraordinarily complex bronze ritual vessels. From Shang times on, the Chinese language has been written in a logographic script, which shaped the ways people have become educated and the value assigned to education.

• How was China governed in the period looked back on as its golden age?

The Zhou Dynasty, which overthrew the Shang in about 1050 B.C.E., parceled out its territory to lords, whose titles gradually became hereditary. The texts transmitted from this period present Heaven as the high god. Kings were called Sons of Heaven because they had to have Heaven's approval to gain the throne. If they did not rule in the interests of the people, Heaven could take the Mandate away from them and confer it on a worthier person.

• What were the consequences of the breakup of Zhou unity and the rise of independent states?

The ties between the Zhou king and his lords gradually weakened, and the domains over time came to act like independent states. After 500 B.C.E. China is best thought of as a multistate realm. Social and cultural change was particularly rapid under these conditions of intense competition. Changes in military technology included the introduction of cavalry, infantry armies, and the crossbow. Iron utensils came into use, as did metal coinage.

• What ideas did Confucius teach, and how were they a response to his times?

This Warring States Period was the golden age of Chinese philosophy. Confucius and his followers advocated a deeply moral view of the way to achieve order through the cultivation of virtues by everyone from the ruler on down. Key virtues were sincerity, loyalty, benevolence, and filial piety. Over the next two centuries Confucius's message was elaborated by important followers, including Mencius, who urged rulers to rule through goodness and argued that human nature is good, and Xunzi, who stressed the power of ritual and argued that human nature is selfish and must be curbed through education.

• What did those who opposed Confucianism argue?

In the contentious spirit of the age, many thinkers countered Confucian principles. Daoists like Laozi and Zhuangzi looked beyond the human realm to the entire cosmos and spoke of the relativity of concepts such as good and bad and life and death. The Legalists were hardheaded men who heaped ridicule on the idea that a ruler could get his people to be good by being good himself and proposed instead clear laws with strict rewards and punishments. Natural philosophers explored issues Confucius had neglected, such as the forces that bring about the changes in the seasons and health and illness.

Suggested Reading

Blunden, Caroline, and Mark Elvin. *Cultural Atlas of China.* 1983. Valuable both for its historical maps and its well-illustrated topical essays.

Chang, Kwang-chih. *Archeology of Ancient China,* 4th ed. 1986. An overview by a leading archaeologist.

de Bary, Wm. Theodore, and Irene Bloom. *Sources of Chinese Tradition.* 1999. Large collection of primary sources for Chinese intellectual history, with lengthy introductions.

Ebrey, Patricia Buckley. *Cambridge Illustrated History of China.* 1996. Well-illustrated brief overview of Chinese history.

Graham, A. C. *Disputers of the Tao: Philosophical Argument in Ancient China.* 1989. A philosophically rich overview of the intellectual flowering of the Warring States Period.

Ledderose, Lothar. *Ten Thousand Things: Module and Mass Production in Chinese Art.* 2000. A new interpretation of Chinese culture in terms of modules; offers fresh perspectives on the Chinese script and the production of bronzes.

Loewe, Michael, and Edward Shaughnessy, eds. *The Cambridge History of Ancient China: From the Origins of Civilization to 221 B.C.* 1999. An authoritative collection of chapters, half by historians, half by archaeologists.

Mote, F. W. *Intellectual Foundations of China.* 1989. Brief but stimulating introduction to early Chinese thought.

Thorp, Robert, and Richard Vinograd. *Chinese Art and Culture.* 2001. Broad coverage of all of China's visual arts.

Yang, Xin, ed. *The Golden Age of Chinese Archaeology.* 1999. The well-illustrated catalogue of a major show of Chinese archaeological finds.

Notes

1. *Chinese Civilization: A Sourcebook,* 2d ed., revised and expanded by Patricia Buckley Ebrey (New York: Free Press/Macmillan, 1993), p. 11. All quotations from this work reprinted and edited with the permission of The Free Press, a Division of Simon & Schuster Adult Publishing Group. Copyright © 1993 by Patricia Buckley Ebrey. All rights reserved.

2. Edward Shaughnessy, "Western Zhou History," in M. Loewe and E. Shaughnessy, eds., *The Cambridge History of Ancient China* (New York: Cambridge University Press, 1999), p. 336. Reprinted with the permission of Cambridge University Press and Edward L. Shaughnessy.

3. Patricia Buckley Ebrey, *The Cambridge Illustrated History of China* (Cambridge: Cambridge University Press, 1996), p. 34.

4. Ebrey, *Chinese Civilization,* p. 21.
5. Ibid., p. 19.
6. Ibid.
7. *Analects* 7.19, 15.30. Translated by Patricia Ebrey.
8. Ebrey, *Chinese Civilization,* p. 26.
9. Ibid., p. 24, modified.
10. Ibid., p. 27.
11. Ibid., p. 28, modified.
12. Ibid., p. 28.
13. Ibid., p. 31.
14. Ibid.
15. Ibid., p. 33.
16. Ibid., p. 35.

Listening to the

PAST

The Book of Mencius

The book that records the teachings of Mencius (ca. 370–ca. 300 B.C.E.) was modeled on the Analects of Confucius. It presents, in no particular order, conversations between Mencius and several rulers, philosophers, and disciples. Unlike the Analects, however, the Book of Mencius includes extended discussions of particular points, suggesting that Mencius had a hand in recording the conversations.

Mencius had an audience with King Hui of Liang. The king said, "Sir, you did not consider a thousand li too far to come. You must have some ideas about how to benefit my state."

Mencius replied, "Why must Your Majesty use the word 'benefit'? All I am concerned with are the benevolent and the right. If Your Majesty says, 'How can I benefit my state?' your officials will say, 'How can I benefit my family,' and officers and common people will say, 'How can I benefit myself?' Once superiors and inferiors are competing for benefit, the state will be in danger.

"When the head of a state of ten thousand chariots is murdered, the assassin is invariably a noble with a fief of a thousand chariots. When the head of a fief of a thousand chariots is murdered, the assassin is invariably head of a subfief of a hundred chariots. Those with a thousand out of ten thousand, or a hundred out of a thousand, had quite a bit. But when benefit is put before what is right, they are not satisfied without snatching it all. By contrast, there has never been a benevolent person who neglected his parents or a righteous person who put his lord last. Your Majesty perhaps will now also say, 'All I am concerned with are the benevolent and the right.' Why mention 'benefit'?"

After seeing King Xiang of Liang, Mencius said to someone, "When I saw him from a distance, he did not look like a ruler, and when I got closer, I saw nothing to command respect. But he asked, 'How can the realm be settled?'

"I answered, 'It can be settled through unity.'

"'Who can unify it?' he asked.

"I answered, 'Someone not fond of killing people.'

"'Who could give it to him?'

"I answered, 'Everyone in the world will give it to him. Your Majesty knows what rice plants are? If there is a drought in the seventh and eighth months, the plants wither, but if moisture collects in the sky and forms clouds and rain falls in torrents, the plants suddenly revive. This is the way it is; no one can stop the process. In the world today there are no rulers disinclined toward killing. If there were a ruler who did not like to kill people, everyone in the world would crane their necks to catch sight of him. This is really true. The people would flow toward him the way water flows down. No one would be able to repress them.'"

After an incident between Zou and Lu, Duke Mu asked, "Thirty-three of my officials died but no common people died. I could punish them, but I could not punish them all. I could refrain from punishing them, but they did angrily watch their superiors die without saving them. What would be the best course for me to follow?"

Mencius answered, "When the harvest failed, even though your granaries were full, nearly a thousand of your subjects were lost—the old and weak among them dying in the gutters, the able-bodied scattering in all directions. Your officials never reported the situation, a case of superiors callously inflicting suffering on their subordinates. Zengzi said, 'Watch out, watch out! What you do will be done to you.' This was the first chance the people had to pay them back. You should not resent them. If Your Highness practices benevolent government, the common people will love their superiors and die for those in charge of them."

King Xuan of Qi asked, "Is it true that Tang banished Jie and King Wu took up arms against Zhou?"

Mencius replied, "That is what the records say."

"Then is it permissible for a subject to assassinate his lord?"

Mencius said, "Someone who does violence to the good we call a villain; someone who does violence to the right we call a criminal. A person who is both a villain and a criminal we call a scoundrel. I have heard that the scoundrel Zhou was killed, but have not heard that a lord was killed."

King Xuan of Qi asked about ministers.

Mencius said, "What sort of ministers does Your Majesty mean?"

The king said, "Are there different kinds of ministers?"

"There are. There are noble ministers related to the ruler and ministers of other surnames."

The king said, "I'd like to hear about noble ministers."

Mencius replied, "When the ruler makes a major error, they point it out. If he does not listen to their repeated remonstrations, then they put someone else on the throne."

The king blanched. Mencius continued, "Your Majesty should not be surprised at this. Since you asked me, I had to tell you truthfully."

After the king regained his composure, he asked about unrelated ministers. Mencius said, "When the king makes an error, they point it out. If he does not heed their repeated remonstrations, they quit their posts."

Bo Gui said, "I'd like a tax of one part in twenty. What do you think?"

Mencius said, "Your way is that of the northern tribes. Is one potter enough for a state with ten thousand households?"

"No, there would not be enough wares."

"The northern tribes do not grow all the five grains, only millet. They have no cities or houses, no ritual sacrifices. They do not provide gifts or banquets for feudal lords, and do not have a full array of officials. Therefore, for them, one part in twenty is enough. But we live in the central states. How could we abolish social roles and do without gentlemen? If a state cannot do without potters, how much less can it do without gentlemen.

"Those who want to make government lighter than it was under Yao and Shun are to some degree barbarians. Those who wish to make government heavier than it was under Yao and Shun are to some degree [tyrants like] Jie."

Gaozi said, "Human nature is like whirling water. When an outlet is opened to the east, it flows east;

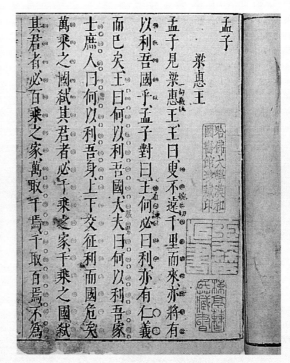

Opening page of a 1617 edition of the Book of Mencius. *(Rare Books Collections, Harvard-Yenching Library, Harvard University)*

when an outlet is opened to the west, it flows west. Human nature is no more inclined to good or bad than water is inclined to east or west."

Mencius responded, "Water, it is true, is not inclined to either east or west, but does it have no preference for high or low? Goodness is to human nature like flowing downward is to water. There are no people who are not good and no water that does not flow down. Still, water, if splashed, can go higher than your head; if forced, it can be brought up a hill. This isn't the nature of water; it is the specific circumstances. Although people can be made to be bad, their natures are not changed."

Questions for Analysis

1. Does Mencius give consistent advice to the kings he talks to?

2. Do you see a link between Mencius's views on human nature and his views on the true king?

3. What role does Mencius see for ministers?

Source: Reprinted and edited with the permission of The Free Press, a Division of Simon & Schuster Adult Publishing Group, from *Chinese Civilization: A Sourcebook,* Second Edition, revised and expanded by Patricia Buckley Ebrey. Copyright © 1993 by Patricia Buckley Ebrey. All rights reserved.

Tetrapylon of Aphrodisias. This monumental gate celebrates the beautiful and rich city of Aphrodisias in modern Turkey. *(John Buckler)*

4

THE GREEK EXPERIENCE (CA. 3500–146 B.C.E.)

The people of ancient Greece developed a culture that fundamentally shaped the civilization of the western part of Eurasia much as the Chinese did for the eastern part. The Greeks were the first in the Mediterranean and neighboring areas to explore most of the questions that still concern thinkers today. Going beyond mythmaking, the Greeks strove to understand the world in logical, rational terms. The result was the birth of philosophy and science, subjects as important to many of them as religion. From daily life they developed the concept of politics. Their contributions to the arts and literature still fertilize intellectual life today.

The history of the Greeks is divided into two broad periods: the Hellenic, roughly the time between the arrival of the Greeks and the triumph of Macedonia in 338 B.C.E.; and the Hellenistic, the years from Alexander the Great (336–323 B.C.E.) to the Roman conquest (200–146 B.C.E.).

HELLAS: THE LAND AND THE POLIS (CA. 3500– CA. 800 B.C.E.)

How did the geography of Greece divide the land so that small communities naturally developed?

Hellas, as the Greeks call their land, encompasses the Greek peninsula and the islands surrounding it, the area known as the Aegean basin. This basin in turn included the Greek settlements in Ionia in Asia Minor, the western coast of modern Turkey. Geography acts as an enormously divisive force in Greek life because the rugged terrain led to political fragmentation. Consequently, no strong central state became permanently dominant.

● **Mycenaean Lion Hunt** The Mycenaeans were a robust, warlike people who enjoyed the thrill and the danger of hunting. This scene on the blade of a dagger depicts hunters armed with spears and protected by shields defending themselves against charging lions. *(National Archaeological Museum/ Archaeological Receipts Fund)*

The Earliest Settlers

At the faint dawn of history, small farming communities worked much of the land. They prospered and expanded in a gradual process still little understood. Historians can, however, describe two well-documented early civilizations. The Minoan culture, the earlier of the two, arose about 3500 B.C.E. on the island of Crete. Its modern discoverers named it after the mythical king Minos. The second society, the Mycenaean, flourished between about 1575 and 1000 B.C.E. Its name, too, is modern, derived from the small Greek town where its remains were first discovered. Because both the Minoans and Mycenaeans used bronze instruments, modern scholars name this the Bronze Age.

At the head of Minoan society stood a king and his nobles governing a society of farmers and maritime merchants. Besides spreading throughout Crete, the Minoans traded with Egypt and the coastal cities of the ancient Near East. Their trading ventures also brought them into contact with the Mycenaeans on the Greek peninsula. The Mycenaeans founded numerous kingdoms from Thessaly in the north to the southern Peloponnesos. The kingdom was the basic Mycenaean political unit, headed by a king and his warrior aristocracy. Owners of most of the land, they relied on non-noble artisans, traders, and farmers to run the economy. Slaves, at the bottom of the social scale, were owned by the king and aristocrats. Mycenaean commerce quickly spread throughout the eastern Mediterranean, reaching Asia Minor, Cyprus, and Egypt. Prosperity, however, did not bring peace, and between 1300 and 1000 B.C.E. various kingdoms ravaged one another in a savage series of wars that destroyed both the Minoan and Mycenaean civilizations.

The fall of these first kingdoms ushered in a period of poverty and disruption usually called Greece's "Dark Age" (ca. 1100–800 B.C.E.). Despite daunting challenges, Greece actually became even more Greek during these years. Some Greeks entered the peninsula for the first time, the most important being the Dorians, who became the historical Spartans, Argives, and Messenians. Others migrated eastward to Asia Minor. By the end of the Dark Age Greeks and their culture had spread throughout the Aegean basin (see Map 4.1).

The Polis (ca. 800 B.C.E.)

polis *Generally translated as "city-state," it was the basic political and institutional unit of Greece.*

During the Dark Age, the Greeks developed the **polis,** which is generally translated as "city-state." More than a political institution, the polis was a community of citizens with their own customs and laws. Even though the physical, religious, and political form of the polis varied from place to place, it was the very badge of Greekness.

acropolis *An elevated point within a city on which stood temples, altars, public monuments, and various dedications to the gods of the polis.*

The polis included the town and its surrounding countryside. The people of the polis typically lived in a compact group of houses within a city, which by the fifth century B.C.E. was generally surrounded by a wall. The city contained a point, usually elevated, called the **acropolis,** and a public square or marketplace, the *agora.* On the acropolis stood the temples, altars, public monuments, and various dedications to the gods of the polis. The agora was originally the place where the warrior assembly met, and it became the political center of the polis. In the agora were porticoes, shops, public buildings, and courts.

The *chora,* which included the arable land, pastureland, and wasteland of the polis, was typically its source of wealth. Farmers left the city each morning to work their fields or tend their flocks of sheep and goats, and they returned at night. On the wasteland people often quarried stone or mined for precious metals. Thus the polis was the scene of both urban and agrarian life.

The size of the polis varied according to geographical circumstances. But regardless of its size or wealth, the polis was fundamental to Greek life. The very smallness of the polis enabled Greeks to see how the individual fit into the overall system—how the human parts made up the social whole. The Greeks were their own magistrates, administrators, and soldiers.

The polis could be governed in several ways. In a **monarchy,** a term derived from the Greek for "the rule of one man," a king represented the community, reigning according to law and respecting the rights of the citizens. The aristocracy could govern the state. A literal political translation of the term *aristocracy* means "power in the hands of the best." Or the running of the polis could be the prerogative of an **oligarchy,** which literally means "the rule of a few"—in this case a small group of wealthy citizens not necessarily of aristocratic birth. Still another form of government was **tyranny,** rule by a man who had seized power by extralegal means. Or the polis could be governed as a **democracy,** through the rule of the people, a concept that in Greece meant that all citizens, regardless of birth or wealth, administered the workings of government.

Because the bonds that held the polis together were so intimate, Greeks were extremely reluctant to allow foreigners to share fully in its life. Nor could women play political roles. Women participated in some religious ceremonies, and served as priestesses, but the polis had no room for them in state affairs. In Greek democracy, citizenship was extended to many but not all males whose families had long lived in the polis.

Although each polis was jealous of its independence, some Greeks banded together to create leagues of city-states. Here was the birth of Greek federalism, a political system in which several states formed a central government while remaining independent in their internal affairs. United in a league, a confederation of city-states was far stronger than any of the individual members and better able to withstand external attack.

The passionate individualism of the polis proved to be another serious weakness. The citizens of each polis were determined to remain free and autonomous. Since the Greeks were rarely willing to unite in larger political bodies, the political result was almost constant warfare. A polis could dominate, but unlike Rome it could not incorporate other cities.

Chronology

ca. 3500–338 B.C.E.　Hellenic period

ca. 3500–ca. 1000 B.C.E.　Minoan and Mycenaean civilizations

ca. 1100–800 B.C.E.　Evolution of the polis; Greece's "Dark Age"

ca. 800–500 B.C.E.　Rise of Sparta and Athens

776 B.C.E.　Foundation of the Olympic games

ca. 750–550 B.C.E.　Greek colonization of the Mediterranean

525–322 B.C.E.　Birth and development of tragedy, historical writing, and philosophy

499–404 B.C.E.　Persian and Peloponnesian Wars

ca. 470–322 B.C.E.　Philosophies of Socrates, Plato, and Aristotle

367–100 B.C.E.　Growth of mystery religions

340–262 B.C.E.　Rise of Epicurean and Stoic philosophies

336–100 B.C.E.　Hellenistic period

336–323 B.C.E.　Reign of Alexander the Great

326–146 B.C.E.　Spread of commerce from the Mediterranean Sea to India

310–212 B.C.E.　Period of scientific advancements

monarchy　*Derived from the Greek for "the rule of one man," it was a type of Greek government in which a king represented the community.*

oligarchy　*"The rule of a few," a type of Greek government in which a small group of wealthy citizens, not necessarily of aristocratic birth, ruled.*

MAP 4.1 **Ancient Greece** In antiquity the home of the Greeks included the islands of the Aegean and the western shore of Turkey as well as the Greek peninsula itself.

Legend:
- Ancient Greece
- Plains
- ★ Major battle of the Persian Wars
- ▲ Mountain
- 🏛 Sanctuary

THE ARCHAIC AGE (CA. 800–500 B.C.E.)

What were the major accomplishments of the Archaic age, and why were they important?

The maturation of the polis coincided with an era that gave rise to two developments of lasting importance. The first was another geographical expansion of Greeks, who now ventured as far east as the Black Sea and as far west as the Atlantic Ocean. The next saw Sparta and Athens, the two poles of the Greek experience, rise to prominence.

Overseas Expansion

With stability and prosperity, the Greek world grew in wealth and numbers, which brought new problems. Given the infertility of Greece, the increase in population led to land hunger. The resulting social and political tensions drove many Greeks to seek new homes outside Greece (see Map 4.2).

tyranny *Rule by a tyrant, a man who used his wealth to gain a political following that could take over the existing government.*

democracy *A type of Greek government in which all citizens, without regard to birth or wealth, administered the workings of government. It is translated as "the power of the people."*

From about 750 to 550 B.C.E. Greeks poured onto the coasts of the northern Aegean and the Black Sea, westward along the north Africa coast, Sicily, southern Italy, and beyond to Spain and the Atlantic. In all these places the Greeks established flourishing cities that turned the Mediterranean into a Greek lake. A later wave of colonization spread Greeks throughout the northern coast of the Black Sea as far east as southern Russia. Colonization on this scale meant that the future culture of this entire area would be Greek, and to this heritage Rome would later fall heir.

The Growth of Sparta

During the Archaic period the Spartans also faced problems of overpopulation and land hunger. They solved both by conquering the rich region of Messene in 715 B.C.E. They made the Messenians *helots,* state slaves, who soon rose in a revolt that took the Spartans thirty years to crush. Afterwards, non-nobles who had shared in the fighting demanded rights equal to those of the nobility. Under intense pressure the aristocrats agreed to remodel the state in a system called the Lycurgan regimen after Lycurgus, a legendary lawgiver. All Spartans were given equal political rights. Two kings ruled, assisted by a council of nobles. Executive power lay in the hands of five *ephors,* overseers, elected by the people. Economically, the helots did all the work, while Spartan citizens devoted their time to military training.

In the Lycurgan system every citizen owed primary allegiance to Sparta. Suppression of the individual together with emphasis on military prowess led to a barracks state. Family life itself was sacrificed to the polis. After long, hard military training that began at age seven, citizen men became lifelong soldiers, the best in Greece. Family life remained important to Spartan society, but it was second to the needs of military

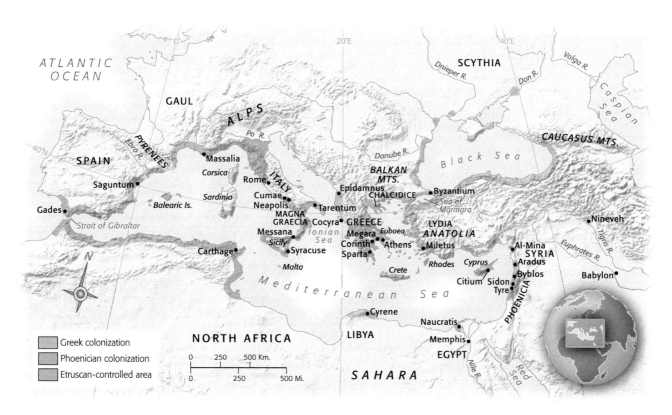

MAP 4.2 **Colonization of the Mediterranean** Though the Greeks and Phoenicians colonized the Mediterranean basin at about the same time, the Greeks spread much farther.

hoplite *The heavily armed infantry man who was the backbone of the Greek army.*

defense. In battle Spartans were supposed to stand and die rather than retreat. **Hoplites,** heavily armed infantrymen, were urged to come back with their shields or be carried dead on them. In the Lycurgan regimen Spartans were expected to train vigorously, do with little, and like it.

In this martial atmosphere women were remarkably free. The Spartans viewed maternal health as crucial for the bearing of healthy children and thus encouraged women to participate in athletics and to eat well. With men in military service much of their lives, citizen women ran the estates and owned land in their own right. They were not physically restricted or secluded. Spartans expected them to be good wives and strict mothers of future soldiers. Not only in time of war but also in peace men often did not see their wives for long periods. Men's most meaningful relations were same-sex ones. The Spartan military leaders viewed such relationships as militarily advantageous because they felt that men would fight even more fiercely for lovers and comrades. Close links among men thus contributed to Spartan civic life, which was admired throughout the Greek world.

The Evolution of Athens

Like Sparta, Athens faced pressing social and economic problems during the Archaic period, but the Athenians eventually extended to all citizens the right and duty of governing the polis. The late seventh century B.C.E. was for Athens a time of turmoil because aristocrats had begun to seize the holdings of smaller landowners. In 621 B.C.E. the aristocrat Draco, under pressure from the peasants and with the consent of the nobles, published the first law code of the Athenian polis. Though harsh, his code nonetheless embodied the ideal that the law belonged to all citizens. Yet the aristocracy still governed Athens oppressively, and by the early sixth century B.C.E. the social and economic situation remained dire, as noble landholders forced small farmers into economic dependence. Many families were sold into slavery, while others were exiled and their land mortgaged to the rich. Solon, an aristocrat and a poet, railed against these injustices in his poems, which he recited in the agora for all to hear. Solon's sincerity and good sense convinced other aristocrats that he was no crazed revolutionary. Moreover, the common people trusted him. Around 594 B.C.E. the nobles elected him *archon,* chief magistrate of the polis, and gave him extraordinary power to reform the state.

Solon immediately freed all people enslaved for debt, recalled all exiles, canceled all debts on land, and made enslavement for debt illegal. He allowed even the poorest men into the old aristocratic assembly, where they could vote in the election of magistrates.

Though solving some immediate problems, Solon's reforms did not bring peace to Athens. Some aristocrats tried to make themselves tyrants, while others opposed them. In 546 B.C.E. Pisistratus, an exiled noble, returned to Athens, defeated his opponent, and became tyrant. Pisistratus reduced the power of the aristocracy while supporting the common people. Under his rule Athens prospered, and his building program made Athens into a splendid city. His reign as tyrant promoted the growth of democratic ideas by arousing rudimentary feelings of equality among many Athenians.

Democracy became reality under the leadership of Cleisthenes, a prominent aristocrat who won the support of ordinary people to emerge triumphant in 508 B.C.E. Cleisthenes created the **deme,** a local unit that kept the roll of citizens within its jurisdiction.

deme *A local unit that served as the basic element of Cleisthenes's political system.*

The democracy functioned on the ideal that all full citizens were sovereign. Yet not all citizens could take time from work to participate in government. They therefore delegated their power to other citizens by creating various offices to run the democracy. The most prestigious of them was the board of ten archons, elected for one year, who handled legal and military affairs. After leaving office, they entered the *Areopagos,* a select council of ex-archons who handled cases involving homicide, wounding, and arson.

Legislation was in the hands of two bodies, the *boule,* or council, composed of five hundred members, and the *ecclesia,* the assembly of all citizens. The boule, separate from the Areopagos, was perhaps the major institution of the democracy. By supervising the various committees of government and proposing bills to the assembly, it guided Athenian political life. It received foreign envoys and forwarded treaties to the assembly for ratification. The ecclesia by a simple majority vote, however, had the final word.

Athenian democracy demonstrated that a large group of people, not just a few, could efficiently run the affairs of state. Because citizens could speak their minds, they were not forced to rebellion or conspiracy to express their views. Like all democracies in ancient Greece, however, the Athenian was limited. Women, slaves, and outsiders could not be citizens. Their opinions were neither recorded nor legally binding.

THE CLASSICAL PERIOD (500–338 B.C.E.)

Although the classical period saw tremendous upheavals, what were its lasting achievements?

In the years between 500 and 338 B.C.E. Greek civilization reached its highest peak in politics, thought, and art. In this period the Greeks beat back the armies of the Persian Empire. Then, turning their spears against one another, they destroyed their own political system in a century of warfare. Some thoughtful Greeks recorded these momentous events. Herodotus (ca. 485–425 B.C.E.), "the father of history," described the Persian War of 490–479 B.C.E., followed by Thucydides (ca. 460–ca. 399 B.C.E.), whose account of the Peloponnesian War remains a literary classic. This era also saw the flowering of philosophy, as thinkers like Socrates (ca. 470–399 B.C.E.), Plato (427–347 B.C.E.), and Aristotle (384–322 B.C.E.) pondered the meaning of the universe and human nature. The Greeks invented drama, and Greek architects reached the zenith of their art. Because of these various intellectual and artistic achievements, this age is called the classical period.

Delian League *A grand naval alliance, created by the Athenians and aimed at liberating Ionia from Persian rule.*

The Deadly Conflicts (499–404 B.C.E.)

Warfare marked the entire classical period. In 499 B.C.E. the Ionian Greeks with feeble Athenian help unsuccessfully rebelled against the Persian Empire. In retaliation the Persians struck at Athens, only to be defeated at Marathon (see Map 4.1). In 480 B.C.E. the Persian king Xerxes invaded Greece on a massive scale. Under the leadership of Sparta by land and Athens by sea, many Greeks united to defeat the Persians in hard-fought battles at the pass of Thermopylae and in the waters off Artemsium in 480 B.C.E. In 479 B.C.E., after the loss of Athens, the Greeks defeated the Persians at the decisive battle of Salamis and finally again at Plataea later that year.

In 478 B.C.E. the victorious Athenians and their allies formed the **Delian League,** a grand naval alliance intended to liberate Ionia from Persian rule. While driving the Persians out of Asia Minor, the Athenians also turned the league into an Athenian empire. Under their great leader Pericles (ca. 494–429 B.C.E.) the Athenians grew so powerful and aggressive that they alarmed Sparta and its allies. In 431 B.C.E. Athenian imperialism finally drove Sparta into the conflict known as the Peloponnesian War. At its outbreak a Spartan ambassador warned the Athenians: "This day will be the beginning of great evils

● **Leonidas at Thermopylae** This heroic statue symbolizes the sacrifice of King Leonidas at the battle. Together with his Spartans, the Thespians, and the Thebans, he heroically died to stop the Persians at the pass of Thermopylae. *(Professor Paul Cartledge)*

● **The Acropolis of Athens**
These buildings embody the noblest spirit of Greek architecture. From the entrance visitors walk through the Propylaea and its pillars. Ahead opens the grand view of the Parthenon, still noble in ruins. To the left stands the Erechtheum, the whole a monument to Athens itself. *(Courtesy, Sotiris Toumbis Editions)*

for the Greeks."[1] Few have ever spoken more prophetically. The Peloponnesian War lasted a generation (431–404 B.C.E.) and brought widespread destruction and huge loss of life. In 404 B.C.E. the Athenians finally surrendered, but not before Greek civilization had been struck a serious blow.

Athenian Arts in the Age of Pericles

In the last half of the fifth century B.C.E. Pericles turned Athens into the showplace of Greece by making the Acropolis a wonder for all time. He appropriated allied money to pay for a huge building program that erected temples and other buildings to honor Athena, the patron goddess of the city, and to show the Greek world the glory of Athens. The Propylaea is a magnificent gateway to a living cultural museum. The nearby temple of Athena Nike (Athena the Victorious) is a small gem. Above all, the Parthenon stands splendidly as a monumental gift to Athena. In many ways the Athenian Acropolis is the epitome of Greek art and its spirit. Although the buildings were dedicated to the gods and most of the sculptures portray gods, they all nonetheless express the Greek fascination with the human form. The Acropolis also exhibits the rational side of Greek art. Greek artists portrayed action in a balanced and restrained fashion, capturing the noblest aspects of human beings: their reason and dignity.

Other aspects of Athenian cultural life were also rooted in the life of the polis. The development of drama was tied to the religious festivals of the city. The polis sponsored the production of plays and required wealthy citizens to pay the expenses of their production. Although many plays were highly controversial, they were neither suppressed nor censored.

Aeschylus (525–456 B.C.E.) was the first dramatist to explore such basic questions as the rights of the individual, the conflict between society and the individual, and the nature of good and evil. In his trilogy of plays, *The Oresteia,* he treats the themes of betrayal, murder, and reconciliation, urging that reason and justice be applied to reconcile fundamental conflicts. The final play concludes with a prayer that civil dissension never be allowed to destroy the city.

Sophocles (496–406 B.C.E.) also deals with matters personal, political, and divine. In *Antigone* he emphasizes the precedence of divine law over political law and family custom. In *Oedipus the King* he tells the story of a good man doomed by the gods to kill his father and marry his mother. When Oedipus fails to avoid his fate, in despair he blinds himself and flees into exile. In *Oedipus at Colonus* Sophocles treats the last days of the broken man, whose patient suffering and uncomplaining piety ultimately win the blessings and honor of the gods. Sophocles urges people to obey the will of the gods even without fully understanding it, for the gods stand for justice and order.

Euripides (ca. 480–406 B.C.E.), the last of the three great tragic dramatists, likewise explored the theme of personal conflict within the polis and sounded the depths of the individual. With Euripides drama entered a new and more personal phase. To him the gods mattered far less than people. The essence of his tragedy is the flaws of people who bring disaster on themselves because their passions overwhelm reason.

Writers of Athenian comedy treated the affairs of the polis bawdily and often coarsely. Even so, their plays too were performed at religious festivals. They used humor as political commentary in an effort to suggest and support the proper policies of the polis. Best known of the comedians is Aristophanes (ca. 445–386 B.C.E.), a merciless critic of cranks, quacks, and fools. He used his art of sarcasm to dramatize his ideas on the right conduct of the citizen and his leaders for the good of the polis.

Despite the undeniable achievements of the Athenians, many modern historians have exaggerated their importance. This Athenocentrism fails to do justice to the other Greeks who also shaped society, culture, and history.

Aspects of Social Life in Athens

The Athenians, like other Greeks, lived comparatively simple lives with few material possessions. The Athenian house was rather simple. It consisted of a series of rooms opening onto a central courtyard that contained a well, an altar, and a washbasin. Larger houses often had a room at the front, where the men of the family ate and entertained guests, and women's quarters at the back. If the family lived in the country, stalls for animals faced the courtyard. Farmers kept oxen for plowing, various animals for food, and donkeys for transportation. Even in the city chickens and perhaps a goat or two roamed the courtyard with dogs and cats.

In the city a man might support himself as a craftsman, potter, bronzesmith, or tanner, or he could contract with the polis to work on public buildings. Certain crafts, including spinning and weaving, were generally done by women. Men and women without skills worked as paid laborers, but competed with slaves, who were usually foreigners or prisoners of war. Citizens and slaves were paid the same amount for their work.

The social conditions of Athenian women have been the subject of much debate and little agreement, in part because the sources are fragmentary. Women rarely played notable roles in public affairs, and we know the names of no female poets, artists, or philosophers from classical Athens. Women did manage the household and attend religious festivals. The status of a free woman was strictly protected by law. Only her children could be citizens. Only she was in charge of the household and the family's possessions, yet the law protected her primarily to protect her husband's interests. Women in Athens and elsewhere in Greece, like those in Mesopotamia, brought dowries to their husbands upon marriage, which legally remained their property.

● **Woman Grinding Grain**   Here a woman takes the grain raised on the family farm and grinds it by hand in a mill. She needed few tools to turn the grain into flour. *(National Archaeological Museum, Athens/Archaeological Receipts Fund)*

● **Sacrificial Scene** Much of Greek religion was simple and festive, as this scene demonstrates. The participants include women and boys dressed in their finest clothes and crowned with garlands. Musicians add to the festivities. Only the sheep will not enjoy the ceremony. *(National Archaeological Museum, Athens/ Archaeological Receipts Fund)*

A citizen woman's main functions were to bear and raise children. Respectable citizen women ideally lived secluded lives in which the only men they usually saw were relatives and tradesmen. How far this ideal was actually a reality is impossible to say, but prosperous women probably spent much of their time at home. There they oversaw domestic slaves and hired labor, and together with servants and friends worked wool into cloth. In a sense, poor and noncitizen women lived freer lives than did wealthier women. They performed manual labor in the fields or sold goods in the agora, going about their affairs much as men did. Prostitution was legal in Athens, and some prostitutes added intellectual accomplishments to physical beauty. These *hetairai* accompanied men in public settings where their wives would not have been welcome, serving men as social as well as sexual partners.

In classical Athens, part of a male adolescent citizen's training in adulthood was supposed to entail a hierarchical sexual and tutorial relationship with an older man, who most likely was married and may have had other female sexual partners as well. These relationships between adolescents and men were often celebrated in literature and art, in part because Athenians regarded perfection as possible only in the male. Women were generally seen as inferior to men, dominated by their bodies rather than their minds.

Same-sex relations did not mean that people did not marry, for Athenians saw the continuation of the family line as essential. Sexual desire and procreation were both important aspects of life, but they were not necessarily linked for ancient Greeks.

Greek Religion

It is extremely difficult to understand Greek religion, since, unlike modern peoples, the ancient Greeks had no uniform faith or creed. Although the Greeks usually worshiped the same deities—Zeus, Hera, Apollo, Athena, and others—the cults of these divinities varied from polis to polis. The Greeks had no sacred books such as the Bible, and Greek religion was often a matter more of ritual than belief. Nor did cults impose an ethical code of conduct. Unlike the Egyptians and Hebrews, the Greeks lacked a priesthood as the modern world understands the term. In Greece priests and priestesses existed to care for temples and sacred property and to conduct the proper rituals, but not to make religious rules or doctrines, much less to enforce them. In short, there existed in Greece no central ecclesiastical authority and no organized creed.

The most important members of the Greek pantheon were Zeus, the king of the gods, and his consort, Hera. Although they were the mightiest and most honored of the deities who lived on Mount Olympus, their divine children were closer to ordinary people. Apollo was especially popular. He represented the epitome of youth, beauty, benevolence, and athletic skill. He was also the god of music and culture, in many ways symbolizing the best of Greek culture. His sister Athena, who patronized women's crafts such as weaving, was also a warrior-goddess who had been born from the head of Zeus without a mother. Best known for her cult at Athens, to which she gave her name, she was highly revered throughout Greece. Besides these Olympian gods, each polis had its own minor deities, each with his or her own local cult. Much religion was local and domestic. Each village possessed its own cults and rituals, and individual families honored various deities in their homes.

Though Greek religion in general was individual or related to the polis, the Greeks also shared some Pan-Hellenic festivals, the chief of which were held at Olympia to honor Zeus and at Delphi to honor Apollo. The festivities at Olympia included the famous athletic contests that have inspired the modern Olympic games. Held every four years, they attracted visitors from all over the Greek world and lasted well into Christian times. The Pythian games at Delphi were also held every four years, but these contests included musical and literary competitions. Both the Olympic and Pythian games were unifying factors in Greek life.

The Flowering of Philosophy

The Greeks, like peoples before them, originally spun myths and epics to explain the origin of the universe. Yet going further, they created philosophy to understand the cosmos in purely physical terms. Some Greeks in Ionia began an intellectual revolution that still flourishes today. These thinkers are called the Pre-Socratics because their rational efforts preceded those of Socrates. Taking individual facts, they wove them into general theories. Despite appearances, they concluded, the universe is actually simple and subject to natural laws. Drawing on their observations, they speculated about the basic building blocks of the universe.

The first of these Pre-Socratic thinkers, Thales (ca. 600 B.C.E.) sought to determine the basic element of the universe from which all else sprang. He surmised that it was water. Although he was wrong, it was the beginning of the scientific method. Another Pre-Socratic, Anaximander (d. 547 B.C.E.) was the first to use general concepts, which are essential to abstract thought. Heraclitus (ca. 500 B.C.E.) declared the primal element to be fire, which is ever changing and eternal. Democritus (ca. 460 B.C.E.) created the atomic theory that the universe is made up of invisible, indestructible particles. The culmination of Pre-Socratic thought was the theory that four simple substances make up the universe: fire, air, earth, and water.

This stream of thought also branched into other directions. Hippocrates (ca. 470–400 B.C.E.), the father of medicine, sought natural explanations for diseases and natural means to treat them. He relied on empirical knowledge rather than religion or magic to further his work. The Sophists took the direction of making a distinction between science and philosophy. While differing on particulars, they all agreed that human beings were the proper subject of study. They also believed that excellence could be taught. They held that nothing is absolute; everything is relative.

Socrates (ca. 470–399 B.C.E.) shared the Sophists' belief that people are the essential subjects of philosophical inquiry. He started with a general topic and narrowed it

Primary Source:
Apologia
Learn why Socrates was condemned to death, and why he refused to stop questioning the wisdom of his countrymen.

to its essentials by posing questions, then sought answers. This is the Socratic method. He felt that through knowledge people could approach the supreme good and thus find happiness. Yet in 399 B.C.E. the Athenians executed him for corrupting the youth and for impiety.

Socrates' student Plato (427–347 B.C.E.) founded the Academy, a school dedicated to philosophy. Plato developed the theory that all tangible things are unreal and temporary, copies of "forms" or "ideas" that are constant and indestructible. The highest form is the idea of good, which he equated with god.

Aristotle (384–322 B.C.E.) went beyond his teacher Plato by using observation and analysis of natural phenomena to explain the cosmos. He argued that the universe was finite, spherical, and eternal. He postulated four principles: matter, form, movement, and goal. His theory of cosmology added ether as one of the building blocks of the universe. He wrongly concluded that the earth is the center of the universe and that the stars and planets revolve around it.

The philosophies of Plato and Aristotle both viewed women as inferior beings. Plato associated women with the body and emotions and men with superior faculties of mind and reason. Aristotle thought that women's primary purpose was to bear children. Even though Athenian philosophers pushed beyond the limited thinking of previous generations, they still reflected the accepted values and concepts of their times.

> **Primary Source:**
> **Aristotle on Politics**
> *Discover the strengths and weaknesses, as Aristotle saw them, of kingdoms, aristocracies, and democracies.*

MAP 4.3 **Alexander's Conquests** This map shows the course of Alexander's invasion of the Persian Empire and the speed of his progress. More important than the great success of his military campaigns was his founding of Hellenistic cities in the East.

From Polis to Monarchy (404–323 B.C.E.)

Immediately after the Peloponnesian War, Sparta began striving for empire over the Greeks. Yet even with Persian help, Sparta could not maintain its hold on Greece. In 371 B.C.E. at Leuctra in Boeotia, a Theban army under Epaminondas destroyed the flower of the Spartans. But the Thebans were unable to bring peace to Greece. In 362 B.C.E. Epaminondas was killed in battle, and a period of stalemate followed. Philip II,

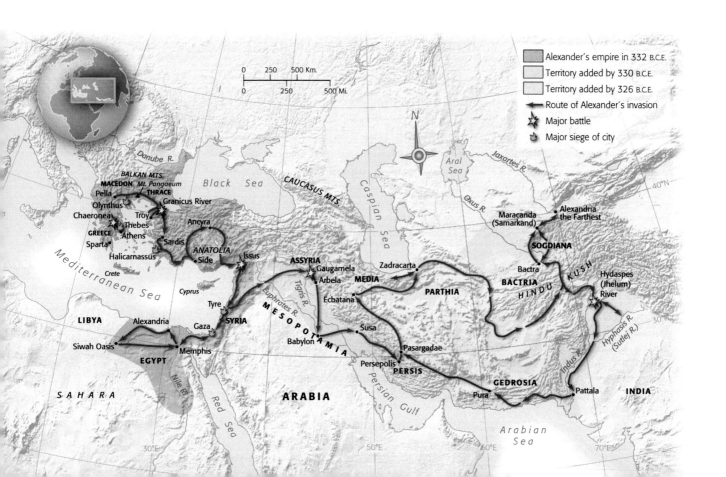

● **Alexander at the Battle of Issus**   At left, Alexander the Great, bareheaded and wearing a breastplate, charges King Darius, who is standing in a chariot. The moment marks the turning point of the battle, as Darius turns to flee from the attack. *(National Museum, Naples/Alinari/Art Resource, NY)*

king of Macedonia (r. 359–336 B.C.E.), turned the situation to his advantage. By clever use of his wealth and superb army, Philip won control of the northern Aegean, awakening fear in Athens. Finally, in 338 B.C.E. he defeated a combined Theban-Athenian army at Chaeronea. He had conquered Greece and become its arbiter. Because the Greeks could not put aside their quarrels, they fell to an invader.

Philip used his victory to unite the Greek states with his Macedonian kingdom to proclaim a crusade to liberate the Ionian Greeks from Persian rule. Before he could launch his crusade, Philip fell to an assassin's dagger in 336 B.C.E. His young son Alexander, soon to be known as "the Great," vowed to carry on Philip's mission. In 334 B.C.E. Alexander led an army of Macedonians and Greeks into western Asia. In the next three years he won three major battles—at the Granicus River, at Issus, and at Gaugamela—on his march to the east (see Map 4.3). Having overthrown the Persian Empire, in 326 B.C.E. he entered India. Finally, at the Hyphasis River his troops refused to go farther. Alexander reluctantly turned south to the Arabian Sea and then back west. In 324 B.C.E. Alexander returned to Susa, and died the next year Babylon.

The political consequence of Alexander's premature death was chaos. Since several of the chief Macedonian officers aspired to Alexander's position as emperor while others opposed them, civil war lasting forty-three years tore Alexander's empire apart. By the end of this conflict, the most successful generals had carved out their own smaller and generally stable monarchies.

Ptolemy immediately seized Egypt and transformed the native system into a Greco-Macedonian kingdom. Seleucus meanwhile won the bulk of Alexander's empire, his monarchy extending from western Asia to India. In the third century B.C.E., however, the eastern parts of Seleucus's monarchy gained their independence. The Parthians, a native people, came to power in Iran, and the Greeks created a monarchy of their own in Bactria. Antigonus maintained control of the Macedonian kingdom in Europe. Until the arrival of the Romans in the eastern Mediterranean in the second century B.C.E., the great monarchies waged frequent wars that brought no lasting results. The Hellenistic monarchy was no improvement on the Greek polis.

• • • • • • • • • • • • • • •

THE SPREAD OF HELLENISM (336–100 B.C.E.)

After Alexander the Great's conquest of the Persian Empire, how did Greek immigrants and the native peoples there create a new society?

When the Greeks and Macedonians entered Asia and Egypt, they encountered civilization older than their own. In some ways the Eastern cultures were more advanced than theirs, in others less so. Thus this third great tide of Greek migration differed from preceding waves that had spread over land inhabited by less-developed peoples. In this process both Greeks and native peoples confronted a new cultural reality. The Greeks saw themselves as "the West," while the peoples of the ancient Near East made up "the East." "East" as yet had no wider meaning for the Greeks, who had only just learned of India and knew nothing of China and lands beyond. Since the Eastern civilization was older and in some ways more sophisticated than the Greek, the newcomers had a great deal to learn from it. Yet the Greeks also proved surprisingly successful in spreading their own vibrant culture among the easterners. The result was the blending of Hellenism and Near Eastern cultures that is now called "Hellenistic." No comparable spread and sharing of cultures had occurred in this area since the days of the Mesopotamians.

Cities and Kingdoms

A major development in this new world was the supremacy of monarchy that for the Greeks replaced the polis as the chief political unit of society. Furthermore, these new kingdoms consisted of numerous different peoples who at first had little in common. Although the native populations found kingdoms traditional and familiar, to the Greeks monarchy was new and somewhat alien. To them civilized life without the polis was unthinkable. Hellenistic kings solved the problem by combining the concepts of monarchy and polis to embrace all their subjects. The kingdom became dominant in political affairs, and the polis, now only a city, served as the administrative and cultural unit. The Greek city thereby became the linchpin of the Hellenistic monarchy.

A problem, however, remained with this solution. The Greek polis had been **sovereign,** and in a monarchy only the king held sovereignty. Unwilling to create a real polis, Hellenistic kings gave their cities all the external trappings of a polis but none of the political power. Consequently, the Hellenistic city resembled a modern city. It was a cultural center with theaters, temples, and libraries—a seat of learning and a place for amusement. The Hellenistic city was also an economic center—a marketplace, a scene of trade and manufacturing. On these terms Hellenistic cities proved remarkably effective.

sovereign *An independent, autonomous state run by its citizens, free of any outside power or restraint.*

Building a Shared Society

Despite difficulties, Hellenistic monarchies successfully spread Greek culture. If the Hellenistic component was sometimes largely a veneer, it at least touched nearly every life. At the same time the Greeks became increasingly influenced by the societies they conquered. These two tendencies produced a mutually recognized common Hellenistic culture, remarkably widespread and healthy. Even so, Hellenistic kingdoms were never entirely unified in language, customs, and thought. Greek culture took firmest hold along the shores of the Mediterranean, where it thrived until the coming of the Arabs. It also prospered farther inland. In Bactria Greek and Iranian settlements led to an independent society that was soundly founded and well integrated. Bactria itself became an outpost of Hellenism, from which the Han Dynasty learned of civilized societies other than the Chinese (see page 137). Greco-Bactrians prospered until invaders from Central Asia overwhelmed their settlements in the first century B.C.E. Nonetheless, its cultural influence lasted another century.

The Seleucid kings most successfully built a shared society by their extensive colonization. Their military settlements spread from western Asia Minor along the banks of the Tigris and Euphrates and father east to India. Although the Seleucids had no elaborate plan for Hellenizing the native population, they nevertheless introduced a large and vigorous Greek population to these lands. Their presence alone had an impact. Seleucid military colonies were generally founded near native villages, thus exposing each to the other's culture. Farther east Greek kings won their independence from the Seleucids and extended their influence into India.

By contrast, the Ptolemies in Egypt at first made no effort to spread their culture, and unlike other Hellenistic kings they were not city builders. Indeed, they founded only the city of Ptolemais near Thebes. The native Egyptian population, the descendants of the pharaoh's people, originally kept their traditional language, religion, and way of life. They also continued to be the foundation of the state. They fed it by their labor in the fields and financed it with their taxes. In the second century B.C.E., however, Greeks and native Egyptians began to intermarry and mingle their cultures and languages. Some natives adopted Greek customs and language and began to play a role in the administration of the kingdom and even to serve in the army. Although more slowly than elsewhere, the overall result was the evolution of a widespread Greco-Egyptian culture.

For natives the prime advantage of Hellenistic culture was its very pervasiveness. The Greek language became the common speech of the entire eastern Mediterranean. A new Greek dialect called the **koine**, which means common, became the speech of the royal court, bureaucracy, and army. Everyone, Greek or easterner, who wanted to find an official position or compete in business had to learn it. As early as the third century B.C.E. some Greek cities granted citizenship to Hellenized natives.

koine *A common dialect of the Greek language that influenced the speech of all Greeks.*

Though Greeks and easterners adapted to each other's ways, there was never a true fusion of cultures. Nonetheless, each found many useful things in the civilization of the other, and they fertilized each other. This mingling of Greek and eastern elements made Hellenistic culture energetic and successful.

The Economic Scope of the Hellenistic World

Alexander's conquest not only changed the political face of the ancient world but also merged it into one broad economic sphere. Yet the period did not see a revolution in the way people lived and worked. The material demands of Hellenistic society remained as simple as before. Yet the spread of Greeks eastward created new markets and stimulated trade. The economic unity of the Hellenistic world, like its cultural bonds, later proved valuable to the Romans.

When Alexander conquered the Persian Empire, he found the royal treasury filled with vast sums of gold, silver, and other treasure. The victors used this wealth to finance the building of roads, the development of harbors, and most especially the founding of new cities. Whole new markets opened to all merchants, who eagerly took advantage of the unforeseen opportunities. In this fresh economic environment Greeks and local residents learned of each other's customs and traditions while forging new contacts. In the process they also spread immediate knowledge of their own cultures.

The Seleucid and Ptolemaic dynasties traded as far afield as India, Arabia, and sub-Saharan Africa. Overland trade with India and Arabia was conducted by caravan that was largely in the hands of easterners. The caravan trade never dealt in bulk goods or essential commodities. Once goods reached the Hellenistic monarchies, Greek merchants took a hand in the trade. Essential to this trade from the Mediterranean to Afghanistan and India was the southern route through Arabia. The desert of Arabia lies west of the Iranian plateau, from which trade routes stretched to the south and farther east to China. Commerce from the east arrived at Egypt and the harbors of Palestine, Phoenicia, and Syria. From these ports goods flowed to Greece, Italy, and Spain.

Over these routes traveled luxury goods that were light, rare, and expensive. In time these luxury items became necessities. This whole development was in part the result of an increased volume of trade. In the prosperity of the period, more people could afford to buy gold, silver, precious stones, and many other easily transportable goods. The most prominent goods in terms of volume were tea and silk. Indeed, the trade in silk gave the major route the name the **Great Silk Road.** In return the peoples of the eastern Mediterranean sent east manufactured items, especially metal weapons, cloth, wine, and olive oil. Although these caravan routes can trace their origins to earlier times, they became far more prominent in the Hellenistic period. Business customs developed and became standardized so that merchants of different nationalities, aided especially by koine, communicated in a way understandable to them all.

Great Silk Road *The name of the major route for the silk trade.*

More economically important than this exotic trade were commercial dealings in essential commodities like raw materials, grain, and industrial products. The Hellenistic monarchies usually raised enough grain for their own needs as well as a surplus for export. For the cities of the Aegean the trade in grain was essential, because many of them could not grow enough. Fortunately for them, abundant wheat supplies were available nearby in Egypt and in the Crimea in southern Russia.

The Greek cities paid for their grain by exporting olive oil and wine. Another significant commodity was fish, which for export was either salted, pickled, or dried. This trade was doubly important because fish provided poor people with an essential element of their diet. Important also was the trade in honey, dried fruit, nuts, and vegetables. Of raw materials wood was high in demand.

Throughout the Hellenistic world slaves almost always found a ready market. Only the Ptolemies discouraged both the trade and slavery itself, but they did so only for economic reasons. Their system had no room for slaves, who only would have competed with inexpensive free labor. Otherwise slave labor could be found in cities and temples, in factories and fields, and in the homes of wealthier people.

Most trade in bulk commodities was seaborne, and the Hellenistic merchant ship was the workhorse of the day. The merchant ship had a broad beam and relied on sails for propulsion. It was far more seaworthy than the Hellenistic warship, which was long, narrow, and built for speed. A small crew of experienced sailors easily handled the merchant vessel. Maritime trade also provided opportunities for workers in many other industries and trades, particularly shipbuilders, dockworkers, teamsters, and pirates. Piracy was a constant factor in the Hellenistic world and remained so until Rome cleared it from the seas.

While demand for goods increased during the period, few new techniques of production appeared. Manual labor far more than machinery continued to turn out agricultural produce, raw materials, and the few manufactured goods the Hellenistic world used. Typical was mining, where slaves, criminals, or forced laborers dug the ore under frightful conditions. The Ptolemies ran their gold mines along harsh lines. One historian gives a grim picture of the miners' lives:

The kings of Egypt condemn [to the mines] those found guilty of wrong-doing and those taken prisoner in war, those who are victims of false accusations and were put into jail because of royal anger. . . . The condemned—and they are very many—all of them are put in chains, and they work persistently and continually, both by day and throughout the night, getting no rest and carefully cut off from escape.[2]

The Ptolemies even condemned women and children to work in the mines. Besides gold and silver, used primarily for coins and jewelry, iron was the most important metal and saw the most varied use. Even so, the method of production never became very sophisticated. Despite these shortcomings, the volume of goods produced increased in this period. Small manufacturing establishments existed nearly everywhere.

All Hellenistic kings paid special attention to agriculture. Much of their revenue came from the produce of royal lands, rents paid by the tenants of royal lands, and taxation of them. The Ptolemies, who made the greatest strides in agriculture, sponsored experiments to improve seed grain. These efforts apart, most people supported themselves in the traditional ways that supplied their basic needs.

HELLENISTIC INTELLECTUAL ADVANCES

How did the intellectual meeting of two vibrant cultures lead to a very fertile intellectual development?

The peoples of the Hellenistic era advanced the ideas and ideals of the classical Greeks to new heights. Their achievements created the religious and intellectual atmosphere that deeply influenced Roman thinking and that of Judaism and early Christianity. Far from being stagnant, this was instead a period of vigorous growth, especially in the areas of philosophy, science, and medicine.

Religion in the Hellenistic World

In religion the most significant new ideas arose outside of Greece. The Hellenistic period saw at first the spread of Greek cults throughout the Near East. When Hellenistic kings founded cities, they also built temples with new cults and priesthoods for the old Olympian gods. Greek cults, as before, sponsored literary, musical, and athletic contests, which were staged in beautiful surroundings among splendid Greek buildings. On the whole, however, the civic cults were primarily concerned with ritual and neither appealed to religious emotions nor embraced matters such as sin and redemption. While lavish in pomp and display, the new cults could not satisfy deep religious feelings or spiritual yearnings.

Greek increasingly sought solace from other sources. Some relied on philosophy as a guide to life, while others turned to superstition, magic, or astrology. Still others shrugged and spoke of **Tyche,** which means "fate," "chance," or "doom"—a capricious and sometimes malevolent force.

Beginning in the second century B.C.E. some individuals were increasingly attracted to new **mystery religions,** so called because they featured a body of ritual and beliefs not divulged to anyone not initiated into the cult. These new mystery cults incorporated aspects of both Greek and Eastern religions and held broad appeal for people who yearned for personal immortality. Already familiar with old mystery cults such as the Eleusinian mysteries in Attica, the new cults did not strike the Greeks as alien. Familiar, too, was the concept of preparation for an initiation. Devotees of the Eleusinian mysteries and other such cults had to prepare themselves mentally, physically, and spiritually before entering the gods' presence. The mystery cults thus fit well with Greek practice.

The new religions enjoyed one tremendous advantage over the old Greek mystery cults. Whereas old Greek cults were tried to particular places, such as Eleusis, the new religions spread

Tyche *The Greek goddess of fate and luck, eventually identified with the Roman goddess Fortuna.*

mystery religions *Any of several religious systems in the Greco-Roman world characterized by secret doctrines and rituals of initiation.*

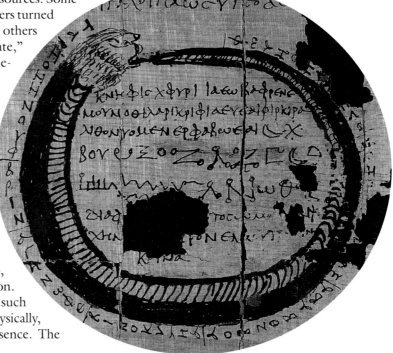

● **Hellenistic Magic** This magical text, written in Greek and Egyptian, displays a snake surrounding the magical incantation. The text is intentionally obscure. *(British Library)*

● **Hellenistic Mystery Cult** The scene depicts part of the ritual of initiation into the cult of Dionysus. The young woman here has just completed the ritual. She now dances in joy as the official with the sacred staff looks on. *(Scala/Art Resource, NY)*

Epicureanism *A Greek system of philosophy founded on the teachings of Epicurus, which emphasized that a life of contentment, free from fear and suffering, was the greatest good.*

throughout the Hellenistic world. People did not have to undertake long and expensive pilgrimages just to become members of the religion. In that sense the mystery religions came to the people, for temples of the new deities sprang up wherever Greeks lived.

The mystery religions all claimed to save their adherents from the worst that fate could do and promised life for the soul after death. They all had a single concept in common: the belief that by the rites of initiation devotees became united with a deity who had also died and risen from the dead. The sacrifice of the god and his victory over death saved the devotee from eternal death. Similarly, all mystery religions demanded a period of preparation in which the converts strove to become holy, that is, to live by the religion's precepts. Once aspirants had prepared themselves, they went through an initiation in which they learned the secrets of the religion. The initiation was usually a ritual of great emotional intensity, symbolizing the entry into a new life.

Among the mystery religions the Egyptian cults of Serapis and Isis took the Hellenistic world by storm. Serapis, who was invented by King Ptolemy, was believed to be the judge of souls who rewarded virtuous and righteous people with eternal life. The cult of Isis enjoyed even wider appeal than that of Serapis. Isis, wife of Osiris, was believed to have conquered Tyche and promised to save any mortal who came to her. She became the most important goddess of the Hellenistic world, especially among women. Her priests claimed that she had bestowed on humanity the gift of civilization and founded law and literature. She was the goddess of marriage, conception, and childbirth. Like Serapis, she promised to save the souls of her believers.

Mystery religions took care of the big things in life, but many people resorted to ordinary magic for daily matters. When a cat walked across their path, they threw three rocks across the road. People often purified their houses to protect them from Hecate, a sinister goddess associated with witchcraft. Many people had dreams that only seers and augurs could interpret. Some of these superstitions are familiar today because some old fears still live.

Philosophy and the People

During the Hellenistic period philosophy touched more people than ever before. Two significant philosophies caught the minds and hearts of many Greeks and easterners, as well as many later Romans. The first was **Epicureanism,** a practical philosophy of serenity in an often tumultuous world. Epicurus (340–270 B.C.E.) taught that the principal good of life is pleasure, which he defined as the absence of pain. He concluded that any violent emotion is undesirable. He advocated instead mild self-discipline and even considered poverty good so long as people had enough food, clothing, and shelter. Epicurus also taught that people can most easily attain peace and serenity by ignoring the outside world and looking instead into their personal feelings. His followers ignored politics, for it led to tumult, which would disturb the soul.

Opposed to the passivity of the Epicureans, Zeno (335–262 B.C.E.) came to Athens, where he formed his own school, **Stoicism,** named after the Stoa, the building where he taught. To the Stoics the important matter was not whether they achieved anything, but whether they lived virtuous lives. In that way they could triumph over Tyche, which could destroy their achievements but not the nobility of their lives. Stoicism became the most popular Hellenistic philosophy and the one that later captured the mind of Rome.

Zeno and his fellow Stoics considered nature an expression of divine will. In their view, people could be happy only when living in accordance with nature. They stressed "the brotherhood of man," the concept that all people were kindred who were obliged to help one another. The Stoics' most lasting practical achievement was the creation of the concept of natural law. The Stoics concluded that as all people were brothers, partook of divine reason, and were in harmony with the universe, one **natural law** governed them all.

Hellenistic Science

Hellenistic culture achieved its greatest triumphs in science. The most notable of the Hellenistic astronomers was Aristarchus of Samos (ca. 310–230 B.C.E.), who was educated at Aristotle's school. Aristarchus concluded that the sun is far larger than the earth and that the stars are enormously distant from the earth. He argued against Aristotle's view that the earth is the center of the universe. Aristarchus instead propounded the **heliocentric theory**—that the earth and planets revolve around the sun. His work is all the more impressive because he lacked even a rudimentary telescope. Aristarchus's theories, however, did not persuade the ancient world. His heliocentric theory lay dormant until resurrected in the sixteenth century by the brilliant astronomer Nicolaus Copernicus.

In geometry Euclid (ca. 300 B.C.E.), a mathematician living in Alexandria, compiled a valuable textbook of existing knowledge. His book *The Elements of Geometry* became the standard introduction to the subject. Generations of students from antiquity to the present have learned the essentials of geometry from it.

Stoicism   *The most popular of Hellenistic philosophies; it considers nature an expression of divine will and holds that people can be happy only when living in accordance with nature.*

natural law   *The belief that the laws governing ethical behavior are written into nature itself and therefore possess universal validity.*

heliocentric theory   *The belief that the earth revolves around the sun.*

● **Tyche**   The statue depicts Tyche as the bringer of bounty to people. Some Hellenistic Greeks worshiped Tyche in the hope that she would be kind to them. Philosophers tried to free people from her whimsies. Others tried to placate her. *(Fatih Cimok, Turkey)*

● **Catapult** This model shows a catapult as its crew would have seen it in action. The arrow was loaded on the long horizontal beam, its point fitting into the housing. There the torsion spring under great pressure released the arrow at the target, which could be some 400 yards away. *(Courtesy, Noel Kavan)*

The greatest thinker of the period was Archimedes (ca. 287–212 B.C.E.). A clever inventor, he devised new artillery for military purposes. In peacetime he created the Archimedian screw to draw water from a lower to a higher level. (See the feature "Individuals in Society: Archimedes and the Practical Application of Science.") He invented the compound pully to lift heavy weights. His chief interest, however, lay in pure mathematics. He founded the science of hydrostatics and discovered the principle that the weight of a solid floating in a liquid is equal to the weight of the liquid displaced by the solid.

Archimedes willingly shared his work with others, among them Eratosthenes (285–ca. 204 B.C.E.), who was the librarian of the vast royal library in Alexandria. Eratosthenes used mathematics to further the geographical studies for which he is most famous. He calculated the circumference of the earth geometrically, estimating it as about 24,675 miles. He was not wrong by much: the earth is actually 24,860 miles in circumference. Eratosthenes further concluded that the earth is a spherical globe and that the ocean surrounds the land mass.

Besides these tools for peace, Hellenistic science applied theories of mechanics to build machines that revolutionized warfare. The catapult shot large arrows and small stones against enemy targets. Engineers also built wooden siege towers as artillery platforms. Generals added battering rams to bring down large portions of walls. If these new engines made warfare more efficient, they also added to the misery of the people. War came to embrace the whole population.

Hellenistic Medicine

The study of medicine flourished during the Hellenistic period, and Hellenistic physicians carried the work of Hippocrates into new areas. Herophilus, who lived in the first half of the third century B.C.E., approached the study of medicine in a systematic, scientific fashion. He dissected corpses and measured what he observed. He discovered the nervous system and concluded that two types of nerves, motor and sensory, existed. Herophilus also studied the brain, which he considered the center of intelligence. In the process he discerned the cerebrum and cerebellum. His other work dealt with the liver, lungs, and uterus.

In about 280 B.C.E. Philinus and Serapion, pupils of Herophilus, concentrated on the observation and cure of illnesses rather than focusing on dissection. They also laid heavier stress on the use of drugs and medicines to treat illnesses. Heraclides of Tarentum (perhaps first century B.C.E.) carried on this tradition by discovering the benefits of opium and other drugs that relieved pain.

The Hellenistic world was also plagued by people who claimed to cure illnesses through incantations and magic. Quacks tried to heal and alleviate pain by administering weird potions and bogus concoctions. The medical abuses that arose during the period were so flagrant that many people developed an intense distrust of physicians. Nevertheless, the work of men like Herophilus and Serapion made valuable contributions to the knowledge of medicine, and the fruits of their work were handed on to posterity.

Individuals IN SOCIETY

Archimedes and the Practical Application of Science

Throughout the ages generals have besieged cities to force them to surrender. Sieges were particularly hard and violent, bringing misery to soldiers and civilians alike. Between 213 and 211 B.C.E. the Roman general Marcellus laid close siege to the strongly walled city of Syracuse, the home of Archimedes. Not a soldier, Archimedes was the greatest scientist of his age. He towered above all others in abstract thought. The Roman siege challenged him to a practical response. Hiero, king of Syracuse and friend of Archimedes, turned to him for help.

The king persuaded Archimedes to prepare for him offensive and defensive engines to be used in every kind of warfare. These he had never used himself, because he spent the greater part of his life in freedom from war and amid the festal rites of peace. But at the present time his apparatus stood the Syracusans in good stead, and, with the apparatus, its fabricator. When, therefore, the Romans assaulted them by sea and land, the Syracusans were stricken dumb with terror. They thought that nothing could withstand so furious an onset by such forces.

Archimedes, however, began to ply his engines, and shot against the land forces of the attackers all sorts of missiles and immense masses of stones, which came down with incredible din and speed. Nothing whatever could ward off their weight, but they knocked down in heaps those who stood in their way, and threw their ranks into confusion. At the same time huge beams were suddenly projected over the ships from the walls, which sank some of them with great weights plunging down from on high. Others were seized at the prow by iron claws, or beaks like the beaks of cranes, drawn straight up into the air, and then plunged stern first into the depths, or were turned round and round by means of enginery within the city, and dashed upon the steep cliffs that jutted out beneath the wall of the city, with great destruction of the fighting men on board, who perished in the wrecks. Frequently, too, a ship would be lifted out of the water into mid-air, whirled here and there as it hung there, a dreadful spectacle, until its crew had been thrown out and hurled in all directions. Then it would fall empty upon the walls, or slip away from the clutch that had held it. As for the engine that Marcellus was bringing up on the bridge of ships, and which was called "sambuca" [large mechanically operated scaling ladders carried on ships].

While it was still some distance off in its approach to the wall, a stone of 500 pounds' weight was discharged at it, then a second and a third. Some of them, falling upon it with great noise and surge of wave, crushed the foundation of the engine, shattered its framework, and dislodged it from the platform, so that Marcellus, in perplexity, ordered his ships to sail back as fast as they could and his land forces to retire. . . .

Many of their ships, too, were dashed together, and they could not retaliate in any way upon their foes. For Archimedes had built most of his engines close behind the wall, and the Romans seemed to be fighting against the gods, now that countless mischiefs were poured out upon them from an invisible source.

At last the Romans became so fearful that whenever they saw a bit of rope or a stick of timber projecting a little over the wall. "There it is," they shouted, "Archimedes is training some engine upon us." They then turned their backs and fled. Seeing this, Marcellus desisted from all the fighting and assault, and thenceforth depended on a long siege.

For all his genius, Archimedes did not survive the siege. His deeds of war done, he returned to his thinking and his mathematical problems, even with the siege still in the background. When Syracuse was betrayed to the Romans, soldiers streamed in, spreading slaughter and destruction throughout the city. A Roman soldier came upon Archimedes in his study and killed him outright, thus ending the life of one of the world's greatest thinkers.

Archimedes' mill. A slave turns a large cylinder fitted with blades to form a screw that draws water from a well. *(Courtesy, Soprintendenza Archeologica di Pompei. Photograph by Penelope M. Allison)*

Questions for Analysis

1. How did Archimedes' engines repulse the Roman attacks?

2. What effect did his weapons have on the Roman attackers?

3. What is the irony of Archimedes' death?

Source: Reprinted by permission of the publishers and the Trustees of the Loeb Classical Library™ from *Plutarch: Volume V,* Loeb Classical Library™ Volume 87, trans. Bernadotte Perrin (Cambridge, Mass.: Harvard University Press), 1917. The Loeb Classical Library™ is a registered trademark of the President and Fellows of Harvard College.

Chapter Summary

To assess your mastery of this chapter, go to
bedfordstmartins.com/mckayworld

• *How did the geography of Greece divide the land so that small communities naturally developed?*

Terrain divided the land of Greece and the Aegean into small parcels that nurtured small communities. Some groups of people joined together in kingdoms, notably the Minoan kingdom in Crete and the Mycenaean on the mainland. The fall of these kingdoms led to a period known as the Greek Dark Age (ca. 1100–ca. 800 B.C.E.). Greek culture survived the collapse and developed the polis in which individuals governed themselves without elaborate political machinery. They created two prominent forms of governing—oligarchy, rule by a few citizens, and democracy, rule by all citizens. The success of the polis made it the ideal Greek government.

• *What were the major accomplishments of the Archaic age, and why were they important?*

In the Archaic period (ca. 800–500 B.C.E.), Greece prospered until it produced a burgeoning population that colonized the Mediterranean from the Atlantic Ocean to the Black Sea. Sparta created the most successful military polis, while the Athenian polis became democratic.

• *Although the classical period saw tremendous upheavals, what were its lasting achievements?*

The Greeks of the classical period (500–338 B.C.E.) successfully defended themselves from Persian invasions but nearly destroyed themselves in the Peloponnesian War. Yet they built comfortable cities decorated with architectural monuments and fine sculpture. They invented drama to explain individuals and their place in society. They refined their religious beliefs and evolved philosophy the better to understand life.

• *After Alexander the Great's conquest of the Persian Empire, how did Greek immigrants and the native peoples there create a new society?*

When Alexander the Great defeated the Persians, he opened western and central Asia to Greek expansion, resulting in the blending of these civilizations. In the Hellenistic period (336–146 B.C.E.) kingdoms and their cities sponsored a common culture linked by a common Greek dialect, the koine. Hellenistic society promoted commerce, and trade routes connected distant places as never before. Larger populations produced more goods, grew wealthier, and enjoyed broader outlooks. These developments led to greater advances in religion, which was marked by new mystery cults that promised eternal life.

• *How did the intellectual meeting of two vibrant cultures lead to a very fertile intellectual development?*

The new philosophies of Epicureanism and Stoicism helped people cope successfully with Tyche and the new demands of life. Hellenistic thinkers furthered knowledge of the earth and the entire universe. Advances in medicine made the Hellenistic world a healthier place. All these advances resulted in a large, generally satisfied, and worldly society.

Suggested Reading

Archibald, Z. H., et al. *Hellenistic Economics.* 2001. A very informative treatment of the subject.

Boardman, J. *The Greeks Overseas.* 2001. Very valuable coverage of Greek colonization.

Bosworth, A. B. *Conquest and Empire.* 1988. The most balanced discussion of Alexander the Great.

Buckler, J. *Aegean Greece in the Fourth Century BC.* 2003. The only modern study of this period.

Hansen, M. H. *Polis.* 2006. Already the classic treatment of the subject.

Hodkinson, S. *Property and Wealth in Classical Sparta.* 2000. Discusses many vital aspects of Spartan life.

Kingsley, P. *Ancient Philosophy.* 1996. A balanced survey of the entire field.

Patterson, C. B. *The Family in Greek History.* 2001. Treats public and private family relations.

Price, S. *Religions of the Ancient Greeks.* 1999. Covers all religions from ca. 800 B.C.E. to 500 C.E.

Thomas, C. G., and C. Conant. *Citadel to City-State.* 2003. An excellent treatment of early Greece and modern ideas about it.

Notes

1. Thucydides 2.12, translated by J. Buckler.
2. Diodoros 3.12.2–3, translated by J. Buckler.

Listening to the PAST

Alexander and the Brotherhood of Man

One historical problem challenged historians throughout the twentieth century and has yet to be solved to everyone's satisfaction. After returning to Opis, north of Babylon in modern Iraq, Alexander found himself confronted with a huge and unexpected mutiny by his Macedonian veterans. He held a banquet to pacify them, and he included in the festivities some Persians and other Asian followers, some nine thousand in all. During the festivities he offered a public prayer for harmony and partnership in rule between the Macedonians and Persians. Many modern scholars have interpreted this prayer as an expression of his desire to establish a "brotherhood of man." The following passage provides the evidence for this view. From it all readers can determine for themselves whether Alexander attempted to introduce a new philosophical ideal or whether he harbored his own political motives for political cooperation.

8. When [Alexander] arrived at Opis, he collected the Macedonians and announced that he intended to discharge from the army those who were useless for military service either from age or from being maimed in the limbs; and he said he would send them back to their own abodes. He also promised to give those who went back as much extra reward as would make them special objects of envy to those at home and arouse in the other Macedonians the wish to share similar dangers and labours. Alexander said this, no doubt, for the purpose of pleasing the Macedonians; but on the contrary they were, not without reason, offended by the speech which he delivered, thinking that now they were despised by him and deemed to be quite useless for military service. Indeed, throughout the whole of this expedition they had been offended at many other things; for his adoption of the Persian dress, thereby exhibiting his contempt for their opinion often caused them grief, as did also his accoutring the foreign soldiers called Epigoni in the Macedonian style, and the mixing of the alien horsemen among the ranks of the Companions. Therefore they could not remain silent and control themselves, but urged him to dismiss all of them from his army; and they advised him to prosecute the war in company with his father, deriding Ammon by

this remark. When Alexander heard this . . . , he ordered the most conspicuous of the men who had tried to stir up the multitude to sedition to be arrested. He himself pointed out with his hand to the shield-bearing guards those whom they were to arrest, to the number of thirteen; and he ordered these to be led away to execution. When the rest, stricken with terror, became silent, he mounted the platform again, and spoke as follows:

9. "The speech which I am about to deliver will not be for the purpose of checking your start homeward, for, so far as I am concerned, you may depart wherever you wish; but for the purpose of making you understand when you take yourselves off, what kind of men you have been to us who have conferred such benefits upon you. . . .

10. . . . Most of you have golden crowns, the eternal memorials of your valour and of the honour you receive from me. Whoever has been killed has met with a glorious end and has been honoured with a splendid burial. Brazen statues of most of the slain have been erected at home, and their parents are held in honour, being released from all public service and from taxation. But no one of you has ever been killed in flight under my leadership. And now I was intending to send back those of you who are unfit for service, objects of envy to those at home; but since you all wish to depart, depart all of you! Go back and report at home that your king Alexander, the conqueror of the Persians, Medes, Bactrians, and Sacians; the man who has subjugated the Uxians, Arachotians, and Drangians; who has also acquired the rule of the Parthians, Chorasmians, and Hyrcanians, as far as the Caspian Sea . . . —report that when you returned to Susa you deserted him and went away, handing him over to the protection of conquered foreigners. Perhaps this report of yours will be both glorious to you in the eyes of men and devout I ween in the eyes of the gods. Depart!"

11. Having thus spoken, he leaped down quickly from the platform, and entered the palace, where he paid no attention to the decoration of his person, nor was any of his Companions admitted to see him. Not

This gilded case for a bow and arrows indicates that Alexander's success came at the price of blood. These vigorous scenes portray more military conflict than philosophical compassion. *(Archaeological Museum Salonica/Dagli-Orti/ The Art Archive)*

even on the morrow was any one of them admitted to an audience; but on the third day he summoned the select Persians within, and among them he distributed the commands of the brigades, and made the rule that only those whom he proclaimed his kinsmen should have the honour of saluting him with a kiss. But the Macedonians who heard the speech were thoroughly astonished at the moment, and remained there in silence near the platform; nor when he retired did any of them accompany the king, except his personal Companions and the confidential body-guards. Though they remained most of them had nothing to do or say; and yet they were unwilling to retire. But when the news was reported to them . . . they were no longer able to restrain themselves; but running in a body to the palace, they cast their weapons there in front of the gates as signs of supplication to the king. Standing in front of the gates, they shouted, beseeching to be allowed to enter, and saying that they were willing to surrender the men who had been the instigators of the disturbance on that occasion, and those who had begun the clamour. They also declared they would not retire from the gates either day or night, unless Alexander would take some pity upon them. When he was informed of this, he came out without delay; and seeing them lying on the ground in humble guise, and hearing most of them lamenting with loud voice, tears began to flow also from his own eyes. He made an effort to say something to them, but they continued their importunate entreaties. At length one of them, Callines by name, a man conspicuous both for his age and because he was a captain of the Companion cavalry, spoke as follows, "O king, what grieves the Macedonians is that you have already made some of the Persians kinsmen to yourself, and that Persians are called Alexander's kinsmen, and have the honour of saluting you with a kiss; whereas none of the Macedonians have as yet enjoyed this honour." Then Alexander, interrupting him, said, "But all of you without exception I consider my kinsmen, and so from this time I shall call you." When he had said this, Callines advanced and saluted him with a kiss, and so did all those who wished to salute him. Then they took up their weapons and returned to the camp, shouting and singing a song of thanksgiving. After this Alexander offered sacrifice to the gods to whom it was his custom to sacrifice, and gave a public banquet, over which he himself presided, with the Macedonians sitting around him; and next to them the Persians; after whom came the men of the other nations, preferred in honour for their personal rank or for some meritorious action. The king and his guests drew wine from the same bowl and poured out the same libations, both the Grecian prophets and the Magians commencing the ceremony. He prayed for other blessings, and especially that harmony and community of rule might exist between the Macedonians and Persians.

Questions for Analysis

1. What was the purpose of the banquet at Opis?

2. Were all of the guests treated equally?

3. What did Alexander gain from bringing together the Macedonians and Persians?

Source: Arrian, *Anabasis of Alexander* 7.8.1–11.9 in F. R. B. Goldophin, ed., *The Greek Historians,* vol. 2. Copyright 1942 and renewed 1970 by Random House, Inc. Used by permission of Random House, Inc.

The Roman Forum. *(Josephine Powell, Photographer, Courtesy of Special Collections, Fine Arts Library, Harvard College Library)*

5

THE WORLD OF ROME
(753 B.C.E.–479 C.E.)

Chapter Preview

The Romans in Italy (ca. 750–290 B.C.E.)
• How did the Romans come to dominate Italy, and what political institutions did they create?

Roman Expansion and Its Repercussions
• How did Rome expand its power beyond Italy, and what were the effects of success on Rome?

The Coming of Christianity
• What was Christianity, and how did it affect life in the empire?

The "Golden Age"
• How did efficient Roman rule lead to a "golden age" for the empire?

Turmoil and Reform (284–337 C.E.)
• How did barbarian invasions and political turmoil shape the Roman Empire in the third and fourth centuries?

Like the Persians under Cyrus and the Macedonians under Alexander, the Romans conquered vast territories in less than a century. Their singular achievement lay in their ability to incorporate conquered peoples into the Roman system. Unlike the Greeks, who refused to share citizenship, the Romans extended theirs first to the Italians and later to the peoples of the provinces. With that citizenship went Roman government and law. Rome created a state that embraced the entire Mediterranean area and extended northward. After a grim period of civil war, in 31 B.C.E. the emperor Augustus restored peace. He extended Roman power and law as far east as the Euphrates River and created the structure that the modern world calls the "Roman Empire."

Roman history is usually divided into two periods: the republic, the age in which Rome grew from a small city-state to ruler of an empire; and the empire, the period when the republican constitution gave way to a constitutional monarchy.

THE ROMANS IN ITALY (CA. 750–290 B.C.E.)

How did the Romans come to dominate Italy, and what political institutions did they create?

While the Greeks pursued their destiny in the eastern Mediterranean, two peoples—the Etruscans and Romans—entered the peninsula of Italy. The Etruscans developed the first cities and a rich cultural life, but the Romans eventually came to dominate the peninsula.

The Etruscans and Rome

The arrival of the Etruscans in the region of Etruria can reasonably be dated to about 750 B.C.E. The Etruscans established permanent settlements that evolved into the first Italian cities, which resembled the

Greek city-states in political organization. They spread their influence over the surrounding countryside, which they farmed and mined for its rich mineral resources. From an early period the Etruscans began to trade natural products, especially iron, with their Greek neighbors in the Mediterranean in exchange for luxury goods. They thereby built a rich cultural life that became the foundation of civilization throughout Italy. In the process they encountered a small collection of villages subsequently called Rome.

The Romans had settled in Italy by the eighth century B.C.E. According to one legend, Romulus and Remus founded the city in 753 B.C.E., Romulus making his home on the Palatine Hill, while Remus chose the Avertine. Under Etruscan influence the Romans prospered, occupying all of Rome's seven hills. Located at an easy crossing point on the Tibur River, Rome stood astride the main avenue of communications between northern and southern Italy. Its seven hills provided safety from attackers and from the floods of the Tibur (see Map 5.1).

From 753 to 509 B.C.E. a line of Etruscan kings ruled the city and introduced numerous customs. The Romans adopted the Etruscan alphabet, which the Etruscans themselves had adoped from the Greeks. The Romans later handed on this alphabet to medieval Europe and thence to the modern Western world. Even the **toga**, the white woolen robe won by citizens, came from the Etruscans. Under the Etruscans Rome enjoyed contacts with the larger Mediterranean world, while the city continued to grow. In the years 753 to 550 B.C.E. temples and public buildings began to grace the city. The **Forum** ceased to be a cemetery and began its history as a public meeting place similar to the Greek agora. Trade in metalwork became common, and wealthier Romans began to import fine Greek vases. The Etruscans had found Rome a collection of villages and made it a city.

toga *The distinctive garment of Roman men, made of a long sash wrapped around the body. The wearing of the toga was forbidden to noncitizens.*

Forum *A public area in the center of Rome that served as focal point of the political, spiritual, and economic life of the city.*

The Roman Conquest of Italy (509–290 B.C.E.)

Legend held that the republic was established when the son of the Etruscan king raped Lucretia, a virtuous Roman wife, who committed suicide at the shame, causing the people to rise up in anger. The republic was actually founded in years after 509, when the Romans fought numerous wars with their Italian neighbors. Not until roughly a century after the founding of the republic did the Romans drive the Etruscans entirely out of Latium. The Romans very early learned the value of alliances with

● **Sarcophagus of Lartie Seianti** The woman portrayed on this lavish sarcophagus is the noble Etruscan Lartie Seianti. Although the sarcophagus is her place of burial, she is portrayed as in life, comfortable and at rest. The influence of Greek art on Etruscan is apparent in almost every feature of the sarcophagus. *(Archaeological Museum, Florence/Nimatallah/ Art Resource, NY)*

the Latin towns around them, which provided them all with security and the Romans with a large reservoir of manpower. These alliances involved the Romans in still other wars that took them farther afield in the Italian peninsula.

Around 390 B.C.E. the Romans suffered a major setback when a new people, the Celts—or Gauls, as the Romans called them—swept aside a Roman army and sacked Rome. More intent on loot than land, they agreed to abandon Rome in return for a thousand pounds of gold. In the century that followed the Romans rebuilt their city and recouped their losses. They brought Latium and their Latin allies fully under their control and conquered the Etruscans. In a series of bitter wars the Romans subdued southern Italy, all the while developing their superior military organization. That and the strength of Roman manpower led them to conquer all of Italy, where they stood unchallenged (see Map 5.1).

All the while, the Romans also spread their religious cults and culture throughout Italy. Although they did not force their beliefs on others, they welcomed their neighbors to religious places of assembly. The Romans and Italians grew closer by the mutual understanding of participation in religious rites.

In politics the Romans shared full Roman citizenship with many of their oldest allies, particularly the Latin cities. In other instances they granted citizenship without the **franchise,** that is, without the right to vote or hold Roman office. These allies were subject to Roman taxes and calls for military service but ran their own local affairs. The Latin allies could acquire full Roman citizenship by moving to Rome. Mundane but vital was Roman road-building. Roman roads, like the Persian Royal Road, facilitated the flow of communication, trade, and armies from the capital to outlying areas. They were the tangible sinews of unity.

The Roman Republic

The Romans summed up their political existence in a single phrase: *senatus populusque Romanus,* "the Roman senate and the people," which they abbreviated "SPQR." This sentiment reflects the republican ideal of shared government rather than power concentrated in a monarchy. It stands for the beliefs, customs, and laws of the republic—its unwritten constitution that evolved over two centuries to meet the demands of the governed.

In the early republic social divisions determined the shape of politics. Political power was in the hands of the aristocracy—the **patricians,** who were wealthy landowners. Patrician families formed clans, as did aristocrats in early Greece. Patricians dominated the affairs of state, provided military leadership in time of war, and monopolized knowledge of law and legal procedure. The common people of Rome, the **plebeians,** were free citizens with a voice in politics, but they could not hold high office or marry into patrician families. While some plebeian merchants rivaled the patricians in wealth, most plebeians were poor artisans, small farmers, and landless urban dwellers.

Chronology

735 B.C.E.   Traditional founding of Rome

ca. 750–509 B.C.E.   Etruscan rule of an evolving Rome

509–290 B.C.E.   Roman conquest of Italy

ca. 494–287 B.C.E.   Struggle of the Orders

264–45 B.C.E.   Punic Wars and conquest of the Mediterranean

88–31 B.C.E.   Civil war

44 B.C.E.   Assassination of Julius Caesar

31 B.C.E.   Triumph of Augustus

27 B.C.E.–68 C.E.   Julio-Claudian emperors, expansion in Europe, prosperity in the empire

ca. 3 B.C.E.–29 C.E.   Life of Jesus

30–312 C.E.   Spread of Christianity

96–180 C.E.   "Golden age" of peace and prosperity, reigns of the five good emperors

193–284 C.E.   Military monarchy, military conflict, and commercial contact with central and eastern Asia

284–337 C.E.   Diocletian and Constantine reconstruct the empire, dividing it into western and eastern halves, construction of Constantinople

380 C.E.   Christianity the official religion of the empire

franchise   *The rights, privileges, and protections of citizenship.*

patricians   *The aristocracy; wealthy landowners who held political power.*

plebeians   *The common people of Rome, who had few of the patricians' advantages.*

praetors *A new office created in 366 B.C.E.; these people acted in place of consuls when the consuls were away, although they primarily dealt with the administration of justice.*

MAP 5.1 **Roman Italy, ca. 265 B.C.E.** The geographical configuration of the Italian peninsula shows how Rome stood astride north-south communication routes and how the state that united Italy stood poised to move into Sicily and northern Africa.

The chief magistrates of the republic were the two consuls, elected for one-year terms. At first the consulship was open only to patrician men. The consuls commanded the army in battle, administered state business, and supervised financial affairs. When the consuls were away from Rome, **praetors** acted in their place. Otherwise, the praetors dealt primarily with the administration of justice. After the age of overseas conquest, the Romans divided the Mediterranean into provinces governed by ex-consuls and ex-praetors. Because of their experience in Roman politics, they were all suited to administer the affairs of the provincials and to fit Roman law and custom into new contexts.

Other officials included *quaestors,* who took charge of the public treasury and prosecuted criminals in the popular courts. *Censors* held many responsibilities including the supervision of public morals, the power to determine who could lawfully sit in the

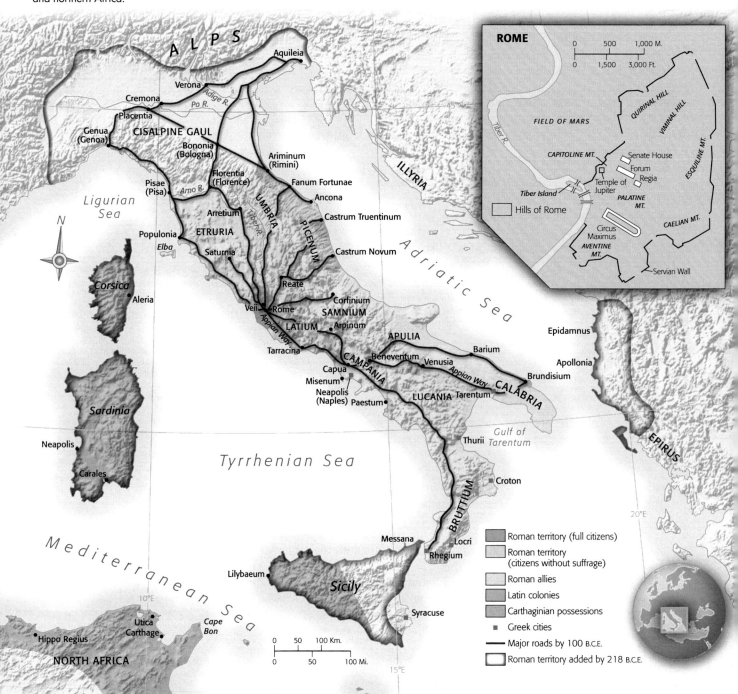

● **Guard Dog** The doorway of the house opened directly onto the street. This entrance is protected by a dog who is always on guard. The notice warns "CAVE CANEM" (beware of the dog). *(Robert Frerck/ Odyssey/Chicago)*

senate, the registration of citizens, and the leasing of public contracts. Lastly, the aediles supervised the streets and markets and presided over public festivals.

Perhaps the greatest institution of the republic was the senate, which had originated under the Etruscans as a council of noble elders who advised the king. During the republic the senate advised the consuls and other magistrates. Because the senate sat year after year, while magistrates changed annually, it provided stability. The senate could not technically pass legislation. It could only offer its advice. Yet increasingly, because of the senate's prestige, its advice came to have the force of law.

A lasting achievement of the Romans was their development of law. Roman civil law, the *ius civile,* consisted of statutes, customs, and forms of procedure that regulated the lives of citizens. As the Romans came into more frequent contact with foreigners, the praetors resorted to the law of equity, the *ius gentium,* the "law of the peoples," which they thought just to all parties. It led to a universal conception of law. By the late republic Roman jurists reached the concept of *ius naturale,* "natural law," based in part on Stoic beliefs, that applied to all societies.

Social Conflict in Rome

Inequality between plebeians and partricians led to a conflict known as the **Struggle of the Orders.** To solve their differences the plebeians nonviolently used the boycott to apply their power as a group. The patricians in turn generally responded peacefully by resorting to practical compromise.

The first showdown between the plebeians and patricians came, according to tradition, in 494 B.C.E. To force the patricians to grant concessions, the plebeians literally walked out of Rome and refused to serve in the army. The plebeians' general strike worked, and the patricians made important concessions. They allowed patricians and plebeians to marry one another. They recognized the right of plebeians to elect their own officials, the tribunes, who could bring plebeian grievances to the senate for resolution. Surrendering their legal monopoly, the patricians codified and published the Law of the

Struggle of the Orders
A great social conflict that developed between patricians and plebeians; the plebeians wanted real political representation and safeguards against patrician domination.

Twelve Tables, so called because they were inscribed on twelve bronze plaques. They also made public legal procedures so that plebeians could argue cases in court.

After a ten-year battle, the plebeians gained the Licinian-Sextian Rogations (or laws) that allowed wealthy plebeians access to all the magistracies of Rome. Once plebeians could hold the consulship, they could also sit in the senate and advise on policy. They also won the right to hold one of the two consulships. Though decisive, this victory did not automatically end the Struggle of the Orders. That happened only in 287 B.C.E. with the passage of the *lex Hortensia* that gave the resolutions of the *concilium plebis,* the Assembly of the People, the force of law for patricians and plebeians alike. This compromise established a new nobility of wealthy plebeians and patricians. Yet the Struggle of the Orders had made all citizens equal before the law, resulting in a Rome stronger and better united than before.

ROMAN EXPANSION AND ITS REPERCUSSIONS

How did Rome expand its power beyond Italy, and what were the effects of success on Rome?

With their internal affairs settled, the Romans turned their attention abroad. In a series of wars they conquered the Mediterranean, creating an overseas empire that brought them unheard of power and wealth. The new situation made many of them more cosmopolitan and comfortable. Yet it also caused social unrest at home and opened unprecedented opportunities for ambitious generals who wanted to rule Rome like an empire. Hard civil war ensued, which Julius Caesar quelled for a moment. Only his grandnephew Octavius, better known to history as Augustus, finally restored peace and order to Rome.

The Age of Overseas Conquest (264–45 B.C.E.)

In 282 B.C.E., when the Romans had reached southern Italy, they embarked upon a series of wars that left them the rulers of the Mediterranean world. Although they sometimes declared war reluctantly, they nonetheless felt the need to dominate, to eliminate any state that could endanger them. Yet they did not map out grandiose strategies to conquer the world. Rather they responded to situations as they arose.

Their presence in southern Italy brought the Romans to Sicily, next door. There they collided with the Carthaginians, Phoenician colonists living in North Africa (see Map 5.2). Conflicting ambitions in Sicily led to the First Punic War, which lasted from 264 to 241 B.C.E. Roman victory led to the island's becoming its first province. Still a formidable enemy, Carthage sent its brilliant general Hannibal (ca. 247–183 B.C.E.) against Rome. During the Second Punic War (218–201 B.C.E.) Hannibal won three major victories, including the devastating blow at Cannae in 216 B.C.E. Carrying the fighting to the very gates of Rome, he spread devastation farther across the Italian countryside. The Roman general Scipio Africanus (ca. 236–ca. 183 B.C.E.) led the counterattack to Carthage itself. In 202 B.C.E., near the town of Zama, Scipio defeated Hannibal in one of history's truly decisive battles. Scipio's victory meant that Rome's heritage would be passed on to posterity.

After defeating Carthage a last time in 146 B.C.E., the Romans turned east. After provocation from the king of Macedonia, Roman legions quickly conquered Macedonia and Greece and defeated the Seleucid monarchy. In 133 B.C.E. the king of Pergamum in Asia Minor willed his kingdom to Rome when he died. The Ptolemies of Egypt meekly obeyed Roman wishes. The Mediterranean had become *mare nostrum,* "our sea."

Old Values and Greek Culture

Rome had conquered the Mediterranean world, but some Romans considered that victory a misfortune. The historian Sallust (86–34 B.C.E.), writing from hindsight, complained that the acquisition of an empire was the beginning of Rome's troubles:

But when through labor and justice our Republic grew powerful . . . then fortune began to be harsh and to throw everything into confusion. The Romans had easily borne labor, danger, and hardship. To them leisure, riches—otherwise desirable—proved to be burdens and torments. So at first money, then desire for power, grew great. These things were a sort of cause of all evils.[1]

Instead, in the second century B.C.E. the Romans learned that they could not return to a simple life. Having become world rulers, they began to build a huge imperial system. They had to change their institutions, social patterns, and way of thinking to shape a new era. In the end Rome triumphed here just as on the battlefield, for out of turmoil came the *pax Romana*—"Roman peace" (see page 112).

Two attitudes represent the major ways in which the Romans met these challenges. One longed for the good old days and an idealized agrarian way of life. The other embraced the new urban culture.

In Roman society, whether traditional or new-fashioned, the head of the family was the **paterfamilias,** the oldest dominant male of the family. He held nearly absolute power over the lives of his wife and children as long as he lived. Until he died, his sons could not legally own property. To deal with important matters, he usually called a council of the adult males. In these councils the women of the family had no formal part, but they could inherit and own property. Romans viewed the family as important and thought that children should be raised by their mothers. Women who fulfilled these ideals were accorded respect. They handled the early education of the children. After the age of seven, sons and often daughters began their formal education.

An influx of slaves came from Rome's conquests. To the Romans slavery was a misfortune that befell some people, but it did not entail any racial theories. Not even later Christians questioned the institution of slavery. For loyal slaves the Romans always held out the possibility of freedom. **Manumission,** the freeing of individual slaves by their masters, became common.

For most Romans religion played an important role in life. Jupiter, the sky-god, and his wife, Juno, became equivalent to the Greek Zeus and Hera. Mars was the god of war but also guaranteed the welfare of the farm. In addition to the great gods, the Romans believed in spirits who haunted fields and even the home itself. Some of the deities were hostile, and only magic could ward them off. Some spirits were ghosts who haunted places where they had lived.

The new feeling of wealth and leisure is most readily seen in Rome, now a great city, where the spoils of war financed the building of baths, theaters, and other places of amusement. Romans developed new tastes and especially a liking for Greek culture. During this period the Greek custom of bathing became a Roman passion. Now large buildings containing pools and exercise rooms became essential parts of the Roman city. The baths were prominent places where men and women went to see and be seen. Despite the objections of the conservatives, these new social customs did not corrupt the Romans. They still continued efficiently to rule their empire.

The Late Republic (133–31 B.C.E.)

The wars of conquest created serious political problems for the Romans. When the legionaries returned home, they found their farms

paterfamilias *A term that means far more than merely "father"; it indicates the oldest dominant male of the family who holds nearly absolute power over the lives of family members as long as he lives.*

manumission *The freeing of individual slaves by their masters.*

● **African Acrobat** Conquest and prosperity brought exotic pleasure to Rome. Every feature of this sculpture is exotic. The young African woman and her daring gymnastic pose would catch anyone's attention. To add to the spice of her act, she performs using a live crocodile as her platform. Americans would have loved it. *(Courtesy of the Trustees of the British Museum)*

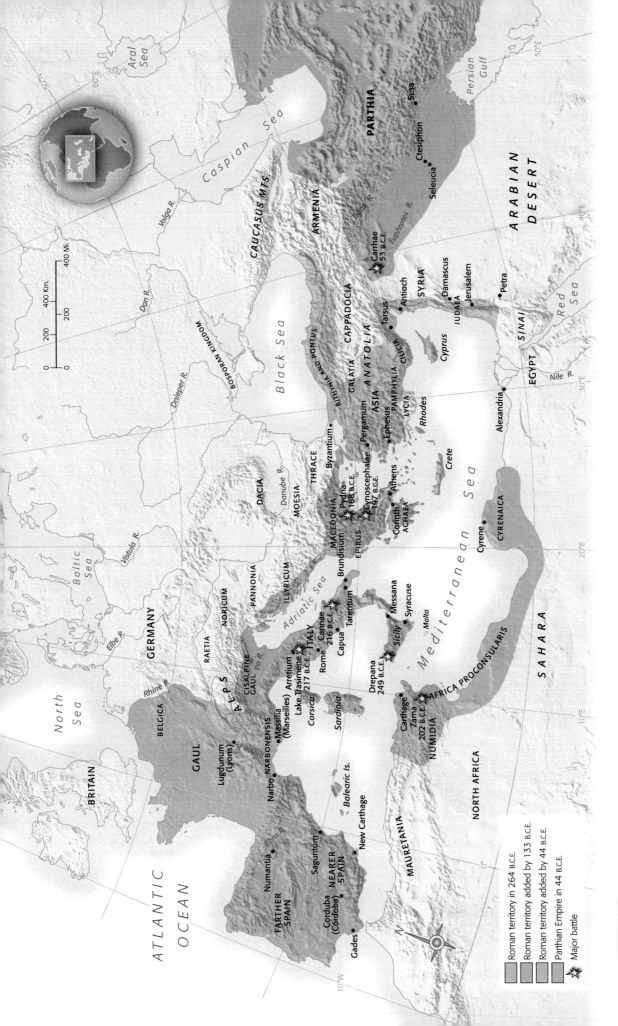

MAP 5.2 Roman Expansion During the Republic The main spurt of Roman expansion occurred between 264 and 133 B.C.E., when most of the Mediterranean fell to Rome, followed by the conquest of Gaul and the eastern Mediterranean by 44 B.C.E.

Roman territory in 264 B.C.E.

Roman territory added by 133 B.C.E.

Roman territory added by 44 B.C.E.

Parthian Empire in 44 B.C.E.

Major battle

ATLANTIC OCEAN

BRITAIN

North Sea

GERMANY

GAUL

BELGICA

NARBONENSIS

Lugdunum (Lyons)

Narbo

Massilia (Marseilles)

Numantia

Saguntum

FARTHER SPAIN

NEARER SPAIN

Corduba (Córdoba)

Gades

New Carthage

Balearic Is.

Ebro R.

Rhine R.

Rhône R.

Elbe R.

Baltic Sea

Vistula R.

RAETIA

NORICUM

PANNONIA

ALPS

CISALPINE GAUL

ITALY

Arretium

Lake Trasimene 217 B.C.E.

Rome

Po R.

Corsica

Sardinia

Capua

Tarentum

Cannae 216 B.C.E.

Brundisium

Drepana 249 B.C.E.

Sicily

Messana

Syracuse

Malta

Carthage

Zama 202 B.C.E.

AFRICA PROCONSULARIS

NUMIDIA

MAURETANIA

NORTH AFRICA

SAHARA

Mediterranean Sea

Adriatic Sea

ILLYRICUM

DACIA

Danube R.

MOESIA

THRACE

MACEDONIA

EPIRUS

Pydna 168 B.C.E.

Cynoscephalae 197 B.C.E.

ACHAEA

Corinth

Athens

Crete

Cyrene

CYRENAICA

Byzantium

BITHYNIA AND PONTUS

GALATIA

ASIA

Pergamum

Ephesus

ANATOLIA

CAPPADOCIA

PAMPHYLIA

LYCIA

CILICIA

Rhodes

Cyprus

Tarsus

Antioch

SYRIA

Damascus

Jerusalem

JUDAEA

Petra

SINAI

Red Sea

EGYPT

Alexandria

Nile R.

Black Sea

CAUCASUS MTS.

ARMENIA

Carrhae 53 B.C.E.

PARTHIA

Susa

Ctesiphon

Seleucia

Persian Gulf

ARABIAN DESERT

Euphrates R.

Tigris R.

Caspian Sea

Aral Sea

Volga R.

Don R.

Dnieper R.

Dniester R.

BOSPORAN KINGDOM

400 Mi.

400 Km.

0   200   400

0   200

N

Roman Table Manners
This mosaic is a floor that can never be swept clean. It whimsically suggests what a dining room floor looked like after a lavish dinner and also tells something about the menu: a chicken head, a wishbone, and remains of various seafood, vegetables, and fruit are easily recognizable. *(Museo Gregoriano Profano, Vatican Museums/Scala/Art Resource, NY)*

looking like those of the people they had conquered. Many were forced to sell their land, and they found ready buyers in those who had grown rich from the wars. These wealthy men created huge estates called **latifundia.** Landless veterans moved to the cities, especially Rome, but could not find work. These developments threatened Rome's army because landless men were forbidden to serve.

latifundia *Huge Roman estates created by buying up several small farms.*

The landless veterans were willing to follow any leader who promised help. Tiberius Gracchus (163–133 B.C.E.), an aristocrat who was appalled by the situation, was elected tribune in 133 B.C.E. Tiberius proposed dividing public land among the poor, but a group of wealthy senators murdered him, launching a long era of political violence that would destroy the republic. Still, Tiberius's brother Gaius Gracchus (153–121 B.C.E.) passed a law providing the urban poor with cheap grain and urged practical reforms. Once again senators tried to stem the tide of reform by murdering him.

The next reformer, Gaius Marius (ca. 157–86 B.C.E.) recruited landless men into the army to put down a rebel king in Africa. He promised them land for their service. But after his victory, the senate refused to honor his promise. From then on, Roman soldiers looked to their commanders, not to the senate or the state, to protect their interests. The turmoil continued until 88 B.C.E., when the Roman general Sulla made himself dictator. Although he voluntarily stepped down nine years later, it was too late to restore the republican constitution. The senate and other institutions of the Roman state had failed to meet the needs of empire. They had lost control of their generals and army. The soldiers put their faith in generals rather than the state, and that doomed the republic.

The history of the late republic is the story of power struggles among many famous Roman figures. Pompey used military success in Spain to force the senate to allow him to run for consul. In 59 B.C.E. he was joined in a political alliance called the **First Triumvirate** by Crassus and Julius Caesar (100–44 B.C.E.). Born of a noble family, Caesar, an able general, was also a brilliant politician with unbridled ambition. Recognizing that military success led to power, he led his troops to victory in Spain and Gaul, modern France. Having later defeated his Roman opponents, he made himself

First Triumvirate *A political alliance between Caesar, Crassus, and Pompey in which they agreed to advance one another's interests.*

Primary Source:
A Man of Unlimited Ambition: Julius Caesar
Find out how Roman attitudes toward kingship led to the assassination of Julius Caesar.

dictator. Using his victory wisely, he enacted basic reforms. He extended citizenship to many provincials outside Italy who had supported him. To relieve the pressure of Rome's huge population, he sent eighty thousand poor people to plant colonies in Gaul, Spain, and North Africa. These new communities—formed of Roman citizens, not subjects—helped spread Roman culture.

In 44 B.C.E. a group of conspirators assassinated Caesar and set off another round of civil war. His grandnephew and heir, the eighteen-year-old Octavian, better known as Augustus, joined with two of Caesar's followers, Marc Antony and Lepidus, in the Second Triumvirate. After defeating Caesar's murderers, they had a falling-out. Octavian forced Lepidus out of office and waged war against Antony, who had become allied with Cleopatra, queen of Egypt. In 31 B.C.E., with the might of Rome at his back, Octavian defeated the combined forces of Antony and Cleopatra at the Battle of Actium in Greece. His victory ended the age of civil war. For his success the senate in 27 B.C.E. voted Octavian the name *Augustus.*

pax Romana *A period during the first and second centuries* C.E. *of security, order, harmony, flourishing culture, and expanding economy.*

The Pax Romana

When Augustus ended the civil wars, he faced the monumental problems of reconstruction. From 29–23 B.C.E. Augustus toiled to heal Rome's wounds. He first had to rebuild the constitution and the organs of government. He next had to demobilize much of the army and care for the welfare of the provinces. Then he had to meet the danger of barbarians on Rome's European frontiers. Augustus was highly successful in meeting these challenges. The world came to know this era as the **pax Romana,** the Roman peace. His gift of peace to a war-torn world sowed the seeds of the empire's golden age.

Augustus claimed that in restoring constitutional government he was also restoring the republic. Yet he had to modify republican forms and offices to meet the new circumstances. While expecting the senate to shoulder heavy administrative burdens, he failed to give it enough actual power to do the job. Many of the senate's prerogatives thus shifted by default to Augustus and his successors.

Augustus also had to fit his own position into the republican constitution. He became **princeps civitatis,** "First Citizen of the State," a prestigious title without power. His real power resided in the multiple magistracies he held and in the powers granted him by the senate. He held the consulship annually. The senate voted him the full power of the tribunes, giving him the right to call the senate into session, present legislation to the people, and defend their rights. He held control of the army, which he made a permanent, standing organization. He kept all this power in the background. Failing to restore the republic, he actually created a constitutional monarchy. Without saying so, he also created the office of emperor. Yet he failed to find a way to institutionalize his position with the army, which remained personal. Although the Augustan principate worked well at first, by the third century C.E. the army would make and break emperors at will.

Augustus put provincial administration on an orderly basis and improved its functioning. He encouraged local self-government and urbanism. As a spiritual bond between the provinces and Rome, Augustus encouraged the

● **Augustus as Imperator** Here Augustus, dressed in breastplate and uniform, emphasizes the imperial majesty of Rome and his role as imperator. The figures on his breastplate represent the restoration of peace, one of Augustus's greatest accomplishments and certainly one that he frequently stressed. *(Erich Lessing/Art Resource, NY)*

cult of *Roma et Augustus,* "Rome and Augustus," as the guardians of the state. The cult spread rapidly and became a symbol of Roman unity.

One of the most momentous aspects of Augustus's reign was Roman expansion into northern and western Europe (see Map 5.3). Augustus completed the conquest of Spain. In Gaul he founded twelve new towns, and the Roman road system linked new settlements with one another and with Italy. After hard fighting, he made the Rhine River and the Roman frontier in Germany. Meanwhile, generals extended the Roman standards as far as the Danube. Roman legions penetrated the areas of modern Austria, southern Bavaria, and western Hungary. The regions of modern Serbia, Bulgaria, and Romania fell. Within this area the legionaries built fortified camps. Roads linked these camps with one another, and settlements grew up around the camps.

Amid the vast expanse of forests, Roman towns, trade, language, and law began to exert a civilizing influence on the barbarians. Many military camps became towns, and many modern European cities owe their origins to the forts of the Roman army. For the first time, the barbarian north came into direct and continuous contact with Mediterranean culture. The Romans maintained peaceful relations with the barbarians whenever possible, but Roman legions remained on the frontier to repel hostile barbarians.

> **princeps civitatis** *A Latin term meaning "first citizen" used as an official title by the early Roman emperors, from Augustus through Diocletian, followed by a Latin term meaning a city under Roman imperial authority possessing some limited degree of autonomy.*

THE COMING OF CHRISTIANITY

What was Christianity, and how did it affect life in the empire?

During the reign of the emperor Tiberius (14–37 C.E.), in the Roman province of Judaea, created out of the Jewish kingdom of Judah, Jesus of Nazareth preached, attracting a following, and was executed on the order of the Roman prefect Pontius Pilate. Much contemporary scholarship has attempted to understand who Jesus was and what he meant by his teachings. Views vary widely. Some see him as a visionary and a teacher, others as a magician and a prophet, and still others as a rebel and a revolutionary. A great many people believe that he was the son of God. The search for the historical Jesus is complicated by many factors. One is the difference between history and faith. History relies on evidence and proof for its conclusions; faith depends on belief. Thus, whether Jesus is divine is not an issue to be decided by historians. Their role is to understand his religious, cultural, social, and historical context.

Unrest in Judaea

The civil wars that destroyed the Roman republic left their mark on Judaea, where Jewish leaders had taken sides in the conflict. The turmoil created a climate of violence throughout the area. Among the Jews two movements spread. First was the rise of the Zealots, who fought to rid Judaea of the Romans. The second movement was the growth of militant apocalypticism, the belief that the coming of the Messiah was near. The Messiah would destroy the Roman legions and then inaugurate a period of happiness and plenty for Jews.

The pagan world played its part in the story of early Christianity. The term **pagan** refers to all those who believed in the Greco-Roman gods. Paganism at the time of Jesus' birth can be broadly divided into three spheres: the official state religion of Rome, the traditional Roman cults of hearth and countryside, and the new mystery religions that arose in the Hellenistic world (see pages 93–94). The mystery religions gave their adherents what neither the official religion nor traditional cults could, but they were exclusive. None of these religious sentiments met many people's spiritual needs.

> **pagan** *From a Latin term meaning "of the country," used to describe followers of a folk religion.*

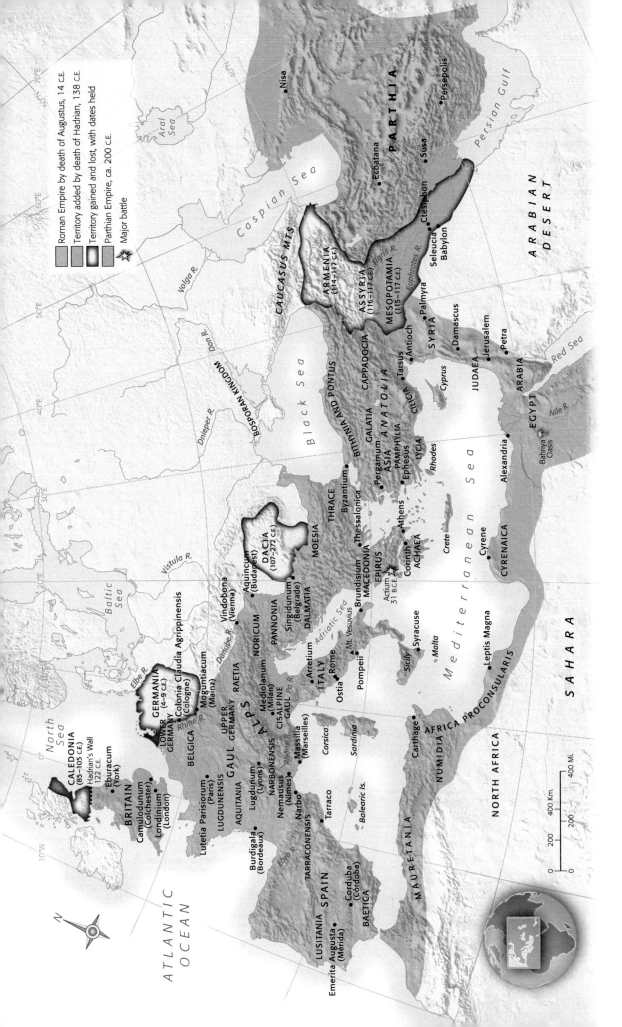

MAP 5.3 **Roman Expansion Under the Empire** Following Roman expansion during the republic, Augustus added vast tracts of Europe to the Roman Empire, which the emperor Hadrian later enlarged by assuming control over parts of central Europe, the Near East, and North Africa.

Roman Empire by death of Augustus, 14 C.E.

Territory added by death of Hadrian, 138 C.E.

Territory gained and lost, with dates held

Parthian Empire, ca. 200 C.E.

Major battle

The Life and Teachings of Jesus

Into this climate of Messianic hope and Roman religious yearning came Jesus of Nazareth (ca. 3 B.C.E.–29 C.E.). He was raised in Galilee, stronghold of the Zealots. The principal evidence for his life and deeds are the four Gospels of the New Testament. These Gospels—their name means "good news"—are records of his teachings and religious doctrines with certain details of his life. They are neither biographies of Jesus nor histories of his life. The earliest Gospels were written some seventy-five years after his death, and there are discrepancies among the four accounts. These differences indicate that early Christians had a diversity of beliefs about Jesus' nature and purpose. Only slowly, as the Christian church became an institution, were lines drawn more clearly between what was considered correct teaching and what was considered incorrect, or **heresy.**

Despite this diversity, there were certain things about Jesus' teachings that almost all the sources agree on: Jesus preached of a heavenly kingdom, one of eternal happiness in a life after death. His teachings were essentially Jewish. His orthodoxy enabled him to preach in the synagogue and the temple. His major deviation from orthodoxy was his insistence that he taught in his own name, not in the name of Yahweh. Was he then the Messiah? A small band of followers thought so, and Jesus claimed that he was. Yet Jesus had his own conception of the Messiah. He would establish a spiritual kingdom, not an earthly one.

● **Pontius Pilate and Jesus** This Byzantine mosaic from Ravenna illustrates a dramatic moment in Jesus' trial and crucifixion. Jesus stands accused before Pilate, but Pilate symbolically washes his hands of the whole affair. *(Scala/Art Resource, NY)*

heresy *A non-orthodox religious practice or belief.*

The prefect Pontius Pilate knew little about Jesus' teachings. He was concerned with maintaining peace and order. The crowds following Jesus at the time of Passover, a highly emotional time in the Jewish year, alarmed Pilate, who faced a volatile situation. Some Jews believed that Jesus was the long-awaited Messiah. Others hated and feared Jesus because they thought him religiously dangerous. To avert riot and bloodshed, Pilate condemned Jesus to death, and his soldiers carried out the sentence. On the third day after Jesus' crucifixion, some of his followers claimed that he had risen from the dead. For the earliest Christians and for generations to come, the resurrection of Jesus became a central element of faith: he had triumphed over death, and his resurrection promised all Christians immortality.

The Spread of Christianity

The memory of Jesus and his teachings survived and flourished. Believers in his divinity met in small assemblies or congregations, often in one another's homes, to discuss the meaning of Jesus' message. These earliest Christians defined their faith to fit the life of Jesus into an orthodox Jewish context. Only later did these congregations evolve into what can be called a church with a formal organization and set of beliefs.

The catalyst in the spread of Jesus' teachings and the formation of the Christian church was Paul of Tarsus, a Hellenized Jew who was comfortable in both the Roman and Jewish worlds. He had begun by persecuting the new sect, but on the road to Damascus he was converted to belief in Jesus. He was the single most important figure responsible for changing Christianity from a Jewish sect into a separate religion. He urged the Jews to include Gentiles, non-Jews, in the faith. His was the first universal message of Christianity.

Many early Christian converts were Gentile women, especially from the wealthier classes, and women were active in spreading Christianity. Paul greeted male and female converts by name in his letters and noted that women often provided financial support for his activities. Missionaries and others spreading the Christian message worked through families and friendship networks. The growing Christian communities differed in their ideas about the proper gender order; some favored giving women a larger role in church affairs, while others were more restrictive.

universalism *The belief that all human beings will ultimately be reconciled to God and achieve salvation.*

● **The Catacombs of Rome** The early Christians used underground crypts and rock chambers to bury their dead. The bodies were placed in these galleries and then sealed up. The catacombs became places of pilgrimage, and in this way the dead continued to be united with the living. *(Catacombe di Priscilla, Rome/Scala/Art Resource, NY)*

Christianity might have remained just another local sect had it not reached Rome, the capital of a far-flung empire. Rome proved to be a dramatic feature in the spread of Christianity for different reasons. First, Jesus had told his followers to spread his word throughout the world, thus making his teachings universal. The pagan Romans also considered their secular empire universal, and the early Christians combined the two concepts of **universalism.** Secular Rome provided another advantage to Christianity. If all roads led to Rome, they also led outward to the provinces. The very stability and extent of the Roman Empire enabled early Christians easily to spread their faith throughout the known world.

The Appeal of Christianity

Christianity offered its adherents the promise of salvation. Christians believed that Jesus had defeated evil and that he would reward his followers with eternal life after death. Christianity also offered the possibility of forgiveness. Human nature was weak, and even the best Christians would fall into sin. But Jesus loved sinners and forgave those who repented. Christianity was also attractive to many because it gave the Roman world a cause. Instead of passivity, Christians stressed the ideal of striving for a goal. By spreading the word of Christ, Christians played their part in God's plan for the triumph of Christianity on earth. They were not discouraged by temporary setbacks, believing Christianity to be invincible. Christianity likewise gave its devotees a sense of community. Believers met regularly to celebrate the **eucharist,** the Lord's Supper. Each individual community was in turn a member of a greater community. And that community, according to Christian Scripture, was indestructible, for Jesus had promised that "the gates of hell shall not prevail against it."[2]

eucharist *A Christian sacrament in which the death of Christ is communally remembered through a meal of bread and wine.*

THE "GOLDEN AGE"

How did efficient Roman rule lead to a "golden age" for the empire?

Augustus's success in creating solid political institutions was tested by the dynasty he created, but later in the first century Rome entered a period of political stability. This era later became known as the "golden age," a time of growing cities and economic well-being.

Politics in the Empire

For fifty years after Augustus's death the dynasty that he established—known as the Julio-Claudians because they were all members of the Julian and Claudian clans—provided the emperors of Rome. Some of the Julio-Claudians, such as Tiberius and Claudius, were sound rulers and able administrators. Others, including Caligula and Nero, were weak and frivolous men. Nonetheless, the Julio-Claudians for the most part gave the empire peace and prosperity.

In 68 C.E. Nero's inept rule led to military rebellion and widespread disruption. Yet only two years later Vespasian (9–79 C.E.), who established the Flavian dynasty, restored order. He also turned Augustus's principate into a monarchy. The Flavians (69–96 C.E.) repaired the damage of civil war to give the Roman world peace, and paved the way for the **five good emperors,** the golden age of the empire (96–180 C.E.). The era of the five good emperors was a period of almost unparalleled prosperity for the empire (see the feature "Individuals in Society: Plutarch of Chaeronea"). Wars generally ended victoriously and were confined to the frontiers. The five good emperors—Nerva, Trajan, Hadrian, Antoninus Pius, and Marcus Aurelius—were among the most dedicated and ablest men in Roman history.

five good emperors *Five consecutive Roman emperors (Nerva, Trajan, Hadrian, Antoninus Pius, and Marcus Aurelius) distinguished by their benevolence and moderation.*

In addition to the full-blown monarchy of the Flavians, other significant changes had occurred in Roman government since Augustus's day. Claudius had created an imperial bureaucracy, which Hadrian, who became emperor in 117 C.E., put on an organized, official basis. He established imperial administrative departments and separated civil from military service. His bureaucracy demanded professionalism from its members. These innovations made for more efficient running of the empire while increasing the authority of the emperor, who was now the ruling power of the bureaucracy.

In these years the Roman army changed from a mobile unit to a defensive force. The frontiers became firmly fixed and defended by a system of forts. Behind them

● **Canopus, Hadrian's Villa** This view of Hadrian's villa embodies sublime and serene beauty. The columns and statues lend dignity, and the pond suggests rest. In the background a spacious house offers a retreat from the cares of imperial duties. (*Mark Edward Smith/ TIPS Images*)

roads were increased and improved both to supply the forts and to reinforce them in times of trouble. The army had evolved into a garrison force, with legions guarding specific areas for long periods.

Life in the Golden Age

This era of peace gave the empire unparalleled prosperity both in Rome and in the provinces. Rome was truly an extraordinary city. It was enormous, with a population somewhere between 500,000 and 750,000. Although it could boast of stately palaces, noble buildings, and beautiful residential areas, most people lived in jerrybuilt houses. Fire and crime were perennial problems even in Augustus's day. Sanitation was a serious problem. Under the five emperors, urban planning and new construction greatly improved the situation. By comparison with later European cities, Rome became a very attractive place to live.

Rome grew so large that it became ever more difficult to feed. The emperor solved the problem by providing citizens with free bread, oil, and wine. By doing so, he also kept their favor. He likewise entertained the people with gladiatorial contests and chariot races. Many gladiators were criminals, some the slaves of gladiatorial schools, others prisoners of war. A few free people, men and women, volunteered for the arena. The Romans actually preferred chariot racing to gladiatorial contests. Two-horse and four-horse chariots ran a course of seven laps, about five miles. Four permanent teams, each with its own color, competed against each other.

In the province and on the frontiers, the era of the five good emperors was one of extensive prosperity. Peace and security opened Britain, Gaul, Germany, and the lands of the Danube to immigration (see Map 5.4). Agriculture flourished in the hands of free tenant farmers. The holders of small parcels of land thrived as never before. Consequently, the small tenant farmer became the backbone of Roman agriculture.

In continental Europe the army was largely responsible for the new burst of expansion. The areas where legions were stationed became Romanized. Upon retirement, legionaries often settled where they had served. Having learned a trade in the army, they brought essential skills to areas that badly needed trained men. These veterans used their retirement pay to set themselves up in business.

Plutarch of Chaeronea

During the era of the five good emperors (96–180 C.E.) people throughout the Roman Empire enjoyed nearly unparalleled peace and prosperity. The five good emperors encouraged Romans and non-Romans alike to embrace concepts and ideas beyond narrow, local boundaries. Plutarch (ca. 50–ca. 120 C.E.) provides an excellent example of this attitude and policy. Born in the small but lovely city of Chaeronea in Greece, he came from a prominent family, but one with only local prestige. He received a typical education in writing, literature, and mathematics. His exploration of the countryside in his spare hours inspired an interest in history. As a youth and later in his life he especially sought out small temples and abandoned battlefields.

When Plutarch reached young manhood, his family sent him to Athens, no longer a mighty military power but instead a center of philosophy and rhetoric. In Athens he polished his innate talents and took advantage of the opportunity to learn about and enjoy the cultural treasures of the city, all the while becoming acquainted with many wealthy and influential young men from elsewhere in the Roman Empire. In the era of the five good emperors, prominent Romans often sent their sons to Athens, not simply to learn but also to become culturally refined. These young men befriended Plutarch and widened his social horizon.

When Plutarch finished his studies, he began a tour of the Roman Empire beyond Athens. With enthusiasm he traveled abroad, forged new friendships, and became acquainted with new-to-him regions and their history. He also avidly read books previously unavailable to him.

Plutarch journeyed to the Peloponnesus, Asia Minor, Crete, and northern Egypt. All along the way he took notes describing what he saw and learned. Like tourists everywhere, he saw the sights; and from his articulate and well-educated friends he encountered information and lore not readily found elsewhere.

At Rome, the political and social center of the empire, Plutarch met leading figures and made many useful social connections. He learned enough Latin to read literary works but never became fluent enough to speak it easily. Consequently he gave public lectures in Greek, which his educated audiences had no difficulty understanding. His good nature opened many doors, and he took advantage of every opportunity to examine official records and other documents to gain information about the early years of the Roman republic and the first Roman emperors. His personal popularity

afforded him an intimate glimpse of life among the Roman elite.

Plutarch returned to Chaeronea where he spent his days writing many influential and compelling biographies of eminent Greeks and Romans, including Themistocles, Pericles, Caesar, and Antony. Both a biographer and a literary artist, he used the careers of his subjects to explore their characters. He made these historical figures human beings. He had also mastered philosophy and wrote extensively on Plato and his teachings. His writings included treatises on moral philosophy as a guide to everyday life. Plutarch was the ideal type of the refined and learned man of his day, a genteel product of Greco-Roman culture. Very popular in his own day, his works hugely influenced the Renaissance and remain popular today.

In the tranquil surroundings of Chaeronea he spent his life. Even now, people visiting the museum at Delphi can see the inscription with which his fellow citizens honored him. Though remaining a lifelong citizen of Chaeronea, Plutarch also symbolizes the urbanity of the Roman Empire in the era of the five good emperors.

This Renaissance popularization of Plutarch depicts one of the favorite writers of that time period and today. *(Courtesy, Antiquity Project/Visual Connection Archive)*

Questions for Analysis

1. What factors helped to propel Plutarch to prominence?

2. What does Plutarch's career indicate about social mobility in the Roman world?

3. Since Plutarch wrote biographies of both Greeks and Romans, does that indicate that he saw a basic unity in classical civilization?

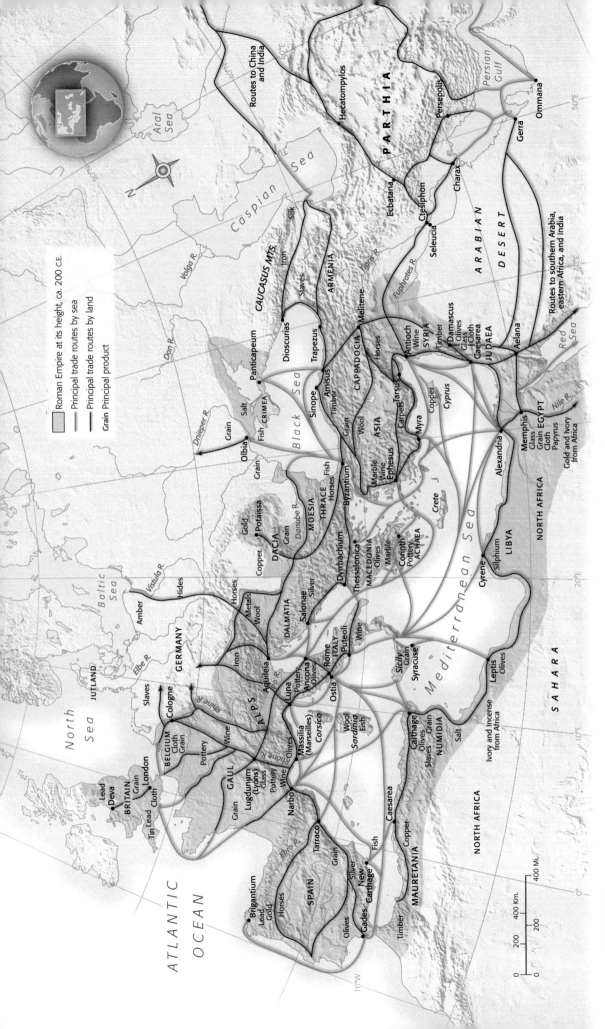

MAP 5.4 The Economic Aspect of the Pax Romana The Roman Empire was not merely a political and military organization but also an intricate economic network through which goods from Armenia and Syria were traded for Western products from as far away as Spain and Britain.

The Roman Provinces

The eastern part of the empire shared in the boom in part by trading with other areas and in part because of local industries. The cities of the east built extensively, beautifying themselves with new amphitheaters, temples, and other public buildings. Especially in the eastern empire this was the heyday of the city.

Trade among the provinces increased dramatically. Britain and Belgium became prime grain producers, much of their harvests going to the armies of the Rhine. Britain's wool industry probably got its start under the Romans. Italy and southern Gaul produced wine in huge quantities. Roman colonists introduced the olive to southern Spain and northern Africa, which soon produced most of the oil consumed in the western empire. In the east the oil production of Syrian farmers reached an all-time high. Egypt produced tons of wheat that fed the Roman populace. The Roman army in Mesopotamia consumed a high percentage of the raw materials and manufactured products of Syria and Asia Minor. During the time of the five good emperors the empire had become an economic as well as a political reality (see Map 5.4).

The growth of industry in the provinces was a striking feature of this period. Cities in Gaul and Germany eclipsed the old Mediterranean manufacturing centers. In the second century C.E. Gaul and Germany took over the pottery market. Lyons in Gaul and later Cologne in Germany became the new centers of the glassmaking industry. The cities of Gaul were nearly unrivaled in the manufacture of bronze and brass. Europe and western Asia had entered fully into a united economic, political, and cultural world.

● **Gladiatorial Games**
Though hardly games, the contests were vastly popular among the Romans. Gladiators were usually slaves, but successful ones could gain their freedom. The fighting was hard but fair, and the gladiators shown here look equally matched. *(Interfoto Pressebildagentur/Alamy)*

Eastward Expansion

Their expansion took the Romans into Central Asia, which had two immediate effects. The first was a long military confrontation between the Romans and their Iranian neighbors. Second, Roman military movement eastward coincided with Chinese expansion to the west, resulting in a period when the major ancient civilizations of the world came into contact with each other (see page 144).

When their expansion took the Romans farther eastward, they encountered the Parthians, who had established a kingdom in Iran in the Hellenistic period (see page 89). The Romans tried unsuccessfully to drive the Parthians out of Armenia and Mesopotamia until the Parthians fell to the Sasanids, a people indigenous to southern Iran, in 226 C.E. When the Romans continued their attacks against this new enemy, the Sasanid king Shapur defeated the Roman legions of the emperor Valerius, whom he took prisoner. Not until the reign of Diocletian and Constantine was Roman rule again firmly established in western Asia.

Although warfare disrupted parts of Asia, it did not stop trade that had prospered from Hellenistic times (see pages 91–93). Rarely did a merchant travel the entire distance from China to Mesopotamia. Protecting their own profits, the Parthians acted as middlemen to prevent the Chinese and Romans from making direct contact. Chinese merchants sold their wares to the Parthians at the Stone Tower, located in modern Tashkughan in Afghanistan. The Parthians then carried the goods overland to Mesopotamia or Egypt, where they were shipped throughout the Roman Empire. Silk was still a major commodity from east to west, along with other luxury goods. In return the Romans traded glassware, precious gems, and slaves. The Parthians added exotic fruits, rare birds, and other products desired by the Chinese (see the feature "Global Trade: Pottery" on pages 124–125).

Contacts Between Rome and China

This was also an era of exciting maritime exploration. Roman ships sailed from Egyptian ports to the mouth of the Indus River, where they traded local merchandise and wares imported by the Parthians. Merchants who made the voyage contended with wind, shoal waters, and pirates. Despite such dangers and discomforts, hardy mariners pushed into the Indian Ocean and beyond, reaching Malaya, Sumatra, and Java, when they traded with equally hardy local sailors.

Maritime trade between Chinese and Roman ports began in the second century C.E., though no merchant traveled the entire distance. The period of this contact coincided with the era of Han greatness in China (see pages 135–144). The Han emperor Wu Ti encouraged trade by land as well as sea, and Chinese merchants traded in the Parthian Empire along what came to be known as the "Great Silk Road." Indeed, a later Han emperor sent an ambassador directly to the Roman Empire by sea. The ambassador, Kan Ying, sailed to the Roman province of Syria during the reign of the emperor Nerva (96–98 C.E.), the first Chinese official to see for himself the Greco-Roman world. Although he left a fascinating report of his travels to his emperor, the Romans paid no attention to the contact. For the Romans China remained more of a mythical than a real place, and they never bothered to learn more about it.

•••••••••••••••

TURMOIL AND REFORM (284–337 C.E.)

How did barbarian invasions and political turmoil shape the Roman Empire in the third and fourth centuries?

The era of the five good emperors gave way to a period of chaos and stress. During the third century C.E. the Roman Empire was stunned by civil war and barbarian invasions. By the time peace was restored, the economy was shattered, cities had shrunk in size, and agriculture was becoming manorial. In the disruption of the third century and the reconstruction of the fourth, the transition from the classical to the medieval world began.

Reconstruction Under Diocletian and Constantine

At the close of the third century C.E. the emperor Diocletian (r. 284–305 C.E.) ended the period of chaos. Repairing the damage done in the third century was the major work of the emperor Constantine (r. 306–337 C.E.) in the fourth. But if the price was high, so was the prize.

Under Diocletian the princeps became *dominus,* "lord." The emperor claimed that he was "the elect of god," that he ruled because of divine favor. To underline the emperor's exalted position, Diocletian and Constantine adopted the court ceremonies and trappings of the Persian Empire.

Diocletian recognized that the empire had become too great for one man to handle and so divided it into a western and an eastern half (see Map 5.5). Diocletian assumed direct control of the eastern part, while giving the rule of the western part to a colleague along with the title *augustus,* which had become synonymous with emperor. Diocletian and his fellow augustus further delegated power by appointing two men to assist them. Each man was given the title of *caesar* to indicate his exalted rank. Although this system is known as the *Tetrarchy* because four men ruled the empire, Diocletian was clearly the senior partner and final source of authority.

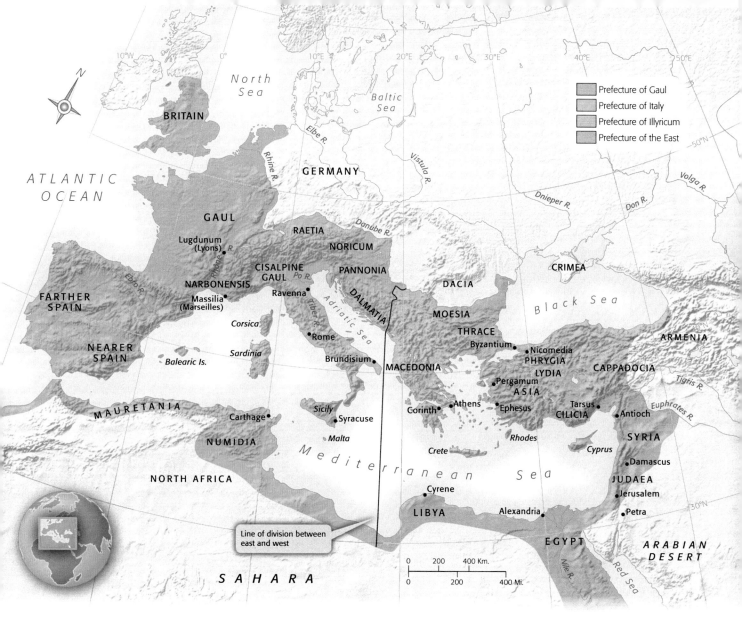

Prefecture of Gaul
Prefecture of Italy
Prefecture of Illyricum
Prefecture of the East

Line of division between east and west

MAP 5.5 The Roman World Divided Under Diocletian, the Roman Empire was first divided into a western and an eastern half, a development that foreshadowed the medieval division between the Latin West and the Byzantine East.

Diocletian's political reforms were a momentous step. The Tetrarchy soon failed, but Diocletian's division of the empire into two parts became permanent. Throughout the fourth century C.E. the eastern and western sections drifted apart. In later centuries the western part witnessed the decline of Roman government and the rise of barbarian kingdoms, while the eastern half evolved into the Byzantine Empire.

Economic Hardship and Consequences

Major economic, social, and religious problems also confronted Diocletian and Constantine. They needed additional revenues to support the army and the imperial court. Yet the wars and invasions had struck a serious blow to Roman agriculture. Christianity had become too strong either to ignore or to crush. The way Diocletian, Constantine, and their successors responded to these problems left a permanent impression on future developments.

The empire itself was less capable of recovery than in earlier times. Wars and invasions had disrupted normal commerce and the means of production. Mines were exhausted in the attempt to supply much-needed ores, especially gold and silver. In the

POTTERY

Today we often consider pottery in utilitarian and decorative terms, but it served a surprisingly large number of purposes in the ancient world. Families used earthen pottery for cooking and tableware, for storing grains and liquids, and for lamps. On a larger scale pottery was used for the transportation and protection of goods traded overseas.

The creation of pottery dates back to the Neolithic period. Pottery required few resources to make, as potters needed only abundant sources of good clay and wheels upon which to throw their vessels. Once made, the pots were baked in specially constructed kilns. Although the whole process was relatively simple, skilled potters formed groups that made utensils for entire communities. Later innovations occurred when the artisans learned to glaze their pots by applying a varnish before baking them in a kiln.

The earliest potters focused on coarse ware: plain plates, cups, and cooking pots that remained virtually unchanged throughout antiquity. Increasingly, however, potters began to decorate these pieces with simple designs. In this way pottery became both functional and decorative. One of the most popular pieces was the amphora, a large two-handled jar with a wide mouth, a round belly, and a base. It became the workhorse of maritime shipping because it protected contents from water and rodents, was easy and cheap to produce, and could be reused. Amphoras contained goods as different as wine and oil, spices and unguents, dried fish and

The Pottery Trade

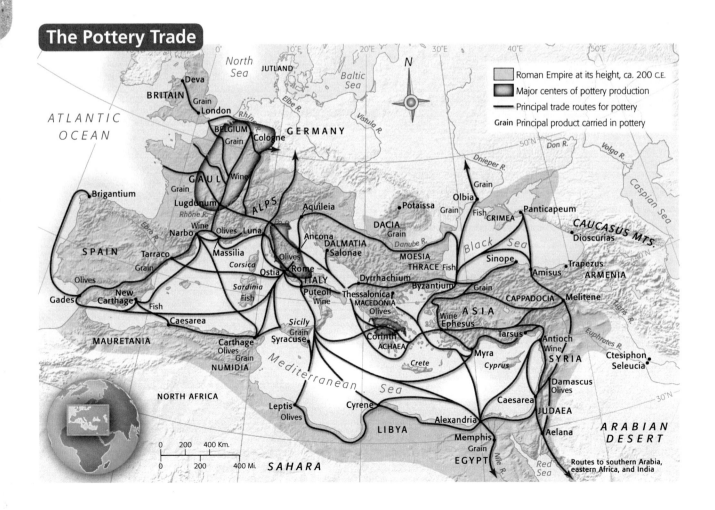

Roman Empire at its height, ca. 200 C.E.

Major centers of pottery production

Principal trade routes for pottery

Grain Principal product carried in pottery

The Greeks captured Troy by concealing themselves in a wooden horse, which the Trojans pulled into the city. On this piece from a pot found in Mykonos, probably dating to the seventh century B.C.E., Greeks have just launched their attack from inside the horse. (Archaeological Receipts Fund, Athens)

pitch. The amphora's dependability and versatility kept it in use from the fourth century B.C.E. to the beginning of the Middle Ages.

In classical Greece individual potters sold their wares directly to local customers or traders; manufacturer and buyer alone determined the quantity of goods for sale and their price. In the Hellenistic and Roman periods amphoras became common throughout the Mediterranean and carried goods eastward to the Black Sea, Persian Gulf, and Red Sea. The Ptolemies of Egypt sent amphoras and their contents even farther, to Arabia, eastern Africa, and India. Thus merchants and mariners who had never seen the Mediterranean depended on these containers.

Other pots proved as useful as the amphora, and all became a medium of decorative art. By the eighth century B.C.E. Greek potters and artists began to decorate their wares by painting them with patterns and scenes from mythology, legend, and daily life. They portrayed episodes such as the chariot race at Patroclus's funeral or battles from the *Iliad.* Some portrayed the gods, such as Dionysos at sea. These images widely spread knowledge of Greek religion and culture. In the West, especially the Etruscans in Italy and the Carthaginians in North Africa eagerly welcomed the pots, their decora-

tion, and their ideas. The Hellenistic kings shipped these pots as far east as China. Pottery thus served as a cultural exchange among people scattered across huge portions of the globe.

The Romans took the manufacture of pottery to an advanced stage by introducing a wider range of vessels for new purposes. The Roman ceramic trade spread from Italy throughout the Mediterranean. The Roman army provides the best example of how this ordinary industry affected the broader culture. Especially on the European frontiers the army used its soldiers to produce the pottery it needed. These soldiers made their own Italian *terra sigallata,* which was noted for its smooth red glaze. Native potters immediately copied this style, thus giving rise to local industries. Indeed, terra sigallata remained the dominant pottery style in northern Europe until the seventh century C.E. When Roman soldiers retired, they often settled where they had served, especially if they could continue their trades. Such ordinary Romans added local ideas to their craft. This exchange resulted in a culture that was becoming European, rather than just Roman, and extended into Britain, France, the Low Countries, and southern Germany.

cities markets, trade, and industry were disrupted, and travel became dangerous. The devastation of the countryside increased the difficulty of feeding and supplying the cities. Merchant and artisan families rapidly left devastated regions. Economic hardship had been met by cutting the silver content of coins until money was virtually worthless. The immediate result was crippling inflation throughout the empire.

Diocletian's attempt to curb inflation illustrates the methods of absolute monarchy. In a move unprecedented in Roman history, Diocletian issued an edict that fixed maximum prices and wages throughout the empire. The emperors dealt with the tax system just as strictly and inflexibly. Taxes became payable in kind, that is, in goods and services instead of money. All those involved in the growing, preparation, and transportation of food and other essentials were locked into their professions. A baker or shipper could not go into any other business, and his son took up the trade at his death. In this period of severe depression, many localities could not pay their taxes. In such cases local tax collectors, who were themselves locked into service, had to make up the difference from their own funds. This system soon wiped out a whole class of moderately wealthy people.

Because of worsening conditions during the third century C.E., many free tenant farmers and their families were killed, fled the land to escape the barbarians or brigands, or abandoned farms ravaged in the fighting. Large tracts of land consequently lay deserted. Great landlords with ample resources began at once to reclaim as much of this land as they could. The huge estates that resulted, called villas, were self-sufficient. Since they produced more than they consumed, they successfully competed with the declining cities by selling their surplus in the countryside. They became islands of stability in an unsettled world.

The rural residents who remained on the land were exposed to the raids of barbarians and brigands and to the tyranny of imperial officials. In return for the protection and security landlords could offer, the small landholders gave over their lands and their freedom. They could no longer decide to move elsewhere. Henceforth, they and their families worked their patrons' land, not their own. Free people were becoming what would later be called serfs.

The Acceptance of Christianity

The Roman attitude toward Christianity evolved as well during this period of empire. At first many pagans genuinely misunderstood Christian practices and rites. They thought that such secret rites as the Lord's Supper, at which Christians said that they ate and drank the body and blood of Jesus, were acts of cannibalism. Pagans thought that Christianity was one of the worst of the mystery cults with immoral and indecent rituals. They also feared that the gods would withdraw their favor from the Roman Empire because of the Christian insistence that the pagan gods either did not exist or were evil spirits.

The Christians also exaggerated the degree of pagan hostility to them, and most of the gory stories about the martyrs are fictitious. There were indeed some cases of pagan persecution of the Christians, but with few exceptions they were local and sporadic in nature. Even Nero's notorious persecution was temporary and limited to Rome. No constant persecution of Christians occurred. As time went on, pagan hostility and suspicion decreased. Pagans realized that Christians were not working to overthrow the state and that Jesus was no rival of Caesar. The emperor Trajan forbade his governors to hunt down Christians. Though admitting that he considered Christianity an abomination, he preferred to leave Christians in peace.

The stress of the third century C.E., however, seemed to some emperors the punishment of the gods. Although the Christians depicted Diocletian as a fiend, he persecuted them in the hope that the gods would restore their blessing on Rome. Yet even his persecutions were never very widespread or long-lived. By the late third century C.E. pagans had become used to Christianity, and Constantine recognized Christianity as a legitimate religion. He himself died a Christian in 337 C.E. In time the Christian triumph would be complete. In 380 C.E. the emperor Theodosius made Christianity the official religion of the Roman Empire. At that point Christians began to persecute the pagans for their religion. History had come full circle.

The Construction of Constantinople

The triumph of Christianity was not the only event that made Constantine's reign a turning point in Roman history. Constantine took the bold step of building a new capital for the empire. Constantinople, the New Rome, was constructed on the site of Byzantium, the old Greek city on the Bosporus. Throughout the third century C.E. emperors had found Rome and western Europe hard to defend. The eastern part of the empire was more easily defensible and so escaped the worst of the barbarian devastation. It was wealthy and its urban life still vibrant. Moreover, Christianity was more widespread in the east than in the west, and the city of Constantinople was intended to be a Christian center.

● **Arch of Constantine**   Though standing in stately surroundings, Constantine's arch in Rome is decorated with art plundered from the arches of Trajan and Marcus Aurelius. He robbed them rather than decorate his own with the inferior work of his own day. *(Michael Reed, photographer/www.mike-reed.com)*

From the Classical World to Late Antiquity

Although Constantine had restored order, he could not undo the past. Too much had changed forever. The two-faced Roman god Janus, who looked both ways, in this case looked both to the past and the future and well symbolizes this period. A great deal of the past remained through these years of change. People still lived under the authority of the emperors and the guidance of Roman law. They still communicated with one another as usual, in Latin throughout the west and Greek in the east. Greco-roman art, architecture, and literature surrounded them as part of daily life.

Yet changes were also underway. Government had evolved from the pagan republic of the past to the Christian monarchy of the new age. The empire itself was split into east and west. The east remained the world of urbanism and empire, while the west became the home of independent barbarian kingdoms built on classical foundations.

Paganism faded into the background as Christianity prevailed. Greek philosophy was replaced by Christian theology, as thinkers tried earnestly to understand Jesus' message. Through all these changes the lives of ordinary people did not change dramatically. They farmed, worked in cities, and nurtured their families. They took new ideas, blended them with the old, and created new cultural forms. The classical world gradually gave way to a new intellectual, spiritual, and political life that forever changed the face of western Eurasia.

Chapter Summary

Key Terms

toga
Forum
franchise
patricians
plebeians
praetors
Struggle of the Orders
paterfamilias
manumission
latifundia
First Triumvirate
pax Romana
princeps civitatis
pagan
heresy
universalism
eucharist
five good emperors

To assess your mastery of this chapter, go to
bedfordstmartins.com/mckayworld

• How did the Romans come to dominate Italy, and what political institutions did they create?

The Etruscans and Romans both settled in Italy and the Etruscans developed the first cities and a rich cultural life. Ruling as kings, the Etruscans introduced Romans to urbanism, industry, trade, and the alphabet. The Romans fought numerous wars with the Etruscans, and in 509 B.C.E. the Romans won their independence and created the republic. The republic functioned through a shared government of the people directed by the senate, summarized by the expression SPQR—*senatus populusque Romanus,* the Roman senate and people. In resolving a social conflict known as the "Struggle of the Orders," Roman nobles and ordinary people created a state administered by magistrates elected from the entire population and a legal code common to all.

• How did Rome expand its power beyond Italy, and what were the effects of success on Rome?

Once united, the Romans launched a series of wars that took them from Spain in the west to Pergamum in Asia Minor. Their empire brought wealth, which led to a grand building program and a rich life for very many Romans. Increased power brought political problems, and during the late republic many poor people sought political and social reforms. Ambitious generals fought for power until Julius Caesar restored order. His adopted son Augustus transformed the republic into the empire by creating a constitutional monarchy in which he was the sole executive of the state. He directed the organs of government and the army, while encouraging local government.

• What was Christianity, and how did it affect life in the empire?

Christians developed as an offshoot of Judaism, when Jesus of Nazareth proclaimed himself the son of God. He taught that belief in his divinity led to eternal life. His followers spread their belief across the empire, transforming it from a Jewish sect into a new religion.

• How did efficient Roman rule lead to a "golden age" for the empire?

Augustus was followed by a series of efficient emperors who created an official bureaucracy to administer the empire. The five good emperors divided civil from military service, and made the army a garrison force to guard the frontiers. During this golden period Rome became the magnificent capital of the empire, increasingly adorned with beautiful buildings and improved urban housing, and harboring a well-fed populace. Rome also became a city of fun, marked by gladiatorial games and chariot racing. This was also a period of thriving agriculture and commercial expansion throughout the empire.

• *How did barbarian invasions and political turmoil shape the Roman Empire in the third and fourth centuries?*

When Rome expanded eastward from Europe, it met opposition, yet even during the fighting, commerce among the Romans, the Iranians, and the Chinese empire thrived through a series of trade routes, the most famous being the Great Silk Road. After the five good emperors, the empire fell prey to civil war and foreign invasion, both of which devastated the land and caused political chaos. Two gifted emperors, Diocletian and Constantine, restored order and then permanently divided the empire into western and eastern halves. Their rigid control of the economy was not successful. Rich landowners reclaimed land and created villas worked by tenants instead of free farmers. Meanwhile, the emperors legalized Christianity. The symbol of change became the new capital of the empire, Constantinople, the New Rome. The classical world gave way to the medieval.

Suggested Reading

Bruun, C., ed. *The Roman Middle Republic, ca. 400–133 B.C.* 2000. Treats the central issues of the period.

Burn, T. S. *Rome and the Barbarians, 100 B.C.–A.D. 400.* 2003. Analyzes the mutual impact of Romans and barbarians.

D'Ambra, E. *Roman Women.* 2007. A comprehensive and learned treatment of all aspects of women's life, private and public.

Esler, P. *The Early Christian World.* 2004. A collection of studies that cover all aspects of the topic.

Goldsworthy, A. *Roman Warfare.* 2000. A concise treatment of warfare from republican to imperial times.

Goodman, M. *The Roman World, 44 B.C.–A.D. 180.* 1997. A solid general treatment of the empire.

Kamm, A. *Julius Caesar.* 2006. An excellent brief biography that deals with all important aspects of his life.

MacMullen, R. *Roman Social Relations, 50 B.C.–A.D. 284.* 1981. Still an excellent discussion of the topic by a leading scholar.

Scullard, H. H. *A History of the Roman World,* 4th ed. 1993. Still the best single account of Roman history.

Turcam, R. *The Gods of Ancient Rome.* 2000. Provides a concise survey of the Roman pantheon.

Notes

1. Sallust, *War with Cataline* 10.1–3, translated by J. Buckler.
2. Matthew 16:18.

Listening to the PAST

Titus Flamininus and the Liberty of the Greeks

After his arrival in Greece in 197 B.C.E., Titus Flamininus defeated the Macedonians in Thessaly. He next sent his recommendations on the terms of the peace agreement to the Roman senate. The following year the senate sent him ten commissioners, who agreed with his ideas. The year 196 B.C.E. was also the occasion when the great Pan-Hellenic Isthmian games were regularly celebrated near Corinth. Many of the dignitaries and the most prominent people of the Hellenistic world were present. Among them was Flamininus, who came neither as a participant in the games nor solely as a spectator of them. Instead, he took the occasion to make a formal announcement about Roman policy. There in Isthmia he officially announced that Rome granted freedom to the Greeks. He assured his audience that Rome had not come as a conqueror. The eminent Greek biographer Plutarch has left a vivid account of the general response to this pronouncement.

Accordingly, at the Isthmian games, where a great throng of people were sitting in the stadium and watching the athletic contests (since, indeed, after many years Greece had at last ceased from wars waged in hopes of freedom, and was now holding festival in time of assured peace), the trumpet signalled a general silence, and the herald, coming forward into the midst of the spectators, made proclamation that the Roman senate and Titus Quinctius Flamininus proconsular general, having conquered King Philip and the Macedonians, restored to freedom, without garrisons and without imposts, and to the enjoyment of their ancient laws, the Corinthians, the Locrians, the Phocians, the Euboeans, the Achaeans of Phthiotis, the Magnesians, the Thessalians, and the Perrhaebians. At first, then, the proclamation was by no means generally or distinctly heard, but there was a confused and tumultuous movement in the stadium of people who wondered what had been said, and asked one another questions about it, and called out to have the proclamation made again; but when silence had been restored, and the herald in tones that were louder

than before and reached the ears of all, had recited the proclamation, a shout of joy arose, so incredibly loud that it reached the sea. The whole audience rose to their feet, and no heed was paid to the contending athletes, but all were eager to spring forward and greet and hail the saviour and champion of Greece.

And that which is often said of the volume and power of the human voice was then apparent to the eye. For ravens which chanced to be flying overhead fell down into the stadium. The cause of this was the rupture of the air; for when the voice is borne aloft loud and strong, the air is rent asunder by it and will not support flying creatures, but lets them fall, as if they were over a vacuum, unless, indeed, they are transfixed by a sort of blow, as of a weapon, and fall down dead. It is possible, too, that in such cases there is a whirling motion of the air, which becomes like a waterspout at sea with a refluent flow of the surges caused by their very volume.

Be that as it may, had not Titus, now that the spectacle was given up, at once foreseen the rush and press of the throng and taken himself away, it would seem that he could hardly have survived the concourse of so many people about him at once and from all sides. But when they were tired of shouting about his tent, and night was already come, then, with greetings and embraces for any friends and fellow citizens whom they saw, they betook themselves to banqueting and carousing with one another. And here, their pleasure naturally increasing, they moved to reason and discourse about Greece, saying that although she had waged many wars for the sake of her freedom, she had not yet obtained a more secure or more delightful exercise of it than now, when others had striven in her behalf, and she herself, almost without a drop of blood or a pang of grief, had borne away the fairest and most enviable of prizes. Verily, they would say, valour and wisdom are rare things among men, but the rarest of all blessings is the just man. For men like Agesilaüs, or Lysander, or Nicias, or Alcibiades could indeed conduct wars well, and understood how to be victorious commanders in battles by land and sea, but they would

This coin provides a contemporary profile of Titus Flamininus, which also illustrates Roman realism in portraiture. *(Courtesy of the Trustees of the British Museum)*

publicly proclaimed freedom to the Greeks. Then he visited the different cities, establishing among them law and order, abundant justice, concord, and mutual friendliness. He quieted their factions and restored their exiles, and plumed himself on his persuading and reconciling the Greeks more than on his conquest of the Macedonians, so that their freedom presently seemed to them the least of his benefactions. . . .

. . . In the case of Titus and the Romans, . . . gratitude for their benefactions to the Greeks brought them, not merely praises, but also confidence among all men and power, and justly too. For men not only received the officers appointed by them, but actually sent for them and invited them and put themselves in their hands. And this was true not only of peoples and cities, nay, even kings who had been wronged by other kings fled for refuge into the hands of Roman officials, so that in a short time—and perhaps there was also divine guidance in this—everything became subject to them. But Titus himself took most pride in his liberation of Greece.

not use their successes so as to win legitimate favour and promote the right. Indeed, if one excepts the action at Marathon, the sea-fight at Salamis, Plataea, Thermopylae, and the achievements of Cimon at the Eurymedon and about Cyprus, Greece has fought all her battles to bring servitude upon herself, and every one of her trophies stands as a memorial of her own calamity and disgrace, since she owed her overthrow chiefly to the baseness and contentiousness of her leaders. Whereas men of another race, who were thought to have only slight sparks and insignificant traces of a common remote ancestry, from whom it was astonishing that any helpful word or purpose should be vouchsafed to Greece—these men underwent the greatest perils and hardships in order to rescue Greece and set her free from cruel despots and tyrants.

So ran the thoughts of the Greeks; and the acts of Titus were consonant with his proclamations. For at once he sent Lentulus to Asia to set Bargylia free, and Stertinius to Thrace to deliver the cities and islands there from Philip's garrisons. Moreover, Publius Villius sailed to have a conference with Antiochus concerning the freedom of the Greeks who were under his sway. Titus himself also paid a visit to Chalcis, and then sailed from there to Magnesia, removing their garrisons and restoring to the peoples their constitutions. He was also appointed master of ceremonies for the Nemeian games at Argos, where he conducted the festival in the best possible manner, and once more

Questions for Analysis

1. Did Titus Flamininus really want peace for the Greeks, or was this a cynical propaganda gesture?

2. What caused Greek political difficulties in the first place?

3. Was the Greek response to Titus Flamininus's proclamation genuine and realistic?

Source: Reprinted by permission of the publishers and the Trustees of the Loeb Classical Library from *Plutarch: Volume X—Parallel Lives.* Loeb Classical Library Volume L 102, trans. B. Perrin (Cambridge, Mass.: Harvard University Press, 1921). The Loeb Classical Library® is a registered trademark of the President and Fellows of Harvard College.

The Chinese Buddhist Monk Ganjin (688–763 C.E.).
Ganjin was blind by the time he finally reached Japan on
the sixth attempt in 754 and began his missionary work.

(Suzanne Perrin/Japan Interlink)

6 EAST ASIA AND THE SPREAD OF BUDDHISM, 256 B.C.E.–800 C.E.

East Asia was transformed over the millennium from 200 B.C.E. to 800 C.E. In 200 B.C.E. only one of the societies in the region had writing, iron technology, large cities, and complex state organizations. Over the course of the next several centuries, this situation changed dramatically as war, trade, diplomacy, missionary activity, and pursuit of learning brought increased contact among the peoples of the region. Buddhism came to provide a common set of ideas and visual images for the entire area. Chinese was widely used as an international language outside its native area.

Increased communication stimulated state formation in Central Asia, Tibet, Korea, Manchuria, and Japan. The new states usually adopted political models from China. Nevertheless, by 800 each of these regions was well on its way to developing a distinct political and cultural identity. Ancient China is treated in Chapter 3; this is the first chapter to treat Korea and Japan.

THE AGE OF EMPIRE IN CHINA

What were the social, cultural, and political consequences of the unification of China under a strong centralized government?

In much the same period in which Rome created a huge empire, the Qin and Han rulers in China created an empire on a similar scale. Like the Roman Empire, the Chinese empire was put together through force of arms and held in place by sophisticated centralized administrative machinery.

The Qin Unification (221–206 B.C.E.)

In 221 B.C.E., after decades of constant warfare, the state of Qin, the state that had adopted Legalist policies (see pages 70–71), succeeded in defeating the last of its rivals. China was unified for the first time in many centuries. The king of Qin decided that the title

● **Army of the First Emperor** The thousands of life-size ceramic soldiers buried in pits about a half mile from the First Emperor's tomb help us imagine the Qin military machine. It was the Qin emperor's concern with the afterlife that led him to construct such a lifelike guard. The soldiers were originally painted in bright colors, and they held real bronze weapons. *(Robert Harding World Imagery)*

"king" was not grand enough and invented the title "emperor" (*huangdi*). He called himself the First Emperor (Shihuangdi) in anticipation of a long line of successors.

Once Qin ruled all of China, the First Emperor and his shrewd Legalist minister Li Si embarked on a sweeping program of centralization that touched the lives of nearly everyone in China. To cripple the nobility of the defunct states, the First Emperor ordered the nobles to leave their lands and move to the capital. To administer the territory that had been seized, he dispatched officials, then controlled them through a long list of regulations, reporting requirements, and penalties for inadequate performance. These officials owed their power and positions entirely to the favor of the emperor and had no hereditary rights to their offices.

To harness the enormous human resources of his people, the First Emperor ordered a census of the population. Census information helped the imperial bureaucracy to plan its activities—to estimate the costs of public works, the tax revenues needed to pay for them, and the labor force available for military service and building projects. To make it easier to administer all regions uniformly, the script was standardized, along with weights, measures, coinage, even the axle lengths of carts. Private possession of arms was outlawed to make it more difficult for subjects to rebel. To make it easier for Qin armies to move rapidly, thousands of miles of roads were built. Most of the labor on these projects came from farmers performing required corvée labor or convicts working their sentences.

Some twentieth-century Chinese historians glorified the First Emperor as a bold conqueror who let no obstacle stop him, but the traditional evaluation of him was almost entirely negative. For centuries Chinese historians castigated him as a cruel, arbitrary, impetuous, suspicious, and superstitious megalomaniac. Hundreds of thousands of subjects were drafted to build the **Great Wall,** a rammed-earth fortification along the northern border between the Qin realm and the land controlled by the

Great Wall *A rammed-earth fortification built along the northern border of China during the reign of the First Emperor.*

nomadic Xiongnu. After Li Si complained that scholars used records of the past to denigrate the emperor's achievements and undermine popular support, the emperor had all writings other than useful manuals on topics such as agriculture, medicine, and divination collected and burned. As a result of this massive book burning, many ancient texts were lost.

Three times assassins tried to kill the First Emperor, and perhaps as a consequence he became obsessed with discovering the secrets of immortality. He spent lavishly on a tomb designed to protect him in the afterlife. Although the central chambers have not yet been excavated, in nearby pits archaeologists have unearthed thousands of life-size terra-cotta figures of armed soldiers and horses lined up to protect him.

After the First Emperor died in 210 B.C.E., the Qin state unraveled. The Legalist institutions designed to concentrate power in the hands of the ruler made the stability of the government dependent on his strength and character. The First Emperor's heir was murdered by his younger brother, and uprisings soon followed.

The Han Dynasty (206 B.C.E.–220 C.E.)

The eventual victor in the struggle for power that ensued was Liu Bang, known in history as Emperor Gaozu (r. 202–195 B.C.E.). The First Emperor of Qin was from the Zhou aristocracy. Gaozu was, by contrast, from a modest family of commoners, so his elevation to emperor is evidence of how thoroughly the Qin Dynasty had destroyed the old order.

Gaozu did not disband the centralized government created by the Qin, but he did remove its most unpopular features. Harsh laws were canceled, taxes were sharply reduced, and a policy of laissez faire was adopted in an effort to promote economic recovery. With policies of this sort, relative peace, and the extension of China's frontiers, the Chinese population grew rapidly in the first two centuries of the Han Dynasty. The census of 2 C.E. recorded a population of 58 million, the earliest indication of the large size of China's population.

In contrast to the Qin promotion of Legalism, the Han came to promote Confucianism and recruit officials on the basis of their Confucian learning or Confucian moral qualities. Under the most activist of the Han emperors, Emperor Wu, the "Martial Emperor" (r. 141–87 B.C.E.), Confucian scholars were given a privileged position. The Han government's efforts to recruit men trained in the Confucian classics marked the beginning of the Confucian scholar-official system, one of the most distinctive features of imperial China. Chinese officials, imbued with Confucian values, did not comply automatically with the policies of the ruler, above all because they saw criticism of the government as one of their duties. Their willingness to stand up to the ruler also reflected the fact that most of the Confucian scholars selected to serve

Chronology

ca. 230–208 B.C.E. Construction of Great Wall to protect against Xiongnu

221 B.C.E. China unified under Qin Dynasty

206 B.C.E.–220 C.E. Han Dynasty

145–ca. 85 B.C.E. Sima Qian, Chinese historian

111 B.C.E. Emperor Wu conquers Nam Viet

108 B.C.E. Han government establishes colonies in Korea

105 C.E. Chinese invention of paper

ca. 200 C.E. Buddhism begins rapid growth in China

220–589 C.E. Age of Division in China

313–668 C.E. Three Kingdoms Period in Korea

372 C.E. Buddhism introduced in Korea

538 C.E. Buddhism introduced in Japan

581–618 C.E. Sui Dynasty

604 C.E. Prince Shōtoku's "Seventeen Principles" in Japan

618–907 C.E. Tang Dynasty

668 C.E. Silla unifies Korea

690 C.E. Empress Wu declares herself emperor, becoming the only Chinese woman emperor

710 C.E. Japan's capital moved to Nara

735–737 C.E. Smallpox epidemic in Japan

845 C.E. Tang emperor begins persecution of Buddhism

as officials came from landholding families, much like those who staffed the Roman government, which gave them some economic independence.

The Han government was supported largely by the taxes and labor service demanded of farmers, but this revenue regularly fell short of the government's needs. To pay for his military campaigns, Emperor Wu took over the minting of coins, confiscated the land of nobles, sold offices and titles, and increased taxes on private businesses. A widespread suspicion of commerce as an unproductive exploitation of the true producers made it easy to levy especially heavy assessments on merchants. The worst blow to businessmen, however, was the government's decision to enter into market competition with them by selling the commodities that had been collected as taxes. In 119 B.C.E. government monopolies were established in the production of iron, salt, and liquor. These enterprises had previously been sources of great profit for private entrepreneurs. Large-scale grain dealing also had been a profitable business, which the government now took over. Grain was to be bought where it was plentiful and its price low and to be either stored in granaries or transported to areas of scarcity. This procedure was supposed to eliminate speculation in grain, provide more constant prices, and bring profit to the government.

Inner Asia and the Silk Road

The difficulty of defending against the nomadic pastoral peoples to the north is a major reason China came to favor a centralized bureaucratic form of government. Resources from the entire subcontinent were needed to maintain control of the northern border.

Beginning long before the Han Dynasty, China's contacts with its northern neighbors had involved both trade and military conflict. China's neighbors sought Chinese products such as silk and lacquer ware. When they did not have goods to trade or when trading relations were disrupted, raiding was considered an acceptable alternative in the tribal cultures of the region. Chinese sources speak of defending against raids of "barbarians" from Shang times (ca. 1500–ca. 1050 B.C.E.) on, but not until the rise of nomadism in the mid-Zhou period (fifth–fourth centuries B.C.E.) did the horsemen of the north become China's main military threat.

The economy of these nomads was based on raising sheep, goats, camels, and horses. Families lived in tents that could be taken down and moved north in summer and south in winter as groups of families moved in search of pasture. Herds were tended on horseback, and everyone learned to ride from a young age. Especially awesome from the Chinese perspective was the ability of nomad horsemen to shoot arrows while riding horseback. The typical social structure of the steppe nomads was fluid, with family and clan units linked through loyalty to tribal chiefs selected for their military prowess. Charismatic tribal leaders could form large coalitions and mobilize the entire society for war.

Chinese farmers and Inner Asian herders had such different modes of life that it is not surprising that they had little respect for each other. For most of the imperial period, Chinese farmers looked on the northern non-Chinese horsemen as gangs of bullies who thought robbing was easier than working for a living. The nomads identified glory with military might and viewed farmers as contemptible weaklings.

● **Xiongnu Metalwork** The metal ornaments of the Xiongnu provide convincing evidence that they were in contact with nomadic pastoralists farther west in Asia, such as the Scythians, who also fashioned metal plaques and buckles in animal designs. This buckle or ornament is made of gold and is about 3 inches tall. *(The Metropolitan Museum of Art, Gift of J. Pierpont Morgan, 1917 [17.190.1672]. Photograph © 1981 The Metropolitan Museum of Art)*

In the late third century B.C.E. the Xiongnu (known in the West as the Huns) formed the first great confederation of nomadic tribes (see Map 6.1). The Qin's Great Wall was built to defend against them, and the Qin sent out huge armies against them. The early Han emperors tried to make peace with them, offering generous gifts of silk, rice, cash, and even imperial princesses as brides. But these policies were controversial, since critics thought they merely strengthened the enemy. Certainly Xiongnu power did not decline, and in 166 B.C.E. 140,000 Xiongnu raided to within a hundred miles of the Chinese capital.

Emperor Wu decided that China had to push the Xiongnu back. He sent several armies of one hundred thousand to three hundred thousand troops deep into Xiongnu territory. These costly campaigns were of limited value since the Xiongnu were a moving target: fighting nomads was not like attacking walled cities. If the Xiongnu did not want to fight the Chinese troops, they simply moved their camps. To try to find allies and horses, Emperor Wu turned his attention west, toward Central Asia. From the envoy he sent into Bactria, Parthia, and Ferghana in 139 B.C.E., the Chinese learned for the first time of other civilized states comparable to China (see Map 6.1). The envoy described Ferghana as an urban society ten thousand *li* (about three thousand miles) west of China, where grapes were grown for wine and the horses were particularly fine. In Parthia, he was impressed by the use of silver coins stamped with the image of the king's face. These regions, he reported, were familiar with Chinese products, especially silk, and did a brisk trade in them.

MAP 6.1 **The Han Empire** The Han Dynasty asserted sovereignty over vast regions from Korea in the east to Central Asia in the west and Vietnam in the south. Once garrisons were established, traders were quick to follow, leading to considerable spread of Chinese material culture in East Asia. Chinese goods, especially silk, were in demand far beyond East Asia, promoting long-distance trade across Eurasia.

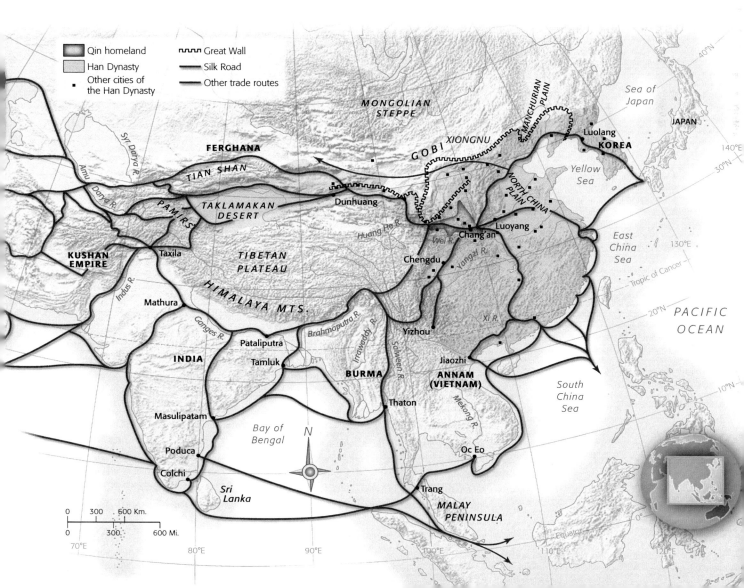

Silk Road *The trade routes across Central Asia through which Chinese silk and other items were traded.*

Emperor Wu sent an army into Ferghana and gained recognition of Chinese overlordship in the area, thus obtaining control over the trade routes across Central Asia commonly called the **Silk Road.** The city-states along this route did not resist the Chinese presence. They could carry out the trade on which they depended more conveniently with Chinese garrisons to protect them than with rival tribes raiding them.

At the same time, Emperor Wu sent troops into northern Korea to establish military districts that would flank the Xiongnu on their eastern border. By 111 B.C.E. the Han government also had extended its rule south into what is now northern Vietnam. Thus during Emperor Wu's reign, the territorial reach of the Han state was vastly extended.

tributary system *A system used by China to regulate contact with foreign powers. States and tribes beyond its borders sent envoys bearing gifts and received gifts in return.*

During the Han Dynasty, China developed a **tributary system** to regulate contact with foreign powers. States and tribes beyond its borders sent envoys bearing gifts and received gifts in return. Over the course of the dynasty the Han government's outlay on these gifts was huge, perhaps as much as 10 percent of state revenue. In 25 B.C.E., for instance, the government gave tributary states twenty thousand rolls of silk cloth and about twenty thousand pounds of silk floss. Although the tribute system was a financial burden to the Chinese, it reduced the cost of defense and offered China confirmation that it was the center of the civilized world.

The silk given to the Xiongnu and other northern tributaries often entered the trading networks of Sogdian, Parthian, and Indian merchants, who carried it by caravans across Asia. There was a market both for skeins of silk thread and for silk cloth woven in Chinese or Syrian workshops. Caravans returning to China carried gold, horses, and occasionally handicrafts of West Asian origin, such as glass beads and cups. Through the trade along the Silk Road, the Chinese learned of new foodstuffs, including walnuts, pomegranates, sesame, and coriander, all of which came to be grown in China. This trade was largely carried by the two-humped Bactrian camel, which had been bred in Central Asia since the first century B.C.E. With a heavy coat of hair to withstand the bitter cold of winter, each camel could carry about five hundred pounds of cargo. (See the feature "Global Trade: Silk" on pages 140–141.)

Maintaining a military presence so far from the center of China was expensive. To cut costs, the government set up self-supporting military colonies, recruited Xiongnu tribes to serve as auxiliary forces, and established vast government horse farms. Still, military expenses threatened to bankrupt the Han government.

Han Intellectual and Cultural Life

Confucianism made a comeback during the Han Dynasty, but it was a changed Confucianism. Although Confucian texts had fed the First Emperor's bonfires, some dedicated scholars had hidden their books, and others had memorized whole works: one ninety-year-old man was able to recite two long books almost in their entirety. The ancient books recovered in this way (called the **Confucian classics**) were revered as repositories of the wisdom of the past. Scholars studied them with piety and attempted to make them more useful as sources of moral guidance by writing commentaries on them. Many Confucian scholars specialized in a single classic, and teachers passed on to their disciples their understanding of each sentence in the work. Other Han Confucians went to the opposite extreme, developing comprehensive cosmological theories that explained the world in terms of cyclical flows of yin and yang and the five phases (fire, water, earth, metal, and wood). Some used these theories to elevate the role of the emperor, who alone had the capacity to link the realms of Heaven, earth, and man. Natural disasters such as floods or earthquakes were viewed as portents that the emperor had failed in his role of maintaining the proper balance among the forces of Heaven and earth.

Confucian classics *The ancient texts recovered during the Han Dynasty that Confucian scholars treated as sacred scriptures.*

Han art and literature reveal a fascination with omens, portents, spirits, immortals, and occult forces. Emperor Wu tried to make contact with the world of gods and immortals through elaborate sacrifices, and he welcomed astrologers, alchemists, seers, and shamans to his court. He marveled at stories of the paradise of the Queen Mother of the West and the exploits of the Yellow Emperor, who had taken his entire court with him when he ascended to the realm of the immortals. Much of this interest in immortality and communicating with the spirit world was absorbed into the emerging religion of Daoism, which also drew on the philosophical ideas of Laozi and Zhuangzi.

A major intellectual accomplishment of the Han Dynasty was history writing. Sima Qian (145–ca. 85 B.C.E.) wrote a comprehensive history of China from the time of the mythical sage-kings of high antiquity to his own day, dividing his account into a chronology recounting political events, biographies of key individuals, and treatises on subjects such as geography, taxation, and court rituals. As an official of the emperor, he had access to important people and documents and to the imperial library. Like the Greeks Herodotus and Thucydides (see page 83), Sima Qian believed fervently in visiting the sites where history was made, examining artifacts, and questioning people about events. He was also interested in China's geography and local history. The result of his research, ten years in the making, was **Records of the Grand Historian,** a massive work of literary and historical genius. In the chapter devoted to "money-makers," he described how the Ping family made its fortune:

Lu people are customarily cautious and miserly, but the Ping family of Cao were particularly so. They started out by smelting iron and in time accumulated a fortune of a hundred million cash. All the members of the family from the father and elder brothers down to the sons and grandsons, however, made a promise that they would "Never look down without picking up something useful; never look up without grabbing something of value." They traveled about to all the provinces and kingdoms, selling goods on credit, lending money and trading. It was because of their influence that so many people in Zou and Lu abandoned scholarship and turned to the pursuit of profit.[1]

From examples like these Sima Qian concluded that wealth has no permanent master: "It finds its way to the man of ability like the spokes of a wheel converging upon the hub, and from the hands of the worthless it falls like shattered tiles."[2] For centuries to come, Sima Qian's work set the standard for Chinese historical writing, although most of the histories modeled after it covered only a single dynasty. The first of these was the work of three members of the Ban family in the first century C.E. (See the feature "Individuals in Society: The Ban Family.")

The circulation of books like Sima Qian's was made easier by the invention of paper, which the Chinese traditionally date to 105 C.E. Scribes had previously written on strips of bamboo and wood or rolls of silk. Cai Lun, to whom the Chinese attribute the invention of paper, worked the fibers of rags, hemp, bark, and other scraps into sheets of paper. Paper, thus, was somewhat similar to the papyrus made from pounded reeds in ancient Egypt. Though much less durable than wood, paper was far cheaper than silk and became a convenient means of conveying the written word. Compared to papyrus, it depended less on a specific source of plant fiber and so could be produced many places.

Records of the Grand Historian A comprehensive history of China written by Sima Qian.

Economy and Society in Han China

How were ordinary people's lives affected by the creation of a huge bureaucratic empire? The lucky ones who lived in Chang'an or Luoyang, the great cities of the empire, got to enjoy the material benefits of increased long-distance trade and a boom in the production of luxury goods.

The government did not promote trade per se. The Confucian elite, like ancient Hebrew wise men, considered trade necessary but lowly. Agriculture and crafts were more honorable because they produced something, but merchants merely took

GLOBAL TRADE

SILK

Silk was one of the earliest commodities to stimulate international trade. By 2500 B.C.E. Chinese farmers had domesticated *Bombyx mori,* the Chinese silkworm, and by 1000 B.C.E. they were making fine fabrics with complex designs. Sericulture (silk making) is labor-intensive. In order for silkworms to spin their cocoons, they have to be fed leaves from mulberry trees. The leaves have to be picked and chopped, then fed to the worms every few hours, day and night, during the month between hatching and spinning. The cocoons consist of a single filament several thousand feet long but a minuscule 0.025 millimeter thick. More than two thousand cocoons are needed to make a pound of silk. After the cocoons are boiled to loosen the natural gum that binds the filament, several strands of filament are twisted together to make yarns.

What made silk the most valued of all textiles was its beauty and versatility. It could be made into sheer gauzes, shiny satins, multicolored brocades, and plush velvets. Fine Han silks have been found in Xiongnu tombs in northern Mongolia. Korea and Japan not only imported silk but also began silk production themselves, and silk came to be used in both places in much the way it was used in China—for the clothes of the elite,

The Silk Trade

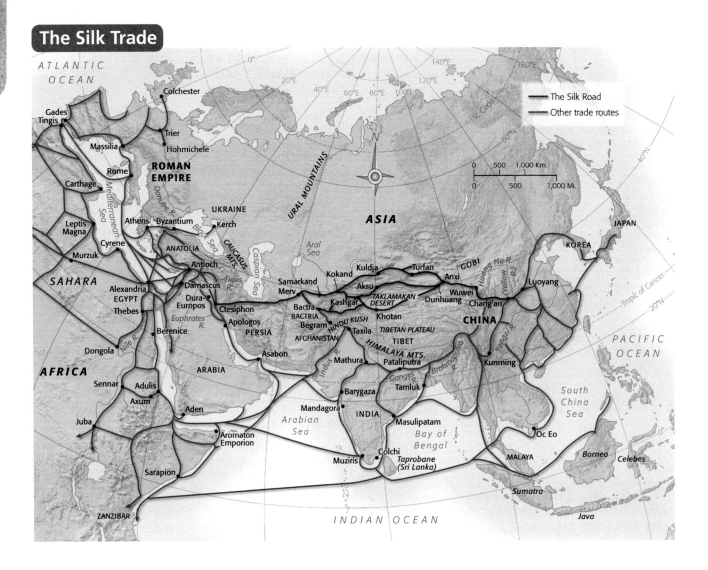

This fragment of a silk damask, about a foot square, was woven in China in the eleventh or twelfth century C.E., then transported by sea to Persia, where it was excavated along with southern Chinese porcelains of similar date. The design on the damask shows baby boys among pomegranates and flowers. Pomegranates have many seeds, making them symbols for ample progeny, a message conveyed even more concretely by the boys. (The Metropolitan Museum of Art. Purchase, Rogers Fund, 1952 [52.8]. Photograph © 1997 The Metropolitan Museum of Art)

for temple banners, and as a surface for writing and painting. Central Asia, Persia, India, and Southeast Asia also became producers of silk in distinctive local styles. Lacking suitable climates to produce silk, Mongolia and Tibet remained major importers of Chinese silks into modern times.

What makes the silk trade famous, however, is not the trade within Asia but the trade across Asia to Europe. In Roman times, silk carried by caravans across Asia or by ships across the Indian Ocean became a high-status luxury item, said to cost its weight in gold. To satisfy Roman taste, imported silk fabrics were unraveled and rewoven in Syrian workshops. Although the techniques of sericulture gradually spread through Asia, they remained a mystery in the West until the Byzantine emperor Justinian in the sixth century had two monks bring back silkworms from China along with knowledge of how to care for them and process their cocoons.

In medieval times, most of the silk imported into Europe came from Persia, the Byzantine Empire, or the Arab world. Venetian merchants handled much of the trade. Some of this fabric still survives in ancient churches, where it was used for vestments and altar clothes and to wrap relics. In the eleventh century, Roger I, king of Sicily, captured groups of silk-workers from Athens and Corinth and moved them to Sicily, initiating the production of silk in western Europe. Over the next couple of centuries, Italy became a major silk producer, joined by France in the fifteenth century.

When Marco Polo traveled across Asia in the late thirteenth century, he found local silk for sale in Baghdad, Georgia, Persia, and elsewhere, but China remained the largest producer. He claimed that more than a thousand cartloads of silk were brought into the capital of China every day.

With the development of the sea route between western Europe and China from the sixteenth century on, Europe began importing large quantities of Chinese silk, much of it as silk floss—raw silk—to supply Italian, French, and English silk weavers. In 1750 almost 70,000 kilograms (77.2 tons) of raw silk and nearly 20,000 lengths of silk cloth were carried from China to Europe. By this period the aristocracy of Europe regularly wore silk clothes, including silk stockings.

Mechanization of silk making began in Europe in the seventeenth century. The Italians developed machines to "throw" the silk—doubling and twisting raw silk into threads having the required strength and thickness. In the early nineteenth century, the introduction of Jacquard looms using punched cards made complex patterns easier to weave.

In the 1920s the silk industry was hit hard by the introduction of synthetic fibers, especially rayon and nylon. In the 1940s women in the United States and Europe switched from silk stockings to the much less expensive nylon stockings. European production of silk almost entirely collapsed.

In the 1980s silk made a comeback as China in the post-Mao era rapidly expanded its silk production. By 2003 there were more than two thousand silk enterprises in China, employing a million workers and supplying 80 percent of the total world trade in silk.

advantage of others' shortages to make profits as middlemen. This attitude justified the government's takeover of the grain, iron, and salt businesses. Still, the government indirectly promoted commerce by building cities and roads.

Markets were the liveliest places in the cities. Besides stalls selling goods of all kinds, markets offered fortunetellers and entertainers. People flocked to puppet shows and performances of jugglers and acrobats. The markets also were used for the execution of criminals, to serve as a warning to onlookers.

Government patronage helped maintain the quality of craftsmanship in the cities. By the beginning of the first century C.E., China had about fifty state-run ironworking factories. Chinese metalworking was the most advanced in the world at the time. In contrast to Roman blacksmiths, who hammered heated iron to make wrought iron tools, the Chinese knew how to liquefy iron and pour it into molds, producing tools with a higher carbon content that were harder and more durable. Han workmen turned out iron plowshares, agricultural tools with wooden handles, and weapons and armor.

Iron was replacing bronze in tools, but bronzeworkers still turned out a host of goods. Bronze was prized for jewelry, mirrors, and dishes. Bronze was also used for minting coins and for precision tools such as carpenters' rules and adjustable wrenches. Surviving bronze gear-and-cog wheels bear eloquent testimony to the sophistication of Han machinery. Han metal-smiths were mass-producing superb crossbows long before the crossbow was dreamed of in Europe.

The bulk of the population in Han times and even into the twentieth century consisted of peasants living in villages of a few hundred households. Since the Han empire, much like the contemporaneous Roman Empire, drew its strength from a large population of free peasants who contributed both taxes and labor services to the state, the government had to try to keep peasants independent and productive. The economic insecurity of small holders was described by one official in 178 B.C.E. in terms that could well have been repeated in most later dynasties:

They labor at plowing in the spring and hoeing in the summer, harvesting in the autumn and storing foodstuff in winter, cutting wood, performing labour service for the local government, all the while exposed to the dust of spring, the heat of summer, the storms of autumn, and the chill of winter. Through all four seasons they never get a day off. They need funds to cover such obligations as entertaining guests, burying the dead, visiting the sick, caring for orphans, and bringing up the young. No matter how hard they work they can be ruined by floods or droughts, or cruel and arbitrary officials who impose taxes at the wrong times or keep changing their orders. When taxes fall due, those with produce have to sell it at half price [to raise the needed cash], and those without [anything to sell] have to borrow [at such high rates] they will have to pay back twice what they borrowed. Some as a consequence sell their lands and houses, even their children and grandchildren.[3]

To fight peasant poverty, the government kept land taxes low (one-thirtieth of the harvest), provided relief in time of famine, and promoted up-to-date agricultural methods. Still, many hard-pressed peasants were left to choose between migration to areas where new lands could be opened and quasi-servile status as the dependents of a magnate. Throughout the Han period, Chinese farmers in search of land to till pushed into frontier areas, expanding Chinese domination at the expense of other ethnic groups, especially in central and south China.

The Chinese family in Han times was much like the Roman (see page 109) and the Indian (see pages 315–316) family. In all three societies, senior males had great authority, marriages were arranged by parents, and brides normally joined their husbands' families. Other practices were more distinctive to China, such as the universality of patrilineal family names, the practice of dividing land equally among the sons in a family, and the great emphasis placed on the virtue of filial piety. The brief *Classic of Filial Piety,* which claimed that filial piety was the root of all virtue, gained wide

The Ban Family

Ban Biao (3–54 C.E.), a successful official from a family with an envied library, had three highly accomplished children: his twin sons, the general Ban Chao (32–102) and the historian Ban Gu (32–92); and his daughter, Ban Zhao (ca. 45–120).

After distinguishing himself as a junior officer in campaigns against the Xiongnu, Ban Chao was sent in 73 C.E. to the Western Regions to see about the possibility of restoring Chinese overlordship there, lost since Wang Mang's time (early first century C.E.). Ban Chao spent most of the next three decades in Central Asia. Through patient diplomacy and a show of force, he reestablished Chinese control over the oasis cities of Central Asia, and in 92 he was appointed protector general of the area.

His twin brother Ban Gu was one of the most accomplished writers of his age, excelling in a distinctive literary form known as the rhapsody (*fu*). His "Rhapsody on the Two Capitals" is in the form of a dialogue between a guest from Chang'an and his host in Luoyang. It describes the palaces, spectacles, scenic spots, local products, and customs of the two great cities. Emperor Zhang (r. 76–88) was fond of literature and often had Ban Gu accompany him on hunts or travels. He also had him edit a record of the court debates he held on issues concerning the Confucian classics.

Ban Biao was working on a history of the Western Han Dynasty when he died in 54. Ban Gu took over this project, modeling it on Sima Qian's *Records of the Grand Historian.* He added treatises on law, geography, and bibliography, the last a classified list of books in the imperial library.

Because of his connection to a general out of favor, Ban Gu was sent to prison in 92, where he soon died. At that time the *History of the Former Han Dynasty* was still incomplete. The emperor called on Ban Gu's widowed sister, Ban Zhao, to finish it. She came to the palace, where she not only worked on the history but also became a teacher of the women of the palace. According to the *History of the Later Han,* she taught them the classics, history, astronomy, and mathematics. In 106 an infant succeeded to the throne, and the widow of an earlier emperor became regent. This empress frequently turned to Ban Zhao for advice on government policies.

Ban Zhao credited her own education to her learned father and cultured mother and became an advocate of the education of girls. In her *Admonitions for*

Ban Zhao continued to be considered the ideal woman teacher into the eighteenth century, when this imaginary portrait depicted her taking up her brush among women and children. *(National Palace Museum, Taipei, Taiwan)*

Women, Ban Zhao objected that many families taught their sons to read but not their daughters. She did not claim girls should have the same education as boys; after all, "just as yin and yang differ, men and women have different characteristics." Women, she wrote, will do well if they cultivate the womanly virtues such as humility. "Humility means yielding and acting respectful, putting others first and oneself last, never mentioning one's own good deeds or denying one's own faults, enduring insults and bearing with mistreatment, all with due trepidation."* In subsequent centuries, Ban Zhao's *Admonitions* became one of the most commonly used texts for the education of girls.

Questions for Analysis

1. What inferences would you draw from the fact that a leading general had a brother who was a literary man?

2. What does Ban Zhao's life tell us about women in her society? How do you reconcile her personal accomplishments with the advice she gave for women's education?

*Patricia Buckley Ebrey, ed., *Chinese Civilization: A Sourcebook,* rev. ed. (New York: Free Press, 1993), p. 75.

Primary Source:
Lessons for Women
*Discover what Ban Zhao, the
foremost female writer in Han
China, had to say about the
proper behavior of women.*

circulation in Han times. The virtues of loyal wives and devoted mothers were extolled in the *Biographies of Exemplary Women,* which told the stories of women from China's past who were notable for giving their husbands good advice, knowing how to educate their sons, and sacrificing themselves when forced to choose between their fathers and husbands. The book also contained a few cautionary tales of scheming, jealous, manipulative women who brought destruction to all around them.

China and Rome

The empires of China and Rome have often been compared. Both were large, complex states governed by monarchs, bureaucracies, and standing armies. Both reached directly to the people through taxation and conscription policies. Both invested in infrastructure such as roads and waterworks. Both had to work hard to keep land from becoming too concentrated in the hands of hard-to-tax wealthy magnates. In both empires people in neighboring areas that came under political domination were attracted to the conquerors' material goods, productive techniques, and other cultural products, resulting in gradual cultural assimilation. Both China and Rome had similar frontier problems and tried similar solutions, such as using "barbarian" auxiliaries and settling soldier-colonists.

Nevertheless, the differences between Rome and Han China are worth as much notice as the similarities. The Roman Empire was linguistically and culturally more diverse than China. In China there was only one written language; but in the Roman Empire people still wrote in Greek and several other languages, and people from the East could claim more ancient civilizations. Politically, the dynastic principle was stronger in China than in Rome. Han emperors were never chosen by the army or by any institution comparable to the Roman senate, nor were there any republican ideals in China. In contrast to the graduated forms of citizenship in Rome, Han China drew no distinctions between original and added territories. The social and economic structures also differed in the two empires. Slavery was much more important in Rome than in China, and merchants were more favored. Over time these differences put Chinese and Roman social and political development on rather different trajectories.

The Fall of the Han and the Age of Division

In the second century C.E. the Han government suffered a series of blows. A succession of child emperors allowed their mothers' relatives to dominate the court. Emperors turned to **eunuchs** (castrated palace servants) for help in ousting the consort families (families of empresses), only to find that they were just as difficult to control. In 166 and 169 scholars who had denounced the eunuchs were arrested, killed, or banished from the capital and official life. Then in 184 a millenarian religious sect rose in massive revolt. The armies raised to suppress the rebels soon took to fighting among themselves. In 189 one general slaughtered two thousand eunuchs in the palace and took the Han emperor captive. After years of fighting, a stalemate was reached, with three warlords each controlling distinct territories in the north, the southeast, and the southwest. In 220 one of them forced the last of the Han emperors to abdicate, formally ending the Han Dynasty.

The period after the fall of the Han Dynasty is often referred to as the **Age of Division** (220–589). A brief reunification from 280 to 316 came to an end when non-Chinese who had been settling in north China since Han times seized the opportunity afforded by the political turmoil to take power. For the next two and a half centuries north China was ruled by one or more non-Chinese dynasty (the Northern Dynasties), and the south was ruled by a sequence of four short-lived Chinese dynasties (the Southern Dynasties) centered in the area of the present-day city of Nanjing.

In the south a hereditary aristocracy entrenched itself in the higher reaches of

eunuchs *Castrated males who played an important role as palace servants.*

Age of Division *The period after the fall of the Han Dynasty, during which time China was politically divided.*

officialdom. These families intermarried only with families of equivalent pedigree and compiled lists and genealogies of the most eminent families. They saw themselves as maintaining the high culture of the Han and looked on the emperors of the successive dynasties as upstarts—as military men rather than men of culture. In this aristocratic culture, the arts of poetry and calligraphy flourished, and people began collecting writings by famous calligraphers.

Establishing the capital at Nanjing, south of the Yangzi River, had a beneficial effect on the economic development of the south. To pay for an army and to support the imperial court and aristocracy in a style that matched their pretensions, the government had to expand the area of taxable agricultural land, whether through settling migrants or converting the local inhabitants into taxpayers. The south, with its temperate climate and ample supply of water, offered nearly unlimited possibilities for such development.

The Northern Dynasties are interesting as the first case of alien rule in China. Ethnic tensions flared from time to time. In the late fifth century the Northern Wei Dynasty (386–534) moved the capital from near the Great Wall to the ancient city of Luoyang, adopted Chinese-style clothing, and made Chinese the official language. The Xianbei tribesmen, who still formed the main military force, saw themselves as marginalized by these policies and rebelled in 524. For the next fifty years north China was torn apart by struggles for power. It had long been the custom of the northern pastoral tribes to enslave those they captured; sometimes the residents of entire cities were enslaved. In 554, when the city of Jiangling was taken, one hundred thousand civilians were enslaved and distributed to generals and officials.

THE SPREAD OF BUDDHISM OUT OF INDIA

How were both Buddhism and China changed by the spread of Buddhism across Asia?

In much the same period that Christianity was spreading out of its original home in ancient Israel, Buddhism was spreading beyond India. Like Christianity, Buddhism was shaped by its contact with cultures in the different areas into which it spread, leading to several distinct forms. The Mahayana form of Buddhism (see page 41) that spread via Central Asia to China, Korea, and Japan is distinct from the Theravada form that spread from India to Sri Lanka and Southeast Asia and the Tantric form that spread to Tibet.

Central Asia is a loose term used to refer to the vast area between the ancient civilizations of Persia, India, and China. Modern political borders are a product of competition among the British, Russians, and Chinese for empire in the mid-nineteenth century and have relatively little to do with the earlier history of the region. Through most of recorded history, the region was ethnically and culturally diverse; it was home to urban centers, especially at the oases along the Silk Road, and to pastoralists in the mountains and grasslands.

Under Ashoka (see pages 45–46) Buddhism began to spread to Central Asia. This continued under the Kushan empire (ca. 50–250 C.E.), especially under the greatest Kushan king, Kanishka I (ca. 100 C.E.). In this region, where the influence of Greek art was strong, artists began to depict the Buddha in human form. Over the next several centuries most of the city-states of Central Asia became centers of Buddhism, from Bamiyan, northwest of Kabul, to Kucha, Khotan, Loulan, Turfan, and Dunhuang (see Map 6.2). Because the remarkable Buddhist civilization of Central Asia was later supplanted by Islam, it was not until early in the twentieth century that European archaeologists discovered its traces. The main sites yielded not only numerous

Buddhist paintings but also thousands of texts in a variety of languages. In Khotan, for instance, an Indian language was used for administrative purposes long after the fall of the Kushan empire. Other texts were in various Persian languages, showing the cultural mix of the region.

The first translators of Buddhist texts into Chinese were not Indians but Parthians, Sogdians, and Kushans from Central Asia. One of the most important interpreters of Buddhism in China was the eminent Central Asian monk Kumarajiva (350–413) from Kucha, who settled in Chang'an and directed several thousand monks in the translation of Buddhist texts.

Why did Buddhism find so many adherents in China during the three centuries after the fall of the Han Dynasty in 220? There were no forced conversions, but still the religion spread rapidly. In the unstable political environment, many people were open to new ideas. To Chinese scholars the Buddhist concepts of the transmigration of souls, karma, and nirvana posed a stimulating intellectual challenge. To rulers the Buddhist religion offered a source of magical power and a political tool to unite

MAP 6.2 **The Spread of Buddhism** Buddhism spread throughout India in Ashoka's time and beyond India in later centuries. The different forms of Buddhism found in Asia today reflect this history. The Mahayana Buddhism of Japan came via Central Asia, China, and Korea, with a secondary later route through Tibet. The Theravada Buddhism of Southeast Asia came directly from India and indirectly through Sri Lanka.

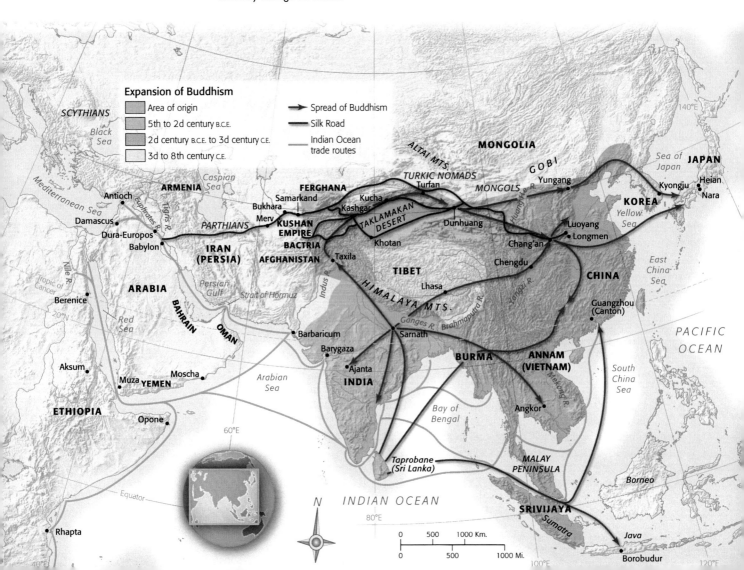

Chinese and non-Chinese. In a rough and tumultuous age Buddhism's emphasis on kindness, charity, and eternal bliss was deeply comforting. As in India, Buddhism posed no threat to the social order, and the elite who were drawn to Buddhism encouraged its spread to people of all classes. (See the feature "Listening to the Past: Copying Buddhist Sutras" on pages 160–161.)

The monastic establishment grew rapidly in China. Like their Christian counterparts in medieval Europe, Buddhist monasteries played an active role in social, economic, and political life. By 477 there were said to be 6,478 Buddhist temples and 77,258 monks and nuns in the north. Some decades later south China had 2,846 temples and 82,700 clerics. Given the importance of family lines in China, becoming a monk was a major decision, since a man had to give up his surname and take a vow of celibacy, thus cutting himself off from the ancestral cult. Those not ready to become monks or nuns could pursue Buddhist goals as pious laypeople by performing devotional acts and making contributions to monasteries. Among the most generous patrons were rulers in both the north and south.

In China women turned to Buddhism as readily as men. Although incarnation as a female was considered lower than incarnation as a male, it was also viewed as temporary, and women were encouraged to pursue salvation on terms nearly equal to men. Joining a nunnery became an alternative for a woman who did not want to marry or did not want to stay with her husband's family in widowhood.

● **Meditating Monk**   This monk, wearing the traditional patchwork robe, sits in the crossed-legged meditation position. His small niche is to the left of the main image of the Buddha in cave 285 at Dunhuang, a cave completed in 539 under the patronage of a prince of the Northern Wei imperial house who was then the local governor. *(Photo: Lois Conner. Courtesy, Dunhuang Academy)*

Buddhism had an enormous impact on the visual arts in China, especially sculpture and painting. Before Buddhism, Chinese had not set up statues of gods in temples, but now they decorated temples with a profusion of images. Inspired by the cave-temples of India and Central Asia, in China, too, caves were carved into rock faces to make temples.

Buddhist temples were just as splendid in the cities. One author described the ceremony held each year on the seventh day of the fourth month at the largest monastery in the northern capital, Luoyang. All the Buddhist statues in the city, more than a thousand altogether, would be brought to the monastery, and the emperor would come in person to scatter flowers as part of the Great Blessing ceremony:

The gold and the flowers dazzled in the sun, and the jewelled canopies floated like clouds; there were forests of banners and a fog of incense, and the Buddhist music of India shook heaven and earth. All kinds of entertainers and trick riders performed shoulder to shoulder. Virtuous hosts of famous monks came, carrying their staves; there were crowds of the Buddhist faithful, holding flowers; horsemen and carriages were packed beside each other in an endless mass.[4]

● **Yungang Colossal Buddha** Beginning about 460 C.E. the Northern Wei rulers constructed a series of caves at Yungang, not far from their capital. The large Buddha shown here in a lotus meditation posture is 45 feet (13.7 meters) tall. Notice the long ears and the robe across the Buddha's shoulders, both features associated with the Buddha. *(Dean Conger/Corbis)*

Not everyone was won over by Buddhist teachings. Critics of Buddhism labeled it immoral, unsuited to China, and a threat to the state since monastery land was not taxed and monks did not perform labor service. Twice in the north orders were issued to close monasteries and force monks and nuns to return to lay life, but these suppressions did not last long, and no attempt was made to suppress belief in Buddhism.

THE CHINESE EMPIRE RE-CREATED: SUI (581–618) AND TANG (618–907)

In what ways was China's second empire different from its first?

In the 570s and 580s, the long period of division in China was brought to an end under the leadership of the Sui Dynasty. Yang Jian, who both founded the Sui Dynasty and oversaw the reunification of China, was from a Chinese family that had intermarried with the non-Chinese elite of the north. His conquest of the south involved naval as well as land battles, with thousands of ships on both sides contending for control of the Yangzi River. The Sui reasserted Chinese control over northern Vietnam and campaigned into Korea and against the new force on the steppe, the Turks. The Sui strengthened central control of the government by curtailing the power of local officials to appoint their own subordinates and by instituting competitive written examinations for the selection of officials.

The crowning achievement of the Sui Dynasty was the **Grand Canal,** which connected the Huang (Yellow) and Yangzi River regions. The canal facilitated the shipping of tax grain from the prosperous Yangzi Valley to the centers of political and military power in north China. Henceforth the rice-growing Yangzi Valley and south China played an ever more influential role in the country's economic and political life, strengthening China's internal cohesion.

Grand Canal *A canal, built during the Sui Dynasty, that connected the Huang (Yellow) and Yangzi Rivers.*

Despite these accomplishments, the Sui Dynasty lasted for only two reigns. The ambitious projects of the two Sui emperors led to exhaustion and unrest, and in the ensuing warfare Li Yuan, a Chinese from the same northwest aristocratic circles as the founder of the Sui, seized the throne.

The Tang Dynasty (618–907)

The dynasty founded by Li Yuan, the Tang, was one of the high points of traditional Chinese civilization. Especially during this dynasty's first century, its capital, Chang'an, was the cultural center of East Asia, drawing in merchants, pilgrims, missionaries, and students to a degree never matched before or after. This position of strength gave the Chinese the confidence to be open to what they could learn from the outside world, leading to a more cosmopolitan culture than in any other period before the twentieth century.

The first two Tang rulers, Gaozu (r. 618–626) and Taizong (r. 626–649), were able monarchs. Adding to their armies auxiliary troops composed of Turks, Tanguts, Khitans, and other non-Chinese led by their own chieftains, they campaigned into Korea, Vietnam, and Central Asia. In 630 the Chinese turned against their former allies, the Turks, gaining territory from them and winning for Taizong the title of Great Khan, so that he was for a short period simultaneously head of both the Chinese and the Turkish empires.

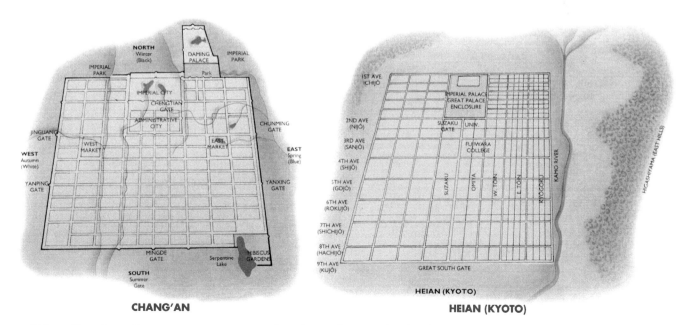

CHANG'AN

HEIAN (KYOTO)

● **Urban Planning**   Chang'an in Tang times attracted merchants, pilgrims, and students from all over East Asia. The city was laid out on a square grid (*left*) and divided into walled wards, the gates to which were closed at night. Temples were found throughout the city, but trade was limited to two government-supervised markets. In the eighth and ninth centuries the Japanese copied the general plan of Chang'an in designing their capitals—first at Nara, then at Heian, shown on the right. *(From* Cradles of Civilization: China *[Weldon Owen Pty Limited, Australia])*

In the civil sphere Tang accomplishments far outstripped anything known in Europe until the growth of national states in the seventeenth century. Tang emperors subdivided the administration of the empire into departments, much like the numerous agencies of modern governments. They built on the Sui precedent of using written examinations to select officials. Although only about thirty men were recruited this way each year, the prestige of passing the examinations became so great that more and more men attempted them. Candidates had to master the Confucian classics and the rules of poetry, and they had to be able to analyze practical administrative and political matters. Government schools were founded to prepare the sons of officials and other young men for service as officials.

The mid-Tang Dynasty saw two women—Empress Wu and Consort Yang Guifei—rise to positions of great political power. Empress Wu was the consort of the weak and sickly Emperor Gaozong. After Gaozong suffered a stroke in 660, she took full charge. She continued to rule after Gaozong's death, summarily deposing her own two sons and dealing harshly with all opponents. In 690 she proclaimed herself emperor, the only woman who took that title in Chinese history. To gain support, she circulated a Buddhist sutra that predicted the imminent reincarnation of the Buddha Maitreya as a female monarch, during whose reign the world would be free of illness, worry, and disaster. Although despised by later historians as an evil usurper, Empress Wu was an effective leader. It was not until she was over eighty that members of the court were able to force her out in favor of her son.

Her grandson, the emperor Xuanzong (r. 713–756), in his early years presided over a brilliant court and patronized leading poets, painters, and calligraphers. In his later years, however, after he became enamored of his consort Yang Guifei, he let things slide. This was a period when ample and rounded proportions were much admired in women, and Yang was said to be such a full-figured beauty. The emperor allowed her to place friends and relatives in important positions in the government. One of her favorites was the general An Lushan, who, after getting into a quarrel with Yang's brother over control of the government, rebelled in 755. Xuanzong had to flee the capital, and the troops that accompanied him forced him to have Yang Guifei executed.

The rebellion of An Lushan was devastating to the Tang Dynasty. Peace was restored only by calling on the Uighurs, a Turkish people allied with the Tang, who looted the capital after taking it from the rebels. After the rebellion was finally suppressed in 763, the central government had to keep meeting the extortionate demands of the Uighurs. Many military governors came to treat their provinces as hereditary kingdoms and withheld tax returns from the central government. In addition, eunuchs gained increasing power at court and were able to prevent both the emperors and Confucian officials from doing much about them.

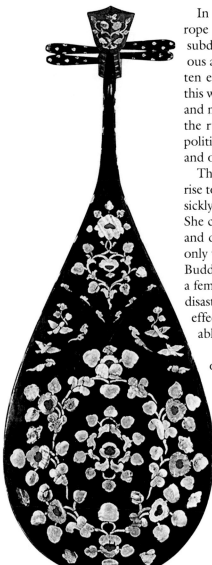

● **Five-Stringed Pipa/Biwa** This musical instrument, decorated with fine wood marquetry, was probably presented by the Tang court to a Japanese envoy. It was among the objects placed in a royal storage house (Shōsōin) in 756. *(Courtesy, Nara National Museum)*

Tang Culture

The reunification of north and south led to cultural flowering. The Tang capital cities of Chang'an and Luoyang became great metropolises; Chang'an and its suburbs grew to more than 2 million inhabitants. The cities were laid out in rectangular grids and contained a hundred-odd walled "blocks" inside their walls.

In these cosmopolitan cities, knowledge of the outside world was stimulated by the presence of envoys, merchants, and pilgrims who came from neighboring states in Central Asia, Japan, Korea, Tibet, and Southeast Asia. Because of the presence of foreign merchants, many religions were practiced, including Nestorian Christianity, Manichaeism, Zoroastrianism, Judaism, and Islam, although none of them spread into the Chinese population the way Buddhism had a few centuries earlier. Foreign fashions in hair and clothing were often copied, and foreign amusements such as polo found followings among the well-to-do. The introduction of new musical instruments

Primary Source: The Christian Monument *An eighth-century inscription tells a remarkable tale: how a Christian sect from Syria was supported by the Chinese emperor.*

● **Woman Playing Polo**   Notions of what makes women attractive have changed over the course of Chinese history. The figurines found in Tang tombs reveal that active women, even women playing polo on horseback like the one shown here, were viewed as appealing. In earlier and later periods, female beauty was identified with slender waists and delicate faces, but in Tang times women were admired for their plump bodies and full faces. *(Chinese. Equestrienne [tomb figure], buff earthenware with traces of polychromy, first half 8th cent., 56.2 x 48.2 cm. Gift of Mrs. Pauline Palmer Wood, 1970.1073. Photograph © 1998, The Art Institute of Chicago)*

and tunes from India, Iran, and Central Asia brought about a major transformation in Chinese music.

The Tang Dynasty was the great age of Chinese poetry. Skill in composing poetry was tested in the civil service examinations, and educated men had to be able to compose poems at social gatherings. The pain of parting, the joys of nature, and the pleasures of wine and friendship were all common poetic topics. One of Li Bo's (701–762) most famous poems describes an evening of drinking with only the moon and his shadow for company:

A cup of wine, under the flowering trees;
I drink alone, for no friend is near.
Raising my cup I beckon the bright moon,
For he, with my shadow, will make three men.
The moon, alas, is no drinker of wine;
Listless, my shadow creeps about at my side.
. . .
Now we are drunk, each goes his way.
May we long share our odd, inanimate feast,
And we meet at last on the cloudy River of the sky.[5]

Primary Source:
Memorial on Buddhism
Read how Han Yu, upset at the growing influence of Buddhism, denigrated that religion as "un-Chinese" in a text addressed to the Tang emperor.

The poet Bo Juyi (772–846) often wrote of more serious subjects. At times he worried about whether he was doing his job justly and well:

From these high walls I look at the town below
Where the natives of Pa cluster like a swarm of flies.
How can I govern these people and lead them aright?
I cannot even understand what they say.
But at least I am glad, now that the taxes are in,
To learn that in my province there is no discontent.[6]

In Tang times Buddhism fully penetrated Chinese daily life. Stories of Buddhist origin became widely known, and Buddhist festivals, such as the festival for feeding hungry ghosts in the summer, became among the most popular holidays. Buddhist monasteries became an important part of everyday life. They ran schools for children. In remote areas they provided lodging for travelers. Merchants entrusted their money and wares to monasteries for safekeeping, in effect transforming the monasteries into banks and warehouses. The wealthy often donated money or land to support temples and monasteries, making monasteries among the largest landlords.

At the intellectual and religious level, Buddhism was developing in distinctly Chinese directions. Two schools that thrived were Pure Land and Chan. **Pure Land** appealed to laypeople. The simple act of calling on the Buddha Amitabha and his chief helper, the compassionate bodhisattva Guanyin, could lead to rebirth in Amitabha's paradise, the Pure Land. Among the educated elite the **Chan** school (known in Japan as Zen) also gained popularity. Chan teachings rejected the authority of the scriptures and claimed the superiority of mind-to-mind transmission of Buddhist truths. The "northern" tradition emphasized meditation and monastic discipline. The "southern" tradition was even more iconoclastic, holding that enlightenment could be achieved suddenly through insight into one's own true nature, even without prolonged meditation.

In the late Tang period, opposition to Buddhism reemerged. In addition to concerns about the fiscal impact of removing so much land from the tax rolls and so many men from the labor service force, there were concerns about Buddhism's foreign origins. As China's international position weakened, xenophobia emerged. During the persecution of 845, more than 4,600 monasteries and 40,000 temples and shrines were destroyed, and more than 260,000 Buddhist monks and nuns were forced to return to secular life. Although this ban was lifted after a few years, the monastic establishment never fully recovered. Among laypeople Buddhism retained a strong hold, and basic Buddhist ideas like karma and reincarnation had become fully incorporated into everyday Chinese thinking. But Buddhism was never again as central to Chinese life.

Pure Land *A school of Buddhism that taught that by paying homage to the Buddha Amitabha and his chief helper, one could achieve rebirth in Amitabha's paradise.*

Chan *A school of Buddhism (known in Japan as Zen) that rejected the authority of the sutras and claimed the superiority of mind-to-mind transmission of Buddhist truths.*

THE EAST ASIAN CULTURAL SPHERE

What elements of Chinese culture were adopted by Koreans, Vietnamese, and Japanese, and how did they adapt them to their own circumstances?

During the millennium from 200 B.C.E. to 800 C.E. China exerted a powerful influence on its immediate neighbors, who began forming states of their own. By Tang times China was surrounded by independent states in Korea, Manchuria, Tibet, the area that is now Yunnan province, Vietnam, and Japan. All of these states were much smaller than China in area and population, making China by far the dominant force politically and culturally until the nineteenth century. Nevertheless, each of these separate states developed a strong sense of uniqueness and independent identity.

The earliest information about each of these countries is found in Chinese sources. Han armies brought Chinese culture to Korea and Vietnam, but even in those cases much cultural borrowing was entirely voluntary as the elite, merchants, and craftsmen adopted the techniques, ideas, and practices they found appealing. In Japan much of the process of absorbing elements of Chinese culture was mediated via Korea. In Korea, Japan, and Vietnam the fine arts—painting, architecture, and ceramics in particular—were all strongly influenced by Chinese models. Tibet, though a thorn in the side of Tang China, was as much in the Indian sphere of influence as in the Chinese and thus followed a somewhat different trajectory. Most significant, it never adopted Chinese characters as its written language, nor was it as influenced by Chinese artistic styles as other areas. Moreover the form of Buddhism that became dominant in Tibet came directly from India, not through Central Asia and China.

In each area, literate Chinese-style culture was at first an upper-level overlay over an indigenous cultural base, but in time many products and ideas adopted from China became incorporated into everyday life, ranging from written language to chopsticks and soy sauce. By the eighth century the Chinese language was a written lingua franca among educated people throughout East Asia. Educated Vietnamese, Koreans, and Japanese could communicate in writing when they could not understand each other's spoken languages, and envoys to Chang'an could carry out "brush conversations" with each other. The books that educated people read included the Chinese classics, histories, and poetry, as well as Buddhist sutras translated into Chinese. The great appeal of Buddhism known primarily through Chinese translation was a powerful force promoting cultural borrowing.

● **Bronze Drum**   By 300 B.C.E. large bronze drums were being cast in what is now northern Vietnam. They were regularly decorated with scenes of daily life, war, and rituals. This drum, called the Ngoc Lu Drum, has depictions of boats carrying warriors on its sides. The three concentric rings on top show birds, deer, houses, and pairs of people pounding rice. *(From A. J. Bernet Kempers, The Kettledrums of South Asia: A Bronze Age World and Its Aftermath [Leiden, The Netherlands: A. A. Balkema, 1988, Tozzer Library, Harvard College Library])*

Vietnam

Vietnam is today classed with the countries to its west as part of Southeast Asia, but its ties are at least as strong to China. The Vietnamese first appear in Chinese sources as a people of south China called the Yue, who gradually migrated farther south as the Chinese state expanded. The people of the Red River valley in northern Vietnam had achieved a relatively advanced level of Bronze Age civilization by the first century B.C.E. The bronze heads of their arrows often were dipped in poison to facilitate killing large animals such as elephants, whose tusks were traded to China for iron. Power was held by hereditary tribal chiefs who served as civil, religious, and military leaders, with the king as the most powerful chief.

The collapse of the Qin Dynasty in 206 B.C.E. had an impact on this area because a former Qin general, Zhao Tuo (Trieu Da in Vietnamese), finding himself in the far south, set up his own kingdom of Nam Viet (Nan Yue in Chinese). This kingdom covered much of south China and was ruled by Trieu Da from his capital near the present site of Guangzhou. Its population consisted chiefly of the Viet people. After killing all officials loyal to the Chinese emperor, Trieu Da adopted the customs of the Viet and made himself the ruler of a vast state that extended as far south as modern-day Da Nang.

After almost a hundred years of diplomatic and military duels between the Han Dynasty and Trieu Da and his successors, Nam Viet was conquered in 111 B.C.E. by Chinese armies. Chinese administrators were assigned to replace the local nobility. Chinese

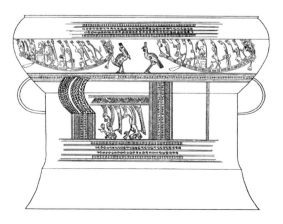

political institutions were imposed, and Confucianism became the official ideology. The Chinese language was introduced as the medium of official and literary expression, and Chinese ideographs were adopted as the written form for the Vietnamese spoken language. The Chinese built roads, waterways, and harbors to facilitate communication within the region and to ensure that they maintained administrative and military control over it. Chinese art, architecture, and music had a powerful impact on their Vietnamese counterparts.

Chinese innovations that were beneficial to the Vietnamese were readily integrated into the indigenous culture, but the local elite were not reconciled to Chinese political domination. The most famous early revolt took place in 39 C.E., when two widows of local aristocrats, the Trung sisters, led an uprising against foreign rule. After overwhelming Chinese strongholds, they declared themselves queens of an independent Vietnamese kingdom. Three years later a powerful army sent by the Han emperor reestablished Chinese rule.

China retained at least nominal control over northern Vietnam through the Tang Dynasty, and there were no real borders between China proper and Vietnam during this time. The local elite became culturally dual, serving as brokers between the Chinese governors and the native people.

Korea

Korea is a mountainous peninsula some 600 miles long extending south from Manchuria and Siberia. At its tip it is about 120 miles from Japan (see Map 6.3). Archaeological, linguistic, and anthropological evidence indicates that the Korean people share a common ethnic origin with other peoples of North Asia, including those of Manchuria, Siberia, and Japan. Linguistically, Korean is not related to Chinese.

Bronze and iron technology spread from China and North Asia in the Zhou period. In about 194 B.C.E. Wiman, an unsuccessful rebel against the Han Dynasty, fled to Korea and set up a state called Chosŏn in what is now northwest Korea and southern Manchuria. In 108 B.C.E. this state was overthrown by the armies of the Han emperor Wu. Four commanderies were established there, and Chinese officials were dispatched to govern them.

The impact of the Chinese commanderies in Korea was similar to that of the contemporaneous Roman colonies in Britain in encouraging the spread of culture and political forms. The commanderies survived not only through the Han Dynasty, but also for nearly a century after the fall of the dynasty, to 313 C.E. The Chinese never controlled the entire Korean peninsula, however. The Han commanderies coexisted with the native Korean kingdom of Koguryŏ, founded in the first century B.C.E. Chinese sources describe this kingdom as a society of aristocratic tribal warriors who had under them a mass of serfs and slaves, mostly from conquered tribes. After the Chinese colonies were finally overthrown, the kingdoms of Paekche and Silla emerged farther south on the peninsula in the third and fourth centuries C.E., leading to what is called the Three Kingdoms Period (313–668 C.E.). In all three Korean kingdoms Chinese was used as the language of government and learning. Each of the three kingdoms had hereditary kings, but their power

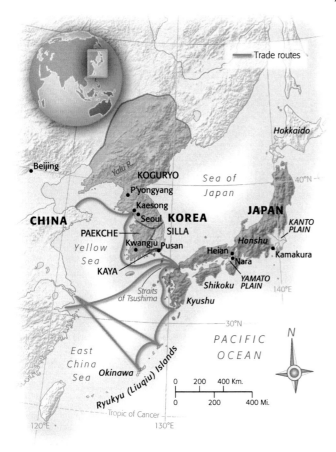

MAP 6.3 **Korea and Japan, ca. 600** Korea and Japan are of similar latitude, but Korea's climate is more continental, with harsher winters. Of Japan's four islands, Kyushu is closest to Korea and mainland Asia.

was curbed by the existence of very strong hereditary elites.

Buddhism was officially introduced in Koguryŏ from China in 372 and in the other states not long after. Buddhism placed Korea in a pan-Asian cultural context. Buddhist monks went back and forth between China and Korea. One even made the journey to India and back, and others traveled on to Japan to aid in the spread of Buddhism there.

When the Sui Dynasty finally reunified China in 589, it tried to establish control of at least a part of Korea. But the Korean kingdoms were much stronger than their predecessors in Han times, and they repeatedly repulsed Chinese attacks. The Tang government then tried allying itself with one state to fight another. Silla and Tang jointly destroyed Paekche in 660 and Koguryŏ in 668. The unification under Silla marks the first political unification of Korea.

Although Silla quickly forced the Tang to withdraw, for the next century Silla embarked on a policy of wholesale borrowing of Chinese culture and institutions. Annual embassies were sent to Chang'an, and large numbers of students studied in China. The Silla government was modeled on the Tang, although modifications were made to accommodate Korea's more aristocratic social structure.

Japan

Japan does not touch China as do Korea, Tibet, and Vietnam. The heart of Japan is four mountainous islands off the coast of Korea (see Map 6.3). Japan's early development was closely tied to that of the mainland, especially to Korea. Physical anthropologists have discerned several major waves of immigrants into Japan. People of the Jōmon culture, established by about 10,000 B.C.E. after an influx of people from Southeast Asia, practiced hunting and fishing and fashioned clay pots. New arrivals from northeast Asia brought agriculture and a distinct culture called Yayoi (ca. 300 B.C.E.–300 C.E.). Later Yayoi communities

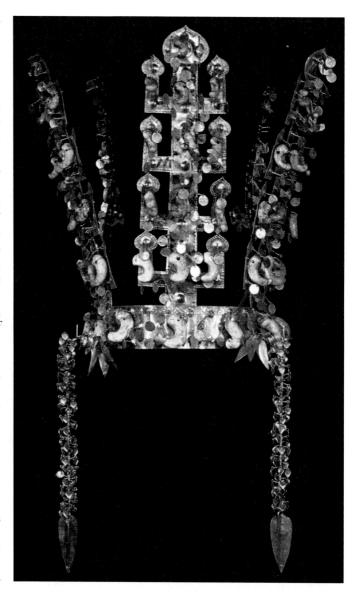

● **Gold Crown** Excavated from a fifth- to sixth-century royal Silla tomb, this magnificent crown reflects metalwork traditions found in scattered places across the Eurasian steppe. The crown is decorated with dangling gold disks and comma-shaped beads of jadeite. The upright bars at the top are thought to represent deer antlers. *(Kyongju National Museum, Kyongju)*

were marked by complex social organization with rulers, soldiers, artisans, and priests. Objects of Chinese and Korean manufacture found their way into Japan, an indication that people were traveling back and forth as well. In the third century C.E. Chinese histories begin to report on the land called Wa made up of mountainous islands. It had numerous communities, markets, granaries, tax collection, and class distinctions. The people ate with their fingers, used body paint, purified themselves by bathing after a funeral, and liked liquor. Of their rulers the Chinese historian wrote:

The country formerly had a man as ruler. For some seventy or eighty years after that there were disturbances and warfare. Thereupon the people agreed upon a woman for their ruler. Her name was Himiko. She occupied herself with magic and sorcery, bewitching the people. Though mature in age, she remained unmarried. She had a younger brother who assisted her in ruling the country. After she became the ruler, there were few who saw her. She had one thousand women as attendants, but only one man. He served her food and drink and acted as a medium of communication. . . .

When Himiko passed away, a great mound was raised, more than a hundred paces in diameter. Over a hundred male and female attendants followed her to the grave. Then a king was placed on the throne, but the people would not obey him. Assassination and murder followed; more than one thousand were thus slain.

A relative of Himiko named Iyo, a girl of thirteen, was then made queen and order was restored.[7]

During the fourth through sixth centuries, new waves of migrants from Korea brought with them the language that evolved into Japanese. They also brought sericulture (silk making), bronze swords, crossbows, iron plows, and the Chinese written language. In this period, a social order similar to Korea's emerged, dominated by a warrior aristocracy organized into clans. Clad in helmet and armor, these warriors wielded swords, battle-axes, and often bows. Some of them rode into battle on horseback. Those vanquished in battle were made slaves. Each clan had its own chieftain, who marshaled clansmen for battle and served as chief priest. Over time the clans fought with each other, and their numbers were gradually reduced through conquest and alliance. By the fifth century the chief of the clan that claimed descent from

● **Hōryūji Temple** Japanese Buddhist temples, like those in China and Korea, consisted of several buildings within a walled compound. The buildings of the Hōryūji Temple (built 670–711; Prince Shōtoku's original temple burned down) include the oldest wooden structures in the world and house some of the best early Buddhist sculpture in Japan. The three main buildings depicted here are the pagoda, housing relics; the main hall, with the temple's principal images; and the lecture hall, for sermons. The five-story pagoda could be seen from far away, much like the steeples of cathedrals in medieval Europe. *(The Orion Press)*

the sun-goddess, located in the Yamato plain around modern Osaka, had come to occupy the position of Great King—or Queen, as female rulers were not uncommon in this period.

The Yamato rulers used their religion to subordinate the gods of their rivals, much as Hammurabi had used Marduk in Babylonia (see page 7). They established the chief shrine of the sun-goddess near the seacoast, where she could catch the first rays of the rising sun. Cults to other gods also were supported as long as they were viewed as subordinate to the sun-goddess. This native religion was later termed **Shinto,** the Way of the Gods.

In the sixth century Prince Shōtoku (574–622) undertook a sweeping reform of the state designed to strengthen Yamato rule by adopting Chinese-style bureaucratic practices. His "Seventeen Principles" of 604 drew from both Confucian and Buddhist teachings. In it he likened the ruler to Heaven and instructed officials to put their duty to the ruler above the interest of their families. He instituted a ladder of official ranks similar to China's, admonished the nobility to avoid strife and opposition, and urged adherence to Buddhist precepts. Near his seat of government, Prince Shōtoku built the magnificent Hōryūji Temple and staffed it with monks from Korea. He also opened direct relations with China, sending four missions during the brief Sui Dynasty.

State-building efforts continued through the seventh century and culminated in the establishment in 710 of Japan's first permanent capital at **Nara,** north of modern Osaka. Nara, which was modeled on the Tang capital of Chang'an, gave its name to an era that lasted until 794 and that was characterized by the avid importation of Chinese ideas and methods. Seven times missions with five hundred to six hundred men were sent on the difficult journey to Chang'an. Chinese and Korean craftsmen were often brought back to Japan, especially to help with the decoration of the many Buddhist temples then under construction. Musical instruments and tunes were imported as well, many originally from Central Asia. Chinese practices were instituted, such as the compilation of histories and law codes, the creation of provinces, and the appointment of governors to collect taxes from them. By 750 some seven thousand men staffed the central government.

Increased contact with the mainland had unwanted effects as well, such as the great smallpox epidemic of 735–737, which is thought to have reduced the population of about 5 million by 30 percent. (Smallpox did not become an endemic childhood disease in Japan until the tenth or eleventh century.)

The Buddhist monasteries that ringed Nara were both religious centers and wealthy landlords, and the monks were active in the political life of the capital. Copying the policy of the Tang Dynasty in China, the government ordered that every province establish a Buddhist temple with twenty monks and ten nuns to chant sutras and perform other ceremonies on behalf of the emperor and the state. When an emperor abdicated in 749 in favor of his daughter, he became a Buddhist priest, a practice many of his successors would later follow.

Many of the temples built during the Nara period still stand, the wood, clay, and bronze statues in them exceptionally well preserved. The largest of these temples was the Tōdaiji, with its huge bronze statue of the Buddha, which stood fifty-three feet tall and was made from more than a million pounds of metal. When the temple and statue were completed in 752, an Indian monk painted the eyes, and the ten thousand monks present for the celebration had a magnificent vegetarian feast. Objects from the dedication ceremony were placed in a special storehouse, the Shōsōin, and about ten thousand of them are still there, including books, weapons, mirrors, screens, and objects of gold, lacquer, and glass, most made in China but some coming from Central Asia and Persia via the Silk Road.

Shinto   *The "Way of the Gods," it was the native religion espoused by the Yamato rulers.*

Nara   *Japan's first true city; it was established in 710 north of modern Osaka.*

**Primary Source:
Chronicles of Japan**
These guidelines for imperial officials show how the Soga clan welcomed Chinese influence in an attempt to increase the authority of the Japanese imperial family.

Chapter Summary

To assess your mastery of this chapter, go to
bedfordstmartins.com/mckayworld

Key Terms

Great Wall
Silk Road
tributary system
Confucian classics
*Records of the Grand
  Historian*
eunuchs
Age of Division
Grand Canal
Pure Land
Chan
Shinto
Nara

• *What were the social, cultural, and political consequences of the unification of China under a strong centralized government?*

The unification of China in 221 B.C.E. by the Qin Dynasty had momentous consequences. During the four centuries of the subsequent Han Dynasty, unified government provided internal peace and promoted Confucian principles. It aided economic development by building roads and providing relief in cases of floods, droughts, and famines. It could draw on its vast resources to send huge armies against the nomadic Xiongnu, who regularly raided settlements in the north. These armies made possible a major expansion of Chinese territory both to the south and into Central Asia. Overlordship in Central Asia allowed trade along the Silk Road to flourish. The Han was so successful that its memory inspired many efforts to reunify China during the four centuries of division that followed.

• *How were both Buddhism and China changed by the spread of Buddhism across Asia?*

In the final years of the Han Dynasty, Buddhism reached China. Conquest had little to do with the spread of Buddhism in East Asia (in contrast with the spread of Christianity and Islam, which often followed a change of rulers). Rather it was merchants and missionaries who brought Buddhism across the Silk Road. By the time it reached China, Buddhism was a religion with a huge body of scriptures, celibate monks and nuns, traditions of depicting Buddhas and bodhisattvas in statues and paintings, and a strong proselytizing tradition, all of which distinguished it from China's indigenous religious traditions. Buddhism brought to China new philosophical concepts, new artistic styles, and the new social roles of celibate monks and nuns.

• *In what ways was China's second empire different from its first?*

After centuries of division, China was reunified in 589 by the Sui and Tang Dynasties. China regained overlordship along the Silk Road into Central Asia and once again had to deal with powerful northern neighbors, this time the Turks and Uighurs. But there was also much that was different between the Han and Tang empires. The south had become a much more major part of the economy, settled by many more Chinese. Perhaps in part because of the enormous popularity of Buddhism, Chinese culture in Tang times was highly receptive to influences from outside during this period, especially from Persia and India. Poetry played a much larger part in intellectual life, and the examination system was becoming steadily more important as well.

• *What elements of Chinese culture were adopted by Koreans, Vietnamese, and Japanese, and how did they adapt them to their own circumstances?*

In this era, China's neighbors, especially Korea, Japan, and Vietnam, began to adopt elements of China's material, political, and religious culture, including the

Chinese writing system. Force of arms helped bring Chinese culture to both Korea and Vietnam. But military might was not the primary means by which culture spread in this period. Particularly in Korea and Japan, ambitious rulers sought out Chinese expertise and Chinese products, believing the adoption of the most advanced ideas and technologies to be to their advantage. They could pick and choose, adopting those elements of the more advanced cultures that suited them while retaining features of their earlier cultures, in the process developing distinctive national styles.

Suggested Reading

Barfield, Thomas. *Perilous Frontier: Nomadic Empires and China, 221 B.C.–A.D. 1757.* 1989. A bold interpretation of the relationship between the rise and fall of dynasties in China and the rise and fall of nomadic confederations that derived resources from them.

Elvin, Mark. *The Pattern of the Chinese Past.* 1973. Analyzes the military dimensions of China's unification.

Farris, Wayne. *Population, Disease, and Land in Early Japan, 645–900.* 1985. Shows the impact of the introduction of smallpox to Japan in the eighth century on the government and rural power structure.

Hardy, Grant. *Worlds of Bronze and Bamboo: Sima Qian's Conquest of History.* 1999. An excellent introduction to the methods of China's earliest historian. Although Sima Qian seems to present just the facts, Hardy shows how he brings out different perspectives and interpretations in different chapters.

Holcomb, Charles. *The Genesis of East Asia, 221 B.C.–A.D. 907.* 2001. A thought-provoking analysis of the connections between China and Korea, Japan, and Vietnam, which emphasizes the use of the Chinese script.

Schafer, Edward. *The Golden Peaches of Samarkand.* 1963. Draws on Tang literature to show the place of the western regions in Tang life and imagination.

Seth, Michael J. *A Concise History of Korea: From the Neolithic Period Through the Nineteenth Century.* 2006. An up-to-date and well-balanced introduction to Korean history.

Totman, Conrad. *A History of Japan.* 1999. A broad and up-to-date history of Japan.

Waley, Arthur. *The Life and Times of Po Chu-i, 772–846 A.D.* 1949. A lively biography of a Tang official, which draws heavily on his poetry.

Wright, Arthur. *Buddhism in Chinese History.* 1959. This short book remains a good introduction to China's encounter with Buddhism and the ways Buddhism was adapted to China.

Notes

1. Burton Watson, trans. *Records of the Grand Historian of China,* vol. 2 (New York: Columbia University Press, 1961), p. 496.
2. Ibid., p. 499.
3. Patricia Buckley Ebrey, *The Cambridge Illustrated History of China* (Cambridge: Cambridge University Press, 1996), p. 74.
4. W. F. Jenner, *Memories of Loyang: Yang Hsüan-chih and the Lost Capital (493–534)* (Oxford: Clarendon Press, 1981), p. 208.
5. Arthur Waley, trans., *More Translations from the Chinese* (New York: Knopf, 1919), p. 27. Reprinted by permission of the Arthur Waley Estate.
6. Ibid., p. 71.
7. *Sources of Japanese Tradition,* by de Bary, Keene, Tanabe, and Varley, eds. Copyright © 2001 by Columbia University Press. Reproduced with permission of COLUMBIA UNIVERSITY PRESS in the format Textbook via Copyright Clearance Center.

Listening to the PAST

Copying Buddhist Sutras

Buddhism was not merely a set of ideas but also a set of practices. In Chinese, Japanese, and Korean monasteries, as in Western ones, monks and nuns, under the direction of an abbot or abbess, would read and copy scriptures as an act of devotion. Pious laypeople might pay to have sutras copied as a means of earning religious merit. Sometimes at the end of a sutra a copyist attached a statement explaining the circumstances that had surrounded the act of copying. Here are two such statements, one from a sutra found in Dunhuang, on the northwest fringe of China proper, dated 550, and the other from Korea, dated 755.

1.

Happiness is not fortuitous: pray for it and it will be found. Results are not born of thin air: pay heed to causes and results will follow. This explains how the Buddhist disciple and nun Daorong—because her conduct in her previous life was not correct—came to be born in her present form, a woman, vile and unclean.

Now if she does not honor the awesome decree of Buddha, how can future consequences be favorable for her? Therefore, having cut down her expenditures on food and clothing, she reverently has had the *Nirvana sutra* copied once. She prays that those who read it carefully will be exalted in mind to the highest realms and that those who communicate its meaning will cause others to be so enlightened.

She also prays that in her present existence she will have no further sickness or suffering, that her parents in seven other incarnations (who have already died or will die in the future) and her present family and close relatives may experience joy in the four elements [earth, water, fire, and air], and that whatever they seek may indeed come to pass. Finally, she prays that all those endowed with knowledge may be included within this prayer. Dated the 29th day of the fourth month of 550.

2.

The copying began on the first day of the eighth month of 754, and was completed on the fourteenth day of the second month of the following year.

One who made a vow to copy the scripture is Dharma master Yongi of Hwangnyong Monastery. His purposes were to repay the love of his parents and to pray for all living beings in the dharma realm to attain the path of the Buddha.

The scripture is made as follows: First scented water is sprinkled around the roots of a paper-bark mulberry tree to quicken its growth; the bark is then peeled and pounded to make paper with a clean surface. The copyists, the artisans who make the centerpiece of the scroll, and the painters who draw the images of buddhas and bodhisattvas all receive the bodhisattva ordination and observe abstinence. After relieving themselves, sleeping, eating, or drinking, they take a bath in scented water before returning to the work. Copyists are adorned with new pure garments, loose trousers, a coarse crown, and a deva crown. Two azure-clad boys sprinkle water on their heads and . . . azure-clad boys and musicians perform music. The processions to the copying site are headed by one who sprinkles scented water on their path, another who scatters flowers, a dharma master who carries a censer, and another dharma master who chants Buddhist verses. Each of the copyists carries incense and flowers and invokes the name of the Buddha as he progresses.

This gilt bronze image of Maitreya, not quite 3 feet tall, was made in Korea in about 600. It depicts the Buddha Maitreya, the Future Buddha who presides over Tushita Heaven. The rounded face, slender body, and gracefully draped robe help convey the idea that the Buddha is neither male nor female but beyond such distinctions. *(Courtesy, Yushin Yoo)*

Upon reaching the site, all take refuge in the three Jewels (the Buddha, the Dharma, and the Order), make three bows, and offer the *Flower Garland Scripture* and others to buddhas and bodhisattvas. Then they sit down and copy the scripture, make the centerpiece of the scroll, and paint the buddhas and bodhisattvas. Thus, azure-clad boys and musicians cleanse everything before a piece of relic is placed in the center.

Now I make a vow that the copied scripture will not break till the end of the future—even when a major chilicosm [millions of universes] is destroyed by the three calamities, this scripture shall be intact as the void. If all living things rely on this scripture, they shall witness the Buddha, listen to his dharma, worship the relic, aspire to enlightenment without backsliding, cultivate the vows of the Universally Worthy Bodhisattva, and achieve Buddhahood.

Questions for Analysis

1. How does the nun who wrote the first note explain her birth as a woman? Whom does she hope to benefit by the act of copying the sutra?

2. What do you make of the emphasis on rituals surrounding copying the sutra in the second statement?

Sources: Patricia Buckley Ebrey, ed., *Chinese Civilization: A Sourcebook* (New York: Free Press, 1993), pp. 102–103; Peter H. Lee, ed., *Sourcebook of Korean Civilization* (New York: Columbia University Press, 1993), pp. 201–202, modified.

Engraved Mississippian Copper Plate. This ornamental copper plate was excavated in Etowah Mound, Georgia, a Mississippian site first settled in about 1000 C.E. The copper may have been mined along the shore of Lake Superior in what is now northern Michigan, the largest source of copper in North America. *(National Museum of American History, Smithsonian Institution, Washington, D.C.)*

10 CIVILIZATIONS OF THE AMERICAS, 2500 B.C.E.–1500 C.E.

From the beginning of recorded history—that is, from the earliest invention of writing systems—the Eastern and Western Hemispheres developed in isolation from one another. In both areas people initially gathered and hunted their food, and then some groups began to plant crops, adapting plants that were native to the areas they settled. Techniques of plant domestication spread, allowing for greater density of population because harvested crops provided a more regular food supply than did gathered food. In certain parts of both hemispheres, efficient production and transportation of food supplies allowed for the development of cities, with monumental buildings constructed to honor divine and human power, specialized production of a wide array of products, and marketplaces where those products were exchanged. New products included improved military equipment, which leaders used to enhance their power and build up the large political entities we call "kingdoms" and "empires." The power of those leaders also often rested on religious ideas, in which providing service to a king was viewed as a way to honor divine power. These large political units did not develop everywhere in either hemisphere, however, nor was settled agriculture the only economic system. In many places, particularly where the climate or environment made growing crops difficult or impossible, gathering and hunting, sometimes combined with raising animals for food, continued to provide for human sustenance.

The separate but parallel paths of the two hemispheres were radically changed by Columbus's voyage and the events that followed. The greater availability of metals, especially iron, in the Eastern Hemisphere meant that the military technology of the Europeans who came to the Western Hemisphere was more deadly than anything indigenous peoples had developed. Even more deadly, however, were the germs Europeans brought with them: measles, mumps, bubonic plague, influenza, and smallpox. Because the two hemispheres had been out of contact for so long, indigenous people had no resistance, and they died in astounding numbers. Population estimates of the Western Hemisphere in the 1400s vary,

MAP 10.1 **The Peoples of Mesoamerica and South America** The major indigenous peoples of Mesoamerica and South America represented a great variety of languages and cultures adapted to a wide range of environments. *(Source: Adapted from* The Times Atlas of World History, *3d ed., p. 149. Reprinted by permission of HarperCollins Publishers Ltd.)*

but many demographers place the total population at about 70 million people. They also estimate that in many parts of the Western Hemisphere, 90 percent of the population died within the first decades of European contact.

Disease often spread ahead of actual groups of conquerors or settlers, when a few or even one native person came into contact with a European landing party and then returned to the village. Germs spread to other people as they did normal things like preparing food, carrying children, or talking about what they had seen. People became sick and died quickly, so that when Europeans got to an area several weeks or months later, they found people who were already weak and fewer in number.

The history of the Western Hemisphere *after* Columbus shapes all the words we use to describe it. About a decade after Columbus's first voyage, another Italian explorer and adventurer, Amerigo Vespucci, wrote a letter to his old employers, the Medici rulers in Italy, trumpeting the wonders of the "new world" he had seen. He claimed to have been the first to see what is now Venezuela on a voyage in 1497, a year before Columbus got there. This letter was published many times in many different languages, and the phrase "New World" began to show up on world maps around 1505. Shortly after that the word *America,* meaning "the land of Amerigo," also appeared, because mapmakers read and believed Vespucci's letter. By just a few years later, mapmakers and others knew that Columbus had been the first to this new world. They wanted to omit the label "America" from future maps, but the name had already stuck.

Our use of the word *Indian* for the indigenous peoples of the Americas stems from another mistake. Columbus was trying to reach Asia by sailing west and thought he was somewhere in the East Indies when he landed, which is why he called the people he met "Indians." They apparently called themselves "Tainos," and people who lived on nearby islands called themselves other things. In many cases people died so fast that we have no idea now what they actually called themselves, so the words we use for various indigenous groups come from other indigenous groups or from European languages and were sometimes originally insulting or derogatory nicknames. Many indigenous groups today are returning to designations from their own languages, and scholars are attempting to use terminology that is historically accurate, so certain groups are known by multiple names. The use of the word *Indian* is itself highly controversial, and various other terms are often used, including Native Americans, Amerindians, and (in Canada) First Peoples. Each of these substitutes has supporters and opponents, including people who are themselves of indigenous background. There is no term for all the inhabitants of the Western Hemisphere that is universally accepted, though in the United States "American Indians" is now preferred. The many peoples of the Americas did not think of themselves as belonging to a single group, any more than the peoples living in sixteenth-century Europe thought of themselves as Europeans (see Map 10.1).

All these issues were in the future in 1492, of course. Columbus's voyage resulted in a devastating chain of events for the inhabitants of the Western Hemisphere and determined the language we use to talk about them. In fact, even Western Hemisphere is a post-Columbus concept, as it requires setting an arbitrary line that divides the two halves of the world. Many different points were proposed over the centuries, and only in the nineteenth century was the current prime meridian at Greenwich—a suburb of London—agreed on.

This huge area had a highly complex history for millennia before Columbus, however, and a great diversity of peoples, cultures, and linguistic groups. New information about these cultures is emerging every year, provoking vigorous debates among scholars. In no other chapter of this book are the basic outlines of what most people agree happened changing as fast as they are for this chapter.

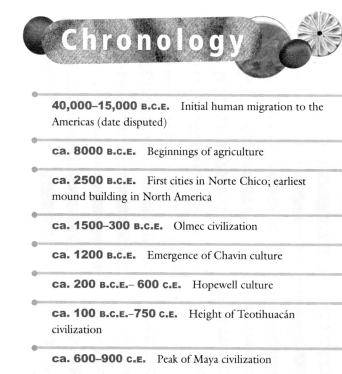

Chronology

40,000–15,000 B.C.E. Initial human migration to the Americas (date disputed)

ca. 8000 B.C.E. Beginnings of agriculture

ca. 2500 B.C.E. First cities in Norte Chico; earliest mound building in North America

ca. 1500–300 B.C.E. Olmec civilization

ca. 1200 B.C.E. Emergence of Chavin culture

ca. 200 B.C.E.–600 C.E. Hopewell culture

ca. 100 B.C.E.–750 C.E. Height of Teotihuacán civilization

ca. 600–900 C.E. Peak of Maya civilization

ca. 1050–1250 Construction of mounds at Cahokia

1325 Construction of Aztec city of Tenochtitlán begins

mid-1400s Height of Aztec culture

ca. 1500 Inca Empire reaches its largest extent

THE EARLY PEOPLES OF THE AMERICAS

How did early peoples in the Americas adapt to their environment as they created economic and political systems?

Mesoamerica *The term used by scholars to designate the area of present-day Mexico and Central America.*

As in the development of early human cultures in Afroeurasia (Chapter 1), the environment shaped the formation of human settlements in the Americas. North America includes arctic tundra, dry plains, coastal wetlands, woodlands, deserts, and temperate rain forests. **Mesoamerica,** a term scholars use to designate the area of present-day Mexico and Central America, is dominated by high plateaus with a temperate climate and good agricultural land bounded by coastal plains. The Caribbean coast of Central America—modern Belize, Guatemala, Honduras, Nicaragua, El Salvador, Costa Rica, and Panama—is characterized by thick jungle lowlands, heavy rainfall, and torrid heat. South America is a continent of extremely varied terrain. The entire western coast is edged by the Andes, the highest mountain range in the Western Hemisphere. Three-fourths of South America—almost the entire interior of the continent—is lowland plains. The Amazon River, at four thousand miles the second-longest river in the world, is bordered by tropical lowland rain forests with dense growth and annual rainfall in excess of eighty inches. All these environments have supported extensive human settlement at various times, though it is easier to learn about those in dryer areas because artifacts survive longer there.

Settling the Americas

The traditions of many American Indian peoples teach that the group originated independently, often through the actions of a divine figure. Many creation accounts, including that of the book of Genesis in the Bible, begin with people who are created out of earth and receive assistance from supernatural beings—who set out certain ways people are supposed to behave. Both Native American and biblical creation accounts continue to have deep spiritual importance for many people.

Archaeological and DNA evidence indicates that the earliest humans came to the Americas from Siberia and East Asia, but exactly when and how this happened is currently being hotly debated. The traditional account is that people crossed the Bering Strait from what is now Russian Siberia to what is now Alaska about fifteen thousand years ago, mostly by walking. This was the end of the last Ice Age, so that more of the world's water was frozen and ocean levels were much lower than they are today. (This situation is the opposite of what is occurring today; global warming is melting polar ice, which will raise water levels around the world.) The people migrated southward through North America between two large ice sheets that were slowly melting and retreating, and relatively quickly they spread through the entire hemisphere. They lived by gathering and hunting, using spears with stone tips that archaeologists term *Clovis points* after the town in New Mexico where they were first discovered.

Clovis points have been found widely throughout the Americas, and many archaeologists see the Clovis people as the ancestors of most indigenous people in the Western Hemisphere. There is some difference of opinion about exactly when the Clovis culture flourished, for various methods of carbon-14 dating produce slightly different results, with some scholars accepting 11,000 B.C.E. as the height of Clovis technology and others 9000 B.C.E. (Carbon-14 dating uses the rate at which the radioactive isotope of carbon—present in all living things—breaks down into a nonradioactive form to determine how old things are.)

Disagreements regarding the age of the Clovis culture are significant because they are part of a much broader debate about the traditional account of migration to the Americas. Archaeologists working at Monte Verde along the coast of Chile have excavated a site that they date to about 9000 B.C.E., and perhaps much earlier. This site is ten thousand miles from the Bering Land bridge, which would have meant a very fast walk. Monte Verde and a few other sites are leading increasing numbers of archaeologists to conclude that migrants over the land bridge were preceded by people who traveled along the coast in skin boats, perhaps as early as forty thousand years ago. They lived by fishing and gathering rather than hunting big game, and they slowly worked their way southward. The coasts that they traveled along are today far under water, so archaeological evidence is difficult to obtain, but DNA and other genetic evidence has lent support to this idea. (DNA evidence has generally not supported various other theories of early migrations from Europe or Australia.)

However and whenever people got to the Western Hemisphere—and a consensus about this may emerge in the next decade—they lived by gathering, fishing, and hunting, as did everyone throughout the world at that point. Some groups were nomadic and followed migrating game, while others did not have to travel to be assured of a regular food supply. Coastal settlements from the Pacific Northwest to the southern end of South America relied on fish and shellfish, and some also hunted seals and other large marine mammals.

The Development of Agriculture

About 8000 B.C.E., people in some parts of the Americas began raising crops as well as gathering wild produce. As in the development of agriculture in Afroeurasia, people initially planted the seeds of native plants. Pumpkins and other members of the gourd family were one of the earliest crops, as were chilies, beans, and avocados. At some point, people living in what is now southern Mexico also began raising what would become the most important crop in the Americas—maize, which we generally call "corn." Exactly how this happened is not clear. In contrast to other grain crops such as wheat and rice, the kernels of maize—which are the seeds as well as the part that is eaten for food—are wrapped in a husk, so that the plant cannot propagate itself easily. In addition, no wild ancestor of maize has been found. What many biologists now think happened is that a related grass called *teosinte* developed mutant forms with large kernels enclosed in husks, and people living in the area quickly realized its benefits. They began to intentionally plant these kernels and crossbred the results to get a better crop each year.

People bred various types of maize for different purposes and for different climates, making it the staple food throughout the highlands of Mesoamerica. They often planted maize along with squash, beans, and other crops in a field called a **milpa;** the beans use the maize stalks for support as they both grow and also fix nitrogen in the soil, acting as a natural fertilizer. Crops can be grown in milpas year after year, in contrast to single-crop planting in which rotation is needed so as not to exhaust the soil. Maize came to have a symbolic and religious meaning; it was viewed as the source of human life and was a prominent feature in sculptures of kings and gods.

In central Mexico, along with milpas, people also built *chinampas,* floating gardens. They dredged soil from the bottom of a lake or pond, placed the soil on mats of woven twigs, and then planted crops in the soil. Chinampas were enormously productive, yielding up to three harvests a year.

Knowledge of maize cultivation, and maize seeds themselves, spread out from Mesoamerica into both North and South America. By 3000 B.C.E. farmers in what is now Peru and Uruguay were planting maize, and by 2000 B.C.E. farmers in southwest North America were as well. The crop then spread into the Mississippi Valley and to northeastern North America, where farmers bred slightly different variants for the different growing conditions. After 1500 C.E. maize cultivation spread to Europe, Africa, and Asia as well, becoming an essential food crop there. (In the twentieth century maize became even more successful; about one-quarter of the nearly fifty thousand items in the average American supermarket now contain corn.)

milpa *A system of effective agriculture used throughout Meso-america that relies on crop rotation and the planting of multiple crops in a single field. The term is derived from a Nahuatl word meaning "field."*

The expansion of maize was the result of contacts between different groups that can be traced through trade goods as well. Copper from the Great Lakes was a particularly valuable item and was traded throughout North America, reaching Mexico by 3000 B.C.E. Obsidian from the Rocky Mountains, used for blades, was traded widely, as were shells and later pottery.

Different cultivars of maize could be developed for many different climates, but maize was difficult to grow in high altitudes. Thus in the high Andes, people relied on potatoes, terracing the slopes with stone retaining walls to keep the hillsides from sliding. High-altitude valleys were connected to mountain life and vegetation to form a single interdependent agricultural system called "vertical archipelagoes" capable of supporting large communities. Such vertical archipelagoes often extended more than thirty-seven miles from top to bottom. The terraces were shored up with earthen walls to retain moisture, enabling the production of bumper crops of many different types of potatoes. Potatoes ordinarily cannot be stored for long periods, but Andean

● **Inca Terraces** In order to create more land for farming and limit soil erosion, Andean peoples built terraces up steep slopes. Later the Incas built systems of aqueducts and canals to bring water to terraced fields. *(Wolfgang Kaehler/Corbis)*

peoples developed a product called *chuñu,* freeze-dried potatoes made by subjecting potatoes alternately to nightly frosts and daily sun. Chuñu will keep unspoiled for several years. Coca (the dried leaves of a plant native to the Andes from which cocaine is derived), chewed in moderation as a dietary supplement, enhanced people's stamina and their ability to withstand the cold.

Maize will also not grow in hot, wet climates very well. In Amazonia, manioc, a tuber that can be cooked in many ways, became the staple food. It was planted along with other crops, including fruits, nuts, and various types of palm trees. People domesticated peach palms, for example, which produce fruit, pulp that is made into flour, heart of palm that is eaten raw, and juice that can be fermented into beer. Just how many people Amazonian agriculture supported before the introduction of European diseases is an issue hotly debated by anthropologists, but increasing numbers see the original tropical rain forest not as a pristine wilderness, but as an ecosystem managed effectively by humans for thousands of years. The oldest known pottery in the Americas has been found along the Amazon River, as well as in the Andes.

Farming in the Americas was not limited to foodstuffs. Beginning about 2500 B.C.E., people living along the coast of Peru used irrigation to raise cotton, and textiles became an important part of Peruvian culture. Agriculture in the Americas was extensive, though it was limited by the lack of an animal that could be harnessed to pull a plow. People throughout the Americas domesticated dogs, and in the Andes they domesticated llamas and alpacas to carry loads through the mountains. But no native species allowed itself to be harnessed as horses, oxen, and water buffalo did in Asia and Europe, which meant that all agricultural labor was human-powered.

● **Colombian Lime Container** The use of coca in rituals and to withstand bodily discomfort is an ancient tradition in South America. Pieces of coca leaves were placed in the mouth with small amounts of powdered lime made from seashells. The lime helped release the hallucinogens in the coca. This 9-inch gold bottle for holding lime shows a seated figure with rings in the ears and beads across the forehead and at the neck, wrists, knees, and ankles. A tiny spatula would be used to secure the lime through the bottle's narrow neck. *(The Metropolitan Museum of Art, Jan Mitchell and Sons Collection, Gift of Jan Mitchell, 1991 [1991.419.22]. Photograph © 1992 The Metropolitan Museum of Art)*

EARLY CIVILIZATIONS

What physical, social, and intellectual features characterized early civilizations in the Americas?

Agricultural advancement had definitive social and political consequences. Careful cultivation of the land brought a reliable and steady food supply, which contributed to a relatively high fertility rate and in turn to a population boom. Population in the Americas grew steadily and may have been about 15 million people by the first century B.C.E. This growth in population allowed for greater concentrations of people and the creation of the first urban societies.

Mounds, Towns, and Trade in North and South America

In North America by 2500 B.C.E., some groups began to build massive earthworks, mounds of earth and stone. The mounds differed in shape, size, and purpose: some were conical, others elongated or wall-like, others pyramidical, and still others, called effigy mounds, in serpentine, bird, or animal form. The Ohio and Mississippi Valleys

● **Inca Khipu, ca. 1400 C.E.** This khipu, a collection of colored, knotted strings, recorded numeric information and allowed Inca administrators to keep track of the flow of money, goods, and people in their large empire. Every aspect of the khipu—the form and position of the knots, the colors and spin of the string—may have provided information. Administrators read them visually and by running their hands through them, as Braille text is read today. *(Museo Arqueologico Rafael Larco Herrera, Lima, Peru)*

Norte Chico *A region along the coast of Peru that possessed a highly developed urban culture characterized by massive stepped pyramids and extensive use of cotton as early as 2500 B.C.E.*

khipu *A intricate system of knotted and colored strings used by early Peruvian cultures to store information such as census and tax records.*

contain the richest concentration of mounds, but they have been found from the Great Lakes down to the Gulf of Mexico (see Map 10.3 on page 273). One early large mound at Poverty Point, Louisiana, on the banks of the Mississippi, dates from about 1300 B.C.E. and consists of six octagonal ramparts, one within the other, that measure 6 feet high and more than 400 yards across. The area was home to perhaps five thousand people and was inhabited for hundreds of years, with trade goods brought in by canoe and carved stone beads exported.

Large structures for political and religious purposes began to be built earlier in South America than in North America. By about 2500 B.C.E. cities grew along river valleys on the coast of Peru in the region called **Norte Chico.** Stepped pyramids, some more than ten stories high, dominated these settlements, which were built at about the same time the pyramids were being constructed in Egypt. Cities in Norte Chico often used irrigation to produce crops of squash, beans, cotton, and other crops. Those along the coast relied extensively on fish and shellfish, which they traded with inland cities for the cotton needed to make nets. The largest city, Caral, had many plazas, houses, and temples, built with quarried stone using woven cotton and grass bags filled with smaller stones for support. Cotton was used in Norte Chico for many things, including the earliest example yet discovered of a **khipu** (also spelled *quipu*), a collection of knotted strings that was used to record information. Later Peruvian cultures, including the Incas, developed ever more complex khipu, using the colors of the string and the style and position of the knots to represent tax obligations, census records, and other numeric data.

Along with khipu, Norte Chico culture also developed religious ideas that may have been adopted by later Andean cultures. The oldest religious image yet found in the Americas, a piece of gourd with a drawing of a fanged god holding a staff, comes from Norte Chico, dating about 2250 B.C.E. This Staff God became a major deity in many Andean cultures, one of a complex pantheon of deities. Religious ceremonies, as well as other festivities, in Norte Chico involved music, as a large number of bone flutes have been discovered.

The earliest cities in the Andes were built by the **Chavin** people beginning about 1200 B.C.E. They built pyramids and other types of monumental architecture, quarrying and trimming huge blocks of stone and assembling them without mortar. They worked gold and silver into human and animal figurines, trading these and other goods to coastal peoples.

The Olmecs

The **Olmecs** created the first society with cities in Mesoamerica. The word *Olmec* comes from an Aztec term for the peoples living in southern Veracruz and western Tabasco, Mexico, between about 1500 and 300 B.C.E. They did not call themselves Olmecs or consider themselves a unified group, but their culture penetrated and influenced all parts of Mesoamerica. Until 1993 knowledge of the Olmecs rested on archaeological evidence—pyramids, jade objects, axes, figurines, and stone monuments—but that year two linguists deciphered Olmec writing. Since then, understanding of Olmec and other contemporary Mesoamerican cultures such as the Zapotecs also comes from the written records they left.

The Olmecs cultivated maize, squash, beans, and other plants and supplemented that diet with wild game and fish. Originally they lived in egalitarian societies that had no distinctions based on status or wealth. After 1500 B.C.E. more complex, hierarchical societies evolved. Most peoples continued to live in small villages along the rivers of the region, while the leaders of the societies resided in the large cities today known as San Lorenzo, La Venta, Tres Zapotes, and Laguna de los Cerros. These cities contained palaces (large private houses) for the elite, large plazas, temples (ritual centers), ball courts, water reservoirs, and carved stone drains for the disposal of wastes. Like the Chavin (with whom they had no contact), the Olmecs created large pyramid-shaped buildings. They also carved huge stone heads of rulers or gods, beginning a tradition of monumental stone sculptures adopted by later Mesoamerican civilizations. In order to trace celestial phenomena—which they believed influenced human life—they developed a complex calendar involving three different ways of counting time. The need to record time led to the development of a writing system. Whereas the earliest written records from Mesopotamia are tax records for payments to the temple (see page 4), the earliest written records from Mesoamerica, dating from about 700 B.C.E., are dates. Many early records also record the deeds of kings, so that the political history of Mesoamerica is becoming more detailed as scholars learn to read various writing systems.

The Olmecs had sacred ceremonial sites where they sometimes practiced human sacrifice, another tradition adopted by later Mesoamerican cultures. They erected special courts on which men played a game with a hard rubber ball that was both religious ritual and sport. Finally, the Olmecs engaged in long-distance trade, exchanging rubber, cacao (from which chocolate is made), pottery, figurines, jaguar pelts, and the services of painters and sculptors for obsidian (a hard, black volcanic glass from which paddle-shaped weapons were made), basalt, iron ore, shells, and various perishable goods. Commercial networks extended as far away as central and western Mexico and the Pacific coast.

Around 900 B.C.E. San Lorenzo, the center of early Olmec culture, was destroyed, probably by migrating peoples from the north, and power passed to La Venta in Tabasco. Archaeological excavation at La Venta has uncovered a huge volcano-shaped pyramid. Standing 110 feet high at an inaccessible site on an island in the Tonala River, the so-called Great Pyramid was the center of the Olmec religion. The upward thrust of this monument, like ziggurats in Mesopotamia or cathedrals of medieval Europe, may have represented the human effort to get closer to the gods. Built of huge stone slabs, the Great Pyramid required, scholars estimated, some eight hundred thousand man-hours of labor. It testifies to the region's bumper harvests, which were able to support a labor force large enough to build such a monument.

• •

CLASSICAL ERA MESOAMERICA AND NORTH AMERICA

How did Mesoamerican and North American peoples develop prosperous and stable societies in the classical era?

The urban culture of the Olmecs and other Mesoamerican peoples influenced subsequent Mesoamerican societies. Especially in what became known as the classical era (300–900 C.E.), various groups developed large states centered on cities, with high levels of technological and intellectual achievement. Of these, the **Maya** were the most long-lasting, but other city-states were significant as well. Peoples living in North America built communities that were smaller than those in Mesoamerica, but many also used irrigation techniques to enhance agricultural production and built earthwork mounds for religious purposes.

Maya *A highly developed Mesoamerican culture centered in the Yucatán peninsula of Mexico. The Maya created the most intricate writing system in the Western Hemisphere.*

Maya Technology and Trade

The word *Maya* seems to derive from *Zamna,* the name of a Maya god. Linguistic evidence leads scholars to believe that the first Maya were a small North American Indian group that emigrated from the area that is now southern Oregon and northern California to the western highlands of Guatemala. Between the third and second millennia B.C.E., various groups, including the Cholans and Tzeltalans, broke away from the parent group and moved north and east into the Yucatán peninsula. The Cholan-speaking Maya, who occupied the area during the time of great cultural achievement, apparently created the culture.

Maya culture rested on agriculture. The staple crop in Mesoamerica was maize, often raised in multiple-crop milpas with other foodstuffs, including beans, squash, chili peppers, some root crops, and fruit trees. The Maya also practiced intensive agriculture in raised, narrow, rectangular plots that they built above the low-lying, seasonally flooded land bordering rivers.

The raised-field and milpa systems of intensive agriculture yielded food sufficient to support large population centers. The entire Maya region could have had as many as 14 million inhabitants. At Uxmal, Uaxactún, Copán, Piedras Negras, Tikal, Palenque, and Chichén Itzá (see Map 10.2), archaeologists have uncovered the palaces of nobles, elaborate pyramids where nobles were buried, engraved *steles* (stone-slab monuments), masonry temples, altars, sophisticated polychrome pottery, and courts for games played with a rubber ball. The largest site, Tikal, may have had forty thousand people and served as a religious and ceremonial center.

Public fairs for trading merchandise accompanied important religious festivals. Jade, obsidian, beads of red spiny oyster shell, lengths of cloth, and cacao beans—all in high demand in the

● **Palace Doorway Lintel at Yaxchilan, Mexico**
Lady Xoc, principal wife of King Shield-Jaguar, who holds a torch over her, pulls a thorn-lined rope through her tongue to sanctify with her blood the birth of a younger wife's child—reflecting the importance of blood sacrifice in Maya culture. The elaborate headdresses and clothes of the couple show their royal status. *(© Justin Kerr 1985)*

Mesoamerican world—served as media of exchange. The extensive trade among Maya communities, plus a common language, promoted the union of the peoples of the region and gave them a common sense of identity. Merchants trading beyond Maya regions, such as with the Zapotecs of the Valley of Oaxaca and the Teotihuacános of the central valley of Mexico, were considered state ambassadors bearing "gifts" to royal neighbors, who reciprocated with their own "gifts." Since this long-distance trade played an important part in international relations, the merchants conducting it were high nobles or even members of the royal family.

The extensive networks of rivers and swamps in the area ruled by the Maya were the main arteries of transportation; over them large canoes carved out of hardwood trees carried cargoes of cloth and maize. Wide roads also linked Maya centers; on the roads merchants and lords were borne in litters, goods and produce on human backs. Trade produced considerable wealth that seems to have been concentrated in a noble class, for the Maya had no distinctly mercantile class. They did have a sharply defined hierarchical society. A hereditary elite owned private land, defended society, carried on commercial activities, exercised political power, and directed religious rituals. Artisans and scribes made up the next social level. The rest of the people were workers, farmers, and slaves, the latter including prisoners of war.

Wars were fought in Maya society for a variety of reasons. Long periods without rain caused crop failure, which led to famine and then war with other centers for food. Certain cities, such as Tikal, extended their authority over larger areas through warfare with neighboring cities. Within the same communities, domestic strife between factions over the succession to the kingship or property led to violence.

MAP 10.2 **The Maya World, 300–900 C.E.** The Maya built dozens of cities, linked together in trading networks of roads and rivers. Only the largest of them are shown here. They developed a complex writing system, using it to record political events, astronomical calculations, and religious ideas.

Maya Science and Religion

The Maya developed the most complex writing system in the Americas, a script with nearly a thousand characters that represent concepts and sounds. They used it to record chronology, religion, and astronomy in books made of bark paper and deerskin, on stone pillars archaeologists term "steles," on pottery, and on the walls of temples and other buildings. The deciphering of this writing over the last fifty years has demonstrated that inscriptions on steles are historical documents recording the births, accessions, marriages, wars, and deaths of Maya kings. The writing and pictorial imagery often represent the same events and have allowed for a fuller understanding of Maya dynastic history.

Learning about Maya religion through written records is more difficult. In the sixteenth century Spanish religious authorities ordered all books of Maya writing to be destroyed, viewing them as demonic. Only three (and part of a fourth) survived, because they were already in Europe. These texts do provide information about religious rituals and practices, as well as astronomical calculations. Further information comes from the **Popul Vuh,** or Book of Council, a book of mythological narratives and dynastic history written in the Maya language but in Roman script in the middle of the sixteenth century. Like the Bible in Judeo-Christian tradition, the *Popul Vuh* gives

Popul Vuh *The Book of Council, a collection of mythological narratives and dynastic histories that constitutes the primary record of the Maya civilization.*

● **Maya Ballplayers** Two teams of two players each face off in this lively scene on a painted ceramic vessel. Note that the ballplayers are wearing deer and vulture headdresses, Maya symbols of hunting and war. War was sometimes called the "hunting of men." (Chrysler Museum of Art, Norfolk, Va., © Justin Kerr)

the Maya view of the creation of the world, concepts of good and evil, and the entire nature and purpose of the living experience. Because almost all religious texts from Mesoamerica—not just Maya texts, but those from other cultures as well—were destroyed by Spanish Christian authorities, its significance is enormous.

Maya religious practice emphasized performing rituals at specific times, which served as an impetus for further refinements of the calendar. From careful observation of the earth's movements around the sun, the Maya devised a calendar of eighteen 20-day months and one 5-day month, for a total of 365 days. Their religious calendar, like that of the Olmecs, was a cycle of 260 days based perhaps on the movement of the planet Venus. When these two calendars coincided, which happened once every fifty-two years, the Maya celebrated a period of feasting, ballgame competitions, and religious observance. These observances—and those at other times as well—included human sacrifice to honor the gods and demonstrate the power of earthly kings.

Using a system of bars (— = 5) and dots (∘ = 1), the Maya devised a form of mathematics based on the vigesimal (20) rather than the decimal (10) system. More unusual was their use of the number zero, which allows for more complex calculations than are possible in number systems without it. The zero may have actually been "discovered" by the Olmecs, who used it in figuring their calendar, but the Maya used it mathematically as well. (At about the same time, mathematicians in India also began using zero.) They proved themselves masters of abstract knowledge—notably in astronomy, mathematics, calendric development, and the recording of history.

Maya civilization lasted about a thousand years, reaching its peak between approximately 600 and 900 C.E., the period when the Tang Dynasty was flourishing in China, Islam was spreading in the Middle East, and Carolingian rulers were extending their sway in Europe. Between the eighth and tenth centuries, the Maya abandoned their cultural and ceremonial centers, and Maya civilization collapsed. Archaeologists and historians attribute the decline to a combination of agricultural failures due to land exhaustion and drought; overpopulation; disease; and constant wars fought as an extension of economic and political goals. These wars brought widespread destruction, which aggravated agrarian problems. Maya royal ideology also played a role in their decline: just as in good times kings attributed moral authority and prosperity to themselves, so in bad times, when military, economic, and social conditions deteriorated, they became the objects of blame.

Teotihuacán and the Toltecs

The Maya were not alone in creating a complex culture in Mesoamerica during the classic period. In the isolated valley of Oaxaca at modern-day Monte Albán in southern Mexico, Zapotecan-speaking peoples established a great religious center whose temples and elaborately decorated tombs testify to the wealth of the nobility. To the north of Monte Albán, **Teotihuacán** in central Mexico witnessed the flowering of a remarkable civilization built by a new people from regions east and south of the Valley of Mexico. The city of Teotihuacán had a population of over two hundred thousand—larger than any European city at the time. The inhabitants were stratified into distinct social classes. The rich and powerful resided in houses of palatial splendor in a special precinct. Ordinary working people, tradespeople, artisans, and obsidian craftsmen lived in apartment compounds, or *barrios,* on the edge of the city. Agricultural laborers lived outside the city. Teotihuacán was a great commercial center, the entrepôt for trade and culture for all of Mesoamerica. It was also the ceremonial center, a capital filled with artworks, a mecca that attracted thousands of pilgrims a year.

Teotihuacán *A city in central Mexico that became a great commercial center during the classic period.*

In the center of the city stood the Pyramids of the Sun and the Moon. The Pyramid of the Sun is built of sun-dried bricks and faced with stone. Each of its sides is seven hundred feet long and two hundred feet high. The smaller Pyramid of the Moon is similar in construction. In lesser temples, natives and outlanders worshiped the rain-god and the feathered serpent later called Quetzalcoatl. These gods were associated with the production of corn, the staple of the people's diet.

Toltecs *An heir to Teotihuacán, this confederation extended its hegemony over most of central Mexico under the reign of Topiltzin.*

Around 750 C.E. less-developed peoples from the southwest burned Teotihuacán, and the city-state fell apart. This collapse, plus that of the Maya, marks the end of the classical period in Mesoamerica for most scholars, just as the end of the Roman Empire in the west marks the end of the classical era in Europe. As in Europe, a period characterized by disorder, militarism, and domination by smaller states followed.

Whereas nature gods and their priests seem to have governed the great cities of the earlier period, militant gods and warriors dominated the petty states that now arose. Among these states, the most powerful heir to Teotihuacán was the Toltec confederation, a weak union of strong states. The **Toltecs** admired the culture of their predecessors and sought to absorb and preserve it. Through intermarriage, they assimilated with the Teotihuacán people. In fact, every new Mesoamerican confederation became the cultural successor of earlier confederations.

Under Topiltzin (r. ca. 980–1000), the Toltecs extended their hegemony over most of central Mexico. Topiltzin established his capital at Tula. Its splendor and power became legendary during his reign. After the reign of Topiltzin, troubles beset the Toltec state. Drought led to crop failure. Northern peoples, the Chichimecas, attacked the borders in waves. Weak, incompetent rulers could not quell domestic uprisings. When the last Toltec king committed suicide in 1174, the Toltec state collapsed.

● **Maya Burial Urn** After tightly wrapping the bodies of royal and noble persons in cloth, the K'iché Maya people of Guatemala placed them in urns and buried them in pyramids or sacred caves. The lid represents a divine being through whose mouth gifts may have been offered to the deceased. The figure with corncobs on top of the lid is the maize-god, a sacred figure to all Mesoamerican peoples. *(Museum of Fine Arts, Boston, Gift of Landon T. Clay [1988.1290]. © 2008 Museum of Fine Arts, Boston)*

● **Zapotec Deity** This Zapotec image of a god was found at Monte Albán, the primary Zapotec religious center. Made to be worn as a breast ornament, it was created through lost-wax casting, in which a mold is made from a wax model, and molten gold poured in to replace the wax. *(Giraudon/The Bridgeman Art Library)*

Hohokam *A Native American culture that emerged around 300 B.C.E. and was centered around the Gila River in Arizona. The Hohokam practiced a system of agriculture that relied on irrigation trenches, dams, and terraces to cultivate their arid land.*

Anasazi *A Native American culture that dominated the Four Corners region of the southwestern United States; remarkable for their construction of numerous cliff-dwellings in the region.*

Hopewell *An important mound-building Native American culture that thrived between 200 B.C.E. and 600 C.E. The culture was centered near the town of Hopewell, Ohio, and was noted for extensive canals and a trade network that extended from the Caribbean to Illinois.*

Hohokam, Hopewell, and Mississippian

Mesoamerican trading networks extended into southwestern North America, where by 300 B.C.E. the **Hohokam** people and other groups were using irrigation canals, dams, and terraces to enhance their farming of the arid land (see Map 10.3). The Hohokam built platforms for ceremonial purposes and played ballgames with rubber balls similar to those of the Olmecs and other Mesoamerican people. The rubber balls themselves were imported, for rubber trees do not grow in the desert, with turquoise and other precious stones exported in return. Religious ideas came along with trade goods, as the feathered serpent god became important to desert peoples. Other groups, including the **Anasazi**, Yuma, and later Pueblo, also built settlements in this area, using large sandstone blocks and masonry to construct thick-walled houses that offered protection from the heat. Mesa Verde, the largest Anasazi town, had a population of about twenty-five hundred living in houses built into and on cliff walls. Roads connected Mesa Verde to other Anasazi towns, allowing timber and other construction materials to be brought in more easily. Drought, deforestation, and soil erosion led to decline in both the Hohokam and Anasazi cultures, increasing warfare between towns.

To the east, the mound building that had first been developed at settlements along the Mississippi around 2000 B.C.E. spread more widely along many river basins. The most important mound-building culture in the first several centuries B.C.E. was the **Hopewell** culture, named for a town in Ohio near where the most extensive mounds were built. Some mounds were burial chambers for priests, leaders, and other high-status individuals, or for thousands of more average people. Others were platforms for the larger houses of important people. Still others were simply huge mounds of earth shaped like animals or geometric figures. Mound building thus had many purposes: it was a way to honor the gods, to remember the dead, and to make distinctions between leaders and common folk

Hopewell earthwork construction also included canals that enabled trading networks to expand, bringing products from the Caribbean far into the interior. Those

MAP 10.3 **Major North American Agricultural Societies, 600–1500 c.e.** Many North American groups used agriculture to increase the available food supply and allow for greater population density and the development of urban centers. Shown here are three of these cultures: the Mississippian, Anasazi, and Hohokam. Most mound-building cultures raised crops, and many were connected in an extensive trading network.

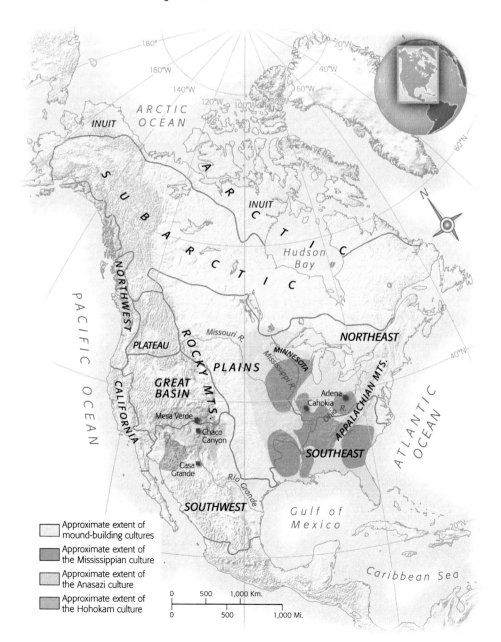

trading networks also carried maize, allowing more intensive agriculture to spread throughout the eastern woodlands of North America.

At Cahokia, near the confluence of the Mississippi and Missouri Rivers in Illinois, archaeologists have uncovered the largest mound of all. Begun about 1050 C.E. and completed about 1250 C.E., the complex at Cahokia covered five and a half square miles and was the ceremonial center for perhaps thirty-eight thousand people. A fence of wooden posts surrounded the core. More than five hundred rectangular mounds or houses, inside and outside the fence, served as tombs and as the bases for temples and palaces. Within the fence, the largest mound rose in four stages to a height of one hundred feet and was more than one thousand feet long, larger than the largest Egyptian pyramid. At its top, a small conical platform supported a wooden fence and a rectangular temple. The mounds at Cahokia represent the culture of the **Mississippian** mound builders.

What do the mounds tell us about Mississippian societies? The largest mounds served as burial chambers for leaders and, in many cases, the women and retainers who were sacrificed in order to assist the leader in the afterlife. Mounds also contain valuable artifacts, such as jewelry made from copper from Michigan, mica (a mineral used in building) from the Appalachians, obsidian from the Rocky Mountains, conch shells from the Caribbean, and pipestone from Minnesota.

From these burial items, archaeologists have deduced that mound culture was hierarchical. The leader had religious responsibilities and also managed long-distance trade and gift-giving. The exchange of goods was not perceived as a form of commerce, but as a means of showing respect and of establishing bonds among diverse groups. Large towns housed several thousand inhabitants and served as political and ceremonial centers. They controlled surrounding villages of a few hundred people, but did not grow into politically unified city-states the way Tikal or Teotihuacán did.

Pottery in the form of bowls, jars, bottles, and effigy pipes in various shapes best reveals Mississippian peoples' art and religious ideas. Designs showing eagles, plumed serpents, warriors decapitating victims, and ceremonially ornamented priests suggest a strong Mesoamerican influence. At its peak, about 1150, Cahokia and its environs probably housed between thirty thousand and fifty thousand people, the largest city north of Mesoamerica. Building the interior wooden fence had denuded much of the

Mississippian *An important mound-building culture that thrived between 800 and 1500 C.E. in a territory that extended from the Mississippi River to the Appalachian Mountains. The largest mound produced by this culture is found at Cahokia, Illinois.*

● **Great Serpent Mound, Adams County, Ohio** Made by people in the Hopewell culture, this 1,254-foot-long mound in the form of a writhing snake has its "head" at the highest point, suggesting an open mouth ready to swallow a huge egg formed by a heap of stones. *(Georg Gerster/ Photo Researchers, Inc.)*

MAP 10.4 **The Aztec (Mexica) Empire** The Mexica migrated into the central valley of what is now Mexico from the north, conquering other groups and establishing an empire, later called the Aztec Empire. The capital of the Aztec Empire was Tenochtitlán, built on islands in Lake Texcoco.

surrounding countryside of trees, however, which made spring floods worse and destroyed much of the city. An earthquake at the beginning of the thirteenth century knocked down more, and the city never recovered. Thus ecological crises appear to have played a part in bringing an end to various North American cultures, though their technologies and religious ideas were often maintained by those that developed later in the same areas.

Mississippian mound builders relied on agriculture to support their complex cultures, and by the time Cahokia was built, maize agriculture had spread to the Atlantic coast. Particularly along riverbanks and the coastline, fields of maize, beans, and squash surrounded large, permanent villages. Hunting provided meat protein, but the bulk of people's foodstuffs came from farming. The earliest European reports from Virginia and New England describe these villages and sometimes show illustrations of rows of houses within walls. By several decades after contact, disease had destroyed village life.

THE AZTECS

How did the Aztecs both build on the achievements of earlier Mesoamerican cultures and develop new traditions to create their large empire?

The **Aztecs** provide a spectacular example of a culture that adopted many things from earlier peoples and also adapted them to create an even more powerful state. Around 1300, a group of **Nahuatl**-speaking people are believed to have migrated southward from what is now northern Mexico, settling on the shores and islands in Lake Texcoco in the central valley of Mexico (see Map 10.4). Here they built the twin cities of Tenochtitlán and Tlatelolco, which by 1500 were probably larger than any city in Europe except Istanbul. As they migrated, these people conquered many neighboring city-states and established an empire. This empire was later termed the "Aztec" Empire and the people called the "Aztecs." This was not a word used at the time,

Aztec *A term coined by nineteenth-century historians to describe the Mexica people.*

Nahuatl *The language of both the Toltecs and the Aztecs.*

Mexica *Another term for Aztec; it is a pre-Columbian term designating the dominant ethnic people of the island capital of Tenochtitlán-Tlatelolco.*

however, and now most scholars prefer the term **Mexica** to refer to the empire and its people; we use both terms here.

Religion and War in Aztec Society

In Mexica society, religion was the dynamic factor that transformed other aspects of the culture: economic security, social mobility, education, and especially war. War was an article of religious faith. The state religion of the Aztecs initially gave them powerful advantages over other groups in central Mexico; it inspired them to conquer vast territories in a remarkably short time. War came to be seen as a religious duty to the Mexicas, through which nobles, and occasionally commoners, honored the gods, gained prestige, and often acquired wealth.

The Mexicas worshiped a number of gods and goddesses as well as some deities that had dual natures as both male and female. The basic conflict in the world was understood as one between order and disorder, though the proper life balances these two, as disorder could never be completely avoided. Disorder was linked to dirt and uncleanness, so temples, shrines, and altars were kept very clean; rituals of purification often involved sweeping or bathing. Like many polytheists, Mexicas took the deities of people they encountered into their own pantheon, or mixed their attributes with those of existing gods. Quetzalcoatl, for example, the feathered serpent god found among many Mesoamerican groups, was generally revered by the Mexicas as a creator deity and source of knowledge.

Huitzilopochtli *The chief among the Aztecs' many gods, who symbolized the sun blazing at high noon.*

Among the deities venerated by Mexica and other Mesoamerican groups was **Huitzilopochtli,** a young warrior god whose name translates fully as "Blue Hummingbird of the South" (or "on the Left") and who symbolized the sun blazing at high noon. The sun, the source of all life, had to be kept moving in its orbit if darkness was not to overtake the world. To keep it moving, Aztecs believed, the sun had to be frequently fed precious fluids—that is, human blood. Human sacrifice was a sacred duty, essential for the preservation and prosperity of humankind. (See the feature "Individuals in Society: Tlacaélel.")

Most victims were war captives, for the Aztecs controlled their growing empire by sacrificing prisoners seized in battle, by taking hostages from among defeated peoples as ransom against future revolt, and by demanding from subject states an annual tribute of people to be sacrificed to Huitzilopochtli. Unsuccessful generals, corrupt judges, and careless public officials, even people who accidentally entered forbidden precincts of the royal palaces, were routinely sacrificed. In some years it was difficult to provide enough war captives, so other types of people, including criminals, slaves, and people supplied as tribute, were sacrificed as well. Such victims did not have the same status as captives, however, and Mexicas engaged in special wars simply to provide victims for sacrifices, termed "flower (or flowery) wars." Flowers were frequently associated metaphorically with warfare in Mexica culture, with blood described as a flower of warfare, swords and banners as blooming like flowers, and a warrior's life as fleeting like a flower's blooming. The objective of flower wars was capturing warriors from the other side, not killing them.

The Mexica state religion required constant warfare for two basic reasons. One was to meet the gods' needs for human sacrifice; the other was to acquire warriors for the next phase of imperial expansion. The sacred campaigns of Huitzilopochtli were synchronized with the political and economic needs of the Mexica nation as a whole. Moreover, defeated peoples had to pay tribute in foodstuffs to support rulers, nobles, warriors, and the imperial bureaucracy. The vanquished supplied laborers for agriculture, the economic basis of Mexica society. Likewise, conquered peoples had to produce workers for the construction and maintenance of the entire Aztec infrastructure—roads, dike systems, aqueducts, causeways, and the royal palaces. Finally, merchants also benefited, for war opened new markets for traders' goods in subject territories.

Tlacaélel

The hummingbird god Huitzilopochtli was originally a somewhat ordinary god of war and of young men, but in the fifteenth century he was elevated in status among the Mexica. He became increasingly associated with the sun and gradually became the Mexicas' most important deity. This change was primarily the work of Tlacaélel, the very long-lived chief adviser to the emperors Itzcóatl (r. 1427–1440), Montezuma I (r. 1440–1469), and Axayacatl (r. 1469–1481). Tlacaélel first gained influence during wars in the 1420s in which the Mexicas defeated the rival Tepanecs, after which he established new systems of dividing military spoils and enemy lands. At the same time, he advised the emperor that new histories were needed in which the destiny of the Mexica people was made clearer. Older historical texts were destroyed, and in these new chronicles the fate of the Mexicas was directly connected to Huitzilopochtli. Mexica writing was primarily pictographic, drawn and then read by specially trained scribes, who used written records as an aid to oral presentation, especially for legal issues, historical chronicles, religious and devotional poetry, and astronomical calculations.

According to these new texts, the Mexicas had been guided to Lake Texcoco by Huitzilopochtli; there they saw an eagle perched on a cactus, which a prophecy had told would mark the site of their new city. Huitzilopochtli kept the world alive by bringing the sun's warmth, but to do this he required the Mexicas, who increasingly saw themselves as the "people of the sun," to provide a steady offering of human blood.

The worship of Huitzilopochtli became linked to cosmic forces as well as daily survival. In Nahua tradition, the universe was understood to exist in a series of five suns, or five cosmic ages. Four ages had already passed, and their suns had been destroyed; the fifth sun, the age in which the Mexicas were now living, would also be destroyed unless the Mexicas fortified the sun with the energy found in blood. Warfare thus not only brought new territory under Mexica control, but also provided sacrificial victims for their collaboration with divine forces. With these ideas, Tlacaélel created what Miguel León-Portilla, a leading contemporary scholar of Nahuatl religion and philosophy, has termed a "mystico-militaristic" conception of Aztec destiny.

Human sacrifice was practiced in many cultures of Mesoamerica, including the Olmec and the Maya as well as the Mexica, before the changes introduced by Tlacaélel, but the number of victims is believed to have

Tlacaélel emphasized human sacrifice as one of the Aztecs' religious duties. *(Scala/Art Resource, NY)*

increased dramatically during the last period of Mexica rule. A huge pyramid-shaped temple in the center of Tenochtitlán, dedicated to Huitzilopochtli and the water god Tlaloc, was renovated and expanded many times, the last in 1487. Each expansion was dedicated by priests sacrificing war captives. Similar ceremonies were held regularly throughout the year on days dedicated to Huitzilopochtli and were attended by many observers, including representatives from neighboring states as well as masses of Mexicas. According to many accounts, victims were placed on a stone slab and their hearts cut out with an obsidian knife; the officiating priest then held the heart up as an offering to the sun. Sacrifices were also made to other gods at temples elsewhere in Tenochtitlán, and perhaps in other cities controlled by the Mexicas.

Estimates about the number of people sacrificed to Huitzilopochtli and other Mexica gods vary enormously and are impossible to verify. Both Mexica and later Spanish accounts clearly exaggerated the numbers, but most historians today assume that between several hundred and several thousand people were killed each year.

Questions for Analysis

1. How did the worship of Huitzilopochtli contribute to Aztec expansion? To hostility toward the Aztecs?

2. Why might Tlacaélel have seen it as important to destroy older texts as he created this new Aztec mythology?

Sources: León-Portilla, Miguel. *Pre-Columbian Literatures of Mexico* (Norman: University of Oklahoma Press, 1969); Clendinnen, Inga. *Mexicas: An Interpretation* (Cambridge: Cambridge University Press, 1991).

● **The Goddess Tlazolteotl** The Aztecs believed that cleanliness was a way to honor the gods, and that Tlazolteotl (sometimes called "Mother of the Gods") consumed the sins of humankind by eating refuse. She was also the goddess of childbirth. Notice the squatting position for childbirth, then common all over the world. (Dumbarton Oaks, Pre-Columbian Collection, Washington, D.C.)

tecuhtli *Provincial governors who exercised full political, judicial, and military authority on the Aztec emperor's behalf.*

The Life of the People

A wealth of information has survived about fifteenth- and sixteenth-century Mexico. The Aztecs wrote many books recounting their history, geography, and religious practices. They loved making speeches, which scribes wrote down. The Aztecs also preserved records of their legal disputes, which alone amounted to vast files. The Spanish conquerors subsequently destroyed much of this material. But enough documents remain to construct a picture of the Mexica people at the time of the Spanish intrusion.

No sharp social distinctions existed among the Aztecs during their early migrations. All were equally poor. The head of a family was both provider and warrior, and a sort of tribal democracy prevailed in which all adult males participated in important decision making. By the early sixteenth century, however, Aztec society had changed. A stratified social structure had come into being, and the warrior aristocracy exercised great authority.

Scholars do not yet understand precisely how this change occurred. According to Aztec legend, the Mexica admired the Toltecs and chose their first king, Acamapichti, from among them. The many children he fathered with Mexica women formed the nucleus of the noble class. At the time of the Spanish intrusion into Mexico, men who had distinguished themselves in war occupied the highest military and social positions in the state. Generals, judges, and governors of provinces were appointed by the emperor from among his servants who had earned reputations as war heroes. These great lords, or **tecuhtli,** dressed luxuriously and lived in palaces. The provincial governors exercised full political, judicial, and military authority on the emperor's behalf. In their territories they maintained order, settled disputes, and judged legal cases; oversaw the cultivation of land; and made sure that tribute—in food or gold—was paid. The governors also led troops in wartime. These functions resembled those of feudal lords in western Europe during the Middle Ages (see pages 367–368). Just as only nobles in France and England could wear fur and carry swords, just as gold jewelry and elaborate hairstyles for women distinguished royal and noble classes in African kingdoms, so in Mexica societies only the tecuhtli could wear jewelry and embroidered cloaks. The growth of a strong mercantile class as the empire expanded led to an influx of tropical wares and luxury goods: cotton, feathers, cocoa, skins, turquoise jewelry, and gold. The upper classes enjoyed an elegant and extravagant lifestyle.

Beneath the great nobility of soldiers and imperial officials was the class of warriors. Theoretically every free man could be a warrior, and parents dedicated their male children to war, burying a male child's umbilical cord with some arrows and a shield on the day of his birth. In actuality the sons of nobles enjoyed advantages deriving from their fathers' position and influence in the state. At the age of six, boys entered a school that trained them for war. Future warriors were taught to fight with a *macana,* a paddle-shaped wooden club edged with bits of obsidian. Youths were also trained in the use of spears, bows and arrows, and lances fitted with obsidian points. They learned to live on little food and sleep and to accept pain without complaint. At about age eighteen, a warrior fought his first campaign. If he captured a prisoner for ritual sacrifice, he acquired the title *iyac,* or warrior. If in later campaigns he succeeded in killing or capturing four of the enemy, he became a *tequiua*—one who shared in the booty and thus was a member of the nobility. If a young man failed in several campaigns to capture the required four prisoners, he joined the **maceualtin,** the plebeian or working class.

The maceualtin were the ordinary citizens—the backbone of Aztec society and the vast majority of the population. The word *maceualti* means "worker" and implies boorish speech and vulgar behavior. Members of this class performed all sorts of agricultural, military, and domestic services and carried heavy public burdens not required of noble warriors. Government officials assigned the maceualtin work on the temples, roads, and bridges. Army officers called them up for military duty, but Mexica considered this an honor and a religious rite, not a burden. Unlike nobles, priests, orphans, and slaves, maceualtin paid taxes. Maceualtin in the capital, however, possessed certain rights: they held their plots of land for life, and they received a small share of the tribute paid by the provinces to the emperor.

Beneath the maceualtin were the *tlalmaitl,* the landless workers or serfs. Some social historians speculate that this class originated during the period of migrations and upheavals following the end of the classical period (see page 271), when weak and defenseless people placed themselves under the protection of strong warriors, just as European peasants had become serfs after the end of the Roman Empire (see page 126). The tlalmaitl provided agricultural labor, paid rents in kind, and were bound to the soil—they could not move off the land. The tlalmaitl resembled in many ways the serfs of western Europe, but unlike serfs they performed military service when called on to do so. They enjoyed some rights as citizens and generally were accorded more respect than slaves.

Slaves were the lowest social class. Like Asian, European, and African slaves, most were prisoners captured in war or kidnapped from enemy tribes. But Aztecs who stole from a temple or private house or plotted against the emperor could also be enslaved, and people in serious debt sometimes voluntarily sold themselves into slavery. Female

maceualtin *The vast majority of the Aztec population; the ordinary citizens or members of the working class.*

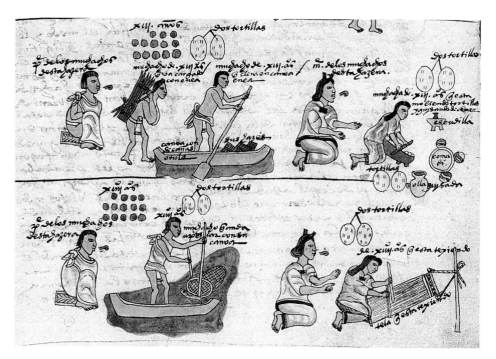

● **Aztec Youth** As shown in this codex, Aztec society had basic learning requirements for each age (indicated by dots) of childhood and youth. In the upper panel, boys of age thirteen gather firewood and collect reeds and herbs in a boat, while girls learn to make tortillas on a terra-cotta grill. At fourteen (*lower panel*), boys learn to fish from a boat, and girls are taught to weave. *(The Bodleian Library, University of Oxford, MS Arch. Selden. A.1, fol. 60r)*

slaves often became their masters' concubines. Mexica slaves, however, differed fundamentally from European ones, for they could possess goods, save money, buy land and houses and even slaves for their own service, and purchase their freedom. If a male slave married a free woman, their offspring were free, and a slave who escaped and managed to enter the emperor's palace was automatically free. Most slaves eventually gained their freedom. Mexica slavery, therefore, had some humane qualities and resembled slavery in Islamic societies (see pages 205–207).

Women of all social classes played important roles in Mexica society, but those roles were restricted entirely to the domestic sphere. As the little hands of the newborn male child were closed around a tiny bow and arrow indicating his warrior destiny, so the infant female's hands were wrapped around miniature weaving instruments and a small broom: weaving was a sacred and exclusively female art; the broom signaled a female's responsibility for the household shrines and for keeping the household swept and free of contamination. Almost all of the Mexica people married, a man at about twenty when he had secured one or two captives, a woman a couple of years earlier. As in premodern Asian and European societies, parents selected their children's spouses, using neighborhood women as go-betweens. Save for the few women vowed to the service of the temple, marriage and the household were a woman's fate; marriage represented social maturity for both sexes. Pregnancy became the occasion for family and neighborhood feasts, and a successful birth launched celebrations lasting from ten to twenty days.

Women were expected to pray for their husbands' success in battle while they were gone. As one prayer to Huitzilopochtli went:

O great Lord of All Things, remember your servant
Who has gone to exalt your honor and the greatness of your name.
He will offer blood in that sacrifice that is war.
Behold, Lord, that he did not go out to work for me
Or for his children . . . He went for your sake,
In your name, to obtain glory for you . . .
Give him victory in this war so that he may return
To rest in his home and so that my children and I may see
His countenance again and feel his presence."[1]

Alongside the secular social classes stood the temple priests. Huitzilopochtli and each of the numerous lesser gods had many priests to oversee the upkeep of the temple, assist at religious ceremonies, and perform ritual sacrifices. The priests also did a brisk business in foretelling the future from signs and omens. Aztecs consulted priests on the selection of wives and husbands, on the future careers of newborn babies, and before leaving on journeys or for war. Temples possessed enormous wealth in gold and silver ceremonial vessels, statues, buildings, and land. From the temple revenues and resources, the priests supported schools, aided the poor, and maintained hospitals. The chief priests had the ear of the emperor and often exercised great power and influence.

At the peak of the social pyramid stood the emperor. The various Aztec historians contradict one another about the origin of the imperial dynasty, but modern scholars tend to accept the verdict of one sixteenth-century authority that the "custom has always been preserved among the Mexicans (that) the sons of kings have not ruled by right of inheritance, but by election."[2] A small oligarchy of the chief priests, warriors, and state officials made the selection. If none of the sons proved satisfactory, a brother or nephew of the emperor was chosen, but election was always restricted to the royal family.

The Aztec emperor was expected to be a great warrior who had led Mexica and allied armies into battle. All his other duties pertained to the welfare of his people. It was up to the emperor to see that justice was done—he was the final court of appeal. He also held ultimate responsibility for ensuring an adequate food supply. The emperor Montezuma I (r. 1440–1467) distributed twenty thousand loads of stockpiled grain when a flood hit Tenochtitlán. The records show that the Aztec emperors took their public duties seriously.

The Cities of the Aztecs

When the Spanish entered **Tenochtitlán** (which they called Mexico City) in November 1519, they could not believe their eyes. According to Bernal Díaz, one of Cortés's companions:

when we saw all those cities and villages built in the water, and other great towns on dry land, and that straight and level causeway leading to Mexico, we were astounded. These great towns and cues (temples) and buildings rising from the water, all made of stone, seemed like an enchanted vision. . . . Indeed, some of our soldiers asked whether it was not all a dream.[3]

Tenochtitlán had about sixty thousand households. The upper class practiced polygamy and had many children, and many households included servants and slaves. The total population probably numbered around 250,000. At the time, no European city and few Asian ones could boast a population even half that size. The total Aztec Empire has been estimated at around 5 million inhabitants, with the total population of Mesoamerica estimated at between 20 and 30 million.

Originally built on salt marshes, Tenochtitlán was approached by four great highways that connected it with the mainland. Bridges stood at intervals (comparable to modern Paris). Stone and adobe walls surrounded the city itself, making it (somewhat like medieval Constantinople; see page 169) highly defensible and capable of resisting

Tenochtitlán *A large and prosperous Aztec city that was admired by the Spanish when they entered in 1519.*

● **Tenochtitlán** The great Mexican archaeologist Ignacio Marquina designed this reconstruction of the central plaza of the Mexica city as it looked in 1519. The temple precinct, an area about 500 square yards, contained more than eighty structures, pyramids, pools, and homes of gods and of the men and women who served them. Accustomed to the clutter and filth of Spanish cities, the Spaniards were amazed by the elegance and cleanliness of Tenochtitlán. *(Enrique Franco-Torrijos)*

a prolonged siege. Wide, straight streets and canals crisscrossed the city. Boats and canoes plied the canals. Lining the roads and canals stood thousands of rectangular one-story houses of mortar faced with stucco. Although space was limited, many small gardens and parks were alive with the colors and scents of flowers.

A large aqueduct whose sophisticated engineering astounded Cortés carried pure water from distant springs and supplied fountains in the parks. Streets and canals opened onto public squares and marketplaces. Tradespeople offered every kind of merchandise. Butchers hawked turkeys, ducks, chickens, rabbits, and deer; grocers sold kidney beans, squash, avocados, corn, and all kinds of peppers. Artisans sold intricately designed gold, silver, and feathered jewelry. Seamstresses offered sandals, loincloths and cloaks for men, and blouses and long skirts for women—the clothing customarily worn by ordinary people—and embroidered robes and cloaks for the rich. Slaves for domestic service, wood for building, herbs for seasoning and medicine, honey and sweets, knives, jars, smoking tobacco, even human excrement used to cure animal skins—all these wares made a dazzling spectacle.

At one side of the central square of Tenochtitlán stood the great temple of Huitzilopochtli. Built as a pyramid and approached by three flights of 120 steps each, the temple was about one hundred feet high and dominated the city's skyline. According to Cortés, it was "so large that within the precincts, which are surrounded by a very high wall, a town of some five hundred inhabitants could easily be built. All round inside this wall there are very elegant quarters with very large rooms and corridors where their priests live."[4]

Travelers, perhaps inevitably, compare what they see abroad with what is familiar to them at home. Tenochtitlán thoroughly astounded Cortés, and in his letter to the emperor Charles V, he describes the city in comparison to his homeland: "the market square," where sixty thousand people a day came to buy and sell, "was twice as big as Salamanca"; the beautifully constructed "towers," as the Spaniards called the pyramids, rose higher "than the cathedral at Seville"; Montezuma's palace was "so marvelous that it seems to me to be impossible to describe its excellence and grandeur[;] . . . in Spain there is nothing to compare with it." Accustomed to the squalor and filth of Spanish cities, the cleanliness of Tenochtitlán dumbfounded the Spaniards, as did all the evidence of its ordered and elegant planning.[5]

• • • • • •

THE INCAS

What were the sources of strength and prosperity, and of problems, for the Incas as they created their enormous empire?

In the center of Peru rise the cold highlands of the Andes. Six valleys of fertile and wooded land at altitudes ranging from eight thousand to eleven thousand feet punctuate highland Peru. The largest of these valleys are the Huaylas, Cuzco, and Titicaca. It was there that Inca civilization developed and flourished. Like the Aztecs, the **Incas** were a small militaristic group that came to power, conquered surrounding groups, and established one of the most extraordinary empires in the world. Gradually, Inca culture spread throughout Peru.

Incas *The Peruvian empire that was at its peak from 1438 until 1532.*

Earlier Peruvian Cultures

Inca achievements built on those of cultures that preceded them in the Andes and the Peruvian coast. These included the Chavin and the **Moche** civilization, which flourished along a 250-mile stretch of Peru's northern coast between 100 and 800 C.E. Rivers that flowed out of the Andes into the valleys allowed the Moche people to develop complex irrigation systems for agricultural development. Each Moche valley contained a large ceremonial center with palaces and pyramids surrounded by settlements of up to ten thousand people. The dazzling gold and silver artifacts, elaborate

Moche *A Native American culture that thrived along Peru's northern coast between 100 and 800 C.E. The culture existed as a series of city-states rather than a single empire and is distinguished by an extraordinarily rich and diverse pottery industry.*

headdresses, and ceramic vessels display a remarkable skill in metalwork and pottery.

Politically, Moche culture was a series of small city-states rather than one unified state, which increased warfare. As in Aztec culture, war provided victims for human sacrifice, frequently portrayed on Moche pottery. Beginning about 500, the Moche suffered several severe *El Niños,* the change in ocean current patterns in the Pacific that brings both searing drought and flooding. Their leaders were not able to respond effectively, and the cities lost population.

In the Andes, various states developed after Chavin that were each able to carve out a slightly larger empire. They built cities around large public plazas, with temples, palaces, and elaborate stonework. Using terraces and other means to increase the amount of arable soil, they grew potatoes and other crops, even at very high altitudes. Enough food was harvested to feed not only the farmers themselves but also massive armies and administrative bureaucracies and thousands of industrial workers. These cultures were skilled at using fibers for a variety of purposes, including building boats to use on Lake Titicaca and bridges for humans and pack llamas to cross steep valleys.

Inca Imperialism

Who were the Incas? *Inca* was originally the name of the governing family of an Amerindian group that settled in the basin of Cuzco (see Map 10.5). From that family, the name was gradually extended to all peoples living in the Andes valleys. The Incas themselves used the word to identify their ruler or emperor. Here the term is used for both the ruler and the people. As with the Aztecs, so with the Incas: religious ideology was the force that transformed the culture. Religious concepts created pressure for imperialist expansion.

MAP 10.5 **The Inca Empire, 1532** Beginning in the fifteenth century, the Incas expanded their holdings through warfare. They built an extensive network of roads to hold their ethnically diverse empire together.

The Incas believed their ruler descended from the sun-god and that the health and prosperity of the state depended on him. Dead rulers were thought to link the people to the sun-god. When the ruler died, his corpse was preserved as a mummy in elaborate clothing and housed in a sacred and magnificent chamber. His royal descendants as a group managed his lands and sources of income for him and used the revenues to care for his mummy, maintain his cult, and support themselves. New rulers did not inherit these riches, so they had to win their own possessions by means of war and imperial expansion.

Around 1000 C.E. the Incas were one of many small groups fighting among themselves for land and water. The cult of royal mummies provided the impetus for expansion. The desire for conquest provided incentives for courageous (or ambitious) nobles: those who were victorious in battle and gained new territories for the state could expect lands, additional wives, servants, herds of llamas, gold, silver, fine clothes, and other symbols of high status. Even common soldiers who distinguished themselves in battle could be rewarded with booty and raised to noble status. The imperial interests of the emperor paralleled those of other social groups. Under Pachacuti Inca (1438–1471) and his successors, Inca domination was gradually extended by warfare to the frontier of present-day Ecuador and Colombia in the north and to the Maule River in present-day Chile in the south (see Map 10.5), an area of about 350,000 square miles. Eighty provinces, scores of ethnic groups, and 16 million people came under Inca control. A remarkable system of roads held the empire together.

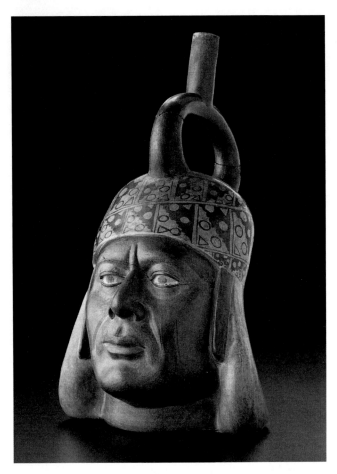

● **Portrait Vessel of a Ruler** Artisans of the Moche culture on the northern coast of Peru produced objects representing many aspects of their world, including this flat-bottomed stirrup-spout jar with a ruler's face. The commanding expression conveys a strong sense of power, as does the elaborate headdress with the geometric designs of Moche textiles worn only by elite persons. *(South America, Peru, North Coast, Moche Culture, Portrait Vessel of a Ruler, earthenware with pigmented clay slip, 300–700, 35.6 x 24.1, Kate S. Buckingham Endowment, 1955.2338, 3/4 view. Photograph by Robert Hashimoto. Photograph © 1999, The Art Institute of Chicago)*

Quechua *First deemed the official language of the Incas under Pachacuti, it is still spoken by most Peruvians today.*

Primary Source: Chronicles
Learn how the Incas used the elaborate knotted ropes called khipus as record-keeping devices that helped them govern a vast and prosperous empire.

Before Inca civilization, each group that entered the Andes valleys had its own distinct language. These languages were not written and have become extinct. Scholars will probably never understand the linguistic condition of Peru before the fifteenth century when Pachacuti made the Inca language, which the Spanish called **Quechua** (pronounced "keshwa"), the official language of his people and administration. Conquered peoples were forced to adopt the language, and Quechua spread the Inca way of life throughout the Andes. Though not written until the Spanish in Peru adopted it as a second official language, Quechua had replaced local languages by the seventeenth and eighteenth centuries and is still spoken by most Peruvians today.

Both the Aztecs and the Incas ruled very ethnically diverse peoples. Whereas the Aztecs tended to control their subject peoples through terror, the Incas governed by means of imperial unification. They imposed not only their language but also their entire panoply of gods. Magnificent temples scattered throughout the expanding empire housed images of these gods. Priests led prayers and elaborate rituals, and on such occasions as a terrible natural disaster or a great military victory, they sacrificed human beings to the gods. Subject peoples were required to worship the state gods.

Imperial unification was also achieved through the forced participation of local chieftains in the central bureaucracy and through a policy of colonization. To prevent rebellion in newly conquered territories, Pachacuti Inca and subsequent rulers transferred all their inhabitants to other parts of the empire, replacing them with workers who had lived longer under Inca rule. They drafted local men for distant wars, breaking up kin groups that had existed in Andean society for centuries.

An excellent system of roads—averaging three feet in width, some paved and others not—facilitated the transportation of armies and the rapid communication of royal orders by runners. The roads followed straight lines wherever possible but also crossed pontoon bridges and tunneled through hills. This great feat of Inca engineering bears striking comparison with Roman roads, which also linked an empire.

Ruling an empire requires a bureaucracy as well as an army, and Inca officials, tax collectors, and accountants traveled throughout the empire. They made increasingly elaborate khipus (see page 266) to record financial and labor obligations, the output of fields, population levels, land transfers, and other numerical records. Scholars have deciphered the way numbers were recorded on khipus, finding a base-ten system. Khipus may also have been used to record narrative history, but this is more speculative, as knowledge of how to read them died out after the Spanish conquest. Just as the Spanish destroyed books in Mesoamerica, they destroyed khipus in the Andes because they thought they might contain religious messages and encourage people to resist Spanish authority. About 750 Inca khipus survive today, more than half in museums in Europe.

Rapid Inca expansion, however, produced stresses. Although the pressure for growth remained unabated, open lands began to be scarce. Attempts to penetrate the tropical Amazon forest east of the Andes led to repeated military disasters. The Incas waged wars with highly trained armies drawn up in massed formation and fought pitched battles on level ground, often engaging in hand-to-hand combat. But in dense jungles, the troops could not maneuver or maintain order against enemies using guerrilla tactics and sniping at them with deadly blowguns. Another source of stress was revolts among subject peoples in conquered territories. Even the system of roads and trained runners eventually caused administrative problems. The average runner could cover about 50 leagues, or 175 miles, per day—a remarkable feat of physical endurance, especially at high altitude—but the larger the empire became, the greater the distances to be covered. The roundtrip from the capital at Cuzco to Quito in Ecuador, for example, took from ten to twelve days, so that an emperor might have to base urgent decisions on incomplete or out-of-date information. The empire was overextended.

When the Inca Huayna Capac died in 1525, his throne was bitterly contested by two of his sons, Huascar and Atauhualpa. Huascar's threat to do away with the cult of royal mummies led the nobles—who often benefited from managing land and wealth for a deceased ruler—to throw their support behind Atauhualpa. In the civil war that began in 1532, Atauhualpa's veteran warriors easily defeated Huascar's green recruits, but the conflict weakened the Incas. On his way to his coronation at Cuzco, Atauhualpa encountered Pizarro and 168 Spaniards who had recently entered the kingdom. The Spaniards quickly became the real victors in the Inca kingdom (see pages 442–443).

● **Machu Picchu** The Inca city of Machu Picchu, surrounded by mountains in the clouds, clings to a spectacular crag in upland Peru. It was built around 1450, at the point that the Inca Empire was at its height, and abandoned about a century later. *(Will McIntyre/Photo Researchers, Inc.)*

● **An Inca Cape** Inca artisans could produce gorgeous textiles, and on ceremonial occasions nobles proudly paraded in brightly colored feathers or in garments made of luxurious alpaca wool. This exquisite cape is fashioned from the feathers of a blue and yellow macaw; the pattern, befitting aristocratic tastes, features lordly pelicans carried on litters by less exalted birds. *(The Textile Museum, Washington, D.C., 91.395. Acquired by George Hewitt Myers in 1941)*

Inca Society

ayllu *A clan; it served as the fundamental social unit of Inca society.*

curacas *The headman of the Inca clan; he was responsible for conducting relations with outsiders.*

The **ayllu,** or clan, served as the fundamental social unit of Inca society. All members of the ayllu owed allegiance to the **curacas,** or headman, who conducted relations with outsiders. The ayllu held specific lands, granted it by village or provincial authorities on a long-term basis, and individual families tended to work the same plots for generations. Cooperation in the cultivation of the land and intermarriage among members of the ayllu wove people there into a tight web of connections.

In return for the land, all men had to perform public duties and pay tribute to the authorities. Their duties included building and maintaining palaces, temples, roads, and irrigation systems. Tribute consisted of potatoes, corn, and other vegetables paid to the village head, who in turn paid them to the provincial governor. A draft rotary system called **mita** (turn) determined when men of a particular village performed public works. As the Inca Empire expanded, this pattern of social and labor organization was imposed on other, newly conquered indigenous peoples. After the conquest, the Spaniards adopted and utilized the Incas' ways of organizing their economy and administration, just as the Incas (and, in Mesoamerica, the Aztecs) had built on earlier cultures.

mita *A draft rotary system that determined when men of a particular hamlet performed public works.*

The Incas had well-established mechanisms for public labor drafts and tribute collection. The emperors sometimes gave newly acquired lands to victorious generals, distinguished civil servants, and favorite nobles. These lords subsequently exercised authority previously held by the native curacas. Whether long-time residents or new colonists, common people had the status of peasant farmers, which entailed heavy agricultural or other obligations. Just as in medieval Europe peasants worked several days each week on their lord's lands, so the Inca people had to work on state lands (that is, the emperor's lands) or on lands assigned to the temple. Peasants also labored on roads and bridges; terraced and irrigated new arable land; served on construction crews for royal palaces, temples, and public buildings such as fortresses; acted as runners on the post roads; and excavated in the imperial gold, silver, and copper mines. The imperial government annually determined the number of laborers needed for these various undertakings, and each district had to supply an assigned quota. The government also made an ayllu responsible for the state-owned granaries and for the production of cloth for army uniforms.

The state required everyone to marry and even decided when and sometimes whom a person should marry. Men married around the age of twenty, women a little younger. The Incas did not especially prize virginity; premarital sex was common. The marriage ceremony consisted of the joining of hands and the exchange of a pair of sandals. This ritual was followed by a large wedding feast at which the state presented the bride and groom with two sets of clothing, one for everyday wear and one for festive occasions. If a man or woman did not find a satisfactory mate, the provincial governor selected one for him or her. Travel was forbidden, so couples necessarily came from the same region. Like most warring societies with high male death rates, the Incas practiced polygamy, though the cost of supporting many wives restricted it largely to the upper classes.

The Incas relied heavily on local authorities and cultural norms for day-to-day matters. In some ways, however, the common people were denied choice and initiative and led regimented lives. The Incas did, however, take care of the poor and aged, distribute grain in times of shortage and famine, and supply assistance in natural disasters. Scholars have debated whether Inca society was socialistic, totalitarian, or a forerunner of the welfare state; it may be merely a matter of definition. Although the Inca economy was strictly regulated, there certainly was not an equal distribution of wealth. Everything above and beyond the masses' basic needs went to the emperor and the nobility.

The backbreaking labor of ordinary people in the fields and mines made possible the luxurious lifestyle of the great Inca nobility. The nobles—called *oregones,* or "big ears," by the Spanish because they pierced their ears and distended the lobes with heavy jewelry—were the ruling Inca's kinsmen. Lesser nobles included the curacas, royal household servants, public officials, and entertainers.

In the fifteenth century Inca rulers superimposed imperial institutions on those of kinship. They ordered allegiance to be paid to the ruler at Cuzco rather than to the curacas and relocated the entire populations of certain regions. Entirely new ayllus were formed, based on residence rather than kinship. As the empire expanded, there arose a noble class of warriors, governors, and local officials whose support the ruling Inca secured with gifts of land, precious metals, and llamas and alpacas (llamas were used as beasts of burden; alpacas were raised for their long fine wool). The nobility was exempt from agricultural work and from other kinds of public service.

Chapter Summary

Key Terms

Mesoamerica
milpa
Norte Chico
khipu
Chavin
Olmecs
Maya
Popul Vuh
Teotihuacán
Toltecs
Hohokam
Anasazi
Hopewell
Mississippian
Aztec
Nahuatl
Mexica
Huitzilopochtli
tecuhtli
maceualtin
Tenochtitlán
Incas
Moche
Quechua
ayllu
curacas
mita

To assess your mastery of this chapter, go to
bedfordstmartins.com/mckayworld

• *How did early peoples in the Americas adapt to their environment as they created economic and political systems?*

The environment shaped the formation of human settlements in the Americas, which began when people crossed into the Western Hemisphere from Asia. All the highly varied environments, from polar tundra to tropical rain forests, came to support human settlement. About 8000 B.C.E., people in some parts of the Americas began raising crops as well as gathering wild produce. Maize became the most important crop, with knowledge about its cultivation spreading out from Mesoamerica into North and South America.

• *What physical, social, and intellectual features characterized early civilizations in the Americas?*

Agricultural advancement led to an increase in population, which allowed for greater concentrations of people and the creation of the first urban societies. In certain parts of North and South America, towns dependent on agriculture flourished, especially in coastal areas and river valleys. Some in North America began to build large earthwork mounds, while those in South America practiced irrigation. The Olmecs created the first society with cities in Mesoamerica, with large ceremonial buildings, an elaborate and accurate calendar, and a system of writing.

• *How did Mesoamerican and North American peoples develop prosperous and stable societies in the classical era?*

The urban culture of the Olmecs and other Mesoamerican peoples influenced subsequent societies. Especially in what became known as the classical era (300–900 C.E.), various groups developed large states centered on cities, with high levels of technological and intellectual achievement. Of these, the Maya were the most long-lasting, creating a complex written language and elegant art. Peoples living in North America built communities that were smaller than those in Mesoamerica, but many also used irrigation techniques to enhance agricultural production and continued to build earthwork mounds for religious purposes.

• *How did the Aztecs both build on the achievements of earlier Mesoamerican cultures and develop new traditions to create their large empire?*

The Aztecs, also known as the Mexica, built a unified culture based heavily on the heritage of earlier Mesoamerican societies and distinguished by achievements in engineering, sculpture, and architecture. In Mexica society, religion was the dynamic factor that transformed other aspects of the culture: economic security, social mobility, education, and especially war. War was an article of religious faith, providing riches and land, and also sacrificial victims for ceremonies honoring the Aztec gods. Aztec society was hierarchical, with nobles and priests having special privileges. The Aztec empire centered on Tenochtitlán, the most spectacular and one of the largest cities in the world in 1500.

• **What were the sources of strength and prosperity, and of problems, for the Incas as they created their enormous empire?**

The Peruvian coast and Andean highlands were home to a series of cultures that cultivated cotton as well as food crops. Of these, the largest empire was created by the Incas, who began as a small militaristic group and conquered surrounding groups. The Incas established a far-flung empire that stretched along the Andes, keeping this together through a system of roads, along which moved armies and administrators. Andean society was dominated by clan groups, and Inca measures to disrupt these and move people great distances created resentment.

Suggested Reading

Clendinnen, I. *Aztecs: An Interpretation*. 1992. Pays particular attention to the role that rituals and human sacrifice played in Aztec culture.

Coe, M. *The Mayas*. 2005. A new edition of a classic survey that incorporates the most recent scholarship.

Conrad, G. W., and A. A. Demarest. *Religion and Empire: The Dynamics of Aztec and Inca Expansionism*. 1993. Compares the two largest American empires.

D'Altroy, T. *The Incas*. 2003. Examines the ways in which the Incas drew on earlier traditions to create their empire; by a leading scholar.

Freidel, D. *A Forest of Kings: The Untold Story of the Ancient Maya*. 1990. A splendidly illustrated work providing expert treatment of the Maya world.

Kehoe, Alice Beck. *America Before the European Invasion*. 2002. An excellent survey of North America before the coming of the Europeans, by an eminent anthropologist.

Knight, A. *Mexico: From the Beginnings to the Spanish Conquest*. 2002. Provides information on many Mesoamerican societies.

León-Portilla, M. *The Aztec Image of Self and Society: An Introduction to Nahua Culture*. 1992. The best appreciation of Aztec religious ritual and symbolism.

Mann, Charles C. *1491: New Revelations of the Americas Before Columbus*. 2005. A thoroughly researched overview of all the newest scholarship, written for a general audience.

Milner, G. *The Moundbuilders: Ancient Peoples of Eastern North America*. 2005. Beautifully illustrated book that discusses the mounds and the societies that built them; could also be used as a tourist guide.

Wright, R. *Time Among the Mayas*. 1989. A highly readable account of Maya agricultural and religious calendars.

Notes

1. Fray Diego Durán, *Mexicas: The History of the Indies of New Spain*, translated, with notes, by Doris Heyden and Fernand Horcasitas (New York: Orion Press, 1964), p. 203.

2. Quoted in J. Soustelle, *Daily Life of the Aztecs on the Eve of the Spanish Conquest*, trans. P. O'Brian (Stanford, Calif.: Stanford University Press, 1970), p. 89.

3. B. Díaz, *The Conquest of New Spain*, trans. J. M. Cohen (New York: Penguin Books, 1978), p. 214.

4. Quoted in J. H. Perry, *The Discovery of South America* (New York: Taplinger, 1979), pp. 161–163.

5. Quoted in I. Clendinnen, *Aztecs: An Interpretation* (New York: Cambridge University Press, 1992), pp. 16–17.

Listening to the PAST

The Death of Inca Yupanque (Pachacuti Inca) in 1471

In 1551 the Spaniard Juan de Betanzos began to write Narrative of the Incas. *Although Betanzos had only the Spanish equivalent of a grade school education when he arrived in Peru, and although he lacked dictionaries and grammar books, he had two powerful assets. First, he learned Quechua and earned a reputation for being the best interpreter and translator in postconquest Peru. Second, Betanzos had married Angelina Yupanque, an Inca noblewoman (her Inca name was Cuxirimay Ocllo) who was the widow of Atahualpa. Through her, Betanzos gained immediate and firsthand access to the Inca oral tradition. When he finished his book six years later, modern scholars believe he had produced "the most authentic chronicle that we have."*

Narrative of the Incas provides a gold mine of information about Inca customs and social history. There is so much description of marriage, childbirth, and raising children—activities that were seen as the realm of women in both Inca and Spanish society—that scholars suspect Angelina Yupanque provided her husband with much of his information. Here is his account of the death of Inca Yupanque (Pachacuti Inca) in 1471.

Since there were instructions for the idolatries and activities that you have heard about, Inca Yupanque ordered that immediately after he died these activities and sacrifices should be done. In addition, as soon as this was done, word should be sent to all the land, and from all the provinces and towns they should bring again all that was necessary for the service of the new lord, including gold, silver, livestock, clothing, and the rest of the things needed to replenish all the storehouses that, because of his death, had been emptied for the sacrifices and things he ordered to be done, and it should be so abundant because he realized that the state of the one who was thus Inca was growing greater.

While Inca Yupanque was talking and ordering what was to be done after he died, he raised his voice in a song that is still sung today in his memory by those of his generation. This song went as follows: "Since I bloomed like the flower of the garden, up to now I

have given order and justice in this life and world as long as my strength lasted. Now I have turned into earth." Saying these words of his song, Inca Yupanque Pachacuti expired, leaving in all the land justice and order, as already stated. And his people were well supplied with idols, idolatries, and activities. After he was dead, he was taken to a town named Patallacta, where he had ordered some houses built in which his body was to be entombed. He was buried by putting his body in the earth in a large new clay urn, with him very well dressed. Inca Yupanque ordered that a golden image made to resemble him be placed on top of his tomb. And it was to be worshiped in place of him by the people who went there. Soon it was placed there. He ordered that a statue be made of his fingernails and hair that had been cut in his lifetime. It was made in that town where his body was kept. They very ceremoniously brought this statue on a litter to the city of Cuzco for the fiestas in the city. This statue was placed in the houses of Topa Inca Yupanque. When there were fiestas in the city, they brought it out for them with the rest of the statues. What is more laughable about this lord Inca Yupanque is that, when he wanted to make some idol, he entered the house of the Sun [the temple to the sun in Cuzco] and acted as though the Sun spoke to him, and he himself answered the Sun to make his people believe that the Sun ordered him to make those idols and *guacas** and so that they would worship them as such.

When the statue was in the city, Topa Inca Yupanque ordered those of his own lineage to bring this statue out for the feasts that were held in Cuzco. When they brought it out like this, they sang about the things that the Inca did in his life, both in the wars and in his city. Thus they served and revered him, changing its garments as he used to do, and serving it as he was served when he was alive. All of which was done thus.

This statue, along with the gold image that was on top of his tomb, was taken by Manco Inca from

---

*Any object, place, or person worshiped as a deity.

ELNOVENOINGA
PACHACVTIINGA
IVPANQVI

Reynobas   tachile y le to   Dasucorsellesa
                                        pachaqh

Revered as a great conqueror and lawgiver, Pachacuti Inca here wears the sacred fringed headband symbolizing his royal authority and the large earrings of the *oregones*, the nobility. *(Pachacuti Inca, from Nueva Coronica & Buen Gobierno, by Guaman Poma de Ayala. Courtesy, Musée du Quai Branly/ Scala Picture Library)*

the city when he revolted. On the advice that Doña Angelina Yupanque gave to the Marquis Don Francisco Pizarro, he got it and the rest of the wealth with it. Only the body is in Patallacta at this time, and judging by it, in his lifetime he seems to have been a tall man. They say that he died at the age of one hundred twenty years. After his father's death, Topa Inca Yupanque ordered that none of the descendants of his father, Inca Yupanque, were to settle the area beyond the rivers of Cuzco. From that time until today the descendants of Inca Yupanque were called *Capacaillo Ynga Yupanque haguaynin,* which means "lineage of kings," "descendants and grandchildren of Inca Yupanque." These are the most highly regarded of all the lineages of Cuzco. These are the ones who were ordered to wear two feathers on their heads.

As time passed, this generation of *orejones* [*oregones*]† multiplied. There were and are today many who became heads of families and renowned as firstborn. Because they married women who were not of their lineage, they took a variety of family names. Seeing this, those of Inca Yupanque ordered that those who had mixed with other people's blood should take

†Nobles.

new family names and extra names so that [only] those of his lineage could clearly be called *Capacaillo* and descendants of Inca Yupanque.

Questions for Analysis

1. Juan de Betanzos clearly shows his disapproval of the cult of the royal mummies through his choice of words, but he also includes details that help explain its power. Judging by his description, why did people honor deceased rulers? Why did rulers (or at least Inca Yupanque) think they deserved such honors?

2. In the last paragraph, Inca Yupanque's descendants seek to limit their special title of *Capacaillo.* Why might they have done this? What effect might this have on marriage patterns among the descendants of an Inca king?

Source: Narrative of the Incas by Juan de Betanzos, trans. and ed. Roland Hamilton and Dana Buchanan from the Palma de Mallorca manuscript (Austin: University of Texas Press, 1996), pp. 138–139. Copyright © 1996. Used by permission of the University of Texas Press.

Wedding Procession of Prince Dara-Shikoh, Agra, February 1633. Female musicians ride atop elephants. *(The Royal Collection © 2007, Her Majesty Queen Elizabeth II)*

19

THE ISLAMIC WORLD POWERS, CA. 1400–1800

Chapter Preview

The Three Turkish Ruling Houses: The Ottomans, Safavids, and Mughals
• How were the three Islamic empires established, and what sorts of governments did they set up?

Cultural Flowering
• What cultural advances occurred under the rule of these three houses?

Non-Muslims Under Muslim Rule
• How did Christians, Jews, Hindus, and other non-Muslims fare under these Islamic states?

Shifting Trade Routes and European Penetration
• How were the Islamic empires affected by the decline in overland trade and the great growth in maritime commerce, and how were European powers able to use trade to make inroads as this period progressed?

Dynastic Decline
• Did any common factors lead to the decline of the Islamic empires in the seventeenth and eighteenth centuries?

After the breakup of the Mongol Empire, new states emerged in south and west Eurasia. By the sixteenth century the Ottoman Empire centered in Anatolia, the Safavid Empire in Persia, and the Mughal Empire in India controlled vast territories from West Africa to Central Asia, from the Balkans to the Bay of Bengal. Their origins were similar (in Turkish tribal polities), and they similarly had to adjust to ruling large sedentary populations. They all adapted to the decline in the supremacy of the mounted archer that resulted from the introduction of firearms.

Lasting almost five hundred years (1453–1918), the Ottoman Empire was one of the largest, best-organized, and most enduring political entities in world history. In Persia the Safavid Dynasty created a Shi'ite state and presided over a brilliant culture. In India the Mughal leader Babur and his successors gained control of much of the Indian subcontinent. Mughal rule inaugurated a period of radical administrative reorganization in India and the flowering of intellectual and architectural creativity. These three states were not allied to each other—the Safavids and Ottomans were divided on theological grounds between Sunni and Shi'ite and competed for control of Mesopotamia. Still they faced similar challenges and responded in similar ways. Culturally they were strongly linked, with ideas, practices, and styles quickly spreading from one society to another.

THE THREE TURKISH RULING HOUSES: THE OTTOMANS, SAFAVIDS, AND MUGHALS

How were the three Islamic empires established, and what sorts of governments did they set up?

Before the Mongols arrived in Central Asia and Persia, another nomadic Central Asian people, the Turks, had gained overlordship in key territories from Anatolia to Delhi in north India. The Turks had been quick to join the Mongols and formed important elements in the armies and administrations of the Mongol states in Persia and Central Asia. In these regions, Turks far outnumbered ethnic Mongols.

As Mongol strength in Persia and Central Asia deteriorated in the late thirteen and fourteenth centuries, the Turks resumed their expansion. In the late fourteenth century, the Turkish leader Tamerlane (1336–1405) built a Central Asian empire from his base in Samarkand, campaigning into India and through Persia to the Black Sea. Tamerlane campaigned continuously from the 1360s till his death in 1405, trying to repeat the achievements of Chinggis Khan. He did not get involved in administering the new territories, but rather appointed lords and let them make use of existing political structures. Thus, when after his death his sons and grandson fought against each other for succession, his empire quickly fell apart, and power devolved to the local level. Sufi orders thrived, and Islam became the most important force integrating the region. It was from the many small Turkish chiefs that the founders of the three main empires emerged.

The Ottoman Turkish Empire

Ottomans *Ruling house of the Turkish empire that lasted from 1453 to 1918.*

Anatolia *The region of modern Turkey.*

The **Ottomans** took their name from Osman (r. 1280–1324), the chief of a band of seminomadic Turks that had migrated into western **Anatolia** during the era when the Mongol Il-khans still held Persia. The Ottomans gradually expanded at the expense of other Turkish statelets and the Byzantine Empire. The Ottoman ruler called himself "border chief," or leader of the *ghazis,* frontier fighters in the *jihad,* or holy war. The earliest Ottoman historical source, a fourteenth-century saga, describes the ghazis as the "instrument of God's religion . . . God's scourge who cleanses the earth from the filth of polytheism . . . God's pure sword."[1] Although temporarily slowed by defeat at the hands of Tamerlane in 1402, the Ottomans quickly reasserted themselves after Tamerlane's death in 1405.

The holy war was intended to subdue, not destroy. The Ottomans built their empire by absorbing the Muslims of Anatolia and by becoming the protector of the Orthodox church and of the millions of Greek Christians in Anatolia and the Balkans. In 1326 they took Bursa in western Anatolia, and in 1352 they gained a foothold in Europe by seizing Gallipoli. Their victories led more men, including recent converts, to join them as ghazi. In 1389 at Kosovo in the Balkans, the Ottomans defeated a combined force of Serbs and Bosnians. In 1396 on the Danube River in modern Bulgaria, they crushed King Sigismund of Hungary, who was supported by French, German, and English knights. After the victories in the Balkans, the Ottomans added to their military through the creation of slave troops (discussed below). These troops were outfitted with guns and artillery and trained to use them effectively.

The reign of Sultan Mehmet II (r. 1451–1481) saw the Ottoman conquest of Constantinople, capital of the Byzantine Empire, which had lasted a thousand years. The Byzantine emperor Constantine IX Palaeologus (r. 1449–1453), with only about ten thousand men, relied on the magnificent system of circular walls and stone fortifications for his defense. Mehmet II had more than one hundred thousand men and a large fleet, but iron chains spanning the harbor kept him out. Turkish ingenuity and Western technology eventually decided the battle. Mehmet's army carried boats over the steep hills to come in behind the chains blocking the harbor, then bombarded the city from the rear. A Transylvanian cannon founder who deserted the Greeks for the Turks cast huge bronze cannon on the spot (bringing raw materials to the scene of military action was easier than moving guns long distances).[2]

Sultan-i-Rum *The name that the Ottoman sultans took as their title; it means "sultan of Rome."*

With the conquest of Constantinople (renamed Istanbul) as a base, the Ottomans quickly absorbed the rest of the Byzantine Empire. They continued to expand through the Middle East and into North Africa in the sixteenth century. Once Constantinople was theirs, the Ottoman sultans considered themselves successors of both the Byzantine and Seljuk emperors, as their title **Sultan-i-Rum** (sultan of Rome) attests.

To begin the transformation of Istanbul into an imperial Ottoman capital, Mehmet ordered the city cleaned up and the walls repaired. He appointed officials to adapt the city administration to Ottoman ways and ordered wealthy residents to participate in building mosques, markets, water fountains, baths, and other public facilities. The population of Istanbul had declined in the decades before the conquest, and warfare, flight, and the sale of many survivors into slavery had decreased the population further. Therefore, Mehmet transplanted to the city inhabitants of other territories, granting them tax remissions and possession of empty houses. He wanted them to start businesses, make the city prosperous, and transform it into a microcosm of the empire.

Gunpowder, invented by the Chinese and adapted to artillery use by the Europeans, played an influential role in the expansion of the Ottoman state. In the first half of the sixteenth century, the Ottomans gained control of shipping in the eastern Mediterranean, eliminated the Portuguese from the Red Sea and Persian Gulf, and supported Andalusian and North African Muslims in their fight against the Spanish reconquista. Under the superb military leadership of Selim (r. 1512–1520), the Ottomans in 1514 turned the Safavids back from Anatolia. The Ottomans also added Syria and Palestine (1516) and Egypt (1517) to the empire, extending their rule across North Africa to Tunisia and Algeria. Selim's rule marks the beginning of four centuries when most Arabs were under Ottoman rule.

Suleiman (r. 1520–1566) extended Ottoman dominion to its widest geographical extent (see Map 19.1). Suleiman's army crushed the Hungarians at Mohács in 1526, killing the king and thousands of his nobles. Three years later, the Turks besieged the Habsburg capital of Vienna. Only an accident—the army's insistence on returning home before winter—prevented Muslim control of all central Europe. The Ottomans' military discipline, ability to coordinate cavalry and infantry, and capability in logistics were usually superior to those of the Europeans.

From the late fourteenth to the early seventeenth century, the Ottoman Empire was a key player in European politics. In 1525 Francis I of France and Suleiman struck an alliance; both believed that only their collaboration could prevent Habsburg hegemony in Europe. The Habsburg emperor Charles V retaliated by seeking an alliance with Safavid Persia. Suleiman renewed the French agreement with Francis's son, Henry II (r. 1547–1559), and the French entente became the cornerstone of Ottoman policy in western Europe. Suleiman also allied with the German Protestant princes, forcing the Catholic Habsburgs to grant concessions to the Protestants. Ottoman pressure proved an important factor in the official recognition of Lutheran Protestants at the Peace of Augsburg in 1555. In addition to the rising tide of Protestantism, the Ottoman threat strengthened the growth of national monarchy in France.

Chronology

1280–1324 Osman, founder of the Ottoman Dynasty

1336–1405 Life of Tamerlane

ca. mid-1400s Coffeehouses become center of Islamic male social life

1453 Ottoman conquest of Constantinople

ca. 1498–1805 Mughal Empire

1501–1722 Safavid Empire

1501–1524 Reign of Shah Ismail

1520–1566 Reign of Ottoman emperor Suleiman I; period of artistic flowering in Ottoman Empire

1520–1558 Hürrem wields influence in Ottoman Empire as Suleiman's wife

1521 Piri Reis, *Book of the Sea,* a navigational map book

1548–1557 Pasha Sinan designs and builds Suleimaniye Mosque in Istanbul

1556–1605 Reign of Akbar in Mughal Empire

1570 Turks take control of Cyprus

1571 First major Ottoman defeat by Christians, at Lepanto

1587–1629 Reign of Shah Abbas; height of Safavid power; carpet weaving becomes major Persian industry

1631–1648 Construction of Taj Mahal under Shah Jahan

1658–1707 Reign of Aurangzeb; Mughal power begins to decline

1668 Bombay leased to British East India Company

1763 Treaty of Paris recognizes British control over much of India

In eastern Europe to the north of Ottoman lands stood the Grand Duchy of Moscow. In the fifteenth century, Ottoman rulers did not regard it as a threat; in 1497 they even gave Russian merchants freedom of trade within the empire. But in 1547 Ivan IV (the Terrible) brought under Russian control the entire Volga region (see Map 19.1). In 1557 Ivan's ally, the Cossack chieftain Dimitrash, tried to take Azov, the northernmost Ottoman fortress. Ottoman plans to recapture the area succeeded in uniting Russia, Persia, and the pope against the Turks.

Though usually victorious on land, the Ottomans did not enjoy complete dominion on the seas. Competition with the Habsburgs and pirates for control of the Mediterranean led the Ottomans to conquer Cyprus in 1570 and settle thousands of Turks from Anatolia there. (Thus began the large Turkish presence on Cyprus that continues to the present day.) In response, Pope Pius V organized a Holy League against the Turks, which had a victory in 1571 at Lepanto with a squadron of more than two hundred Spanish, Venetian, and papal galleys. Still, the Turks remained supreme on land and quickly rebuilt their entire fleet.

To the east, war with Persia occupied the sultans' attention throughout the sixteenth century. Several issues lay at the root of the long and exhausting conflicts:

MAP 19.1 **The Ottoman Empire at Its Height, 1566** The Ottomans, like their great rivals the Habsburgs, rose to rule a vast dynastic empire encompassing many different peoples and ethnic groups. The army and the bureaucracy served to unite the disparate territories into a single state.

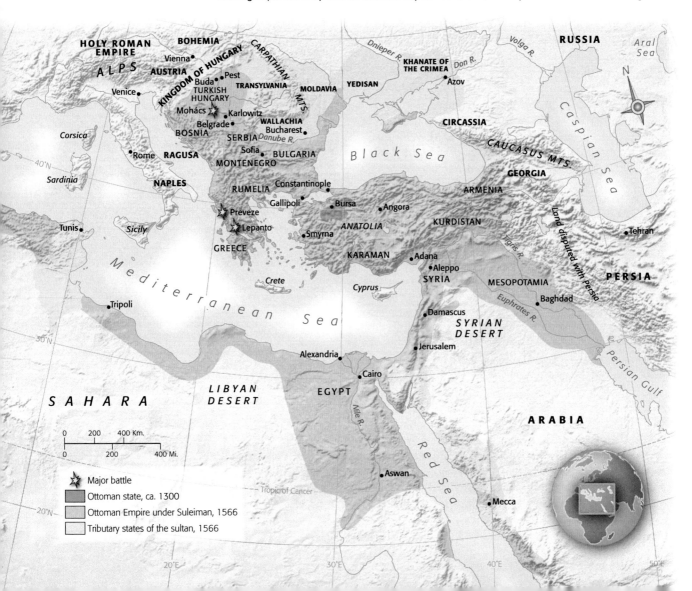

● **Battle of Mohács** The *Süleymanname* (Book of Suleiman), a biography, contains these wonderful illustrations of the battle that took place in Hungary on August 29, 1526. In the right panel, Suleiman in a white turban sits on a black horse surrounded by his personal guard, while janissaries fire cannon at the enemy. In the left panel, the Europeans are in disarray, in contrast to the Turks' discipline and order. Suleiman inflicted a crushing defeat and absorbed Hungary into the Ottoman Empire. The artist attempted to show the terrain and battle tactics. *(Topkapi Saray Museum, Istanbul)*

religious antagonism between the Sunni Ottomans and the Shi'ite Persians, competition to expand at each other's expense in Mesopotamia, desires to control trade routes, and European alliances. Finally, in 1638, the Ottomans captured Baghdad, and the treaty of Kasr-I-Shirim established a permanent border between the two powers.

The Ottoman political system reached its classic form under Suleiman I. All authority flowed from the **sultan** to his public servants: provincial governors, police officers, military generals, heads of treasuries, viziers. In Turkish history, Suleiman is known as the Lawgiver because of his profound influence on the civil law. He ordered Lütfi Paşa (d. 1562), a poet and juridical scholar of slave origin, to draw up a new general code of laws. This code prescribed penalties for routine criminal acts such as robbery, adultery, and murder. It also sought to reform bureaucratic and financial corruption in areas such as harem intervention in administrative affairs, foreign merchants' payment of bribes to avoid customs duties, imprisonment without trial, and promotion in the provincial administration because of favoritism rather than ability. The legal code also introduced the idea of balanced financial budgets. The head of the religious establishment was given the task of reconciling sultanic law with Islamic law. Suleiman's legal acts influenced many legal codes, including that of the United States. Today, Suleiman's image, along with the images of Solon, Moses, and Thomas Jefferson, appears in the chamber of the U.S. House of Representatives.

sultan *An Arabic word originally used by the Seljuk Turks to mean authority or dominion; it was used by the Ottomans to connote political and military supremacy.*

devshirme *A process whereby the sultan's agents swept the provinces for Christian youths to become slaves.*

janissaries *Turkish for "recruits"; they formed the elite army corps.*

concubine *A woman who is a recognized spouse but of lower status than a wife.*

Slavery was widespread in the Ottoman empire. Slaves were purchased from Spain, North Africa, and Venice; captured in battle; or drafted through the system known as **devshirme,** by which the sultan's agents compelled Christian families in the Balkans to turn over their boys. As the Ottoman frontier advanced in the fifteenth and sixteenth centuries, Albanian, Bosnian, Wallachian, and Hungarian slave boys filled Ottoman imperial needs. The slave boys were converted to Islam and trained for the imperial civil service and the standing army. The brightest 10 percent entered the palace school, where they learned to read and write Arabic, Ottoman Turkish, and Persian. Other boys were sent to Turkish farms, where they acquired physical toughness in preparation for military service. Known as **janissaries** (Turkish for "recruits"), they formed the elite army corps. Thoroughly indoctrinated and absolutely loyal to the sultan, the janissary slave corps eliminated the influence of old Turkish families and played a central role in Ottoman military affairs in the sixteenth century.

The Ottoman ruling class consisted in part of descendants of Turkish families that had formerly ruled parts of Anatolia and in part of people of varied ethnic origins who rose through the bureaucratic and military ranks, many beginning as the sultan's slaves. All were committed to the Ottoman way: Islamic in faith, loyal to the sultan, and well versed in the Turkish language and the culture of the imperial court. In return for their services to the sultan, they held landed estates for the duration of their lives. The ruling class had the legal right to use and enjoy the profits, but not the ownership, of the land. Since all property belonged to the sultan and reverted to him on the holder's death, Turkish nobles, unlike their European counterparts, did not have a local base independent of the ruler. The absence of a hereditary nobility and private ownership of agricultural land differentiates the Ottoman system from European feudalism.

By the reign of Selim I, the principle was established that the sultan did not contract legal marriage but perpetuated the ruling house through concubinage. A slave **concubine** could have none of the political aspirations or leverage that a native or foreign-born noblewoman had (with a notable exception; see the feature "Individuals in

● **Music in a Garden**
This illustration of a courtly romance depicts several women in a garden, intently listening to a musician, cups of a beverage in their hands. *(Biblioteca Vaticana Apostolica)*

Individuals IN SOCIETY

Hürrem

Hürrem (1505?–1558) was born in the western Ukraine (then part of Poland), the daughter of a Ruthenian priest, and was given the Polish name Aleksandra Lisowska. When Tartars raided, they captured and enslaved her. In 1520 she was given as a gift to Suleiman on the occasion of his accession to the throne. The Venetian ambassador (probably relying on secondhand or thirdhand information) described her as "young, graceful, petite, but not beautiful." She was given the Turkish name Hürrem, meaning "joyful."

Hürrem apparently brought joy to Suleiman. Their first child was born in 1521; by 1525 they had four sons and a daughter; sources note that by that year Suleiman visited no other woman. But he waited eight or nine years before breaking Ottoman dynastic tradition by making Hürrem his legal wife, the first slave concubine so honored. For the rest of her life, Hürrem played a highly influential role in the political, diplomatic, and philanthropic life of the Ottoman state. First, great power flowed from her position as mother of the prince, the future sultan Selim II (r. 1566–1574). Then, as the intimate and most trusted adviser of the sultan, she was Suleiman's closest confidant. He was frequently away in the far-flung corners of his multiethnic empire. Hürrem wrote him long letters filled with her love and longing for him, her prayers for his safety in battle, and political information about affairs in Istanbul, the activities of the grand vizier, and the attitudes of the janissaries. At a time when some people believed that the sultan's absence from the capital endangered his hold on the throne, Hürrem acted as his eyes and ears for potential threats.

Hürrem was the sultan's contact with her native Poland, which sent more embassies to Istanbul than any other power. Through her correspondence with King Sigismund I, peace between Poland and the Ottomans was maintained. When Sigismund II succeeded his father in 1548, Hürrem sent congratulations on his accession, along with two pairs of pajamas (originally a Hindu garment, but commonly worn in southwestern Asia) and six handkerchiefs. By sending the shah of Persia gold-embroidered sheets and shirts she had sewn herself, Hürrem sought to display the wealth of the sultanate and to keep peace between the Ottomans and the Safavids.

The enormous stipend that Suleiman gave Hürrem permitted her to participate in his vast building program. In Jerusalem (in the Ottoman province of Palestine), she founded a hospice for fifty-five pilgrims

Hürrem and her ladies in the harem.
(Bibliothèque nationale de France)

that included a soup kitchen that fed four hundred pilgrims a day. In Istanbul Suleiman built and Hürrem endowed the Haseki (meaning "royal favorite concubine") mosque complex and a public bath for women near the Women's Market.

Perhaps Hürrem tried to fulfill two functions hitherto distinct in Ottoman political theory: those of the sultan's favorite and mother of the prince. She also performed the conflicting roles of slave concubine and imperial wife. Turks, however, reviled Hürrem and thought she had bewitched Suleiman.

Questions for Analysis

1. Compare Hürrem to other powerful fifteenth- or sixteenth-century women, such as Isabella of Castile, Catherine de' Medici of France, Elizabeth of England, and Mary Queen of Scots.

2. What was Hürrem's "nationality"? What role did it play in her life?

Source: Leslie P. Pierce, *The Imperial Harem: Women and Sovereignty in the Ottoman Empire* (New York: Oxford University Press, 1993).

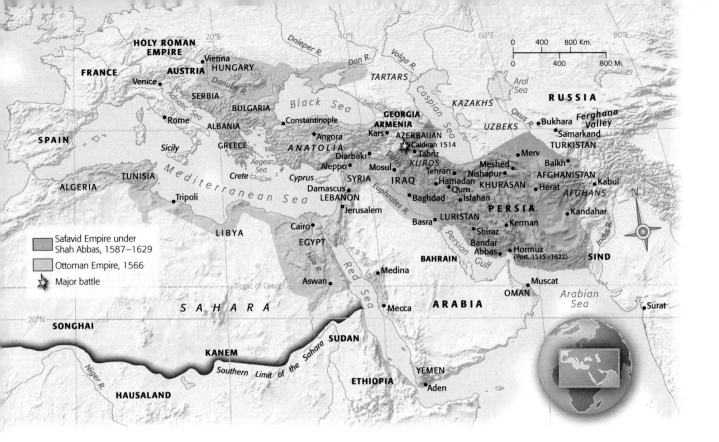

MAP 19.2 **The Safavid Empire** In the late sixteenth century, the power of the Safavid kingdom of Persia rested on its strong military force, its Shi'ite Muslim faith, and its extraordinarily rich trade in rugs and pottery. Many of the cities on the map, such as Tabriz, Qum, and Shiraz, were great rug-weaving centers.

Society: Hürrem"). When one of the sultan's concubines became pregnant, her status and her salary increased. If she delivered a boy, she raised him until the age of ten or eleven. Then the child was given a province to govern under his mother's supervision. She accompanied him there, was responsible for his good behavior, and worked through imperial officials and the janissary corps to promote his interests. Since succession to the throne was open to all the sultan's sons, at his death fratricide often resulted, and the losers were blinded or executed.

Slave concubinage paralleled the Ottoman development of slave soldiers and slave viziers. All held positions entirely at the sultan's pleasure, owed loyalty solely to him, and thus were more reliable than a hereditary nobility, as existed in Europe. Great social prestige, as well as the opportunity to acquire power and wealth, was attached to being a slave of the imperial household. Suleiman even made it a practice to marry his daughters to top-ranking slave-officials.

The Safavid Theocracy in Persia

After the collapse of Tamerlane's empire in 1405, Persia was controlled by Turkish lords, no single one dominant until 1501 when fourteen-year-old Ismail led a Turkish army to capture Tabriz and declared himself **shah** (king) and a particular Shi'ia sect the official and compulsory religion of his new empire. In the early twenty-first century, Iran remains the only Muslim state in which Shi'ism is the official religion.

The strength of the early **Safavid** state rested on three crucial features. First, it had the loyalty and military support of Turkish Sufis known as **Qizilbash** (a Turkish word meaning "redheads" that was applied to these people because of the red hats they

---

Primary Source:
Letter to Shah Ismail of Persia
Ottoman sultan Selim I, a Sunni Muslim, threatens war against the Persian shah, his Shia enemy.

---

shah *Persian word for "king."*

Safavid *The dynasty that encompassed all of Persia and other regions; its state religion was Shi'ism.*

Qizilbash *Nomadic tribesmen who were Sufis and loyal to and supportive of the early Safavid state.*

wore). The shah secured the loyalty of the Qizilbash by granting them vast grazing lands, especially on the troublesome Ottoman frontier. In return, the Qizilbash supplied him with troops. Second, the Safavid state utilized the skills of urban bureaucrats and made them an essential part of the civil machinery of government. The third source of Safavid strength was the Shi'ite faith. The Shi'ites claimed descent from Ali, Muhammad's cousin and son-in-law, and believed that leadership among Muslims rightfully belonged to them as the Prophet's descendants. Ismail claimed descent from a line of twelve infallible *imams* (leaders) beginning with Ali and was officially regarded as their representative on earth.

Shi'ism gradually shaped the cultural and political identity of Persia (and later Iran). Recent scholarship asserts that Ismail was not "motivated by cynical notions of political manipulation."[3] He imported Shi'ite *ulama* (scholars outstanding in learning and piety) from other Arab lands to instruct and guide his people, and he persecuted and exiled Sunni ulama. With its puritanical emphasis on the holy law and on self-flagellation in penance for any disloyalty to Ali, the Safavid state represented theocracy triumphant throughout the first half century of its existence.

Safavid power reached its height under Shah Abbas (r. 1587–1629), whose military achievements, support for trade and commerce, and endowment of the arts earned him the epithet "the Great." He moved the capital to Isfahan. He adopted the Ottoman practice of building an army of slaves, primarily captives from the Caucuses (especially Armenians and Georgians), who could serve as a counterweight to the Qizilbash. He increased the use of gunpowder weapons and made alliances with European powers against the Ottomans and Portuguese. In his campaigns against the Ottomans, Shah Abbas captured Baghdad, Mosul, and Diarbakr in Mesopotamia (see Map 19.2).

The Mughal Empire in India

Of the three great Islamic empires of the early modern world, the **Mughal** Empire of India was the largest, wealthiest, and most populous. Extending over 1.2 million square miles at the end of the seventeenth century, with a population between 100 million and 150 million, and with fabulous wealth and resources, the Mughal Empire surpassed Safavid Persia and Ottoman Turkey. Among the Mughal ruler's world contemporaries, only the Ming emperor of China could compare with him.

In 1504 Babur (r. 1483–1530), the Turkish ruler of a small territory in Central Asia, captured Kabul and established a kingdom in Afghanistan. An adventurer who claimed descent from Chinggis Khan and Tamerlane, Babur moved southward into India when he could not expand in Afghanistan. In 1526, with a force of only twelve thousand men, Babur defeated the sultan of Delhi at Panipat. Babur's capture of the cities of Agra and Delhi, key fortresses of the north, paved the way for further conquests in northern India. Although many

● **Persian "Ardabil" Carpet from the Safavid Period** The Persians were among the first carpet weavers of ancient times and perfected the art over thousands of years. This carpet, reputably from the Safavid shrine at Ardabil, is one of only three signed and dated (around 1539–1540) carpets from the Safavid period, when Persian carpet making was at its zenith. Hand-knotted and hand-dyed, this wool carpet was royally commissioned with a traditional medallion design, consisting of a central sunburst medallion surrounded by radiating pendants. Mosque lamps project from the top and bottom of the medallion. Inscribed on the carpet is an ode by the fourteenth-century poet Hafiz: "I have no refuge in this world other than thy threshold / My head has no resting place other than this doorway." *(Victoria & Albert Museum/The Art Archive)*

Mughal *A term meaning "Mongol," used to refer to the Muslim empire of India, although its founders were primarily Turks, Afghans, and Persians.*

badshah *Persian word for highest ruler; it was the title that Akbar took at the age of thirteen.*

Primary Source: Akbarnama
These selections from the history of the house of Akbar offer a glimpse inside the policies and religious outlook of the Mughal emperor.

of his soldiers wished to return north with their spoils, Babur decided to stay in India. A gifted writer, Babur wrote an autobiography in Turkish that recounts his military campaigns, describes places and people he encountered, recounts his difficulties giving up wine, and shows his wide-ranging interests in everything from a Turkish general who excelled at leapfrog to his own love of fruit and swimming. He was not particularly impressed by India, complaining that the country lacked good horses, bread, grapes, and meat, and that people were neither kind, friendly, nor clever.

During the reign of Babur's son Humayun (r. 1530–1540 and 1555–1556), the Mughals lost most of their territories in Afghanistan. Humayun went into temporary exile in Persia, where he developed a deep appreciation for Persian art and literature. The reign of Humayun's son Akbar (r. 1556–1605) may well have been the greatest in the history of India. Under his dynamic leadership, the Mughal state took definite form. A boy of thirteen when he became **badshah,** or imperial ruler, Akbar pursued expansionist policies. The Mughal Empire under Akbar eventually included most of the subcontinent north of the Godavari River (see Map 19.3). No kingdom or coalition of kingdoms could long resist Akbar's armies. The once independent states of northern India were forced into a centralized political system under the sole authority of the Mughal emperor.

Akbar replaced Turkish with Persian as the official language of the Mughal Empire. Persian remained the official language until the British replaced it with English in 1835. To govern this vast region, Akbar developed an administrative bureaucracy centered on four co-equal ministers: for finance and revenue; the army and intelligence; the judiciary and religious patronage; and the imperial household, which included roads, bridges, and infrastructure throughout the empire. Under Akbar's Hindu finance minister, Raja Todar Mal, a uniform system of taxes was put in place. In the provinces, imperial governors, appointed by and responsible solely to the emperor, presided over administrative branches modeled on those of the central government. The government, however, rarely interfered in the life of village communities. Whereas the Ottoman sultans and Safavid shahs made extensive use of slaves acquired from non-Muslim lands for military and administrative positions, Akbar used the services of royal princes, nobles, and warrior-aristocrats. Initially these men were Muslims from Central Asia, but to reduce their influence, Akbar vigorously recruited Persians and Hindus. No single ethnic or religious faction could challenge the emperor.

Akbar's descendants extended the Mughal empire further. His son Jahangir (r. 1605–1628) lacked his father's military abilities and administrative genius, but he did succeed in consolidating Mughal rule in Bengal. Jahangir's son Shah Jahan (r. 1628–1658) launched fresh territorial expansion. Faced with dangerous revolts by the Muslims in Ahmadnagar and the resistance of the newly arrived Portuguese in Bengal, Shah Jahan not only crushed them but also strengthened his northwestern frontier. Shah Jahan's son Aurangzeb (r. 1658–1707) deposed his father and confined him for years in a small cell. A puritanically devout and strictly orthodox Muslim, as well as a skillful general and a clever diplomat, Aurangzeb ruled more of India than did any previous badshah, having extended the realm deeper into south India (see Map 19.3).

• • • • • • • • • • • •

CULTURAL FLOWERING

What cultural advances occurred under the rule of these three houses?

All three Islamic imperial houses were great patrons and presided over extraordinary artistic flowering. There was much in common across their court cultures, probably because of the common Persian influence on the Turks since the tenth century. In

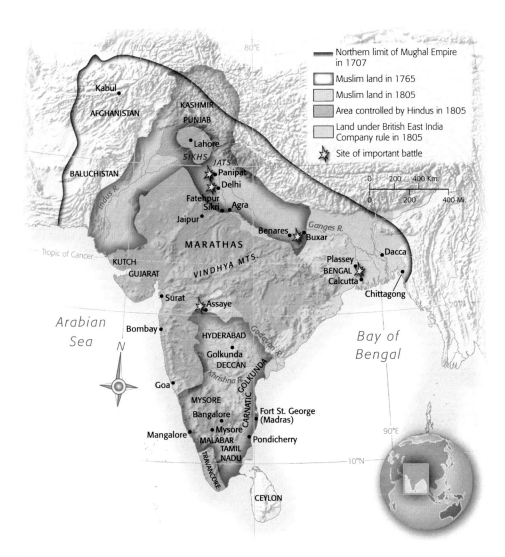

MAP 19.3 **India, 1707–1805**   In the eighteenth century, Mughal power gradually yielded to the Hindu Marathas and to the British East India Company.

addition, artistic styles and intellectual and religious trends would spread from one to the other. This was aided by common languages. Persian was used as the administrative language by the Mughals in India, and Arabic was a lingua franca of the entire region because of its centrality in Islam.

One of the arts all three shared was carpets. Carpet designs and weaving techniques demonstrate both cultural integration and local distinctiveness. Turkic migrants carried their weaving traditions with them as they moved but also readily adopted new motifs, especially from Persia. In Anatolia the town of Usak began its rise as a center of commercial carpet production in the fifteenth century. In Safavid Persia, Shah Abbas was determined to improve his country's export trade and built the small cottage business of carpet weaving into a national industry. In the capital city of Isfahan alone, factories employed more than twenty-five thousand weavers, who produced woolen carpets, brocades, and silks of brilliant color, design, and quality. Because the small hands of women and children can tie tinier knots than the large hands of men, women and children have often been used (and exploited) in the manufacture of expensive rugs.

Another art that spread from Persia to both Ottoman and Mughal lands was miniature painting, especially for book illustration. This tradition had been enriched by the many Chinese artists brought to Persia during the Mongol period. There was also an interplay between carpets and miniature painting. The naturalistic reproduction of lotus blossoms, peonies, chrysanthemums, birds, and even dragons, as well as tulips and carnations, appear in both book illustrations and carpets.

Akbar enthusiastically supported artists who produced magnificent paintings and books in the Indo-Persian style. In Mughal India, as throughout the Muslim world, books were regarded as precious objects. Time, talent, and expensive materials went into their production, and they were highly coveted because they reflected wealth, learning, and power. Akbar reportedly possessed twenty-four thousand books when he died. Abu-l-Fazl describes Akbar's library and love of books:

His Majesty's library is divided into several parts. . . . Prose works, poetical works, Hindi, Persian, Greek, Kashmirian, Arabic, are all separately placed. In this order they are also inspected. Experienced people bring them daily and read them before His Majesty, who hears every book from beginning to end . . . and rewards the readers with presents of cash either in gold or silver, according to the number of leaves read out by them. . . . There are no historical facts of past ages, or curiosities of science, or interesting points of philosophy, with which His Majesty, a leader of impartial sages, is unacquainted.[4]

City and Palace Building

In all three empires, strong rulers built capital cities and imperial palaces as visible expressions of dynastic majesty. Europeans called Suleiman "the Magnificent" because of the grandeur of his court. With annual state revenues of about $80 million (at a time when Elizabeth I of England could expect $150,000 and Francis I of France perhaps $1 million) and thousands of servants, he had a lifestyle no European monarch could begin to rival. He used his fabulous wealth to adorn Istanbul with palaces, mosques, schools, and libraries. The building of hospitals, roads, and bridges and the reconstruction of the water systems of the great pilgrimage sites at Mecca and Jerusalem benefited his subjects. Safavid Persia and Mughal India produced rulers with similar ambitions.

The greatest builder under the Ottomans was Pasha Sinan (1491–1588), a Greek-born devshirme recruit who rose to become imperial architect under Suleiman. A contemporary of Michelangelo, Sinan designed 312 public buildings—mosques, schools, hospitals, public baths, palaces, and burial chapels. His masterpieces, the Shehzade and Suleimaniye mosques in Istanbul, which rivaled the Byzantine church of Hagia Sophia, represented solutions to spatial problems unique to domed buildings and expressed the discipline, power, and devotion to Islam that characterized the Ottoman Empire under Suleiman. Istanbul became a prosperous, bustling city of more than a million people.

Shah Abbas made his capital, Isfahan, the jewel of the Safavid empire. A seventeenth-century English visitor described Isfahan's bazaar as "the surprisingest piece of Greatness in Honour of commerce the world can boast of." Besides splendid rugs, stalls displayed pottery and fine china, metalwork of exceptionally high quality, and silks and velvets of stunning weave and design. A city of perhaps 750,000 people, Isfahan contained 162 mosques, 48 schools where future members of the ulama learned the sacred Muslim sciences, 273 public baths, and the vast imperial palace. Private houses had their own garden courts, and public gardens, pools, and parks adorned the wide streets. Tales of the beauty of Isfahan circulated worldwide, attracting thousands of tourists annually in the seventeenth and eighteenth centuries.

Akbar in India was also a great builder. The birth of a long-awaited son, Jahangir, inspired Akbar to build a new city, Fatehpur-Sikri, to symbolize the regime's Islamic

● **Suleimaniye Mosque** Designed and built (1548–1557) by Sinan, a janissary who became the greatest architect in Ottoman history, and surrounded by madrasas, a hospital, and shops, this mosque asserts the dynasty's power, religious orthodoxy, and the sultan's position as "God's shadow on earth." Suleiman, who financed it, is buried here. *(Robert Frerck/Odyssey/Chicago)*

foundations. He personally supervised the construction of the city, which combined the Muslim tradition of domes, arches, and spacious courts with the Hindu tradition of flat stone beams, ornate decoration, and solidity. According to the historian Abu-l-Fazl, "His Majesty plans splendid edifices, and dresses the work of his mind and heart in the garment of stone and clay."[5] Completed in 1578, the city included an imperial palace, a mosque, lavish gardens, and a hall of worship, as well as thousands of houses for ordinary people. Unfortunately because of its bad water supply, the city was soon abandoned.

Of Akbar's successors, Shah Jahan had the most sophisticated interest in architecture. Because his capital at Agra was cramped, in 1639 he decided to found a new capital city at Delhi. Hindus considered the area especially sacred, and the site reflects their influence. In the design and layout of the buildings, however, Persian ideas predominated, an indication of the numbers of Persian architects and engineers who had flocked to the subcontinent. The walled palace-fortress alone extended over 125 acres. Built partly of red sandstone, partly of marble, it included private chambers for the emperor; mansions for the wives, widows, and concubines of the imperial household; huge audience rooms for the conduct of public business (treasury, arsenal, and military); baths; and vast gardens filled with flowers, trees, and thirty silver fountains spraying water. In 1650, with living quarters for guards, military officials, merchants, dancing girls, scholars, and hordes of cooks and servants, the palace-fortress housed 57,000 people. It also boasted a covered public bazaar (comparable to a modern

● **Isfahan Tiles** The embellishment of Isfahan under Shah Abbas I created an unprecedented need for tiles—as had the rebuilding of imperial Istanbul after 1453, the vast building program of Suleiman the Magnificent, and a huge European demand. Persian potters learned their skills from the Chinese. By the late sixteenth century, Italian and Austrian potters had imitated the Persian and Ottoman tile makers. *(Courtesy of the Trustees of the Victoria & Albert Museum)*

mall), 270 feet long and 27 feet wide, with arcaded shops. It was probably the first roofed shopping center in India, although such centers were common in western Asia. The sight of the magnificent palace left contemporaries speechless, and the words of an earlier poet were inscribed on the walls:

If there is a paradise on the face of the earth,
It is this, it is this.

Beyond the walls, princes and aristocrats built mansions and mosques on a smaller scale. With a population between 375,000 and 400,000, Delhi gained the reputation of being one of the great cities of the Muslim world.

For his palace, Shah Jahan ordered the construction of the Peacock Throne. (See the feature "Listening to the Past: The Weighing of Shah Jahan on His Forty-Second Lunar Birthday" on pages 572–573.) This famous piece was encrusted with emeralds, diamonds, pearls, and rubies. It took seven years to fashion and cost the equivalent of $5 million. It served as the imperial throne of India until 1739, when the Persian warrior Nadir Shah seized it as plunder and carried it to Persia.

Shah Jahan's most enduring monument is the Taj Mahal. Twenty thousand workers toiled eighteen years to build this memorial in Agra to Shah Jahan's favorite wife, who died giving birth to their fifteenth child. One of the most beautiful structures in the world, the Taj Mahal is both an expression of love and a superb architectural blending of Islamic and Indian culture.

Gardens

Many of the architectural masterpieces of this age had splendid gardens attached to them as well. Gardens represent a distinctive and highly developed feature of Persian culture. From the second century, and with the model of the biblical account of the

Garden of Eden (Genesis 2 and 3), a continuous tradition of gardening had existed in Persia. A garden was a walled area with a pool in the center and geometrically laid-out flowering plants, especially roses. "In Arabic, paradise is simply *al janna*, the garden,"[6] and often as much attention was given to flowers as to food crops. First limited to the ruler's court, gardening soon spread among the wealthy citizens. Gardens served not only as centers of prayer and meditation but also as places of revelry and sensuality. A ruler might lounge near his pool as he watched the ladies of his harem bathe in it.

After the Abbasid conquest of Persia in 636–637, formal gardening spread west and east through the Islamic world, as illustrated by the magnificent gardens of Muslim Spain, southern Italy, and later southeastern Europe. The Mongol followers of Tamerlane took landscape architects from Persia back to Samarkand and adapted their designs to nomad encampments. In 1396 Tamerlane ordered the construction of a garden in a meadow, called House of Flowers. When Tamerlane's descendant Babur established the Mughal Dynasty in India, he adapted the Persian garden to the warmer southern climate. Gardens were laid out near palaces, mosques, shrines, and mausoleums, including the Taj Mahal, which had four water channels symbolizing the four rivers of paradise.

Because it represented paradise, the garden played a large role in Muslim literature. Some scholars hold that to understand Arabic poetry, one must study Arabic gardening. The literary genres of flowers and gardens provided basic themes for Hispano-Arab poets and a model for medieval Christian Europe. The secular literature of Muslim Spain, rife with references such as "a garland of verses," influenced the lyric poetry of southern France, the troubadours, and the courtly love tradition.

Gardens, of course, are seasonal. To remind themselves of "paradise" during the cold winter months, rulers, city people, and nomads ordered Persian carpets, which flower all year. Most Persian carpets of all periods use floral patterns and have a formal garden design.

Intellectual and Religious Trends

During the centuries from 1400 to 1800, there were many advances in mathematics, geographical literature, astronomy, medicine, and the religious sciences in the Islamic empires. Building on the knowledge of earlier Islamic writers and stimulated by Ottoman naval power, the geographer and cartographer Piri Reis produced a map incorporating Islamic and Western knowledge that showed all the known world (1513); another of his maps detailed Columbus's third voyage to the New World. Piri Reis's *Book of the Sea* (1521) contained 129 chapters, each with a map incorporating all Islamic (and Western) knowledge of the seas and navigation and describing harbors, tides, dangerous rocks and shores, and storm

● **Polo** Two teams of four on horseback ride back and forth on a grass field measuring 200 by 400 yards, trying to hit a 4½-ounce wooden ball with a 4-foot mallet through the opponents' goal. Because a typical match involves many high-speed collisions among the horses, each player has to maintain a string of expensive ponies in order to change mounts several times during the game. Students of the history of sports believe the game originated in Persia, as shown in this eighteenth-century miniature, whence it spread to India, China, and Japan. Brought from India to England, where it became very popular among the aristocracy in the nineteenth century, polo is a fine example of cross-cultural influences. *(Private Collection)*

areas. Takiyuddin Mehmet (1521–1585), who served as the sultan's chief astronomer, built an observatory at Istanbul. His *Instruments of the Observatory* catalogued astronomical instruments and described an astronomical clock that fixed the location of heavenly bodies with greater precision than ever before.

There were also advances in medicine. Under Suleiman, however, the imperial palace itself became a center of medical science, and the large number of hospitals established in Istanbul and throughout the empire testifies to his support for medical research and his concern for the sick. Abi Ahmet Celebi (1436–1523), the chief physician of the empire, produced a study on kidney and bladder stones and supported the research of the Jewish doctor Musa Colinus ul-Israil on the application of drugs. Celebi founded the first Ottoman medical school, which served as a training institution for physicians of the empire. The sultans and the imperial court relied on a cadre of elite Jewish physicians.

● **Religious Scholar Filling a Wine Cup** This seventeenth-century Persian painting on paper illustrates four lines of poetry that make fun of a religious scholar who was persuaded to overcome his usual avoidance of wine. *(Freer Gallery of Art, Smithsonian Institution, Washington, D.C., Gift of Charles Lang Freer, F1907.2)*

Ottoman physicians made less progress on one of the great scourges of the period, recurrent outbreaks of plague. Muhammed had once said not to go to a country where an epidemic existed but also not to leave a place because an epidemic broke out. As a consequence, when European cities began enforcing quarantines to control the spread of plague, Ottoman rulers dismissed their efforts, leading, some scholars believe, to great loss of life from the plague there.[7]

In the realm of religion, the rulers of all three empires were Muslims and drew legitimacy from their support for Islam, at least among their Muslim subjects. The Sunni-Shi'ia split between the Ottomans and Safavids led to efforts to define and enforce religious orthodoxy on both sides. For the Safavids this entailed suppressing Sufi movements and Sunnis, even marginalizing—sometimes massacring—the original Qizilbash warriors.

Sufi fraternities thrived throughout the Muslim world, even when the states tried to limit them. In India, Sufi orders also influenced non-Muslims. The mystical Bhakti movement among Hindus involved dances, poems, and songs reminiscent of Sufi orders. The development of the new religion of the Sikhs also was influenced by Sufis. The Sikhs traced themselves back to a teacher in the sixteenth century who argued that God did not distinguish between Muslims and Hindus but saw everyone as his children. Sikhs rejected the caste system and forbade alcohol and tobacco, and men did not cut their hair (covering it instead with a turban). The Sikh movement was most successful in northwest India, where Sikh men armed themselves to defend their communities.

Despite all the signs of cultural vitality in the three Islamic empires, none of them adopted the printing press or went through the sorts of cultural expansion associated with it in China and Europe. Until 1729, the Ottoman authorities prohibited printing books in Turkish or Arabic (but Jews, Armenians, and

Greeks could establish presses and print in their own languages). Printing was not banned in Mughal India, but neither did the technology spread, even after Jesuit missionaries printed Bibles in Indian languages beginning in the 1550s. The Islamic authorities in each of these empires did not want to see writings circulate that might unsettle society and religious teachings.

Coffeehouses

In the mid-fifteenth century, a new social convention spread throughout the Islamic world—drinking coffee. Arab writers trace the origins of coffee to Yemen, where the mystical Sufis drank coffee in their *dhiks,* or "devotional services." Sufis sought a trancelike concentration on God to the exclusion of everything else, and the use of coffee helped them stay awake. Most Sufis were not professional holy men but were employed as tradesmen and merchants. Therefore, the use of coffee for pious purposes led to its use as a business lubricant—an extension of hospitality to a potential buyer in a shop. Merchants carried the Yemenite practice to Mecca in about 1490. From Mecca, where pilgrims were introduced to it, drinking coffee spread to Egypt and Syria. In 1555 two Syrians opened a coffeehouse in Istanbul.

Coffeehouses provided a place for conversation and male sociability; there a man could entertain his friends cheaply and more informally than at home. But coffeehouses encountered religious and governmental opposition, which are indistinguishable under the shari'a, or holy law. Opponents of coffeehouses rested their arguments on four grounds: (1) because of its chemical composition, coffee is intoxicating and physically harmful; (2) coffee drinking was an innovation, and therefore a violation of Islamic law; (3) the coffeehouse encouraged political discussions that could be dangerous to the sultan; and (4) patrons of coffeehouses tended to be low types who engaged in immoral behavior, such as gambling, using drugs, soliciting prostitutes, and engaging in sodomy. The musical entertainment that coffeehouses provided, critics said, lent an atmosphere of debauchery. Thus coffeehouses drew the attention of government officials, who were also the guardians of public morality.

Although debate over the morality of coffeehouses continued through the sixteenth century, the acceptance of them represented a revolution in Islamic life: socializing was no longer confined to the home. Since the medical profession remained divided on coffee's harmful effects, and since the religious authorities could not prove that coffeehouses violated the shari'a, drinking coffee could not be forbidden. In the seventeenth century, coffee and coffeehouses spread to Europe.

● **Turkish Coffeehouse** This sixteenth-century miniature depicts many activities typical of coffeehouses: patrons enter (*upper left*); some sit drinking coffee in small porcelain cups (*center*); the manager makes fresh coffee (*right*). In the center, on a low sofa, men sit reading and talking. At bottom appear activities considered disreputable: musicians playing instruments, others playing games such as backgammon, a board game where moves are determined by rolls of dice. (*Reproduced by kind permission of the Trustees of the Chester Beatty Library, Dublin, Ms 439, folio 9*)

NON-MUSLIMS UNDER MUSLIM RULE

How did Christians, Jews, Hindus, and other non-Muslims fare under these Islamic states?

Drawing on Qur'anic teachings, Muslims had long practiced a religious toleration unknown in Christian Europe. On the promise of obedience and the payment of a poll tax, the Muslim rulers guaranteed the lives and property of Christians and Jews. In the case of the Ottomans, this included not only the Christians and Jews who had been living under Muslim rule for centuries, but also the Serbs, Bosnians, Croats, and other Orthodox Christians in the newly conquered Balkans. The Ottoman conqueror of Constantinople, Mehmet, nominated the Greek patriarch as official representative of the Greek population. This and other such appointments recognized non-Muslims as functioning parts of Ottoman society and economy. In 1454 one Jewish resident, Isaac Sarfati, sent a circular letter to his coreligionists in the Rhineland, Swabia, Moravia, and Hungary praising the happy conditions of the Jews under the crescent in contrast to the "great torture chamber" under Christian rulers and urging them to come to Turkey.[8] A massive migration to Ottoman lands followed. When Ferdinand and Isabella of Spain expelled the Jews in 1492, many immigrated to the Ottoman Empire.

Babur and his successors acquired even more non-Muslim subjects with their conquests in India, which had not only Hindus, but substantial numbers also of Jains, Zoroastrians, Christians, and Sikhs. Over time, the number of Indians who converted to Islam increased, but the Mughal rulers did not force conversion. The Ganges plain, the geographical area of the subcontinent most intensely exposed to Mughal rule and for the longest span of time, had, when the first reliable census was taken in 1901, a Muslim population of only 10 to 15 percent. In fact, "in the subcontinent as a whole there is an inverse relationship between the degree of Muslim political penetration and the degree of Islamization."[9]

Akbar went the furthest in promoting Muslim-Hindu accommodation. He celebrated important Hindu festivals, such as Diwali, the festival of lights. He wore his uncut hair in a turban "as a concession to Indian usage and to please his Indian subjects."[10] Twice Akbar married Hindu princesses, one of whom became the mother of his heir, Jahangir. He appointed the Spanish Jesuit Antonio Monserrate (1536–1600) as tutor to his second son, Prince Murad. Hindus eventually totaled 30 percent of the

● **Emperor Akbar and Fatehpur-Sikri** In 1569 Akbar founded the city of Fatehpur-Sikri (the City of Victory) to honor the Muslim holy man Shaykh Salim Chishti, who had foretold the birth of Akbar's son and heir Jahangir. Akbar is shown here seated on the cushion in the center overseeing the construction of the city. The image is contained in the *Akbarnama*, a book of illustrations Akbar commissioned to officially chronicle his reign. *(Victoria & Albert Museum/The Bridgeman Art Library)*

imperial bureaucracy. In 1579 Akbar abolished the **jitza,** the tax on non-Muslims. These actions, especially the abolition of the jitza, infuriated the ulama, and serious conflict erupted between them and the emperor. Ultimately, Akbar issued an imperial decree declaring that the Mughal emperor had supreme authority, even above the ulama, in all religious matters. This statement, resting on a policy of benign toleration, represented a severe defeat for the Muslim religious establishment.

Some of Akbar's successors sided more with the ulama. A combination of religious zeal and financial necessity seems to have prompted Aurangzeb to promote stricter forms of Islam. He appointed censors of public morals in important cities to enforce Islamic laws against gambling, prostitution, drinking, and the use of narcotics. He forbade sati—the self-immolation of widows on their husbands' funeral pyres—and the castration of boys to be sold as eunuchs. He also abolished all taxes not authorized by Islamic law. This measure led to a serious loss of state revenues. To replace them, Aurangzeb in 1679 reimposed the jitza, the tax on non-Muslims.

Regulating Indian society according to Islamic law meant modifying the religious toleration and cultural cosmopolitanism instituted by Akbar. Aurangzeb ordered the destruction of some Hindu temples and tried to curb Sikhism. He required Hindus to pay higher customs duties than Muslims. Out of fidelity to Islamic law, he even criticized his mother's tomb, the Taj Mahal: "The lawfulness of a solid construction over a grave is doubtful, and there can be no doubt about the extravagance involved."[11] Aurangzeb employed more Hindus in the imperial administration than had any previous Mughal ruler, but his religious policy proved highly unpopular with the majority of his subjects.

SHIFTING TRADE ROUTES AND EUROPEAN PENETRATION

How were the Islamic empires affected by the decline in overland trade and the great growth in maritime commerce, and how were European powers able to use trade to make inroads as this period progressed?

The economic foundation of all three Islamic empires was agriculture, and taxes on farmers supported the government and armies. Some new crops, including coffee, sugar, and tobacco, became important in this period, but new world crops do not seem to have led to population increases that were as rapid as elsewhere in Eurasia. By 1800, the population of India was about 190 million, that of Safavid lands about 8 million, and that of Ottoman lands about 24 million (the three together thus less than China, about 300 million in 1800).

Trade was also a crucial element in the economies of these three empires. In 1450 all the great highways of international trade were in Muslim hands, and the wealth of the Muslim states rested heavily on commerce. In the early seventeen century, worldwide economic depression and silver shortages had a devastating effect on the East-West overland trade, from which it never recovered. By 1750 the Muslims had lost control of the trade, which probably contributed to the political decline of these empires (discussed below).

European colonial expansion and shifting trade patterns isolated the Ottomans and the Safavids from the centers of growth in the Western Hemisphere and the East Indies. European trade with the Americas, Africa, and Asia by means of the Atlantic also meant that the old southwestern Asian trade routes were bypassed. To try to revive trade with Europe, the Ottomans signed a series of agreements known as **capitulations.** A trade compact signed in 1536 and renewed in 1569 virtually exempted French merchants from Ottoman law and allowed them to travel and buy and sell throughout the sultan's dominions and to pay low customs duties on French imports and exports.

jitza *A tax on non-Muslims.*

capitulations *A series of agreements that basically surrender the rights of one party. The Ottoman government signed these with European powers and gave them a stranglehold on Ottoman trade and commerce.*

● **Kalamkari Textile from Golconda** Golconda, in southeast India, is the site of a great fortress complex and many palaces, mosques, and Hindu temples that were destroyed in 1687 and left in ruins. This textile is called *kalamkari*, meaning pen or brushed work, and represents a style of design and manufacture unique to the region. Containing a rich variety of Persian, Hindu, and Muslim motifs, this superb example of seventeenth-century painted cotton, depicting various scenes of life in the palace and gardens, suggests the beauty and complexity of Indian textile manufacture. *(The Bridgeman Art Library)*

In 1590, in spite of strong French opposition, a group of English merchants gained the right to trade in Ottoman territory in return for supplying the sultan with iron, steel, brass, and tin for his war with Persia. In 1615, as part of a twenty-year peace treaty, the capitulation rights already given to French and English businessmen were extended to the Habsburgs. These capitulations progressively gave European merchants an economic stranglehold on Ottoman trade and commerce.

Whereas trade between Europe and the Ottomans declined as trade routes shifted, direct trade with India expanded greatly. The Mughal period witnessed the growth of a thriving capitalist commercial economy on the Indian subcontinent. Although most people were engaged in agriculture, from which most imperial revenue was derived, a manufacturing industry supported by a money economy and mercantile capitalism expanded.

Block-printed cotton cloth, produced by artisans working at home, was India's chief export. Through an Islamic business device involving advancing payment to artisans, banker-brokers supplied the material for production and the money that the artisans could live on while they worked; the cloth brokers specified the quality, quantity, and design of the finished product. This procedure resembles the later English "domestic" or "putting-out" system (see page 647), for the very good reason that the English took the idea from the Indians. Within India, the demand for cotton cloth, as well as for food crops, was so great that Akbar had to launch a wide-scale road-building campaign. From Gujarat, Indian merchant bankers shipped their cloth worldwide: across the Indian Ocean to Aden and the Muslim-controlled cities on the east coast of Africa; across the Arabian Sea to Muscat and Hormuz and up the Persian Gulf to the cities of Persia; up the Red Sea to the Mediterranean; by sea also to Malacca, Indonesia, China, and Japan; by land across Africa to Ghana on the west coast; and to Astrakhan, Poland, Moscow, and even the Russian cities on the distant Volga River. In many of these places, Indian businessmen had branch offices. All this activity represented enormous trade, which produced fabulous wealth for some Indian merchants. Some scholars have compared India's international trade in the sixteenth century with that of Italian firms, such as the Medici. The Indian trade actually extended over a far wider area. Indian merchants were often devout Hindus, Muslims, Buddhists, or Jains, evidence that undermines the argument of some Western writers, notably Karl Marx (see page 681), that religion retarded Asia's economic development.

European Rivalry for the Indian Trade

Shortly before Babur's invasion of India, the Portuguese under the navigator Pedro Alvares Cabral had opened the subcontinent to Portuguese trade. In 1510 they established the port of Goa on the Arabian Sea as their headquarters and through a policy of piracy and terrorism took control of Muslim shipping in the Indian and Arabian Oceans (see Map 19.3), charging high fees for passage. The Portuguese historian Barrões attempted to justify Portugal's seizure of commercial traffic that the Muslims had long dominated:

It is true that there does exist a common right to all to navigate the seas and in Europe we recognize the rights which others hold against us; but the right does not extend beyond Europe and therefore the Portuguese as Lords of the Sea are justified in confiscating the goods of all those who navigate the seas without their permission.[12]

In short, Western principles of international law should not restrict them in Asia. For almost a century, the Portuguese controlled the spice trade over the Indian Ocean.

In 1602 the Dutch formed the Dutch East India Company with the stated goal of wresting the enormously lucrative spice trade from the Portuguese. The Dutch concentrated their efforts in Indonesia. The scent of fabulous profits also attracted the English. With a charter signed by Queen Elizabeth, eighty London merchants organized the British East India Company. In 1619 Emperor Jahangir granted a British mission important commercial concessions at Surat on the west coast of India. Gifts, medical services, and bribes to Indian rulers enabled the British to set up twenty-seven other coastal forts. Fort St. George on the east coast became the modern city of Madras. In 1668 the city of Bombay—given to England when the Portuguese princess Catherine of Braganza married King Charles II—was leased to the company, marking the virtually total British absorption of Portuguese power in India. In 1690 the company founded a fort that became the city of Calcutta. Thus the three places that later became centers of British economic and political imperialism—Madras, Bombay, and Calcutta (today called Chennai, Mumbai, and Kolkata)—date back to before 1700.

Factory-Fort Societies

The British called their trading post at Surat a **factory-fort** and the term was later used for all European settlements in India. The term did not signify manufacturing; it

factory-fort *A term first used by the British for their trading post at Surat, it was later applied to all European walled settlements in India.*

● **English Factory-Fort at Surat** The factory-fort began as a storage place for goods before they were bought and transported abroad; it gradually expanded to include merchants' residences and some sort of fortification. By 1650 the English had twenty-three factory-forts in India. Surat, in the Gujarat region on the Gulf of Cambay, was the busiest factory-fort and port until it was sacked by the Marathas in 1664. *(Mansell Collection)*

designated the walled compound containing the residences, gardens, and offices of British East India Company officials and the warehouses where goods were stored before being shipped to Europe. The company president exercised political authority over all residents.

Factory-forts existed to make profits from the Asian-European trade, and they evolved into flourishing sources of economic profit. The British East India Company sold silver, copper, zinc, lead, and fabrics to the Indians and bought cotton goods, silks, pepper and other spices, sugar, and opium from them. By the late seventeenth century, the company was earning substantial profits. Profitability increased after 1700 when the company began to trade with China. Some Indian merchants in Calcutta and Bombay made gigantic fortunes from trade within Asia.

Because the directors of the British East India Company in London discouraged all unnecessary expenses and financial risks, they opposed any interference in local Indian politics and even missionary activities. Political instability in India in the early eighteenth century caused the company's factories to evolve into defensive installations manned by small garrisons of native troops (**sepoys**) trained in Western military drill and tactics. When warlords appeared or an uprising occurred, people from the

sepoys *The native Indian troops who were trained as infantrymen.*

surrounding countryside flocked into the fort, and the company factory-forts gradually came to exercise political authority over the territories around them.

Indian and Chinese wares enjoyed great popularity in England and on the European continent in the late seventeenth and early eighteenth centuries. The middle classes wanted Indian textiles, which were colorful, durable, cheap, and washable. The upper classes desired Chinese wallpaper and porcelains and Indian silks and brocades. Europeans had to pay for everything they bought from Asia with precious metals because Asians had little interest in European manufactured articles. Thus there was insistent pressure in England, France, and the Netherlands against the importation of Asian goods because of the fear that the drain of gold would hurt their economies.

The Rise of the British East India Company

The French were the last to arrive in India. In the 1670s the French East India Company established factories at Chandernagore in Bengal, Pondicherry, and elsewhere. Joseph Dupleix (1697–1764), who was appointed governor general at Pondicherry in 1742, made allies of Indian princes and built an army of native troops who were trained as infantrymen.

From 1740 to 1763, Britain and France were almost continually engaged in a tremendous global struggle. India, like North America in the Seven Years' War, became a battlefield and a prize. The French won land battles, but English sea power decided the first phase of the war. Then a series of brilliant victories destroyed French power

● **Taj Mahal at Agra**   This tomb is the finest example of Muslim architecture in India. Its white marble exterior is inlaid with semiprecious stones in Arabic inscriptions and floral designs. The oblong pool reflects the building, which asserts the power of the Mughal Dynasty. *(John Elk/Stock, Boston)*

in southern India. By preventing French reinforcements from arriving, British sea power again proved to be the determining factor, and British jurisdiction soon extended over the important northern province of Bengal. The Treaty of Paris of 1763 recognized British control of much of India, and scholars view the treaty as the beginning of the British Empire in India.

How was the vast subcontinent to be governed? Parliament believed that the British East India Company had too much power and considered the company responsible for the political disorders in India, which were bad for business. The Regulating Act of 1773 created the office of governor general, with an advisory council, to exercise political authority over the territory controlled by the company. The India Act of 1784 required that the governor general be chosen from outside the company, and it made company directors subject to parliamentary supervision.

Implementation of these reforms fell to three successive governors, Warren Hastings, (r. 1774–1785), Lord Charles Cornwallis (r. 1786–1794), and the marquess Richard Wellesley (r. 1797–1805). Hastings sought allies among Indian princes, laid the foundations for the first Indian civil service, abolished tolls to facilitate internal trade, placed the salt and opium trades under government control, and planned a codification of Muslim and Hindu laws. Cornwallis introduced the British style of property relations, in effect converting a motley collection of former Mughal officers, tax collectors, and others into English-style landlords. The result was a new system of landholding in which the rents of tenant farmers supported the landlords. Wellesley was victorious over local rulers who resisted British rule and vastly extended British influence in India. Like most nineteenth-century British governors of India, Wellesley believed that British rule strongly benefited the Indians. With supreme condescension, he wrote that British power should be established over the Indian princes in order

to deprive them of the means of prosecuting any measure or of forming any confederacy hazardous to the security of the British empire, and to enable us to preserve the tranquility of India by exercising a general control over the restless spirit of ambition and violence which is characteristic of every Asiatic government.[13]

● ● ● ● ● ● ● ● ●

DYNASTIC DECLINE

Did any common factors lead to the decline of the Islamic empires in the seventeenth and eighteenth centuries?

By the eighteenth century, all three of the major Islamic empires were on the defensive. They faced some common problems—succession difficulties, financial strain, loss of military superiority—but their circumstances differed in significant ways as well.

The first to fall was the Safavid Empire. Shah Abbas was succeeded by inept rulers whose heavy indulgence in wine and the pleasures of the harem weakened the monarchy and fed the slow disintegration of the state. Shi'ite religious institutions grew stronger. Decline in the military strength of the army encouraged increased foreign aggression. In 1722 the Afghans invaded from the east, seized Isfahan, and were able to repulse an Ottoman invasion from the west. In Isfahan thousands of officials and members of the shah's family were executed. In the following centuries some strong men emerged, but no leader was able to reunite all of Persia.

The Ottoman throne also suffered from a series of weak sultans. In the fifteenth and early sixteenth centuries, Turkish practice guaranteed that the sultans would be forceful men. The sultan's sons gained administrative experience as governors of provinces and military experience on the battlefield as part of their education. After the sultan died, any son who wanted to succeed had to contest his brothers to claim the throne, after which the new sultan would have his defeated brothers executed. Although bloody, this system led to the succession of capable, determined men. After Suleiman's reign, however, this tradition was abandoned. To prevent threats of usurpation, sons of the sultan were brought up in the harem and confined there as adults, denied a role in government. After years of indolence and dissipation, not surprisingly, few of these princes turned out to be strong military leaders. Selim II (r. 1566–1574), whom the Turks called "Selim the Drunkard," left the conduct of public affairs to his vizier while he pursued the pleasures of the harem. Turkish sources attribute his death to a fall in his bath caused by dizziness when he tried to stop drinking. A series of rulers who were incompetent or minor children left power in the hands of leading bureaucratic officials and the mothers of the heirs. Political factions formed around viziers, military leaders, and palace women. In the contest for political favor, the devshirme was abandoned, and political and military ranks were filled by Muslims.

As in parts of Europe, rising population without corresponding economic growth caused serious social problems. A long period of peace in the late sixteenth century and again in the mid-eighteenth century and a decline in the frequency of visits of the plague led to a doubling of the population. The land could not sustain so many people, nor could the towns provide jobs for the thousands of agricultural workers who fled to them. The return of demobilized soldiers aggravated the problem. Inflation, famine, and widespread revolts resulted. The economic center of gravity shifted from the capital to the provinces, and politically the empire began to decentralize as well. Local notables and military men, rather than central officials, exercised political power. Provincial autonomy brought more people into political participation, thus laying a foundation for later nationalism.

Ottoman armies began losing wars and territory along their European borders. The army was depending more on mercenaries, and military technology fell behind. The Ottomans did not keep up with the innovations in drill and command and control that were then transforming European armies. By the terms of the peace treaty with Austria signed at Karlowitz (1699), the Ottomans lost the major European provinces of Hungary and Transylvania, along with the tax revenues they had provided.

In Mughal India the old Turkish practice of letting the heirs fight for the throne persisted, leading to frequent struggles over succession, but also to strong rulers. Yet military challenges proved daunting there as well. After defeating his father and brothers, Aurangzeb pushed the conquest of the south. The stiffest opposition came from the Marathas, a militant Hindu group centered in the western Deccan. From 1681 until his death in 1707, Aurangzeb led repeated sorties through the Deccan. He took many forts and won several battles, but total destruction of the Maratha guerrilla bands eluded him. After his death, they played an important role in the collapse of the Mughal Empire.

Aurangzeb's death led to thirteen years of succession struggles, shattering the empire. His eighteenth-century successors were less successful than the Ottomans in making the dynasty the focus of loyalty. Mughal provincial governors began to rule independently, giving only minimal allegiance to the badshah at Delhi. The Marathas, who pressed steadily northward, constituted the gravest threat to Mughal authority. No ruler could defeat them.

In 1739 the Persian adventurer Nadir Shah invaded India, defeated the Mughal army, looted Delhi, and after a savage massacre carried off a huge amount of treasure, including the Peacock Throne. When Nadir Shah withdrew to Afghanistan, he took with him the Mughal government's prestige. Constant skirmishes between the Afghans and the Marathas for control of the Punjab and northern India ended in 1761 at Panipat, where the Marathas were crushed by the Afghans. At that point, India no longer had any power capable of imposing order on the subcontinent or checking the penetration of the rapacious Europeans.

Chapter Summary

To assess your mastery of this chapter, go to
bedfordstmartins.com/mckayworld

• *How were the three Islamic empires established, and what sorts of governments did they set up?*

After the decline of the Mongols in Central Asia and Persia, many small Turkic-ruled states emerged. Three of them went on to establish large empires: the Ottomans in Anatolia, the Safavids in Persia, and the Mughals in India. In each case, the state steadily expanded for several generations, though it did eventually run up against foes it could not defeat. All three empires responded to the shift in military technology away from the mounted archer toward the use of gunpowder weapons. The Ottomans in particular made effective use of guns and artillery.

• *What cultural advances occurred under the rule of these three houses?*

The wealth of these empires provided the material basis for a great cultural efflorescence. Royal patronage was especially important in the building of palaces and cities. Other major arts of the period included carpets and book illustrations. Intellectually, this was a fertile period for both natural science and religious speculation. Islam received special protection and support from all three governments, but there were key differences: The Ottomans and Mughals supported the Sunni tradition, the Safavids, the Shi'ite tradition.

• *How did Christians, Jews, Hindus, and other non-Muslims fare under these Islamic states?*

All of the Islamic empires had substantial non-Muslim subjects. The Ottomans ruled over the Balkans, where most of the people were Christian. In India, Muslims were outnumbered by Hindus. Following Islamic teachings, Christians and Jews were not persecuted in these empires, and Hindus in India came to be treated as though they too were "protected" people.

• *How were the Islamic empires affected by the decline in overland trade and the great growth in maritime commerce, and how were European powers able to use trade to make inroads as this period progressed?*

The Islamic regions of Eurasia had been the crossroads of East-West and North-South trade for many centuries, but with the great expansion of European maritime trade in the late fifteenth and sixteenth centuries, trade between Europe and India, China, and Southeast Asia shifted decisively to the maritime route. Indian textiles, much desired in Southeast Asia and China, attracted European businessmen. The inability of Indian leaders in the eighteenth century to resolve their domestic differences led first to British intervention and then to British rule of several parts of the Indian subcontinent.

• *Did any common factors lead to the decline of the Islamic empires in the seventeenth and eighteenth centuries?*

The eighteenth century saw the destruction of the Safavid Empire and the great decline in the reach of the Mughal Empire. The Ottomans, too, suffered major setbacks in the seventeenth and eighteenth centuries (though they would make a comeback in the nineteenth century). Some of the common problems these empires faced were the end of expansion, difficulties with succession, tendencies toward decentralization, and population growth not matched by economic growth. In India, the Mughals faced not only tendencies toward decentralization but also the appearance of new foes, traders from Europe backed by their governments.

Suggested Reading

Atil, Esin. *The Age of Sultan Suleyman the Magnificent.* 1987. A splendidly illustrated celebration of the man and his times.

Dale, Stephen Frederic. *The Garden of the Eight Paradises: Babur and the Culture of Empire in Central Asia, Afghanistan and India, 1483–1750.* 2004. A scholarly biography that draws on and analyzes Babur's autobiography.

Findley, Carter Vaughn. *The Turks in World History.* 2005. Takes a macro look at the three Islamic empires as part of the history of the Turks.

Finkel, Caroline. *Osman's Dream: A History of the Ottoman Empire.* 2006. A new interpretation that views the Ottomans from their own perspective.

Inalcik, Halil, and Renda Günsel. *Ottoman Civilization.* 2002. A huge, beautifully illustrated, government-sponsored overview, with emphasis on the arts and culture.

Jackson, Peter, and Lawrence Lockhart, eds. *The Cambridge History of Iran,* Vol. 6, *The Timurid and Safavid*

Periods. 1986. A set of essays on the social and cultural as well as political and economic history of Iran by leading scholars.

Lapidus, Ira M. *A History of Islamic Societies,* 2nd ed. 2002. A comprehensive yet lucid survey.

Mukhia, Harbans. *The Mughals of India: A Framework for Understanding.* 2004. A short but thoughtful analysis of the Mughal society and state.

Pierce, Leslie. *The Imperial Harem: Women and Sovereignty in the Ottoman Empire.* 1993. A fresh look at the role of elite women under the Ottomans.

Richards, John F. *The Mughal Empire.* 1993. Offers a coherent narrative history of the period 1526–1720.

Ruthven, Malise, and Azim Nanji. *Historical Atlas of Islam.* 2004. Provides numerous maps illustrating the shifting political history of Islamic states.

Notes

1. Quoted in B. Lewis, *The Muslim Discovery of Europe* (New York: W. W. Norton, 1982), p. 29.
2. W. H. McNeill, *The Pursuit of Power: Technology, Armed Force, and Society Since A.D. 1000* (Chicago: University of Chicago Press, 1982), p. 87.
3. D. Morgan, *Medieval Persia, 1040–1797* (New York: Longman, 1988), pp. 112–113.
4. Quoted in M. C. Beach, *The Imperial Image: Paintings for the Mughal Court* (Washington, D.C.: Freer Gallery of Art, Smithsonian Institution, 1981), pp. 9–10.
5. Quoted in V. A. Smith, *The Oxford History of India* (Oxford: Oxford University Press, 1967), p. 398.
6. J. Goody, *The Culture of Flowers* (Cambridge: Cambridge University Press, 1993), p. 103.
7. See William McNeill, *Plagues and Peoples* (New York: Anchor Books, 1998), pp. 198–199.

8. F. Babinger, *Mehmed the Conqueror and His Times,* trans. R. Manheim (Princeton, N.J.: Princeton University Press, 1978), p. 107.
9. R. M. Eaton, *The Rise of Islam and the Bengal Frontier, 1204–1760* (Berkeley: University of California Press, 1993), p. 115.
10. J. F. Richards, *The New Cambridge History of India: The Mughal Empire* (Cambridge: Cambridge University Press, 1995), p. 45.
11. Quoted in S. K. Ikram, *Muslim Civilization in India* (New York: Columbia University Press, 1964), p. 202.
12. Quoted in K. M. Panikkar, *Asia and Western Domination* (London: George Allen & Unwin, 1965), p. 35.
13. Quoted in W. Bingham, H. Conroy, and F. W. Iklé, *A History of Asia,* vol. 2 (Boston: Allyn and Bacon, 1967), p. 74.

Listening to the PAST

The Weighing of Shah Jahan on His Forty-Second Lunar Birthday*

In 1799 the nawab (provincial governor) of Oudh in northern India sent to King George III of Great Britain the Padshahnama, or official history of the reign of Shah Jahan. A volume composed of 239 folios on very high-quality gold-flecked tan paper with forty-four stunningly beautiful paintings illustrating the text, the Padshahnama represents both a major historical chronicle of a Mughal emperor's reign and an extraordinary artistic achievement. One of the great art treasures of the world, it now rests in the Royal Library at Windsor.

All the Mughal emperors had a strong historical sense and the desire to preserve records of their reigns. They brought to India the traditional Muslim respect for books as sources of secular and religious knowledge and as images of their wealth and power. The Padshahnama, in stressing Shah Jahan's descent from Tamerlane and his right to the throne, in celebrating his bravery and military prowess, and in magnifying his virtues, is one long glorification of Jahan's rule. The Persian scholar and calligrapher Abdul-Hamid Lahawri wrote the text. Many Persian artists painted the illustrations with detailed precision and an exactitude that art historians consider sensitive and faithful to the original.

Since alms are beneficial for repelling bodily and psychic harm and for attracting spiritual and corporeal benefits, as all peoples, religions, and nations are agreed, His Majesty Arsh-Ashyani [Akbar] established the custom of weighing and had himself weighed twice [a year], once after the end of the solar year and the other after the end of the lunar year. In the solar weighing he was weighed twelve times, first against gold and then eleven other items, while in the lunar weighing he was weighed eight times, first against silver and then seven other items. . . . The amounts from the weighings were given away in alms.

. . . Inasmuch as it benefited the needy, His Majesty Jahanbani [Shah Jahan] has his perfect self weighed twice, and in his generosity he has ordered that gold and silver be used each time. . . .

The lunar weighing ceremony for the end of the forty-third year of the Emperor's life was held. The Emperor, surrounded by a divine aura, was weighed against gold and the other usual things, and the skirt of the world was held out in expectation of gold and silver. On this auspicious day Muhammad-Ali Beg, the ambassador of Iran, was awarded a gold-embroidered robe of honor, a jeweled belt, an elephant, a female elephant, and four large ashrafis, one weighing 400 tolas [a measure of weight, slightly more than two mithcals], the second 300 tolas, the third 200 tolas, and the fourth 100 tolas, and four rupees also of the weights given above, and he was given leave to depart. From the time he paid homage until the time he set out to return he had been given 316,000 rupees in cash and nearly a lac of rupees in goods.

An earlier weighing ceremony of the Emperor Jahangir, on 1 September 1617, was described by the always observant, and usually skeptical, first English ambassador to the Mughal court, Sir Thomas Roe: "Was the Kings Birthday, and the solemnitie of his weighing, to which I went, and was carryed into a very large and beautifull Garden; the square within all water; on the sides flowres and trees. . . . Here attended the Nobilitie, all sitting about it on Carpets, vntill the King came; who at last appeared clothed, or rather loden with Diamonds, Rubies, Pearles, and other precious vanities, so great, so glorious! . . . Suddenly hee entered into the scales, sate like a woman on his legges, and there was put against him many bagges to fit his weight, which were changed sixe times, and they say was siluer, and that I vnderstood his weight to be nine thousand Rupias, which are almost one thousand pound sterling."

Another official history of Shah Jahan's reign, the 'Amal-i-Salih, describes the ceremonial weighing that took place another year.

*A solar year is the time required for the earth to make one complete revolution around the sun (365 days). A lunar year equals 12 lunar months.

The "Weighing of Shah Jahan," who sits cross-legged on one plate of the scales, as bags of gold and silver wait to be placed on the other side. *(The Royal Collection © 2007, Her Majesty Queen Elizabeth II)*

Since it is His Majesty's custom and habit to have beggars sought out, and his generous nature is always looking for a pretext to relieve those who are in need, therefore twice a year he sits, like the orient sun in majesty, in the pan of the scale of auspiciousness in the solar and lunar weighing ceremonies. Twice a year by solar and lunar calculation a magnificent celebration and a large-scale banquet is arranged by order of His Majesty. An amount equal to his weight in gold and silver is distributed among the destitute and the poor according to their deservedness and merits. Although this type of alms is not mentioned in the religious law, nonetheless since scholars of this country are all in agreement that such alms are the most perfect type of alms for repelling corporeal and spiritual catastrophes and calamities, therefore this pleasing method was chosen and established by His Majesty Arsh-Ashyani, whose personality was, like the world-illuminating sun, based upon pure effulgence. By this means the poor attained their wishes, and in truth the custom of *aqiqa*—which is an established custom in the law

of the Prophet and his Companions, and in which on the seventh day after birth the equivalent weight of an infant's shaven hair in silver is given in alms, and a sacrificial animal is divided and distributed among the poor—has opened the way to making this custom permissible.

Questions for Analysis

1. Consider Shah Jahan's motives for the practice of ceremonial weighing. Does it have any theological basis?

2. Compare the Mughal practice to something similar in Ottoman, European, and South American societies.

Source: King of the World. The Padshahnama. An Imperial Mughal Manuscript from the Royal Library, Windsor Castle, ed. Milo Cleveland Beach and Ebba Koch, trans. Wheeler Thackston (Washington, D.C.: Azimuth Editions—Sackler Gallery, 1997, pp. 39–43). Reprinted by permission of W. M. Thackston, translator.

Voltaire, the renowned Enlightenment thinker, leans forward on the left to exchange ideas and witty conversation with Frederick the Great, king of Prussia. *(Bildarchiv Preussischer Kulturbesitz/ Art Resource, NY)*

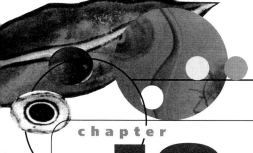

18

chapter preview

The Scientific Revolution
- *What was revolutionary in new attitudes toward the natural world?*

The Enlightenment
- *How did the new worldview affect the way people thought about society and human relations?*

The Enlightenment and Absolutism
- *What impact did this new way of thinking have on political developments and monarchical absolutism?*

TOWARD A NEW WORLDVIEW, 1540–1789

The intellectual developments of the seventeenth and eighteenth centuries created the modern worldview that the West continues to hold—and debate—to this day. In the seventeenth century fundamentally new ways of understanding the natural world emerged. Those leading the changes saw themselves as philosophers and referred to their field of study as "natural philosophy." In the nineteenth century scholars hailed their achievements as a "scientific revolution" that produced modern science as we know it. The new "science" created in the seventeenth century entailed the search for precise knowledge of the physical world based on the union of experimental observations with sophisticated mathematics. Whereas medieval scholars looked to authoritative texts like the Bible or the classics, seventeenth-century natural philosophers performed experiments and relied on increasingly complex mathematical calculations. The resulting conception of the universe and its laws remained in force until Einstein's discoveries in the first half of the twentieth century.

In the eighteenth century philosophers extended the use of reason from nature to human society. They sought to bring the light of reason to bear on the darkness of prejudice, outmoded traditions, and ignorance. Self-proclaimed members of an "Enlightenment" movement, they wished to bring the same progress to human affairs as their predecessors had brought to the understanding of the natural world. While the scientific revolution ushered in modern science, the Enlightenment created concepts of human rights, equality, progress, universalism, and tolerance that still guide Western societies today.

While many view the scientific revolution and the Enlightenment as bedrocks of the achievement of Western civilization, others have seen a darker side. For these critics, the mastery over nature permitted by the scientific revolution threatens to overwhelm the earth's fragile equilibrium, and the belief in the universal application of "reason" can lead to arrogance and intolerance, particularly intolerance of other people's spiritual values. Such vivid debates about the legacy of these intellectual and cultural developments testify to their continuing importance in today's world.

Book Companion Site

This icon will direct you to primary sources and study materials available at **bedfordstmartins.com/mckaywest**

The Scientific Revolution

The emergence of modern science was a development of tremendous long-term significance. A noted historian has even said that the scientific revolution of the late sixteenth and seventeenth centuries "outshines everything since the rise of Christianity and reduces the Renaissance and Reformation to the rank of mere episodes, mere internal displacements, within the system of medieval Christendom." The scientific revolution was "the real origin both of the modern world and the modern mentality."[1] This statement is an exaggeration, but not much of one. Of all the great civilizations, only that of the West developed modern science. With the scientific revolution Western society began to acquire its most distinctive traits.

• *What was revolutionary in new attitudes toward the natural world?*

Scientific Thought in 1500

Since developments in astronomy and physics were at the heart of the scientific revolution, one must begin with the traditional European conception of the universe. It is important to remember that the practitioners of the scientific revolution did not consider their field *science* but rather **natural philosophy**. Their intention was not to create modern science but to ask fundamental questions about the nature of the universe, its purpose, and how it functioned. They did not set supernatural questions aside, as do modern scientists, but incorporated them in their speculations, which made reference not only to Christian theology but often to magic, alchemy, and astrology as well. The dividing line between matter and spirit, or reason and faith, was much less rigid for participants in the scientific revolution than it is for scientists today.

In the early 1500s natural philosophy was still based primarily on the ideas of Aristotle,

the great Greek philosopher of the fourth century B.C. These ideas had gradually been recovered during the Middle Ages. Medieval theologians such as Thomas Aquinas brought Aristotelian philosophy into harmony with Christian doctrines. According to this revised Aristotelian view, a motionless earth was fixed at the center of the universe. Around it moved ten separate transparent crystal spheres. In the first eight spheres were embedded, in turn, the moon, the sun, the five known planets, and the fixed stars. Then followed two spheres added during the Middle Ages to account for slight changes in the positions of the stars over the centuries. Beyond the tenth sphere was Heaven, with the throne of God and the souls of the saved. Angels kept the spheres moving in perfect circles.

Aristotle's views, suitably revised by medieval philosophers, also dominated thinking about physics and motion on earth. Aristotle had distinguished sharply between the world of the celestial spheres and that of the earth—the sublunar world. The spheres consisted of a perfect, incorruptible "quintessence," or fifth essence. The sublunar world, however, was made up of four imperfect, changeable elements. The "light" elements (air and fire) naturally moved upward, while the "heavy" elements (water and earth) naturally moved downward. These nat-

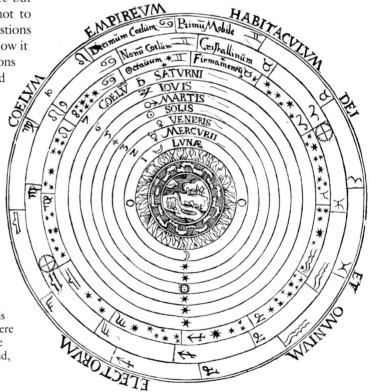

The Aristotelian Universe as Imagined in the Sixteenth Century A round earth is at the center, surrounded by spheres of water, air, and fire. Beyond this small nucleus, the moon, the sun, and the five planets were embedded in their own rotating crystal spheres, with the stars sharing the surface of one enormous sphere. Beyond, the heavens were composed of unchanging ether. (*Image Select/Art Resource, NY*)

ural directions of motion did not always prevail, however, for elements were often mixed together and could be affected by an outside force such as a human being. Aristotle and his followers also believed that a uniform force moved an object at a constant speed and that the object would stop as soon as that force was removed.

Aristotle's ideas about astronomy and physics were accepted with minor revisions for two thousand years, and with good reason. First, they offered an understandable, commonsense explanation for what the eye actually saw. Second, Aristotle's science as interpreted by Christian theologians fit neatly with Christian doctrines. It established a home for God and a place for Christian souls. It put human beings at the center of the universe and made them the critical link in a "great chain of being" that stretched from the throne of God to the most lowly insect on earth. Thus examination of the natural world was primarily a branch of theology, and it reinforced religious thought.

The Copernican Hypothesis

The desire to explain and thereby glorify God's handiwork led to the first great departure from the medieval system. This departure was the work of the Polish clergyman and astronomer Nicolaus Copernicus (1473–1543). As a young man Copernicus studied church law and astronomy in various European universities. He saw how professional astronomers still depended for their most accurate calculations on the second century B.C. work of Ptolemy. Author of a geographical synthesis that profoundly influenced European voyages of exploration (see page 494), Ptolemy was also a great astronomer. His achievement had been to work out complicated rules to explain the minor irregularities in the movement of the planets. These rules enabled stargazers and astrologers to track the planets with greater precision. Many people then (and now) believed that the changing relationships between planets and stars influenced events on earth.

The young Copernicus was uninterested in astrology and felt that Ptolemy's cumbersome and occasionally inaccurate rules detracted from the majesty of a perfect Creator. He preferred an old Greek idea being discussed in Renaissance Italy: that the sun, rather than the earth, was at the center of the universe. Finishing his university studies and returning to a church position in East Prussia, Copernicus worked on his hypothesis from 1506 to 1530. Never questioning the Aristotelian belief in crystal spheres or the idea that circular motion was most perfect and divine, Copernicus theorized that the stars and planets, including the earth, revolved around a fixed sun.

Chronology

ca 1540–1690	Scientific revolution
1543	Copernicus, *On the Revolutions of the Heavenly Spheres*
1564–1642	Life of Galileo
1571–1630	Life of Kepler
1662	Royal Society of London founded
1687	Newton, *Principia* and law of universal gravitation
1690	Locke, *Essay Concerning Human Understanding*
ca 1690–1780	Enlightenment
1694–1778	Life of Voltaire
1700–1789	Growth of book publishing
1720–1780	Rococo style in art and decoration
ca 1740–1780	Salons led by elite women
1740–1786	Reign of Frederick the Great of Prussia
ca 1750–1790	Enlightened absolutists
1751–1765	Diderot and d'Alembert, *Encyclopedia*
1762	Rousseau, *The Social Contract*
1762–1796	Reign of Catherine the Great of Russia
1780–1790	Reign of Joseph II of Austria

Yet Copernicus was a cautious man. Fearing the ridicule of other astronomers, he did not publish his *On the Revolutions of the Heavenly Spheres* until 1543, the year of his death.

The **Copernican hypothesis** had enormous scientific and religious implications, many of which the conservative Copernicus did not anticipate. First, it put the stars at rest, their apparent nightly movement simply a result of the earth's rotation. Thus it destroyed the main reason for believing in crystal spheres capable of moving the stars around the earth. Second, Copernicus's theory suggested a universe of staggering size. If in the course of a year the earth moved around the sun and yet the stars appeared to remain in the same place, then the universe was unthinkably large. Finally, by characterizing the earth as just another planet, Copernicus destroyed the basic idea of Aristotelian physics—that the earthly world was quite different from the heavenly one. Where, then, was the realm of perfection? Where were Heaven and the throne of God?

Book Companion Site

Primary Source: Commentariolus: Copernicus Outlines His Thesis

The Copernican hypothesis brought sharp attacks from religious leaders, especially Protestants. Martin Luther spoke of him as the "new astrologer who wants to prove that the earth moves and goes round. . . . The fool wants to turn the whole art of astronomy upside down." Luther noted that "as the Holy Scripture tells us, so did Joshua bid the sun stand still and not the earth."[2] John Calvin also condemned Copernicus. Catholic reaction was milder at first. The Catholic Church had never held to literal interpretations of the Bible, and not until 1616 did it officially declare the Copernican hypothesis false.

This slow reaction also reflected the slow progress of Copernicus's theory for many years. Other events were almost as influential in creating doubts about traditional astronomical ideas. In 1572 a new star appeared and shone very brightly for almost two years. The new star, which was actually a distant exploding star, made an enormous impression on people. It seemed to contradict the idea that the heavenly spheres were unchanging and therefore perfect. In 1577 a new comet suddenly moved through the sky, cutting a straight path across the supposedly impenetrable crystal spheres. It was time, as a typical scientific writer put it, for "the radical renovation of astronomy."[3]

From Brahe to Galileo

One astronomer who agreed was Tycho Brahe (1546–1601). Born into a prominent Danish noble family, Brahe was tremendously impressed by a partial eclipse of the sun at an early age. Completing his studies abroad and returning to Denmark, he established himself as Europe's leading astronomer with his detailed observations of the new star of 1572. Aided by generous grants from the king of Denmark, Brahe built the most sophisticated observatory of his day. For twenty years he meticulously observed the stars and planets with the naked eye. An imposing man who had lost a piece of his nose in a duel and replaced it with a special bridge of gold and silver alloy, a noble who exploited his peasants arrogantly and approached the heavens humbly, Brahe contributed a great mass of data. His limited understanding of mathematics prevented him, however, from making much sense out of his data. Part Ptolemaic, part Copernican, he

believed that all the planets revolved around the sun and that the entire group of sun and planets revolved in turn around the earth-moon system.

It was left to Brahe's brilliant young assistant, Johannes Kepler (1571–1630), to go much further. Kepler was a medieval figure in many ways. Coming from a minor German noble family and trained for the Lutheran ministry, he long believed that the universe was built on mystical mathematical relationships and a musical harmony of the heavenly bodies. Working and reworking Brahe's mountain of observations in a staggering effort after the Dane's death, this brilliant mathematician eventually went beyond mystical intuitions.

Kepler formulated three famous laws of planetary motion. First, building on Copernican theory, he demonstrated in 1609 that the orbits of the planets around the sun are elliptical rather than circular. Second, he demonstrated that the planets do not move at a uniform speed in their orbits. Third, in 1619 he showed that the time a planet takes to make its complete orbit is precisely related to its distance from the sun. Kepler's contribution was monumental. Whereas Copernicus had speculated, Kepler proved mathematically the precise relations of a sun-centered (solar) system. His work demolished the old system of Aristotle and Ptolemy, and in his third law he came close to formulating the idea of universal gravitation.

While Kepler was unraveling planetary motion, a young Florentine named Galileo Galilei (1564–1642) was challenging all the old ideas about motion. Like so many early scientists, Galileo was a poor nobleman first marked for a religious career. However, he soon became fascinated by mathematics. A brilliant student, in 1589 Galileo became a professor of mathematics at age twenty-five. He proceeded to examine motion and mechanics in a new way. Indeed, his great achievement was the elaboration and consolidation of the **experimental method.** That is, rather than speculate about what might or should happen, Galileo conducted controlled experiments to find out what actually *did* happen. In his famous acceleration experiment, he showed that a uniform force—in this case, gravity—produced a uniform acceleration. Here is how Galileo described his pathbreaking method and conclusion in his *Two New Sciences:*

A piece of wooden moulding . . . was taken; on its edge was cut a channel a little more than one finger in breadth. Having made this groove very straight, smooth and polished, and having lined it with parchment, also as smooth and polished as possible, we rolled along it a hard, smooth and very round bronze ball. . . . Noting . . . the time required to make the descent . . . we now rolled the ball only one-quarter the length of the channel; and having measured the time of its descent, we found it precisely one-half of the former. . . . In such experiments [over many distances], repeated a full hundred times, we always found that the spaces traversed were to each other as the squares of the times, and that this was true for all inclinations of the plane.[4]

With this and other experiments, Galileo formulated the **law of inertia.** Rest was not the natural state of objects. Rather, an object continues in motion forever unless stopped by some external force. Aristotelian physics was in shambles.

In the tradition of Brahe, Galileo also applied the experimental method to astronomy. On hearing details about the invention of the telescope in Holland, Galileo made one for himself and trained it on the heavens. He quickly discovered the first four moons of Jupiter, which clearly suggested that Jupiter could not possibly be embedded in any impenetrable crystal sphere. This discovery provided new evidence for the Copernican theory, in which Galileo already believed. Galileo then pointed his telescope at the moon. He wrote in 1610 in *Siderus Nuncius:*

I feel sure that the moon is not perfectly smooth, free from inequalities, and exactly spherical, as a large school of philosophers considers with regard to the moon and the other heavenly bodies. On the contrary, it is full of inequalities, uneven, full of hollows and protuberances, just like the surface of the earth itself, which is varied. . . . The next object which I have observed is the essence or substance of the Milky Way. By the aid of a telescope anyone may behold this in a manner which so distinctly appeals to the senses that all the disputes which have tormented philosophers through so many ages are exploded by the irrefutable evidence of our eyes, and we are freed from wordy disputes upon the subject. For the galaxy is nothing else but a mass of innumerable stars planted together in clusters.[5]

Reading these famous lines, one feels a crucial corner in Western civilization being turned. The traditional religious worldview, which rested on determining and accepting the proper established authority, was beginning to give way to a new method. This new method of learning and investigating was the greatest accomplishment of the entire scientific revolution, for it proved capable of great extension. A historian investigating documents of

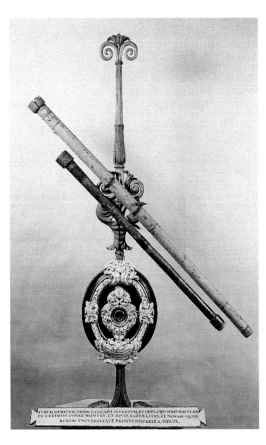

Galileo's Paintings of the Moon When Galileo published the results of his telescopic observations of the moon, he added these paintings to illustrate the marvels he had seen. Galileo made two telescopes, which are shown here. The larger one magnifies fourteen times, the smaller one twenty times. *(Biblioteca Nazionale Centrale, Florence/Art Resource, NY; Museum of Science, Florence/Art Resource, NY)*

the past, for example, is not so different from a Galileo studying stars and rolling balls.

Galileo was employed in Florence by the Medici grand dukes of Tuscany, and his work eventually aroused the ire of some theologians. The issue was presented in 1624 to Pope Urban VIII, who permitted Galileo to write about different possible systems of the world as long as he did not presume to judge which one actually existed. After the publication in Italian of his widely read *Dialogue on the Two Chief Systems of the World* in 1632, which openly lampooned the traditional views of Aristotle and Ptolemy and defended those of Copernicus, Galileo was tried for heresy by the papal Inquisition. Imprisoned and threatened with torture, the aging Galileo recanted, "renouncing and cursing" his Copernican errors.

Newton's Synthesis

The accomplishments of Kepler, Galileo, and other scientists had taken effect by about 1640. The old astronomy and physics were in ruins, and several fundamental breakthroughs had been made. The new findings had not, however, been fused together in a new synthesis, a single explanatory system that would comprehend motion both on earth and in the skies. That synthesis, which prevailed until the twentieth century, was the work of Isaac Newton (1642–1727).

Newton was born into lower English gentry and attended Cambridge University. A genius who spectacularly united the experimental and theoretical-mathematical sides of modern science, Newton was also fascinated by alchemy. He sought the elixir of life and a way to change base metals into gold and silver. Newton was also intensely religious. He was far from being the perfect rationalist so endlessly eulogized by writers in the eighteenth and nineteenth centuries.

Of his intellectual genius and incredible powers of concentration there can be no doubt. Arriving at some of his most basic ideas about physics in 1666 at age twenty-four, but unable to prove these theories mathematically, he attained a professorship and studied optics for many years. In 1684 Newton returned to physics for eighteen extraordinarily intensive months. For weeks on end he seldom left his room except to read his lectures. His meals were sent up, but he usually forgot to eat them, his mind fastened like a vise on the laws of the universe. He opened the third book of his immortal *Mathematical Principles of Natural Philosophy,* published in Latin in 1687 and generally known as the *Principia,* with these lines:

Isaac Newton   This portrait suggests the depth and complexity of the great genius. Is the powerful mind behind those piercing eyes thinking of science or of religion, or perhaps of both? *(Scala/Art Resource, NY)*

In the preceding books I have laid down the principles of philosophy [that is, science]. . . . These principles are the laws of certain motions, and powers or forces, which chiefly have respect to philosophy. . . . It remains that from the same principles I now demonstrate the frame of the System of the World.

Newton made good his grandiose claim. His towering accomplishment was to integrate in a single explanatory system the astronomy of Copernicus, as corrected by Kepler's laws, with the physics of Galileo and his predecessors. Newton did this by means of a set of mathematical laws that explain motion and mechanics. These laws of dynamics are complex, and it took scientists and engineers two hundred years to work out all their implications. Nevertheless, the key feature of the Newtonian synthesis was the **law of universal gravitation.** According to this law, every body in the universe attracts every other body in the universe in a precise mathematical relationship, whereby the force of attraction is proportional to the quantity of matter of the objects and inversely proportional to the square of the distance between them. The whole universe—from Kepler's elliptical orbits to Galileo's rolling balls—was unified in one majestic system.

Causes of the Scientific Revolution

The scientific revolution drew on long-term developments in European culture. The first was the development of the medieval university. By the thirteenth century permanent universities with professors and large student bodies had been established in western Europe to train the lawyers, doctors, and church leaders society required. By 1300 philosophy had taken its place alongside law, medicine, and theology. Medieval philosophers developed a limited but real independence from theologians and a sense of free inquiry. They nobly pursued a body of knowledge and tried to arrange it meaningfully by means of abstract theories.

Within this framework what we now think of as science was able to emerge as a minor but distinct branch of philosophy. In the fourteenth and fifteenth centuries leading universities established new professorships of mathematics, astronomy, and physics (natural philosophy) within their faculties of philosophy. Although the prestige of the new fields was low, critical thinking was now applied to scientific problems by a permanent community of scholars. And an outlet existed for the talents of a Galileo or a Newton: all the great pathfinders either studied or taught at universities.

Second, the Renaissance also stimulated scientific progress. The recovery of the finest works of Greek mathematics—a byproduct of Renaissance humanism's ceaseless search for the knowledge of antiquity—greatly improved European mathematics. The recovery of more texts also showed that classical mathematicians had their differences; Europeans were thus forced to try to resolve these ancient controversies by means of their own efforts. Finally, Renaissance patrons, especially in Italy, often supported scientists as well as artists and writers. Various rulers and wealthy business people funded scientific investigations, as the Medicis of Florence did for Galileo.

The navigational problems of long sea voyages in the age of overseas expansion were a third factor in the scientific revolution. Ship captains on distant shores needed to be able to chart their positions as accurately as possible so that reliable maps could be drawn and the risks of international trade reduced. As early as 1484 the king of Portugal appointed a commission of mathematicians to perfect tables to help seamen find their latitude. This resulted in the first European navigation manual. Navigational problems were also critical in the development of many new scientific instruments, such as the telescope, barometer, thermometer, pendulum clock, microscope, and air pump. Better instruments, which permitted more accurate observations, often led to important new knowledge. Galileo with his telescope was by no means unique.

Better instruments were part of a fourth factor in the scientific revolution: the development of better ways of obtaining knowledge about the world. Two important thinkers, Francis Bacon (1561–1626) and René Descartes (1596–1650), represented key aspects of this improvement in scientific methodology.

The English politician and writer Francis Bacon was the greatest early propagandist for the new experimental method. Rejecting the Aristotelian and medieval method of using speculative reasoning to build general theories, Bacon argued that new knowledge had to be pursued through empirical experimental research. The researcher who wants to learn more about leaves or rocks should not speculate about the subject but should rather collect a multitude of specimens and then compare and analyze them, he said. General principles will then emerge. Bacon's contribution was to formalize the empirical method, which had already been used by Brahe and Galileo, into the general theory of inductive reasoning known as **empiricism**.

Book Companion Site
Primary Source: Francis Bacon Rejects Superstition and Extols the Virtue of Science

The French philosopher René Descartes was a true genius who made his first great discovery in mathematics. As a twenty-three-year-old soldier serving in the Thirty Years' War, he experienced a life-changing intellectual vision on a single night in 1619. Descartes saw that there was a perfect correspondence between geometry and algebra and that geometrical, spatial figures could be expressed as algebraic equations and vice versa. A major step forward in the history of mathematics, Descartes's discovery of analytic geometry provided scientists with an important new tool.

Descartes's greatest achievement was to develop his initial vision into a whole philosophy of knowledge and science. He decided it was necessary to doubt everything that could reasonably be doubted and then, as in geometry, to use deductive reasoning from self-evident principles to ascertain scientific laws. Descartes's reasoning ultimately reduced all substances to "matter" and

The Observatory at Nuremberg The quest for scientific knowledge in the seventeenth century was already an expensive undertaking that required teamwork and government support, as this encyclopedic illustration suggests. Nuremberg was a historic center of commerce and culture in southern Germany, and its observatory played a pioneering role in early astronomical advances. *(Kunstsammlungen der Veste Coburg)*

"mind"—that is, to the physical and the spiritual. His view of the world as consisting of two fundamental entities is known as **Cartesian dualism.** Descartes was a profoundly original and extremely influential thinker.

Bacon's inductive experimentalism and Descartes's deductive, mathematical reasoning are combined in the modern scientific method, which began to crystallize in the late seventeenth century. Neither man's extreme approach was sufficient by itself. Bacon's inability to appreciate the importance of mathematics and his obsession with practical results clearly showed the limitations of antitheoretical empiricism. Likewise, some of Descartes's positions—he believed, for example, that it was possible to deduce the whole science of medicine from first principles—demonstrated the inadequacy of rigid, dogmatic rationalism. Thus the modern scientific method has joined precise observations and experimentalism with the search for general laws that may be expressed in rigorously logical, mathematical language.

Finally, there is the question of the role of religion in the development of science. Just as some historians have argued that Protestantism led to the rise of capitalism, others have concluded that Protestantism was a fundamental factor in the rise of modern science. Protestantism, particularly in its Calvinist varieties, supposedly made scientific inquiry a question of individual conscience and not of religious doctrine. The Catholic Church, in contrast, supposedly suppressed scientific theories that conflicted with its teachings and thus discouraged scientific progress. The truth is more complicated. *All* Western religious authorities—Catholic, Protestant, and Jewish—opposed the Copernican system to a greater or lesser extent until about 1630, by which time the scientific revolution was definitely in progress. The Catholic Church was initially less hostile than Protestant and Jewish religious leaders, and Italian scientists played a crucial role in scientific progress right up to the trial of Galileo in 1633. Thereafter, the Counter-Reformation church became more hostile to science, a change that helped account for the decline of science in Italy (but not in Catholic France) after 1640. At the same time, Protestant countries such as the Netherlands and Denmark became quite "pro-science," especially countries that lacked a strong religious authority capable of imposing religious orthodoxy on scientific questions.

This was certainly the case with Protestant England after 1630. English religious conflicts became so intense that the authorities could not impose religious unity on anything, including science. Significantly, the forerunners of the Royal Society agreed to discuss only "neutral" scientific questions so as not to come to blows over closely related religious and political disputes. The work of Bacon's many followers during Oliver Cromwell's commonwealth helped solidify the neutrality and independence of science. Bacon advocated the experimental approach precisely because it was open-minded and independent of preconceived religious and philosophical ideas. Neutral and useful, science became an accepted part of life and developed rapidly in England after about 1640.

Science and Society

The rise of modern science had many consequences, some of which are still unfolding. First, it went hand in hand with the rise of a new and expanding social group—the international **scientific community.** Members of this community were linked together by common interests and shared values as well as by journals and the learned scientific societies founded in many countries in the later seventeenth and eighteenth centuries. Expansion of knowledge was the primary goal of this community, and scientists' material and psychological rewards depended on their success in this endeavor. Thus science became competitive, and even more scientific advance was inevitable. Second, as governments intervened to support and sometimes direct research, the new scientific community became closely tied to the state and its agendas. National academies of science were created under state sponsorship in London in 1662, Paris in 1666, Berlin in 1700, and later across Europe.

Third, the scientific revolution introduced not only new knowledge about nature but also a new and revolutionary way of obtaining such knowledge—the modern scientific method. In addition to being both theoretical and experimental, this method was highly critical. It refused to base its conclusions on tradition and established sources, on ancient authorities and sacred texts. This critical attitude to established authority would inspire thinkers to question traditions in other domains as well.

Some things did not change in the scientific revolution. New "rational" methods for approaching nature did not question traditional inequalities between the sexes—and may have worsened them in some ways. When Renaissance courts served as centers of learning, talented noblewomen could find niches in study and research. The rise of a professional scientific community raised barriers for women because the new academies that furnished professional credentials did not accept female members. (This continued for a long time. Marie Curie, the first person to win two Nobel prizes, was rejected by the French Academy of Science in 1911 because she was a woman.[6])

There were, however, a number of noteworthy exceptions. In Italy, universities and academies did offer posts to women, attracting some foreigners spurned by their own countries. In addition, some sectors of accomplishment were more accessible to women, with fine arts being the most important. Women excelled as makers of wax anatomical models and as botanical and zoological illustrators. Because the new scientific method relied on precise observation, illustration became a highly valued skill. Women were also very much involved in informal scientific communities, attending salons, participating in scientific experiments, and writing learned treatises. Some female intellectuals were recognized as full-fledged members of the philosophical dialogue. In England, Margaret Cavendish, Anne Conway, and Mary Astell all con-

Metamorphoses of the Caterpillar and Moth Maria Sibylla Merian (1647–1717), the stepdaughter of a Dutch painter, became a celebrated scientific illustrator in her own right. Her finely observed pictures of insects in the South American colony of Surinam introduced many new species, shown in their various stages of development. For Merian, science was intimately tied with art: she not only painted but also bred caterpillars and performed experiments on them. Her two-year stay in Surinam, accompanied by a teenage daughter, was a daring feat for a seventeenth-century woman. *(Bildarchiv Preussischer Kulturbesitz/Art Resource, NY)*

tributed to debates about Descartes's mind-body dualism, among other issues. Descartes himself conducted an intellectual correspondence with the princess Elizabeth of Bohemia, of whom he stated: "I attach more weight to her judgement than to those messieurs the Doctors, who take for a rule of truth the opinions of Aristotle rather than the evidence of reason."[7]

If women themselves played a limited role in scientific discovery, scholars have recently emphasized the importance of representations of femininity and masculinity in the scientific revolution. Nature was often depicted as a female, whose veil of secrecy needed to be stripped away and penetrated by male experts. In the same time period, the Americas were similarly depicted as a female terrain whose potentially fertile lands needed to be controlled and impregnated by male colonists.

The scientific revolution had few consequences for economic life and the living standards of the masses until the late eighteenth century. True, improvements in the techniques of navigation facilitated overseas trade and helped enrich states and merchant companies. But science had relatively few practical economic applications. Thus the scientific revolution of the seventeenth century was first and foremost an intellectual revolution. For more than a hundred years its greatest impact was on how people thought and believed.

The Enlightenment

The scientific revolution was the single most important factor in the creation of the new worldview of the eighteenth-century **Enlightenment.** This worldview, which has played a large role in shaping the modern mind, grew out of a rich mix of diverse and often conflicting ideas. For the talented (and not-so-talented) writers who espoused them, these ideas competed vigorously for the attention of a growing public of well-educated but fickle readers, who remained a minority of the population. Despite the diversity, three central concepts stand at the core of Enlightenment thinking. The most important and original idea was that the methods of natural science could and should be used to examine and understand all aspects of life. This was what intellectuals meant by *reason,* a favorite word of Enlightenment thinkers. Nothing was to be accepted on faith. Everything was to be submitted to **rationalism,** a secular, critical way of thinking. A second important Enlightenment concept was that the scientific method was capable of discovering the laws of human society as well as those of nature. Thus was social science born. Its birth led to the third key idea, that of

progress. Armed with the proper method of discovering the laws of human existence, Enlightenment thinkers believed that it was at least possible for human beings to create better societies and better people. Their belief was strengthened by some modest improvements in economic and social life during the eighteenth century.

● *How did the new worldview affect the way people thought about society and human relations?*

The Emergence of the Enlightenment

Loosely united by certain key ideas, the European Enlightenment was a broad intellectual and cultural movement that gained strength gradually and did not reach its maturity until about 1750. Yet it was the generation that came of age between the publication of Newton's *Principia* in 1687 and the death of Louis XIV in 1715 that tied the crucial knot between the scientific revolution and a new outlook on life. Talented writers of that generation popularized hard-to-understand scientific achievements for the educated elite.

The most famous and influential popularizer was a versatile French man of letters, Bernard de Fontenelle (1657–1757), who set out to make science witty and entertaining—as easy to read as a novel—for a broad nonscientific audience. This was a tall order, but Fontenelle largely succeeded. His most famous work, *Conversations on the Plurality of Worlds* (1686), begins with two elegant figures walking in the gathering shadows of a large park. One is a woman, a sophisticated aristocrat, and the other is her friend, perhaps even her lover. They gaze at the stars, and their talk turns to a passionate discussion of . . . astronomy! The man confides that "each star may well be a different world," then gently stresses how error is giving way to truth. At one point he explains:

There came on the scene . . . one Copernicus, who made short work of all those various circles, all those solid skies, which the ancients had pictured to themselves. . . . Fired with the noble zeal of a true astronomer, he took the earth and spun it very far away from the center of the universe, where it had been installed, and in that center he put the sun, which had a far better title to the honor.[8]

Rather than despair at this dismissal of traditional understanding, Fontenelle's lady rejoices in the knowledge that the human mind is capable of making great progress.

This concept of progress was essentially a creation of the later seventeenth century. Medieval and Reformation thinkers had been concerned primarily with sin and salvation. The humanists of the Renaissance had emphasized worldly matters, but they had looked backward. They had believed it might be possible to equal the magnificent accomplishments of the ancients, but they did not ask for more. Fontenelle and like-minded writers had come to believe that, at least in science and mathematics, their era had gone far beyond antiquity. Progress, at least intellectual progress, was very possible.

Fontenelle and other writers of his generation were also instrumental in bringing science into conflict with religion. This was a major innovation because many seventeenth-century scientists, both Catholic and Protestant, did not draw antireligious implications from their scientific findings and believed that their work exalted God. The greatest scientist of them all, Isaac Newton, was a devout, if unorthodox, Christian who saw all his studies as directed toward explaining God's message. Fontenelle, in contrast, was skeptical about absolute truth and cynical about the claims of organized religion. Since such unorthodox views could not be stated openly in an absolute monarchy like Louis XIV's France, Fontenelle made his point through subtle editorializing about science. His depiction of the cautious Copernicus as a self-conscious revolutionary was typical. In *Eulogies of Scientists,* Fontenelle exploited with endless variations the fundamental theme of rational, progressive scientists versus prejudiced, reactionary priests.

The progressive and antireligious implications that writers such as Fontenelle drew from the scientific revolution reflected a very real crisis in European thought at the end of the seventeenth century. This crisis had its roots in several intellectual uncertainties and dissatisfactions, of which the demolition of Aristotelian-medieval science was only one.

A second uncertainty involved the whole question of religious truth. The destructive wars of religion that culminated in the Thirty Years' War (1618–1648) had been fought, in part, because religious freedom was an intolerable idea in Europe in the early seventeenth century. Both Catholics and Protestants had believed that religious truth was absolute and therefore worth fighting and dying for. Most Catholics and Protestants also believed that a strong state required unity in religious faith. Yet the disastrous results of the many attempts to impose such religious unity, such as Louis XIV's brutal expulsion of the French Huguenots in 1685, led some people to ask whether ideological conformity in religious matters was really necessary. Others skeptically asked if religious truth could ever be known with absolute certainty and concluded that it could not.

The most famous of these skeptics was Pierre Bayle (1647–1706), a French Huguenot who despised Louis

Popularizing Science   The frontispiece illustration of Fontenelle's *Conversations on the Plurality of Worlds* invites the reader to share the pleasures of astronomy with an elegant lady and an entertaining teacher. The drawing shows the planets revolving around the sun. *(By permission of the Syndics of Cambridge University Library)*

XIV and found refuge in the Netherlands. A teacher by profession and a crusading journalist by inclination, Bayle took full advantage of the toleration and intellectual freedom of his adopted land. He critically examined the religious beliefs and persecutions of the past in his *Historical and Critical Dictionary,* written in French and published in the Netherlands in 1697. Demonstrating that human beliefs had been extremely varied and very often mistaken, Bayle concluded that nothing can ever be known beyond all doubt. In religion as in philosophy, humanity's best hope was open-minded toleration. Bayle's **skepticism** was very influential. Reprinted frequently in the Netherlands and in England, his four-volume *Dictionary* was found in more private libraries of eighteenth-century France than was any other book.

The rapidly growing travel literature on non-European lands and cultures was a third cause of uncertainty. In the wake of the great discoveries, Europeans were learning that the peoples of China, India, Africa, and the Americas all had their own very different beliefs and customs. Europeans shaved their faces and let their hair grow. Turks shaved their heads and let their beards grow. In Europe a man bowed before a woman to show respect. In Siam a man turned his back on a woman when he met her because it was disrespectful to look directly at her. Countless similar examples discussed in the travel accounts helped change the perspective of educated Europeans. They began to look at truth and morality in relative, rather than absolute, terms. If anything was possible, who could say what was right or wrong?

A fourth cause and manifestation of European intellectual turmoil was John Locke's epoch-making *Essay Concerning Human Understanding*. Published in 1690—the same year Locke published his famous *Second Treatise of Civil Government* (see page 548)—Locke's essay brilliantly set forth a new theory about how human beings learn and form their ideas. In doing so, he rejected the prevailing view of Descartes, who had held that all people are born with certain basic ideas and ways of thinking. Locke insisted that all ideas are derived from experience. The human mind at birth is like a blank tablet, or **tabula rasa,** on which the environment writes the individual's understanding and beliefs. Human development is therefore determined by education and social institutions, for good or for evil. Locke's *Essay Concerning Human Understanding* passed through many editions and translations. Along with Newton's *Principia,* it was one of the dominant intellectual inspirations of the Enlightenment.

The Philosophes and the Public

By the time Louis XIV died in 1715, many of the ideas that would soon coalesce into the new worldview had been assembled. Yet Christian Europe was still strongly attached to its traditional beliefs, as witnessed by the powerful revival of religious orthodoxy in the first half of the eighteenth century (see pages 672–673). By the outbreak of the American Revolution in 1775, however, a large portion of western Europe's educated elite had embraced many of the new ideas. This acceptance was the work of one of history's most influential groups of intellectuals, the **philosophes.** It was the philosophes who proudly proclaimed that they, at long last, were bringing the light of knowledge to their ignorant fellow creatures in an Age of Enlightenment.

Philosophe is the French word for "philosopher," and it was in France that the Enlightenment reached its highest development. There were at least three reasons for this. First, French was the international language of the educated classes in the eighteenth century, and the education of the rich and the powerful across Europe often lay in the hands of French tutors espousing Enlightenment ideas. France's cultural leadership was reinforced by the fact that it was still the wealthiest and most populous country in Europe.

Second, after the death of Louis XIV, French absolutism and religious orthodoxy remained strong, but not too strong. Critical books were often banned by the censors, and their authors were sometimes jailed or exiled—but they were not tortured or burned. Intellectual radicals battled against powerful opposition in France, but they did not face the overwhelming restraints generally found in eastern and east-central Europe.

Third, the French philosophes were indeed philosophers, asking fundamental philosophical questions about the meaning of life, God, human nature, good and evil, and cause and effect. But in the tradition of Bayle and Fontenelle, they were not content with abstract arguments or ivory-tower speculations. They were determined to reach and influence all the French (and European) economic and social elites, many of which were joined together in the eighteenth-century concept of the "republic of letters," an imaginary, transnational realm constituted by all members of the educated or enlightened public.

Suspicious of the people but intensely committed to reason, reform, and slow, difficult progress, the great philosophes and their imitators were not free to write as they wished, since it was illegal in France to openly criticize either church or state. Their most radical works had to circulate in manuscript form. Knowing that direct attacks would probably be banned or burned, the philosophes wrote novels and plays, histories and philosophies, dictionaries and encyclopedias, all filled with satire and double meanings to spread their message to the public. One of the greatest philosophes, the baron de Montesquieu (1689–1755), brilliantly pioneered this approach in *The Persian Letters,* an extremely influential social satire published in 1721. This work consisted of amusing letters supposedly written by two Persian travelers, Usbek and Rica, who see European customs in unique ways and thereby allow Montesquieu to cleverly criticize existing practices and beliefs.

Like many Enlightenment philosophes, Montesquieu saw relations between men and women as particularly representative of overall social and political systems. He used the oppression of women in the Persian harem, described in letters from Usbek's wives, to symbolize Eastern political tyranny. At the end of the book, the rebellion of Usbek's harem against the cruel eunuchs he left in charge of them demonstrates that despotism must ultimately fail. Montesquieu also uses the Persians' observations of habitual infidelity among French wives and the strength of female power behind the throne to poke fun at European social and political customs. As Rica remarks:

The thing is that, for every man who has any post at court, in Paris, or in the country, there is a woman through whose hands pass all the favours and sometimes the injustices that he does. These women are all in touch with one another, and compose a sort of commonwealth whose members are always busy giving each other mutual help and support.

Montesquieu was exaggerating, but he echoed other critics of the informal power women gained in an absolutist system, where royal mistresses and female courtiers could have more access to the king than government ministers.

Having gained fame by using wit as a weapon against cruelty and superstition, Montesquieu settled down on his family estate to study history and politics. His interest was partly personal, for, like many members of the French robe nobility, he was disturbed by the growth in royal absolutism under Louis XIV. But Montesquieu was also inspired by the example of the physical sciences, and he set out to apply the critical method to the problem of government in *The Spirit of Laws* (1748). The result was a complex comparative study of republics, monarchies, and despotisms—a great pioneering inquiry in the emerging social sciences.

Showing that forms of government were shaped by history, geography, and customs, Montesquieu focused on the conditions that would promote liberty and prevent tyranny. He argued that despotism could be avoided if there was a **separation of powers,** with political power divided and shared by a variety of classes and legal estates holding unequal rights and privileges. A strong, independent upper class was especially important, according to Montesquieu, because in order to prevent the abuse of power "it is necessary that by the arrangement of things, power checks power." Admiring greatly the English balance of power among the king, the houses of Parliament, and the independent courts, Montesquieu believed that in France the thirteen high courts—the *parlements*—were

frontline defenders of liberty against royal despotism. Apprehensive about the uneducated poor, Montesquieu was clearly no democrat, but his theory of separation of powers had a great impact on France's wealthy, well-educated elite. The constitutions of the young United States in 1789 and of France in 1791 were based in large part on this theory.

Book Companion Site
Primary Source: Montesquieu Identifies the Necessity for the Separation of Governmental Powers

The most famous and in many ways most representative philosophe was François Marie Arouet, who was known by the pen name Voltaire (1694–1778). In his long career, this son of a comfortable middle-class family wrote more than seventy witty volumes, hobnobbed with kings and queens, and died a millionaire because of shrewd business speculations. His early career, however, was turbulent. In 1717 Voltaire was imprisoned for eleven months in the Bastille in Paris for insulting the regent of France. In 1726 a barb from his sharp tongue led a great French nobleman to have him beaten and arrested. This experience made a deep impression on Voltaire. All his life he struggled against legal injustice and unequal treatment before the law. Released from prison after promising to leave the country, Voltaire lived in England for three years and came to share Montesquieu's enthusiasm for English institutions.

Returning to France and soon threatened again with prison in Paris, Voltaire had the great fortune of meeting Gabrielle-Emilie Le Tonnelier de Breteuil, marquise du Châtelet (1706–1749), an intellectually gifted woman from the high aristocracy with a passion for science. Inviting Voltaire to live in her country house at Cirey in Lorraine and becoming his long-time companion (under the eyes of her tolerant husband), Madame du Châtelet studied physics and mathematics and published scientific articles and translations.

Perhaps the finest representative of a small number of elite Frenchwomen and their intellectual accomplishments during the Enlightenment, Madame du Châtelet suffered nonetheless because of her gender. Excluded on principle from the Royal Academy of Sciences, she depended on private tutors for instruction and became uncertain of her ability to make important scientific discoveries. Madame du Châtelet therefore concentrated on spreading the ideas of others, and her translation with an accompanying commentary of Newton's *Principia* into French for the first (and only) time was her greatest work. But she, who had patiently explained Newton's

Madame du Châtelet The marquise du Châtelet was fascinated by the new world system of Isaac Newton. She helped
spread Newton's ideas in France by translating his *Principia*
and by influencing Voltaire, her companion for fifteen years
until her death. *(Giraudon/Art Resource, NY)*

complex mathematical proofs to Europe's foremost
philosophe, had no doubt that women's limited scientific
contributions in the past were due to limited and unequal education. She once wrote that if she were a ruler,
"I would reform an abuse which cuts off, so to speak, half
the human race. I would make women participate in all
the rights of humankind, and above all in those of the
intellect."[9]

While living at Cirey, Voltaire wrote various works
praising England and popularizing English scientific
progress. Newton, he wrote, was history's greatest man,
for he had used his genius for the benefit of humanity. "It
is," wrote Voltaire, "the man who sways our minds by the
prevalence of reason and the native force of truth, not
they who reduce mankind to a state of slavery by force
and downright violence . . . that claims our reverence and
admiration."[10] In the true style of the Enlightenment,
Voltaire mixed the glorification of science and reason with
an appeal for better individuals and institutions.

Yet like almost all of the philosophes, Voltaire was a reformer, not a revolutionary, in social and political matters.
He was eventually appointed royal historian in 1743, and
his *Age of Louis XIV* portrayed Louis as the dignified
leader of his age. Voltaire also began a long correspondence with Frederick the Great and, after the death of his
beloved Emilie, accepted Frederick's invitation to come
brighten up the Prussian court in Berlin. The two men
later quarreled, but Voltaire always admired Frederick as
a free thinker and an enlightened monarch.

Unlike Montesquieu, Voltaire pessimistically concluded that the best one could hope for in the way of
government was a good monarch, since human beings
"are very rarely worthy to govern themselves." Nor did
he believe in social and economic equality in human affairs. The idea of making servants equal to their masters
was "absurd and impossible." The only realizable equality, Voltaire thought, was that "by which the citizen only
depends on the laws which protect the freedom of the
feeble against the ambitions of the strong."[11]

Voltaire's philosophical and religious positions were
much more radical. In the tradition of Bayle, his volumi-
nous writings challenged, often indirectly, the Catholic
Church and Christian theology at almost every point.
Though he was considered by many devout Christians to
be a shallow blasphemer, Voltaire's religious views were
ambiguous and quite typical of the complex attitudes
toward religion held by Enlightenment thinkers. Voltaire
clearly believed in God, but his was a distant, deistic God,
the great Clockmaker who built an orderly universe and
then stepped aside and let it run. Above all, Voltaire and
most of the philosophes hated all forms of religious intolerance, which they believed often led to fanaticism and
savage, inhuman action. Simple piety and human kindness—as embodied in Christ's great commandments to
"love God and your neighbor as yourself"—were religion enough, as may be seen in Voltaire's famous essay
on religion. (See the feature "Listening to the Past:
Voltaire on Religion" on pages 618–619.)

The ultimate strength of the French philosophes lay in
their number, dedication, and organization. The philosophes felt keenly that they were engaged in a common
undertaking that transcended individuals. Their greatest
and most representative intellectual achievement was,
quite fittingly, a group effort—the seventeen-volume *Encyclopedia: The Rational Dictionary of the Sciences, the
Arts, and the Crafts,* edited by Denis Diderot (1713–1784)
and Jean le Rond d'Alembert (1717–1783). They were
a curious pair. Diderot began his career as a hack writer,
first attracting attention with a skeptical tract on religion that was quickly burned by the judges of Paris.

D'Alembert was one of Europe's leading scientists and mathematicians, the orphaned and illegitimate son of celebrated aristocrats. From different circles and with different interests, the two men set out to find coauthors who would examine the rapidly expanding whole of human knowledge. Even more fundamentally, they set out to teach people how to think critically and objectively about all matters. As Diderot said, he wanted the *Encyclopedia* to "change the general way of thinking."[12]

The editors of the *Encyclopedia* had to conquer innumerable obstacles. After the appearance in 1751 of the first volume, which dealt with such controversial subjects as atheism, the soul, and blind people (all words beginning with *a* in French), the government temporarily banned publication. The pope later placed the work on the Catholic Church's index of forbidden works and pronounced excommunication on all who read or bought it. In an attempt to appease the authorities, the timid publisher watered down some of the articles in the last ten volumes without the editors' consent. Yet Diderot's unwavering belief in the importance of his mission held the encyclopedists together for fifteen years, and the enormous work was completed in 1765. Hundreds of thousands of articles by leading scientists, famous writers, skilled workers, and progressive priests treated every aspect of life and knowledge.

Not every article was daring or original, but the overall effect was little short of revolutionary. Science and the industrial arts were exalted, religion and immortality questioned. Intolerance, legal injustice, and out-of-date social institutions were openly criticized. More generally, the writers of the *Encyclopedia* showed that human beings could use the process of reasoning to expand human knowledge. The encyclopedists were convinced that greater knowledge would result in greater human happiness, for knowledge was useful and made possible economic, social, and political progress. The *Encyclopedia* was widely read, especially in less-expensive reprint editions published in Switzerland, and it was extremely influential in France and throughout western Europe as well. It summed up the new worldview of the Enlightenment.

The Enlightenment Outside of France

For all the importance of Paris as a center of Enlightenment thought, historians now recognize the existence of important strands of Enlightenment thought in other areas of Europe. They have identified distinctive Enlightenment movements in eighteenth-century Italy, Greece, the Balkans, Poland, Hungary, and Russia.

Different areas followed different strands of Enlightenment thinking. In England and Germany, scholars have described a more conservative Enlightenment that tried to integrate the findings of the scientific revolution with religious faith and practices. After the Act of Union with England and Ireland in 1707, Scotland was freed from political crisis to experience a vigorous period of intellectual growth. The Scottish Enlightenment, centered in Edinburgh, was marked by an emphasis on pragmatic and scientific reasoning. Intellectual revival was stimulated by the creation of the first public educational system in Europe. The most important figure in Edinburgh was David Hume (1711–1776), whose carefully argued religious skepticism had a powerful impact at home and abroad.

Building on Locke's teachings on learning, Hume argued that the human mind is really nothing but a bundle of impressions. These impressions originate only in sense experiences and our habits of joining these experiences together. Since our ideas ultimately reflect only our sense experiences, our reason cannot tell us anything about questions that cannot be verified by sense experience (in the form of controlled experiments or mathematics), such as the origin of the universe or the existence of God. Paradoxically, Hume's rationalistic inquiry ended up undermining the Enlightenment's faith in the power of reason.

Urban Culture and the Public Sphere

Enlightenment ideas did not float on air. A series of new institutions and practices emerged in the late seventeenth and eighteenth centuries to facilitate the spread of Enlightenment ideas. First, the European production and consumption of books grew dramatically in the eighteenth century. In Germany the number of new titles appearing annually grew substantially, from roughly six hundred new titles in 1700 to about eleven hundred in 1764 and about twenty-six hundred in 1780. France also witnessed an explosive growth in book consumption. The number of books in the hands of elite readers increased eightfold to tenfold between the 1690s and the 1780s, when the private library of the typical noble contained more than three hundred volumes.

Moreover, the types of books people read changed dramatically. The proportion of religious and devotional books published in Paris declined precipitously, from one-half of the total in the 1690s to one-tenth of the total in the 1780s. History and law held constant, while the proportion of published books treating the arts and sciences surged.

Even these figures understate the shift in French taste because France's unpredictable but pervasive censorship

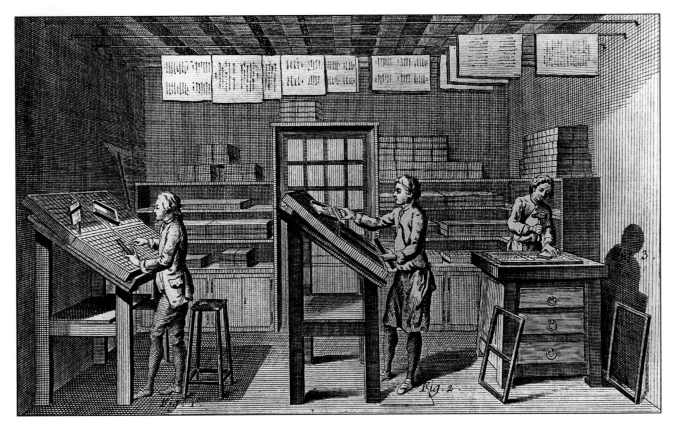

Illustrating the *Encyclopedia*: "The Print Shop" Diderot wanted to present all valid knowledge—that is, knowledge based on reason and the senses and not on tradition and authority. This plate, one of 3,000 detailed illustrations accompanying the 70,000 essays in the *Encyclopedia,* shows (*from left to right*) compositors setting type, arranging lines, and blocking down completed forms. Printed sheets dry above. *(Division of Rare & Manuscript Collections, Cornell University Library)*

caused many books to be printed abroad and smuggled back into the country for "under-the-cloak" sale. Experts believe that perhaps the majority of French books produced between 1750 and 1789 came from publishing companies outside of France. These publishers, located primarily in the Netherlands and Switzerland but also in England and a few small west German principalities, also smuggled forbidden books in French and other languages into the absolutist states of central, southern, and eastern Europe.

The illegal book trade in France also featured an astonishing growth of scandalmongering denunciations of high political figures and frankly pornographic works. These literary forms frequently came together in scathing pornographic accounts of the moral and sexual depravity of the French court, allegedly mired in luxury, perversion, and adultery. Echoing Montesquieu, a favorite theme was the way that some beautiful but immoral aristocratic

women used their sexual charms to gain power over weak rulers and high officials, thereby corrupting the process of government. These tracts included graphic accounts and images of sexual debauchery among aristocrats and even by the queen herself. Spurred by repeated royal directives, the French police did their best to stamp out this underground literature, but new slanders kept cropping up, with corrosive effects on public confidence in the monarchy.

Reading more books on many more subjects, the educated public in France and throughout Europe increasingly approached reading in a new way. The result was what some scholars have called a **reading revolution.** The old style of reading in Europe had been centered on sacred texts, full of authority, inspiring reverence and teaching earthly duty and obedience to God. Reading had been patriarchal and communal, with the father of the family slowly reading the text aloud and the audience savoring each word. Now reading involved many texts, which were constantly changing and commanded no special respect. Reading became individual, silent, and rapid. The well-educated classes were reading insatiably, skeptically, and carelessly. Subtle but profound, the reading revolution ushered in new ways of relating to the written word.

Conversation, discussion, and debate also played a critical role in the Enlightenment. Paris set the example, and other French and European cities followed. In Paris a number of talented, wealthy women presided over regular social gatherings of the great and near-great in their elegant private drawing rooms, or **salons.** There they encouraged a d'Alembert and a Fontenelle to exchange witty, uncensored observations on literature, science, and philosophy with great aristocrats, wealthy middle-class financiers, high-ranking officials, and noteworthy foreign-

ers. (D'Alembert himself was the illegitimate son of a well-known salon hostess, Madame de Tencin, who abandoned him on the steps of a Parisian church.) Talented hostesses, or *salonnières,* brought the various French elites together and mediated the public's freewheeling examination of Enlightenment thought.

Elite women also exercised an unprecedented feminine influence on artistic taste. Soft pastels, ornate interiors, sentimental portraits, and starry-eyed lovers protected by hovering cupids were all hallmarks of the style they favored. This style, known as **rococo,** was popular throughout Europe in the eighteenth century. It has been argued that feminine influence in the drawing room went hand in hand with the emergence of polite society and the general attempt to civilize a rough military nobility. Similarly, some philosophes championed greater rights and expanded education for women, claiming that the

Selling Books, Promoting Ideas   This appealing bookshop with its intriguing ads for the latest works offers to put customers "Under the Protection of Minerva," the Roman goddess of wisdom. Large packets of books sit ready for shipment to foreign countries. Book consumption surged in the eighteenth century. *(Musée des Beaux-Arts, Dijon/Art Resource, NY)*

Enlightenment Culture An actor performs the first reading of a new play by Voltaire at the salon of Madame Geoffrin. Voltaire, then in exile, is represented by a bust statue. *(Réunion des Musées Nationaux/Art Resource, NY)*

position and treatment of women were the best indicators of a society's level of civilization and decency.[13] To be sure, for these male philosophes greater rights for women did not mean equal rights, and the philosophes were not particularly disturbed by the fact that elite women remained legally subordinate to men in economic and political affairs. Elite women lacked many rights, but so did most men.

One of the most famous salons was that of Madame Geoffrin, the unofficial godmother of the *Encyclopedia*. Having lost her parents at an early age, she was married at fifteen by her well-meaning grandmother to a rich and boring businessman of forty-eight. After dutifully raising her children, Madame Geoffrin broke out of her gilded cage. With the aid of an aristocratic neighbor and in spite of her husband's loud protests, she developed a twice-weekly salon that counted Fontenelle and Montesquieu among its regular guests. Inheriting a large fortune after her husband's death, Madame Geoffrin gave the encyclopedists generous financial aid and helped save

their enterprise from collapse. Corresponding with the king of Sweden and Catherine the Great of Russia, Madame Geoffrin remained her own woman, a practicing Christian who would not tolerate attacks on the church in her house.

The salon also provided an informal apprenticeship for younger women who aspired to lead salons of their own. One such woman was Julie de Lespinasse. Eventually forming her own highly informal salon and attracting the keenest minds in France and Europe, Lespinasse epitomized the skills of the Enlightenment hostess. As one philosophe wrote:

She could unite the different types, even the most antagonistic, sustaining the conversation by a well-aimed phrase, animating and guiding it at will. . . . Politics, religion, philosophy, news: nothing was excluded. Her circle met daily from five to nine. There one found men of all ranks in the State, the Church, and the Court, soldiers and foreigners, and the leading writers of the day.[14]

As this passage suggests, the salons created a cultural realm free from religious dogma and political censorship. There a diverse but educated public could debate issues and form its own ideas. Through their invitation lists, salon hostesses brought together members of the intellectual, economic, and social elites. In such an atmosphere, the philosophes, the French nobility, and the prosperous middle classes intermingled and influenced one another. Thinking critically about almost any question became fashionable and flourished alongside hopes for human progress through greater knowledge and enlightened public opinion.

Membership at the salons was restricted to the well-born, the well-connected, and the exceptionally talented. A number of institutions emerged for those who aspired to follow, rather than lead, the Enlightenment. Lending libraries served an important function for people who could not afford to buy their own books. The coffeehouses that first appeared in the late seventeenth century became meccas of philosophical discussion. Then, as now, one could linger for hours to read or debate for the price of a cup of coffee. In addition to these institutions, book clubs, Masonic lodges, and journals all played roles in the creation of a new **public sphere** that celebrated open debate informed by critical reason. The public sphere was an idealized space where members of society came together as individuals to discuss issues relevant to the society, economics, and politics of the day.

What of the common people? Did they participate in the Enlightenment? Enlightenment philosophes did not direct their message to peasants or urban laborers. Whether of middling or noble origin, intellectuals sought patronage from the wealthy and powerful. They believed that the masses had no time or talent for philosophical speculation and that elevating them would be a long, slow, potentially dangerous process. Deluded by superstitions and driven by violent passions, they thought, the people were like little children in need of firm parental guidance. French philosophe d'Alembert characteristically made a sharp distinction between "the truly enlightened public" and "the blind and noisy multitude."[15]

There is some evidence, however, that the people were not immune to the words of the philosophes. At a time of rising literacy, book prices were dropping in cities and towns, and many philosophical ideas were popularized in cheap pamphlets. Moreover, even illiterate people had access to written material, through the practice of public reading. The Parisian glass-worker Jacques-Louis Ménétra, whose education consisted of a few years of schooling and his trade apprenticeship, claimed in his autobiography to have cultivated a friendship with Jean-Jacques Rousseau and to have enjoyed a game of chess and a philosophical discussion with the writer. Although they were barred from salons and academies, ordinary people were not immune to the new ideas in circulation.

Late Enlightenment

After about 1770 a number of thinkers and writers began to attack the Enlightenment's faith in reason, progress, and moderation. The most famous of these was the Swiss Jean-Jacques Rousseau (1712–1778), a brilliant and difficult thinker and an appealing but neurotic individual. Born into a poor family of watchmakers in Geneva, Rousseau went to Paris and was greatly influenced by Diderot and Voltaire. Always extraordinarily sensitive and suspicious, he came to believe that his philosophe friends and the women of the Parisian salons were plotting against him. In the mid-1750s he broke with them personally and intellectually, living thereafter as a lonely outsider with his uneducated common-law wife and going in his own highly original direction.

Like other Enlightenment thinkers, Rousseau was passionately committed to individual freedom. Unlike them, however, he attacked rationalism and civilization as destroying, rather than liberating, the individual. Warm, spontaneous feeling had to complement and correct cold intellect. Moreover, the basic goodness of the individual and the unspoiled child had to be protected from the cruel refinements of civilization. Rousseau's ideals greatly influenced the early romantic movement (see pages 660–661), which rebelled against the culture of the Enlightenment in the late eighteenth century.

Reconfirming Montesquieu's critique of women's influence in public affairs, Rousseau called for a rigid division of gender roles. According to Rousseau, women and men were radically different beings. Destined by nature to assume a passive role in sexual relations, women should also be passive in social life. A woman's role was to care for her children at home and to please her husband with good housekeeping, a modest demeanor, and a fresh, natural appearance. Women's passion for fashion, attending salons, and pulling the strings of power was unnatural and had a corrupting effect on both politics and society. Rousseau thus rejected the sophisticated way of life of elite Parisian women. Against them, he rearticulated conventional stereotypes as a form of natural law, against which debate was impossible. These views had a strong impact on both men and women in the late eighteenth century, contributing to calls for privileged women to abandon their stylish corsets and to breast-feed their children.

Rousseau's contribution to political theory in *The Social Contract* (1762) was equally significant. His contribution was based on two fundamental concepts: the general will and popular sovereignty. According to Rousseau, the **general will** is sacred and absolute, reflecting the common interests of all the people, who have displaced the monarch as the holder of sovereign power. The general will is not necessarily the will of the majority, however. At times the general will may be the authentic, long-term needs of the people as correctly interpreted by a farseeing minority. Little noticed before the French Revolution, Rousseau's concept of the general will appealed greatly to democrats and nationalists after 1789. (The concept has since been used by many dictators who have claimed that they, rather than some momentary majority of the voters, represent the general will.) Rousseau was both one of the most influential voices of the Enlightenment and, in his rejection of rationalism and social discourse, a harbinger of reaction against Enlightenment ideas.

Book Companion Site
Primary Source: Rousseau Espouses Popular Sovereignty and the General Will

As the reading public developed, it joined forces with the philosophes to call for the autonomy of the printed word. Immanuel Kant (1724–1804), a professor in East Prussia and the greatest German philosopher of his day, posed the question of the age when he published a pamphlet in 1784 entitled *What Is Enlightenment?* Kant answered, "*Sapere Aude!* [dare to know] Have courage to use your own understanding!—that is the motto of enlightenment." He argued that if serious thinkers were granted the freedom to exercise their reason publicly in print, enlightenment would almost surely follow. Kant was no revolutionary; he also insisted that in their private lives, individuals must obey all laws, no matter how unreasonable, and should be punished for "impertinent" criticism. Kant thus tried to reconcile absolute monarchical authority with a critical public sphere. This balancing act characterized experiments with "enlightened absolutism" in the eighteenth century.

Race and the Enlightenment

In addition to criticizing their own societies and political systems, Enlightenment thinkers wrote about society and human nature outside their borders. In recent years, historians have found in the scientific revolution and the Enlightenment a crucial turning point in European ideas about race. Many of the most important thinkers of the Enlightenment devoted substantial attention to comparisons of European and non-European cultures, deriving their understanding of people at home from differences with people abroad. The result was the formation of highly influential new understandings of **racial difference.** As with other strands of Enlightenment thought, the new scientific method, and its apparently neutral, rational thinking, provided intellectual legitimacy for their findings.

A primary catalyst for new ideas about race was the urge to classify nature unleashed by the scientific revolution's insistence on careful empirical observation. In *The System of Nature* (1735) Swedish botanist Carl von Linné argued that nature was organized into a God-given hierarchy, which mankind must uncover and chart meticulously. As scientists developed more elaborate taxonomies of plant and animal species, they also began to classify humans into hierarchically ordered "races" and to investigate the origins of race. The Comte de Buffon argued that humans originated with one species that then developed into distinct races due largely to climactic conditions. In *A Natural History* he describes experiments conducted on African bodies to determine the cause of their "blackness," which was assumed to be an acquired variation from humans' originally white skin.

Using the word *race* to designate biologically distinct groups of humans, akin to distinct animal species, was new. Previously, Europeans grouped other peoples into "nations" based on their historical, political, and cultural affiliations, rather than on supposedly innate physical differences. Unsurprisingly, when European thinkers drew up a hierarchical classification of human species, their own "race" was placed at the top. Europeans had long believed they were culturally superior to "barbaric" peoples in Africa and, since 1492, the New World. Now emerging ideas about racial difference taught them they were biologically superior as well.

Enlightenment thinkers such as David Hume and Immanuel Kant helped popularize these ideas. In *Of Natural Characters* (1748), Hume wrote:

I am apt to suspect the negroes and in general all other species of men (for there are four or five different kinds) to be naturally inferior to the whites. There never was a civilized nation of any other complexion than white, nor even any individual eminent amongst them, no arts, no sciences. . . . Such a uniform and constant difference could not happen, in so many countries and ages if nature had not made an original distinction between these breeds of men.[16]

The Prussian philosopher Immanuel Kant taught and wrote as much about "anthropology" and "geography" as he did about standard philosophical themes such as logic, metaphysics, and moral philosophy. He shared and elaborated Hume's views about race in *On the Different Races of Man* (1775), claiming that there were four human races, each of which had derived from an original race of "white brunette" people. According to Kant, the closest descendants of the original race were the white inhabitants of northern Germany. In deriving new physical characteristics, the other races had degenerated both physically and culturally from this origin.

These ideas did not go unchallenged. James Beattie responded directly to Hume's claims of white superiority by pointing out that Europeans had started out as savage as nonwhites and that many non-European peoples in the Americas, Asia, and Africa had achieved high levels of civilization. Johann von Herder criticized Kant, arguing that humans could not be classified into races based on skin color and that each culture was as intrinsically worthy as any other. These challenges to emerging scientific notions of racial inequality, however, were in the minority. Many other Enlightenment voices agreeing with Kant and Hume—Thomas Jefferson among them—may be found.

Scholars are only at the beginning of efforts to understand links between Enlightenment ideas about race and its notions of equality, progress, and reason. There are clear parallels, though, between the use of science to propagate racial hierarchies and its use to defend social inequalities between men and women. As Rousseau used women's "natural" passivity to argue for their passive role in society, so a Hume and a Kant used non-Europeans' "natural" inferiority to defend slavery and colonial domination. The new powers of science and reason were thus marshaled to imbue traditional stereotypes with the force of natural law.

The Enlightenment and Absolutism

How did the Enlightenment influence political developments? To this important question there is no easy answer. Most Enlightenment thinkers outside of England and the Netherlands believed that political change could best come from above—from the ruler—rather than from below, especially in central and eastern Europe. Royal absolutism was a fact of life, and the kings and queens of Europe's leading states clearly had no intention of giving up their great power. Therefore, the philosophes and their sympathizers realistically concluded that a benevolent absolutism offered the best opportunities for improving society. Critical thinking was

turning the art of good government into an exact science. It was necessary to educate and "enlighten" the monarch, who could then make good laws and promote human happiness.

The philosophes' influence was heightened by the fact that many government officials were attracted to and interested in philosophical ideas. They were among the best-educated and best-informed members of society, and their daily involvement in complex affairs of state made them naturally interested in ideas for improving or reforming human society. Encouraged and instructed by these officials, some absolutist rulers of the later eighteenth century tried to govern in an "enlightened" manner. Yet the actual programs and accomplishments of these rulers varied greatly. It is necessary to examine the evolution of monarchical absolutism at close range before trying to judge the Enlightenment's effect and the meaning of what historians have often called the **enlightened absolutism** of the later eighteenth century.

Enlightenment teachings inspired European rulers in small as well as large states in the second half of the eighteenth century. Absolutist princes and monarchs in several west German and Italian states, as well as in Scandinavia, Spain, and Portugal, proclaimed themselves more enlightened. A few smaller states were actually the most successful in making reforms, perhaps because their rulers were not overwhelmed by the size and complexity of their realms. Denmark, for example, carried out extensive and progressive land reform in the 1780s that practically abolished serfdom and gave Danish peasants secure tenure on their farms. Yet by far the most influential of the new-style monarchs were in Prussia, Russia, and Austria, and they deserve primary attention.

• *What impact did this new way of thinking have on political developments and monarchical absolutism?*

Frederick the Great of Prussia

Frederick II (r. 1740–1786), commonly known as Frederick the Great, built masterfully on the work of his father, Frederick William I (see page 571). This was somewhat surprising, for, like many children with tyrannical parents, he rebelled against his family's wishes in his early years. Rejecting the crude life of the barracks, Frederick embraced culture and literature, even writing poetry and fine prose in French, a language his father detested. After trying unsuccessfully to run away in 1730 at age eighteen, he was virtually imprisoned and compelled to watch as his companion in flight was beheaded at his father's command. Yet like many other rebellious youths, Frederick eventually reconciled with his father, and by the time he came to the throne ten years later Frederick was determined to use the splendid army that his father had left him.

Therefore, when the ruler of Austria, Charles VI, also died in 1740 and his young and charismatic daughter Maria Theresa inherited the Habsburg dominions, Frederick suddenly and without warning invaded her rich, mainly German province of Silesia. This action defied solemn Prussian promises to respect the Pragmatic Sanction, which guaranteed Maria Theresa's succession. Maria Theresa's disunited army was no match for Prussian precision; in 1742, as other greedy powers were falling on her lands in the general European War of the Austrian Succession (1740–1748), she was forced to cede almost all of Silesia to Prussia (see Map 17.2 on page 570). In one stroke Prussia had doubled its population to six million people. Now Prussia unquestionably towered above all the other German states and stood as a European Great Power.

Though successful in 1742, Frederick had to spend much of his reign fighting against great odds to save Prussia from total destruction. Maria Theresa was determined to regain Silesia, and when the ongoing competition between Britain and France for colonial empire brought another great conflict in 1756 (see page 635), Austria fashioned an aggressive alliance with France and Russia. During the Seven Years' War (1756–1763), the aim of the alliance was to conquer Prussia and divide up its territory. Frederick led his army brilliantly, striking repeatedly at vastly superior forces invading from all sides. At times he believed all was lost, but he fought on with stoic courage. In the end he was miraculously saved: Peter III came to the Russian throne in 1762 and called off the attack against Frederick, whom he greatly admired.

In the early years of his reign Frederick II had kept his enthusiasm for Enlightenment culture strictly separated from a brutal concept of international politics. He wrote:

Of all States, from the smallest to the biggest, one can safely say that the fundamental rule of government is the principle of extending their territories. . . . The passions of rulers have no other curb but the limits of their power. Those are the fixed laws of European politics to which every politician submits.[17]

But the terrible struggle of the Seven Years' War tempered Frederick and brought him to consider how more humane policies for his subjects might also strengthen the state. Thus Frederick went beyond a superficial commitment to Enlightenment culture for himself and his circle. He tolerantly allowed his subjects to believe as they wished in religious and philosophical matters. He promoted the advancement of knowledge, improving his country's schools and permitting scholars to publish their findings. Moreover, Frederick tried to improve the lives of his subjects more directly. As he wrote his friend Voltaire, "I must enlighten my people, cultivate their manners and morals, and make them as happy as human beings can be, or as happy as the means at my disposal permit."

The legal system and the bureaucracy were Frederick's primary tools. Prussia's laws were simplified, torture of prisoners was abolished, and judges decided cases quickly and impartially. Prussian officials became famous for their hard work and honesty. After the Seven Years' War ended in 1763, Frederick's government energetically promoted the reconstruction of agriculture and industry in his war-torn country. Frederick himself set a good example. He worked hard and lived modestly, claiming that he was "only the first servant of the state." Thus Frederick justified monarchy in terms of practical results and said nothing of the divine right of kings.

Frederick's dedication to high-minded government went only so far, however. He never tried to change Prussia's existing social structure. True, he condemned serfdom in the abstract, but he accepted it in practice and did not even free the serfs on his own estates. He accepted and extended the privileges of the nobility, which he saw as his primary ally in the defense and extension of his realm. The Junker nobility remained the backbone of the army and the entire Prussian state.

Nor did Frederick listen to thinkers like Moses Mendelssohn (1729–1786), who urged that Jews be given freedom and civil rights. (See the feature "Individuals in Society: Moses Mendelssohn and the Jewish Enlightenment.") As in other German states, Jews in Prussia remained an oppressed group. The vast majority were confined to tiny, overcrowded ghettos, were excluded by law from most business and professional activities, and could be ordered out of the kingdom at a moment's notice. A very few Jews in Prussia did manage to succeed and to obtain the right of permanent settlement, usually by performing some special service for the state. But they were the exception, and Frederick firmly opposed any general emancipation for the Jews, as he did for the serfs.

Catherine the Great of Russia

Catherine the Great of Russia (r. 1762–1796) was one of the most remarkable rulers of her age, and the French philosophes adored her. Catherine was a German princess from Anhalt-Zerbst, a totally insignificant principality sandwiched between Prussia and Saxony. Her father commanded a regiment of the Prussian army, but

Individuals in Society

Moses Mendelssohn and the Jewish Enlightenment

In 1743 a small, humpbacked Jewish boy with a stammer left his poor parents in Dessau in central Germany and walked eighty miles to Berlin, the capital of Frederick the Great's Prussia. According to one story, when the boy reached the Rosenthaler Gate, the only one through which Jews could pass, he told the inquiring watchman that his name was Moses and that he had come to Berlin "to learn." The watchman laughed and waved him through. "Go Moses, the sea has opened before you."* Embracing the Enlightenment and seeking a revitalization of Jewish religious thought, Moses Mendelssohn did point his people in a new and uncharted direction.

Turning in Berlin to a learned rabbi he had previously known in Dessau, the young Mendelssohn studied Jewish law and eked out a living copying Hebrew manuscripts in a beautiful hand. But he was soon fascinated by an intellectual world that had been closed to him in the Dessau ghetto. There, like most Jews throughout central Europe, he had spoken Yiddish— a mixture of German, Polish, and Hebrew. Now, working mainly on his own, he mastered German; learned Latin, Greek, French, and English; and studied mathematics and Enlightenment philosophy. Word of his exceptional abilities spread in Berlin's Jewish community (1,500 of the city's 100,000 inhabitants). He began tutoring the children of a wealthy Jewish silk merchant, and he soon became the merchant's clerk and later his partner. But his great passion remained the life of the mind and the spirit, which he avidly pursued in his off hours.

Gentle and unassuming in his personal life, Mendelssohn was a bold thinker. Reading eagerly in Western philosophy since antiquity, he was, as a pious Jew, soon convinced that Enlightenment teachings need not be opposed to Jewish thought and religion. Indeed, he concluded that reason could complement and strengthen religion, although each would retain its integrity as a separate sphere.[†] Developing this idea in his first great work, "On the Immortality of the Soul" (1767), Mendelssohn used the neutral setting of a philosophical dialogue between Socrates and his followers in ancient Greece to argue that the human soul lived forever. In refusing to bring religion and critical thinking into conflict, he was strongly influenced by contemporary German philosophers who argued similarly on behalf of Christianity. He reflected the way the German Enlightenment generally supported established religion, in contrast to the French Enlightenment, which attacked it. This was the most important difference in Enlightenment thinking between the two countries.

Mendelssohn's treatise on the human soul captivated the educated German public, which marveled that a Jew could have written a philosophical masterpiece. In the excitement, a Christian zealot named Lavater challenged Mendelssohn in a pamphlet to accept Christianity or to demonstrate how the Christian faith was not "reasonable." Replying politely but passionately, the Jewish philosopher affirmed that all his studies had only strengthened him in the faith of his fathers, although he certainly did not seek to convert anyone not born into Judaism. Rather, he urged toleration in religious matters. He spoke up courageously for his fellow Jews and decried the oppression they endured, and he continued to do so for the rest of his life.

Orthodox Jew and German philosophe, Moses Mendelssohn serenely combined two very different worlds. He built a bridge from the ghetto to the dominant culture over which many Jews would pass, including his novelist daughter Dorothea and his famous grandson, the composer Felix Mendelssohn.

Lavater (right) *attempts to convert Mendelssohn, in a painting by Moritz Oppenheim of an imaginary encounter.* (Collection of the Judah L. Magnes Museum, Berkeley)

Questions for Analysis

1. How did Mendelssohn seek to influence Jewish religious thought in his time?
2. How do Mendelssohn's ideas compare with those of the French Enlightenment?

*H. Kupferberg, *The Mendelssohns: Three Generations of Genius* (New York: Charles Scribner's Sons, 1972), p. 3.
[†]D. Sorkin, *Moses Mendelssohn and the Religious Enlightenment* (Berkeley: University of California Press, 1996), pp. 8 ff.

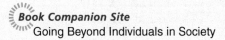
Book Companion Site
Going Beyond Individuals in Society

Catherine the Great as Equestrian and Miniature of Count Grigory Grigoryevich Orlov
Catherine conspired with her lover Count Orlov to overthrow her husband Peter III and became empress of Russia. Strongly influenced by the Enlightenment, she cultivated the French philosophes and instituted moderate reforms, only to reverse them in the aftermath of Pugachev's rebellion. This equestrian portrait now hangs above her throne in the palace throne room. *(left: Musée des Beaux-Arts, Chartres/The Bridgeman Art Library; right: © The State Hermitage Museum, St. Petersburg)*

her mother was related to the Romanovs of Russia, and that proved to be Catherine's chance.

Peter the Great had abolished the hereditary succession of tsars so that he could name his successor and thus preserve his policies. This move opened a period of palace intrigue and a rapid turnover of rulers until Peter's youngest daughter, Elizabeth, came to the Russian throne in 1741. A shrewd but crude woman, Elizabeth named her nephew Peter heir to the throne and chose Catherine to be his wife in 1744. It was a mismatch from the beginning. The fifteen-year-old Catherine was intelligent and attractive; her husband shared neither of these qualities. Ignored by her husband, Catherine carefully studied Russian, endlessly read writers such as Bayle and Voltaire, and made friends at court. Soon she knew what she wanted: "I did not care about Peter," she wrote in her *Memoirs,* "but I did care about the crown."[18]

As the old empress Elizabeth approached death, Catherine plotted against her unpopular husband. She selected as her new lover a dashing young officer named Grigory Orlov, who with his four officer brothers commanded considerable support among the soldiers stationed in St. Petersburg. When Peter came to the throne in 1762, his decision to withdraw Russian troops from the coalition against Prussia alienated the army. At the end of six months Catherine and her conspirators deposed Peter III in a palace revolution, and the Orlov brothers murdered him. The German princess became empress of Russia.

Catherine had drunk deeply at the Enlightenment well. Never questioning the common assumption that absolute monarchy was the best form of government, she set out to rule in an enlightened manner. She had three main goals. First, she worked hard to continue Peter the Great's effort to bring the culture of western Europe to backward Russia. To do so, she imported Western architects, sculptors, musicians, and intellectuals. She bought masterpieces of Western art in wholesale lots and patronized the philosophes. An enthusiastic letter writer, she corresponded extensively with Voltaire and praised him as the "champion of the human race." When the French government banned the *Encyclopedia,* she offered to publish it in St. Petersburg, and she sent money to Diderot when he needed it. With these and countless similar actions, Catherine won good press in the West for herself and for her country. Moreover, this intellectual ruler, who wrote plays and loved good talk, set the tone for the entire Russian nobility. Peter the Great westernized Russian armies, but it was Catherine who westernized the imagination of the Russian nobility.

Catherine's second goal was domestic reform, and she began her reign with sincere and ambitious projects. Better laws were a major concern. In 1767 she appointed a special legislative commission to prepare a new law code. No new unified code was ever produced, but Catherine did restrict the practice of torture and allowed limited religious toleration. She also tried to improve education and strengthen local government. The philosophes applauded these measures and hoped more would follow.

Book Companion Site
Primary Source: Catherine the Great's Grand Instruction to the Legislative Commission

Such was not the case. In 1773 a common Cossack soldier named Emelian Pugachev sparked a gigantic uprising of serfs, very much as Stenka Razin had done a century earlier (see page 576). Proclaiming himself the true tsar, Pugachev issued "decrees" abolishing serfdom, taxes, and army service. Thousands joined his cause, slaughtering landlords and officials over a vast area of southwestern Russia. Pugachev's untrained forces eventually proved no match for Catherine's noble-led regular army. Betrayed by his own company, Pugachev was captured and savagely executed.

Pugachev's rebellion was a decisive turning point in Catherine's domestic policy. On coming to the throne, she had condemned serfdom in theory, but Pugachev's rebellion put an end to any intentions she might have had about reforming the system. The peasants were clearly dangerous, and her empire rested on the support of the nobility. After 1775 Catherine gave the nobles absolute control of their serfs. She extended serfdom into new areas, such as Ukraine. In 1785 she formalized the nobility's privileged position, freeing nobles forever from taxes and state service. Under Catherine the Russian nobility attained its most exalted position, and serfdom entered its most oppressive phase.

Catherine's third goal was territorial expansion, and in this respect she was extremely successful. Her armies subjugated the last descendants of the Mongols, the Crimean Tatars, and began the conquest of the Caucasus. Her greatest coup by far was the partition of Poland (see Map 18.1). By 1700 Poland had become a weak and decentralized republic with an elected king (see page 567), and Poland's fate in the late eighteenth century demonstrated the dangers of failing to build a strong absolutist state. All important decisions continued to require the unanimous agreement of all nobles elected to the Polish Diet, which meant that nothing could ever be done to strengthen the state. When, between 1768 and 1772, Catherine's armies scored unprecedented victories against the Turks and thereby threatened to disturb the balance of power between Russia and Austria in eastern Europe, Frederick of Prussia obligingly came forward with a deal. He proposed that Turkey be let off easily and that Prussia, Austria, and Russia each compensate itself by taking a gigantic slice of Polish territory. Catherine jumped at the chance. The first partition of Poland took place in 1772. Two more partitions, in 1793 and 1795, gave all three powers more Polish territory, and the ancient republic of Poland vanished from the map.

Expansion helped Catherine keep the nobility happy, for it provided her with vast new lands to give to her faithful servants. Until the end this remarkable woman—who always believed that, in spite of her domestic setbacks, she was slowly civilizing Russia—kept her zest for life. Fascinated by a new twenty-two-year-old flame when she was a grandmother in her sixties, she happily reported her good fortune to a favorite former lover: "I have come back to life like a frozen fly; I am gay and well."[19]

The Austrian Habsburgs

In Austria two talented rulers did manage to introduce major reforms, although traditional power politics was more important than Enlightenment teachings. One was Joseph II (r. 1780–1790), a fascinating individual. For an earlier generation of historians, he was the "revolutionary emperor," a tragic hero whose lofty reforms were undone by the landowning nobility he dared to challenge. More recent scholarship has revised this romantic interpretation and has stressed how Joseph II continued the state-building work of his mother, the empress Maria Theresa (1740–1780), a remarkable but old-fashioned absolutist.

Mapping the Past

MAP 18.1 The Partition of Poland and Russia's Expansion, 1772–1795 During the sixteenth century the Polish nobility confirmed its right to elect the kings of Poland. The parliament could be blocked by the veto of a single member. In the seventeenth century warfare with Sweden and Russian Cossacks resulted in Poland's loss of the Baltic areas and Ukraine. In 1772 war threatened between Russia and Austria over Russian gains from the Ottoman Empire. To satisfy desires for expansion without fighting, Prussia's Frederick the Great proposed that parts of Poland be divided among Austria, Prussia, and Russia. In 1793 and 1795 the three powers partitioned the remainder, and the ancient republic of Poland vanished from the map. ❶ Why was Poland vulnerable to partition in the latter half of the eighteenth century? What does it say about European politics at the time that a country could simply cease to exist on the map? Could that happen today? ❷ Of the three powers that divided the kingdom of Poland, which benefited the most? How did the partition affect the geographical boundaries of each state, and what was the significance? ❸ What border with the former Poland remained unchanged? Why do you think this was the case?

Emerging from the long War of the Austrian Succession in 1748 with the serious loss of Silesia, Maria Theresa and her closest ministers were determined to introduce reforms that would make the state stronger and more efficient. Three aspects of these reforms were most important. First, Maria Theresa introduced measures aimed at limiting the papacy's political influence in her realm. Second, a whole series of administrative reforms strengthened the central bureaucracy, smoothed out some provincial differences, and revamped the tax system, taxing even the lands of nobles without special exemptions. Third, the government sought to improve the lot of the agricultural population, cautiously reducing the power of lords over their hereditary serfs and their partially free peasant tenants.

Maria Theresa The empress and her husband pose with eleven of their sixteen children at Schönbrunn palace in this family portrait by court painter Martin Meytens (1695–1770). Joseph, the heir to the throne, stands at the center of the star pattern. Wealthy women often had very large families, in part because they, unlike poor women, seldom nursed their babies. *(Réunion des Musées Nationaux/Art Resource, NY)*

to re-establish order. Peasants once again were required to do forced labor for their lords.

Evaluating "Enlightened Absolutism"

Despite differences, the leading eastern European monarchs of the later eighteenth century all claimed that they were acting on the principles of the Enlightenment. The philosophes generally agreed with this assessment and cheered them on. Beginning in the mid-nineteenth century historians developed the idea of a common "enlightened despotism" or "enlightened absolutism," and they canonized Frederick, Catherine, and Joseph as its most outstanding examples. More recent research has raised doubts about this old interpretation and has led to a fundamental revaluation.

There is general agreement that these absolutists, especially Catherine and Frederick, did encourage and spread the cultural values of the Enlightenment. Perhaps this was their greatest achievement. Skeptical in religion and intensely secular in basic orientation, they unabashedly accepted the here and now and sought their happiness in the enjoyment of it. At the same time, they were proud of their intellectual accomplishments and good taste, and they supported knowledge, education, and the arts. No wonder the philosophes felt that these monarchs were kindred spirits.

Historians also agree that the absolutists believed in change from above and tried to enact needed reforms. Yet the results of these efforts brought only very modest improvements, and the life of the peasantry remained very hard in the eighteenth century. Thus some historians have concluded that these monarchs were not really sincere in their reform efforts. Others disagree, arguing that powerful nobilities blocked the absolutists' genuine commitment to reform. (The old interpretation of Joseph II as the tragic revolutionary emperor forms part of this argument.)

The emerging answer to this controversy is that the later Eastern absolutists were indeed committed to reform but that humanitarian objectives were of secondary importance. Above all, the absolutists wanted reforms that would strengthen the state and allow them to com-

Coregent with his mother from 1765 onward and a strong supporter of change, Joseph II moved forward rapidly when he came to the throne in 1780. He controlled the established Catholic Church even more closely in an attempt to ensure that it produced better citizens. He granted religious toleration and civic rights to Protestants and Jews—a radical innovation that impressed his contemporaries. In even more spectacular peasant reforms, Joseph abolished serfdom in 1781, and in 1789 he decreed that all peasant labor obligations be converted into cash payments. This measure was violently rejected not only by the nobility but also by the peasants it was intended to help since their primitive barter economy was woefully lacking in money. When a disillusioned Joseph died prematurely at forty-nine, the entire Habsburg empire was in turmoil. His brother Leopold II (r. 1790–1792) canceled Joseph's radical edicts in order

pete militarily with their neighbors. Modern scholarship has therefore stressed how Catherine, Frederick, and Joseph were in many ways simply continuing the state-building of their predecessors, reorganizing armies and expanding bureaucracies to raise more taxes and troops. The reason for this continuation was simple. The international political struggle was brutal, and the stakes were high. First Austria under Maria Theresa and then Prussia under Frederick the Great had to engage in bitter fighting to escape dismemberment, while decentralized Poland was coldly divided and eventually liquidated.

Yet in this drive for more state power, the later absolutists were also innovators, and the idea of an era of enlightened absolutism retains a certain validity. Sharing the Enlightenment faith in critical thinking and believing that knowledge meant power, these absolutists really were more enlightened than their predecessors because they put state-building reforms in a new, broader perspective. Above all, the later absolutists considered how more humane laws and practices could help their populations become more productive and satisfied and thus able to contribute more substantially to the welfare of the state. It was from this perspective that they introduced many of their most progressive reforms, tolerating religious minorities, simplifying legal codes, and promoting practical education.

The primacy of state over individual interests also helps explain some puzzling variations in social policies. For example, Catherine the Great took measures that worsened the peasants' condition because she looked increasingly to the nobility as her natural ally and sought to strengthen it. Frederick the Great basically favored the status quo, limiting only the counterproductive excesses of his trusted nobility against its peasants. Joseph II believed that greater freedom for peasants was the means to strengthen his realm, and he acted accordingly. Each enlightened absolutist sought greater state power, but each believed that a different policy would attain it.

The eastern European absolutists of the later eighteenth century combined old-fashioned state-building with the culture and critical thinking of the Enlightenment. In doing so, they succeeded in expanding the role of the state in the life of society. They perfected bureaucratic machines that were to prove surprisingly adaptive and capable of enduring into the twentieth century. Their failure to implement policies we would recognize as humane and enlightened—such as abolishing serfdom—may reveal inherent limitations in Enlightenment thinking about equality and social justice, rather than in their execution of an Enlightenment program. The fact that leading philosophes supported rather than criticized Eastern rulers' policies suggests some of the blinders of the era.

Chapter Summary

Book Companion Site
To assess your mastery of this chapter, visit **bedfordstmartins.com/mckaywest**

• *What was revolutionary in new attitudes toward the natural world?*

• *How did the new worldview affect the way people thought about society and human relations?*

• *What impact did this new way of thinking have on political developments and monarchical absolutism?*

Decisive breakthroughs in astronomy and physics in the seventeenth century demolished the imposing medieval synthesis of Aristotelian philosophy and Christian theology. These developments had only limited practical consequences at the time, but the impact of new scientific knowledge on intellectual life was enormous. The emergence of modern science was a distinctive characteristic of

Western civilization and became a key element of Western identity. During the eighteenth century scientific thought fostered new ideas about racial differences and provided justifications for belief in Western superiority.

Interpreting scientific findings and Newtonian laws in a manner that was both antitradition and antireligion, Enlightenment philosophes extolled the superiority of rational, critical thinking. This new method, they believed, promised not just increased knowledge but even the discovery of the fundamental laws of human society. Although they reached different conclusions when they turned to social and political realities, they did stimulate absolute monarchs to apply reason to statecraft and the search for useful reforms. Above all, the philosophes succeeded in shaping an emerging public opinion and spreading their radically new worldview.

The ideas of the Enlightenment were an inspiration for monarchs, particularly absolutist rulers in central and eastern Europe who saw in them important tools for reforming and rationalizing their governments. Their primary goal was to strengthen their states and increase the efficiency of their bureaucracies and armies. Enlightened absolutists believed that these reforms would ultimately improve the lot of ordinary people, but this was not their chief concern. With few exceptions, they did not question the institution of serfdom. The fact that leading philosophes supported rather than criticized Eastern rulers' policies suggests some of the limitations of the era.

Key Terms

natural philosophy	skepticism
Copernican hypothesis	tabula rasa
experimental method	philosophes
law of inertia	separation of powers
law of universal gravitation	reading revolution
empiricism	salons
Cartesian dualism	rococo
scientific community	public sphere
Enlightenment	general will
rationalism	racial difference
progress	enlightened absolutism

Suggested Reading

Alexander, John T. *Catherine the Great: Life and Legend.* 1989. The best biography of the famous Russian tsarina.

Beales, Derek. *Joseph II.* 1987. A fine biography of the reforming Habsburg ruler.

Chartier, Roger. *The Cultural Origins of the French Revolution.* 1991. An imaginative analysis of the changing attitudes of the educated public.

Eze, E. Chukwudi, ed. *Race and the Enlightenment: A Reader.* 1997. A pioneering source on the origins of modern racial thinking in the Enlightenment.

Goodman, Dena. *The Republic of Letters: A Cultural History of the Enlightenment.* 1994. An innovative study of the role of salons and salon hostesses in the rise of the Enlightenment.

MacDonogh, Giles. *Frederick the Great.* 2001. An outstanding biography of the Prussian king.

Munck, Thomas. *The Enlightenment: A Comparative History.* 2000. Compares developments in Enlightenment thought in different countries.

Muthu, Sankar. *Enlightenment Against Empire.* 2003. Examines Enlightenment figures' opposition to colonialism.

Outram, Dorinda. *The Enlightenment*, 2d ed. 2006. An outstanding and accessible introduction to Enlightenment debates that emphasizes the Enlightenment's social context and global reach.

Schiebinger, Londa. *The Mind Has No Sex? Women in the Origins of Modern Science.* 1998. Discusses how the new science excluded women.

Shapin, Steven. *The Scientific Revolution.* 2001. A concise and well-informed general introduction to the scientific revolution.

Sorkin, David. *Moses Mendelssohn and the Religious Enlightenment.* 1996. A brilliant study of the Jewish philosopher and of the role of religion in the Enlightenment.

Notes

1. H. Butterfield, *The Origins of Modern Science* (New York: Macmillan, 1951), p. viii.
2. Quoted in A. G. R. Smith, *Science and Society in the Sixteenth and Seventeenth Centuries* (New York: Harcourt Brace Jovanovich, 1972), p. 97.
3. Quoted in Butterfield, *The Origins of Modern Science*, p. 47.
4. Ibid., pp. 115–116.
5. Ibid., p. 120.
6. L. Schiebinger, *The Mind Has No Sex? Women in the Origins of Modern Science* (Cambridge, Mass.: Harvard University Press, 1989), p. 2.
7. Jacqueline Broad, *Women Philosophers of the Seventeenth Century* (Cambridge: Cambridge University Press, 2003), p. 17.
8. Quoted in P. Hazard, *The European Mind, 1680–1715* (Cleveland: Meridian Books, 1963), pp. 304–305.
9. Schiebinger, *The Mind Has No Sex?* p. 64.
10. Quoted in L. M. Marsak, ed., *The Enlightenment* (New York: John Wiley & Sons, 1972), p. 56.
11. Quoted in G. L. Mosse et al., eds., *Europe in Review* (Chicago: Rand McNally, 1964), p. 156.
12. Quoted in P. Gay, "The Unity of the Enlightenment," *History* 3 (1960): 25.
13. See E. Fox-Genovese, "Women in the Enlightenment," in *Becoming Visible: Women in European History*, 2d ed., ed. R. Bridenthal, C. Koonz, and S. Stuard (Boston: Houghton Mifflin, 1987), esp. pp. 252–259, 263–265.
14. Quoted in G. P. Gooch, *Catherine the Great and Other Studies* (Hamden, Conn.: Archon Books, 1966), p. 149.
15. Jean Le Rond d'Alembert, *Eloges lus dans les séances publiques de l'Académie française* (Paris, 1779), p. ix, quoted in Mona Ozouf, "'Public Opinion' at the End of the Old Regime," *The Journal of Modern History* 60, Supplement: Rethinking French Politics in 1788 (September 1988), p. S9.
16. Quoted in Emmanuel Chukwudi Eze, ed., *Race and the Enlightenment: A Reader* (Oxford: Blackwell, 1997), p. 33. This section draws heavily on this reader.
17. Quoted in L. Krieger, *Kings and Philosophers, 1689–1789* (New York: W. W. Norton, 1970), p. 257.
18. Quoted in Gooch, *Catherine the Great*, p. 15.
19. Ibid., p. 53.

Voltaire on Religion

Voltaire was the most renowned and probably the most influential of the French philosophes. His biting satirical novel Candide *(1759) is still widely assigned in college courses, and his witty yet serious* Philosophical Dictionary *remains a source of pleasure and stimulation. The* Dictionary *consists of a series of essays on topics ranging from Adam to Zoroaster, from certainty to circumcision. The following passage is taken from the essay on religion.*

Voltaire began writing the Philosophical Dictionary *in 1752, at the age of fifty-eight, after arriving at the Prussian court in Berlin. Frederick the Great applauded Voltaire's efforts, but Voltaire put the project aside after leaving Berlin, and the first of several revised editions was published anonymously in 1764. It was an immediate and controversial success. Snapped up by an "enlightened" public, it was denounced by religious leaders as a threat to the Christian community and was burned in Geneva and Paris.*

I meditated last night; I was absorbed in the contemplation of nature; I admired the immensity, the course, the harmony of those infinite globes which the vulgar do not know how to admire.

I admired still more the intelligence which directs these vast forces. I said to myself: "One must be blind not to be dazzled by this spectacle; one must be stupid not to recognize its author; one must be mad not to worship the Supreme Being. What tribute of worship should I render Him? Should not this tribute be the same in the whole of space, since it is the same Supreme Power which reigns equally in all space?

"Should not a thinking being who dwells on a star in the Milky Way offer Him the same homage as a thinking being on this little globe of ours? Light is the same for the star Sirius as for us; moral philosophy must also be the same. If a feeling, thinking animal on Sirius is born of a tender father and mother who have been occupied with his happiness, he owes them as much love and care as we owe to our parents. If someone in the Milky Way sees a needy cripple, and if he can aid him and does not do so, then he is guilty toward all the globes.

"Everywhere the heart has the same duties: on the steps of the throne of God, if He has a throne; and in the depths of the abyss, if there is an abyss."

I was deep in these ideas when one of those genii who fill the spaces between the worlds came down to me. I recognized the same aerial creature who had appeared to me on another occasion to teach me that the judgments of God are different from our own, and how a good action is preferable to a controversy.

The genie transported me into a desert all covered with piles of bones. . . . He began with the first pile. "These," he said, "are the twenty-three thousand Jews who danced before a calf, together with the twenty-four thousand who were killed while fornicating with Midianitish women. The number of those massacred for such errors and offences amounts to nearly three hundred thousand.

"In the other piles are the bones of the Christians slaughtered by each other because of metaphysical disputes. They are divided into several heaps of four centuries each. One heap would have mounted right to the sky; they had to be divided."

"What!" I cried, "brothers have treated their brothers like this, and I have the misfortune to be of this brotherhood!"

"Here," said the spirit, "are the twelve million native Americans killed in their own land because they had not been baptized."

"My God! . . . Why assemble here all these abominable monuments to barbarism and fanaticism?"

An impish Voltaire, by the French sculptor Houdon. *(Courtesy of Board of Trustees of the Victoria & Albert Museum)*

"To instruct you. . . . Follow me now." [The genie takes Voltaire to the "heroes of humanity, who tried to banish violence and plunder from the world," and tells Voltaire to question them.]

[At last] I saw a man with a gentle, simple face, who seemed to me to be about thirty-five years old. From afar he looked with compassion upon those piles of whitened bones, through which I had been led to reach the sage's dwelling place. I was astonished to find his feet swollen and bleeding, his hands likewise, his side pierced, and his ribs laid bare by the cut of the lash. "Good God!" I said to him, "is it possible for a just man, a sage, to be in this state? I have just seen one who was treated in a very hateful way, but there is no comparison between his torture and yours. Wicked priests and wicked judges poisoned him; is it by priests and judges that you were so cruelly assassinated?"

With great courtesy he answered, "Yes."

"And who were these monsters?"

"They were hypocrites."

"Ah! that says everything; I understand by that one word that they would have condemned you to the cruelest punishment. Had you then proved to them, as Socrates did, that the Moon was not a goddess, and that Mercury was not a god?"

"No, it was not a question of planets. My countrymen did not even know what a planet was; they were all arrant ignoramuses. Their superstitions were quite different from those of the Greeks."

"Then you wanted to teach them a new religion?"

"Not at all; I told them simply: 'Love God with all your heart and your neighbor as yourself, for that is the whole of mankind's duty.' Judge yourself if this precept is not as old as the universe; judge yourself if I brought them a new religion." . . .

"But did you say nothing, do nothing that could serve them as a pretext?"

"To the wicked everything serves as pretext."

"Did you not say once that you were come not to bring peace, but a sword?"

"It was a scribe's error; I told them that I brought peace and not a sword. I never wrote anything; what I can't have been changed without evil intention."

"You did not then contribute in any way by your teaching, either badly reported or badly interpreted, to those frightful piles of bones which I saw on my way to consult with you?"

"I have only looked with horror upon those who have made themselves guilty of all these murders."

. . . [Finally] I asked him to tell me in what true religion consisted.

"Have I not already told you? Love God and your neighbor as yourself."

"Is it necessary for me to take sides either for the Greek Orthodox Church or the Roman Catholic?"

"When I was in the world I never made any difference between the Jew and the Samaritan."

"Well, if that is so, I take you for my only master." Then he made a sign with his head that filled me with peace. The vision disappeared, and I was left with a clear conscience.

Questions for Analysis

1. Why did Voltaire believe in a Supreme Being? Does this passage reflect the influence of Isaac Newton's scientific system? If so, how?

2. Was Voltaire trying to entertain, teach, or do both? Was he effective? Why?

3. If Voltaire was trying to convey serious ideas about religion and morality, what were those ideas? What was he attacking?

4. If a person today thought and wrote like Voltaire, would that person be called a defender or a destroyer of Christianity? Why?

Source: F. M. Arouet de Voltaire, *Oeuvres complètes,* vol. 8, trans. J. McKay (Paris: Firmin-Didot, 1875), pp. 188–190.

In this painting by the female artist Nanine Vallain, the figure of Liberty bears a copy of the Declaration of the Rights of Man and of the Citizen in one hand and a pike to defend them in the other. The painting hung in the Jacobin club until its fall from power. *(Musée de la Revolution Française, Vizille/The Bridgeman Art Library)*

THE REVOLUTION IN POLITICS, 1775–1815

The last years of the eighteenth century were a time of great upheaval. A series of revolutions and revolutionary wars challenged the old order of monarchs and aristocrats. The ideas of freedom and equality, ideas that have not stopped shaping the world since that era, flourished and spread. The revolutionary era began in North America in 1775. Then in 1789 France, the most influential country in Europe, became the leading revolutionary nation. It established first a constitutional monarchy, then a radical republic, and finally a new empire under Napoleon. Inspired by both the ideals of the Revolution and internal colonial conditions, the slaves of Saint-Domingue rose up in 1791. Their rebellion led to the creation of the new independent nation of Haiti in 1805.

The armies of France violently exported revolution beyond the nation's borders in an effort to establish new governments throughout much of Europe. The world of modern domestic and international politics was born.

Background to Revolution

Since July 1789 the origins of the French Revolution have been one of the most debated topics in history. Historians long explained the Revolution as a clash between the rising bourgeoisie and the entrenched nobility in which the former asserted its right to political power commensurate with its new economic strength. It is now apparent that such a simplistic explanation cannot account for the complexity of an event that spanned several decades and involved millions of people and numerous nations. In uncovering the path to revolution, numerous interrelated factors must be taken into account. These include deep social changes in France, a long-term political crisis that eroded monarchical legitimacy, the impact of new political ideas derived from the Enlightenment, the emergence of a "public sphere" in which such opinions were formed and shared, and, perhaps most importantly, a financial crisis created by France's participation in expensive overseas wars.

Book Companion Site

This icon will direct you to primary sources and study materials available at **bedfordstmartins.com/mckaywest**

While these developments built a thirst for fundamental political reform, there was nothing inevitable in the unfolding of the Revolution. As in many historical events, chance played a significant role in leading the French to revolution and in the course of events after its outbreak. Examining the background of institutions, events, and ideas helps explain how the fascinating and complex phenomenon known as the French Revolution came into being.

• *What social, political, and economic factors formed the background to the French Revolution?*

Legal Orders and Social Change

As in the Middle Ages, France's 25 million inhabitants were still legally divided into three orders, or **estates**— the clergy, the nobility, and everyone else. As the nation's first estate, the clergy numbered about one hundred thousand and had important privileges. It owned about 10 percent of the land and paid only a "voluntary gift," rather than regular taxes, to the government every five years. Moreover, the church levied a tax (the tithe) on landowners, which averaged somewhat less than 10 percent.

The second estate consisted of some four hundred thousand nobles, the descendants of "those who fought" in the Middle Ages. Nobles owned about 25 percent of the land in France outright, and they too were lightly taxed. Moreover, nobles continued to enjoy certain **manorial rights,** or privileges of lordship, that dated back to medieval times. These included exclusive rights to hunt and fish, village monopolies on baking bread and pressing grapes for wine, fees for justice, and a host of other "useful privileges." In addition, nobles had "honorific privileges" such as the right to precedence on public occasions and the right to wear swords. These rights conspicuously proclaimed the nobility's legal superiority and exalted social position.

Everyone else was a commoner, legally a member of the third estate. A few commoners—prosperous merchants, lawyers, and officials—were well educated and rich, and they might even have purchased manorial rights as a way of obtaining profit and social honor. The vast majority of the third estate consisted of peasants and agricultural workers in the countryside and urban artisans and unskilled day laborers. Thus the third estate was a conglomeration of very different social groups united only by their shared legal status as distinct from the nobility and clergy.

A FAUT ESPERER Q'EU JEU LA FINIRA BEN TOT.

The Three Estates In this political cartoon from 1789 a peasant of the third estate struggles under the crushing burden of a happy clergyman and a plumed nobleman. The caption—"Let's hope this game ends soon"—sets forth a program of reform that any peasant could understand. (*Réunion des Musées Nationaux/Art Resource, NY*)

In discussing the origins of the French Revolution, historians long focused on growing tensions between the nobility and the comfortable members of the third estate, the *bourgeoisie* or upper middle class. Increasing in size, wealth, culture, and self-confidence, this rising bourgeoisie became progressively exasperated by archaic "feudal" laws restraining the economy and by the pretensions of a reactionary nobility that was closing ranks against middle-class aspirations. As a result, the French bourgeoisie eventually rose up to lead the entire third estate in a great social revolution that destroyed feudal privileges and established a capitalist order based on individualism and a market economy.

In recent years, a flood of new research has challenged these accepted views. Above all, revisionist historians have questioned the existence of growing social conflict between a progressive capitalistic bourgeoisie and a reactionary feudal nobility in eighteenth-century France. Instead, they see both bourgeoisie and nobility as highly fragmented, riddled with internal rivalries. The ancient sword nobility, for example, was profoundly separated from the newer robe nobility by differences in wealth, education, and worldview. Differences within the bourgeoisie—between wealthy financiers and local lawyers, for example—were no less profound. Rather than standing as unified blocs against each other, nobility and bourgeoisie formed two parallel social ladders increasingly linked together at the top by wealth, marriage, and Enlightenment culture.

Revisionist historians stress three developments in particular. First, the nobility remained a fluid and relatively open order. Throughout the eighteenth century substantial numbers of successful commoners continued to seek and obtain noble status through government service and purchase of expensive positions conferring nobility. Second, key sections of the nobility were no less liberal than the middle class, and until revolution actually began, both groups generally supported the judicial opposition to the government led by the Parlement of Paris. Third, the nobility and the bourgeoisie were not really at odds in the economic sphere. Investment in land and government service were the preferred activities of both groups, and the ideal of the merchant capitalist was to gain enough wealth to retire from trade, purchase an estate, and live nobly as a large landowner. At the same time, wealthy nobles often acted as aggressive capitalists, investing especially in mining, metallurgy, and foreign trade.

Revisionists have clearly shaken the belief that the bourgeoisie and the nobility were inevitably locked in growing conflict before the Revolution. But in stressing the similarities between the two groups, especially at the top, revisionists have also reinforced the view that the Old Regime had ceased to correspond with social reality by the 1780s. Legally, society was still based on rigid orders inherited from the Middle Ages. In reality, France had already moved far toward being a society based on wealth and education in which an emerging elite that included both aristocratic and bourgeois notables was frustrated by a bureaucratic monarchy that continued to claim the right to absolute power.

Chronology

1773	Boston Tea Party
1775	Paine, *Common Sense*
1775–1783	American Revolution
1786–1789	Financial crisis in France
1789	Feudalism abolished in France; ratification of U.S. Constitution; storming of the Bastille
1789–1799	French Revolution
1790	Burke, *Reflections on the Revolution in France*
1791	Slave insurrection in Saint-Domingue
1792	Wollstonecraft, *A Vindication of the Rights of Woman*
1793	Execution of Louis XVI
1793–1794	Economic controls to help poor in France; Robespierre's Reign of Terror
1794	Robespierre deposed and executed
1794–1799	Thermidorian reaction
1799–1815	Napoleonic era
1805	Haitian republic declares independence
1812	Napoleon invades Russia
1814–1815	Napoleon defeated and exiled

The Crisis of Political Legitimacy

Overlaying these social changes was a century-long political and fiscal struggle between the monarchy and its opponents that was primarily enacted in the law courts. When Louis XIV finally died in 1715 and was succeeded by his five-year-old great-grandson, Louis XV (r. 1715–1774), the Sun King's elaborate system of absolutist rule was challenged. Favored by the duke of Orléans (1674–1723), who governed as regent until 1723, a number of institutions retrieved powers they had lost under Louis XIV. Instead of assuming personal rule, the regent reinstated councils of state to aid in decision making.

Most important, in 1715 the duke restored to the high courts of France—the parlements—the ancient right to evaluate royal decrees publicly in writing before they were registered and given the force of law. The restoration of this right, which had been suspended under Louis XIV, was a fateful step. The magistrates of the parlements were leaders of the robe nobility. In 1604 Henry IV had created the paulette (see page 528) on royal offices as a way to raise desperately needed revenue. The unintended consequence of this act was to transform royal offices, including judicial positions, into a form of private property passed down from father to son. By allowing a well-entrenched and highly articulate branch of the nobility to evaluate the king's decrees before they became law, the duke of Orléans sanctioned a counterweight to absolute power.

These implications became clear when the heavy expenses of the War of the Austrian Succession plunged France into financial crisis. In 1748 Louis XV appointed a finance minister who decreed a 5 percent income tax on every individual regardless of social status. Exemption from most taxation had long been a hallowed privilege of the nobility, and other important groups—the clergy, the large towns, and some wealthy bourgeoisie—had also gained special tax advantages over time. The result was a vigorous protest from many sides led by the influential Parlement of Paris. The monarchy retreated; the new tax was dropped.

Following the disastrously expensive Seven Years' War (see pages 635–637), the conflict re-emerged. The government tried to maintain emergency taxes after the war ended; the Parlement of Paris protested and even challenged the basis of royal authority, claiming that the king's power had to be limited to protect liberty. Once again the government caved in and withdrew the taxes. The judicial opposition then asserted that the king could not levy taxes without the consent of the Parlement of Paris, which was acting as the representative of the entire nation.

After years of attempting to compromise with the parlements, Louis XV roused himself for a determined defense of his absolutist inheritance. "The magistrates," he angrily told the Parlement of Paris in a famous face-to-face confrontation, "are my officers. . . . In my person only does the sovereign power rest."[1] In 1768 Louis appointed a tough career official named René de Maupeou as chancellor and ordered him to crush the judicial opposition.

Maupeou abolished the existing parlements and exiled the vociferous members of the Parlement of Paris to the provinces. He created a new and docile parlement of royal officials, known as the **Maupeou parlements,** and he began once again to tax the privileged groups. A few

philosophes applauded these measures: the sovereign was using his power to introduce badly needed reforms that had been blocked by a self-serving aristocratic elite. Most philosophes, and public opinion as a whole, sided with the old parlements, however, and there was widespread criticism of "royal despotism."

Learned dissent was accompanied by scandalous libels. Known as Louis le bien-aimé (beloved Louis) in his youth, the king found his people turning against him for moral as well as political reasons. Kings had always maintained mistresses who were invariably chosen from the court nobility. Louis XV broke that pattern with Madame de Pompadour, daughter of a disgraced bourgeois financier. As favorite from 1745 to 1750, Pompadour exercised tremendous influence over literature, art, and the decorative arts, using her patronage to support Voltaire and promote the rococo style. Even after their love affair ended, Pompadour wielded considerable influence over the king, helping bring about the alliance with Austria that resulted in the Seven Years' War. Pompadour's low birth and hidden political influence generated a stream of resentful pamphleteering.

After Pompadour, the king appeared to sink ever lower in licentiousness; his last favorite, Madame du Barry, was derided as a common streetwalker, and the king was accused of maintaining a brothel of teenage girls at Versailles to serve his lusts. The illegal stream of scandal-mongering became a torrent. Lurid and pornographic depictions of the court ate away at the foundations of royal authority, especially among the common people in turbulent Paris. The king was being stripped of the sacred aura of God's anointed on earth and was being reinvented in the popular imagination as a degenerate.

Despite this progressive **desacralization** of the monarchy, its power was still great enough to ride over the opposition, and Louis XV would probably have prevailed if he had lived to a ripe old age, but he died in 1774. The new king, Louis XVI (r. 1774–1792), was a shy twenty-year-old with good intentions. Taking the throne, he is reported to have said, "What I should like most is to be loved."[2] The eager-to-please monarch yielded in the face of vehement opposition from France's educated elite. He dismissed chancellor Maupeou and repudiated the strong-willed minister's work. Louis also waffled on the economy, dismissing controller-general Turgot when his attempts to liberalize the economy drew fire. A weakened but unreformed monarchy now faced a judicial opposition that claimed to speak for the entire French nation. Increasingly locked in stalemate, the country was drifting toward renewed financial crisis and political upheaval.

The Impact of the American Revolution

Coinciding with the first years of Louis XVI's reign, the American Revolution had an enormous impact on France both in practical and ideological terms. French expenses to support the colonists bankrupted the Crown, while the ideals of liberty and equality provided heady inspiration for political reform.

Like the French Revolution, the American Revolution had its immediate origins in struggles over increased taxes. The high cost of the Seven Years' War—fought with little financial contribution from the colonies—doubled the British national debt. When the government tried to recoup some of the losses in increased taxes on the colonies in 1765, the colonists reacted with anger.

The key questions were political rather than economic. To what extent could the home government assert its power while limiting the authority of colonial legislatures and their elected representatives? Accordingly, who should represent the colonies, and who had the right to make laws for Americans? The British government replied that Americans were represented in Parliament, albeit indirectly (like most British people themselves), and that the absolute supremacy of Parliament throughout the empire could not be questioned. Many Americans felt otherwise.

In 1773 the dispute over taxes and representation flared up again after the British government awarded a monopoly on Chinese tea to the East India Company, suddenly excluding colonial merchants from a lucrative business. In response, Boston men disguised as Indians held a rowdy "tea party" and threw the company's tea into the harbor. This led to extreme measures. The so-called Coercive Acts closed the port of Boston, curtailed local elections, and greatly expanded the royal governor's power. County conventions in Massachusetts protested vehemently and urged that the acts be "rejected as the attempts of a wicked administration to enslave America." Other colonial assemblies joined in the denunciations. In September 1774 the First Continental Congress met in Philadelphia, where the more radical members argued successfully against concessions to the Crown. Compromise was also rejected by the British Parliament, and in April 1775 fighting began at Lexington and Concord.

The fighting spread, and the colonists moved slowly but inevitably toward open rebellion and a declaration of independence. The uncompromising attitude of the British government and its use of German mercenaries dissolved long-standing loyalties to the home country and rivalries among the separate colonies. Some colonists

Toward Revolution in Boston The Boston Tea Party was only one of many angry confrontations between British officials and Boston patriots. On January 27, 1774, an angry crowd seized a British customs collector and tarred and feathered him. This French engraving of 1784 commemorates the defiant and provocative action. *(The Granger Collection, New York)*

remained loyal to the Crown; large numbers of these Loyalists emigrated to the northern colonies of Canada.

On July 4, 1776, the Second Continental Congress adopted the Declaration of Independence. Written by Thomas Jefferson, it boldly listed the tyrannical acts committed by George III (r. 1760–1820) and confidently proclaimed the natural rights of mankind and the **sovereignty** of the American states. Sometimes called the world's greatest political editorial, the Declaration of Independence in effect universalized the traditional rights of English people and made them the rights of all mankind. It stated that "all men are created equal. . . . They are endowed by their Creator with certain unalienable rights. . . . Among these are life, liberty, and the pursuit of happiness."

On the international scene, the French wanted revenge for the humiliating defeats of the Seven Years' War.

They sympathized with the rebels and supplied guns and gunpowder from the beginning. By 1777 French volunteers were arriving in Virginia, and a dashing young nobleman, the marquis de Lafayette (1757–1834), quickly became one of George Washington's most trusted generals. In 1778 the French government offered a formal alliance to the American ambassador in Paris, Benjamin Franklin, and in 1779 and 1780 the Spanish and Dutch declared war on Britain. Catherine the Great of Russia helped organize the League of Armed Neutrality in order to protect neutral shipping rights, which Britain refused to recognize.

Thus by 1780 Great Britain was engaged in an imperial war against most of Europe as well as against the thirteen colonies. In these circumstances, and in the face of severe reverses, a new British government decided to cut its losses and offered peace on extremely generous terms. By the Treaty of Paris of 1783, Britain recognized the independence of the thirteen colonies and ceded all its territory between the Allegheny Mountains and the Mississippi River to the Americans. Out of the bitter rivalries of the Old World, the Americans snatched dominion over a vast territory.

Europeans who dreamed of a new era were fascinated by the political lessons of the American Revolution. The Americans had begun with a revolutionary defense against tyrannical oppression, and they had been victorious. They had then shown how rational beings could assemble together to exercise sovereignty and write a permanent constitution—a new social contract. All this gave greater reality to the concepts of individual liberty and representative government and reinforced one of the primary ideas of the Enlightenment: that a better world was possible.

No country felt the consequences of the American Revolution more directly than France. Hundreds of French officers served in America and were inspired by the experience, the marquis de Lafayette chief among them. French intellectuals and publicists engaged in passionate analysis of the new federal Constitution as well as the constitutions of the various states of the new United States. Perhaps more importantly, the expenses of supporting the revolutionary forces provided the last nail in the coffin for the French treasury.

Financial Crisis

The French Revolution thus had its immediate origins in the financial difficulties of the government. The efforts of Louis XV's ministers to raise taxes had been thwarted by the high courts, led by the Parlement of Paris, which was strengthened in its opposition by widespread popular support. When renewed efforts to reform the tax system met a similar fate in 1776, the government was forced to finance all of its enormous expenditures during the American war with borrowed money. As a result, the national debt and the annual budget deficit soared.

By the 1780s, fully 50 percent of France's annual budget went for interest payments on the debt. Another 25 percent went to maintain the military, while 6 percent was absorbed by the king and his court at Versailles. Less than 20 percent of the entire national budget was available for the productive functions of the state, such as transportation and general administration. This was an impossible financial situation.

One way out would have been for the government to declare partial bankruptcy, forcing its creditors to accept greatly reduced payments on the debt. The Spanish monarchy had regularly repudiated large portions of its debt in earlier times, and France had done likewise after an attempt to establish a national bank ended in financial disaster in 1720. Yet by the 1780s the French debt was being held by an army of aristocratic and bourgeois creditors, and the French monarchy, though absolute in theory, had become too weak for such a drastic and unpopular action.

Nor could the king and his ministers print money and create inflation to cover their deficits. Unlike England and Holland, which had far larger national debts relative to their populations, France had no central bank, no paper currency, and no means of creating credit. French money was good gold coin. Therefore, when a depressed economy and public distrust made it increasingly difficult for the government to obtain new gold loans in 1786, it had no alternative but to try to increase taxes. Since France's tax system was unfair and out-of-date, increased revenues were possible only through fundamental reform. Such reforms, which would affect all groups in France's complex and fragmented society, opened a Pandora's box of social and political demands.

The Revolution was looming by 1787, though no one could have realized what was to follow. Spurred by a depressed economy and falling tax receipts, Louis XVI's minister of finance revived old proposals to impose a general tax on all landed property as well as to form provincial assemblies to help administer the tax, and he convinced the king to call an **Assembly of Notables** to gain support for the idea. The notables, who were mainly important noblemen and high-ranking clergy, opposed the new tax. In exchange for their support, they demanded that control over all government spending be given to the provincial assemblies. When the government refused, the notables responded that such sweeping tax changes required the approval of the Estates General, the representative body of all three estates, which had not met since 1614.

Facing imminent bankruptcy, the king tried to reassert his authority. He dismissed the notables and established new taxes by decree. In stirring language, the judges of the Parlement of Paris promptly declared the royal initiative null and void. When the king tried to exile the judges, a tremendous wave of protest swept the country. Frightened investors also refused to advance more loans to the state. Finally, in July 1788, Louis XVI bowed to public opinion and called for a spring session of the Estates General.

Revolution in Metropole and Colony, 1789–1791

Although inspired by the ideals of the American Revolution, the French Revolution did not mirror the American example. It was more radical and more complex, more influential and more controversial, more loved and more hated. For Europeans and most of the rest of the world, it was the great revolution of the eighteenth century, *the* revolution that opened the modern era in politics. In turn, the slave insurrection in Saint-Domingue—which ultimately resulted in the second independent republic of the Americas—inspired liberation movements across the world.

- *What were the immediate events that sparked the Revolution, and how did they result in the formation of a constitutional monarchy in France? How did the ideals and events of the early Revolution raise new aspirations in the colonies?*

The Formation of the National Assembly

Once Louis had agreed to hold the **Estates General**, following precedent, he set elections for the three orders. As at previous meetings of the Estates General, local assemblies were to prepare a list of grievances for their representatives to bring to the next electoral level. This request, as traditional as it was, set off a flood of debate, criticism, and demands throughout France. All across the country, clergy, nobles, and commoners came together in their respective orders to draft petitions for change and to elect delegates to the Estates General. These documents reveal the main complaints French subjects had on the eve of revolution. The local assemblies of the clergy showed considerable dissatisfaction with the church hierarchy. The nobles were politically divided. A conservative majority was drawn from the poorer and more numerous provincial nobility, but fully one-third of the nobility's representatives were liberals committed to major changes.

As for the third estate, there was great popular participation in the elections. Almost all male commoners twenty-five years of age and older had the right to vote. However, most of the representatives selected by the third estate were well-educated, prosperous members of the middle class. Most were not businessmen but rather lawyers and government officials. Social status and prestige were matters of particular concern to this economic elite. No delegates from the great mass of laboring poor—the peasants and urban artisans—were elected.

The petitions for change coming from the three estates showed a surprising degree of consensus. There was general agreement that royal absolutism should give way to a constitutional monarchy in which laws and taxes would require the consent of the Estates General in regular meetings. All agreed that individual liberties would have to be guaranteed by law and that economic regulations should be loosened. The striking similarities in the grievance petitions of the clergy, nobility, and third estate reflected a shared commitment to a basic reform platform among the educated elite.

Book Companion Site
Primary Source: The Third Estate Speaks: The Cahier de Doleances of the Carcassonne

Yet an increasingly bitter quarrel undermined this consensus during the intense electoral campaign: *how* would the Estates General vote, and precisely *who* would lead in the political reorganization that was generally desired? The Estates General of 1614 had sat as three separate houses. Each house held one vote, despite the enormous numerical discrepancies between the estates in the general population. Given the close ties between them, the nobility and clergy would control all decisions. As soon as the estates were called, the aristocratic Parlement of Paris, mainly out of respect for tradition but partly out of a desire to enhance the nobility's political position, ruled that the Estates General should once again sit separately. The ruling was quickly denounced by some intellectuals, who demanded instead a single assembly dominated by the third estate to ensure fundamental reforms. In his famous 1789 pamphlet *What Is the Third Estate?* the abbé Emmanuel Joseph Sieyès argued that the nobility was a tiny, overprivileged minority and that the neglected third estate constituted the true strength of the French nation. When the government agreed that the third estate should have as many delegates as the clergy and the nobility combined but then rendered this act meaningless by upholding voting by separate order, reform-minded critics saw fresh evidence of an aristocratic conspiracy.

In May 1789 the twelve hundred delegates of the three estates paraded in medieval pageantry through the streets of Versailles to an opening session resplendent with feudal magnificence. The estates were almost immediately deadlocked. Delegates of the third estate refused to transact any business until the king ordered the clergy and nobility to sit with them in a single body. Finally, after a six-week war of nerves, a few parish priests began to go over to the third estate, which on June 17 voted to call itself the **National Assembly.** On June 20 the delegates of the third estate, excluded from their hall because of "repairs," moved to a large indoor tennis court. There they swore the famous Oath of the Tennis Court, pledging not to disband until they had written a new constitution.

The king's response was ambivalent. On June 23 he made a conciliatory speech urging reforms to a joint session, and four days later he ordered the three estates to meet together. At the same time, the vacillating and indecisive monarch apparently followed the advice of relatives and court nobles who urged him to dissolve the Estates General by force. The king called an army of eighteen thousand troops toward Versailles, and on July 11 he dismissed his finance minister and his other more liberal ministers. As Louis XVI belatedly reasserted his "divine right" to rule, middle-class delegates and their allies from the liberal nobility resigned themselves to being disbanded at bayonet point. One third-estate delegate reassured a worried colleague, "You won't hang—you'll only have to go back home."[3]

The Revolt of the Poor and the Oppressed

While delegates of the third estate pressed for political rights, economic hardship gripped the common people. Grain was the basis of the diet of ordinary people in the eighteenth century, and in 1788 the harvest had been extremely poor. The price of bread began to soar. In Paris, where bread was regularly subsidized by the government in an attempt to prevent popular unrest, the price rose to 4 sous. The poor could scarcely afford to pay 2 sous per pound, for even at that price a laborer with a wife and three children had to spend half his wages on the family's bread.

Harvest failure and high bread prices unleashed a classic economic depression of the preindustrial age. With food so expensive and with so much uncertainty, the demand for manufactured goods collapsed. Thousands of artisans and small traders were thrown out of work. By the end of 1789 almost half of the French people would be in need of relief. One person in eight was a pauper living in extreme want. In Paris perhaps 150,000 of the city's 600,000 people were without work in July 1789.

Against this background of poverty and ongoing political crisis, the people of Paris entered decisively onto the revolutionary stage. They believed in a general, though ill-defined, way that the economic distress had human causes. They believed that they should have steady work and enough bread at fair prices to survive. Specifically, they feared that the dismissal of the king's moderate finance minister would put them at the mercy of aristocratic landowners and grain speculators. Rumors that the king's troops would sack the city began to fill the air. Angry crowds formed, and passionate voices urged action. On July 13 the people began to seize arms for the defense of the city as the king's armies moved toward Paris, and on July 14 several hundred people marched to the Bastille to search for weapons and gunpowder.

A medieval fortress with walls ten feet thick and eight great towers each one hundred feet high, the Bastille had long been used as a royal prison. It was guarded by eighty retired soldiers and thirty Swiss mercenaries. The governor of the fortress-prison refused to hand over the powder, panicked, and ordered his men to resist, killing ninety-eight people attempting to enter. Cannon were brought to batter the main gate, and fighting continued until the prison surrendered. The governor of the prison was later hacked to death, and his head was stuck on a pike and paraded through the streets. The next day a committee of citizens appointed the marquis de Lafayette commander of the city's armed forces. Paris was lost to the king, who was forced to recall the finance minister and disperse his troops. The popular uprising had broken the power monopoly of the royal army and thereby saved the National Assembly.

Book Companion Site
Primary Source: The Taking of the Bastille and Its Aftermath: An English Perspective

As the delegates resumed their inconclusive debates at Versailles, the countryside sent them a radical and unmistakable message. Throughout France peasants began to rise in insurrection against their lords, ransacking manor houses and burning feudal documents that recorded their obligations. In some areas peasants reinstated traditional village practices, undoing recent enclosures and reoccupying old common lands. They seized forests, and taxes went unpaid. Fear of vagabonds and outlaws—called the **Great Fear** by contemporaries—seized the countryside and fanned the flames of rebellion. The long-suffering peasants were doing their best to free themselves from manorial rights and exploitation.

Faced with chaos, yet afraid to call on the king to restore order, some liberal nobles and middle-class delegates at Versailles responded to peasant demands with a surprise maneuver on the night of August 4, 1789. The duke of Aiguillon, also notably one of France's greatest noble landowners, declared that

in several provinces the whole people forms a kind of league for the destruction of the manor houses, the ravaging of the lands, and especially for the seizure of the archives where the title deeds to feudal properties are kept. It seeks to throw off at last a yoke that has for many centuries weighted it down.[4]

He urged equality in taxation and the elimination of feudal dues. In the end, all the old noble privileges—peasant serfdom where it still existed, exclusive hunting rights, fees for justice, village monopolies, the right to make peasants work on the roads, and a host of other dues—were abolished. Thus the French peasantry, which already owned about 30 percent of all the land, achieved an unprecedented victory in the early days of revolutionary upheaval. Henceforth, French peasants would seek mainly to protect and consolidate their triumph. As the Great Fear subsided in the countryside, they became a force for order and stability.

A Limited Monarchy

The National Assembly moved forward. On August 27, 1789, it issued the Declaration of the Rights of Man and of the Citizen, which stated, "Men are born and remain free and equal in rights." The declaration also maintained that mankind's natural rights are "liberty, property, security, and resistance to oppression" and that "every man is presumed innocent until he is proven guilty." As for law, "it is an expression of the general will; all citizens have the right to concur personally or through their representatives in its formation. . . . Free expression of thoughts and opinions is one of the most precious rights of mankind: every citizen may therefore speak, write, and publish freely." In short, this clarion call of the liberal revolutionary ideal guaranteed equality before the law, representative government for a sovereign people, and individual freedom. This revolutionary credo, only two pages long, was disseminated throughout France and Europe and around the world.

Book Companion Site
Primary Source: The Declaration of the Rights of Man and of the Citizen

Moving beyond general principles to draft a constitution proved difficult. The questions of how much power the king should retain and whether he could permanently veto legislation led to another deadlock. Once again the decisive answer came from the poor—in this instance, the poor women of Paris.

Women customarily bought the food and managed the poor family's slender resources. In Paris great numbers of women also worked for wages, making garments and luxury items destined for an aristocratic and international clientele. Immediately after the fall of the Bastille, many of France's great court nobles began to leave Versailles for foreign lands, so that a plummeting demand for luxuries intensified the general economic crisis. International markets also declined. The church was no longer able to give its traditional grants of food and money to the poor. Increasing unemployment and hunger put tremendous pressure on household managers, and the result was another popular explosion.

On October 5 some seven thousand desperate women marched the twelve miles from Paris to Versailles to demand action. A middle-class deputy looking out from the Assembly saw "multitudes arriving from Paris including fishwives and bullies from the market, and these people wanted nothing but bread." This great crowd invaded the Assembly, "armed with scythes, sticks and pikes." One tough old woman defiantly shouted into the debate, "Who's that talking down there? Make the chatterbox shut up. That's not the point: the point is that we want bread."[5] Hers was the genuine voice of the people, essential to any understanding of the French Revolution.

The women invaded the royal apartments, slaughtered some of the royal bodyguards, and furiously searched for the queen, Marie Antoinette, who was widely despised for her frivolous and supposedly immoral behavior. "We are going to cut off her head, tear out her heart, fry her liver, and that won't be the end of it," they shouted, surging through the palace in a frenzy. It seems likely that only the intervention of Lafayette and the National Guard saved the royal family. But the only way to calm the disorder was for the king to live in Paris, as the crowd demanded.

The next day the royal family left for Paris in the midst of a strange procession. The heads of two aristocrats, stuck on pikes, led the way. They were followed by the

The Women of Paris March to Versailles   On October 5, 1789, a large group of Parisian market women marched to Versailles to protest the price of bread. For the people of Paris, the king was the baker of last resort, responsible for feeding his people during times of scarcity. The crowd forced the royal family to return with them and to live in Paris, rather than remain isolated from their subjects at court. *(Erich Lessing/Art Resource, NY)*

remaining members of the royal bodyguard, unarmed and mocked by fierce men holding sabers and pikes. A mixed and victorious multitude surrounded the carriage of the captured royal family, hurling crude insults at the queen. There was drinking and eating among the women, who had emerged as a major element in the Parisian revolutionary crowd.[6]

The National Assembly followed the king to Paris, and the next two years, until September 1791, saw the consolidation of the liberal revolution. Under middle-class leadership, the National Assembly abolished the French nobility as a legal order and pushed forward with the creation of a **constitutional monarchy,** which Louis XVI reluctantly agreed to accept in July 1790. In the final constitution, the king remained the head of state, but all lawmaking power was placed in the hands of the National Assembly, elected by the economic upper half of French males.

New laws broadened women's rights to seek divorce, to inherit property, and to obtain financial support for illegitimate children from fathers. But women were not allowed to vote or hold political office for at least two

reasons. First, the great majority of comfortable, well-educated males in the National Assembly believed that women should be limited to child rearing and domestic duties and should leave politics and most public activities to men, as Rousseau had advocated in his influential writings (see page 607). Second, the delegates to the National Assembly were convinced that political life in absolutist France had been profoundly corrupt and that a prime example of this corruption was the way that some talented but immoral aristocratic women had used their sexual charms to manipulate weak rulers and their ministers. Thus delegates argued that excluding women from politics would help create the civic virtue that had been missing: pure, home-focused wives would raise the high-minded sons needed to govern the nation.

The National Assembly replaced the complicated patchwork of historic provinces with eighty-three departments of approximately equal size. The jumble of weights and measures that varied from province to province was reformed, leading to the introduction of the metric system in 1793. Monopolies, guilds, and workers' associations were prohibited, and barriers to trade within France were abolished in the name of economic liberty. Thus the National Assembly applied the critical spirit of the Enlightenment in a thorough reform of France's laws and institutions.

The Assembly also imposed a radical reorganization on the country's religious life. It granted religious freedom to the small minority of French Jews and Protestants. Of greater impact, it then nationalized the Catholic Church's property and abolished monasteries as useless relics of a distant past. The government used all former church property as collateral to guarantee a new paper currency, the assignats, and then sold the property in an attempt to put the state's finances on a solid footing. Although the church's land was sold in large blocks, peasants eventually purchased much when it was subdivided. These purchases strengthened their attachment to the new revolutionary order in the countryside.

The religious reorganization of France brought the new government into conflict with the Catholic Church and many sincere Christians, especially in the countryside. Imbued with the rationalism and skepticism of the eighteenth-century philosophes, many delegates distrusted popular piety and "superstitious religion." Thus they established a national church, with priests chosen by voters. The National Assembly then forced the Catholic clergy to take a loyalty oath to the new government. The pope formally condemned this attempt to subjugate the church, and only half the priests of France swore the oath. The result was a deep religious divide within the country and the clergy. The attempt to remake the Catholic Church, like the Assembly's abolition of guilds and workers associations, sharpened the conflict between the educated classes and the common people that had been emerging in the eighteenth century. This policy toward the church was the revolutionary government's first important failure.

Revolutionary Aspirations in Saint-Domingue

The French Revolution radically transformed not only the territorial nation of France but its overseas colonies as well. On the eve of the Revolution, Saint-Domingue—the most profitable of all Caribbean colonies—was even more rife with social tensions than France itself. In addition to distinctions between noble and commoner or rich and poor, Saint-Domingue harbored divisions between free and unfree and a racial spectrum that included black, mixed race, and white people.

The colony's slave population was at least five hundred thousand, in comparison to a white population of approximately forty thousand. Because the brutal conditions created very high death rates among slaves, traders brought a constant stream of new arrivals from Africa. In 1789 up to two-thirds of slaves in Saint-Domingue had been born in Africa, most in the west-central region of the continent. Many were veterans of wars in Africa.

The free population was divided by color and by wealth. The European population included French colonial officials, wealthy planters and merchants, and poor immigrants. A sizable population of free people of African and mixed African European descent also existed, who referred to themselves as "free coloreds" or **free people of color.** They varied from modest artisans, to plantation managers and clerks, to wealthy established planters who owned slaves themselves. Failing to achieve their dreams of a colonial fortune, poor whites bitterly resented the privileges of the others, especially the free-colored elite. The white elite harbored its own grudges against France's monopoly on colonial trade and the royal government's attempts in the 1780s to impose legislation requiring humane treatment of slaves.

The 1685 *Code noir* (Black Code) that set the parameters of slavery had granted free people of color the same legal status as whites: they could own property, live where they wished, and pursue any education or career they desired. From the 1760s on, however, colonial administrators began rescinding these rights, and by the time of the Revolution, myriad aspects of free coloreds' lives—from the professions they could practice, to the names they could adopt, to the clothes they could wear—were ruled by discriminatory laws. White planters eagerly welcomed these laws, convinced that the best defense of slavery was a rigid color line.

The political and intellectual turmoil of the 1780s, with its growing rhetoric of liberty, equality, and fraternity, raised new challenges and possibilities for each of these groups. For slaves, news of abolitionist movements in France, and the royal government's own attempts to rein in the worst abuses of slavery, led to hopes that the mother country might grant them freedom. Free people of color found in such rhetoric the principles on which to base a defense of their legal and political rights. They looked to political reforms in Paris as a means of gaining political enfranchisement and reasserting equal status with whites. The white elite, not surprisingly, saw matters very differently. Infuriated by talk of abolition and determined to protect their way of life, they looked to revolutionary ideals of representative government for the chance to gain control of their own affairs, as had the American colonists before them. The meeting of the Estates General and the Declaration of the Rights of Man and of the Citizen raised these conflicting colonial aspirations to new levels.

The National Assembly, however, frustrated the hopes of all these groups. Cowed by colonial representatives who claimed that support for free coloreds would result in slave insurrection and independence, the Assembly refused to extend French constitutional safeguards to the colonies. Instead, it ruled that each colony would draft its own constitution, with free rein over decisions on slavery and the enfranchisement of free people of color. After dealing this blow to the aspirations of slaves and free coloreds, the committee also reaffirmed French monopolies over colonial trade, thereby angering planters as well.

In July 1790 Vincent Ogé, a free man of color, returned to Saint-Domingue from Paris determined to redress these issues. He raised an army of several hundred, occupied the town of Grande-Rivière, and sent letters to the new Provincial Assembly of Saint-Domingue demanding political rights for all free citizens, a statute already passed in France. After initial victories, his army was defeated, and Ogé himself was tortured and executed. In an attempt to forge compromise, in May 1791 the National Assembly granted political rights to free people of color born to two free parents who possessed sufficient property. When news of this legislation arrived in Saint-Domingue, the white elite was furious and the colonial governor refused to enact it. Violence now erupted between groups of whites and free coloreds in parts of the colony. The liberal revolution had failed to satisfy the contradictory ambitions in the colonies.

World War and Republican France, 1791–1799

When Louis XVI accepted the final version of the National Assembly's constitution in September 1791, a young and still obscure provincial lawyer and delegate named Maximilien Robespierre (1758–1794) concluded, "The Revolution is over." Robespierre was both right and wrong. He was right in the sense that the most constructive and lasting reforms were in place. Nothing substantial in the way of liberty and fundamental reform would be gained in the next generation. He was wrong in the sense that a much more radical stage lay ahead. New heroes and new ideologies were to emerge in revolutionary wars and international conflict in which Robespierre himself would play a central role.

● *How and why did the Revolution take a radical turn at home and in the colonies?*

Foreign Reactions and the Beginning of War

The outbreak and progress of revolution in France produced great excitement and a sharp division of opinion in Europe and the United States. Liberals and radicals saw a mighty triumph of liberty over despotism. In Great Britain especially, they hoped that the French example would lead to a fundamental reordering of Parliament, which was in the hands of the aristocracy and a few wealthy merchants. After the French Revolution began, conservative leaders such as Edmund Burke (1729–1797) were deeply troubled by the aroused spirit of reform. In 1790 Burke published *Reflections on the Revolution in France,* one of the great defenses of European conservatism. He defended inherited privileges in general and those of the English monarchy and aristocracy. He glorified the unrepresentative Parliament and predicted that thoroughgoing reform like that occurring in France would lead only to chaos and tyranny. Burke's work sparked much debate.

One passionate rebuttal came from a young writer in London, Mary Wollstonecraft (1759–1797). Born into the middle class, Wollstonecraft was schooled in adversity by a mean-spirited father who beat his wife and squandered his inherited fortune. Determined to be independent in a society that expected women of her class to become obedient wives, she struggled for years to earn her living as a governess and a teacher—practically the only acceptable careers for single, educated women—before attaining success as a translator and author. Incensed by Burke's book, Wollstonecraft immediately wrote a blistering, widely read attack, *A Vindication of the Rights of Man* (1790).

Then she made a daring intellectual leap, developing for the first time the logical implications of natural-law philosophy in her masterpiece, *A Vindication of the Rights of Woman* (1792). To fulfill the still-unrealized potential of the French Revolution and to eliminate the sexual inequality she had felt so keenly, she demanded that

the Rights of Women be respected . . . [and] JUSTICE for one-half of the human race. . . . It is time to effect a revolution in female manners, time to restore to them their lost dignity, and make them, as part of the human species, labor, by reforming themselves, to reform the world.

Setting high standards for women—"I wish to persuade women to endeavor to acquire strength, both of mind and body"—Wollstonecraft broke with those who had a low opinion of women's intellectual potential. She advocated rigorous coeducation, which would make women better wives and mothers, good citizens, and economically independent. Women could manage businesses and enter politics if only men would give them the chance. Men themselves would benefit from women's rights, for Wollstonecraft believed that "the two sexes mutually corrupt and improve each other."[7] Wollstonecraft's analysis testified to the power of the Revolution to excite and inspire outside of France. Paralleling ideas put forth independently in France by Olympe de Gouges (1748–1793), a self-taught writer and woman of the people (see the feature "Listening to the Past: Revolution and Women's Rights" on pages 714–715), Wollstonecraft's work marked the birth of the modern women's movement for equal rights, and it was ultimately very influential.

Book Companion Site
Primary Source: A Feminist Analysis of Natural Law and the Rights of Women

The kings and nobles of continental Europe, who had at first welcomed the revolution in France as weakening a competing power, began to feel no less threatened than did Burke and his supporters. In June 1791, Louis XVI and Marie Antoinette were arrested and returned to Paris after trying unsuccessfully to slip out of France. The shock of this arrest led the monarchs of Austria and Prussia to issue the Declaration of Pillnitz in August 1791. This carefully worded statement declared their willingness to intervene in France in certain circumstances and was expected to have a sobering effect on revolutionary France without causing war.

But the crowned heads of Europe misjudged the revolutionary spirit in France. When the National Assembly disbanded, it sought popular support by decreeing that none of its members would be eligible for election to the new Legislative Assembly. This meant that when the new representative body convened in October 1791, it had a different character. The great majority of the legislators were still prosperous, well-educated middle-class men, but they were younger and less cautious than their predecessors. Many of the deputies belonged to a political club called the **Jacobin club,** after the name of the former monastery in which they held their meetings. Such clubs had proliferated in Parisian neighborhoods since the beginning of the Revolution, drawing men and women to debate the burning political questions of the day.

The Capture of Louis XVI, June 1791 This painting commemorates a dramatic turning point in the French Revolution, the midnight arrest of Louis XVI and the royal family as they tried to flee France in disguise and reach counter-revolutionaries in the Austrian Netherlands. Recognized and stopped at Varennes, just forty miles from the border, the king still nearly succeeded, telling municipal officers that dangerous mobs controlled Paris and securing promises of safe passage. But within hours the local leaders reversed themselves, and by morning Louis XVI was headed back to Paris. *(Bibliothèque nationale de France)*

The new representatives to the Assembly were passionately committed to the Revolution and distrustful of monarchy after Louis's attempted flight. They increasingly lumped "useless aristocrats" and "despotic monarchs" together, and they whipped themselves into a patriotic fury with bombastic oratory. If the courts of Europe were attempting to incite a war of kings against France, then "we will incite a war of people against kings. . . . Ten million Frenchmen, kindled by the fire of liberty, armed with the sword, with reason, with eloquence would be able to change the face of the world and make the tyrants tremble on their thrones."[8] Only Robespierre and a very few others argued that people would not welcome liberation at the point of a gun. Such warnings were brushed aside. France would "rise to the full height of her mission," as one deputy urged. In April 1792 France declared war on Francis II, the Habsburg monarch.

France's crusade against tyranny went poorly at first. Prussia joined Austria in the Austrian Netherlands (present-day Belgium), and French forces broke and fled at their first encounter with armies of this First Coalition. The road to Paris lay open, and it is possible that only conflict between the Eastern monarchs over the division of Poland saved France from defeat.

Military reversals and patriotic fervor led the Legislative Assembly to declare the country in danger. Volunteer armies from the provinces streamed through Paris, fraternizing with the people and singing patriotic songs like the stirring "Marseillaise," later the French national anthem. In this supercharged wartime atmosphere, rumors of treason by the king and queen spread in Paris. On August 10, 1792, a revolutionary crowd attacked the royal palace at the Tuileries, capturing it after heavy fighting with the Swiss Guards. The king and his family fled for their lives to the nearby Legislative Assembly, which suspended the king from all his functions, imprisoned him, and called for a new National Convention to be elected by universal male suffrage. Monarchy in France was on its deathbed, mortally wounded by war and popular upheaval.

The Second Revolution

The fall of the monarchy marked a rapid radicalization of the Revolution, a phase that historians often call the **second revolution.** Louis's imprisonment was followed by the September Massacres. Wild stories that imprisoned counter-revolutionary aristocrats and priests were plotting with the allied invaders seized the city. As a result, angry crowds invaded the prisons of Paris and slaughtered half the men and women they found. In late September 1792 the new, popularly elected National Convention proclaimed France a republic.

The republic sought to create a new popular culture, fashioning compelling symbols that broke with the past and glorified the new order. It adopted a brand-new revolutionary calendar, which eliminated saints' days and renamed the days and the months after the seasons of the year. The republic energetically promoted broad, open-air, democratic festivals. These spectacles brought the entire population together and sought to redirect the people's traditional enthusiasm for Catholic religious celebrations to secular holidays instilling republican virtue and a love of nation. These spectacles were less successful in villages than in cities, where popular interest in politics was greater and Catholicism was weaker.

All the members of the National Convention were republicans, and at the beginning almost all belonged to the Jacobin club of Paris. But the Jacobins themselves were increasingly divided into two bitterly competitive groups—the **Girondists,** named after a department in southwestern France that was home to several of their leaders, and **the Mountain,** led by Robespierre and another young lawyer, Georges Jacques Danton. The Mountain was so called because its members sat on the uppermost benches on the left side of the assembly hall. A majority of the indecisive Convention members, seated in the "Plain" below, floated back and forth between the rival factions.

This division emerged clearly after the National Convention overwhelmingly convicted Louis XVI of treason. The Girondists accepted his guilt but did not wish to put the king to death. By a narrow majority, the Mountain carried the day, and Louis was executed on January 21, 1793, on the newly invented guillotine. One of his last statements was "I am innocent and shall die without fear. I would that my death might bring happiness to the French, and ward off the dangers which I foresee."[9]

Both the Girondists and the Mountain were determined to continue the "war against tyranny." The Prussians had been stopped at the Battle of Valmy on September 20, 1792, one day before the republic was proclaimed. French armies then invaded Savoy and captured Nice, moved into the German Rhineland, and by November 1792 were occupying the entire Austrian Netherlands. Everywhere they went French armies of occupation chased the princes, "abolished feudalism," and found support among some peasants and middle-class people.

But the French armies also lived off the land, requisitioning food and supplies and plundering local treasures. The liberators looked increasingly like foreign invaders.

International tensions mounted. In February 1793 the National Convention, at war with Austria and Prussia, declared war on Britain, Holland, and Spain as well. Republican France was now at war with almost all of Europe, a great war that would last almost without interruption until 1815.

As the forces of the First Coalition drove the French from the Austrian Netherlands, peasants in western France revolted against being drafted into the army. They were supported and encouraged in their resistance by devout Catholics, royalists, and foreign agents. In Paris the National Convention was locked in a life-and-death political struggle between the Girondists and the Mountain. Both groups were sincere republicans, hating privilege and wanting to temper economic liberalism with social concern. Yet personal hatreds ran deep. The Girondists feared a bloody dictatorship by the Mountain, and the Mountain was no less convinced that the more moderate Girondists would turn to conservatives and even royalists in order to retain power.

With the middle-class delegates so bitterly divided, the laboring poor of Paris emerged as the decisive political factor. The laboring men and women of Paris always constituted—along with the peasantry in the summer of 1789—the elemental force that drove the Revolution forward. It was the artisans, day laborers, market women, and garment workers who had stormed the Bastille, marched on Versailles, driven the king from the Tuileries, and carried out the September Massacres. The laboring poor and the petty traders were often known as the **sans-culottes,** "without breeches," because sans-culottes men wore trousers instead of the knee breeches of the aristocracy and the solid middle class. The immediate interests of the sans-culottes were mainly economic, and in spring 1793 rapid inflation, unemployment, and food shortages were again weighing heavily on poor families.

Moreover, by spring 1793 the sans-culottes had become keenly interested in politics. Encouraged by the so-called angry men, such as the passionate young ex-priest and journalist Jacques Roux, sans-culottes men and women were demanding radical political action to guarantee them their daily bread. At first the Mountain joined the Girondists in rejecting these demands. But in the face of military defeat, peasant revolt, and hatred of the Girondists, the Mountain and especially Robespierre became more sympathetic. The Mountain joined with sans-culottes activists in the city government to engineer a popular uprising that forced the Convention to arrest thirty-one Girondist deputies for treason on June 2. All power passed to the Mountain.

Robespierre and others from the Mountain joined the recently formed Committee of Public Safety, to which the Convention had given dictatorial power to deal with the national emergency. These developments in Paris triggered revolt in leading provincial cities, such as Lyons and Marseilles, where moderates denounced Paris and demanded a decentralized government. The peasant revolt spread, and the republic's armies were driven back on all fronts. By July 1793 only the areas around Paris and on the eastern frontier were firmly held by the central government. Defeat seemed imminent.

Total War and the Terror

A year later, in July 1794, the Austrian Netherlands and the Rhineland were once again in the hands of conquering French armies, and the First Coalition was falling apart. This remarkable change of fortune was due to the revolutionary government's success in harnessing, for perhaps the first time in history, the explosive forces of a planned economy, revolutionary terror, and modern nationalism in a total war effort.

Robespierre and the Committee of Public Safety advanced with implacable resolution on several fronts in 1793 and 1794. First, they collaborated with the fiercely patriotic and democratic sans-culottes, who retained the common people's traditional faith in fair prices and a moral economic order and who distrusted most wealthy capitalists and all aristocrats. Thus Robespierre and his coworkers established, as best they could, a **planned economy** with egalitarian social overtones. Rather than let supply and demand determine prices, the government set maximum allowable prices for key products. Though the state was too weak to enforce all its price regulations, it did fix the price of bread in Paris at levels the poor could afford. Rationing was introduced, and bakers were permitted to make only the "bread of equality"—a brown bread made of a mixture of all available flours. White bread and pastries were outlawed as luxuries. The poor of Paris may not have eaten well, but at least they ate.

They also worked, mainly to produce arms and munitions for the war effort. The government told craftsmen what to produce, nationalized many small workshops, and requisitioned raw materials and grain. Sometimes planning and control did not go beyond orders to meet the latest emergency. But failures to control and coordinate were failures of means and not of desire. The second revolution and the ascendancy of the sans-culottes had produced an embryonic emergency socialism, which thoroughly frightened Europe's propertied classes and

Contrasting Visions of the Sans-Culottes   The woman on the left, with her playful cat and calm simplicity, suggests how the French sans-culottes saw themselves as democrats and virtuous citizens. The ferocious sans-culotte harpy on the right, a creation of wartime England's vivid counter-revolutionary imagination, screams for more blood, more death: "I am the Goddess of Liberty! Long live the guillotine!" *(Bibliothèque nationale de France)*

had great influence on the subsequent development of socialist ideology.

Second, while radical economic measures supplied the poor with bread and the armies with weapons, the **Reign of Terror** (1793–1794) used revolutionary terror to solidify the home front. Special revolutionary courts responsible only to Robespierre's Committee of Public Safety tried rebels and "enemies of the nation" for political crimes. Drawing on popular support centered in the local Jacobin clubs, these local courts ignored normal legal procedures and judged severely. Some forty thousand French men and women were executed or died in prison. Another three hundred thousand suspects were arrested.

Robespierre's Reign of Terror is one of the most controversial phases of the French Revolution. Most historians now believe that the Reign of Terror was not directed against any single class. Rather, it was a political weapon directed impartially against all who might oppose the revolutionary government. For many Europeans of the time, however, the Reign of Terror represented a frightening perversion of the generous ideals of 1789, strengthening the belief that France had foolishly replaced a weak king with a bloody dictatorship.

The third and perhaps most decisive element in the French republic's victory over the First Coalition was its ability to draw on the explosive power of patriotic dedication to a national state and a national mission. An essential part of modern **nationalism,** this commitment was something new in history. With a common language and a common tradition newly reinforced by the ideas of popular sovereignty and democracy, large numbers of French people were stirred by a common loyalty. They developed an intense emotional commitment to the defense of the nation, and they imagined the nation as a great loving family that included all right-thinking patriots. In such circumstances war was no longer the gentlemanly game of the eighteenth century, but rather total war, a life-and-death struggle between good and evil.

The French Revolution

May 5, 1789	Estates General convene at Versailles.
June 17, 1789	Third estate declares itself the National Assembly.
June 20, 1789	Oath of the Tennis Court is sworn.
July 14, 1789	Storming of the Bastille occurs.
July–August 1789	Great Fear ravages the countryside.
August 4, 1789	National Assembly abolishes feudal privileges.
August 27, 1789	National Assembly issues Declaration of the Rights of Man and of the Citizen.
October 5, 1789	Women march on Versailles and force royal family to return to Paris.
November 1789	National Assembly confiscates church lands.
July 1790	Civil Constitution of the Clergy establishes a national church. Louis XVI reluctantly agrees to accept a constitutional monarchy.
June 1791	Royal family is arrested while attempting to flee France.
August 1791	Austria and Prussia issue the Declaration of Pillnitz. Slave insurrections break out in Saint-Domingue.
April 1792	France declares war on Austria. Legislative Assembly enfranchises free people of color.
August 1792	Parisian mob attacks the palace and takes Louis XVI prisoner.
September 1792	September Massacres occur. National Convention declares France a republic and abolishes monarchy.
January 1793	Louis XVI is executed.
February 1793	France declares war on Britain, Holland, and Spain. Revolts take place in some provincial cities.
March 1793	Bitter struggle occurs in the National Convention between Girondists and the Mountain.
April–June 1793	Robespierre and the Mountain organize the Committee of Public Safety and arrest Girondist leaders.
September 1793	Price controls are instituted to aid the sans-culottes and mobilize the war effort. British troops invade Saint-Domingue.
1793–1794	Reign of Terror darkens Paris and the provinces.
February 1794	National Convention abolishes slavery in all French territories.
Spring 1794	French armies are victorious on all fronts.
July 1794	Robespierre is executed. Thermidorian reaction begins.
1795–1799	The Directory rules.
1795	Economic controls are abolished, and suppression of the sans-culottes begins. Toussaint L'Ouverture named brigadier general.
1797	Napoleon defeats Austrian armies in Italy and returns triumphant to Paris.
1798	Austria, Great Britain, and Russia form the Second Coalition against France.
1799	Napoleon overthrows the Directory and seizes power.

(Handwritten annotations: "Pre Revolution" next to May 5, 1789–June 20, 1789; "Liberal Rev." next to August 27, 1789; "Radical Revolution" next to March 1793–April–June 1793.)

Everyone had to participate in the national effort. According to a famous decree of August 23, 1793:

The young men shall go to battle and the married men shall forge arms. The women shall make tents and clothes, and shall serve in the hospitals; children shall tear rags into lint. The old men will be guided to the public places of the cities to kindle the courage of the young warriors and to preach the unity of the Republic and the hatred of kings.

The all-out mobilization of French resources under the Terror combined with the fervor of modern nationalism to create an awesome fighting machine. After August 1793 all unmarried young men were subject to the draft, and by January 1794 the French had about eight hundred thousand soldiers on active duty in fourteen armies. A force of this size was unprecedented in the history of European warfare, and recent research concludes that the French armed forces outnumbered their enemies almost four to one.[10] Well trained, well equipped, and constantly indoctrinated, the enormous armies of the re-

public were led by young, impetuous generals. These generals often had risen from the ranks, and they personified the opportunities the Revolution offered gifted sons of the people. Following orders from Paris to attack relentlessly, French generals used mass assaults at bayonet point to overwhelm the enemy. "No maneuvering, nothing elaborate," declared the fearless General Hoche. "Just cold steel, passion and patriotism."[11] By spring 1794 French armies were victorious on all fronts. The republic was saved.

Revolution in Saint-Domingue

The second stage of revolution in Saint-Domingue also resulted from decisive action from below. In August 1791 slaves, previously fettered witnesses to the confrontation between whites and free coloreds, took events into their own hands. Groups of slaves held a series of nighttime meetings to plan a mass insurrection. These meetings reportedly included religious ceremonies in

Slave Revolt on Saint-Domingue Starting in August 1791 the slaves of Saint-Domingue rose in revolt. *(Giraudon/Art Resource, NY)*

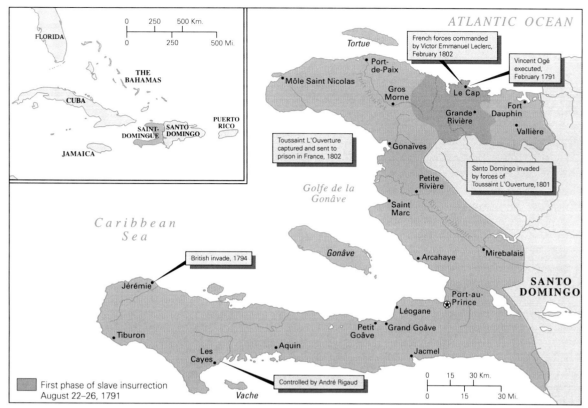

MAP 21.1 The Haitian Revolution   Neighbored by the Spanish colony of Santo Domingo, Saint-Domingue was the most profitable European colony in the Caribbean. In 1770 the French transferred the capital from Le Cap to Port-au-Prince, which became capital of the newly independent Haiti in 1804. Slave revolts erupted in the north, near Le Cap, in 1791.

Slave revolution

which participants made ritual offerings and swore a sacred oath of secrecy and revenge. The rituals belonged to the religious practices, later known as "voodoo," that slaves had created on Saint-Domingue plantations from a combination of Catholicism and African cults. French soldiers later reported that religious incantations and African songs accompanied rebel slaves into combat. African culture thus played an important role in the Saint-Domingue revolution, alongside Enlightenment ideals of freedom and equality.

Revolts began on a few plantations on the night of August 22; within a few days the uprising had swept much of the northern plain, creating a slave army estimated at around 2,000 individuals. By August 27 it was "10,000 strong, divided into 3 armies, of whom 700 or 800 are on horseback, and tolerably well-armed."[12] During the

Slave Army!

next month slaves attacked and destroyed hundreds of sugar and coffee plantations.

On April 4, 1792, as war loomed with the European states, the National Assembly issued a new decree enfranchising all free blacks and free people of color, but not slaves. The loyalty of free men of color, the Paris government reasoned, was crucial to defeating the slave rebellion and stabilizing the colony.

Warfare in Europe soon spread to Saint-Domingue (see Map 21.1), adding another complicating factor to its racial and political conflicts. Since the beginning of the slave insurrection, the Spanish in neighboring Santo Domingo had supported rebel slaves, and in early 1793 they began to bring slave leaders and their soldiers into the Spanish army. Toussaint L'Ouverture, a freed slave who had joined the slave revolt, was named a Spanish officer. The British navy also blockaded the colony, and invading British troops captured French territory on the island. For the Spanish and British, revolutionary chaos provided a tempting opportunity to capture a profitable colony.

Desperate for forces to oppose France's enemies, the commissioners sent by the newly elected National Convention turned to slaves. They began by promising freedom to those who fought for France. By October 1793 they had abolished slavery throughout the colony. On February 4, 1794, the Convention ratified the **abolition of slavery** and extended it to all French territories, including the Caribbean colonies of Martinique and Guadeloupe. The new constitution of 1795 reaffirmed abolition and the principle that the same laws would apply in the colonies as in metropolitan France. In just four years insurgent slaves had ended centuries of bondage in the French Caribbean and won full political rights.

For the future, the problem loomed of how these rights would be applied. The most immediate question, however, was whether France would be able to retain the colony, which was still under attack by Spanish and British forces. The tide began to turn when Toussaint L'Ouverture switched sides, bringing his military and political skills, along with four thousand well-trained soldiers, to support the French war effort.

By 1796 the French had gradually regained control of the colony, and L'Ouverture had emerged as the key leader of the combined slave and free colored forces. In May 1796 he was named commander of the western province of Saint-Domingue (see Map 21.1). The increasingly conservative nature of the French government during the Thermidorian reaction, however, threatened to undo the gains made by former slaves and free people of color. As exiled planters gained a stronger voice in French policymaking, L'Ouverture and other local leaders grew ever more wary of what the future might hold.

Book Companion Site
Primary Source: A Black Revolutionary Leader in Haiti: Toussaint L'Ouverture

The Thermidorian Reaction and the Directory, 1794–1799

The success of the French armies led Robespierre and the Committee of Public Safety to relax the emergency economic controls, but they extended the political Reign of Terror. In March 1794, to the horror of many sans-culottes, Robespierre's Terror wiped out many of the angry men who had been criticizing Robespierre for being

soft on the wealthy and who were led by the radical social democrat Jacques Hébert. Two weeks later, Robespierre sent many of his long-standing collaborators, including the famous orator Danton, up the steps to the guillotine. A strange assortment of radicals and moderates in the Convention, knowing that they might be next, organized a conspiracy. They howled down Robespierre when he tried to speak to the National Convention on 9 Thermidor (July 27, 1794). The next day it was Robespierre's turn to be shaved by the revolutionary razor.

As Robespierre's closest supporters followed their leader to the guillotine, France unexpectedly experienced a thorough reaction to the despotism of the Reign of Terror. In a general way, this **Thermidorian reaction** recalled the early days of the Revolution. The respectable middle-class lawyers and professionals who had led the liberal revolution of 1789 reasserted their authority, drawing support from their own class, the provincial

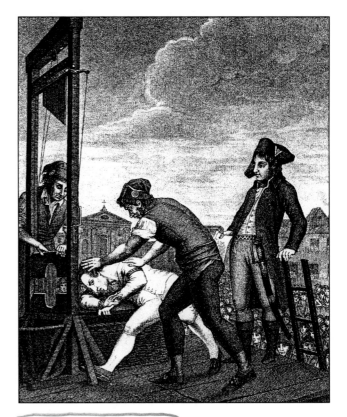

The Execution of Robespierre The guillotine was painted red and was completely wooden except for the heavy iron blade. Large crowds witnessed the executions in a majestic public square in central Paris, then known as the Place de la Revolution and now called the Place de la Concorde (Harmony Square). *(Snark/Art Resource, NY)*

cities, and the better-off peasants. The National Convention abolished many economic controls, let prices rise sharply, and severely restricted the local political organizations in which the sans-culottes had their strength.

The collapse of economic controls, coupled with runaway inflation, hit the working poor very hard. The sans-culottes accepted private property, but they believed passionately in small business, decent wages, and economic justice. Increasingly disorganized after Robespierre purged radical leaders, the common people of Paris finally revolted against the emerging new order in early 1795. The Convention quickly used the army to suppress these insurrections and made no concessions to the poor. In the face of all these reversals, the revolutionary fervor of the laboring poor in Paris finally subsided. Excluded and disillusioned, the urban poor would have little interest in and influence on politics until 1830.

In villages and small towns there arose a great cry for peace and a turning toward religion, especially from women, who had seldom experienced the political radicalization of sans-culottes women in the big cities. Instead, these women had tenaciously defended their culture and religious beliefs against the often heavy-handed attacks of antireligious revolutionary officials after 1789. As the government began to retreat on the religious question from 1796 to 1801, the women of rural France brought back the Catholic Church and the open worship of God.

As for the middle-class members of the National Convention, in 1795 they wrote yet another constitution that they believed would guarantee their economic position and political supremacy. As in previous elections, the mass of the population voted only for electors, whose number was cut back to men of substantial means. Electors then elected the members of a reorganized legislative assembly as well as key officials throughout France. The new assembly also chose a five-man executive—the Directory.

The Directory continued to support French military expansion abroad. War was no longer so much a crusade as a means to meet ever-present, ever-unsolved economic problems. Large, victorious French armies reduced unemployment at home and were able to live off the territories they conquered and plundered.

The unprincipled action of the Directory reinforced widespread disgust with war and starvation. This general dissatisfaction revealed itself clearly in the national elections of 1797, which returned a large number of conservative and even monarchist deputies who favored peace at almost any price. The members of the Directory, fearing for their skins, used the army to nullify the elections and began to govern dictatorially. Two years later Napoleon Bonaparte ended the Directory in a coup d'état and substituted a strong dictatorship for a weak one. The effort to establish stable representative government had failed.

The Napoleonic Era, 1799–1815

For almost fifteen years, from 1799 to 1814, France was in the hands of a keen-minded military dictator of exceptional ability. One of history's most fascinating leaders, Napoleon Bonaparte (1769–1821) realized the need to put an end to civil strife in France in order to create unity and consolidate his rule. And he did. But Napoleon saw himself as a man of destiny, and the glory of war and the dream of universal empire proved irresistible. For years he spiraled from victory to victory, but in the end he was destroyed by a mighty coalition united in fear of his restless ambition.

• *Why did Napoleon Bonaparte assume control of France, and what factors led to his downfall? How did the new republic of Haiti gain independence from France?*

Napoleon's Rule of France

In 1799 when he seized power, young General Napoleon Bonaparte was a national hero. Born in Corsica into an impoverished noble family in 1769, Napoleon left home and became a lieutenant in the French artillery in 1785. After a brief and unsuccessful adventure fighting for Corsican independence in 1789, he returned to France as a French patriot and a dedicated revolutionary. Rising rapidly in the new army, Napoleon was placed in command of French forces in Italy and won brilliant victories there in 1796 and 1797. His next campaign, in Egypt, was a failure, but Napoleon returned to France before the fiasco was generally known, and his reputation remained intact.

Napoleon soon learned that some prominent members of the legislature were plotting against the Directory. The dissatisfaction of these plotters stemmed not so much from the fact that the Directory was a dictatorship as from the fact that it was a weak dictatorship. Ten years of upheaval and uncertainty had made firm rule much more appealing than liberty and popular politics to these disillusioned revolutionaries. The abbé Sieyès personified this evolution in thinking. In 1789 he had written that the nobility was grossly overprivileged and that the entire people should rule the French nation. Now Sieyès's

The Napoleonic Era

November 1799	Napoleon overthrows the Directory.
December 1799	French voters overwhelmingly approve Napoleon's new constitution.
1800	Napoleon founds the Bank of France.
1801	France defeats Austria and acquires Italian and German territories in the Treaty of Lunéville. Napoleon signs the Concordat with the pope.
1802	France signs the Treaty of Amiens with Britain. French forces arrive in Saint-Domingue.
April 1803	Toussaint L'Ouverture dies in France.
January 1804	Jean Jacques Dessalines declares Haitian independence.
March 1804	Napoleonic Code comes into force.
December 1804	Napoleon crowns himself emperor.
May 1805	First Haitian constitution promulgated.
October 1805	Britain defeats the French and Spanish fleet at the Battle of Trafalgar.
December 1805	Napoleon defeats Austria and Russia at the Battle of Austerlitz.
1807	Napoleon redraws the map of Europe in the treaties of Tilsit.
1810	The Grand Empire is at its height.
June 1812	Napoleon invades Russia with 600,000 men.
Fall–Winter 1812	Napoleon makes a disastrous retreat from Russia.
March 1814	Russia, Prussia, Austria, and Britain sign the Treaty of Chaumont, pledging alliance to defeat Napoleon.
April 1814	Napoleon abdicates and is exiled to Elba.
February–June 1815	Napoleon escapes from Elba and rules France until he is defeated at the Battle of Waterloo.

motto was "Confidence from below, authority from above."

Like the other members of his group, Sieyès wanted a strong military ruler. The flamboyant thirty-year-old Napoleon was ideal. Thus the conspirators and Napoleon organized a takeover. On November 9, 1799, they ousted the Directors, and the following day soldiers disbanded the legislature at bayonet point. Napoleon was named first consul of the republic, and a new constitution consolidating his position was overwhelmingly approved in a plebiscite in December 1799. Republican appearances were maintained, but Napoleon was already the real ruler of France.

The essence of Napoleon's domestic policy was to use his great and highly personal powers to maintain order and end civil strife. He did so by working out unwritten agreements with powerful groups in France whereby the groups received favors in return for loyal service. Napoleon's bargain with the solid middle class was codified in the famous Civil Code of 1804, which reasserted two of the fundamental principles of the liberal and essentially moderate revolution of 1789: equality of all male citizens before the law and absolute security of wealth and private property. Napoleon and the leading bankers of Paris established the privately owned Bank of France, which loyally served the interests of both the state and the financial oligarchy. Napoleon's defense of the new economic order also appealed successfully to peasants, who had gained both land and status from the revolutionary changes. Thus Napoleon reconfirmed the gains of the peasantry and reassured the solid middle class, which had lost a large number of its revolutionary illusions in the face of social upheaval.

At the same time Napoleon accepted and strengthened the position of the French bureaucracy. Building on the solid foundations that revolutionary governments had inherited from the Old Regime, he perfected a thoroughly centralized state. As recent scholarship shows, Napoleon consolidated his rule by recruiting disillusioned revolutionaries for the network of ministers, prefects, and centrally appointed mayors that depended on him and came to serve him well. Only former revolutionaries who leaned too far to the left or to the right were pushed to the sidelines.[13] Nor were members of the old nobility slighted. In 1800 and again in 1802 Napoleon granted amnesty to one hundred thousand émigrés on the condition that they return to France and take a loyalty oath. Members of this returning elite soon ably occupied many high posts in the expanding centralized state. Only one thousand die-hard monarchists were exempted and remained abroad. Napoleon also created a new imperial nobility in order to reward his most talented generals and officials.

Napoleon's skill in gaining support from important and potentially hostile groups is illustrated by his treatment of the Catholic Church in France. In 1800 the French clergy was still divided into two groups: those who had taken an oath of allegiance to the revolutionary government and those in exile or hiding who had refused to do so. Personally uninterested in religion, Napoleon wanted to heal the religious division so that a united Catholic Church could serve as a bulwark of order and social peace in France. After arduous negotiations, Napoleon and Pope Pius VII (1800–1823) signed the Concordat of 1801. The pope gained the precious right for French Catholics to practice their religion freely, but Napoleon gained political power: his government now nominated bishops, paid the clergy, and exerted great influence over the church in France.

The domestic reforms of Napoleon's early years were his greatest achievement. Much of his legal and administrative reorganization has survived in France to this day. More generally, Napoleon's domestic initiatives gave the great majority of French people a welcome sense of stability and national unity.

Order and unity had a price: Napoleon's authoritarian rule. Women, who had often participated in revolutionary politics without having legal equality, lost many of the gains they had made in the 1790s. Under the law of the new Napoleonic Code, women were dependents of either their fathers or their husbands, and they could

not make contracts or even have bank accounts in their own names. Indeed, Napoleon and his advisers aimed at re-establishing a family monarchy, where the power of the husband and father was as absolute over the wife and the children as that of Napoleon was over his subjects.

Free speech and freedom of the press were continually violated. By 1811 only four newspapers were left, and they were little more than organs of government propaganda. The occasional elections were a farce. Later laws prescribed harsh penalties for political offenses. These changes in the law were part of the creation of a police state in France. Since Napoleon was usually busy making war, this task was largely left to Joseph Fouché, an unscrupulous opportunist who had earned a reputation for brutality during the Reign of Terror. As minister of police, Fouché organized a ruthlessly efficient spy system that kept thousands of citizens under continual police surveillance. People suspected of subversive activities were arbitrarily detained, placed under house arrest, or consigned to insane asylums. After 1810 political suspects were held in state prisons, as they had been during the Terror. There were about twenty-five hundred such political prisoners in 1814.

Napoleon's Expansion in Europe

Napoleon was above all a military man, and a great one. After coming to power in 1799 he sent peace feelers to Austria and Great Britain, the two remaining members of the Second Coalition that had been formed against France in 1798. When these overtures were rejected, French armies led by Napoleon decisively defeated the Austrians. In the Treaty of Lunéville (1801) Austria accepted the loss of almost all its Italian possessions, and German territory on the west bank of the Rhine was incorporated into France. Once more, as in 1797, the British were alone, and war-weary, like the French.

Still seeking to consolidate his regime domestically, Napoleon concluded the Treaty of Amiens with Great Britain in 1802. France remained in control of Holland, the Austrian Netherlands, the west bank of the Rhine, and most of the Italian peninsula. The Treaty of Amiens was clearly a diplomatic triumph for Napoleon, and peace with honor and profit increased his popularity at home.

In 1802 Napoleon was secure but unsatisfied. Ever a romantic gambler as well as a brilliant administrator, he could not contain his power drive. Aggressively redrawing the map of Germany so as to weaken Austria and encourage the secondary states of southwestern Germany to side with France, Napoleon tried to restrict British trade with all of Europe. After deciding to renew war

The Coronation of Napoleon, 1804 (detail) In this grandiose painting by Jacques-Louis David, Napoleon prepares to crown his wife, Josephine, in an elaborate ceremony in Notre Dame Cathedral. Napoleon, the ultimate upstart, also crowned himself. Pope Pius VII, seated glumly behind the emperor, is reduced to being a spectator. *(Louvre/Réunion des Musées Nationaux/Art Resource, NY)*

with Britain in May 1803, Napoleon concentrated his armies in the French ports on the Channel in the fall and began making preparations to invade England. Great Britain remained dominant on the seas, and when Napoleon tried to bring his Mediterranean fleet around Gibraltar to northern France, a combined French and Spanish fleet was virtually annihilated by Lord Nelson at the Battle of Trafalgar on October 21, 1805. Invasion of England was henceforth impossible. Renewed fighting had its advantages, however, for the first consul used the wartime atmosphere to have himself proclaimed emperor in late 1804.

Austria, Russia, and Sweden joined with Britain to form the Third Coalition against France shortly before the Battle of Trafalgar. Actions such as Napoleon's assumption of the Italian crown had convinced both Alexander I of Russia and Francis II of Austria that

Napoleon was a threat to their interests and to the European balance of power. Yet the Austrians and the Russians were no match for Napoleon, who scored a brilliant victory over them at the Battle of Austerlitz in December 1805. Alexander I decided to pull back, and Austria accepted large territorial losses in return for peace as the Third Coalition collapsed.

Napoleon then proceeded to reorganize the German states to his liking. In 1806 he abolished many of the tiny German states as well as the ancient Holy Roman Empire and established by decree the German Confederation of the Rhine, a union of fifteen German states minus Austria, Prussia, and Saxony. Naming himself "protector" of the confederation, Napoleon firmly controlled western Germany.

Napoleon's intervention in German affairs alarmed the Prussians, who mobilized their armies after more than a decade of peace with France. Napoleon attacked and won two more brilliant victories in October 1806 at Jena and Auerstädt, where the Prussians were outnumbered two to one. The war with Prussia, now joined by Russia, continued into the following spring, and after Napoleon's larger armies won another victory, Alexander I of Russia wanted peace.

For several days in June 1807 the young tsar and the French emperor negotiated face to face on a raft anchored in the middle of the Niemen River. All the while, the helpless Frederick William III of Prussia rode back and forth on the shore anxiously awaiting the results. As the German poet Heinrich Heine said later, Napoleon had but to whistle and Prussia would have ceased to exist. In the subsequent treaties of Tilsit, Prussia lost half of its population, while Russia accepted Napoleon's reorganization of western and central Europe and promised to enforce Napoleon's economic blockade against British goods.

The War of Haitian Independence

In the midst of these victories, Napoleon was forced to accept defeat overseas. With Toussaint L'Ouverture acting increasingly as an independent ruler of the western province of Saint-Domingue, another general, André Rigaud, set up his own government in the southern peninsula, which had long been more isolated from France than the rest of the colony. Both leaders maintained policies, initially established by the French, of requiring former slaves to continue to work on their plantations. They believed that reconstructing the plantation economy was crucial to maintaining their military and political victories, and they harshly suppressed resistance from former slaves.

Tensions mounted, however, between L'Ouverture and Rigaud. While L'Ouverture was a freed slave of African descent, Rigaud belonged to the free colored elite. This elite resented the growing power of former slaves like L'Ouverture, who in turn accused them of adopting the racism of white settlers. Civil war broke out between the two sides in 1799, when L'Ouverture's forces, led by his lieutenant Jean Jacques Dessalines, invaded the south. Victory over Rigaud gave Toussaint control of the entire colony. (See the feature "Individuals in Society: Toussaint L'Ouverture.")

This victory was soon challenged by Napoleon's arrival in power. Napoleon intended to reinvigorate the Caribbean plantation economy as a basis for expanding French power. His new constitution of 1799 opened the way for a re-establishment of slavery much feared in the colony. When the colonial assembly of Saint-Domingue, under L'Ouverture's direction, drafted its own constitution—which reaffirmed the abolition of slavery and granted L'Ouverture governorship for life—Napoleon viewed it as a seditious act. He ordered his brother-in-law General Charles-Victor-Emmanuel Leclerc to lead an expedition to the island to crush the new regime. Napoleon placed a high premium on bringing the colony to heel, writing to Leclerc: "Once the blacks have been disarmed and the principal generals sent to France, you will have done more for the commerce and civilization of Europe than we have done in our most brilliant campaigns." An officer sent to serve in the colony had a more cynical interpretation, writing that he was being sent to "fight with the Negroes for their own sugar."[14]

In 1802 Leclerc landed in Saint-Domingue. Although Toussaint L'Ouverture cooperated with the French and turned his army over to them, Leclerc had him arrested and deported to France, along with his family, where he died in 1803. After arresting L'Ouverture, Leclerc moved to defuse the threat posed by former slaves by taking away their arms. This effort aroused armed resistance on the plantations and led to the defection of the remnants of L'Ouverture's army. Jean Jacques Dessalines united the resistance under his command and led them to a crushing victory over the French forces. Of the fifty-eight thousand French soldiers, fifty thousand were lost in combat and to disease. On January 1, 1804, Dessalines formally declared the independence of Saint-Domingue and the creation of the new sovereign nation of Haiti, the name used by the pre-Columbian inhabitants of the island. (The remaining French Caribbean colonies—Guadeloupe, Martinique, and French Guiana—remained part of France. Slavery was re-established and remained in force until 1848.)

Haiti, the second independent state in the Americas and the first in Latin America, was thus born from the first successful large-scale slave revolt in history. Fearing the spread of slave rebellion to the United States, President Thomas Jefferson refused to recognize Haiti. Both the American and the French Revolutions thus exposed their limits by acting to protect economic interests at the expense of revolutionary ideals of freedom and equality. Yet, Haitian independence had fundamental repercussions for world history. As one recent historian of the Haitian revolution commented:

The slave insurrection of Saint-Domingue led to the expansion of citizenship beyond racial barriers despite the massive political and economic investment in the slave system at the time. If we live in a world in which democracy is meant to exclude no one, it is in no small part because of the actions of those slaves in Saint-Domingue who insisted that human rights were theirs too.[15]

The Grand Empire and Its End

Napoleon resigned himself to the loss of Saint-Domingue, but he still maintained imperial ambitions in Europe. Increasingly, he saw himself as the emperor of Europe and not just of France. The so-called **Grand Empire** he built had three parts. The core, or first part, was an ever-expanding France, which by 1810 included Belgium, Holland, parts of northern Italy, and much German territory on the east bank of the Rhine. Beyond French borders Napoleon established the second part: a number of dependent satellite kingdoms, on the thrones of which he placed (and replaced) the members of his large family. The third part comprised the independent but allied states of Austria, Prussia, and Russia. After 1806 both satellites and allies were expected to support Napoleon's continental system and to cease trade with Britain.

The impact of the Grand Empire on the peoples of Europe was considerable. In the areas incorporated into France and in the satellites (see Map 21.2), Napoleon introduced many French laws, abolishing feudal dues and serfdom where French revolutionary armies had not already done so. Some of the peasants and middle class benefited from these reforms. Yet Napoleon had to put the prosperity and special interests of France first in order to safeguard his power base. Levying heavy taxes in money and men for his armies, he came to be regarded more as a conquering tyrant than as an enlightened liberator. Thus French rule sparked patriotic upheavals and encouraged the growth of reactive nationalism, for individuals in different lands learned to identify emotionally with their own embattled national families as the French had done earlier.

The first great revolt occurred in Spain. In 1808 a coalition of Catholics, monarchists, and patriots rebelled against Napoleon's attempts to make Spain a French satellite with a Bonaparte as its king. French armies occupied Madrid, but the foes of Napoleon fled to the hills and waged uncompromising guerrilla warfare. Spain was a clear warning: resistance to French imperialism was growing.

Yet Napoleon pushed on, determined to hold his complex and far-flung empire together. In 1810, when the Grand Empire was at its height, Britain still remained at war with France, helping the guerrillas in Spain and Portugal. The continental system, organized to exclude British goods from the continent and force that "nation of shopkeepers" to its knees, was a failure. Instead, it was France that suffered from Britain's counter-blockade, which created hard times for French artisans and the middle class. Perhaps looking for a scapegoat, Napoleon turned on Alexander I of Russia, who in 1811 openly repudiated Napoleon's war of prohibitions against British goods.

Napoleon's invasion of Russia began in June 1812 with a force that eventually numbered 600,000, probably the largest force yet assembled in a single army. Only one-third of this Great Army was French, however; nationals of all the satellites and allies were drafted into the operation. Originally planning to winter in the Russian city of Smolensk if Alexander did not sue for peace, Napoleon reached Smolensk and recklessly pressed on toward Moscow. The great Battle of Borodino that followed was a draw, and the Russians retreated in good order. Alexander ordered the evacuation of Moscow, which then burned in part, and he refused to negotiate. Finally, after five weeks in the abandoned city, Napoleon ordered a retreat. That retreat was one of the greatest military disasters in history. The Russian army, the Russian winter, and starvation cut Napoleon's army to pieces. When the frozen remnants staggered into Poland and Prussia in December, 370,000 men had died and another 200,000 had been taken prisoner.[16]

Leaving his troops to their fate, Napoleon raced to Paris to raise yet another army. Possibly he might still have saved his throne if he had been willing to accept a France reduced to its historical size—the proposal offered by Austria's foreign minister, Prince Klemens von Metternich. But Napoleon refused. Austria and Prussia deserted Napoleon and joined Russia and Great Britain in the Treaty of Chaumont in March 1814, by which the four powers pledged allegiance to defeat the French emperor. All across Europe patriots called for a "war of liberation" against Napoleon's oppression, and the well-disciplined regular armies of Napoleon's enemies closed in for the kill. Less than a month later, on April 4, 1814, a defeated Napoleon abdicated his throne. After this unconditional abdication, the victorious allies granted Napoleon the island of Elba off the coast of Italy as his own tiny state. Napoleon was even allowed to keep his imperial title, and France was required to pay him a yearly income of 2 million francs.

The allies also agreed to the restoration of the Bourbon dynasty, in part because demonstrations led by a few

Individuals in Society

Toussaint L'Ouverture

Little is known of the early life of the brilliant military and political leader Toussaint L'Ouverture. He was born in 1743 on a plantation outside Le Cap owned by the Count de Bréda. According to tradition, Toussaint was the eldest son of a captured African prince from modern-day Benin. Toussaint Bréda, as he was then called, occupied a privileged position among slaves. Instead of performing backbreaking labor in the fields, he served his master as a coachman and livestock keeper. He also learned to read and write French and some Latin, but he was always more comfortable with the Creole dialect.

During the 1770s the plantation manager emancipated Toussaint, who subsequently leased his own small coffee plantation, worked by slaves. He married Suzanne Simone, who already had one son, and the couple had another son during their marriage.

Toussaint L'Ouverture entered history in 1791 when he joined the slave uprisings that swept Saint-Domingue. (At some point he took on the cryptic *nom de guerre* "l'ouverture" meaning "the opening.") Toussaint rose to prominence among rebel slaves allied with Spain and by early 1794 controlled his own army. In 1794 he defected to the French side and led his troops to a series of victories against the Spanish. In 1795 the National Convention promoted L'Ouverture to brigadier general.

Over the next three years L'Ouverture successively eliminated rivals for authority on the island. First he freed himself of the French commissioners sent to govern the colony. With a firm grip on power in the northern province, Toussaint defeated General André Rigaud in 1800 to gain control in the south. His army then marched on the capital of Spanish Santo Domingo on the eastern half of the island, meeting little resistance. The entire island of Hispaniola was now under his command.

As one historian has described him, L'Ouverture was a "small, wiry man, very black, with mobile, penetrating eyes; he greatly impressed most who met him, even those who thought him ugly. He had lost his upper set of front teeth in battle and his ears were deformed by wearing heavy gold earrings, but his presence was commanding and suggested enormous self-control."[*] A devout Catholic who led a frugal and ascetic life, L'Ouverture impressed others with his enormous physical energy, intellectual acumen, and air of mystery.

Equestrian portrait of Toussaint L'Ouverture. (Réunion des Musées Nationaux/Art Resource, NY)

With control of Saint-Domingue in his hands, L'Ouverture was confronted with the challenge of building a post-emancipation society, the first of its kind. The task was made even more difficult by the chaos wreaked by war, the destruction of plantations, and bitter social and racial tensions. For L'Ouverture the most pressing concern was to re-establish the plantation economy. Without revenue to pay his army, the gains of the rebellion could be lost. He therefore encouraged white planters to return and reclaim their property. He also adopted harsh policies toward former slaves, forcing them back to their plantations and restricting their ability to acquire land. When they resisted, he sent troops across the island to enforce submission.

In 1801 L'Ouverture convened a colonial assembly to draft a new constitution that reaffirmed his draconian labor policies. The constitution named L'Ouverture governor for life, leaving Saint-Domingue as a colony in name alone. When news of the constitution arrived in France, an angry Napoleon dispatched General Leclerc to re-establish French control. In June 1802 Leclerc's forces arrested L'Ouverture and took him to France. He was jailed at Fort de Joux in the Jura Mountains near the Swiss border, where he died of pneumonia on April 7, 1803. It was left to his lieutenant, Jean Jacques Dessalines, to win independence for the new Haitian nation.

Questions for Analysis

1. Toussaint L'Ouverture was both slave and slave owner. How did each experience shape his life and actions?
2. Despite their differences, what did Toussaint L'Ouverture and Napoleon Bonaparte have in common? Why did they share a common fate?

[*] David Patrick Geggus, *Haitian Revolutionary Studies* (Bloomington: Indiana University Press, 2002), p. 22.

Book Companion Site
Going Beyond Individuals in Society

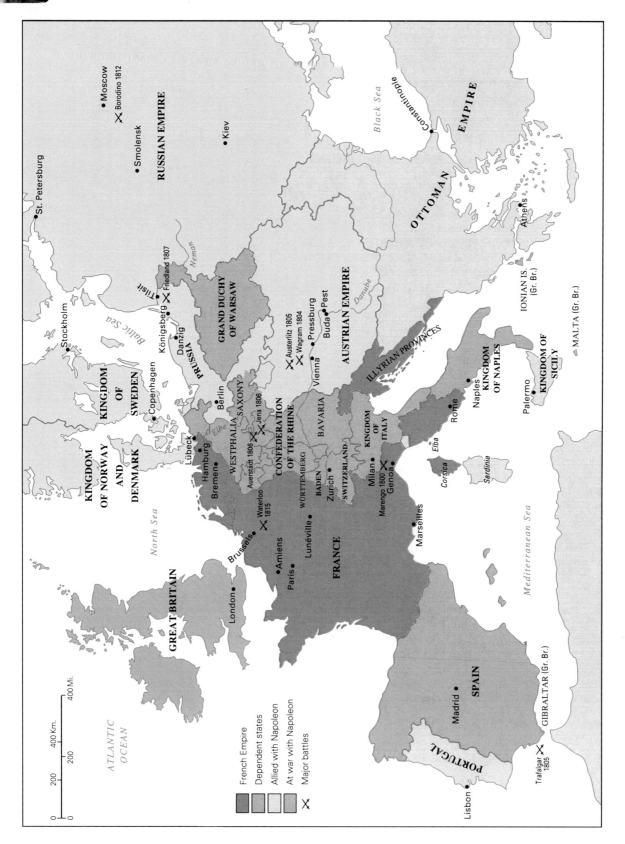

ATLANTIC
OCEAN

400 Mi.
400 Km.

French Empire
Dependent states
Allied with Napoleon
At war with Napoleon
Major battles

GREAT BRITAIN

London

North Sea

KINGDOM
OF NORWAY
AND
DENMARK

Stockholm

KINGDOM
OF
SWEDEN

Copenhagen

St. Petersburg

Baltic Sea

Königsberg
Danzig
Tilsit
Friedland 1807
Neman

PRUSSIA

Berlin

Lübeck
Hamburg
Bremen
Elbe

WESTPHALIA
SAXONY
Auerstädt 1806
Jena 1806

Brussels
Waterloo
1815

Amiens
Paris
Lunéville

FRANCE

BADEN
WÜRTTEMBERG
Zurich
SWITZERLAND

CONFEDERATION
OF THE RHINE

BAVARIA

KINGDOM
OF
ITALY

Milan
Genoa
Marengo 1800

Marseilles

GRAND DUCHY
OF WARSAW

Austerlitz 1805
Wagram 1804
Pressburg
Vienna
Buda
Pest

AUSTRIAN EMPIRE

Danube

ILLYRIAN PROVINCES

Smolensk
Kiev

RUSSIAN EMPIRE

Moscow
Borodino 1812

Black Sea

Constantinople

OTTOMAN
EMPIRE

Athens

IONIAN IS.
(Gr. Br.)

MALTA (Gr. Br.)

Elba
Corsica
Sardinia

Rome
Naples

KINGDOM OF NAPLES

Palermo

KINGDOM OF
SICILY

Mediterranean Sea

SPAIN

Madrid

PORTUGAL

Lisbon

Trafalgar
1805

GIBRALTAR (Gr. Br.)

The War in Spain This unforgettable etching by the Spanish painter Francisco Goya (1746–1828) comes from his famous collection "The Disasters of the War." A French firing squad executes captured Spanish rebels almost as soon as they are captured, an everyday event in a war of atrocities on both sides. Do you think these rebels are "terrorists" or "freedom fighters"? (*Foto Marburg/Art Resource, NY*)

Mapping the Past

MAP 21.2 Napoleonic Europe in 1810 Only Great Britain remained at war with Napoleon at the height of the Grand Empire. Many British goods were smuggled through Helgoland, a tiny but strategic British possession off the German coast. Compare this map with Map 16.2, which shows the division of Europe in 1715. ❶ How had the balance of power shifted in Europe from 1715 to 1810? What changed, and what remained the same? ❷ Why did Napoleon succeed in achieving vast territorial gains where Louis XIV did not? ❸ In comparing Map 16.2 with this map, what was the impact of Napoleon's wars on Germany and the Italian peninsula? What significance do you think this had for these regions in the nineteenth century?

dedicated French monarchists indicated some support among the French people for that course of action. The new monarch, Louis XVIII (r. 1814–1824), tried to consolidate that support by issuing the Constitutional Charter, which accepted many of France's revolutionary changes and guaranteed civil liberties. Indeed, the charter gave France a constitutional monarchy roughly similar to that established in 1791, although far fewer people had the right to vote for representatives to the resurrected Chamber of Deputies. Moreover, in an attempt to strengthen popular support for Louis XVIII's new government, France was treated leniently by the allies, which agreed to meet in Vienna to work out a general peace settlement.

Yet Louis XVIII—old, ugly, and crippled by gout—totally lacked the glory and magic of Napoleon. Hearing of political unrest in France and diplomatic tensions in Vienna, Napoleon staged a daring escape from Elba in February 1815. Landing in France, he issued appeals for support and marched on Paris with a small band of followers. French officers and soldiers who had fought so long for their emperor responded to the call. Louis XVIII fled, and once more Napoleon took command. But Napoleon's gamble was a desperate long shot, for the allies were united against him. At the end of a frantic period known as the Hundred Days, they crushed his forces at Waterloo on June 18, 1815, and imprisoned him on the rocky island of St. Helena, far off the western coast of Africa. Louis XVIII returned again and recommenced his reign. The allies now dealt more harshly with the apparently incorrigible French. As for Napoleon, he took revenge by writing his memoirs, skillfully nurturing the myth that he had been Europe's revolutionary liberator, a romantic hero whose lofty work had been undone by oppressive reactionaries. An era had ended.

Chapter Summary

- *What social, political, and economic factors formed the background to the French Revolution?*
- *What were the immediate events that sparked the Revolution, and how did they result in the formation of a constitutional monarchy in France? How did the ideals and events of the early Revolution raise new aspirations in the colonies?*
- *How and why did the Revolution take a radical turn at home and in the colonies?*
- *Why did Napoleon Bonaparte assume control of France, and what factors led to his downfall? How did the new republic of Haiti gain independence from France?*

Book Companion Site
To assess your mastery of this chapter, visit **bedfordstmartins.com/mckaywest**

The French Revolution was forged by multiple and complex factors. Whereas an earlier generation of historians was convinced that the origins of the Revolution lay in class struggle between the entrenched nobility and the rising bourgeoisie, it is now clear that many other factors were involved. Certainly, French society had undergone significant transformations during the eighteenth century, which dissolved many economic and social differences among elites without removing the legal distinction between them. These changes were accompanied by political struggles between the monarchy and its officers, particularly in the high law courts. Emerging public opinion focused on the shortcomings of monarchical rule, and a rising torrent of political theory, cheap pamphlets, gossip, and innuendo offered scathing and even pornographic depictions of the king and his court. With their sacred royal aura severely tarnished, Louis XV and his successor Louis XVI found themselves unable to respond to the financial crises generated by French involvement in the Seven Years' War and the American Revolution. Louis XVI's half-hearted efforts to redress the situation were quickly overwhelmed by elite and popular demands for fundamental reform.

Forced to call a meeting of the Estates General for the first time in almost two centuries, Louis XVI fell back on the traditional formula of one vote for each of the three orders of society. Debate over the composition of the assembly called forth a bold new paradigm: that the Third Estate in itself constituted the French nation. By 1791 the National Assembly had eliminated Old Regime privileges and had established a constitutional monarchy. Talk in France of liberty, equality, and fraternity raised new and contradictory aspirations in the colony of Saint-Domingue. White planters lobbied for increased colonial autonomy; free people of color sought the return of legal equality; slaves of African birth or descent took direct action on revolutionary ideals by rising in rebellion against their masters.

With the execution of the royal couple and the declaration of terror as the order of the day, the French Revolution took an increasingly radical turn from the end of 1792. Popular fears of counter-revolutionary conspiracy combined with the outbreak of war against a mighty alliance of European monarchs convinced many that the Revolution was vulnerable and must be defended against its multiple enemies. In a spiraling cycle of accusations and executions, the Jacobins eliminated political opponents and then factions within its own party. The Directory government that took power after the fall of Robespierre restored political equilibrium at the cost of the radical platform of social equality he had pursued.

Wearied by the weaknesses of the Directory, a group of conspirators gave Napoleon Bonaparte control of France. His brilliant reputation as a military leader and his charisma and determination made him seem ideal to lead France to victory over its enemies. As is so often the case in history, Napoleon's relentless ambitions ultimately led to his downfall. His story is paralleled by that of Toussaint L'Ouverture, another soldier who emerged to the political limelight from the chaos of revolution only to endure exile and defeat.

As complex as its origins are the legacies of the French Revolution. These include liberalism, assertive nationalism, radical democratic republicanism, embryonic socialism, self-conscious conservatism, abolitionism, decolonization, and movements for racial and sexual equality. The Revolution also left a rich and turbulent history of electoral competition, legislative assemblies, and even mass politics. Thus the French Revolution and conflicting interpretations of its significance presented a whole range of political options and alternative visions of the future. For this reason, it was truly the revolution in modern European politics.

Key Terms

estates
manorial rights
Maupeou parlements
desacralization
sovereignty
Assembly of Notables
Estates General
National Assembly
Great Fear
constitutional
  monarchy
free people of color

Jacobin club
second revolution
Girondists
the Mountain
sans-culottes
planned economy
Reign of Terror
nationalism
abolition of slavery
Thermidorian
  reaction
Grand Empire

Suggested Reading

Bell, David A. *The Cult of the Nation in France: Inventing Nationalism, 1680–1800*. 2001. Traces early French nationalism through its revolutionary culmination.

Blanning, T. C. W. *The French Revolutionary Wars (1787–1802)*. 1996. A masterful account of the revolutionary wars that also places the French Revolution in its European context.

Broers, Michael. *Europe Under Napoleon*. 2002. Probes Napoleon's impact on the territories he conquered.

Connelly, Owen. *The French Revolution and Napoleonic Era*. 1991. An excellent introduction to the French Revolution and Napoleon.

Desan, Suzanne. *The Family on Trial in Revolutionary France*. 2004. Studies the effects of revolutionary law on the family, including the legalization of divorce.

Dubois, Laurent. *Avengers of the New World: The Story of the Haitian Revolution*. 2004. An excellent and highly readable account of the revolution that transformed the French colony of Saint-Domingue into the independent state of Haiti.

Englund, Steven. *Napoleon: A Political Life*. 2004. A good biography of the French emperor.

Hunt, Lynn. *Politics, Culture and Class in the French Revolution*, 2d ed. 2004. A pioneering examination of the French Revolution as a cultural phenomenon that generated new festivals, clothing, and songs and even a new calendar.

Landes, John B. *Visualizing the Nation: Gender, Representation, and Revolution in Eighteenth-Century France*. 2001. Analyzes images of gender and the body in revolutionary politics.

Schechter, Ronald. *Obstinate Hebrews: Representations of Jews in France, 1715–1815*. 2003. An illuminating study of Jews and attitudes toward them in France from Enlightenment to emancipation.

Sutherland, Donald. *France, 1789–1815*. 1986. An overview of the French Revolution that emphasizes its many opponents, as well as its supporters.

Tackett, Timothy. *When the King Took Flight*. 2003. An exciting re-creation of the royal family's doomed effort to escape from Paris.

Notes

1. Quoted in R. R. Palmer, *The Age of Democratic Revolution*, vol. 1 (Princeton, N.J.: Princeton University Press, 1959), pp. 95–96.
2. Quoted in G. Wright, *France in Modern Times*, 4th ed. (New York: W. W. Norton, 1987), p. 34.
3. G. Lefebvre, *The Coming of the French Revolution* (New York: Vintage Books, 1947), p. 81.
4. P. H. Beik, ed., *The French Revolution* (New York: Walker, 1970), p. 89.
5. G. Pernoud and S. Flaisser, eds., *The French Revolution* (Greenwich, Conn.: Fawcett, 1960), p. 61.
6. O. Hufton, *Women and the Limits of Citizenship in the French Revolution* (Toronto: University of Toronto Press, 1992), pp. 3–22.
7. Quotations from Wollstonecraft are drawn from E. W. Sunstein, *A Different Face: The Life of Mary Wollstonecraft* (New York: Harper & Row, 1975), pp. 208, 211; and H. R. James, *Mary Wollstonecraft: A Sketch* (London: Oxford University Press, 1932), pp. 60, 62, 69.
8. Quoted in L. Gershoy, *The Era of the French Revolution, 1789–1799* (New York: Van Nostrand, 1957), p. 150.
9. Pernoud and Flaisser, *The French Revolution*, pp. 193–194.
10. T. Blanning, *The French Revolutionary Wars, 1787–1802* (London: Arnold, 1996), pp. 116–128.
11. Quoted ibid., p. 123.
12. Quoted in Laurent Dubois, *Avengers of the New World: The Story of the Haitian Revolution* (Cambridge: Harvard University Press, 2004), p. 97.
13. I. Woloch, *Napoleon and His Collaborators: The Making of a Dictatorship* (New York: W. W. Norton, 2001), pp. 36–65.
14. Quoted in Dubois, *Avengers of the New World*, pp. 255–256.
15. Ibid., p. 3.
16. D. Sutherland, *France, 1789–1815: Revolution and Counterrevolution* (New York: Oxford University Press, 1986), p. 420.

Listening to the Past

Revolution and Women's Rights

The 1789 Declaration of the Rights of Man and of the Citizen was a revolutionary call for legal equality, representative government, and individual freedom. But the new rights were strictly limited to men; Napoleon tightened further the subordination of French women. Among those who saw the contradiction in granting supposedly universal rights to only half the population was Marie Gouze (1748–1793), known to history as Olympe de Gouges. The daughter of a provincial butcher and peddler, she pursued a literary career in Paris after the death of her husband. Between 1790 and 1793 she wrote more than two dozen political pamphlets under her new name. De Gouges's great work was her "Declaration of the Rights of Woman" (1791). Excerpted here, de Gouges's manifesto went beyond the 1789 Rights of Man. It called on males to end their oppression of women and to give women equal rights. A radical on women's issues, de Gouges sympathized with the monarchy and criticized Robespierre in print. Convicted of sedition, she was guillotined in November 1793.

. . . Man, are you capable of being just? . . . Tell me, what gives you sovereign empire to oppress my sex? Your strength? Your talents? Observe the Creator in his wisdom . . . and give me, if you dare, an example of this tyrannical empire. Go back to animals, consult the elements, study plants . . . and distinguish, if you can, the sexes in the administration of nature. Everywhere you will find them mingled; everywhere they cooperate in harmonious togetherness in this immortal masterpiece.

Man alone has raised his exceptional circumstances to a principle. . . . [H]e wants to command as a despot a sex which is in full possession of its intellectual faculties; he pretends to enjoy the Revolution and to claim his rights to equality in order to say nothing more about it.

DECLARATION OF THE RIGHTS OF WOMAN AND THE FEMALE CITIZEN

For the National Assembly to decree in its last sessions, or in those of the next legislature:

Preamble

Mothers, daughters, sisters and representatives of the nation demand to be constituted into a national assembly. Believing that ignorance, omission, or scorn for the rights of woman are the only causes of public misfortunes and of the corruption of governments, [the women] have resolved to set forth in a solemn declaration the natural, inalienable, and sacred rights of woman. . . .

. . . the sex that is as superior in beauty as it is in courage during the sufferings of maternity recognizes and declares in the presence and under the auspices of the Supreme Being, the following Rights of Woman and of Female Citizens:

I. Woman is born free and lives equal to man in her rights. Social distinctions can be based only on the common utility.

II. The purpose of any political association is the conservation of the natural and imprescriptible rights of woman and man; these rights are liberty, property, security, and especially resistance to oppression.

III. The principle of all sovereignty rests essentially with the nation, which is nothing but the union of woman and man. . . .

IV. Liberty and justice consist of restoring all that belongs to others; thus, the only limits on the exercise of the natural rights of woman are perpetual male tyranny; these limits are to be reformed by the laws of nature and reason.

V. Laws of nature and reason proscribe all acts harmful to society. . . .

VI. The law must be the expression of the general will; all female and male citizens must contribute either personally or through their representatives to its formation; it must be the same for all: male and female citizens, being equal in the eyes of the law, must be equally admitted to all honors, positions, and public employment according to their capacity and without other distinctions besides those of their virtues and talents.

VII. No woman is an exception; she is accused, arrested, and detained in cases determined by law. Women, like men, obey this rigorous law.

VIII. The law must establish only those penalties that are strictly and obviously necessary. . . .

IX. Once any woman is declared guilty, complete rigor is [to be] exercised by the law.

X. No one is to be disquieted for his very basic opinions; woman has the right to mount the scaffold; she must equally have the right to mount the rostrum, provided that her demonstrations do not disturb the legally established public order.

XI. The free communication of thoughts and opinions is one of the most precious rights of woman, since that liberty assures the recognition of children by their fathers. Any female citizen thus may say freely, I am the mother of a child which belongs to you, without being forced by a barbarous prejudice to hide the truth. . . .

XIII. For the support of the public force and the expenses of administration, the contributions of woman and man are equal; she shares all the duties . . . and all the painful tasks; therefore, she must have the same share in the distribution of positions, employment, offices, honors, and jobs. . . .

XIV. Female and male citizens have the right to verify, either by themselves or through their representatives, the necessity of the public contribution. This can only apply to women if they are granted an equal share, not only of wealth, but also of public administration. . . .

XV. The collectivity of women, joined for tax purposes to the aggregate of men, has the right to demand an accounting of his administration from any public agent.

XVI. No society has a constitution without the guarantee of rights and the separation of powers; the constitution is null if the majority of individuals comprising the nation have not cooperated in drafting it.

XVII. Property belongs to both sexes whether united or separate; for each it is an inviolable and sacred right. . . .

Postscript

Women, wake up. . . . Discover your rights. . . . Oh, women, women! When will you cease to be

Olympe de Gouges in 1784; aquatint by Madame Aubry (1748–1793). *(Musée de la Ville de Paris, Musée Carnavalet, Paris, France/The Bridgeman Art Library)*

blind? What advantage have you received from the Revolution? A more pronounced scorn, a more marked disdain. . . . [If men persist in contradicting their revolutionary principles,] courageously oppose the force of reason to the empty pretensions of superiority . . . and you will soon see these haughty men, not groveling at your feet as servile adorers, but proud to share with you the treasure of the Supreme Being. Regardless of what barriers confront you; it is in your power to free yourselves; you have only to want to. . . .

Questions for Analysis

1. On what basis did de Gouges argue for gender equality? Did she believe in natural law?

2. What consequences did "scorn for the rights of woman" have for France, according to de Gouges?

3. Did de Gouges stress political rights at the expense of social and economic rights? If so, why?

Source: Olympe de Gouges, "Declaration of the Rights of Woman," in Darline G. Levy, Harriet B. Applewhite, and Mary D. Johnson, eds., *Women in Revolutionary Paris, 1789–1795* (Urbana: University of Illinois Press, 1979), pp. 87–96. Copyright © 1979 by the Board of Trustees, University of Illinois. Used with permission.

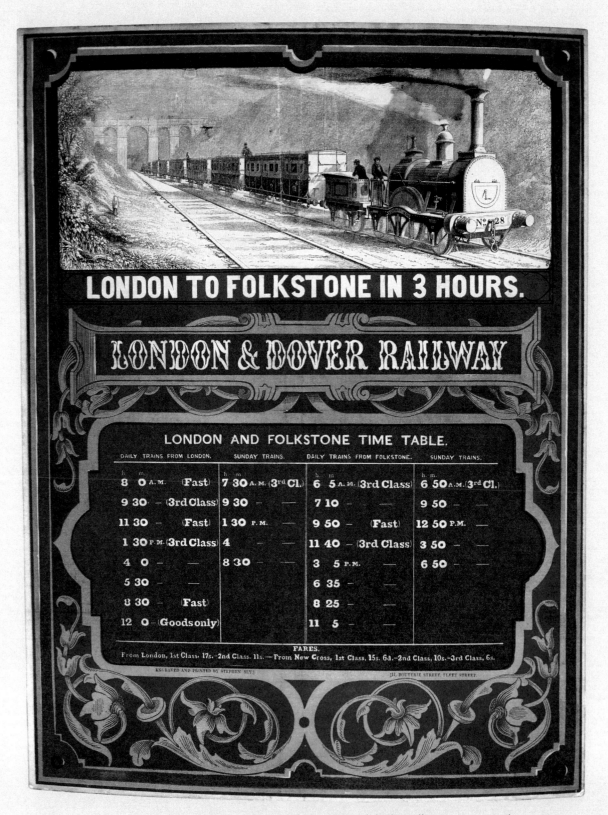

A colorful timetable poster lists the trains from London to Folkstone, the English Channel's gateway port to the European continent, and proudly proclaims the speed of the journey. *(Private Collection/The Bridgeman Art Library)*

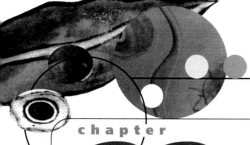

chapter

22

chapter preview

The Industrial Revolution in Britain

• *What were the origins of the Industrial Revolution in Britain, and how did it develop between 1780 and 1850?*

Industrialization in Continental Europe

• *How after 1815 did continental countries respond to the challenge of industrialization?*

Relations Between Capital and Labor

• *How did the Industrial Revolution affect social classes, the standard of living, and patterns of work? What measures were taken to improve the conditions of workers?*

THE REVOLUTION IN ENERGY AND INDUSTRY, CA 1780–1860

While the revolution in France was opening a new political era, another revolution was beginning to transform economic and social life. This was the Industrial Revolution, which began in Great Britain around the 1780s and started to influence continental Europe after 1815. Because the Industrial Revolution was less dramatic than the French Revolution, some historians see industrial development as basically moderate and evolutionary. But from a longer perspective, it was rapid and brought about numerous radical changes. Quite possibly only the development of agriculture during Neolithic times had a comparable impact and significance.

The Industrial Revolution profoundly modified much of human experience. It changed patterns of work, transformed the social class structure and the way people thought about class, and eventually even altered the international balance of political power. The Industrial Revolution also helped ordinary people gain a higher standard of living as the widespread poverty of the preindustrial world was gradually reduced.

Unfortunately, the improvement in the European standard of living was quite limited until about 1850 for at least two reasons. First, even in Britain, only a few key industries experienced a technological revolution. Many more industries continued to use old methods, especially on the continent, and this held down the increase in total production. Second, the increase in total population, which began in the eighteenth century (see pages 625–628), continued all across Europe as the era of the Industrial Revolution unfolded. As a result, the rapid growth in population threatened to eat up the growth in production and to leave most individuals poorer than ever. As a consequence, rapid population growth provided a somber background for European industrialization and made the wrenching transformation all the more difficult.

Book Companion Site

This icon will direct you to primary sources and study materials available at **bedfordstmartins.com/mckaywest**

The Industrial Revolution in Britain

The Industrial Revolution began in Great Britain, that historic union of Scotland, Wales, and England—the wealthiest and the dominant part of the country. It was something new in history, and it was quite unplanned. With no models to copy and no idea of what to expect, Britain had to pioneer not only in industrial technology but also in social relations and urban living. Between 1793 and 1815, these formidable tasks were complicated by almost constant war with France. As the trailblazer in economic development, as France was in political change, Britain must command special attention.

● *What were the origins of the Industrial Revolution in Britain, and how did it develop between 1780 and 1850?*

Eighteenth-Century Origins

Although many aspects of the British Industrial Revolution are still matters for scholarly debate, it is generally agreed that the industrial changes that did occur grew out of a long process of development. First, the expanding Atlantic economy of the eighteenth century served mercantilist Britain remarkably well. The colonial empire that Britain aggressively built, augmented by a strong position in Latin America and in the African slave trade, provided a growing market for British manufactured goods. So did the domestic market. In an age when it was much cheaper to ship goods by water than by land, no part of England was more than twenty miles from navigable water. Beginning in the 1770s, a canal-building boom greatly enhanced this natural advantage (see Map 22.1). Rivers and canals provided easy movement of England's and Wales's enormous deposits of iron and coal, resources that would be critical raw materials in Europe's early industrial age. Nor were there any tariffs within the country to hinder trade, as there were in France before 1789 and in politically fragmented Germany.

Second, agriculture played a central role in bringing about the Industrial Revolution in Britain. English farmers in particular were second only to the Dutch in productivity in 1700, and they were continually adopting new methods of farming as the century went on. The result, especially before 1760, was a period of bountiful crops and low food prices. The ordinary English family did not have to spend almost everything it earned just to

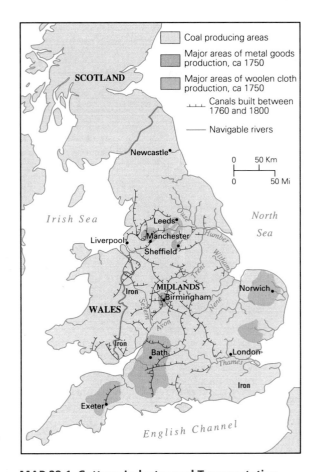

MAP 22.1 Cottage Industry and Transportation in Eighteenth-Century England England had an unusually good system of navigable rivers. From about 1770 to 1800 a canal-building boom linked these rivers together and greatly improved inland transportation.

buy bread. It could spend more on, for example, manufactured goods—leather shoes or a razor for the man, a bonnet or a shawl for the woman, toy soldiers for the son, and a doll for the daughter. Thus demand for goods within the country complemented the demand from the colonies.

Third, Britain had other assets that helped give rise to industrial leadership. Unlike eighteenth-century France, Britain had an effective central bank and well-developed credit markets. The monarchy and the aristocratic oligarchy, which had jointly ruled the country since 1688, provided stable and predictable government. At the same time, the government let the domestic economy operate

Working-class people

with few controls, encouraging personal initiative, technical change, and a free market. Finally, Britain had long had a large class of hired agricultural laborers, rural proletarians, whose numbers were further increased by the second great round of enclosures in the late eighteenth century. These rural wage earners were relatively mobile—compared to village-bound peasants in France and western Germany, for example—and along with cottage workers they formed a potential industrial labor force for capitalist entrepreneurs.

All these factors combined to initiate the Industrial Revolution, a term first coined by awed contemporaries in the 1830s to describe the burst of major inventions and technical changes they had witnessed in certain industries. This technical revolution went hand in hand with an impressive quickening in the annual rate of industrial growth in Britain. Whereas industry had grown at only 0.7 percent between 1700 and 1760 (before the Industrial Revolution), it grew at the much higher rate of 3 percent between 1801 and 1831 (when industrial transformation was in full swing).[1] The decisive quickening of growth probably came in the 1780s, after the American War of Independence and just before the French Revolution.

Therefore, the great economic and political revolutions that shaped the modern world occurred almost simultaneously, though they began in different countries. The Industrial Revolution was, however, a longer process than the political upheavals. It was not complete in Britain until 1850 at the earliest, and it had no real impact on continental countries until after 1815.

The First Factories

The pressure to produce more goods for a growing market was directly related to the first decisive breakthrough of the Industrial Revolution—the creation of the world's first large factories in the British cotton textile industry. Technological innovations in the manufacture of cotton cloth led to a new system of production and social relationships. Since no other industry experienced such a rapid or complete transformation before 1830, these trailblazing developments deserve special consideration.

Although the putting-out system of merchant capitalism (see page 629) was expanding all across Europe in the eighteenth century, this pattern of rural industry was most fully developed in Britain. There, under the pressure of growing demand, the system's limitations began to outweigh its advantages for the first time. This was especially true in the British textile industry after about 1760.

Chronology

ca 1765	Hargreaves invents spinning jenny
1769	Watt creates modern steam engine
1775–1783	American Revolution
1780s–1850	Industrial Revolution
1780–1851	Population boom in England
1789–1799	French Revolution
1798	Malthus, *Essay on the Principle of Population*
1799	Combination Acts passed
1810	Strike of Manchester cotton spinners
1824	Combination Acts repealed
1830s	Industrial banks in Belgium
1830	Stephenson's *Rocket*; first important railroad
1833	Factory Act
1841	List, *National System of Political Economy*
1842	Mines Act
1844	Engels, *The Condition of the Working Class in England*
1851	Great Exhibition held at Crystal Palace

A constant shortage of thread in the textile industry focused attention on ways of improving spinning. Many a tinkering worker knew that a better spinning wheel promised rich rewards. It proved hard to spin the traditional raw materials—wool and flax—with improved machines, but cotton was different. Cotton textiles had first been imported into Britain from India by the East India Company, and by 1760 there was a tiny domestic industry in northern England. After many experiments over a generation, a gifted carpenter and jack-of-all-trades, James Hargreaves, invented his cotton-spinning jenny about 1765. At almost the same moment, a barber-turned-manufacturer named Richard Arkwright invented (or possibly pirated) another kind of spinning machine, the water frame. These breakthroughs produced an explosion in the infant cotton textile industry in the 1780s, when it was increasing the value of its output at an unprecedented rate of about 13 percent each year. By 1790 the new machines were producing ten times as much cotton yarn as had been made in 1770.

Woman Working a Hargreaves's Spinning Jenny The loose cotton strands on the slanted bobbins passed up to the sliding carriage and then on to the spindles in back for fine spinning. The worker, almost always a woman, regulated the sliding carriage with one hand, and with the other she turned the crank on the wheel to supply power. By 1783 one woman could spin by hand a hundred threads at a time on an improved model. *(Mary Evans Picture Library)*

Book Companion Site
Primary Source: Manchester Becomes a Thriving Industrial City

Hargreaves's **spinning jenny** was simple and inexpensive. In early models, from six to twenty-four spindles were mounted on a sliding carriage, and each spindle spun a fine, slender thread. The woman moved the carriage back and forth with one hand and turned a wheel to supply power with the other. Now it was the male weaver who could not keep up with the vastly more efficient female spinner.

Arkwright's **water frame** employed a different principle. It quickly acquired a capacity of several hundred spindles and demanded much more power—waterpower. The water frame thus required large specialized mills, factories that employed as many as one thousand workers from the very beginning. The water frame could spin only coarse, strong thread, which was then put out for respinning on hand-powered cottage jennies. Around 1790 an alternative technique invented by Samuel Crompton also began to require more power than the human arm could supply. After that time, all cotton spinning was gradually concentrated in factories.

The first consequences of these revolutionary developments were more beneficial than is generally believed.

Cotton goods became much cheaper, and they were bought and treasured by all classes. In the past, only the wealthy could afford the comfort and cleanliness of underwear, which was called **body linen** because it was made from expensive linen cloth. Now millions of poor people, who had earlier worn nothing underneath their coarse, filthy outer garments, could afford to wear cotton slips and underpants as well as cotton dresses and shirts.

Families using cotton in cottage industry were freed from their constant search for adequate yarn from scattered, part-time spinners, since all the thread needed could be spun in the cottage on the jenny or obtained from a nearby factory. The wages of weavers, now hard-pressed to keep up with the spinners, rose markedly until about 1792. Weavers were among the best-paid workers in England. They were known to walk proudly through the streets with 5-pound notes stuck in their hatbands, and they dressed like the middle class. As a result, large numbers of agricultural laborers became hand-loom weavers, while mechanics and capitalists sought to invent a power loom to save on labor costs. This Edmund Cartwright achieved in 1785. But the power looms of the factories worked poorly at first, and hand-loom weavers continued to receive good wages until at least 1800.

Working conditions in the early factories were less satisfactory than those of cottage weavers and spinners, and people were reluctant to work in them. Therefore, factory owners often turned to young children who had been abandoned by their parents and put in the care of local parishes. Parish officers often "apprenticed" such unfortunate foundlings to factory owners. The parish thus saved money, and the factory owners gained workers over whom they exercised almost the authority of slave owners.

Apprenticed as young as five or six years of age, boy and girl workers were forced by law to labor for their "masters" for as many as fourteen years. Housed, fed, and locked up nightly in factory dormitories, the young workers received little or no pay. Hours were appalling—commonly thirteen or fourteen hours a day, six days a week. Harsh physical punishment maintained brutal discipline. To be sure, poor children typically worked long hours and frequently outside the home for brutal masters. But the wholesale coercion of orphans as factory apprentices constituted exploitation on a truly unprecedented scale. This exploitation ultimately piqued the conscience of reformers and reinforced more humanitarian attitudes toward children and their labor in the early nineteenth century.

The creation of the world's first modern factories in the British cotton textile industry in the 1770s and 1780s, which grew out of the putting-out system of cottage production, was a major historical development. Both symbolically and substantially, the big new cotton mills marked the beginning of the Industrial Revolution in Britain. By 1831 the largely mechanized cotton textile industry towered above all others, accounting for fully 22 percent of the country's entire industrial production.

The Problem of Energy

The growth of the cotton textile industry might have been stunted or cut short, however, if water from rivers and streams had remained the primary source of power for the new factories. But this did not occur. Instead, an epoch-making solution was found to the age-old problem of energy and power. This solution permitted continued rapid development in cotton textiles, the gradual generalization of the factory system, and the triumph of the Industrial Revolution in Britain.

Human beings have long used their toolmaking abilities to construct machines that convert one form of energy into another for their own benefit. In the medieval period, people began to develop water mills to grind their grain and windmills to pump water and drain swamps. More efficient use of water and wind in the sixteenth and seventeenth centuries enabled human beings to accomplish more; intercontinental sailing ships were a prime example. Nevertheless, even into the eighteenth century,

society continued to rely for energy mainly on plants, and human beings and animals continued to perform most work. This dependence meant that Western civilization remained poor in energy and power.

Lack of power lay at the heart of the poverty that afflicted the large majority of people. The man behind the plow and the woman at the spinning wheel could employ only horsepower and human muscle in their labor. No matter how hard they worked, they could not produce very much.

The shortage of energy had become particularly severe in Britain by the eighteenth century. Because of the growth of population, most of the great forests of medieval Britain had long ago been replaced by fields of grain and hay. Wood was in ever-shorter supply, yet it remained tremendously important. It served as the primary source of heat for all homes and industries and as a basic raw material. Processed wood (charcoal) was the fuel that was mixed with iron ore in the blast furnace to produce pig iron. The iron industry's appetite for wood was enormous, and by 1740 the British iron industry was stagnating. Vast forests enabled Russia to become the world's leading producer of iron, much of which was exported to Britain. But Russia's potential for growth was limited, too, and in a few decades Russia would reach the barrier of inadequate energy that was already holding England back.

The Steam Engine Breakthrough

As this early energy crisis grew worse, Britain looked toward its abundant and widely scattered reserves of coal as an alternative to its vanishing wood. Coal was first used in Britain in the late Middle Ages as a source of heat. By 1640 most homes in London were heated with it, and it also provided heat for making beer, glass, soap, and other products. Coal was not used, however, to produce mechanical energy or to power machinery. It was there that coal's potential was enormous, as a simple example shows.

A hard-working miner can dig out 500 pounds of coal a day using hand tools. Even an extremely inefficient converter, which transforms only 1 percent of the heat energy in coal into mechanical energy, will produce 27 horsepower-hours of work from that 500 pounds of coal. The miner, by contrast, produces only about 1 horsepower-hour in the course of a day. Early steam engines were powerful but still inefficient converters of energy.

As more coal was produced, mines were dug deeper and deeper and were constantly filling with water. Mechanical pumps, usually powered by animals walking in circles at the surface, had to be installed. At one mine, fully five hundred horses were used in pumping. Such power was expensive and bothersome. In an attempt to

Manchester, England, 1851 The development of the steam engine enabled industry to concentrate in towns and cities. Manchester mushroomed from a town of 20,000 in 1750 into "Cotton-opolis," cotton city, with 400,000 inhabitants in 1850. In this painting the artist contrasts the smoky city and its awesome power with the idealized beauty of the suburbs, where the new rich settled and built their mansions. (*The Royal Collection, © 2007 Her Majesty Queen Elizabeth II*)

overcome these disadvantages, Thomas Savery in 1698 and Thomas Newcomen in 1705 invented the first primitive **steam engines.** Both engines were extremely inefficient. Both burned coal to produce steam, which was then used to operate a pump. However, by the early 1770s, many of the Savery engines and hundreds of the Newcomen engines were operating successfully, though inefficiently, in English and Scottish mines.

In the early 1760s, a gifted young Scot named James Watt (1736–1819) was drawn to a critical study of the steam engine. Watt was employed at the time by the University of Glasgow as a skilled craftsman making scientific instruments. The Scottish universities were pioneers in practical technical education, and in 1763 Watt was called on to repair a Newcomen engine being used in a physics course. After a series of observations, Watt saw that the Newcomen engine's waste of energy could be reduced by adding a separate condenser. This splendid

invention, patented in 1769, greatly increased the efficiency of the steam engine.

To invent something in a laboratory is one thing; to make it a practical success is quite another. Watt needed skilled workers, precision parts, and capital, and the relatively advanced nature of the British economy proved essential. A partnership with a wealthy English toymaker provided risk capital and a manufacturing plant. In the craft tradition of locksmiths, tinsmiths, and millwrights, Watt found skilled mechanics who could install, regulate, and repair his sophisticated engines. From ingenious manufacturers such as the cannonmaker John Wilkinson, Watt was gradually able to purchase precision parts. This support allowed him to create an effective vacuum and regulate a complex engine. In more than twenty years of constant effort, Watt made many further improvements. By the late 1780s, the steam engine had become a practical and commercial success in Britain.

The steam engine of Watt and his followers was the Industrial Revolution's most fundamental advance in technology. For the first time in history, humanity had, at least for a few generations, almost unlimited power at its disposal. For the first time, inventors and engineers could devise and implement all kinds of power equipment to aid people in their work. For the first time, abundance was at least a possibility for ordinary men and women.

The steam engine was quickly put to use in several industries in Britain. It drained mines and made possible the production of ever more coal to feed steam engines elsewhere. The steam-power plant began to replace waterpower in the cotton-spinning mills during the 1780s, contributing greatly to that industry's phenomenal rise. Steam also took the place of waterpower in flour mills, in the malt mills used in breweries, in the flint mills supplying the china industry, and in the mills exported by Britain to the West Indies to crush sugar cane.

Steam power promoted important breakthroughs in other industries. The British iron industry was radically transformed. The use of powerful, steam-driven bellows in blast furnaces helped ironmakers switch over rapidly from limited charcoal to unlimited coke (which is made from coal) in the smelting of pig iron after 1770. In the 1780s, Henry Cort developed the puddling furnace, which allowed pig iron to be refined in turn with coke. Strong, skilled ironworkers—the puddlers—"cooked" molten pig iron in a great vat, raking off globs of refined iron for further processing. Cort also developed heavy-duty, steam-powered rolling mills, which were capable of spewing out finished iron in every shape and form.

The economic consequence of these technical innovations was a great boom in the British iron industry. In 1740 annual British iron production was only 17,000 tons. With the spread of coke smelting and the first impact of Cort's inventions, production reached 68,000 tons in 1788, 125,000 tons in 1796, and 260,000 tons in 1806. In 1844 Britain produced 3 million tons of iron. This was a truly amazing expansion. Once scarce and expensive, iron became the cheap, basic, indispensable building block of the economy.

The Coming of the Railroads

The second half of the eighteenth century saw extensive construction of hard and relatively smooth roads, particularly in France before the Revolution. Yet it was passenger traffic that benefited most from this construction. Overland shipment of freight, relying solely on horsepower, was still quite limited and frightfully expensive;

James Nasmyth's Mighty Steam Hammer Nasmyth's invention was the forerunner of the modern pile driver, and its successful introduction in 1832 epitomized the rapid development of steam power technology in Britain. In this painting by the inventor himself, workers manipulate a massive iron shaft being hammered into shape at Nasmyth's foundry near Manchester. *(Science & Society Picture Library, London)*

The Saltash Bridge Railroad construction presented innumerable challenges, such as the building of bridges to span rivers and gorges. Civil engineers responded with impressive feats, and their profession bounded ahead. This painting portrays the inauguration of I. K. Brunel's Saltash Bridge, where the railroad crosses the Tamar River into Cornwall in southwest England. The high spans allow large ships to pass underneath. *(Elton Collection, Ironbridge Gorge Museum Trust)*

shippers used rivers and canals for heavy freight whenever possible. It was logical, therefore, that inventors would try to use steam power.

As early as 1800, an American ran a "steamer on wheels" through city streets. Other experiments followed. In the 1820s, English engineers created steam cars capable of carrying fourteen passengers at ten miles an hour—as fast as the mail coach. But the noisy, heavy steam automobiles frightened passing horses and damaged themselves as well as the roads with their vibrations. For the rest of the century, horses continued to reign on highways and city streets.

The coal industry had long been using plank roads and rails to move coal wagons within mines and at the surface. Rails reduced friction and allowed a horse or a human being to pull a heavier load. Thus once a rail capable of supporting a heavy locomotive was developed in 1816, all sorts of experiments with steam engines on rails went forward. In 1825 after ten years of work, George

Stephenson built an effective locomotive. In 1830 his *Rocket* sped down the track of the just-completed Liverpool and Manchester Railway at sixteen miles per hour. This was the world's first important railroad, fittingly steaming in the heart of industrial England. The line from Liverpool to Manchester was a financial as well as a technical success, and many private companies were quickly organized to build more rail lines. Within twenty years, they had completed the main trunk lines of Great Britain. Other countries were quick to follow.

The significance of the railroad was tremendous. The railroad dramatically reduced the cost and uncertainty of shipping freight overland. This advance had many economic consequences. Previously, markets had tended to be small and local; as the barrier of high transportation costs was lowered, markets became larger and even nationwide. Larger markets encouraged larger factories with more sophisticated machinery in a growing number of industries. Such factories could make goods more cheaply and gradually subjected most cottage workers and many urban artisans to severe competitive pressures.

In all countries, the construction of railroads created a strong demand for unskilled labor and contributed to the growth of a class of urban workers. Hard work on construction gangs was done in the open air with animals and hand tools. Many landless farm laborers and poor peasants, long accustomed to leaving their villages for temporary employment, went to build railroads. By the time the work was finished, life back home in the village often seemed dull and unappealing, and many men drifted to towns in search of work. By the time they sent for their wives and sweethearts to join them, they had become urban workers.

The railroad changed the outlook and values of the entire society. The last and culminating invention of the Industrial Revolution, the railroad dramatically revealed the power and increased the speed of the new age. Racing down a track at sixteen miles per hour or, by 1850, at a phenomenal fifty miles per hour was a new and awesome experience. As a French economist put it after a ride on the Liverpool and Manchester in 1833, "There are certain impressions that one cannot put into words!"

Some great painters, notably Joseph M. W. Turner (1775–1851) and Claude Monet (1840–1926), succeeded in expressing this sense of power and awe. So did the massive new train stations, the cathedrals of the industrial age. Leading railway engineers such as Isambard Kingdom Brunel and Thomas Brassey, whose tunnels pierced mountains and whose bridges spanned valleys, became public idols—the astronauts of their day. Everyday speech absorbed the images of railroading. After you got up a "full head of steam," you "highballed" along. And if you didn't "go off the track," you might "toot your own whistle." The railroad fired the imagination.

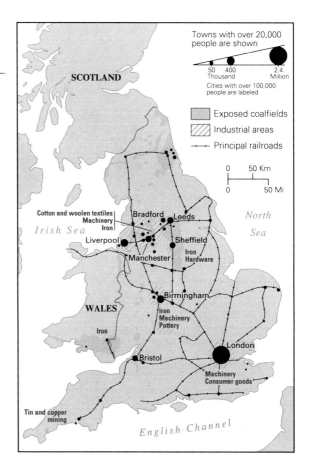

MAP 22.2 The Industrial Revolution in England, ca 1850 Industry concentrated in the rapidly growing cities of the north and the Midlands, where rich coal and iron deposits were in close proximity.

Industry and Population

In 1851 London was the site of a famous industrial fair. This Great Exhibition was held in the newly built **Crystal Palace,** an architectural masterpiece made entirely of glass and iron, both of which were now cheap and abundant. For the millions who visited, one fact stood out: the little island of Britain was the "workshop of the world." It alone produced two-thirds of the world's coal and more than one-half of its iron and cotton cloth. More generally, it has been carefully estimated that in 1860 Britain produced a truly remarkable 20 percent of the entire world's output of industrial goods, whereas it had produced only about 2 percent of the world total in 1750.[2] Experiencing revolutionary industrial change, Britain became the first industrial nation (see Map 22.2).

As the British economy significantly increased its production of manufactured goods, the gross national product (GNP) rose roughly fourfold at constant prices between 1780 and 1851. In other words, the British people as a whole increased their wealth and their national income dramatically. At the same time, the population of Britain boomed, growing from about 9 million in 1780 to almost 21 million in 1851. Thus growing numbers consumed much of the increase in total production. According to one important study, average consumption per person increased by only 75 percent between 1780 and 1851, as the growth in the total population ate up a large part of the fourfold increase in GNP in those years.[3]

Although the question is still debated, many economic historians now believe that rapid population growth in

The Crystal Palace   The Great Exhibition of 1851 attracted more than six million visitors, many of whom journeyed to London on the newly built railroads. Countries and companies from all over the world displayed their products and juries awarded prizes in the strikingly modern Crystal Palace, an architectural marvel built using the cheap iron and glass of the industrial age. In this illustration visitors stroll through the domed hall and peruse the 1500 exhibits. *(Courtesy of the Trustees of the British Museum)*

Great Britain was not harmful because it facilitated industrial expansion. More people meant a more mobile labor force, with a wealth of young workers in need of employment and ready to go where the jobs were. Contemporaries were much less optimistic. In his famous and influential *Essay on the Principle of Population* (1798), Thomas Malthus (1766–1834) argued that population would always tend to grow faster than the food supply. In Malthus's opinion, the only hope of warding off such "positive checks" to population growth as war, famine, and disease was "prudential restraint." That is, young men and women had to limit the growth of population by the old tried-and-true means of marrying late in life. But Malthus was not optimistic about this possibility. The powerful attraction of the sexes would cause most people to marry early and have many children.

Book Companion Site
Primary Source: Malthus Predicts Gloomy Prospects for the Human Condition

Wealthy English stockbroker and leading economist David Ricardo (1772–1823) coldly spelled out the pessimistic implications of Malthus's thought. Ricardo's depressing **iron law of wages** posited that because of the pressure of population growth, wages would always sink to subsistence level. That is, wages would be just high enough to keep workers from starving. With Malthus and Ricardo setting the tone, economics was soon dubbed "the dismal science."

Malthus, Ricardo, and their many followers were proved wrong—in the long run. However, until the 1820s, or even the 1840s, contemporary observers might reasonably have concluded that the economy and the total population were racing neck and neck, with the outcome very much in doubt. The closeness of the race added to the difficulties inherent in the journey toward industrial civilization.

There was another problem as well. Perhaps workers, farmers, and ordinary people did not get their rightful share of the new wealth. Perhaps only the rich got richer, while the poor got poorer or made no progress. We will turn to this great issue after looking at the process of industrialization in continental countries.

Industrialization in Continental Europe

The new technologies developed in the British Industrial Revolution were adopted rather slowly by businesses in continental Europe. Yet by the end of the nineteenth century, several European countries as well as the United States had also industrialized their economies to a considerable but variable degree. This meant that the process of Western industrialization proceeded gradually, with uneven jerks and national (and regional) variations.

Scholars are still struggling to explain these variations, especially since good answers may offer valuable lessons in our own time for poor countries seeking to improve their material condition through industrialization and economic development. The latest findings on the Western experience are encouraging. They suggest that there were alternative paths to the industrial world in the nineteenth century and that, today as then, there was no need to follow a rigid, predetermined British model.

• **How after 1815 did continental countries respond to the challenge of industrialization?**

National Variations

European industrialization, like most economic developments, requires some statistical analysis as part of the effort to understand it. Comparative data on industrial production in different countries over time help give us an overview of what happened. One set of data, the work of a Swiss scholar, compares the level of industrialization on a per capita basis in several countries from 1750 to 1913. These data are far from perfect because there are gaps in the underlying records. But they reflect basic trends and are presented in Table 22.1 for closer study.

As the heading of Table 22.1 makes clear, this is a per capita comparison of levels of industrialization—a comparison of how much industrial product was produced, on average, for each person in a given country in a given year. Therefore, all the numbers in Table 22.1 are expressed in terms of a single index number of 100, which equals the per capita level of industrial goods in Great Britain (and Ireland) in 1900. Every number in the table is thus a percentage of the 1900 level in Britain and is directly comparable with other numbers. The countries are listed in roughly the order that they began to use large-scale, power-driven technology.

What does this overview of European industrialization tell us? First, and very significantly, one sees in the first column that in 1750 all countries were fairly close together and that Britain was only slightly ahead of its archenemy, France. Second, the column headed 1800 shows that Britain had opened up a noticeable lead over all continental countries by 1800, and that gap progressively widened as the British Industrial Revolution accelerated to 1830 and reached full maturity by 1860. The British level of per capita industrialization was twice the French level in 1830, for example, and more than three times the French level in 1860. All other large countries (except the United States) had fallen even further behind Britain than France had at both dates.

Third, variations in the timing and in the extent of industrialization in the continental powers and the United States are also apparent. Belgium, independent in 1831 and rich in iron and coal, led in adopting Britain's new technology, and it experienced a truly revolutionary surge between 1830 and 1860. France developed factory production more gradually, and most historians now detect no burst in French mechanization and no acceleration in the growth of overall industrial output that may accurately be called revolutionary. They stress instead France's relatively good pattern of early industrial growth, which was unjustly tarnished by the spectacular rise of Germany and the United States after 1860. In general, eastern and southern Europe began the process of modern industrialization later than northwestern and central Europe. Nevertheless, these regions made real progress in the late nineteenth century, as growth after 1880 in Austria-Hungary, Italy, and Russia suggests.

Finally, the late but substantial industrialization in eastern and southern Europe meant that all European states (as well as the United States, Canada, and Japan) managed to raise per capita industrial levels in the nineteenth century. These continent-wide increases stood in stark contrast to the large and tragic decreases that occurred at the same time in many non-Western countries, most notably in China and India, as Table 22.1 clearly shows. European countries industrialized to a greater or lesser extent even as most of the non-Western world *de*-industrialized. Thus differential rates of wealth- and power-creating industrial development, which heightened disparities within Europe,

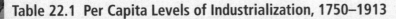

Table 22.1 Per Capita Levels of Industrialization, 1750–1913

	1750	1800	1830	1860	1880	1900	1913
Great Britain	10	16	25	64	87	100	115
Belgium	9	10	14	28	43	56	88
United States	4	9	14	21	38	69	126
France	9	9	12	20	28	39	59
Germany	8	8	9	15	25	52	85
Austria-Hungary	7	7	8	11	15	23	32
Italy	8	8	8	10	12	17	26
Russia	6	6	7	8	10	15	20
China	8	6	6	4	4	3	3
India	7	6	6	3	2	1	2

Note: All entries are based on an index value of 100, equal to the per capita level of industrialization in Great Britain in 1900. Data for Great Britain are actually for the United Kingdom, thereby including Ireland with England, Wales, and Scotland.

Source: P. Bairoch, "International Industrialization Levels from 1750 to 1980," *Journal of European Economic History* 11 (Spring 1982): 294. Reprinted with permission.

also greatly magnified existing inequalities between Europe and the rest of the world. We shall return to this momentous change in world economic relationships in Chapter 26.

The Challenge of Industrialization

The different patterns of industrial development suggest that the process of industrialization was far from automatic. Indeed, building modern industry was an awesome challenge. To be sure, throughout Europe the eighteenth century was an era of agricultural improvement, population increase, expanding foreign trade, and growing cottage industry. Thus when the pace of British industry began to accelerate in the 1780s, continental businesses began to adopt the new methods as they proved their profitability. British industry enjoyed clear superiority, but at first the continent was close behind.

By 1815, however, the situation was quite different. In spite of wartime difficulties, British industry maintained the momentum of the 1780s and continued to grow and improve between 1789 and 1815. On the continent, the upheavals that began with the French Revolution had another effect: they disrupted trade, created runaway inflation, and fostered social anxiety. War severed normal communications between Britain and the continent, severely handicapping continental efforts to use new British machinery and technology. Moreover, the years from 1789 to 1815 were, even for the privileged French economy receiving special favors from Napoleon, a time of "national catastrophe"—in the graphic words of a famous French scholar.[4] Thus France and the rest of Europe were further behind Britain in 1815 than in 1789.

This widening gap made it more difficult, if not impossible, for other countries to follow the British pattern in energy and industry after peace was restored in 1815. Above all, in the newly mechanized industries, British goods were being produced very economically, and these goods had come to dominate world markets completely while the continental states were absorbed in war between 1792 and 1815. In addition, British technology had become so advanced and complicated that very few engineers or skilled technicians outside England understood it. Moreover, the technology of steam power had grown much more expensive. It involved large investments in the iron and coal industries and, after 1830, required the existence of railroads, which were very costly. Continental business people had great difficulty finding the large sums of money the new methods demanded, and there was a shortage of laborers accustomed to working in factories. All these disadvantages slowed the spread of modern industry (see Map 22.3).

After 1815, however, when continental countries began to face up to the British challenge, they had at least three important advantages. First, most continental countries had a rich tradition of putting-out enterprise, merchant capitalists, and skilled urban artisans. Such a tradition gave continental firms the ability to adapt and survive in the face of new market conditions. Second, continental capitalists did not need to develop their own

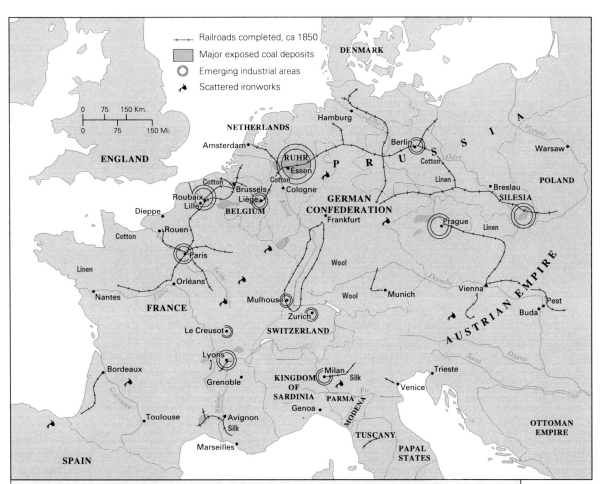

Mapping the Past

MAP 22.3 Continental Industrialization, ca 1850 Although continental countries were beginning to make progress by 1850, they still lagged far behind Britain. For example, continental railroad building was still in an early stage, whereas the British rail system was essentially complete (review Map 22.2, page 725). Coal played a critical role in nineteenth-century industrialization both as a power source for steam engines and as a raw material for making iron and steel. ❶ Locate the major exposed (that is, known) coal deposits in 1850. Which countries and areas appear rich in coal resources, and which appear poor? Is there a difference between northern and southern Europe? ❷ What is the relationship between known coal deposits and emerging industrial areas?

advanced technology. Instead, they could simply "borrow" the new methods developed in Great Britain, as well as engineers and some of the financial resources these countries lacked. European countries such as France and Russia also had a third asset that many non-Western areas lacked in the nineteenth century. They had strong independent governments, which did not fall under foreign political control. These governments could fashion economic policies to serve their own interests, as they proceeded to do. They would eventually use the power of the state to promote industry and catch up with Britain.

Agents of Industrialization

The British realized the great value of their technical discoveries and tried to keep their secrets to themselves. Until 1825 it was illegal for artisans and skilled mechanics to leave Britain; until 1843 the export of textile machinery and other equipment was forbidden. Many talented, ambitious workers, however, slipped out of the country illegally and introduced the new methods abroad.

One such man was William Cockerill, a Lancashire carpenter. He and his sons began building cotton-spinning equipment in French-occupied Belgium in 1799. In 1817 the most famous son, John Cockerill, purchased the old summer palace of the deposed bishops of Liège in southern Belgium. Cockerill converted the palace into a large industrial enterprise, which produced machinery, steam engines, and then railway locomotives. He also established modern ironworks and coal mines.

Cockerill's plants in the Liège area became an industrial nerve center, continually gathering new information and transmitting it across Europe. Many skilled British workers came illegally to work for Cockerill, and some went on to found their own companies throughout Europe. Newcomers brought the latest plans and secrets, so Cockerill could boast that ten days after an industrial advance occurred in Britain, he knew all about it in Belgium. Thus British technicians and skilled workers were a powerful force in the spread of early industrialization.

A second agent of industrialization were talented entrepreneurs such as Fritz Harkort, a business pioneer in the German machinery industry. Serving in England as a Prussian army officer during the Napoleonic wars, Harkort was impressed and enchanted with what he saw. He concluded that Germany had to match all these English achievements as quickly as possible. Setting up shop in an abandoned castle in the still-tranquil Ruhr Valley, Harkort felt an almost religious calling to build steam engines and become the "Watt of Germany."

Harkort's basic idea was simple, but it was enormously difficult to carry out. Lacking skilled laborers to do the job, Harkort turned to England for experienced, though expensive, mechanics. Getting materials also posed a great problem. He had to import the thick iron boilers that he needed from England at great cost. In spite of all these problems, Harkort built and sold engines, winning fame and praise. His ambitious efforts over sixteen years also resulted in large financial losses for himself and his partners, and in 1832 he was forced out of his company by his financial backers, who cut back operations to reduce losses. His career illustrates both the great efforts of a few important business leaders to duplicate the British achievement and the difficulty of the task.

Entrepreneurs like Harkort were obviously exceptional. Most continental businesses adopted factory technology slowly, and handicraft methods lived on. Indeed, continental industrialization usually brought substantial but uneven expansion of handicraft industry in both rural and urban areas for a time. Artisan production of luxury items grew in France as the rising income of the international middle class created foreign demand for silk scarfs, embroidered needlework, perfumes, and fine wines.

Government Support and Corporate Banking

Another major force in continental industrialization was government, which often helped business people in continental countries to overcome some of their difficulties. **Tariff protection** was one such support. For example, after Napoleon's wars ended in 1815, France was suddenly flooded with cheaper and better British goods. The French government responded by laying high tariffs on many British imports in order to protect the French economy. After 1815 continental governments bore the cost of building roads and canals to improve transportation.

They also bore to a significant extent the cost of building railroads. Belgium led the way in the 1830s and 1840s. In an effort to tie the newly independent nation together, the Belgian government decided to construct a state-owned system. Built rapidly as a unified network, Belgium's state-owned railroads stimulated the development of heavy industry and made the country an early industrial leader. Several of the smaller German states also built state systems.

The Prussian government provided another kind of invaluable support. It guaranteed that the state treasury would pay the interest and principal on railroad bonds if the closely regulated private companies in Prussia were

A German Ironworks, 1845   This big business enterprise, the Borsig ironworks in Berlin, mastered the new British method of smelting iron ore with coke. Germany, and especially the state of Prussia, was well endowed with both iron and coal, and the rapid exploitation of these resources after 1840 transformed a poor agricultural country into an industrial powerhouse. *(akg-images)*

unable to do so. Thus railroad investors in Prussia ran little risk, and capital was quickly raised. In France the state shouldered all the expense of acquiring and laying roadbed, including bridges and tunnels. Finished roadbed was leased to a carefully supervised private company, which usually benefited from a state guarantee of its debts. In short, governments helped pay for railroads, the all-important leading sector in continental industrialization.

The career of German journalist and thinker Friedrich List (1789–1846) reflects government's greater role in industrialization on the continent than in England. List considered the growth of modern industry of the utmost importance because manufacturing was a primary means of increasing people's well-being and relieving their poverty. Moreover, List was a dedicated nationalist. He wrote that the "wider the gap between the backward and advanced nations becomes, the more dangerous it is to remain behind." An agricultural nation was not only poor but

also weak, increasingly unable to defend itself and maintain its political independence. To promote industry was to defend the nation.

The practical policies that List focused on in articles and in his influential *National System of Political Economy* (1841) were railroad building and the tariff. List supported the formation of a customs union, or *Zollverein,* among the separate German states. Such a tariff union came into being in 1834, allowing goods to move between the German member states without tariffs, while erecting a single uniform tariff against other nations. List wanted a high protective tariff, which would encourage infant industries, allowing them to develop and eventually hold their own against their more advanced British counterparts. List denounced the British doctrine of free trade as little more than Britain's attempt "to make the rest of the world, like the Hindus, its serfs in all industrial and commercial relations." By the 1840s List's

economic nationalism had become increasingly popular in Germany and elsewhere.

Finally, banks, like governments, also played a larger and more creative role on the continent than in Britain. Previously, almost all banks in Europe had been private, organized as secretive partnerships. Because of the possibility of unlimited financial loss, the partners of private banks tended to be quite conservative and were content to deal with a few rich clients and a few big merchants. They generally avoided industrial investment as being too risky.

In the 1830s, two important Belgian banks pioneered in a new direction. They received permission from the growth-oriented government to establish themselves as corporations enjoying limited liability. That is, a stockholder could lose only his or her original investment in the bank's common stock and could not be assessed for any additional losses. Publicizing the risk-reducing advantage of limited liability, these Belgian banks were able to attract many shareholders, large and small. They mobilized impressive resources for investment in big companies, became industrial banks, and successfully promoted industrial development.

Similar corporate banks became important in France and Germany in the 1850s and 1860s. Usually working in collaboration with governments, they established and developed many railroads and many companies working in heavy industry, which were increasingly organized as limited liability corporations. The most famous such bank was the Crédit Mobilier of Paris, founded by Isaac and Emile Pereire, two young Jewish journalists from Bordeaux. The Crédit Mobilier advertised extensively. It used the savings of thousands of small investors as well as the resources of big ones. The activities of the bank were far-reaching; it built railroads all over France and Europe. As Emile Pereire had said in 1835, "It is not enough to outline gigantic programs on paper. I must write my ideas on the earth."

The combined efforts of skilled workers, entrepreneurs, governments, and industrial banks meshed successfully between 1850 and the financial crash of 1873. This was a period of unprecedentedly rapid economic growth on the continent. In Belgium, Germany, and France, key indicators of modern industrial development—such as railway mileage, iron and coal production, and steam-engine capacity—increased at average annual rates of 5 to 10 percent. As a result, rail networks were completed in western and much of central Europe, and the leading continental countries mastered the industrial technologies that had first been developed in Great Britain. In the early 1870s, Britain was still Europe's most industrial nation, but a select handful of countries were closing the gap that had been opened up by the Industrial Revolution.

Relations Between Capital and Labor

Industrial development brought new social relations and intensified long-standing problems between capital and labor in both urban workshops and cottage industry (see pages 628–631). A new group of factory owners and industrial capitalists arose. These men and women and their families strengthened the wealth and size of the middle class, which had previously been made up mainly of merchants and professional people. The nineteenth century became the golden age of the middle class. Modern industry also created a much larger group, the factory workers. For the first time, large numbers of men, women, and children came together under one roof to work with complicated machinery for a single owner or a few partners in large companies.

The growth of new occupational groups in industry stimulated new thinking about social relations. Often combined with reflections on the French Revolution, this thinking led to the development of a new overarching interpretation—a new paradigm—regarding social relationships (see Chapter 23). Briefly, this paradigm argued, with considerable success, that individuals were members of economically determined classes, which had conflicting interests. Accordingly, the comfortable, well-educated "public" of the eighteenth century came increasingly to see itself as the backbone of the middle class (or the middle classes), and the "people" gradually transformed themselves into the modern working class (or working classes). And if the new class interpretation was more of a deceptive simplification than a fundamental truth for some critics, it appealed to many because it seemed to explain what was happening. Therefore, conflicting classes existed, in part, because many individuals came to believe they existed and developed an appropriate sense of class feeling—what Marxists call **class-consciousness.**

• *How did the Industrial Revolution affect social classes, the standard of living, and patterns of work? What measures were taken to improve the conditions of workers?*

The New Class of Factory Owners

Early industrialists operated in a highly competitive economic system. As the careers of Watt and Harkort illus-

Ford Maddox Brown: Work   This midcentury painting provides a rich visual representation of the new concepts of social class that became common by 1850. The central figures are the colorful laborers, endowed by the artist with strength and nobility. Close by, a poor girl minds her brother and sister for her working mother. On the right, a middle-class minister and a social critic observe and do intellectual work. What work does the couple on horseback perform? *(Birmingham Museums and Art Gallery/ The Bridgeman Art Library)*

trate, there were countless production problems, and success and large profits were by no means certain. Manufacturers therefore waged a constant battle to cut their production costs and stay afloat. Much of the profit had to go back into the business for new and better machinery. "Dragged on by the frenzy of this terrible life," according to one of the dismayed critics, the struggling manufacturer had "no time for niceties. He must conquer or die, make a fortune or drown himself."[5]

Most early industrialists drew upon their families and friends for labor and capital, but they came from a variety of backgrounds. Many, such as Harkort, were from well-established merchant families, which provided a rich network of contacts and support. Others, such as Watt and Cockerill, were of modest means, especially in the early days. Artisans and skilled workers of exceptional ability had unparalleled opportunities. Members of ethnic and religious groups who had been discriminated against in the traditional occupations controlled by the landed aristocracy jumped at the new chances and often helped each other. Scots, Quakers, and other Protestant dissenters were tremendously important in Britain; Protestants and Jews dominated banking in Catholic France. Many of the industrialists were newly rich, and, not surprisingly, they were very proud and self-satisfied.

As factories and firms grew larger, opportunities declined, at least in well-developed industries. It became considerably harder for a gifted but poor young mechanic to start a small enterprise and end up as a wealthy manufacturer. Formal education (for sons and males) became more important as a means of success and advancement, and formal education at the advanced level was expensive. In Britain by 1830 and in France and Germany by 1860, leading industrialists were more likely to have inherited their well-established enterprises, and they were financially much more secure than their struggling fathers and mothers had been. They also had a greater sense of class-consciousness, fully aware that ongoing industrial development had widened the gap between themselves and their workers.

The wives and daughters of successful businessmen also found fewer opportunities for active participation in Europe's increasingly complex business world. Rather than contributing as vital partners in a family-owned enterprise, as so many middle-class women such as Elizabeth Strutt had done (see the feature "Individuals in Society: The Strutt Family"), these women were increasingly valued for their ladylike gentility. By 1850 some influential women writers and most businessmen assumed that middle-class wives and daughters should steer clear of undignified work in offices and factories. Rather, a middle-class lady should protect and enhance her femininity. She should concentrate on her proper role as wife and mother, preferably in an elegant residential area far removed from ruthless commerce and the volatile working class.

The New Factory Workers

The social consequences of the Industrial Revolution have long been hotly debated. The condition of British workers during the transformation has always generated the most controversy among historians because Britain was the first country to industrialize and because the social consequences seemed harshest there. Before 1850 other countries had not proceeded very far with industrialization, and almost everyone agrees that the economic conditions of European workers improved after 1850. Thus the experience of British workers to about 1850 deserves special attention. (Industrial growth also promoted rapid urbanization, with its own awesome problems, as will be shown in Chapter 24.)

From the beginning, the Industrial Revolution in Britain had its critics. Among the first were the romantic poets. William Blake (1757–1827) called the early factories "satanic mills" and protested against the hard life of the Lon-

don poor. William Wordsworth (1770–1850) lamented the destruction of the rural way of life and the pollution of the land and water. Some handicraft workers—notably the **Luddites,** who attacked whole factories in northern England in 1812 and after—smashed the new machines, which they believed were putting them out of work. Doctors and reformers wrote eloquently of problems in the factories and new towns, while Malthus and Ricardo concluded that workers would earn only enough to stay alive.

Book Companion Site
Primary Source: Yorkshire Luddites Threaten the Owner of a Mechanized Factory

This pessimistic view was accepted and reinforced by Friedrich Engels (1820–1895), the future revolutionary and colleague of Karl Marx. After studying conditions in northern England, this young middle-class German published in 1844 *The Condition of the Working Class in England,* a blistering indictment of the middle classes. "At the bar of world opinion," he wrote, "I charge the English middle classes with mass murder, wholesale robbery, and all the other crimes in the calendar." The new poverty of industrial workers was worse than the old poverty of cottage workers and agricultural laborers, according to Engels. The culprit was industrial capitalism, with its relentless competition and constant technical change. Engels's extremely influential charge of middle-class exploitation and increasing worker poverty was embellished by Marx and later socialists.

Meanwhile, other observers believed that conditions were improving for the working people. Andrew Ure wrote in 1835 in his study of the cotton industry that conditions in most factories were not harsh and were even quite good. Edwin Chadwick, a great and conscientious government official well acquainted with the problems of the working population, concluded that the "whole mass of the laboring community" was increasingly able "to buy more of the necessities and minor luxuries of life."[6] Nevertheless, if all the contemporary assessments had been counted up, those who thought conditions were getting worse for working people would probably have been the majority.

In an attempt to go beyond the contradictory judgments of contemporaries, some historians have looked at different kinds of sources. Statistical evidence is one such source. If working people suffered a great economic decline, as Engels and later socialists asserted, then the purchasing power of the working person's wages must have declined drastically.

Scholarly statistical studies have weakened the idea that the condition of the working class got much worse

Individuals in Society

The Strutt Family

For centuries economic life in Europe revolved around hundreds of thousands of small family enterprises. These family enterprises worked farms, crafted products, and traded goods. They built and operated the firms and factories of the early industrial era, with the notable exceptions of the capital-hungry railroads and a few big banks. Indeed, until late in the nineteenth century, close-knit family groups continued to control most successful businesses, including those organized as corporations.

One successful and fairly well-documented family enterprise began with the marriage of Jedediah Strutt (1726–1797) and Elizabeth Woollat (1729–1774) in Derbyshire in northern England in 1755. The son of a farmer, Jedediah fell in love with Elizabeth when he was apprenticed away from home as a wheelwright and lodged with her parents. Both young people grew up in the close-knit dissenting Protestant community, which did not accept the doctrines of the state-sponsored Church of England, and the well-educated Elizabeth worked in a local school for dissenters and then for a dissenter minister in London. Indecisive and self-absorbed, Jedediah inherited in 1754 a small stock of animals from an uncle and finally married Elizabeth the following year.

Aided by Elizabeth, who was "obviously a very capable woman" and who supplied some of the drive her husband had previously lacked, Jedediah embarked on a new career.* He invented a machine to make handsome, neat-fitting ribbed silk stockings, which had previously been made by hand. He secured a patent, despite strong opposition from competitors, and went into production. Elizabeth helped constantly in the enterprise, which was nothing less than an informal partnership between husband and wife.†

In 1757, for example, when Jedediah was fighting to uphold his patent in the local court, Elizabeth left her son of nine months and journeyed to London to seek a badly needed loan from her former employer. She also canvassed her London relatives and dissenter friends for orders for stockings and looked for sales agents and sources of capital. Elizabeth's letters reveal a detailed knowledge of ribbed stockings and the prices and quality of different kinds of thread. The family biographers, old-line economic historians writing without a trace of feminist concerns, conclude that her husband "owed much of his success to her energy and counsel." Elizabeth was always "active in the business—a partner in herself."‡ Historians have often overlooked such invaluable contributions from wives like Elizabeth, partly because the legal rights and consequences of partnership were denied to married women in Britain and Europe in the eighteenth and nineteenth centuries.

The Strutt enterprise grew and gradually prospered, but it always retained its family character. The firm built a large silk mill and then went into cotton spinning in partnership with Richard Arkwright, the inventor of the water frame (see page 720). The brothers of both Jedediah and Elizabeth worked for the firm, and their eldest daughter worked long hours in the warehouse. Bearing three sons, Elizabeth fulfilled yet another vital task because the typical family firm looked to its own members for managers and continued success. All three sons entered the business and became cotton textile magnates. Elizabeth never saw these triumphs. The loyal and talented wife in the family partnership died suddenly at age forty-five while in London with Jedediah on a business trip.

Jedediah Strutt (ca 1790), by Joseph Wright of Derby. (Derby Museum & Art Gallery/ The Bridgeman Art Library)

Questions for Analysis

1. How and why did the Strutts succeed?
2. What does Elizabeth's life tell us about the role of British women in the early Industrial Revolution?

*R. Fitton and A. Wadsworth, *The Strutts and the Arkwrights, 1758–1830: A Study of the Early Factory System* (Manchester, England: Manchester University Press, 1958), p. 23.
†See the excellent discussion by C. Hall, "Strains in the 'Firm of Wife, Children and Friends'? Middle-Class Women and Employment in Early Nineteenth-Century England," in P. Hudson and W. Lee, eds., *Women's Work and the Family Economy in Historical Perspective* (Manchester, England: Manchester University Press, 1990), pp. 106–132.
‡Fitton and Wadsworth, *The Strutts*, pp. 110–111.

Book Companion Site
Going Beyond Individuals in Society

with industrialization. But the most recent studies also confirm the view that the early years of the Industrial Revolution were hard ones for British workers. There was little or no increase in the purchasing power of the average British worker from about 1780 to about 1820. The years from 1792 to 1815, a period of almost constant warfare with France, were particularly difficult. Food prices rose faster than wages, and the living conditions of the laboring poor declined. Only after 1820, and especially after 1840, did real wages rise substantially, so that the average worker earned and consumed roughly 50 percent more in real terms in 1850 than in 1770.[7] In short, there was considerable economic improvement for workers throughout Great Britain by 1850, but that improvement was hard won and slow in coming.

This important conclusion must be qualified, however. First, the hours in the average workweek increased, as some economic historians now believe it had been increasing in parts of northern Europe since the seventeenth century. Thus, to a large extent, workers earned more simply because they worked more. Indeed, significant recent research shows that in England nonagricultural workers labored about 250 days per year in 1760 as opposed to 300 days per year in 1830, while the normal workday remained an exhausting eleven hours throughout the entire period. In 1760 nonagricultural workers still observed many religious and public holidays by not working, and Monday was popularly known as "Saint Monday" because so many workers took the day off. These days of leisure and relaxation declined rapidly after 1760, and by 1830 nonagricultural workers had joined landless agricultural laborers in toiling six rather than five days a week.[8]

Second, the wartime decline in the average worker's standard of living was very important. The difficult war years were formative years for the new factory labor force, and they colored the early experience of modern industrial life in somber tones.

Another way to consider the workers' standard of living is to look at the goods that they purchased. Again the evidence is somewhat contradictory. Speaking generally, workers ate somewhat more food of higher nutritional quality as the Industrial Revolution progressed, except during wartime. Diets became more varied; people ate more potatoes, dairy products, fruits, and vegetables. Clothing improved, but housing for working people probably deteriorated somewhat. In short, per capita use of specific goods supports the position that the standard of living of the working classes rose, at least moderately, after the long wars with France.

Conditions of Work

What about working conditions? Did workers eventually earn more only at the cost of working longer and harder? Were workers exploited harshly by the new factory owners?

The first factories were cotton mills, which began functioning along rivers and streams in the 1770s. Cottage workers, accustomed to the putting-out system, were reluctant to work in the new factories even when they received relatively good wages because factory work was unappealing. In the factory, workers had to keep up with the machine and follow its tempo. They had to show up every day and work long, monotonous hours. Factory workers had to adjust their daily lives to the shrill call of the factory whistle.

Cottage workers were not used to that kind of life and discipline. All members of the family worked hard and long, but in spurts, setting their own pace. They could interrupt their work when they wanted to. Women and children could break up their long hours of spinning with other tasks. On Saturday afternoon the head of the family delivered the week's work to the merchant manufacturer and got paid. Saturday night was a time of relaxation and drinking, especially for the men. Recovering from his hangover on Tuesday, the weaver bent to his task on Wednesday and then worked frantically to meet his deadline on Saturday. Like some students today, he might "pull an all-nighter" on Thursday or Friday in order to get his work in.

Also, early factories resembled English poorhouses, where totally destitute people went to live at public expense. Some poorhouses were industrial prisons, where the inmates had to work in order to receive their food and lodging. The similarity between large brick factories and large stone poorhouses increased the cottage workers' fear of factories and their hatred of factory discipline.

It was cottage workers' reluctance to work in factories that prompted the early cotton mill owners to turn to abandoned and pauper children for their labor. As we have seen, these owners contracted with local officials to employ large numbers of these children, who had no say in the matter. Pauper children were often badly treated and terribly overworked in the mills, as they were when they were apprenticed as chimney sweeps, market girls, shoemakers, and so forth. In the eighteenth century, semiforced child labor seemed necessary and was socially accepted. From our modern point of view, it was cruel exploitation and a blot on the record of the new industrial system.

Workers at a Large Cotton Mill This 1833 engraving shows adult women operating power looms under the supervision of a male foreman, and it accurately reflects both the decline of family employment and the emergence of a gender-based division of labor in many English factories. The jungle of belts and shafts connecting the noisy looms to the giant steam engine on the ground floor created a constant din. *(Time Life Pictures/Getty Images)*

By 1790 the early pattern was rapidly changing. The use of pauper apprentices was in decline, and in 1802 it was forbidden by Parliament. Many more factories were being built, mainly in urban areas, where they could use steam power rather than waterpower and attract a workforce more easily than in the countryside. The need for workers was great. Indeed, people came from near and far to work in the cities, both as factory workers and as laborers, builders, and domestic servants. Yet as they took these new jobs, working people did not simply give in to a system of labor that had formerly repelled them. Rather, they helped modify the system by carrying over old, familiar working traditions.

For one thing, they often came to the mills and the mines as family units. This was how they had worked on farms and in the putting-out system. The mill or mine owner bargained with the head of the family and paid him or her for the work of the whole family. In the cotton mills, children worked for their mothers or fathers, collecting scraps and "piecing" broken threads together. In the mines, children sorted coal and worked the ventilation equipment. Their mothers hauled coal in the tunnels below the surface, while their fathers hewed with pick and shovel at the face of the seam.

The preservation of the family as an economic unit in the factories from the 1790s on made the new surroundings more tolerable, both in Great Britain and in other countries, during the early stages of industrialization. Parents disciplined their children, making firm measures socially acceptable, and directed their upbringing.

The presence of the whole family meant that children and adults worked the same long hours (twelve-hour shifts were normal in cotton mills in 1800). In the early years, some very young children were employed solely to keep the family together. For example, Jedediah Strutt (see page 735) believed children should be at least ten years old to work in his mills, but he reluctantly employed seven-year-olds to satisfy their parents. Adult workers were not particularly interested in limiting the minimum working age or hours of their children as long as family members worked side by side. Only when technical changes threatened to place control and discipline in the hands of impersonal managers and overseers did adult workers protest against inhuman conditions in the name of their children.

Some enlightened employers and social reformers in Parliament definitely felt otherwise. They argued that more humane standards were necessary, and they used widely circulated parliamentary reports to influence public opinion. For example, Robert Owen (1771–1858), a very successful manufacturer in Scotland, testified in 1816 before an investigating committee on the basis of his experience. He stated that "very strong facts" demonstrated that employing children under ten years of age as factory workers was "injurious to the children, and not beneficial to the proprietors."[9] Workers also provided graphic testimony at such hearings as the reformers pressed Parliament to pass corrective laws. They scored some important successes.

Their most significant early accomplishment was the **Factory Act of 1833**. It limited the factory workday for children between nine and thirteen to eight hours and that of adolescents between fourteen and eighteen to twelve hours, although the act made no effort to regulate the hours of work for children at home or in small businesses. Children under nine were to be enrolled in the elementary schools that factory owners were required to establish. The employment of children declined rapidly. Thus the Factory Act broke the pattern of whole families working together in the factory because efficiency required standardized shifts for all workers.

Ties of blood and kinship were important in other ways in Great Britain in the formative years between about 1790 and 1840. Many manufacturers and builders hired workers through subcontractors. They paid the subcontractors on the basis of what the subcontractors and their crews produced—for smelting so many tons of pig iron or moving so much dirt or gravel for a canal or roadbed. Subcontractors in turn hired and fired their own workers, many of whom were friends and relations. The subcontractor might be as harsh as the greediest capitalist, but the relationship between subcontractor and work crew was close and personal. This kind of personal relationship had traditionally existed in cottage industry and in urban crafts, and it was more acceptable to many workers than impersonal factory discipline. This system also provided people with an easy way to find a job. Even today, a friend or relative who is a supervisor is frequently worth a host of formal application forms.

Ties of kinship were particularly important for newcomers, who often traveled great distances to find work. Many urban workers in Great Britain were from Ireland. Forced out of rural Ireland by population growth and deteriorating economic conditions from 1817 on, Irish in search of jobs could not be choosy; they took what they could get. As early as 1824, most of the workers in the Glasgow cotton mills were Irish; in 1851 one-sixth of the population of Liverpool was Irish. Like many other immigrant groups held together by ethnic and religious ties, the Irish worked together, formed their own neighborhoods, and not only survived but also thrived.

The Sexual Division of Labor

The era of the Industrial Revolution witnessed major changes in the sexual division of labor. In preindustrial Europe most people generally worked in family units. By tradition, certain jobs were defined by gender—women and girls for milking and spinning, men and boys for plowing and weaving—but many tasks might go to either sex. Family employment carried over into early factories and subcontracting, but it collapsed as child labor was restricted and new attitudes emerged. A different sexual division of labor gradually arose to take its place. The man emerged as the family's primary wage earner, while the woman found only limited job opportunities. Generally denied good jobs at good wages in the growing urban economy, women were expected to concentrate on unpaid housework, child care, and craftwork at home.

This new pattern of "separate spheres" had several aspects. First, all studies agree that married women from the working classes were much less likely to work full-time for wages outside the house after the first child arrived, although they often earned small amounts doing putting-out handicrafts at home and taking in boarders. Second, when married women did work for wages outside the house, they usually came from the poorest families, where the husbands were poorly paid, sick, unemployed, or missing. Third, these poor married (or widowed) women were joined by legions of young unmarried women, who worked full-time but only in certain jobs. Fourth, all women were generally confined to low-paying, dead-end jobs. Virtually no occupation open to women paid a wage sufficient for a person to live independently. Men predominated in the better-paying, more promising employments. Evolving gradually, but largely in place by 1850, the new sexual division of labor in Britain constituted a major development in the history of women and of the family.

If the reorganization of paid work along gender lines is widely recognized, there is no agreement on its causes. One school of scholars sees little connection with industrialization and finds the answer in the deeply ingrained sexist attitudes of a "patriarchal tradition," which predated the economic transformation. These scholars stress the role of male-dominated craft unions in denying working women access to good jobs and relegating them to unpaid housework. Other scholars, stressing that the gender roles of women and men can vary enormously with time and culture, look more to a combination of economic and biological factors in order to explain the emergence of a sex-segregated division of labor.

Three ideas stand out in this more recent interpretation. First, the new and unfamiliar discipline of the clock and the machine was especially hard on married women of the laboring classes. Above all, relentless factory discipline conflicted with child care in a way that labor on the farm or in the cottage had not. A woman operating ear-splitting spinning machinery could mind a child of seven or eight working beside her (until such work was outlawed), but she could no longer pace herself through pregnancy or breast-feed her baby on the job. Thus a working-class woman had strong incentives to concentrate on child care within her home if her family could afford it.

Second, running a household in conditions of primitive urban poverty was an extremely demanding job in its own right. There were no supermarkets or public transportation. Everything had to be done on foot. Shopping and feeding the family constituted a never-ending challenge. The woman marched from one tiny shop to another, dragging her tired children (for who was to watch them?) and struggling valiantly with heavy sacks and tricky shopkeepers. Yet another brutal job outside the house—a "second shift"—had limited appeal for the average married woman. Thus women might well have accepted the emerging division of labor as the best available strategy for family survival in the industrializing society.[10]

Third, why were the women who did work for wages outside the home segregated and confined to certain "women's jobs"? No doubt the desire of males to monopolize the best opportunities and hold women down provides part of the answer. Yet as some feminist scholars have argued, sex-segregated employment was also a collective response to the new industrial system. Previously, at least in theory, young people worked under a watchful parental eye. The growth of factories and mines brought unheard-of opportunities for girls and boys to mix on the job, free of familial supervision. Continuing to mix after work, they were "more likely to form liaisons, initiate courtships, and respond to advances."[11] Such intimacy also led to more unplanned pregnancies and fueled the illegitimacy explosion that had begun in the late eighteenth century and that gathered force until at least 1850 (see pages 656–657). Thus segregation of jobs by gender was partly an effort by older people to help control the sexuality of working-class youths.

Investigations into the British coal industry before 1842 provide a graphic example of this concern. (See the feature "Listening to the Past: The Testimony of Young Mine Workers" on pages 744–745.) The middle-class men leading the inquiry, who expected their daughters and wives to pursue ladylike activities, often failed to appreciate the physical effort of the girls and women who dragged with belt and chain the unwheeled carts of coal along narrow underground passages. But they professed horror at the sight of girls and women working without shirts, which was a common practice because of the heat, and they quickly assumed the prevalence of licentious sex with the male miners, who also wore very little clothing. In fact, most girls and married women worked for related males in a family unit that provided considerable protection and restraint. Yet many witnesses from the working class also believed that "blackguardism and debauchery" were common and that "they are best out of the pits, the lasses." Some miners stressed particularly the danger of sexual aggression for girls working past puberty. As one explained: "I consider it a scandal for girls to work in the pits. Till they are 12 or 14 they may work very well but after that it's an abomination. . . . The work of the pit does not hurt them, it is the effect on their morals that I complain of."[12] The **Mines Act of 1842** prohibited underground work for all women as well as for boys under ten.

Some women who had to support themselves protested against being excluded from coal mining, which paid higher wages than most other jobs open to working-class women. But provided they were part of families that could manage economically, the girls and the women who had worked underground were generally pleased with the law. In explaining her satisfaction in 1844, one mother of four provided a real insight into why many women accepted the emerging sexual division of labor:

While working in the pit I was worth to my [miner] husband seven shillings a week, out of which we had to pay 2½ shillings to a woman for looking after the younger children. I used to take them to her house at 4 o'clock in the morning, out of their own beds, to put them into hers. Then there was one shilling a week for washing; besides, there was mending to pay for, and other things. The house was not guided. The other children broke things; they did not go to school when they were sent; they would be playing about, and get ill-used by other children, and their clothes torn. Then when I came home in the evening, everything was to do after the day's labor, and I was so tired I had no heart for it; no fire lit, nothing cooked, no water fetched, the house dirty, and nothing comfortable for my husband. It is all far better now, and I wouldn't go down again.[13]

The Early Labor Movement in Britain

Many kinds of employment changed slowly during and after the Industrial Revolution in Great Britain. In 1850 more British people still worked on farms than in any other occupation. The second-largest occupation was domestic service, with more than one million household servants, 90 percent of whom were women. Thus many old, familiar jobs outside industry lived on and provided alternatives for individual workers. This helped ease the transition to industrial civilization.

Within industry itself, the pattern of artisans working with hand tools in small shops remained unchanged in many trades, even as some others were revolutionized by technological change. For example, as in the case of cotton and coal, the British iron industry was completely dominated by large-scale capitalist firms by 1850. Many large ironworks had more than one thousand people on their payrolls. Yet the firms that fashioned iron into small metal goods, such as tools, tableware, and toys, employed on average fewer than ten wage workers, who used time-honored handicraft skills. Only gradually after 1850 did some owners find ways to reorganize some handicraft industries with new machines and new patterns of work. The survival of small workshops gave many workers an alternative to factory employment.

Working-class solidarity and class-consciousness developed in small workshops as well as in large factories. In the northern factory districts, where thousands of "hired hands" looked across at a tiny minority of managers and owners, anticapitalist sentiments were frequent by the 1820s. Commenting in 1825 on a strike in the woolen center of Bradford and the support it had gathered from other regions, one paper claimed with pride that "it is all the workers of England against a few masters of Bradford."[14] Modern technology had created a few versus a many.

The transformation of some traditional trades by organizational changes, rather than technological innovations, could also create ill will and class feeling. The liberal concept of economic freedom gathered strength in the late eighteenth and early nineteenth centuries. As in France during the French Revolution, the British government attacked monopolies, guilds, and workers combinations in the name of individual liberty. In 1799 Parliament passed the **Combination Acts,** which outlawed unions and strikes. In 1813 and 1814, Parliament repealed the old and often disregarded law of 1563 regulating the wages of artisans and the conditions of apprenticeship. As a result of these and other measures, certain skilled artisan workers, such as bootmakers and high-quality tailors, found aggressive capitalists ignoring traditional work rules and flooding their trades with unorganized women workers and children to beat down wages.

Celebrating Skilled Labor This handsome engraving embellished the membership certificate of the British carpenters union, one of the leading "new model unions" that represented skilled workers effectively after 1850. The upper panel shows carpenters building the scaffolding for a great arch; the lower panel captures the spirit of a busy workshop. *(HIP/Art Resource, NY)*

The liberal capitalist attack on artisan guilds and work rules was bitterly resented by many craftworkers, who subsequently played an important part in Great Britain and in other countries in gradually building a modern labor movement to improve working conditions and to serve worker needs. The Combination Acts were widely disregarded by workers. Printers, papermakers, carpenters, tailors, and other such craftsmen continued to take collective action, and societies of skilled factory workers also organized unions. Unions sought to control the number of skilled workers, limit apprenticeship to members' own children, and bargain with owners over wages. They were not afraid to strike; there was, for example, a general strike of adult cotton spinners in Manchester in 1810. In the face of widespread union activity, Parliament repealed the Combination Acts in 1824, and unions were tolerated, though not fully accepted, after 1825.

The next stage in the development of the British trade-union movement was the attempt to create a single large national union. This effort was led not so much by working people as by social reformers such as Robert Owen. Owen, a self-made cotton manufacturer (see page 738), had pioneered in industrial relations by combining firm discipline with concern for the health, safety, and hours of his workers. After 1815 he experimented with cooper-

ative and socialist communities, including one at New Harmony, Indiana. Then in 1834 Owen organized one of the largest and most visionary of the early national unions, the **Grand National Consolidated Trades Union.** When this and other grandiose schemes collapsed, the British labor movement moved once again after 1851 in the direction of craft unions. The most famous of these "new model unions" was the Amalgamated Society of Engineers, which represented skilled machinists. These unions won real benefits for members by fairly conservative means and thus became an accepted part of the industrial scene.

British workers also engaged in direct political activity in defense of their own interests. After the collapse of Owen's national trade union, many working people went into the Chartist movement, which sought political democracy. The key Chartist demand—that all men be given the right to vote—became the great hope of millions of aroused people. Workers were also active in campaigns to limit the workday in factories to ten hours and to permit duty-free importation of wheat into Great Britain to secure cheap bread. Thus working people developed a sense of their own identity and played an active role in shaping the new industrial system. They were neither helpless victims nor passive beneficiaries.

Chapter Summary

Book Companion Site
To assess your mastery of this chapter, visit **bedfordstmartins.com/mckaywest**

• *What were the origins of the Industrial Revolution in Britain, and how did it develop between 1780 and 1850?*

• *How after 1815 did continental countries respond to the challenge of industrialization?*

• *How did the Industrial Revolution affect social classes, the standard of living, and patterns of work? What measures were taken to improve the conditions of workers?*

Western society's industrial breakthrough grew out of a long process of economic and social change in which the rise of capitalism, overseas expansion, and the growth of rural industry stood out as critical preparatory developments. Eventually taking the lead in all of these developments, and also profiting from stable government,

abundant natural resources, and a flexible labor force, Britain experienced between the 1780s and the 1850s an epoch-making transformation, one that is still aptly termed the Industrial Revolution.

Building on technical breakthroughs, power-driven equipment, and large-scale enterprise, the Industrial Revolution in England greatly increased output in certain radically altered industries, stimulated the large handicraft and commercial sectors, and speeded up overall economic growth. Rugged Scotland industrialized at least as fast as England, and Great Britain became the first industrial nation. By 1850 the level of British per capita industrial production was surpassing continental levels by a growing margin, and Britain savored a near monopoly in world markets for mass-produced goods.

Continental countries inevitably took rather different paths to the urban industrial society. They relied more on handicraft production in both towns and villages. Only in the 1840s did railroad construction begin to create the strong demand for iron, coal, and railway equipment that speeded up the process of industrialization in the 1850s and 1860s.

The rise of modern industry had a profound impact on people and their lives. In the early stages, Britain again led the way, experiencing in a striking manner the long-term social changes accompanying the economic transformation. Factory discipline and Britain's stern capitalist economy weighed heavily on working people, who, however, actively fashioned their destinies and refused to be passive victims. Improvements in the standard of living came slowly, but they were substantial by 1850. The era of industrialization fostered new attitudes toward child labor, encouraged protective factory legislation, and called forth a new sense of class feeling and an assertive labor movement. It also promoted a more rigid division of roles and responsibilities within the family that was detrimental to women, another gradual but profound change of revolutionary proportions.

Key Terms

Industrial Revolution	economic
spinning jenny	nationalism
water frame	class-consciousness
body linen	Luddites
steam engines	Factory Act of 1833
coke	Mines Act of 1842
Rocket	Combination Acts
Crystal Palace	Grand National
iron law of wages	Consolidated
tariff protection	Trades Union

Suggested Reading

Cameron, Rondo, and Larry Neal. *A Concise Economic History of the World,* 4th ed. 2003. Provides an introduction to key issues related to the Industrial Revolution and has a carefully annotated bibliography.

Clapham, J. H. *Economic Development of France and Germany.* 1963. A classic study.

Davidoff, Leonore, and Catherine Hall. *Family Fortunes: Men and Women of the English Middle Class, 1750–1850,* rev. ed. 2003. Examines both economic activities and cultural beliefs with great skill.

Fuchs, Rachel G. *Gender and Poverty in Nineteenth-Century Europe.* 2005. Provides a broad comparative perspective.

Gaskell, Elizabeth. *Mary Barton.* 1848. Gaskell's novel offers a realistic portrayal of the new industrial society.

Goodman, Jordan, and Katrina Honeyman. *Gainful Pursuits: The Making of Industrial Europe, 1600–1914.* 1988. An excellent general treatment of European industrial growth.

Kemp, Tom. *Industrialization in Europe,* 2d ed. 1985. A useful overview.

Landes, David. *Dynasties: Fortunes and Misfortunes of the World's Great Family Businesses.* 2006. A collection offering fascinating and insightful histories of famous enterprises and leading capitalists.

Pomeranz, Kenneth. *The Great Divergence: China, Europe, and the Making of the Modern World Economy.* 2000. A sophisticated reconsideration of why western Europe underwent industrialization and China did not.

Stearns, Peter N. *The Industrial Revolution in World History,* 3d ed. 2007. A useful brief survey.

Thompson, E. P. *The Making of the English Working Class.* 1963. A fascinating book in the Marxian tradition that is rich in detail and early working-class lore.

Valenze, Deborah. *The First Industrial Woman.* 1995. A gender study that reinvigorates the debate between "optimists" and "pessimists" about the consequences of industrialization in Britain.

Walton, Whitney. *France and the Crystal Palace: Bourgeois Taste and Artisan Manufacture in the 19th Century.* 1992. Examines the gradual transformation of handicraft techniques and their persistent importance in the international economy.

Wrigley, E. A. *Continuity, Chance and Change: The Character of the Industrial Revolution in England.* 1994. An important reconsideration stressing resources and population.

Notes

1. N. F. R. Crafts, *British Economic Growth During the Industrial Revolution* (Oxford: Oxford University Press, 1985), p. 32.
2. P. Bairoch, "International Industrialization Levels from 1750 to

1980," *Journal of European Economic History* 11 (Spring 1982): 269–333.

3. Crafts, *British Economic Growth,* pp. 45, 95–102.

4. M. Lévy-Leboyer, *Les banques européennes et l'industrialisation dans la première moitié du XIXe siècle* (Paris: Presses Universitaires de France, 1964), p. 29.

5. J. Michelet, *The People,* trans. with an introduction by J. P. McKay (Urbana: University of Illinois Press, 1973; original publication, 1846), p. 64.

6. Quoted in W. A. Hayek, ed., *Capitalism and the Historians* (Chicago: University of Chicago Press, 1954), p. 126.

7. Crafts, *British Economic Growth,* p. 95.

8. H-J. Voth, *Time and Work in England, 1750–1830* (Oxford: Oxford University Press, 2000), pp. 268–270; also pp. 118–133.

9. Quoted in E. R. Pike, *"Hard Times": Human Documents of the Industrial Revolution* (New York: Praeger, 1966), p. 109.

10. See especially J. Brenner and M. Rama, "Rethinking Women's Oppression," *New Left Review* 144 (March–April 1984): 33–71, and sources cited there.

11. J. Humphries, ". . . 'The Most Free from Objection' . . . : The Sexual Division of Labor and Women's Work in Nineteenth-Century England," *Journal of Economic History* 47 (December 1987): 948.

12. Ibid., p. 941; Pike, *"Hard Times,"* p. 266.

13. Pike, *"Hard Times,"* p. 208.

14. Quoted in D. Geary, ed., *Labour and Socialist Movements in Europe Before 1914* (Oxford: Berg, 1989), p. 29.

Listening to the Past

The Testimony of Young Mine Workers

The use of child labor in British industrialization quickly attracted the attention of humanitarians and social reformers. This interest led to investigations by parliamentary commissions, which resulted in laws limiting the hours and the ages of children working in large factories. Designed to build a case for remedial legislation, parliamentary inquiries gave large numbers of workers a rare chance to speak directly to contemporaries and to historians.

The moving passages that follow are taken from testimony gathered in 1841 and 1842 by the Ashley Mines Commission. Interviewing employers and many male and female workers, the commissioners focused on the physical condition of the youth and on the sexual behavior of workers far underground. The subsequent Mines Act of 1842 sought to reduce immoral behavior and sexual bullying by prohibiting underground work for all women (and for boys younger than ten).

Mr. Payne, coal master:

That children are employed generally at nine years old in the coal pits and sometimes at eight. In fact, the smaller the vein of coal is in height, the younger and smaller are the children required; the work occupies from six to seven hours per day in the pits; they are not ill-used or worked beyond their strength; a good deal of depravity exists but they are certainly not worse in morals than in other branches of the Sheffield trade, but upon the whole superior; the morals of this district are materially improving; Mr. Bruce, the clergyman, has been zealous and active in endeavoring to ameliorate their moral and religious education. . . .

Ann Eggley, hurrier, 18 years old:

I'm sure I don't know how to spell my name. We go at four in the morning, and sometimes at half-past four. We begin to work as soon as we get down. We get out after four, sometimes at five, in the evening. We work the whole time except an hour for dinner, and sometimes we haven't time to eat. I hurry [move coal wagons underground] by myself, and have done so for long. I know the corves [small coal wagons] are very heavy, they are the biggest corves anywhere about. The work is far too hard for me; the sweat runs off me all over sometimes. I am very tired at night. Sometimes when we get home at night we have not power to wash us, and then we go to bed. Sometimes we fall asleep in the chair. Father said last night it was both a shame and a disgrace for girls to work as we do, but there was naught else for us to do. I began to hurry when I was seven and I have been hurrying ever since. I have been 11 years in the pits. The girls are always tired. I was poorly twice this winter; it was with headache. I hurry for Robert Wiggins; he is not akin to me. . . . We don't always get enough to eat and drink, but we get a good supper. I have known my father go at two in the morning to work . . . and he didn't come out till four. I am quite sure that we work constantly 12 hours except on Saturdays. We wear trousers and our shifts in the pit and great big shoes clinkered and nailed. The girls never work naked to the waist in our pit. The men don't insult us in the pit. The conduct of the girls in the pit is good enough sometimes and sometimes bad enough. I never went to a day-school. I went a little to a Sunday-school, but I soon gave it over. I thought it too bad to be confined both Sundays and week-days. I walk about and get the fresh air on Sundays. I have not learnt to read. I don't know my letters. I never learnt naught. I never go to church or chapel; there is no church or chapel at Gawber, there is none nearer than a mile. . . . I have never heard that a good man came into the world who was God's son to save sinners. I never

This illustration of a girl dragging a coal wagon was one of several that shocked public opinion and contributed to the Mines Act of 1842. *(The British Library)*

heard of Christ at all. Nobody has ever told me about him, nor have my father and mother ever taught me to pray. I know no prayer; I never pray.

Patience Kershaw, aged 17:

My father has been dead about a year; my mother is living and has ten children, five lads and five lasses; the oldest is about thirty, the youngest is four; three lasses go to mill; all the lads are colliers, two getters and three hurriers; one lives at home and does nothing; mother does nought but look after home.

All my sisters have been hurriers, but three went to the mill. Alice went because her legs swelled from hurrying in cold water when she was hot. I never went to day-school; I go to Sunday-school, but I cannot read or write; I go to pit at five o'clock in the morning and come out at five in the evening; I get my breakfast of porridge and milk first; I take my dinner with me, a cake, and eat it as I go; I do not stop or rest any time for the purpose; I get nothing else until I get home, and then have potatoes and meat, not every day meat. I hurry in the clothes I have now got on, trousers and ragged jacket; the bald place upon my head is made by thrusting the corves; my legs have never swelled, but sisters' did when they went to mill; I hurry the corves a mile and more under ground and back; they weigh 300; I hurry 11 a day; I wear a belt and chain at the workings to get the corves out; the putters [miners] that I work for are *naked* except their caps; they pull off all their clothes; I see them at work when I go up; sometimes they beat me, if I am not quick enough, with their hands; they strike me upon my back; the boys take liberties with me, sometimes, they pull me about; I am the only girl in the pit; there are about 20 boys and 15 men; all the men are naked; I would rather work in mill than in coal-pit.

Isabel Wilson, 38 years old, coal putter:

When women have children thick [fast] they are compelled to take them down early. I have been married 19 years and have had 10 bairns [children]; seven are in life. When on Sir John's work was a carrier of coals, which caused me to miscarry five times from the strains, and was gai [very] ill after each. Putting is no so oppressive; last child was born on Saturday morning, and I was at work on the Friday night.

Once met with an accident; a coal brake my cheek-bone, which kept me idle some weeks.

I have wrought below 30 years, and so has the guid man; he is getting touched in the breath now.

None of the children read, as the work is no regular. I did read once, but no able to attend to it now; when I go below lassie 10 years of age keeps house and makes the broth or stir-about.

Questions for Analysis

1. To what extent are the testimonies of Ann Eggley and Patience Kershaw in harmony with that of Payne?

2. Describe the work of Eggley and Kershaw. What do you think of their work? Why?

3. What strikes you most about the lives of these workers?

4. The witnesses were responding to questions from middle-class commissioners. What did the commissioners seem interested in? Why?

Source: J. Bowditch and C. Ramsland, eds., *Voices of the Industrial Revolution.* Copyright © 1961, 1989 by the University of Michigan. Reprinted by permission.

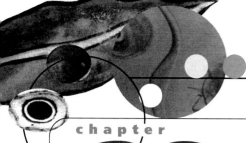

26

THE WEST AND THE WORLD, 1815–1914

While industrialization and nationalism were transforming urban life and Western society, Western society itself was reshaping the world. At the peak of its power and pride, the West entered the third and most dynamic phase of the aggressive expansion that had begun with the Crusades and continued with the great discoveries and the rise of seaborne colonial empires. An ever-growing stream of products, people, and ideas flowed out of Europe in the nineteenth century. Hardly any corner of the globe was left untouched. The most spectacular manifestations of Western expansion came in the late nineteenth century when the leading European nations established or enlarged their far-flung political empires. The political annexation of territory in the 1880s—the "new imperialism," as it is often called by historians—was the capstone of a profound underlying economic and technological process.

Industrialization and the World Economy

The Industrial Revolution created, first in Great Britain and then in continental Europe and North America, a growing and tremendously dynamic economic system. In the course of the nineteenth century, that system was extended across the face of the earth. Some of this extension into non-Western areas was peaceful and beneficial for all concerned, for the West had many products and techniques the rest of the world desired. If peaceful methods failed, however, Europeans did not stand on ceremony. They used their superior military power to force non-Western nations to open their doors to Western economic interests. In general, Westerners fashioned the global economic system so that the largest share of the ever-increasing gains from trade, technology, and migration flowed to the West and its propertied classes.

• *What were some of the global consequences of European industrialization between 1815 and 1914?*

Book Companion Site

This icon will direct you to primary sources and study materials available at **bedfordstmartins.com/mckaywest**

The Rise of Global Inequality

The Industrial Revolution in Europe marked a momentous turning point in human history. Indeed, only by placing Europe's economic breakthrough in a global perspective can one truly appreciate its revolutionary implications and consequences.

From such a global perspective, the ultimate significance of the Industrial Revolution was that it allowed those regions of the world that industrialized in the nineteenth century to increase their wealth and power enormously in comparison to those that did not. As a result, a gap between the industrializing regions (mainly Europe and North America) and the nonindustrializing ones (mainly Africa, Asia, and Latin America) opened up and grew steadily throughout the nineteenth century. Moreover, this pattern of uneven global development became institutionalized, or built into the structure of the world economy. Thus we evolved a "lopsided world," a world of rich lands and poor.

In recent years historical economists have begun to chart the long-term evolution of this gap with some precision. Figure 26.1 summarizes the important findings of one such study. It compares the long-term evolution of average income per person in today's "developed" (or industrialized) regions—defined as Europe, North America, and Japan—with that found in Africa, Asia, and Latin America, also often known as the **Third World.** To get these individual income figures, researchers estimate a country's gross national product (GNP) at different points in time, convert those estimates to some common currency, and divide by the total population.

Figure 26.1 highlights three main points. First, in 1750 the average standard of living was no higher in Europe as a whole than in the rest of the world. In 1750 Europe was still a poor agricultural society. By 1970, however, the average person in the wealthiest countries had an income fully twenty-five times as great as that received by the average person in the poorest countries of Africa and Asia.

Second, it was industrialization that opened the gaps in average wealth and well-being among countries and regions. One sees that Great Britain had jumped well above the European average by 1830, when the first industrial nation was well in advance of its continental competitors. One also sees how Great Britain's lead gradually narrowed as other European countries and the United States successfully industrialized in the course of the nineteenth century.

Third, income per person stagnated in the Third World before 1913, in striking contrast to the industrializing regions. Only after 1945, in the era of political indepen-

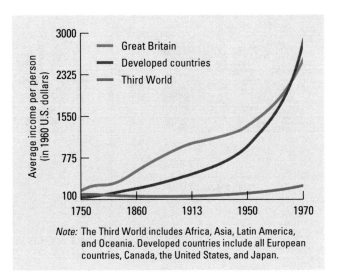

FIGURE 26.1 The Growth of Average Income per Person in the Third World, Developed Countries, and Great Britain, 1750–1970   Growth is given in 1960 U.S. dollars and prices. *(Source: P. Bairoch and M. Lévy-Leboyer, eds.,* Disparities in Economic Development Since the Industrial Revolution. *Copyright © 1981. Reprinted by permission of Palgrave Macmillan, UK.)*

dence and decolonization, did Third World countries finally make some real economic progress, beginning in their turn the critical process of industrialization.

The rise of these enormous income disparities, which are poignant indicators of equal disparities in food and clothing, health and education, life expectancy and general material well-being, has generated a great deal of debate. One school of interpretation stresses that the West used science, technology, capitalist organization, and even its critical worldview to create its wealth and greater physical well-being. Another school argues that the West used its political and economic power to steal much of its riches, continuing in the nineteenth (and twentieth) century the rapacious colonialism born of the era of expansion.

These issues are complex, and there are few simple answers. As noted in Chapter 22, the wealth-creating potential of technological improvement and more intensive capitalist organization was indeed great. At the same time, those breakthroughs rested, in part, on Great Britain's having already used political force to dominate part of the world economy by the late eighteenth century. In the nineteenth century other industrializing countries joined with Britain to extend Western domination over the entire world economy. Wealth—unprecedented wealth—was indeed created, but the lion's share of that new wealth flowed to the West and its propertied classes.

The World Market

Commerce between nations has always been a powerful stimulus to economic development. Never was this more true than in the nineteenth century, when world trade grew prodigiously. In 1913 the value of world trade was roughly $38 billion, or about *twenty-five* times what it had been in 1800, even though prices of both manufactured goods and raw materials were lower in 1913 than in 1800. In a general way, the enormous increase in international commerce summed up the growth of an interlocking world economy centered in and directed by Europe.

Great Britain played a key role in using trade to tie the world together economically. In 1815 Britain already had a colonial empire, for India, Canada, Australia, and other scattered areas remained British possessions after American independence. The technological breakthroughs of the Industrial Revolution allowed Britain to manufacture cotton textiles, iron, and other goods more cheaply and to far outstrip domestic demand for such products. Thus British manufacturers sought export markets first in Europe and then around the world.

Take the case of cotton textiles. By 1820 Britain was exporting 50 percent of its production. Europe bought 50 percent of these cotton textile exports, while India bought only 6 percent. Then as European nations and the United States erected protective tariff barriers and promoted domestic industry, British cotton textile manufacturers aggressively sought and found other foreign markets in non-Western areas. By 1850 India was buying 25 percent and Europe only 16 percent of a much larger total. As a British colony, India could not raise tariffs to protect its ancient cotton textile industry, and thousands of Indian weavers lost their livelihoods.

After the repeal of the Corn Laws in 1846 (see page 764), Britain became the world's single best market. Until 1914 Britain remained the world's emporium, where not only agricultural products and raw materials but also manufactured goods entered freely. Free access to Britain's market stimulated the development of mines and plantations in many non-Western areas.

The growth of trade was facilitated by the conquest of distance. The earliest railroad construction occurred in Europe (including Russia) and in America north of the Rio Grande; other parts of the globe saw the building of rail lines after 1860. By 1920 more than one-quarter of the world's railroads were in Latin America, Asia, Africa, and Australia. Wherever railroads were built, they drastically reduced transportation costs, opened new economic opportunities, and called forth new skills and attitudes. Much of the railroad construction undertaken in Latin America, Asia, and Africa connected seaports with inland cities and regions, as opposed to linking and developing cities and regions within a given country. Thus railroads dovetailed admirably with Western economic interests, facilitating the inflow and sale of Western manufactured goods and the export and the development of local raw materials.

The power of steam revolutionized transportation by sea as well as by land. Steam power, long used to drive paddle wheelers on rivers, particularly in Russia and North America, finally began to supplant sails on the oceans of the world in the late 1860s. Lighter, stronger, cheaper steel replaced iron, which had replaced wood. Screw propellers superseded paddle wheels, while mighty compound steam engines cut fuel consumption by half. Passenger and freight rates tumbled, and the intercontinental shipment of low-priced raw materials became feasible.

An account of an actual voyage by a typical tramp freighter highlights nineteenth-century developments in global trade. The ship left England in 1910 carrying rails and general freight to western Australia. From there it carried lumber to Melbourne in southeastern Australia, where it took on harvester combines for Argentina. In Buenos Aires it loaded wheat for Calcutta, and in Calcutta it took on jute for New York. From New York it carried a variety of industrial products to Australia before returning to England with lead, wool, and wheat after a voyage of approximately seventy-two thousand miles to six continents in seventeen months.

The revolution in land and sea transportation helped European pioneers open up vast new territories and produce agricultural products and raw materials there for sale in Europe. Improved transportation enabled Asia, Africa, and Latin America to ship not only the traditional tropical products—

Chronology

1853	Perry "opens" Japan for trade
1863–1879	Reign of Ismail in Egypt
1865–1909	Reign of Leopold II in Belgium
1867	Meiji Restoration in Japan
1869	Completion of Suez Canal
1898	United States takes over Philippines; hundred days of reform in China
1899	Kipling, "The White Man's Burden"
1902	Conrad, *Heart of Darkness*; Hobson, *Imperialism*

British Ships and Shipbuilders The British continued to dominate international trade before the First World War. This handsome membership certificate of the British shipbuilders union features the vessels that drew the world together and were Britain's pride. Britain's thriving shipbuilding industry was concentrated in southern Scotland along the Clyde. *(Trade Union Congress, London/The Bridgeman Art Library)*

spices, tea, sugar, coffee—but also new raw materials for industry, such as jute, rubber, cotton, and coconut oil.

Intercontinental trade was enormously facilitated by the Suez and Panama Canals. Of great importance, too, was large and continual investment in modern port facilities, which made loading and unloading cheaper, faster, and more dependable. Finally, transoceanic telegraph cables inaugurated rapid communications among the financial centers of the world. While a British tramp freighter steamed from Calcutta to New York, a broker in London was arranging by telegram for it to carry an American

cargo to Australia. World commodity prices were also instantaneously conveyed by the same network of communications.

The growth of trade and the conquest of distance encouraged the expanding European economy to make massive foreign investments beginning about 1840. By the outbreak of World War I in 1914, Europeans had invested more than $40 billion abroad. Great Britain, France, and Germany were the principal investing countries (see Map 26.1). The great gap between rich and poor within Europe meant that the wealthy and moderately well-to-do could and did send great sums abroad in search of interest and dividends.

Most of the capital exported did not go to European colonies or protectorates in Asia and Africa. About three-quarters of total European investment went to other European countries, the United States and Canada, Australia and New Zealand, and Latin America. Europe found its most profitable opportunities for investment in construction of the railroads, ports, and utilities that were necessary to settle and develop the almost-vacant lands in such places as Australia and the Americas. By lending money for a foreign railroad, Europeans also enabled white settlers to buy European rails and locomotives and developed sources of cheap food and raw materials. Much of this investment was peaceful and mutually beneficial for lenders and borrowers. The victims were Native American Indians and Australian aborigines, who were decimated by the diseases, liquor, and weapons of an aggressively expanding Western society.

The Opening of China and Japan

Europe's relatively peaceful development of robust offshoots in sparsely populated North America, Australia, and much of Latin America absorbed huge quantities of goods, investments, and migrants. From a Western point of view, that was the most important aspect of Europe's global thrust. Yet Europe's economic and cultural penetration of old, densely populated civilizations was also profoundly significant, especially for the non-European peoples affected by it. With such civilizations Europeans also increased their trade and profit, and they were prepared to use force, if necessary, to attain their desires. This was what happened in China and Japan, two crucial examples of the general pattern of intrusion into non-Western lands.

Traditional Chinese civilization was self-sufficient. For centuries China had sent more goods and inventions to Europe than it had received, and this was still the case in the early nineteenth century. Trade with Europe was care-

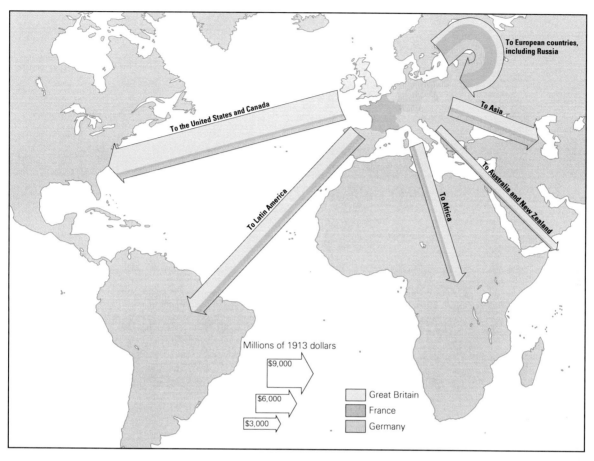

Millions of 1913 dollars

$9,000

$6,000

$3,000

Great Britain
France
Germany

MAP 26.1 European Investment to 1914   Foreign investment grew rapidly after 1850, and Britain, France, and Germany were the major investing nations. As this map suggests, most European investment was not directed to the African and Asian areas seized by the "new imperialism" after 1880.

fully regulated by the Chinese imperial government—the Qing (or Manchu) Dynasty—which required all foreign merchants to live in the southern city of Canton and to buy from and sell to only the local merchant monopoly. Practices considered harmful to Chinese interests, such as the sale of opium, were strictly forbidden.

For years the little community of foreign merchants in Canton had to accept the Chinese system. By the 1820s, however, the dominant group, the British, were flexing their muscles. Moreover, in the smoking of opium—that "destructive and ensnaring vice" denounced by Chinese decrees—they had found something the Chinese really wanted. Grown legally in British-occupied India, opium was smuggled into China by means of fast ships and bribed officials. By 1836 the aggressive goal of the British merchants in Canton was an independent British colony in

China and "safe and unrestricted liberty" in trade. Spurred on by economic motives, they pressured the British government to take decisive action and enlisted the support of British manufacturers with visions of vast Chinese markets to be opened.

At the same time, the Qing government decided that the **opium trade** had to be stamped out. It was ruining the people and stripping the empire of its silver, which was going to British merchants to pay for the opium. The government began to prosecute Chinese drug dealers vigorously and in 1839 it ordered the foreign merchants to obey China's laws. The British merchants refused and were expelled, whereupon war soon broke out.

Using troops from India and being in control of the seas, the British occupied several coastal cities and forced China to surrender. In the Treaty of Nanking in 1842,

Britain and China at War, 1841 Britain capitalized on its overwhelming naval superiority, and this British aquatint celebrates a dramatic moment in a crucial battle near Guangzhou. Having received a direct hit from a steam-powered British ironclad, a Chinese sailing ship explodes into a wall of flame. The Chinese lost eleven ships and five hundred men in the two-hour engagement; the British suffered only minor damage. *(National Maritime Museum, London)*

the imperial government was forced to cede the island of Hong Kong to Britain forever, pay an indemnity of $100 million, and open up four large cities to foreign trade with low tariffs.

Thereafter the opium trade flourished, and Hong Kong developed rapidly as an Anglo-Chinese enclave. China continued to accept foreign diplomats in Beijing (Peking), the imperial capital. Finally, there was a second round of foreign attack between 1856 and 1860, culminating in the occupation of Beijing by seventeen thousand British and French troops and the intentional burning of the emperor's summer palace. Another round of harsh treaties gave European merchants and missionaries greater privileges and protection and forced the Chinese to accept trade and investment on unfavorable terms for several more cities. Thus did Europeans use military aggression to blow a hole in the wall of Chinese seclusion and open the country to foreign trade and foreign ideas.

China's neighbor Japan had its own highly distinctive civilization and even less use for Westerners. European traders and missionaries first arrived in Japan in the sixteenth century. By 1640 Japan had reacted quite negatively to their presence. The government decided to seal off the country from all European influences in order to preserve traditional Japanese culture and society. When American and British whaling ships began to appear off Japanese coasts almost two hundred years later, the policy of exclusion was still in effect. An order of 1825 commanded Japanese officials to "drive away foreign vessels without second thought."[1]

Japan's unbending isolation seemed hostile and barbaric to the West, particularly to the United States. It complicated the practical problems of shipwrecked American sailors and the provisioning of whaling ships and China traders sailing in the eastern Pacific. It also thwarted the hope of trade and profit. Moreover, Americans shared the self-confidence and dynamism of expanding Western society, and they felt destined to play a great role in the

Pacific. To Americans it seemed the duty of the United States to force the Japanese to share their ports and behave as a "civilized" nation.

After several unsuccessful American attempts to establish commercial relations with Japan, Commodore Matthew Perry steamed into Edo (now Tokyo) Bay in 1853 and demanded diplomatic negotiations with the emperor. Japan entered a grave crisis. Some Japanese warriors urged resistance, but senior officials realized how defenseless their cities were against naval bombardment. Shocked and humiliated, they reluctantly signed a treaty with the United States that opened two ports and permitted trade. Over the next five years, more treaties spelled out the rights and privileges of the Western nations and their merchants in Japan. Japan was "opened." What the British had done in China with war, the Americans had done in Japan with only the threat of war.

Western Penetration of Egypt

Egypt's experience illustrates not only the explosive power of the expanding European economy and society but also their seductive appeal in non-Western lands. European involvement in Egypt also led to a new model of formal political control, which European powers applied widely in Africa and Asia after 1882.

Of great importance in African and Middle Eastern history, the ancient land of the pharaohs had since 525 B.C. been ruled by a succession of foreigners, most recently by the Ottoman Turks. In 1798 French armies under young General Napoleon Bonaparte invaded the Egyptian part of the Ottoman Empire and occupied the territory for three years. Into the power vacuum left by the French withdrawal stepped an extraordinary Albanian-born Turkish general, Muhammad Ali (1769–1849).

First appointed governor of Egypt by the Turkish sultan, Muhammad Ali set out to build his own state on the strength of a large, powerful army organized along European lines. He drafted for the first time the illiterate, despised peasant masses of Egypt, and he hired French and Italian army officers to train these raw recruits and their Turkish officers. The government was also reformed, new lands were cultivated, and communications were improved. By the time of his death in 1849, Muhammad Ali had established a strong and virtually independent Egyptian state, to be ruled by his family on a hereditary basis within the Turkish empire.

Muhammad Ali's policies of modernization attracted large numbers of Europeans to the banks of the Nile. The port city of Alexandria had more than fifty thousand Europeans by 1864. Europeans served not only as army officers but also as engineers, doctors, government officials, and police officers. Others turned to trade, finance, and shipping.

To pay for his ambitious plans, Muhammad Ali encouraged the development of commercial agriculture. This development had profound implications. Egyptian peasants were poor but largely self-sufficient, growing food for their own consumption on state-owned lands allotted to them by tradition. Faced with the possibility of export agriculture, high-ranking officials and members of Muhammad Ali's family began carving large private land-holdings out of the state domain. The new landlords made the peasants their tenants and forced them to grow cash crops geared to European markets. Thus Egyptian landowners "modernized" agriculture, but to the detriment of peasant well-being.

These trends continued under Muhammad Ali's grandson Ismail, who in 1863 began his sixteen-year rule as Egypt's **khedive,** or prince. Educated at France's leading military academy, Ismail was a westernizing autocrat. The large irrigation networks he promoted caused cotton production and exports to Europe to boom, and with his support the Suez Canal was completed by a French company in 1869. The Arabic of the masses replaced the Turkish of the conquerors as the official language. Young Egyptians educated in Europe spread new skills, and Cairo acquired modern boulevards and Western hotels. As Ismail proudly declared, "My country is no longer in Africa, we now form part of Europe."[2]

Yet Ismail was too impatient and reckless. His projects were enormously expensive, and by 1876 Egypt owed foreign bondholders a colossal debt that it could not pay. Rather than let Egypt go bankrupt and repudiate its loans, the governments of France and Great Britain intervened politically to protect the European bondholders. They forced Ismail to appoint French and British commissioners to oversee Egyptian finances so that the Egyptian debt would be paid in full. This momentous decision implied direct European political control and was a sharp break with the previous pattern of trade and investment. Throughout most of the nineteenth century, Europeans had used military might and political force primarily to make sure that non-Western lands would accept European trade and investment. Now Europeans were going to determine the state budget and effectively rule Egypt.

Foreign financial control evoked a violent nationalistic reaction among Egyptian religious leaders, young intellectuals, and army officers. In 1879, under the leadership of Colonel Ahmed Arabi, they formed the Egyptian

The Opening of the Suez Canal   A long procession of eighty ships passed through the Suez Canal when it was opened in November 1869, and thousands of spectators lined the shores and joined in the celebrations. The building of the hundred-mile canal was a momentous event, cutting in half the length of the journey between Europe and Asia. *(Archives Charmet/The Bridgeman Art Library)*

Nationalist Party. Continuing diplomatic pressure, which forced Ismail to abdicate in favor of his weak son, Tewfiq (r. 1879–1892), resulted in bloody anti-European riots in Alexandria in 1882. A number of Europeans were killed, and Tewfiq and his court had to flee to British ships for safety. When the British fleet bombarded Alexandria, more riots swept the country, and Colonel Arabi led a revolt. But a British expeditionary force put down the rebellion and occupied all of Egypt.

The British said their occupation was temporary, but British armies remained in Egypt until 1956. They maintained the façade of the khedive's government as an autonomous province of the Ottoman Empire, but the khedive was a mere puppet. British rule did result in tax reforms and somewhat better conditions for peasants, while foreign bondholders received their interest and Egyptian nationalists nursed their injured pride.

British rule in Egypt provided a new model for European expansion in densely populated lands. Such expansion was based on military force, political domination, and a self-justifying ideology of beneficial reform. This model was to predominate until 1914. Thus did Europe's Industrial Revolution lead to tremendous political as well as economic expansion throughout the world after 1880.

The Great Migration

A poignant human drama was interwoven with economic expansion: millions of people pulled up stakes and left their ancestral lands in the course of history's greatest migration. To millions of ordinary people, for whom the opening of China and the interest on the Egyptian debt had not the slightest significance, this great movement was the central experience in the saga of Western expansion. It was, in part, because of this **great migration** that the West's impact on the world in the nineteenth century was so powerful and many-sided.

• *How was massive migration an integral part of Western expansion?*

The Pressure of Population

In the early eighteenth century, the growth of European population entered its third and decisive stage, which continued unabated until the early twentieth century (see Figure 26.2). Birthrates eventually declined in the nineteenth century, but so did death rates, mainly because of the rising standard of living and secondarily because of the medical revolution. Thus the population of Europe (including Asiatic Russia) more than doubled, from approximately 188 million in 1800 to roughly 432 million in 1900.

These figures actually understate Europe's population explosion, for between 1815 and 1932 more than 60 million people left Europe. These migrants went primarily to the "areas of European settlement"—North and South America, Australia, New Zealand, and Siberia—where they contributed to a rapid growth in numbers. Since population grew more slowly in Africa and Asia than in Europe and the Americas, as Figure 26.2 shows, Europeans and people of predominately European origin jumped from about 22 percent of the world's total to about 38 percent on the eve of World War I.

The growing number of Europeans provided further impetus for Western expansion. It was a driving force behind emigration. As in the eighteenth century, the rapid increase in numbers put pressure on the land and led to land hunger and relative overpopulation in area after area. In most countries, migration increased twenty years after a rapid growth in population, as many children of the baby boom grew up, saw little available land and few opportunities, and migrated. This pattern was especially prevalent when rapid population increase predated extensive industrial development, which offered the best long-term hope of creating jobs within the country and reducing poverty. Thus millions of country folk went abroad as well as to nearby cities in search of work and economic opportunity.

Before looking at the people who migrated, let us consider three facts. First, the number of men and women who left Europe increased rapidly before World War I. As Figure 26.3 shows, more than 11 million left in the first decade of the twentieth century, over five times the number departing in the 1850s. The outflow of migrants was clearly an enduring characteristic of European society for the entire period.

Second, different countries had very different patterns of movement. As Figure 26.3 also shows, people left Britain and Ireland (which are not distinguished in the British figures) in large numbers from the 1840s on. This

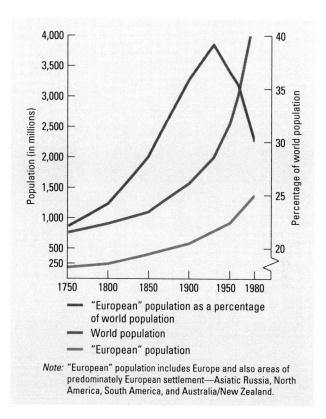

FIGURE 26.2 The Increase of European and World Populations, 1750–1980   (Sources: W. Woodruff, Impact of Western Man: A Study of Europe's Role in the World Economy. St. Martin's Press, New York, 1967, p. 103; United Nations, Statistical Yearbook, 1982, 1985, pp. 2–3.)

emigration reflected not only rural poverty but also the movement of skilled, industrial technicians and the preferences shown to British migrants in the British Empire. Ultimately, about one-third of all European migrants between 1840 and 1920 came from the British Isles. German migration was quite different. It grew irregularly after about 1830, reaching a first peak in the early 1850s and another in the early 1880s. Thereafter it declined rapidly, for Germany's rapid industrialization was providing adequate jobs at home. This pattern contrasted sharply with that of Italy. More and more Italians left the country right up to 1914, reflecting severe problems in Italian villages and relatively slow industrial growth. Thus migration patterns mirrored social and economic conditions in the various European countries and provinces.

Third, although the United States absorbed the largest number of European migrants, less than half of all migrants went to the United States. Asiatic Russia, Canada, Argentina, Brazil, Australia, and New Zealand also attracted

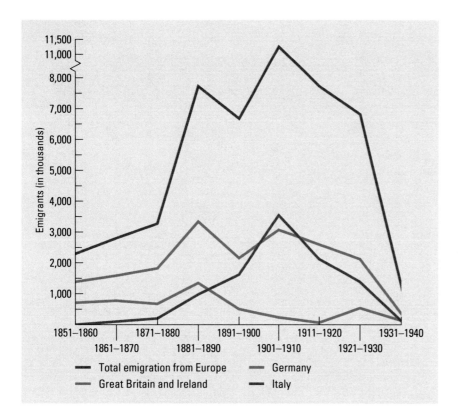

FIGURE 26.3 Emigration from Europe by Decades, 1851–1940
(*Source: Copyright © W. Woodruff, from* Impact of Western Man, *by W. Woodruff, 1982. Reprinted with permission of University Press of America.*)

large numbers, as Figure 26.4 shows. Moreover, migrants accounted for a larger proportion of the total population in Argentina, Brazil, and Canada than in the United States. The common American assumption that European migration meant migration to the United States is quite inaccurate.

European Migrants

What kind of people left Europe, and what were their reasons for doing so? The European migrant was most often a small peasant landowner or a village craftsman whose traditional way of life was threatened by too little land, estate agriculture, and cheap, factory-made goods. German peasants who left the Rhineland and southwestern Germany between 1830 and 1854, for example, felt trapped by what Friedrich List called the "dwarf economy," with its tiny landholdings and declining craft industries. Selling out and moving to buy much cheaper land in the American Midwest became a common response. Thus the European migrant was generally an energetic small farmer or skilled artisan trying hard to stay ahead of poverty, not a desperately impoverished landless peasant or urban proletarian.

Determined to maintain or improve their status, mi-

grants were a great asset to the countries that received them. This was doubly so because the vast majority were young and very often unmarried. They came in the prime of life and were ready to work hard in the new land, at least for a time. Many Europeans moved but remained within Europe, settling temporarily or permanently in another European country. Jews from eastern Europe and peasants from Ireland migrated to Great Britain, Russians and Poles sought work in Germany, and Latin peoples from Spain, Portugal, and Italy entered France. Many Europeans were truly migrants as opposed to immigrants— that is, they returned home after some time abroad. One in two migrants to Argentina and probably one in three to the United States eventually returned to their native land.

The likelihood of repatriation varied greatly by nationality. People who migrated from the Balkans, for instance, were much more likely to return to their countries than people from Ireland and eastern European Jews. Once again, the possibility of buying land in the old country was of central importance. In Ireland (as well as in England and Scotland) land was tightly held by large, often absentee landowners, and little land was available for purchase. In Russia most land was held by non-Jews. Therefore, when Russian Jewish artisans began in the 1880s to escape both factory competition and oppression by mi-

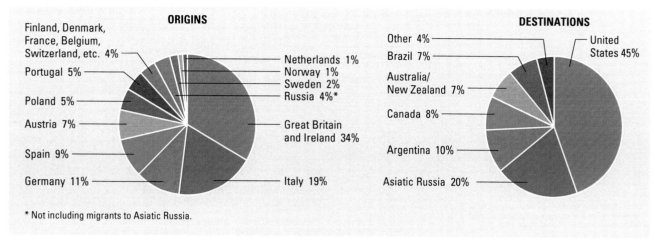

FIGURE 26.4 Origins and Destinations of European Emigrants, 1851–1960 *(Source: Copyright © W. Woodruff, from* Impact of Western Man, *by W. Woodruff, 1982. Reprinted with permission of University Press of America.)*

grating, it was basically a once-and-for-all departure. Non-Jewish migrants from Russia had access to land and returned much more frequently to their peasant villages in central Russia, Poland, and Ukraine.

The mass movement of Italians illustrates many of the characteristics of European migration. As late as the 1880s, three of every four Italians depended on agriculture. With the influx of cheap North American wheat, many small

An Italian Custom in Argentina Italian immigrants introduced the game of boccia to Argentina, where it took hold and became a popular recreation for men. Dressed up in their Sunday best, these Argentinian laborers are totally focused on the game, which is somewhat like horseshoes or shuffleboard. *(Hulton Archive/ Getty Images)*

landowning peasants whose standard of living was falling began to leave their country. Many Italians went to the United States, but before 1900 more went to Argentina and Brazil. In Brazil the large coffee planters, faced with the collapse of black slavery, attracted Italians to their plantations with subsidized travel and promises of relatively high wages.

Many Italians had no intention of settling abroad permanently. Some called themselves **swallows.** After harvesting their own wheat and flax in Italy, they "flew" to Argentina to harvest wheat between December and April. Returning to Italy for the spring planting, they repeated this exhausting process. This was a very hard life, but a frugal worker could save $250 to $300 in the course of a season.

Ties of family and friendship played a crucial role in the movement of peoples. Many people from a given province or village settled together in rural enclaves or tightly knit urban neighborhoods thousands of miles away. Very often a strong individual—a businessman, a religious leader—

would blaze the way and others would follow, forming a "migration chain."

Many landless young European men and women were spurred to leave by a spirit of revolt and independence. In Sweden and in Norway, in Jewish Russia and in Italy, these young people felt frustrated by the small privileged classes, which often controlled both church and government and resisted demands for change and greater opportunity. Many a young Norwegian seconded the passionate cry of Norway's national poet, Martinius Bjørnson: "Forth will I! Forth! I will be crushed and consumed if I stay."[3] Thus for many, migration was a radical way to "get out from under." Migration slowed down when the people won basic political and social reforms, such as the right to vote and social security.

Asian Migrants

Not all migration was from Europe. A substantial number of Chinese, Japanese, Indians, and Filipinos—to name

Vaccinating Migrants Bound for Hawaii, 1904 First Chinese, then Japanese, and finally Koreans and Filipinos went in large numbers across the Pacific to labor in Hawaii on American-owned sugar plantations in the late nineteenth century. The native Hawaiians had been decimated by disease, preparing the way for the annexation of Hawaii by the United States in 1898. *(Corbis)*

only four key groups—responded to rural hardship with temporary or permanent migration. At least 3 million Asians (as opposed to more than 60 million Europeans) moved abroad before 1920. Most went as indentured laborers to work under incredibly difficult conditions on the plantations or in the gold mines of Latin America, southern Asia, Africa, California, Hawaii, and Australia. White estate owners very often used Asians to replace or supplement blacks after the suppression of the slave trade.

In the 1840s, for example, there was a strong demand for field hands in Cuba, and the Spanish government actively recruited Chinese laborers. Between 1853 and 1873, when such migration was stopped, more than 130,000 Chinese laborers went to Cuba. The majority spent their lives as virtual slaves. The great landlords of Peru also brought in more than 100,000 workers from China in the nineteenth century, and there were similar movements of Asians elsewhere.

Such migration from Asia would undoubtedly have grown to much greater proportions if planters and mine owners in search of cheap labor had been able to hire as many Asian workers as they wished. But they could not. Asians fled the plantations and gold mines as soon as possible, seeking greater opportunities in trade and towns. There they came into conflict with local populations, whether in Malaya, East Africa, or areas settled by Europeans. These European settlers demanded a halt to Asian migration. By the 1880s, Americans and Australians were building **great white walls**—discriminatory laws designed to keep Asians out.

A crucial factor in the migrations before 1914 was, therefore, the general policy of "whites only" in the open lands of possible permanent settlement. This, too, was part of Western dominance in the increasingly lopsided world. Largely successful in monopolizing the best overseas opportunities, Europeans and people of European ancestry reaped the main benefits from the great migration. By 1913 people in Australia, Canada, and the United States all had higher average incomes than people in Great Britain, still Europe's wealthiest nation.

Western Imperialism, 1880–1914

The expansion of Western society reached its apex between about 1880 and 1914. In those years, the leading European nations not only continued to send massive streams of migrants, money, and manufactured goods around the world, but also rushed to create or enlarge vast *political* empires abroad. This political empire build-ing contrasted sharply with the economic penetration of non-Western territories between 1816 and 1880, which had left a China or a Japan "opened" but politically independent. By contrast, the empires of the late nineteenth century recalled the old European colonial empires of the seventeenth and eighteenth centuries and led contemporaries to speak of the **new imperialism.**

Characterized by a frantic rush to plant the flag over as many people and as much territory as possible, the new imperialism had momentous consequences. It resulted in new tensions among competing European states, and it led to wars and rumors of war with non-European powers. The new imperialism was aimed primarily at Africa and Asia. It put millions of black, brown, and yellow peoples directly under the rule of whites.

• *How and why after 1875 did European nations rush to build political empires in Africa and Asia?*

The Scramble for Africa

The most spectacular manifestation of the new imperialism was the seizure of Africa, which broke sharply with previous patterns and fascinated contemporary Europeans and Americans. As late as 1880, European nations controlled only 10 percent of the African continent, and their possessions were hardly increasing. The French had begun conquering Algeria in 1830, and by 1880 substantial numbers of French, Italian, and Spanish colonists had settled among the overwhelming Arab majority.

At the other end of the continent, in South Africa, the British had taken possession of the Dutch settlements at Cape Town during the wars with Napoleon I. This takeover had led disgruntled Dutch cattle ranchers and farmers in 1835 to make their so-called Great Trek into the interior, where they fought the Zulu and Xhosa peoples for land. After 1853, while British colonies such as Canada and Australia were beginning to evolve toward self-government, the Boers, or **Afrikaners** (as the descendants of the Dutch in the Cape Colony were beginning to call themselves), proclaimed their political independence and defended it against British armies. By 1880 Afrikaner and British settlers, who detested each other, had wrested control of much of South Africa from the Zulu, Xhosa, and other African peoples.

European trading posts and forts dating back to the Age of Discovery and the slave trade dotted the coast of West Africa. The Portuguese proudly but ineffectively held their old possessions in Angola and Mozambique. Elsewhere over the great mass of the continent, Europeans did not rule.

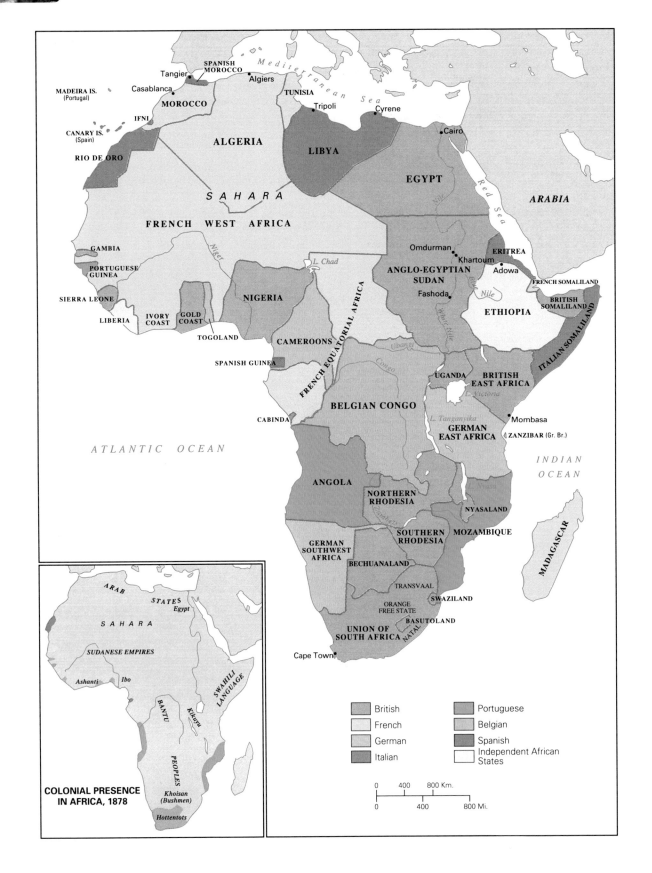

Mediterranean Sea

SPANISH MOROCCO
Tangier
Casablanca
Algiers
MOROCCO
TUNISIA
Tripoli
Cyrene
MADEIRA IS. (Portugal)
IFNI
CANARY IS. (Spain)
Cairo
RIO DE ORO
ALGERIA
LIBYA
EGYPT
ARABIA
Nile
Red Sea
SAHARA
FRENCH WEST AFRICA
Niger
GAMBIA
PORTUGUESE GUINEA
L. Chad
Omdurman
Khartoum
ERITREA
SIERRA LEONE
NIGERIA
ANGLO-EGYPTIAN SUDAN
Adowa
FRENCH SOMALILAND
IVORY COAST
GOLD COAST
LIBERIA
Fashoda
Blue Nile
BRITISH SOMALILAND
TOGOLAND
CAMEROONS
ETHIOPIA
White Nile
SPANISH GUINEA
FRENCH EQUATORIAL AFRICA
Ubangi
ITALIAN SOMALILAND
Congo
UGANDA
BRITISH EAST AFRICA
CABINDA
BELGIAN CONGO
L. Victoria
ATLANTIC OCEAN
L. Tanganyika
Mombasa
GERMAN EAST AFRICA
ZANZIBAR (Gr. Br.)
INDIAN OCEAN
ANGOLA
NORTHERN RHODESIA
Nyasa
NYASALAND
MOZAMBIQUE
MADAGASCAR
GERMAN SOUTHWEST AFRICA
SOUTHERN RHODESIA
Zambezi
BECHUANALAND
TRANSVAAL
SWAZILAND
ORANGE FREE STATE
BASUTOLAND
UNION OF SOUTH AFRICA
NATAL
Cape Town

COLONIAL PRESENCE IN AFRICA, 1878

ARAB STATES
Egypt
SAHARA
SUDANESE EMPIRES
Ashanti
Ibo
BANTU
Kikuyu
SWAHILI LANGUAGE
PEOPLES
Khoisan (Bushmen)
Hottentots

	British		Portuguese
	French		Belgian
	German		Spanish
	Italian		Independent African States

0   400   800 Km.
0   400   800 Mi.

Between 1880 and 1900, the situation changed drastically. Britain, France, Germany, and Italy scrambled for African possessions as if their national livelihoods depended on it (see Map 26.2). By 1900 nearly the whole continent had been carved up and placed under European rule: only Ethiopia in northeast Africa, which repulsed Italian invaders, and Liberia on the West African coast, which had been settled by freed slaves from the United States, remained independent. In the years before 1914, the European powers tightened their control and established colonial governments to rule their gigantic empires.

Book Companion Site
Primary Source: European Imperialism in Africa: A Veteran Explains the Rules of the Game

The Dutch settler republics also succumbed to imperialism, but the final outcome was quite different. The British, led by Cecil Rhodes in the Cape Colony, leapfrogged over the Afrikaner states in the early 1890s and established protectorates over Bechuanaland (now Botswana) and Rhodesia (now Zimbabwe and Zambia), named in honor of its freelance imperial founder. Trying unsuccessfully to undermine the stubborn Afrikaners in the Transvaal, where English-speaking capitalists like Rhodes were developing fabulously rich gold mines, the British conquered their white rivals in the bloody South African War (1899–1902). In 1910 their territories were united with the old Cape Colony and the eastern province of Natal in a new Union of South Africa, established—unlike any other territory in Africa—as a largely "self-governing" colony. This enabled the defeated Afrikaners to use their numerical superiority over the British settlers to gradually take political power, as even the most

educated nonwhites lost the right to vote outside the Cape Colony. (See the feature "Individuals in Society: Cecil Rhodes.")

In the complexity of the European seizure of Africa, certain events and individuals stand out. Of enormous importance was the British occupation of Egypt in 1882, which established the new model of formal political control. There was also the role of Leopold II of Belgium (r. 1865–1909), an energetic, strong-willed monarch with a lust for distant territory. "The sea bathes our coast, the world lies before us," he had exclaimed in 1861. "Steam and electricity have annihilated distance, and all the non-appropriated lands on the surface of the globe can become the field of our operations and of our success."[4] By 1876 Leopold was focusing on central Africa. Subsequently, he formed a financial syndicate under his personal control to send Henry M. Stanley, a sensation-seeking journalist and part-time explorer, to the Congo basin. Stanley was able to establish trading stations, sign "treaties" with African chiefs, and plant Leopold's flag. Leopold's actions alarmed the French, who quickly sent out an expedition under Pierre de Brazza. In 1880 de Brazza signed a treaty of protection with the chief of the large Teke tribe and began to establish a French protectorate on the north bank of the Congo River.

Leopold's buccaneering intrusion into the Congo area raised the question of the political fate of Africa. By 1882 Europe had caught "African fever." There was a gold rush mentality, and the race for territory was on.

To lay down some basic rules for this new and dangerous game of imperialist competition in sub-Saharan Africa, Jules Ferry of France and Otto von Bismarck of Germany arranged an international conference on Africa in Berlin in 1884 and 1885. The conference established the principle that European claims to African territory had to rest on "effective occupation" in order to be recognized by other states. This meant that Europeans would push relentlessly into interior regions from all sides and that no single European power would be able to claim the entire continent. The conference recognized Leopold's personal rule over a neutral Congo free state and agreed to work to stop slavery and the slave trade in Africa.

The **Berlin conference** coincided with Germany's sudden emergence as an imperial power. Prior to about 1880, Bismarck, like many other European leaders at the time, had seen little value in colonies. Colonies reminded him, he said, of a poor but proud nobleman who wore a fur coat when he could not afford a shirt underneath. Then in 1884 and 1885, as political agitation for expansion increased, Bismarck did an abrupt about-face, and Germany established protectorates over a number of

Mapping the Past

MAP 26.2 The Partition of Africa The European powers carved up Africa after 1880 and built vast political empires. European states also seized territory in Asia in the nineteenth century, although some Asian states and peoples managed to maintain their political independence, as may be seen on Map 26.3, page 864. The late nineteenth century was the high point of European imperialism. Compare the patterns of European imperialism in Africa and Asia, using this map and Map 26.3. ❶ What European countries were leading imperialist states in both Africa and Asia, and what lands did they hold? ❷ What countries in Africa and Asia maintained their political independence? ❸ From an imperialist perspective, what in 1914 did the United States and Japan, two very different countries, have in common in Africa and Asia?

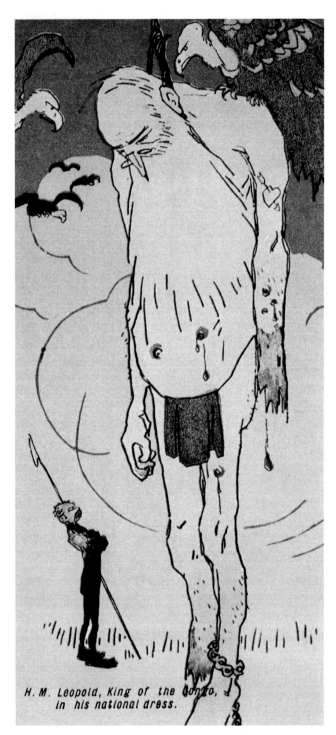

European Imperialism at Its Worst This 1908 English cartoon, "Leopold, King of the Congo, in his national dress," focuses on the barbaric practice of cutting off the hands and feet of Africans who refused to gather as much rubber as Leopold's company demanded. In 1908 an international human rights campaign forced the Belgian king to cede his personal fief to the Belgian state. *(The Granger Collection, New York)*

small African kingdoms and tribes in Togo, Cameroons, southwest Africa, and, later, East Africa. In acquiring colonies, Bismarck cooperated against the British with France's Ferry, who was as ardent for empire as he was for education. With Bismarck's tacit approval, the French pressed southward from Algeria, eastward from their old forts on the Senegal coast, and northward from their protectorate on the Congo River.

Meanwhile, the British began enlarging their West African enclaves and impatiently pushing northward from the Cape Colony and westward from Zanzibar. Their thrust southward from Egypt was blocked in Sudan by fiercely independent Muslims who massacred a British force at Khartoum in 1885.

A decade later, another British force, under General Horatio H. Kitchener, moved cautiously and more successfully up the Nile River, building a railroad to supply arms and reinforcements as it went. Finally, in 1898 these British troops met their foe at Omdurman (see Map 26.2), where Muslim tribesmen armed with spears charged time and time again, only to be cut down by the recently invented machine gun. For one smug participant, the young British officer Winston Churchill, it was "like a pantomime scene" in a play. "These extraordinary foreign figures . . . march up one by one from the darkness of Barbarism to the footlights of civilization . . . and their conquerors, taking their possessions, forget even their names." For another, more somber English observer, "It was not a battle but an execution. The bodies were not in heaps . . . but they spread evenly over acres and acres."[5] In the end, eleven thousand brave Muslim tribesmen lay dead, while only twenty-eight Britons had been killed.

Continuing up the Nile after the Battle of Omdurman, Kitchener's armies found that a small French force had already occupied the village of Fashoda. Locked in imperial competition with Britain ever since the British occupation of Egypt, France had tried to beat the British to one of Africa's last unclaimed areas—the upper reaches of the Nile. The result was a serious diplomatic crisis and even the threat of war. Eventually, wracked by the Dreyfus affair (see page 834) and unwilling to fight, France backed down and withdrew its forces, allowing the British to take over.

The British conquest of Sudan exemplifies the general process of empire building in Africa. The fate of the Muslim force at Omdurman was eventually inflicted on all native peoples who resisted European rule: they were blown away by vastly superior military force. But however much the European powers squabbled for territory and privilege around the world, they always had the sense

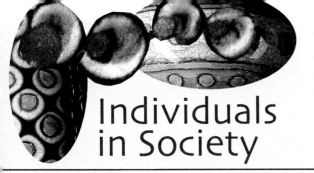

Individuals in Society

Cecil Rhodes

Cecil Rhodes (1853–1902) epitomized the dynamism and the ruthlessness of the new imperialism. He built a corporate monopoly, claimed vast tracts in Africa, and established the famous Rhodes scholarships to develop colonial (and American) leaders who would love and strengthen the British Empire. But to Africans, he left a bitter legacy.

Rhodes came from a large middle-class family and at seventeen went to southern Africa to seek his fortune. He soon turned to diamonds, newly discovered at Kimberley, picked good partners, and was wealthy by 1876. But Rhodes, often called a dreamer, wanted more. He entered Oxford University, while returning periodically to Africa, and his musings crystallized in a belief in progress through racial competition and territorial expansion. "I contend," he wrote, "that we [English] are the finest race in the world and the more of the world we inhabit the better it is for the human race."*

Rhodes's belief in British expansion never wavered. In 1880 he formed the De Beers Mining Company, and by 1888 his firm monopolized southern Africa's diamond production and earned fabulous profits. Rhodes also entered the Cape Colony's legislature and became the all-powerful prime minister from 1890 to 1896. His main objective was to dominate the Afrikaner republics and to impose British rule on as much land as possible beyond their northern borders. Working through a state-approved private company financed in part by De Beers, Rhodes's agents forced and cajoled African kings to accept British "protection," then put down rebellions with Maxim machine guns. Britain thus obtained a great swath of empire on the cheap.

But Rhodes, like many high achievers obsessed with power and personal aggrandizement, went too far. He backed, and then in 1896 declined to call back, a failed invasion of the Transvaal, which was designed to topple the Dutch-speaking republic. Repudiated by top British leaders who had encouraged his plan, Rhodes had to resign as prime minister. In declining health, he continued to agitate against the Afrikaner republics. He died at age forty-nine as the South African War (1899–1902) ended.

In accounting for Rhodes's remarkable but flawed achievements, both sympathetic and critical biographers stress his imposing size, enormous energy, and powerful personality. His ideas were commonplace, but he believed in them passionately, and he could persuade and inspire others to follow his lead. Rhodes the idealist was nonetheless a born negotiator, a crafty

Cecil Rhodes, after crushing the last African revolt in Rhodesia in 1896.
(Brown Brothers)

dealmaker who believed that everyone could be had for a price. According to his best biographer, Rhodes's homosexuality—discreet, partially repressed, and undeniable—was also "a major component of his magnetism and his success."† Never comfortable with women, he loved male companionship. He drew together a "band of brothers," both gay and straight, to share in the pursuit of power.

Rhodes cared nothing for the rights of blacks. Ever a combination of visionary and opportunist, he looked forward to an eventual reconciliation of Afrikaners and British in a united white front. Therefore, as prime minister of the Cape Colony, he broke with the colony's liberal tradition and supported Afrikaner demands to reduce drastically the number of black voters and limit black freedoms. This helped lay the foundation for the Union of South Africa's brutal policy of racial segregation known as *apartheid* after 1948.

Questions for Analysis

1. How did Rhodes relate to Afrikaners and to black Africans? How do you account for the differences and the similarities?
2. In what ways does Rhodes's career throw additional light on the debate over the causes of the new imperialism?

*Robert Rotberg, *The Founder: Cecil Rhodes and the Pursuit of Power* (New York: Oxford University Press, 1988), p. 150.
†Ibid., p. 408.

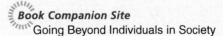
Book Companion Site
Going Beyond Individuals in Society

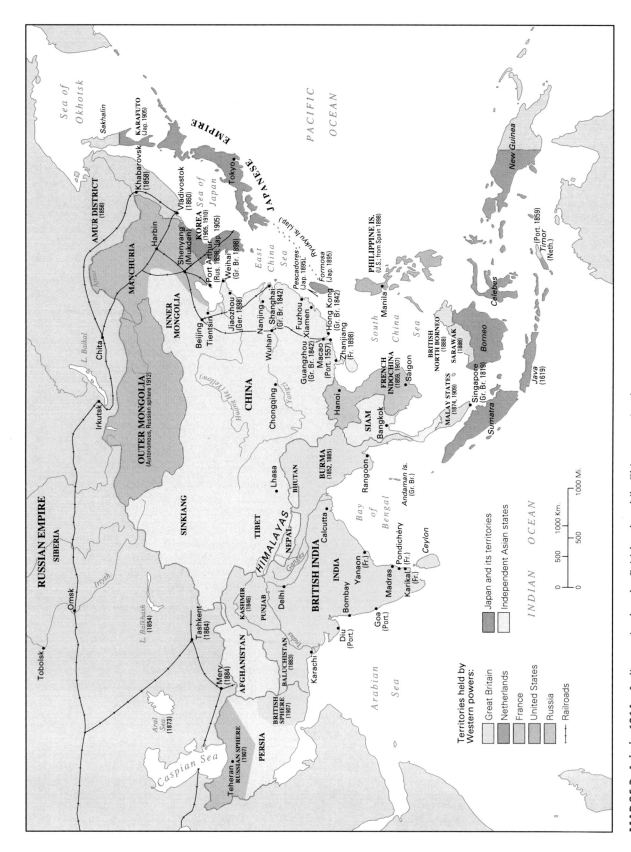

MAP 26.3 Asia in 1914 India remained under British rule, while China precariously preserved its political independence. The Dutch empire in modern-day Indonesia was old, but French control of Indochina was a product of the new imperialism.

to stop short of actually fighting each other. Imperial ambitions were not worth a great European war.

Imperialism in Asia

Although the sudden division of Africa was more spectacular, Europeans also extended their political control in Asia. In 1815 the Dutch ruled little more than the island of Java in the East Indies. Thereafter they gradually brought almost all of the three-thousand-mile archipelago under their political authority, though—in good imperialist fashion—they had to share some of the spoils with Britain and Germany. In the critical decade of the 1880s, the French under the leadership of Ferry took Indochina. India, Japan, and China also experienced a profound imperialist impact (see Map 26.3).

Two other great imperialist powers, Russia and the United States, also acquired rich territories in Asia. Russia moved steadily forward on two fronts throughout the nineteenth century. Russians conquered Muslim areas to the south in the Caucasus and in Central Asia and also proceeded to nibble greedily on China's outlying provinces in the Far East, especially in the 1890s.

The United States's great conquest was the Philippines, taken from Spain in 1898 after the Spanish-American War. When it quickly became clear that the United States had no intention of granting independence, Philippine patriots rose in revolt and were suppressed only after long, bitter fighting. Some Americans protested the taking of the Philippines, but to no avail. Thus another great Western power joined the imperialist ranks in Asia.

Causes of the New Imperialism

Many factors contributed to the late-nineteenth-century rush for territory and empire, which was in turn one aspect of Western society's generalized expansion in the age of industry and nationalism. It is little wonder that controversies have raged over interpretation of the new imperialism, especially since authors of every persuasion have often exaggerated particular aspects in an attempt to prove their own theories. Yet despite complexity and controversy, basic causes are clearly identifiable.

Economic motives played an important role in the extension of political empires, especially the British Empire. By the late 1870s, France, Germany, and the United States were industrializing rapidly behind rising tariff barriers. Great Britain was losing its early lead and facing increasingly tough competition in foreign markets. In this new economic situation, Britain came to value old possessions, especially its vast colony of India, which it

had exploited most profitably for more than a century. When continental powers began to grab territory in the 1880s, the British followed suit immediately. They feared that France and Germany would seal off their empires with high tariffs and restrictions and that future economic opportunities would be lost forever.

Actually, the overall economic gains of the new imperialism proved quite limited before 1914. The new colonies were simply too poor to buy much, and they offered few immediately profitable investments. Nonetheless, even the poorest, most barren desert was jealously prized, and no territory was ever abandoned. Colonies became important for political and diplomatic reasons. Each leading country saw colonies as crucial to national security, military power, and international prestige. For instance, safeguarding the Suez Canal played a key role in the British occupation of Egypt, and protecting Egypt in turn led to the bloody conquest of Sudan. Far-flung possessions guaranteed ever-growing navies the safe havens and the dependable coaling stations they needed in time of crisis or war.

Many people were convinced that colonies were essential to great nations. "There has never been a great power without great colonies," wrote one French publicist in 1877. "Every virile people has established colonial power," echoed the famous nationalist historian of Germany, Heinrich von Treitschke. "All great nations in the fullness of their strength have desired to set their mark upon barbarian lands and those who fail to participate in this great rivalry will play a pitiable role in time to come."[6]

Treitschke's harsh statement reflects not only the increasing aggressiveness of European nationalism after Bismarck's wars of German unification but also Social Darwinian theories of brutal competition among races. As one prominent English economist argued, the "strongest nation has always been conquering the weaker . . . and the strongest tend to be best." Thus European nations, which were seen as racially distinct parts of the dominant white race, had to seize colonies to show they were strong and virile. Moreover, since racial struggle was nature's inescapable law, the conquest of "inferior" peoples was just. "The path of progress is strewn with the wreck . . . of inferior races," wrote one professor in 1900. "Yet these dead peoples are, in very truth, the stepping stones on which mankind has risen to the higher intellectual and deeper emotional life of today."[7] Social Darwinism and harsh racial doctrines fostered imperialist expansion.

So did the industrial world's unprecedented technological and military superiority. Three aspects were crucial. First, the rapidly firing machine gun, so lethal at Omdurman in Sudan, was an ultimate weapon in many another unequal battle. Second, newly discovered quinine proved no less effective in controlling attacks of malaria, which had previously decimated whites in the tropics whenever they left breezy coastal enclaves and dared to venture into mosquito-infested interiors. Third, the combination of the steamship and the international telegraph permitted Western powers to quickly concentrate their firepower in a given area when it was needed. Never before—and never again after 1914—would the technological gap between the West and non-Western regions of the world be so great.

Social tensions and domestic political conflicts also contributed mightily to overseas expansion. In Germany, in Russia, and in other countries to a lesser extent, contemporary critics of imperialism charged conservative political leaders with manipulating colonial issues in order to divert popular attention from the class struggle at home and to create a false sense of national unity. Thus imperial propagandists relentlessly stressed that colonies benefited workers as well as capitalists, providing jobs and cheap raw materials that raised workers' standard of living. Government leaders and their allies in the tabloid press successfully encouraged the masses to savor foreign triumphs and glory in the supposed increase in national prestige. In short, conservative leaders defined imperialist development as a national necessity, which they used to justify the status quo and their hold on power.

Finally, certain special-interest groups in each country were powerful agents of expansion. Shipping companies wanted lucrative subsidies. White settlers demanded more land and greater protection. Missionaries and humanitarians wanted to spread religion and stop the slave trade. Military men and colonial officials, whose role has often been overlooked, foresaw rapid advancement and high-paid positions in growing empires. The actions of such groups pushed the course of empire forward.

A Missionary School   A Swahili schoolboy leads his classmates in a reading lesson in Dar es Salaam in German East Africa before 1914, as portraits of Emperor William II and his wife look down on the classroom. Europeans argued that they were spreading the benefits of a superior civilization with schools like this one, which is unusually solid because of its strategic location in the capital city. *(Ullstein Bilderdienst/The Granger Collection, New York)*

A "Civilizing Mission"

Western society did not rest the case for empire solely on naked conquest and a Darwinian racial struggle or on power politics and the need for naval bases on every ocean. Imperialists developed additional arguments in order to satisfy their consciences and answer their critics.

A favorite idea was that Europeans could and should "civilize" more primitive, nonwhite peoples. According to this view, nonwhites would eventually receive the benefits of modern economies, cities, advanced medicine, and higher standards of living. In time, they might be ready for self-government and Western democracy. Thus the French spoke of their sacred "civilizing mission." In 1899 Rudyard Kipling (1865–1936), who wrote masterfully of Anglo-Indian life and was perhaps the most influential British writer of the 1890s, exhorted Europeans (and Americans in the United States) to unselfish service in distant lands:

Take up the White Man's Burden—
Send forth the best ye breed—
Go bind your sons to exile
To serve your captives' need,
To wait in heavy harness,
On fluttered folk and wild—
Your new-caught, sullen peoples
Half-devil and half-child.[8]

Many Americans accepted the ideology of the **white man's burden.** It was an important factor in the decision to rule, rather than liberate, the Philippines after the Spanish-American War. Like their European counterparts, these Americans sincerely believed that their civilization had reached unprecedented heights and that they had unique benefits to bestow on all "less advanced" peoples. Another argument was that imperial government protected natives from tribal warfare as well as cruder forms of exploitation by white settlers and business people.

Peace and stability under European control also facilitated the spread of Christianity. In Africa Catholic and Protestant missionaries competed with Islam south of the Sahara, seeking converts and building schools to spread the Gospel. Many Africans' first real contact with whites was in mission schools. Some peoples, such as the Ibo in Nigeria, became highly Christianized.

Such occasional successes in black Africa contrasted with the general failure of missionary efforts in India, China, and the Islamic world. There Christians often preached in vain to peoples with ancient, complex religious beliefs. Yet the number of Christian believers around the world did increase substantially in the nineteenth century, and mission-

ary groups kept trying. Unfortunately, "many missionaries had drunk at the well of European racism," and this probably prevented them from doing better.[9]

Critics of Imperialism

The expansion of empire aroused sharp, even bitter, critics. A forceful attack was delivered in 1902, after the unpopular South African War, by radical English economist J. A. Hobson (1858–1940) in his *Imperialism,* a work that influenced Lenin and others. Hobson contended that the rush to acquire colonies was due to the economic needs of unregulated capitalism, particularly the need of the rich to find outlets for their surplus capital. Yet, Hobson argued, imperial possessions did not pay off economically for the country as a whole. Only unscrupulous special-interest groups profited from them, at the expense of both the European taxpayer and the natives. Moreover, Hobson argued that the quest for empire diverted popular attention away from domestic reform and the need to reduce the great gap between rich and poor. These and similar arguments were not very persuasive, however. Most people then (and now) were sold on the idea that imperialism was economically profitable for the homeland, and a broad and genuine enthusiasm for empire developed among the masses.

Hobson and many other critics struck home, however, with their moral condemnation of whites imperiously ruling nonwhites. They rebelled against crude Social Darwinian thought. "O Evolution, what crimes are committed in thy name!" cried one foe. Another sardonically coined a new beatitude: "Blessed are the strong, for they shall prey on the weak."[10] Kipling and his kind were lampooned as racist bullies whose rule rested on brutality, racial contempt, and the Maxim machine gun. Henry Labouchère, a member of Parliament and prominent spokesman for this position, mocked Kipling's famous poem:

Pile on the Brown Man's burden!
And if ye rouse his hate,
Meet his old-fashioned reasons
With Maxims up to date,
With shells and Dum-Dum bullets
A hundred times plain
The Brown Man's loss must never
Imply the White Man's gain.[11]

Similarly, in 1902 in *Heart of Darkness* Polish-born novelist Joseph Conrad (1857–1924) castigated the "pure selfishness" of Europeans in "civilizing" Africa; the main character, once a liberal scholar, turns into a savage brute.

Critics charged Europeans with applying a degrading double standard and failing to live up to their own noble ideals. At home Europeans had won or were winning representative government, individual liberties, and a certain equality of opportunity. In their empires, Europeans imposed military dictatorships on Africans and Asians; forced them to work involuntarily, almost like slaves; and discriminated against them shamelessly. Only by renouncing imperialism, its critics insisted, and giving captive peoples the freedoms Western society had struggled for since the French Revolution would Europeans be worthy of their traditions. Europeans who denounced the imperialist tide provided colonial peoples with a Western ideology of liberation.

Responding to Western Imperialism

To peoples in Africa and Asia, Western expansion represented a profoundly disruptive assault. Everywhere it threatened traditional ruling classes, traditional economies, and traditional ways of life. Christian missionaries and European secular ideologies challenged established beliefs and values. Non-Western peoples experienced a crisis of identity, one made all the more painful by the power and arrogance of the white intruders.

• *What was the general pattern of non-Western responses to Western expansion, and how did India, Japan, and China meet the imperialist challenge?*

The Pattern of Response

Generally, the initial response of African and Asian rulers to aggressive Western expansion was to try to drive the unwelcome foreigners away. This was the case in China, Japan, and upper Sudan, as we have seen. Violent anti-foreign reactions exploded elsewhere again and again, but the superior military technology of the industrialized West almost invariably prevailed. Beaten in battle, many Africans and Asians concentrated on preserving their cultural traditions at all costs. Others found themselves forced to reconsider their initial hostility. Some (such as Ismail of Egypt) concluded that the West was indeed superior in some ways and that it was therefore necessary to reform their societies and copy some European achievements, especially if they wished to escape full-blown Western political rule. Thus it is possible to think of responses to the Western impact as a spectrum, with "traditionalists" at one end, "westernizers" or "modernizers" at the other, and many shades of opinion in between. Both before and after European domination, the struggle among these groups was often intense. With

time, however, the modernizers tended to gain the upper hand.

When the power of both the traditionalists and the modernizers was thoroughly shattered by superior force, the great majority of Asians and Africans accepted imperial rule. Political participation in non-Western lands was historically limited to small elites, and the masses were used to doing what their rulers told them. In these circumstances Europeans, clothed in power and convinced of their righteousness, governed smoothly and effectively. They received considerable support from both traditionalists (local chiefs, landowners, religious leaders) and modernizers (Western-educated professional classes and civil servants).

Nevertheless, imperial rule was in many ways an imposing edifice built on sand. Support for European rule among the conforming and accepting millions was shallow and weak. Thus the conforming masses followed with greater or lesser enthusiasm a few determined personalities who came to oppose the Europeans. Such leaders always arose, both when Europeans ruled directly and when they manipulated native governments, for at least two basic reasons.

First, the nonconformists—the eventual anti-imperialist leaders—developed a burning desire for human dignity. They came to feel that such dignity was incompatible with foreign rule. Second, potential leaders found in the Western world the ideologies and justification for their protest. They discovered liberalism, with its credo of civil liberty and political self-determination. They echoed the demands of anti-imperialists in Europe and America that the West live up to its own ideals. Above all, they found themselves attracted to modern nationalism, which asserted that every people had the right to control its own destiny. After 1917 anti-imperialist revolt would find another weapon in Lenin's version of Marxian socialism. Thus the anti-imperialist search for dignity drew strength from Western thought and culture, as is apparent in the development of three major Asian countries—India, Japan, and China.

Empire in India

India was the jewel of the British Empire, and no colonial area experienced a more profound British impact. Unlike Japan and China, which maintained a real or precarious independence, and unlike African territories, which were annexed by Europeans only at the end of the nineteenth century, India was ruled more or less absolutely by Britain for a very long time.

Arriving in India on the heels of the Portuguese in the seventeenth century, the British East India Company had conquered the last independent native state by 1848. The

Imperial Complexities in India Britain permitted many native princes to continue their rule, if they accepted British domination. This photo shows a road-building project designed to facilitate famine relief in a southern native state. Officials of the local Muslim prince and their British "advisers" watch over workers drawn from the Hindu majority. *(Nizam's Good Works Project—Famine Relief: Road Building, Aurangabad 1895–1902, from Judith Mara Gutman,* Through Indian Eyes. *Courtesy, Private Collection)*

last "traditional" response to European rule—the attempt by the established ruling classes to drive the white man out by military force—was broken in India in 1857 and 1858. Those were the years of the **Great Rebellion** (which the British called a "mutiny"), when an insurrection by Muslim and Hindu mercenaries in the British army spread throughout northern and central India before it was finally crushed, primarily by loyal native troops from southern India. Thereafter Britain ruled India directly.

After 1858 India was ruled by the British Parliament in London and administered by a tiny, all-white civil service in India. In 1900 this elite consisted of fewer than 3,500 top officials, for a population of 300 million. The white elite, backed by white officers and native troops, was competent and generally well-disposed toward the welfare of the Indian peasant masses. Yet it practiced strict job discrimination and social segregation, and most of its members quite frankly considered the jumble of Indian peoples and castes to be racially inferior. As Lord Kitchener, one of the most distinguished top military commanders in India, stated:

It is this consciousness of the inherent superiority of the European which has won for us India. However well educated and clever a native may be, and however brave he may prove himself, I believe that no rank we can bestow on him would cause him to be considered an equal of the British officer.[12]

British women played an important part in the imperial enterprise, especially after the opening of the Suez Canal in 1869 made it much easier for civil servants and businessmen to bring their wives and children with them to India. These British families tended to live in their own separate communities, where they occupied large houses with well-shaded porches, handsome lawns, and a multitude of servants. It was the wife's responsibility to manage this complex household. Many officials' wives learned to relish their duties, and they directed their households and servants with the same self-confident authoritarianism that characterized British political rule in India. (See the feature "Listening to the Past: A British Woman in India" on pages 876–877.)

A small minority of British women—many of them feminists, social reformers, or missionaries, both married and single—sought to go further and shoulder the "white women's burden" in India, as one historian has described it.[13] These women tried especially to improve the lives of Indian women, both Hindu and Muslim, and to move them closer through education and legislation to the better conditions that they believed Western women had attained. Their greatest success was educating some elite Hindu women who took up the cause of reform.

With British men and women sharing a sense of mission as well as strong feelings of racial and cultural superiority, the British acted energetically and introduced many desirable changes to India. Realizing that they needed well-educated Indians to serve as skilled subordinates in the government and army, the British established a modern system of progressive secondary education in which all instruction was in English. Thus through education and government service, the British offered some Indians excellent opportunities for both economic and social advancement. High-caste Hindus, particularly quick to respond, emerged as skillful intermediaries between the British rulers and the Indian people, and soon they formed a new elite profoundly influenced by Western thought and culture.

This new bureaucratic elite played a crucial role in modern economic development, which was a second result of British rule. Irrigation projects for agriculture, the world's third-largest railroad network for good communications, and large tea and jute plantations geared to the world economy were all developed. Unfortunately, the lot of the Indian masses improved little, for the increase in production was eaten up by population increase.

Finally, with a well-educated, English-speaking Indian bureaucracy and modern communications, the British created a unified, powerful state. They placed under the same general system of law and administration the different Hindu and Muslim peoples and the vanquished kingdoms of the entire subcontinent—groups that had fought each other for centuries and had been repeatedly conquered by Muslim and Mongol invaders. It was as if Europe, with its many states and varieties of Christianity, had been conquered and united in a single great empire.

In spite of these achievements, the decisive reaction to European rule was the rise of nationalism among the Indian elite. No matter how anglicized and necessary a member of the educated classes became, he or she could never become the white ruler's equal. The top jobs, the best clubs, the modern hotels, and even certain railroad compartments were sealed off to brown-skinned Indians. The peasant masses might accept such inequality as the latest version of age-old oppression, but the well-educated, English-speaking elite eventually could not. For the elite, racial discrimination meant injured pride and bitter injustice. It flagrantly contradicted those cherished Western concepts of human rights and equality. Moreover, it was based on dictatorship, no matter how benign.

By 1885, when educated Indians came together to found the predominately Hindu Indian National Congress, demands were increasing for the equality and self-government that Britain had already granted white-settler colonies, such as Canada and Australia. By 1907, emboldened in part by Japan's success (see the next section), the radicals in the Indian National Congress were calling for complete independence. Even the moderates were demanding home rule for India through an elected parliament. Although there were sharp divisions between Hindus and Muslims, Indians were finding an answer to the foreign challenge. The common heritage of British rule and Western ideals, along with the reform and revitalization of the Hindu religion, had created a genuine movement for national independence.

The Example of Japan

When Commodore Matthew Perry arrived in Japan in 1853 with his crude but effective gunboat diplomacy,

Japan was a complex feudal society. At the top stood a figurehead emperor, but real power was in the hands of a hereditary military governor, the **shogun.** With the help of a warrior nobility known as **samurai,** the shogun governed a country of hard-working, productive peasants and city dwellers. Often poor and restless, the intensely proud samurai were humiliated by the sudden American intrusion and the unequal treaties with Western countries.

When foreign diplomats and merchants began to settle in Yokohama, radical samurai reacted with a wave of antiforeign terrorism and antigovernment assassinations between 1858 and 1863. The imperialist response was swift and unambiguous. An allied fleet of American, British, Dutch, and French warships demolished key forts, further weakening the power and prestige of the shogun's government. Then in 1867, a coalition led by patriotic samurai seized control of the government with hardly any bloodshed and restored the political power of the emperor. This was the Meiji Restoration, a great turning point in Japanese development.

The immediate, all-important goal of the new government was to meet the foreign threat. The battle cry of the Meiji reformers was "Enrich the state and strengthen the armed forces." Yet how were these tasks to be done? In an about-face that was one of history's most remarkable chapters, the young but well-trained, idealistic but flexible leaders of Meiji Japan dropped their antiforeign attacks. Convinced that Western civilization was indeed superior in its military and industrial aspects, they initiated from above a series of measures to reform Japan along modern lines. In the broadest sense, the Meiji leaders tried to harness the power inherent in Europe's dual revolution in order to protect their country and catch up with the West.

In 1871 the new leaders abolished the old feudal structure of aristocratic, decentralized government and formed a strong unified state. Following the example of the French Revolution, they dismantled the four-class legal system and declared social equality. They decreed freedom of movement in a country where traveling abroad had been a most serious crime. They created a free, competitive, government-stimulated economy. Japan began to build railroads and modern factories. Thus the new generation adopted many principles of a free, liberal society, and, as in Europe, such freedom resulted in a tremendously creative release of human energy.

Yet the overriding concern of Japan's political leadership was always a powerful state, and to achieve this, more than liberalism was borrowed from the West. A powerful modern navy was created, and the army was completely reorganized along European lines, with three-year military service for all males and a professional officer corps.

The Rapid Modernization of the Japanese Army This woodcut from about 1870 shows Japanese soldiers outfitted in Western uniforms and marching in Western formation. Japanese reformers, impressed by Prussian discipline and success on the battlefield, looked to Germany for their military models. *(Ryogoku Tsuneo Tamba Collection/Laurie Platt Winfrey)*

This army of draftees effectively put down disturbances in the countryside, and in 1877 it was used to crush a major rebellion by feudal elements protesting the loss of their privileges. Japan also borrowed rapidly and adapted skillfully the West's science and modern technology, particularly in industry, medicine, and education. Many Japanese were encouraged to study abroad, and the government paid large salaries to attract foreign experts. These experts were always carefully controlled, however, and replaced by trained Japanese as soon as possible.

By 1890, when the new state was firmly established, the

wholesale borrowing of the early restoration had given way to more selective emphasis on those things foreign that were in keeping with Japanese tradition. Following the model of the German Empire, Japan established an authoritarian constitution and rejected democracy. The power of the emperor and his ministers was vast, that of the legislature limited.

Japan successfully copied the imperialism of Western society. Expansion not only proved that Japan was strong; it also cemented the nation together in a great mission. Having "opened" Korea with the gunboat diplomacy of imperialism in 1876, Japan decisively defeated China in a war over Korea in 1894 and 1895 and took Formosa (modern-day Taiwan). In the next years, Japan competed aggressively with the leading European powers for influence and territory in China, particularly Manchuria. There Japanese and Russian imperialism met and collided. In 1904 Japan attacked Russia without warning, and after a bloody war, Japan emerged with a valuable foothold in China, Russia's former protectorate over Port Arthur (see Map 26.3). By 1910, with the annexation of Korea, Japan had become a major imperialist power.

Japan became the first non-Western country to use an ancient love of country to transform itself and thereby meet the many-sided challenge of Western expansion. Moreover, Japan demonstrated convincingly that a modern Asian nation could defeat and humble a great Western power. Many Chinese nationalists were fascinated by Japan's achievement. A group of patriots in French-ruled southern Vietnam sent Vietnamese students to Japan to learn the island empire's secret of success. Japan provided patriots throughout Asia and Africa with an inspiring example of national recovery and liberation.

Toward Revolution in China

In 1860 the two-hundred-year-old Qing Dynasty in China appeared on the verge of collapse. Efforts to repel foreigners had failed, and rebellion and chaos wracked the country. Yet the government drew on its traditional strengths and made a surprising comeback that lasted more than thirty years.

Two factors were crucial in this reversal. First, the traditional ruling groups temporarily produced new and effective leadership. Loyal scholar-statesmen and generals quelled disturbances such as the great Tai Ping rebellion. The empress dowager Tzu Hsi, a truly remarkable woman, governed in the name of her young son and combined shrewd insight with vigorous action to revitalize the bureaucracy.

Second, destructive foreign aggression lessened, for the Europeans had obtained their primary goal of commercial and diplomatic relations. Indeed, some Europeans contributed to the dynasty's recovery. A talented Irishman effectively reorganized China's customs office and increased the government tax receipts, while a sympathetic American diplomat represented China in foreign lands and helped strengthen the central government. Such efforts dovetailed with the dynasty's efforts to adopt some aspects of Western government and technology while maintaining traditional Chinese values and beliefs.

The parallel movement toward domestic reform and limited cooperation with the West collapsed under the blows of Japanese imperialism. The Sino-Japanese War of 1894 to 1895 and the subsequent harsh peace treaty revealed China's helplessness in the face of aggression, triggering a rush for foreign concessions and protectorates in China. At the high point of this rush in 1898, it appeared that the European powers might actually divide China among themselves, as they had recently divided Africa. Probably only the jealousy each nation felt toward its imperialist competitors saved China from partition, although the U.S. Open Door policy, which opposed formal annexation of Chinese territory, may have helped tip the balance. In any event, the tempo of foreign encroachment greatly accelerated after 1894.

So, too, did the intensity and radicalism of the Chinese reaction. Like the leaders of the Meiji Restoration, some modernizers saw salvation in Western institutions. In 1898 the government launched a desperate **hundred days of reform** in an attempt to meet the foreign challenge. More radical reformers, such as the revolutionary Sun Yat-sen (1866–1925), who came from the peasantry and was educated in Hawaii by Christian missionaries, sought to overthrow the dynasty altogether and establish a republic.

On the other side, some traditionalists turned back toward ancient practices, political conservatism, and fanatical hatred of the "foreign devils." "Protect the country, destroy the foreigner" was their simple motto. Such conservative, antiforeign patriots had often clashed with foreign missionaries, whom they charged with undermining reverence for ancestors and thereby threatening the Chinese family and the entire society. In the agony of defeat and unwanted reforms, secret societies such as the Boxers rebelled. In northeastern China, more than two hundred foreign missionaries and several thousand Chinese Christians were killed. Once again the imperialist response was swift and harsh. Peking was occupied and plundered by foreign armies. A heavy indemnity was imposed.

The years after the Boxer Rebellion (1900–1903) were

The Empress Dowager Tzu Hsi (1835–1908) Tzu Hsi drew on conservative forces, like the court eunuchs surrounding her here, to maintain her power. Three years after her death in 1908, a revolution broke out and forced the last Chinese emperor, a boy of six, to abdicate. *(Freer Gallery of Art and Arthur M. Sackler Gallery Archives, Smithsonian Institution. Photographer: Hsun-ling. Negative no. 261)*

ever more troubled. Anarchy and foreign influence spread as the power and prestige of the Qing Dynasty declined still further. Antiforeign, antigovernment revolutionary groups agitated and plotted. Finally in 1912, a spontaneous uprising toppled the Qing Dynasty. After thousands of years of emperors and empires, a loose coalition of revolutionaries proclaimed a Western-style republic and called for an elected parliament. The transformation of China under the impact of expanding Western society entered a new phase, and the end was not in sight.

Chapter Summary

- *What were some of the global consequences of European industrialization between 1815 and 1914?*
- *How was massive migration an integral part of Western expansion?*
- *How and why after 1875 did European nations rush to build political empires in Africa and Asia?*
- *What was the general pattern of non-Western responses to Western expansion, and how did India, Japan, and China meet the imperialist challenge?*

Book Companion Site
To assess your mastery of this chapter, visit **bedfordstmartins.com/mckaywest**

Key Terms

Third World	Afrikaners
opium trade	Berlin conference
khedive	white man's burden
great migration	Great Rebellion
swallows	shogun
great white walls	samurai
new imperialism	hundred days of reform

In the nineteenth century, the industrializing West entered the third and most dynamic phase of its centuries-old expansion into non-Western lands. In so doing, Western nations promoted a prodigious growth of world trade, forced reluctant countries such as China and Japan into the globalizing economy, and profitably subordinated many lands to their economic interests. Western nations also sent forth millions of emigrants to the sparsely populated areas of European settlement, which generally limited migration from Asia.

After 1875, Western countries grabbed vast political empires in Africa and rushed to establish political influence in Asia. The reasons for this culminating surge were many, but the economic thrust of robust industrial capitalism, an ever-growing lead in technology, and the competitive pressures of European nationalism were particularly important.

Western expansion had far-reaching consequences. For the first time in human history, the world became in many ways a single unit. Moreover, European expansion diffused the ideas and techniques of a highly developed civilization. Yet the West relied on force to conquer and rule, and it treated non-Western peoples as racial inferiors. Thus non-Western elites, often armed with Western doctrines, gradually responded to the Western challenge. As the histories of India, Japan, and China show, non-Western elites launched a national, anti-imperialist struggle for dignity, genuine independence, and modernization. This struggle would emerge as a central drama of world history after the great European civil war of 1914 to 1918, which reduced the West's technological advantage and shattered its self-confidence and complacent moral superiority.

Suggested Reading

Aldrich, Robert. *Greater France: A History of French Overseas Expansion.* 1996. A well-balanced study.

Bagchi, Amiya Kumar. *Perilous Passage: Mankind and the Ascendancy of Capital.* 2005. A spirited radical critique of the "rise of the West."

Conklin, Alice. *A Mission to Civilize: The French Republican Ideal and West Africa, 1895–1930.* 1997. An outstanding examination of French imperialism.

Conrad, Joseph. *Heart of Darkness.* A novel that unforgettably probes European imperial motives.

Cook, Scott B. *Colonial Encounters in the Age of High Imperialism.* 1996. A stimulating overview with a very readable account of the explorer Stanley and central Africa.

Crews, Robert. *For Prophet and Tsar: Islam and Empire in Russia and Central Asia.* 2006. Considers neglected aspects of Russian imperialism.

Curtin, P., et al. *African History: From Earliest Times to Independence,* 2d ed. 1995. An excellent brief introduction to Africa in the age of imperialism.

Ebrey, Patricia Buckley. *The Cambridge Illustrated History of China.* 1999. A lively and beautiful work by a leading specialist.

Fage, J. D. *A History of Africa,* 3d ed. 1995. A highly recommended account.

Goodlad, Graham. *British Foreign and Imperial Policy, 1865–1919*. 2000. A lively examination of Britain's leading position in European imperialism.

Hochshild, Adam. *King Leopold's Ghost: A Story of Greed, Terror, and Heroism in Colonial Africa, 1895–1930*. 1997. A chilling account of Belgian imperialism in the Congo.

Maier, Charles S. *Among Empires: American Ascendancy and Its Predecessors*. 2006. Examines imperial power in history and how well America measures up.

Marshall, P. J., ed. *Cambridge Illustrated History of the British Empire*. 1996. A stunning pictorial history.

Midgley, Clare, ed. *Gender and Imperialism*. 1998. Examines the complex questions related to European women and imperialism.

Rotberg, Robert I. *The Founder: Cecil Rhodes and the Pursuit of Power*. 1988. Examines the imperialist's mind and times with great acuity.

Said, Edward. *Orientalism*. 1978. An exceedingly influential cultural study of imperialism and non-Europeans.

Notes

1. Quoted in J. W. Hall, *Japan, from Prehistory to Modern Times* (New York: Delacorte Press, 1970), p. 250.
2. Quoted in Earl of Cromer, *Modern Egypt* (London, 1911), p. 48.
3. Quoted in T. Blegen, *Norwegian Migration to America,* vol. 2 (Northfield, Minn.: Norwegian-American Historical Association, 1940), p. 468.
4. Quoted in W. L. Langer, *European Alliances and Alignments, 1871–1890* (New York: Vintage Books, 1931), p. 290.
5. Quoted in J. Ellis, *The Social History of the Machine Gun* (New York: Pantheon Books, 1975), pp. 86, 101.
6. Quoted in G. H. Nadel and P. Curtis, eds., *Imperialism and Colonialism* (New York: Macmillan, 1964), p. 94.
7. Quoted in W. L. Langer, *The Diplomacy of Imperialism,* 2d ed. (New York: Alfred A. Knopf, 1951), pp. 86, 88.
8. Rudyard Kipling, *The Five Nations* (London, 1903).
9. E. H. Berman, "African Responses to Christian Mission Education," *African Studies Review* 17 (1974): 530.
10. Quoted in Langer, *The Diplomacy of Imperialism,* p. 88.
11. Quoted in Ellis, *The Social History of the Machine Gun,* pp. 99–100.
12. Quoted in K. M. Panikkar, *Asia and Western Dominance: A Survey of the Vasco da Gama Epoch of Asian History* (London: George Allen & Unwin, 1959), p. 116.
13. A. Burton, "The White Women's Burden: British Feminists and 'The Indian Women,' 1865–1915," in *Western Women and Imperialism: Complicity and Resistance,* ed. N. Chauduri and M. Strobel (Bloomington: Indiana University Press, 1992), pp. 137–157.

A British Woman in India

Guides for housekeeping became popular in Europe in the nineteenth century as middle-class women funneled great energy into their homes. A British woman in India probably consulted The Complete Indian Housekeeper and Cook by Flora Annie Steel and Grace Gardiner, a bestseller published in 1888 and frequently updated.

Steel (1847–1929) moved to India in 1867 with her husband, a civil engineer, and lived there until the family returned to England in 1889. Accustomed to directing a large household with several Indian servants, Steel believed herself well qualified to offer advice "to English girls to whom fate may assign the task of being house-mothers in our Eastern empire." The following passage focuses on how the British mistress should manage her Indian servants, and along with practical suggestions it lays bare some basic attitudes and assumptions of Europeans in colonial settings. Steel subsequently wrote books on India, education, and women's issues.

Housekeeping in India, when once the first strangeness has worn off, is a far easier task in many ways than it is in England, though it none the less requires time, and, in this present transitional period, an almost phenomenal patience. . . .

And, first it must be distinctly understood that it is not necessary, or in the least degree desirable, that an educated woman should waste the best years of her life in scolding and petty supervision. Life holds higher duties, and it is indubitable that friction and over-zeal is a sure sign of a bad housekeeper. . . .

Easy, however, as the actual housekeeping is in India, the personal attention of the mistress is quite as much needed here as at home. The Indian servant, it is true, learns more readily, and is guiltless of the sniffiness with which Mary Jane [the servant in England] receives suggestions, but a few days of absence or neglect on the part of the mistress, results in the servants falling into their old habits with the inherited conservatism of dirt. This is, of course, disheartening, but it has to be faced as a necessary condition of life, until a few generations of training shall have started the Indian servant on a new inheritance of habit. It must never be forgotten that at present those mistresses who aim at anything beyond keeping a good table are in the minority, and that pioneering is always arduous work.

The first duty of a mistress is, of course, to be able to give intelligible orders to her servants; therefore it is necessary she should learn to speak Hindustani. No sane Englishwomen would dream of living, say, for twenty years, in Germany, Italy, or France, without making the *attempt,* at any rate, to learn the language. . . .

The next duty is obviously to insist on her orders being carried out. And here we come to the burning question: "How is this to be done?" Certainly, there is at present very little to which we can appeal in the average Indian servant, but then, until it is implanted by training, there is very little sense of duty in a child; yet in some well-regulated nurseries obedience is a foregone conclusion. The secret lies in making rules, and *keeping to them.* The Indian servant is a child in everything save age, and should be treated as a child; that is to say, kindly, but with the greatest firmness. The laws of the household should be those of the Medes and Persians, and first faults should never go unpunished. By overlooking a first offence, we lose the only opportunity we have of preventing it becoming a habit.

But it will be asked, How are we to punish our servants when we have no hold either on their minds or bodies? . . .

In their own experience the authors have found a system of rewards and punishments perfectly easy of attainment. One of them has for years adopted the plan of engaging her servants at so much a month—the lowest rate at which such servant is obtainable—and so much extra as *buksheesh* [a bonus], conditional on good service. For instance, a *khitmutgâr* [male table servant] is engaged permanently on Rs. 9 a month, but the additional rupee which makes the wage up to that usually demanded by good servants is a fluctuating assessment! . . . That plan has never been objected to, and . . . the household quite enters into the spirit of the idea, infinitely preferring it to volcanic eruptions of fault-finding. . . .

In regard to actual housekeeping, the authors emphatically deny the common assertion that it must necessarily run on different lines to what it does in England. Economy, prudence, efficiency are the same all over the world, and because butcher meat is cheap, that is no excuse for its being wasted. Some modification, of course, there must be, *but as little as possible.* . . .

A good mistress in India will try to set a good example to her servants in routine, method, and tidiness. Half-an-hour after breakfast should be sufficient for the whole arrangements for the day; but that half-hour should be given as punctually as possible. An untidy mistress invariably has *untidy,* a weak one, *idle* servants. It should never be forgotten that—though it is true in both hemispheres that if you want a thing done you should do it yourself—still, having to do it is a distinct confession of failure in your original intention. Anxious housewifes are too apt to accept defeat in this way; the result being that the lives of educated women are wasted in doing the work of lazy servants.

The authors' advice is therefore—

"Never do work which an ordinarily good servant ought to be able to do. If the one you have will not or cannot do it, get another who can." . . .

Having thus gone generally into the duties of the mistress, we may detail what in our opinion should be the daily routine.

The great object is to secure three things—smooth working, quick ordering, and subsequent peace and leisure to the mistress. It is as well, therefore, with a view to the preservation of temper, to eat your breakfast in peace before venturing into the pantry and cookroom; it is besides a mistake to be constantly on the worry.

Inspection parade should begin, then, immediately after breakfast, or as near ten o'clock as circumstances will allow. The cook should be waiting—in clean raiment—with a pile of plates, and his viands for the day spread out on a table. With everything *en evidence,* it will not take five minutes to decide on what is best, while a very constant occurrence at Indian tables—the serving up of stale, sour, and unwholesome food—will be avoided. It is perhaps *not* pleasant to go into such details, but a good mistress will remember the breadwinner who requires blood-forming nourishment, and the children whose constitutions are

An English lady attended by her Indian servants. *(Stapleton Collection, UK/The Bridgeman Art Library)*

being built up day by day, sickly or healthy, according to the food given them; and bear in mind the fact that, in India especially, half the comfort of life depends on clean, wholesome, digestible food. . . .

We do not wish to advocate an unholy haughtiness; but an Indian household can no more be governed peacefully, without dignity and prestige, than an Indian Empire. For instance, if the mistress wishes to teach the cook a new dish, let her give the order for everything, down to charcoal, to be ready at a given time, and the cook in attendance; and let her do nothing herself that the servants can do, if only for this reason, that the only way of teaching is to *see* things done, not to let others see *you* do them.

Questions for Analysis

1. What challenges does the British housekeeper face in India? How, according to Steel, should she meet them?

2. In what ways do Steel's comments and housekeeping policies reflect the attitudes of European imperialism?

Source: F. A. Steel and G. Gardiner, *The Complete Indian Housekeeper and Cook* (London: William Heinemann, 1902), chap. 1. Reprinted in L. DiCaprio and M. Wiesner, eds., *Lives and Voices: Sources in European Women's History* (Boston: Houghton Mifflin, 2001), pp. 323–328.

French soldiers in the trenches man a machine gun, the weapon that killed so many, in this chilling work by Christopher Nevinson. *(© Tate, London 2007/Art Resource, NY)*

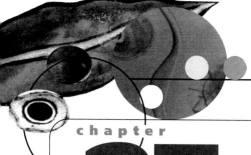

THE GREAT BREAK: WAR AND REVOLUTION, 1914–1919

In the summer of 1914, the nations of Europe went willingly to war. They believed they had no other choice. Moreover, both peoples and governments confidently expected a short war leading to a decisive victory. Such a war, they believed, would "clear the air," and European society would be able to go on as before.

These expectations were almost totally mistaken. The First World War was long, indecisive, and tremendously destructive. To the shell-shocked generation of survivors, it was known simply as the Great War: the war of unprecedented scope and intensity. From today's perspective, it is clear that the First World War marked a great break in the course of Western historical development since the French and Industrial Revolutions. A noted British political scientist has gone so far as to say that even in victorious and relatively fortunate Great Britain, the First World War was *the* great turning point in government and society, "as in everything else in modern British history. . . . There's a much greater difference between the Britain of 1914 and, say, 1920, than between the Britain of 1920 and today."[1] This strong statement contains a great amount of truth, for all of Europe as well as for Britain. World War I was a revolutionary conflict of gigantic proportions.

The First World War

The First World War was extremely long and destructive because it involved all the Great Powers and because it quickly degenerated into a senseless military stalemate. Like evenly matched boxers in a championship bout, the two sides tried to wear each other down. But there was no referee to call a draw, only the blind hammering of a life-or-death struggle.

• *What caused the Great War, and why did it have such revolutionary consequences?*

Book Companion Site

This icon will direct you to primary sources and study materials available at **bedfordstmartins.com/mckaywest**

The Bismarckian System of Alliances

The Franco-Prussian War and the founding of the German Empire opened a new era in international relations. France was decisively defeated in 1871 and forced to pay a large war indemnity and give up Alsace-Lorraine. In ten short years, from 1862 to 1871, Bismarck had made Prussia-Germany—traditionally the weakest of the Great Powers—the most powerful nation in Europe (see pages 821–825).

Yet, as Bismarck never tired of repeating after 1871, Germany was a "satisfied" power. Within Europe, Germany had no territorial ambitions and wanted only peace.

But how was peace to be preserved? Bismarck's first concern was to keep an embittered France diplomatically isolated and without military allies. His second concern was the threat to peace posed from the east, from Austria-Hungary and from Russia. Those two enormous multinational empires had many conflicting interests, particularly

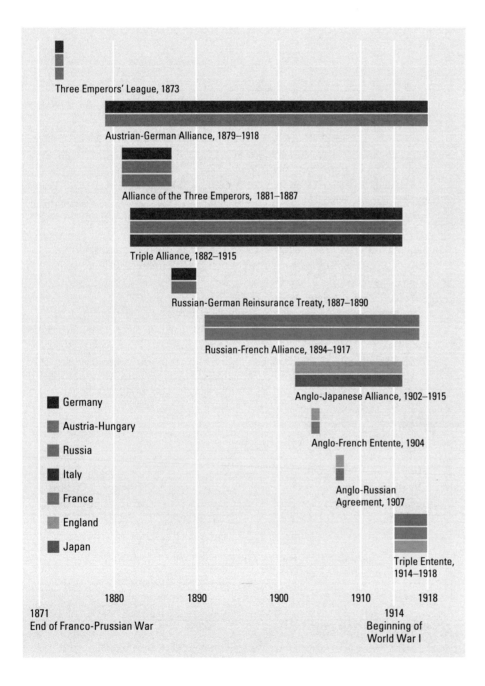

FIGURE 27.1 The Alliance System After 1871 Bismarck's subtle diplomacy maintained reasonably good relations among the eastern monarchies—Germany, Russia, and Austria-Hungary—and kept France isolated. The situation changed dramatically in 1891, when the Russian-French Alliance divided the Great Powers into two fairly equal military blocs.

Three Emperors' League, 1873

Austrian-German Alliance, 1879–1918

Alliance of the Three Emperors, 1881–1887

Triple Alliance, 1882–1915

Russian-German Reinsurance Treaty, 1887–1890

Russian-French Alliance, 1894–1917

Anglo-Japanese Alliance, 1902–1915

Anglo-French Entente, 1904

Anglo-Russian Agreement, 1907

Triple Entente, 1914–1918

■ Germany
■ Austria-Hungary
■ Russia
■ Italy
■ France
■ England
■ Japan

1880   1890   1900   1910   1918

1871
End of Franco-Prussian War

1914
Beginning of World War I

in southeastern Europe, where the strength of the Ottoman Empire was ebbing fast. There was a real threat that Germany might be dragged into a great war between the two rival empires. Bismarck's solution was a system of alliances (see Figure 27.1) to restrain both Russia and Austria-Hungary, to prevent conflict between them, and to isolate a hostile France, which could never forget the loss of Alsace-Lorraine.

A first step was the creation in 1873 of the conservative **Three Emperors' League,** which linked the monarchs of Austria-Hungary, Germany, and Russia in an alliance against radical movements. In 1877 and 1878, when Russia's victories in a war with the Ottoman Empire threatened the balance of Austrian and Russian interests in the Balkans and the balance of British and Russian interests in the entire Middle East, Bismarck played the role of sincere peacemaker. But his balancing efforts at the Congress of Berlin in 1878 infuriated Russian nationalists, and this led Bismarck to conclude a defensive military alliance with Austria against Russia in 1879. This alliance lasted until 1918 and the end of World War I. Motivated by tensions with France, Italy joined Germany and Austria in 1882, thereby forming what became known as the Triple Alliance.

Bismarck continued to work for peace in eastern Europe, seeking to neutralize tensions between Austria-Hungary and Russia. In 1881 he capitalized on their mutual fears and cajoled them both into a secret alliance with Germany. This Alliance of the Three Emperors lasted until 1887.

Bismarck also maintained good relations with Britain and Italy, while encouraging France in Africa but keeping France isolated in Europe. In 1887 Russia declined to renew the Alliance of the Three Emperors because of new tensions in the Balkans. Bismarck craftily substituted the Russian-German Reinsurance Treaty, by which both states promised neutrality if the other was attacked.

Bismarck's accomplishments in foreign policy after 1871 were great. For almost a generation, he maintained German leadership in international affairs, and he worked successfully for peace by managing conflicts and by restraining Austria-Hungary and Russia with defensive alliances.

The Rival Blocs

In 1890 the young, impetuous Emperor William II dismissed Bismarck, in part because of the chancellor's friendly policy toward Russia since the 1870s. William then adamantly refused to renew the Russian-German Reinsurance Treaty, in spite of Russian willingness to do so. This fateful departure in foreign affairs prompted long-

Chronology

1912	First Balkan War
1914	Assassination of Archduke Francis Ferdinand
1914–1918	World War I
1915	Italy and Bulgaria enter World War I; Ministry of Munitions established in Britain
1916	German males between seventeen and sixty required to work only for war effort; Rasputin murdered
1916–1918	Growth of antiwar movement throughout Europe
1917	Russian Revolution
1919	Treaty of Versailles

isolated republican France to court absolutist Russia, offering loans, arms, and friendship. In both countries, there were enthusiastic public demonstrations of friendship in 1891, and in early 1894 France and Russia became military allies. This alliance (see Figure 27.1) was to remain in effect as long as the Triple Alliance of Austria, Germany, and Italy existed. As a result, continental Europe was dangerously divided into two rival blocs.

Book Companion Site
Primary Source: Bismarck's Worst Nightmare: A Franco-Russian Rapprochement

Great Britain's foreign policy became increasingly crucial. Long content with "splendid isolation" and no permanent alliances, Britain after 1891 was the only uncommitted Great Power. Could Britain afford to remain isolated, or would it feel compelled to take sides? Many Germans and some Britons felt that a "natural alliance" united the advanced, racially related Germanic and Anglo-Saxon peoples. However, the generally good relations that had prevailed between Prussia and Great Britain ever since the mid-eighteenth century gave way to a bitter Anglo-German rivalry.

There were several reasons for this tragic development. Commercial rivalry in world markets between Germany and Great Britain increased sharply in the 1890s, and Germany's pursuit of world power unsettled the British. Above all, Germany's decision in 1900 to expand greatly its battle fleet posed a challenge to Britain's long-standing naval supremacy. This decision coincided with the hard-fought South African War (1899–1902) between the British and the tiny Dutch republics of southern Africa,

German Warships Under Full Steam As these impressive ships engaged in battle exercises in 1907 suggest, Germany did succeed in building a large modern navy. But Britain was equally determined to maintain its naval superiority, and the spiraling arms race helped poison relations between the two countries. *(Archives Charmet/Bibliothèque des Arts Décoratifs/ Archives Charmet/The Bridgeman Art Library)*

which brought into the open widespread anti-British feeling, as editorial writers in many nations denounced this latest manifestation of British imperialism. Thus British leaders prudently set about shoring up their exposed position with alliances and agreements.

Britain improved its often-strained relations with the United States and in 1902 concluded a formal alliance with Japan (see Figure 27.1). Britain then responded favorably to the advances of France's skillful foreign minister, Théophile Delcassé, who wanted better relations with Britain and was willing to accept British rule in Egypt in return for British support of French plans to dominate Morocco. The resulting Anglo-French Entente of 1904 settled all outstanding colonial disputes between Britain and France.

Frustrated by Britain's turn toward France in 1904,

Germany's leaders decided to test the strength of the entente. They foolishly rattled their swords by insisting in 1905 on an international conference on the whole Moroccan question. But Germany's crude bullying forced France and Britain closer together, and the conference left Germany empty-handed and isolated (except for Austria-Hungary).

The result of the Moroccan crisis was something of a diplomatic revolution. Britain, France, Russia, and even the United States began to see Germany as a potential threat, a would-be intimidator that might seek to dominate all Europe. At the same time, German leaders began to see sinister plots to "encircle" Germany and block its development as a world power. In 1907 Russia, battered by its disastrous war with Japan and the revolution of 1905, agreed to settle its quarrels with Great Britain in

Persia and Central Asia with the Anglo-Russian Agreement (see Figure 27.1).

Germany's decision to add a large, enormously expensive fleet of big-gun battleships to its already expanding navy also heightened tensions after 1907. German nationalists, led by the extremely persuasive Admiral Alfred von Tirpitz, saw a large navy as the legitimate mark of a great world power and as a source of pride and patriotic unity. But British leaders such as David Lloyd George saw it as a detestable military challenge, which forced them to spend the "People's Budget" (see page 835) on battleships rather than social welfare. Unscrupulous journalists and special-interest groups in both countries also portrayed healthy competition in foreign trade and investment as a form of economic warfare. In 1909 the mass-circulation London *Daily Mail* hysterically informed its readers in a series of reports that "Germany is deliberately preparing to destroy the British Empire."[2] By then Britain was psychologically, if not officially, in the Franco-Russian camp. The leading nations of Europe were divided into two hostile blocs, both ill-prepared to deal with upheaval on Europe's southeastern frontier.

The Outbreak of War

In the early years of the twentieth century, war in the Balkans was as inevitable as anything can be in human history. The reason was simple: nationalism was destroying the Ottoman Empire in Europe and threatening to break up the Austro-Hungarian Empire. The only questions were what kinds of wars would occur and where they would lead.

Greece had long before led the struggle for national liberation, winning its independence in 1832. In 1875 widespread nationalist rebellion in the European provinces of the sprawling Ottoman Empire had resulted in Turkish repression, Russian intervention, and Great Power tensions. Bismarck had helped resolve this crisis at the 1878 Congress of Berlin, which worked out the partial division of Turkish possessions in Europe. Austria-Hungary obtained the right to "occupy and administer" Bosnia and Herzegovina. Serbia and Romania won independence, and a part of Bulgaria won local autonomy. The Ottoman Empire retained important Balkan holdings, for Austria-Hungary and Russia each feared the other's domination of totally independent states in the area (see Map 27.1).

By 1903, however, nationalism in southeastern Europe was on the rise once again. Serbia led the way, becoming openly hostile toward both Austria-Hungary and the Ottoman Empire. The Serbs, a Slavic people, looked to Slavic Russia for support of their national aspirations. To block Serbian expansion and to take advantage of

Russia's weakness after the revolution of 1905, Austria in 1908 formally annexed Bosnia and Herzegovina, with their large Serbian, Croatian, and Muslim populations. The kingdom of Serbia erupted in rage but could do nothing without Russian support.

Then, in 1912, in the First Balkan War, Serbia joined Greece and Bulgaria to attack the Ottoman Empire and then quarreled with Bulgaria over the spoils of victory—a dispute that led in 1913 to the Second Balkan War. Austria intervened in 1913 and forced Serbia to give up Albania. After centuries, nationalism had finally destroyed the Ottoman Empire in Europe (see Map 27.2). This sudden but long-awaited event elated the Balkan nationalists and dismayed the leaders of multinational Austria-Hungary. The former hoped and the latter feared that Austria might be next to be broken apart.

Within this tense context, Archduke Francis Ferdinand, heir to the Austrian and Hungarian thrones, and his wife, Sophie, were assassinated by Serbian revolutionaries living in Bosnia on June 28, 1914, during a state visit to the Bosnian capital of Sarajevo. After some hesitation, the leaders of Austria-Hungary concluded that Serbia was implicated and had to be severely punished once and for all. On July 23 Austria-Hungary finally presented Serbia with an unconditional ultimatum. The Serbian government had forty-eight hours in which to agree to demands that would amount to ceding control of the Serbian state. When Serbia replied moderately but evasively, Austria began to mobilize and then declared war on Serbia on July 28. Thus a desperate multinational Austria-Hungary deliberately chose war in a last-ditch attempt to stem the rising tide of hostile nationalism within its borders and save the existing state. The "Third Balkan War" had begun.

Of prime importance in Austria-Hungary's fateful decision was Germany's unconditional support. Emperor William II and his chancellor, Theobald von Bethmann-Hollweg, realized that war between Austria and Russia was the most probable result, for a resurgent Russia could not stand by, as in the Bosnian crisis, and simply watch the Serbs be crushed. Yet Bethmann-Hollweg apparently hoped that while Russia (and therefore France) would go to war, Great Britain would remain neutral, unwilling to fight for "Russian aggression" in the distant Balkans.

In fact, the diplomatic situation was already out of control. Military plans and timetables began to dictate policy. Russia, a vast country, would require much longer to mobilize its armies than Germany and Austria-Hungary. All the complicated mobilization plans of the Russian general staff had assumed a war with both Austria and Germany: Russia could not mobilize against one without

MAP 27.1 The Balkans After the Congress of Berlin, 1878 The Ottoman Empire suffered large territorial losses but remained a power in the Balkans.

MAP 27.2 The Balkans in 1914 Ethnic boundaries did not follow political boundaries, and Serbian national aspirations threatened Austria-Hungary.

mobilizing against the other. Therefore, on July 29 Tsar Nicholas II ordered full mobilization and in effect declared general war.

The German general staff had also thought only in terms of a two-front war. The staff's plan for war called for knocking out France first with a lightning attack through neutral Belgium before turning on Russia. So German armies attacked Belgium, whose neutrality had been solemnly guaranteed in 1839 by all the great states including Prussia. Thus Germany's terrible, politically disastrous response to a war in the Balkans was an all-out invasion of France by way of the plains of neutral Belgium on August 3. In the face of this act of aggression, Great Britain joined France and declared war on Germany the following day. The First World War had begun.

Book Companion Site
Primary Source: The British Rationale for Entering World War I

Reflections on the Origins of the War

In reflecting on the origins of the First World War, it seems clear that Austria-Hungary deliberately started the Third Balkan War. A war for the right to survive was Austria-Hungary's desperate, though understandable, response to the aggressive, yet understandable, revolutionary drive of Serbian nationalists to unify their people in a single state. Moreover, in spite of Russian intervention in the quarrel, it is clear that from the beginning of the crisis, Germany not only pushed and goaded Austria-Hungary but also was re-

Nationalist Opposition in the Balkans   This band of well-armed and determined guerrillas from northern Albania was typical of groups fighting against Ottoman rule in the Balkans. Balkan nationalists succeeded in driving the Ottoman Turks out of most of Europe, but their victory increased tensions with Austria-Hungary and among the Great Powers. *(Roger-Viollet/Getty Images)*

sponsible for turning a little war into the Great War by means of a sledgehammer attack on Belgium and France. Why Germany was so aggressive in 1914 is less certain.

Diplomatic historians stress that German leaders lost control of the international system after Bismarck's resignation in 1890. They felt increasingly that Germany's status as a world power was declining, while that of Britain, France, Russia, and the United States was growing. Indeed, the powers of what officially became in August 1914 the **Triple Entente**—Great Britain, France, and Russia—were checking Germany's vague but real aspirations as well as working to strangle Austria-Hungary, Germany's only real ally. Germany's aggression in 1914 reflected the failure of all European leaders, not just those in Germany, to incorporate Bismarck's mighty empire permanently and peacefully into the international system.

A more controversial interpretation argues that domestic conflicts and social tensions lay at the root of German aggression. Determined to hold on to power and frightened by the rising socialist movement, the German ruling class was willing to gamble on diplomatic victory and even on war as the means of rallying the masses to its side and preserving its privileged position. Historians have also discerned similar, if less clear-cut, behavior in Great Britain, where leaders faced civil war in northern Ireland, and in Russia, where the revolution of 1905 had brought tsardom to its knees.

This debate over social tensions and domestic political factors correctly suggests that the triumph of nationalism was a crucial underlying precondition of the Great War. Nationalism was at the heart of the Balkan wars, in the form of Serbian aspirations and the grandiose pan-German versus pan-Slavic racism of some fanatics. Nationalism also drove the spiraling arms race. Broad popular commitment

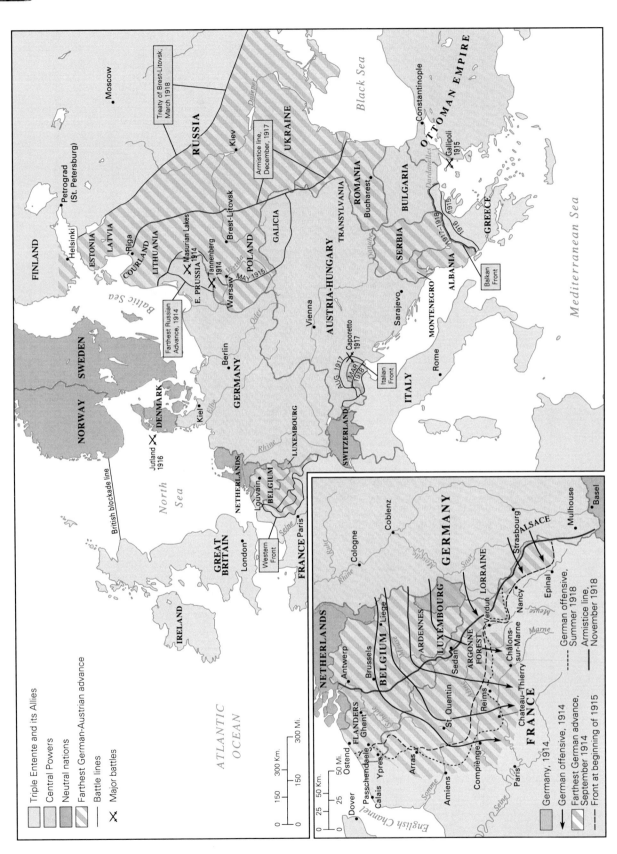

MAP 27.3 The First World War in Europe Trench warfare on the western front was concentrated in Belgium and northern France, while the war in the east encompassed an enormous territory.

"Never Forget!" This 1915 French poster with its passionate headline dramatizes Germany's brutal invasion of Belgium in 1914. Neutral Belgium is personified as a traumatized mother, assaulted and ravished by savage outlaws. The "rape of Belgium" featured prominently—and effectively—in anti-German propaganda. *(Mary Evans Picture Library)*

to "my country right or wrong" weakened groups that thought in terms of international communities and consequences. In each country, the great majority of the population enthusiastically embraced the outbreak of war in August 1914. In each country, people believed that their country had been wronged, and they rallied to defend it. Patriotic nationalism brought unity in the short run.

In all of this, the wealthy governing classes certainly underestimated the risk of war to themselves in 1914. They had forgotten that great wars and great social revolutions very often go hand in hand. Metternich's alliance of conservative forces in support of international peace and the social status quo had become only a distant memory.

Stalemate and Slaughter

When the Germans invaded Belgium in August 1914, they and everyone else believed that the war would be short, for urban society rested on the food and raw materials of the world economy: "The boys will be home by Christmas." The Belgian army heroically defended its homeland, however, and fell back in good order to join a rapidly landed British army corps near the Franco-Belgian border. Instead of quickly capturing Paris in a vast encircling movement, by the end of August dead-tired German soldiers were advancing along an enormous front in the scorching summer heat.

On September 6 the French attacked a gap in the German line at the Battle of the Marne. For three days, France threw everything into the attack. At one point, the French government desperately requisitioned all the taxis of Paris to rush reserves to the troops at the front. Finally, the Germans fell back. Paris and France had been miraculously saved (see Map 27.3).

Soon, with the armies stalled, both sides began to dig trenches to protect themselves from machine-gun fire. By November 1914, an unbroken line of trenches extended from the Belgian ports through northern France, past the fortress of Verdun, and on to the Swiss frontier. In the face of this unexpected stalemate, slaughter on the western front began in earnest. The defenders on both sides dug in behind rows of trenches, mines, and barbed wire. For days and even weeks, ceaseless shelling by heavy artillery supposedly "softened up" the enemy in a given area (and also signaled the coming attack). Then young draftees and their junior officers went "over the top" of the trenches in frontal attacks on the enemy's line.

The cost in lives of this **trench warfare** was staggering, the gains in territory minuscule. The massive French and British offensives during 1915 never gained more than 3 miles of blood-soaked earth from the enemy. In the Battle of the Somme in the summer of 1916, the British and French gained an insignificant 125 square miles at the cost of 600,000 dead or wounded, while the Germans lost 500,000 men. In that same year the unsuccessful German campaign against Verdun cost 700,000 lives on both sides. British poet Siegfried Sassoon (1886–1967) wrote of the Somme offensive, "I am staring at a sunlit picture of Hell."

The year 1917 was equally terrible. The hero of Erich Remarque's great novel *All Quiet on the Western Front* (1929) describes one attack:

We see men living with their skulls blown open; we see soldiers run with their two feet cut off. . . . Still the little piece of convulsed earth in which we lie is held. We have yielded no

The Tragic Absurdity of Trench Warfare   Soldiers charge across a scarred battlefield and overrun an enemy trench. The dead defender on the right will fire no more. But this is only another futile charge that will yield much blood and little land. A whole generation is being decimated by the slaughter. *(By courtesy of the Trustees of the Imperial War Museum)*

more than a few hundred yards of it as a prize to the enemy. But on every yard there lies a dead man.

Such was war on the western front.

Trench warfare shattered an entire generation of young men. Millions who could have provided political creativity and leadership after the war were forever missing. Moreover, those who lived through the slaughter were maimed, shell-shocked, embittered, and profoundly disillusioned. The young soldiers went to war believing in the world of their leaders and elders—the pre-1914 world of order, progress, and patriotism. Then, in Remarque's words, the

"first bombardment showed us our mistake, and under it the world as they had taught it to us broke in pieces."

The Widening War

On the eastern front, slaughter did not degenerate into suicidal trench warfare. With the outbreak of the war, the "Russian steamroller" immediately moved into eastern Germany. Very badly damaged by the Germans under Generals Paul von Hindenburg and Erich Ludendorff at the Battles of Tannenberg and the Masurian Lakes in August and September 1914, Russia never threatened

The Armenian Atrocities When in 1915 some Armenians welcomed Russian armies as liberators after years of persecution, the Ottoman government ordered a genocidal mass deportation of its Armenian citizens from their homeland in the empire's eastern provinces. This photo, taken in Kharpert in 1915 by a German businessman from his hotel window, shows Turkish guards marching Armenian men off to a prison, where they will be tortured to death. A million Armenians died from murder, starvation, and disease during World War I. *(Courtesy of the Armenian Library, Watertown, Mass.)*

Germany again. On the Austrian front, enormous armies seesawed back and forth, suffering enormous losses. Austro-Hungarian armies were repulsed twice by Serbia in bitter fighting. But with the help of German forces, they reversed the Russian advances of 1914 and forced the Russians to retreat deep into their own territory in the eastern campaign of 1915. A staggering 2.5 million Russians were killed, wounded, or taken prisoner that year.

These changing tides of victory and hopes for territorial gains brought neutral countries into the war (see Map 27.3). Italy, a member of the Triple Alliance since 1882, had declared its neutrality in 1914 on the grounds that Austria had launched a war of aggression. Then in May 1915, Italy joined the Triple Entente of Great Britain, France, and Russia in return for promises of Austrian territory. In October 1914 the Ottoman Empire joined with Austria and Germany, by then known as the Central Powers. The following September Bulgaria decided to follow the Ottoman Empire's lead in order to settle old scores with Serbia. The Balkans, with the exception of Greece, came to be occupied by the Central Powers.

The entry of the Ottoman Turks carried the war into the Middle East. Heavy fighting between the Ottomans and the Russians saw battle lines seesawing back and forth and enveloping the Armenians, who lived on both sides of the border and had experienced brutal repression by the Turks in 1909 (see Map 27.5 on page 906). When in 1915 some Armenians welcomed Russian armies as liberators, the Ottoman government ordered a genocidal mass deportation of its Armenian citizens from their homeland. A million Armenians died from murder, starvation, and disease during World War I. In 1915 British forces tried to take the Dardanelles and Constantinople from the Ottomans but were badly defeated.

The British were more successful at inciting the Arabs to revolt against their Turkish overlords. They bargained with the foremost Arab leader, Hussein ibn-Ali (1856–1931), who was a direct descendant of the prophet Muhammad and the chief magistrate (*sharif*) of Mecca, the holiest city in the Muslim world. Controlling much of the Ottoman Empire's territory along the Red Sea, an area known as the Hejaz (see Map 27.5), Hussein managed in 1915 to win vague British commitments for an independent Arab kingdom. Thus in 1916 Hussein revolted against the Turks, proclaiming himself king of the Arabs. He joined forces with the British under T. E. Lawrence, who in 1917 led Arab tribesmen and Indian soldiers in a highly successful guerrilla war against the Turks on the Arabian peninsula.

Similar victories were eventually scored in the Ottoman province of Iraq. Britain occupied the southern Iraqi city of Basra in 1914 and captured Baghdad in 1917. In September 1918 British armies and their Arab allies rolled into Syria. This offensive culminated in the triumphal entry of Hussein's son Faisal into Damascus. Throughout Syria and Iraq there was wild Arab rejoicing. Many patriots expected a large, unified Arab nation-state to rise from the dust of the Ottoman collapse.

As world war engulfed and revolutionized the Middle East, it also spread to some parts of East Asia and Africa. Instead of revolting as the Germans hoped, the colonial subjects of the British and French generally supported their foreign masters, providing crucial supplies and fighting in Europe and the Ottoman Empire. They also helped local British and French commanders seize Germany's colonies around the globe. The Japanese, allied in Asia with the British since 1902, similarly used the war to grab German outposts in the Pacific Ocean and on the Chinese mainland, infuriating Chinese patriots and heightening long-standing tensions between China and Japan. More than a million Africans and Asians served in the various armies of the warring powers; more than double that number served as porters to carry equipment. The French, facing a shortage of young men, made especially heavy use of colonial troops.

In April 1917 the United States declared war on Germany, another crucial development in the expanding conflict. American intervention grew out of the war at sea, sympathy for the Triple Entente, and the increasing desperation of total war. At the beginning of the war, Britain and France had established a total naval blockade to strangle the Central Powers. No neutral ship was permitted to sail to Germany with any cargo. In early 1915 Germany retaliated with a counter-blockade using the murderously effective submarine, a new weapon that violated traditional niceties of fair warning under international law. In May 1915 a German submarine sank the British passenger liner **Lusitania,** claiming more than 1,000 lives, among them 139 Americans. President Woodrow Wilson protested vigorously. Germany was forced to relax its submarine warfare for almost two years; the alternative was almost certain war with the United States.

Early in 1917, the German military command—confident that improved submarines could starve Britain into submission before the United States could come to its rescue—resumed unrestricted submarine warfare. Like the invasion of Belgium, this was a reckless gamble. "German submarine warfare against commerce," President Wilson had told a sympathetic Congress and people, "is a warfare against mankind." Thus the last uncommitted great nation, as fresh and enthusiastic as Europe had been in 1914, entered the world war in April 1917, almost three years after it began. Eventually the United States was to tip the balance in favor of the Triple Entente and its allies.

The Home Front

Before looking at the last year of the Great War, let us turn our attention to the people on the home front. They were tremendously involved in the titanic struggle. War's impact on them was no less massive than on the men crouched in the trenches.

● *What was the impact of total war on civilian populations?*

Mobilizing for Total War

In August 1914, most people greeted the outbreak of hostilities enthusiastically. In every country, the masses believed that their nation was in the right and defending itself from aggression. With the exception of a few extreme left-wingers, even socialists supported the war. Everywhere the support of the masses and working class contributed to national unity and an energetic war effort.

By mid-October generals and politicians had begun to realize that more than patriotism would be needed to win the war, whose end was not in sight. Each country experienced a relentless, desperate demand for men and weapons. In each country, economic life and organization had to change and change fast to keep the war machine from sputtering to a stop. And change they did.

In each country, a government of national unity began to plan and control economic and social life in order to wage **total war.** Free-market capitalism was abandoned, at least "for the duration." Instead, government planning boards established priorities and decided what was to be produced and consumed. Rationing, price and wage controls, and even restrictions on workers' freedom of movement were imposed by government. Only through such regimentation could a country make the greatest possible military effort. Thus, though there were national variations, the great nations all moved toward planned economies commanded by the established political leadership.

The economy of total war blurred the old distinction between soldiers on the battlefield and civilians at home. The war was a war of whole peoples and entire populations. Based on tremendously productive industrial economies not confined to a single nation, total war yielded an effective—and therefore destructive—war effort on all sides.

However awful the war was, the ability of governments to manage and control highly complicated economies strengthened the cause of socialism. With the First World War, state socialism became for the first time a realistic economic blueprint rather than a utopian program. Germany illustrates the general trend. It also went furthest in developing a planned economy to wage total war.

As soon as war began, Walter Rathenau, the talented, foresighted Jewish industrialist in charge of Germany's largest electric company, convinced the government to set up the **War Raw Materials Board** to ration and distribute raw materials. Under Rathenau's direction, every useful material from foreign oil to barnyard manure was inventoried and rationed. Moreover, the board launched successful attempts to produce substitutes such as synthetic rubber and synthetic nitrates, needed to make explosives and essential to the blockaded German war machine. An aggressive recycling campaign, including everything from fruit peels to women's hair, augmented these efforts.

Food was also rationed in accordance with physical need. Men and women doing hard manual work were given extra rations. During the last two years of the war, only children and expectant mothers received milk rations. At the same time, Germany failed to tax the war profits of private firms heavily enough. This failure contributed to massive deficit financing, inflation, the growth of a black market, and the eventual re-emergence of class conflict.

Following the terrible Battles of Verdun and the Somme in 1916, Chancellor Bethmann-Hollweg was driven from office in 1917 by military leaders Hindenburg and Ludendorff, who became the real rulers of Germany. They

Hair for the War Effort Blockaded and cut off from overseas supplies, Germany mobilized effectively to find substitutes at home. This poster calls on German women—especially young women with long flowing tresses—to donate their hair, which was used to make rope. Children were organized by their teachers into garbage brigades to collect every scrap of useful material. *(akg-images)*

decreed the ultimate mobilization for total war. Germany, said Hindenburg, could win only "if all the treasures of our soil that agriculture and industry can produce are used exclusively for the conduct of War. . . . All other considerations must come second."[3] Thus in December 1916, military leaders rammed through the Reichstag the Auxiliary Service Law, which required all males between seventeen and sixty to work only at jobs considered critical to the war effort.

Although women and children were not specifically mentioned, this forced-labor law was also aimed at them. Many women already worked in war factories, mines, and steel mills, where they labored, like men, at the heaviest and most dangerous jobs. With the passage of the Auxiliary Service Law, many more women followed. People averaged little more than one thousand calories a day. Thus in Germany total war led to the establishment of history's first "totalitarian" society, and war production increased while some people starved to death.

Great Britain mobilized for total war less rapidly and less completely than Germany, for it could import materials from its empire and from the United States. By 1915, however, a serious shortage of shells had led to the establishment of the Ministry of Munitions under David Lloyd George. The ministry organized private industry to produce for the war, controlled profits, allocated labor, fixed wage rates, and settled labor disputes. By December 1916, when Lloyd George became prime minister, the British economy was largely planned and regulated. Great Britain had followed successfully in Germany's footsteps.

The Social Impact

The social impact of total war was no less profound than the economic impact, though again there were important national variations. The millions of men at the front and the insatiable needs of the military created a tremendous demand for workers. Jobs were available for everyone. This situation—seldom, if ever, seen before 1914, when unemployment and poverty had been facts of urban life—brought about momentous changes.

One such change was greater power and prestige for labor unions. Having proved their loyalty in August 1914, labor unions cooperated with war governments on work rules, wages, and production schedules in return for real participation in important decisions. This entry of labor leaders and unions into policymaking councils paralleled the entry of socialist leaders into the war governments.

The role of women changed dramatically. In every country, large numbers of women left home and domestic service to work in industry, transportation, and offices. Moreover, women became highly visible—not only as munitions workers but as bank tellers, mail carriers, even police officers. Women also served as nurses and doctors at the front. (See the feature "Individuals in Society: Vera Brittain.") In general, the war greatly expanded the range of women's activities and changed attitudes toward women. As a direct result of women's many-sided war ef-

Waging Total War A British war plant strains to meet the insatiable demand for trench-smashing heavy artillery shells. Quite typically, many of these defense workers are women. *(By courtesy of the Trustees of the Imperial War Museum)*

Individuals in Society

Vera Brittain

Although the Great War upended millions of lives, it struck Europe's young people with the greatest force. For Vera Brittain (1893–1970), as for so many in her generation, the war became life's defining experience, which she captured forever in her famous autobiography, *Testament of Youth* (1933).

Brittain grew up in a wealthy business family in northern England, bristling at small-town conventions and discrimination against women. Very close to her brother Edward, two years her junior, Brittain read voraciously and dreamed of being a successful writer. Finishing boarding school and beating down her father's objections, she prepared for Oxford's rigorous entry exams and won a scholarship to its women's college. Brittain also fell in love with Roland Leighton, an equally brilliant student from a literary family and her brother's best friend. All three, along with two more close friends, Victor Richardson and Geoffrey Thurlow, confidently prepared to enter Oxford in late 1914.

When war suddenly approached in July 1914, Brittain shared with millions of Europeans a thrilling surge of patriotic support for her government, a pro-war enthusiasm she later played down in her published writings. She wrote in her diary that her "great fear" was that England would declare its neutrality and commit the "grossest treachery" toward France.* She seconded Roland's decision to enlist, agreeing with her sweetheart's glamorous view of war as "very ennobling and very beautiful." Later, exchanging anxious letters in 1915 with Roland in France, Vera began to see the conflict in personal, human terms. She wondered if any victory or defeat could be worth Roland's life.

Struggling to quell her doubts, Brittain redoubled her commitment to England's cause and volunteered as an army nurse. For the next three years she served with distinction in military hospitals in London, Malta, and northern France, repeatedly torn between the vision of noble sacrifice and the reality of human tragedy. She lost her sexual inhibitions caring for mangled male bodies, and she longed to consummate her love with Roland. Awaiting his return on leave on Christmas Day in 1915, she was greeted instead with a telegram: Roland had been killed two days before.

Roland's death was the first of the devastating blows that eventually overwhelmed Brittain's idealistic patriotism. In 1917, first Geoffrey and then Victor died from gruesome wounds. In early 1918, as the last great German offensive covered the floors of her war-zone hospital with maimed and dying German prisoners, the bone-weary Vera felt a common humanity and saw only more victims. A few weeks later brother Edward—her last hope—died in action. When the war ended, she was, she said, a "complete automaton," with "my deepest emotions paralyzed if not dead."

Returning to Oxford and finishing her studies, Brittain gradually recovered. She formed a deep, restorative friendship with another talented woman writer, Winifred Holtby, published novels and articles, and became a leader in the feminist campaign for gender equality. She also married and had children. But her wartime memories were always there. Finally, Brittain succeeded in coming to grips with them in *Testament of Youth,* her powerful antiwar autobiography. The unflinching narrative spoke to the experiences of an entire generation and became a runaway bestseller. Above all perhaps, Brittain captured the ambivalent, contradictory character of the war, when millions of young people found excitement, courage, and common purpose but succeeded only in destroying their lives with their superhuman efforts and futile sacrifices. Becoming ever more committed to pacifism, Brittain opposed England's entry into World War II.

Vera Brittain, marked forever by her wartime experiences.
(Vera Brittain Archive, William Ready Division of Archives and Research Collections, McMaster University Library)

Questions for Analysis

1. What were Brittain's initial feelings toward the war? How did they change as the conflict continued? Why did they change?
2. Why did Brittain volunteer as a nurse, as many women did? Judging from her account, how might wartime nursing have influenced women of her generation?
3. In portraying the ambivalent, contradictory character of World War I for Europe's youth, was Brittain describing the contradictory character of all modern warfare?

*Quoted in the excellent study by P. Berry and M. Bostridge, *Vera Brittain: A Life* (London: Virago Press, 2001), p. 59; additional quotes are from pp. 80 and 136. This work is highly recommended.

Book Companion Site
Going Beyond Individuals in Society

fort, Britain, Germany, and Austria granted women the right to vote immediately after the war. Women also showed a growing spirit of independence during the war, as they started to bob their hair, shorten their skirts, and smoke in public.

Book Companion Site
Primary Source: A British Feminist Analyzes the Impact of the War on Women

War promoted greater social equality, blurring class distinctions and lessening the gap between rich and poor. This blurring was most apparent in Great Britain, where wartime hardship was never extreme. In fact, the bottom third of the population generally lived *better* than they ever had, for the poorest gained most from the severe shortage of labor. In continental countries, greater equality was reflected in full employment, rationing according to physical needs, and a sharing of hardships. There, too, society became more uniform and more egalitarian, in spite of some war profiteering.

Finally, death itself had no respect for traditional social distinctions. It savagely decimated the young aristocratic officers who led the charge, and it fell heavily on the mass of drafted peasants and unskilled workers who followed. Yet death often spared the aristocrats of labor, the skilled workers and foremen. Their lives were too valuable to squander at the front, for they were needed to train the newly recruited women and older unskilled men laboring valiantly in war plants at home.

Growing Political Tensions

During the first two years of war, most soldiers and civilians supported their governments. Belief in a just cause, patriotic nationalism, the planned economy, and a sharing of burdens united peoples behind their various national leaders.

Each government employed rigorous censorship to control public opinion, and each used both crude and subtle propaganda to maintain popular support. German propaganda hysterically pictured black soldiers from France's African empire raping German women, while German atrocities in Belgium and elsewhere were ceaselessly recounted and exaggerated by the French and British. Patriotic posters and slogans, slanted news, and biased editorials inflamed national hatreds and helped sustain superhuman efforts.

By the spring of 1916, however, people were beginning to crack under the strain of total war. In April 1916, Irish nationalists in Dublin tried to take advantage of this situation and rose up against British rule in their great Easter Rebellion. A week of bitter fighting passed before the rebels were crushed and their leaders executed. On May 1, 1916, several thousand demonstrators in Berlin heard the radical socialist leader Karl Liebknecht (1871–1919) shout, "Down with the government! Down with the war!" Liebknecht was immediately arrested and imprisoned, but his daring action electrified Europe's far left. Strikes and protest marches over inadequate food began to flare up on every home front.

Soldiers' morale also began to decline. Italian troops mutinied. Numerous French units refused to fight after the disastrous French offensive of May 1917. Only tough military justice for leaders and a tacit agreement with the troops that there would be no more grand offensives enabled the new general in chief, Henri Philippe Pétain, to restore order. A rising tide of war-weariness and defeatism also swept France's civilian population before Georges Clemenceau emerged as a ruthless and effective wartime leader in November 1917. Clemenceau (1841–1929) established a virtual dictatorship, pouncing on strikers and jailing without trial journalists and politicians who dared to suggest a compromise peace with Germany.

The strains were worse for the Central Powers. In October 1916, the chief minister of Austria was assassinated by a young socialist crying, "Down with Absolutism! We want peace!"[4] The following month, when feeble old Emperor Francis Joseph died, a symbol of unity disappeared. In spite of absolute censorship, political dissatisfaction and conflicts among nationalities grew. In April 1917, Austria's chief minister summed up the situation in the gloomiest possible terms. The country and army were exhausted. Another winter of war would bring revolution and disintegration. Both Czech and Yugoslav leaders demanded autonomous democratic states for their peoples. The British blockade kept tightening; people were starving.

The strain of total war and of the Auxiliary Service Law was also evident in Germany. In the winter of 1916 to 1917, Germany's military position appeared increasingly desperate. Stalemates and losses in the west were matched by temporary Russian advances in the east: hence the military's insistence on an all-or-nothing gamble of unrestricted submarine warfare when the Triple Entente refused in December 1916 to consider peace on terms favorable to the Central Powers.

Also, the national political unity of the first two years of war was collapsing as the social conflict of prewar Germany re-emerged. A growing minority of moderate socialists in the Reichstag called for a compromise "peace without annexations or reparations." Such a peace was unthinkable for conservatives and military leaders. So also was the surge in revolutionary agitation and strikes by war-weary workers that occurred in early 1917. When the bread ration was further reduced in April, more than 200,000 workers struck and demonstrated for a week in Berlin, returning to work only under the threat of prison and military discipline. Thus militaristic Germany, like its ally Austria-Hungary (and its enemy France), was beginning to crack in 1917. Yet it was Russia that collapsed first and saved the Central Powers—for a time.

The Russian Revolution

The Russian Revolution of 1917 was one of modern history's most momentous events. Directly related to the growing tensions of World War I, it had a significance far beyond the wartime agonies of a single European nation. The Russian Revolution opened a new era. For some, it was Marx's socialist vision come true; for others, it was the triumph of dictatorship. To all, it presented a radically new prototype of state and society.

- *Why did World War I bring socialist revolution in Russia?*

The Fall of Imperial Russia

Like its allies and its enemies, Russia embraced war with patriotic enthusiasm in 1914. At the Winter Palace, while throngs of people knelt and sang, "God save the tsar," Tsar Nicholas II (r. 1894–1917) repeated the oath Alexander I had sworn in 1812 and vowed never to make peace as long as the enemy stood on Russian soil. Russia's lower house, the Duma, voted war credits. Conservatives anticipated expansion in the Balkans, while liberals and most socialists believed alliance with Britain and France would bring democratic reforms. For a moment, Russia was united.

Unprecedented artillery barrages used up Russia's supplies of shells and ammunition, and better-equipped German armies inflicted terrible losses. In 1915 substantial numbers of Russian soldiers were sent to the front without rifles; they were told to find their arms among the dead. There were 2 million Russian casualties in 1915 alone. Nevertheless, Russia's battered peasant army did not collapse but continued to fight courageously, and Russia moved toward full mobilization on the home front. The Duma and organs of local government took the lead, setting up special committees to coordinate defense, industry, transportation, and agriculture. These efforts improved the military situation. Yet there were many failures, and Russia mobilized less effectively for total war than the other warring nations.

The great problem was leadership. Under the constitution resulting from the revolution of 1905 (see pages 828–829), the tsar had retained complete control over the bureaucracy and the army. Legislation proposed by the Duma, which was weighted in favor of the wealthy and conservative classes, was subject to the tsar's veto. Moreover, Nicholas II fervently wished to maintain the sacred inheritance of supreme royal power. A kindly, slightly stupid man, Nicholas failed to form a close partnership with his citizens in order to fight the war more effectively. He came to rely instead on the old bureaucratic apparatus, distrusting the moderate Duma, rejecting popular involvement, and resisting calls to share power.

As a result, the Duma, the educated middle classes, and the masses became increasingly critical of the tsar's leadership. In September 1915 parties ranging from conservative to moderate socialist formed the Progressive bloc, which called for a completely new government responsible to the Duma instead of the tsar. In answer, Nicholas temporarily adjourned the Duma and announced that he was traveling to the front in order to lead and rally Russia's armies.

His departure was a fatal turning point. With the tsar in the field with the troops, control of the government was taken over by the hysterical empress, Tsarina Alexandra, and a debauched adventurer and self-proclaimed holy man, Rasputin. Nicholas's wife was a strong-willed woman with a hatred of parliaments. Having constantly urged her husband to rule absolutely, Alexandra tried to do so herself in his absence. She seated and unseated the top ministers. Her most trusted adviser was "our Friend Grigori," an uneducated Siberian preacher who was appropriately nicknamed "Rasputin"—the "Degenerate."

Rasputin's influence rested on mysterious healing powers. Alexis, Alexandra's fifth child and heir to the throne, suffered from the rare blood disease hemophilia, and only Rasputin could miraculously stop the bleeding, perhaps through hypnosis.

In a desperate attempt to right the situation and end unfounded rumors that Rasputin was the empress's lover, three members of the high aristocracy murdered Rasputin in December 1916. The empress went into semipermanent shock. Food shortages in the cities worsened; morale declined. On March 8, women calling for bread in Petrograd (formerly St. Petersburg) started riots, which spontaneously spread to the factories and then elsewhere throughout the city. From the front, the tsar ordered troops to restore order, but discipline broke down, and the soldiers joined the revolutionary crowd. The Duma responded by declaring a provisional government on March 12, 1917. Three days later, Nicholas abdicated.

"The Russian Ruling House" This wartime cartoon captures the ominous, spellbinding power of Rasputin over Tsar Nicholas II and his wife, Alexandra. Rasputin's manipulations disgusted Russian public opinion and contributed to the monarchy's collapse. *(Stock Montage)*

The Provisional Government

The March revolution was the result of an unplanned uprising of hungry, angry people in the capital, but it was joyfully accepted throughout the country. The patriotic upper and middle classes rejoiced at the prospect of a more determined and effective war effort, while workers happily anticipated better wages and more food. All classes and political parties called for liberty and democracy. They were not disappointed. As Vladimir Lenin said, Russia became the freest country in the world. After generations of arbitrary authoritarianism, the provisional government quickly established equality before the law; freedom of religion,

speech, and assembly; the right of unions to organize and strike; and the rest of the classic liberal program.

Yet both liberal and moderate socialist leaders of the provisional government rejected social revolution. The reorganized government formed in May 1917 included the fiery agrarian socialist Alexander Kerensky, who became prime minister in July. He refused to confiscate large landholdings and give them to peasants, fearing that such drastic action in the countryside would only complete the disintegration of Russia's peasant army. For the patriotic Kerensky, as for other moderate socialists, the continuation of war was still the all-important national duty. Human suffering and war-weariness grew, sapping the limited strength of the provisional government.

From its first day, the provisional government had to share power with a formidable rival—the **Petrograd Soviet** (or council) of Workers' and Soldiers' Deputies. Modeled on the revolutionary soviets of 1905, the Petrograd Soviet was a huge, fluctuating mass meeting of two thousand to three thousand workers, soldiers, and socialist intellectuals. Seeing itself as a true grassroots revolutionary democracy, this counter- or half-government suspiciously watched the provisional government and issued its own radical orders, further weakening the provisional government. Most famous of these was **Army Order No. 1,** issued to all Russian military forces as the provisional government was forming.

Army Order No. 1 stripped officers of their authority and placed power in the hands of elected committees of common soldiers. Designed primarily to protect the revolution from some counter-revolutionary Bonaparte on horseback, the order instead led to a total collapse of army discipline. Many an officer was hanged for his sins. Meanwhile, following the foolhardy summer offensive, masses of peasant soldiers began "voting with their feet," to use Lenin's graphic phrase. That is, they began returning to their villages to help their families get a share of the land, which peasants were simply seizing as they settled old scores in a great agrarian upheaval. All across the country, liberty was turning into anarchy in the summer of 1917. It was an unparalleled opportunity for the most radical and most talented of Russia's many socialist leaders, Vladimir Ilyich Lenin (1870–1924).

Lenin and the Bolshevik Revolution

From his youth, Lenin's whole life had been dedicated to the cause of revolution. Born into the middle class, Lenin became an implacable enemy of imperial Russia when his older brother was executed for plotting to kill the tsar in

The Russian Revolution

1914	Russia enthusiastically enters the First World War.
1915	Russia suffers 2 million casualties.
	Progressive bloc calls for a new government responsible to the Duma rather than to the tsar.
	Tsar Nicholas adjourns the Duma and departs for the front; Alexandra and Rasputin exert a strong influence on the government.
December 1916	Rasputin is murdered.
March 8, 1917	Bread riots take place in Petrograd (St. Petersburg).
March 12, 1917	Duma declares a provisional government.
March 15, 1917	Tsar Nicholas abdicates without protest.
April 3, 1917	Lenin returns from exile and denounces the provisional government.
May 1917	Reorganized provisional government, including Kerensky, continues the war.
	Petrograd Soviet issues Army Order No. 1, granting military power to committees of common soldiers.
Summer 1917	Agrarian upheavals: peasants seize estates; peasant soldiers desert the army to participate.
October 1917	Bolsheviks gain a majority in the Petrograd Soviet.
November 6, 1917	Bolsheviks seize power; Lenin heads the new "provisional workers' and peasants' government."
November 1917	Lenin accepts peasant seizure of land and worker control of factories; all banks are nationalized.
January 1918	Lenin permanently disbands the Constituent Assembly.
February 1918	Lenin convinces the Bolshevik Central Committee to accept a humiliating peace with Germany in order to safeguard the revolution.
March 1918	Treaty of Brest-Litovsk: Russia loses one-third of its population.
	Trotsky as war commissar begins to rebuild the Russian army.
	Government moves from Petrograd to Moscow.
1918–1920	Great civil war takes place.
Summer 1918	Eighteen regional governments compete for power.
	White armies oppose the Bolshevik Revolution.
1919	White armies are on the offensive but divided politically; they receive little benefit from Allied intervention.
1920	Lenin and the Red Army are victorious, retaking Belorussia and Ukraine.

1887. As a law student, Lenin found a revolutionary faith in Marxian socialism, which began to win converts among radical intellectuals as industrialization surged forward in Russia in the 1890s. Exiled to Siberia for three years, Lenin studied Marxian doctrines with religious intensity. After his release, this young priest of socialism then joined fellow socialists in western Europe and developed his own revolutionary interpretations of the body of Marxian thought.

Three interrelated ideas were central for Lenin. First, like other eastern European radical socialists after 1900, he turned to the early fire-breathing Marx of 1848 and *The Communist Manifesto* for inspiration. Thus Lenin stressed that capitalism could be destroyed only by violent revolution. He tirelessly denounced all revisionist theories of a peaceful evolution to socialism as betraying Marx's message of unending class conflict. Lenin's second, more original idea was that under certain conditions a socialist revolution was possible even in a relatively backward country like Russia. There the industrial working class was small, but peasants were poor and thus potential revolutionaries.

Lenin believed that at a given moment revolution was determined more by human leadership than by vast historical laws. Thus was born his third basic idea: the necessity of a highly disciplined workers' party, strictly controlled by a dedicated elite of intellectuals and full-time revolutionaries like Lenin himself. Unlike ordinary workers and trade-union officials, this elite would never be seduced by short-term gains. It would not stop until revolution brought it to power.

Lenin's theories and methods did not go unchallenged by other Russian Marxists. At meetings of the Russian Social Democratic Labor Party in London in 1903, matters came to a head. Lenin demanded a small, disciplined, elitist party, while his opponents wanted a more democratic party with mass membership. The Russian party of Marxian socialism promptly split into two rival factions. Lenin's camp was called **Bolsheviks,** or "majority group"; his opponents were *Mensheviks,* or "minority group." Lenin's majority did not last, but Lenin did not care. He kept the fine-sounding name Bolshevik and developed the party he wanted: tough, disciplined, revolutionary.

Book Companion Site
Primary Source: What Is to Be Done with Russia?

Unlike most other socialists, Lenin did not rally round the national flag in 1914. Observing events from neutral Switzerland, he saw the war as a product of imperialistic rivalries and as a marvelous opportunity for class war and socialist upheaval. After the March revolution the German government provided the impatient Lenin, his wife, and about twenty trusted colleagues with safe passage across Germany and back into Russia in April 1917. The Germans hoped that Lenin would undermine the sagging war effort of the world's freest society. They were not disappointed.

Arriving triumphantly at Petrograd's Finland Station on April 3, Lenin attacked at once. To the great astonishment of the local Bolsheviks, he rejected all cooperation with the "bourgeois" provisional government of the liberals and moderate socialists. His slogans were radical in the extreme: "All power to the soviets"; "All land to the peasants"; "Stop the war now." Never a slave to Marxian determinism, the brilliant but not unduly intellectual Lenin was a superb tactician. The moment was now.

Yet Lenin almost overplayed his hand. An attempt by the Bolsheviks to seize power in July collapsed, and Lenin fled and went into hiding. He was charged with being a German agent, and indeed he and the Bolsheviks were getting money from Germany.[5] But no matter. Intrigue between Kerensky, who became prime minister in July, and his commander in chief, General Lavr Kornilov, resulted in Kornilov's leading a feeble attack against the provisional government in September. In the face of this rightist "counter-revolutionary" threat, the Bolsheviks were rearmed and redeemed. Kornilov's forces disintegrated, but Kerensky lost all credit with the army, the only force that might have saved him and democratic government in Russia.

Trotsky and the Seizure of Power

Throughout the summer, the Bolsheviks had appealed very effectively to the workers and soldiers of Petrograd, markedly increasing their popular support. Party membership had soared from 50,000 to 240,000, and in October the Bolsheviks gained a fragile majority in the Petrograd Soviet. It was now Lenin's supporter Leon Trotsky (1879–1940), a spellbinding revolutionary orator and independent radical Marxist, who brilliantly executed the Bolshevik seizure of power.

Painting a vivid but untruthful picture of German and counter-revolutionary plots, Trotsky first convinced the Petrograd Soviet to form a special military-revolutionary committee in October and make him its leader. Military power in the capital passed into Bolshevik hands. Then, on the night of November 6, militants from Trotsky's committee joined with trusty Bolshevik soldiers to seize government buildings and pounce on members of the provisional government. Then they went on to the congress of soviets. There a Bolshevik majority—roughly 390 of 650 turbulent delegates—declared that all power had passed to the soviets and named Lenin head of the new government.

The Bolsheviks came to power for three key reasons. First, by late 1917 democracy had given way to anarchy: power was there for those who would take it. Second, in Lenin and Trotsky the Bolsheviks had an utterly determined and truly superior leadership, which both the tsarist government and the provisional government lacked. Third, in 1917 the Bolsheviks succeeded in appealing to many soldiers and urban workers, people who were exhausted by war and eager for socialism. With time, many workers would become bitterly disappointed, but for the moment they had good reason to believe that they had won what they wanted.

Dictatorship and Civil War

History is full of short-lived coups and unsuccessful revolutions. The truly monumental accomplishment of Lenin, Trotsky, and the rest of the Bolsheviks was not taking power but keeping it. In the next four years, the Bolsheviks went on to conquer the chaos they had helped create, and they began to build their kind of dictatorial socialist society. The conspirators became conquerors. How was this done?

Lenin had the genius to profit from developments over which he and the Bolsheviks had no control. Since summer, a peasant revolution had been sweeping across Russia as the tillers of the soil invaded and divided among themselves the estates of the landlords and the church. Peasant seizure of the land—a Russian 1789—was not very Marxian, but it was quite unstoppable in 1917. Thus Lenin's first law, which supposedly gave land to the peasants, actually merely approved what peasants were already doing. Urban workers' great demand in November was direct control of individual factories by local workers committees. This, too, Lenin ratified with a decree in November.

Unlike many of his colleagues, Lenin acknowledged that Russia had lost the war with Germany and that the only realistic goal was peace at any price. That price was very high. Germany demanded in December 1917 that the Soviet government give up all its western territories. These areas were inhabited by Poles, Finns, Lithuanians, and other non-Russians—all those people who had been conquered by the tsars over three centuries and put into the "prisonhouse of nationalities," as Lenin had earlier called the Russian empire.

At first, Lenin's fellow Bolsheviks would not accept such great territorial losses. But when German armies resumed their unopposed march into Russia in February 1918, Lenin had his way in a very close vote in the Central Committee of the party. "Not even his greatest enemy can deny that at this moment Lenin towered like a giant over his Bolshevik colleagues."[6] A third of old Russia's population was sliced away by the German meat ax in the Treaty of Brest-Litovsk in March 1918. With peace, Lenin had escaped the certain disaster of continued war and could pursue his goal of absolute political power for the Bolsheviks—now renamed Communists—within Russia.

In November 1917, the Bolsheviks had cleverly proclaimed their regime only a "provisional workers' and peasants' government," promising that a freely elected

Lenin Rallies Worker and Soldier Delegates At a midnight meeting of the Petrograd Soviet, the Bolsheviks rise up and seize power on November 6, 1917. This painting from the 1940s idealizes Lenin, but his great talents as a revolutionary leader are undeniable. In this re-creation Stalin, who actually played only a small role in the uprising, is standing behind Lenin, already his trusty right-hand man. *(Sovfoto)*

Constituent Assembly would draw up a new constitution. But free elections produced a stunning setback for the Bolsheviks, who won less than one-fourth of the elected delegates. The Socialist Revolutionaries—the peasants' party—had a clear majority. The Constituent Assembly met for only one day, on January 18, 1918. It was then permanently disbanded by Bolshevik soldiers acting under Lenin's orders. Thus even before the peace with Germany, Lenin was forming a one-party government.

The destruction of the democratically elected Constituent Assembly helped feed the flames of civil war. People who had risen up for self-rule in November saw that once again they were getting dictatorship from the capital. For the next three years, "Long live the [democratic] soviets; down with the Bolsheviks" was to be a popular slogan. The officers of the old army took the lead in organizing the so-called White opposition to the Bolsheviks in southern Russia, Ukraine, Siberia, and west of Petrograd. The

"You! Have You Volunteered?" A Red Army soldier makes a compelling direct appeal to the ordinary citizen and demands all-out support for the Bolshevik cause in this 1920 poster by Dmitri Moor, a popular Soviet artist. Lenin recognized the importance of visual propaganda in a vast country with limited literacy, and mass-produced posters like this one were everywhere during the civil war of 1918–1920. *(Stephen White, University of Glasgow)*

Whites came from many social groups and were united only by their hatred of the Bolsheviks—the Reds.

By the summer of 1918, fully eighteen self-proclaimed regional governments—several of which represented minority nationalities—were competing with Lenin's Bolsheviks in Moscow. By the end of the year, White armies were on the attack. In October 1919, it appeared they might triumph, as they closed in on Lenin's government from three sides. Yet they did not. By the spring of 1920, the White armies had been almost completely defeated, and the Bolshevik Red Army had retaken Belorussia and Ukraine. The following year, the Communists also reconquered the independent nationalist governments of the Caucasus. The civil war was over; Lenin had won.

Lenin and the Bolsheviks won for several reasons. Strategically, they controlled the center, while the Whites were always on the fringes and disunited. Moreover, the poorly defined political program of the Whites was vaguely conservative, and it did not unite all the foes of the Bolsheviks under a progressive, democratic banner. Most important, the Communists quickly developed a better army, an army for which the divided Whites were no match.

Once again, Trotsky's leadership was decisive. The Bolsheviks had preached democracy in the army and elected officers in 1917. But beginning in March 1918, Trotsky as war commissar re-established the draft and the most drastic discipline for the newly formed Red Army. Soldiers deserting or disobeying an order were summarily shot. Moreover, Trotsky made effective use of former tsarist army officers, who were actively recruited and given unprecedented powers of discipline over their troops. In short, Trotsky formed a disciplined and effective fighting force.

The Bolsheviks also mobilized the home front. Establishing **war communism**—the application of the total war concept to a civil conflict—they seized grain from peasants, introduced rationing, nationalized all banks and industry, and required everyone to work. Although these measures contributed to a breakdown of normal economic activity, they also served to maintain labor discipline and to keep the Red Army supplied.

"Revolutionary terror" also contributed to the Communist victory. The old tsarist secret police was re-established as the **Cheka,** which hunted down and executed thousands of real or supposed foes, such as the tsar and his family and other "class enemies." Moreover, people were shot or threatened with being shot for minor nonpolitical failures. The terror caused by the secret police became a tool of the government. The Cheka sowed fear, and fear silenced opposition.

Finally, foreign military intervention in the civil war ended up helping the Communists. After Lenin made peace with Germany, the Allies (United States, Britain, Japan) sent troops to Archangel and Vladivostok to prevent war materiel they had sent the provisional government from being captured by the Germans. After the Soviet government nationalized all foreign-owned factories without compensation and refused to pay all of Russia's foreign debts, Western governments, particularly France, began to support White armies in the south and west. Yet these efforts were small and halfhearted. In 1919 Western peoples were sick of war, and few Western politicians believed in a military crusade against the Bolsheviks. Thus Allied intervention in the civil war did not aid the Whites effectively, though it did permit the Communists to appeal to the patriotic nationalism of ethnic Russians, in particular former tsarist army officers. Allied intervention was both too little and too much.

Together, the Russian Revolution and the Bolshevik triumph were one of the reasons the First World War was such a great turning point in modern history. A radically new government, based on socialism and one-party dictatorship, came to power in a great European state, maintained power, and eagerly encouraged worldwide revolution. Although halfhearted constitutional monarchy in Russia was undoubtedly headed for some kind of political crisis before 1914, it is hard to imagine the triumph of the most radical proponents of change and reform except in a situation of total collapse. That was precisely what happened to Russia in the First World War.

The Peace Settlement

Victory over revolutionary Russia boosted sagging German morale, and in the spring of 1918 the Germans launched their last major attack against France. Yet this offensive failed, just as those before it had. With breathtaking rapidity, the United States, Great Britain, and France decisively defeated Germany militarily. The guns of world war finally fell silent. Then as civil war spread in Russia and as chaos engulfed much of eastern Europe, the victorious Western Allies came together in Paris to establish a lasting peace.

Expectations were high; optimism was almost unlimited. The Allies labored intensively and soon worked out terms for peace with Germany and for the creation of the peacekeeping League of Nations. Nevertheless, the hopes of peoples and politicians were soon disappointed, for the peace settlement of 1919 turned out to be a failure. Rather than creating conditions for peace, it sowed the seeds of another war. Surely this was the ultimate tragedy of the Great War, a war that directly and indirectly cost $332 billion and left 10 million dead and another 20 million wounded.

• *How did the Allies fashion a peace settlement, and why was it unsuccessful?*

The End of the War

In early 1917, the strain of total war was showing everywhere. After the Russian Revolution in March, there were major strikes in Germany. In July a coalition of moderates passed a "peace resolution" in the Reichstag, calling for peace without territorial annexations. To counter this moderation born of war-weariness, the German military established a virtual dictatorship. The military also aggressively

exploited the collapse of Russian armies, winning great concessions in the Treaty of Brest-Litovsk in March 1918.

With victory in the east quieting German moderates, General Ludendorff and company fell on France once more in the great spring offensive of 1918. For a time, German armies pushed forward, coming within thirty-five miles of Paris. But Ludendorff's exhausted, overextended forces never broke through. They were decisively stopped in July at the second Battle of the Marne, where 140,000 fresh American soldiers saw action. Adding 2 million men in arms to the war effort by August, the late but massive American intervention decisively tipped the scales in favor of Allied victory.

By September British, French, and American armies were advancing steadily on all fronts, and a panicky General Ludendorff realized that Germany had lost the war. Yet he insolently insisted that moderate politicians shoulder the shame of defeat, and on October 4 the emperor formed a new, more liberal German government to sue for peace. As negotiations over an armistice dragged on, an angry and frustrated German people finally rose up. On November 3, sailors in Kiel mutinied, and throughout northern Germany soldiers and workers began to establish revolutionary councils on the Russian soviet model. The same day, Austria-Hungary surrendered to the Allies and began breaking apart. Revolution broke out in Germany, and masses of workers demonstrated for peace in Berlin. With army discipline collapsing, the emperor abdicated and fled to Holland. Socialist leaders in Berlin proclaimed a German republic on November 9 and simultaneously agreed to tough Allied terms of surrender. The armistice went into effect on November 11, 1918. The war was over.

Revolution in Germany

Military defeat brought political revolution to Germany and Austria-Hungary, as it had to Russia. In Austria-Hungary the revolution was primarily nationalistic and republican in character. Having started the war to preserve an antinationalistic dynastic state, the Habsburg empire had perished in the attempt. In its place, independent Austrian, Hungarian, and Czechoslovakian republics were proclaimed, while a greatly expanded Serbian monarchy united the South Slavs and took the name Yugoslavia. The prospect of firmly establishing the new national states overrode class considerations for most people in east-central Europe.

The German Revolution of November 1918 resembled the Russian Revolution of March 1917. In both cases, a genuine popular uprising welled up from below, toppled an authoritarian monarchy, and brought the establishment of a liberal provisional republic. In both countries, liberals and moderate socialists took control of the central government, while workers' and soldiers' councils formed a counter-government. In Germany, however, the moderate socialists and their liberal allies won, and the Lenin-like radical revolutionaries in the councils lost. In communist terms, the liberal, republican revolution in Germany in 1918 was only half a revolution: a bourgeois political revolution without a communist second installment. It was Russia without Lenin's Bolshevik triumph.

There were several reasons for the German outcome. The great majority of Marxian socialist leaders in the Social Democratic Party were, as before the war, really pink and not red. They wanted to establish real political democracy and civil liberties, and they favored the gradual elimination of capitalism. They were also German nationalists, appalled by the prospect of civil war and revolutionary terror. Moreover, there was less popular support among workers, soldiers, and peasants.

Of crucial importance was the fact that the moderate German Social Democrats, unlike Kerensky and company, accepted defeat and ended the war the day they took power. This act ended the decline in morale among soldiers and prevented the regular army, with its conservative officer corps, from disintegrating. When radicals headed by Karl Liebknecht and Rosa Luxemburg and their supporters in the councils tried to seize control of the government in Berlin in January, the moderate socialists called on the army to crush the uprising. Liebknecht and Luxemburg were arrested and then brutally murdered by army leaders. Their murders, widely believed to have had government support, caused many working-class activists in the Social Democratic Party to break away in anger and join the pro-Lenin German Communist Party that Liebknecht's group had just founded. Finally, even if the moderate socialists had followed Liebknecht and Luxemburg on the Leninist path, it is very unlikely they would have succeeded. Civil war in Germany would certainly have followed. And the Allies, who were already occupying western Germany according to the terms of the armistice, would have marched on to Berlin and ruled Germany directly.

The Treaty of Versailles

The peace conference opened in Paris in January 1919 with seventy delegates representing twenty-seven victorious nations. There were great expectations. A young British diplomat later wrote that the victors "were convinced that they would never commit the blunders and iniquities of the Congress of Vienna [of 1815]." Then the "misguided, reactionary, pathetic aristocrats" had cynically shuffled populations; now "we believed in nationalism, we believed in the self-determination of peoples." Indeed, "we were journeying to Paris . . . to found a new order in Europe. We were preparing not Peace only, but Eternal Peace."[7] This general optimism and idealism had been greatly strengthened by President Wilson's January 1918 peace proposal, the Fourteen Points, which stressed national self-determination and the rights of small countries.

Book Companion Site
Primary Source: A New Diplomacy: The Fourteen Points

The real powers at the conference were the United States, Great Britain, and France, for Germany was not allowed to participate and Russia was locked in civil war and did not attend. Italy was considered part of the Big Four, but its role was quite limited. Almost immediately the three great Allies began to quarrel. President Wilson, who was wildly cheered by European crowds as the spokesman for a new idealistic and democratic international cooperation, was almost obsessed with creating the **League of Nations.** Wilson insisted that this question come first, for he passionately believed that only a permanent international organization could protect member states from aggression and avert future wars. Wilson had his way, although Lloyd George of Great Britain and especially Clemenceau of France were unenthusiastic. They were primarily concerned with punishing Germany.

Playing on British nationalism, Lloyd George had already won a smashing electoral victory in December on the popular platform of making Germany pay for the war. "We shall," he promised, "squeeze the orange until the pips squeak." Personally inclined to make a somewhat moderate peace with Germany, Lloyd George was to a considerable extent a captive of demands for a total victory worthy of the sacrifices of total war against a totally depraved enemy. As Kipling summed up the general British feeling at the end of the war, the Germans were "a people with the heart of beasts."[8]

France's Georges Clemenceau, "the Tiger" who had broken wartime defeatism and led his country to victory, wholeheartedly agreed. Like most French people, Clemenceau wanted old-fashioned revenge. He also wanted lasting security for France. This, he believed, required the creation of a buffer state between France and Germany, the permanent demilitarization of Germany, and vast German reparations. He feared that sooner or later Germany with its 60 million people would attack France with its 40 million unless the Germans were permanently weakened. Moreover, France had no English Channel (or Atlantic Ocean) as a reassuring barrier against German aggression. Wilson, supported by Lloyd George, would hear none of this. Clemenceau's demands seemed vindictive, violating morality and the principle of national self-determination. By April the countries attending the conference were deadlocked on the German question, and Wilson packed his bags to go home.

In the end, convinced that France could not afford to face Germany alone in the future, Clemenceau agreed to a compromise. He gave up the French demand for a Rhineland buffer state in return for a formal defensive alliance with the United States and Great Britain. Under the terms of this alliance, both Wilson and Lloyd George promised that their countries would come to France's aid in the event of a German attack. Thus Clemenceau appeared to win his goal of French security, as Wilson had won his of a permanent international organization. The Allies moved quickly to finish the settlement, believing that any adjustments would later be possible within the dual framework of a strong Western alliance and the League of Nations (see Map 27.4).

The **Treaty of Versailles** between the Allies and Germany was the key to the settlement, and the terms were not unreasonable as a first step toward re-establishing international order. Had Germany won, it seems certain that France and Belgium would have been treated with greater severity, as Russia had been at Brest-Litovsk. Germany's colonies were given to France, Britain, and Japan as League of Nations mandates. Germany's territorial losses within Europe were minor, thanks to Wilson. Alsace-Lorraine was returned to France. Parts of Germany inhabited primarily by Poles were ceded to the new Polish state, in keeping with the principle of national self-determination. Predominately German Danzig was also placed within the Polish tariff lines, but as a self-governing city under League of Nations protection. Germany had to limit its army to 100,000 men and agree to build no military fortifications in the Rhineland.

More harshly, the Allies declared that Germany (with Austria) was responsible for the war and had therefore to pay reparations equal to all civilian damages caused by the war. This unfortunate and much-criticized clause expressed inescapable popular demands for German blood, but the actual figure was not set, and there was the clear possibility that reparations might be set at a reasonable level in the future when tempers had cooled.

When presented with the treaty, the German government protested vigorously. But there was no alternative, especially considering that Germany was still starving because the Allies had not yet lifted their naval blockade. On June 28, 1919, German representatives of the ruling moderate Social Democrats and the Catholic Party signed the treaty in the Sun King's Hall of Mirrors at Versailles, where Bismarck's empire had been joyously proclaimed almost fifty years before.

Book Companion Site
Primary Source: A Defeated Germany Contemplates the Peace Treaty

Separate peace treaties were concluded with the other defeated European powers—Austria, Hungary, and Bulgaria. For the most part, these treaties merely ratified the existing situation in east-central Europe following the breakup of the Austro-Hungarian Empire. Like Austria, Hungary was a particularly big loser, as its "captive" nationalities (and some interspersed Hungarians) were ceded to Romania, Czechoslovakia, Poland, and Yugoslavia. Italy got some Austrian territory.

The Peace Settlement in the Middle East

Although Allied leaders at Versailles focused mainly on European questions, they also imposed a political settlement on what had been the Ottoman Empire. This settlement brought radical changes to the Middle East, and it became very controversial. Basically, the Ottoman Empire was broken up, Britain and France expanded their power and influence in the Middle East, and Arab nationalists felt cheated and betrayed.

The British government had encouraged the wartime Arab revolt against the Ottoman Turks (see page 890) and had even made vague promises of an independent Arab kingdom. However, when the fighting stopped, the British and the French chose instead to honor secret wartime agreements to divide and rule the Ottoman lands. Most important, in 1916 Britain and France had agreed that France would receive modern-day Lebanon and Syria, and much of southern Turkey, and Britain would receive Palestine, Transjordan, and Iraq. This agreement contradicted British (and later Wilsonian) promises concerning Arab independence after the war. When Britain and France set about implementing their secret plans after the armistice, Arab nationalists felt they were being double-crossed.

British plans for the old Ottoman province of Palestine also angered Arab nationalists. The **Balfour Declaration** of November 1917, made by the British foreign secretary Arthur Balfour, had declared that Britain favored a "National Home for the Jewish People" in Palestine, but without prejudicing the civil and religious rights of the non-Jewish communities already living in Palestine.

Mapping the Past

MAP 27.4 Shattered Empires and Territorial Changes After World War I The Great War brought tremendous changes in eastern Europe. New nations and new boundaries were established, generally on the principle of national self-determination. A dangerous power vacuum was created by the new, usually small states established between Germany and Soviet Russia. ❶ Identify the boundaries of Germany, Austria-Hungary, and Russia in 1914, and note carefully the changes caused by the war. ❷ What territory did Germany lose, and why did France, Poland, and even Denmark receive it? Why was Austria sometimes called a head without a body in the 1920s? ❸ What new independent states (excluding disputed Bessarabia) were formed from the old Russian empire, and what nationalities lived in these states?

Some members of the British cabinet believed the declaration would appeal to German, Austrian, and American Jews and thus help the British war effort. Others sincerely supported the Zionist vision of a Jewish homeland (pages 838–839), which they hoped would also help Britain maintain control of the Suez Canal. In any event, Palestinian Arabs were dismayed.

In 1914 Jews accounted for about 11 percent of the predominately Arab population in the three Ottoman administrative units that would subsequently be lumped together by the British to form Palestine. The "National Home for the Jewish People" mentioned in the Balfour Declaration implied to the Arabs—and to the Zionist Jews as well—the establishment of some kind of Jewish state that would be incompatible with majority rule. Moreover, a state founded on religious and ethnic exclusivity was out of keeping with both Islamic and Ottoman tradition, which had historically been more tolerant of religious diversity and minorities than had the Christian monarchs or nation-states in Europe.

Despite strong French objections, Hussein of the Hejaz (see page 890) was allowed to send his son Faisal (1885–1933) as his representative to the Versailles Peace Conference. Yet Hussein's efforts to secure Arab independence came to nothing. President Wilson wanted to give the Arab case serious consideration, but the British and the French were determined to rule Syria, Iraq, Transjordan, and Palestine as League of Nations mandates, and they confirmed only the independence of Hussein's kingdom of Hejaz (see Map 27.5). In response Arab nationalists came together in Damascus as the General Syrian Congress in 1919 and unsuccessfully called again for political independence. (See the feature "Listening to the Past: Arab Political Aspirations in 1919" on pages 910–911.) Brushing aside Arab opposition, the British mandate in Palestine formally incorporated the Balfour Declaration and its commitment to a Jewish national home. When Faisal returned to Syria, his followers repudiated the agreement he had reluctantly accepted. In March 1920 they met as the Syrian National Congress and proclaimed Syria independent, with Faisal as king. A similar congress declared Iraq an independent kingdom.

Prince Faisal at the Versailles Peace Conference, 1919 Standing in front, Faisal is supported by his allies and black slave. Nur-as-Said, an officer in the Ottoman army who joined the Arab revolt, is second from the left, and the British officer T. E. Lawrence—popularly known as Lawrence of Arabia—is fourth from the left in back. Faisal failed to win political independence for the Arabs, as the British backed away from the vague promises they had made during the war. *(Courtesy of the Trustees of the Imperial War Museum)*

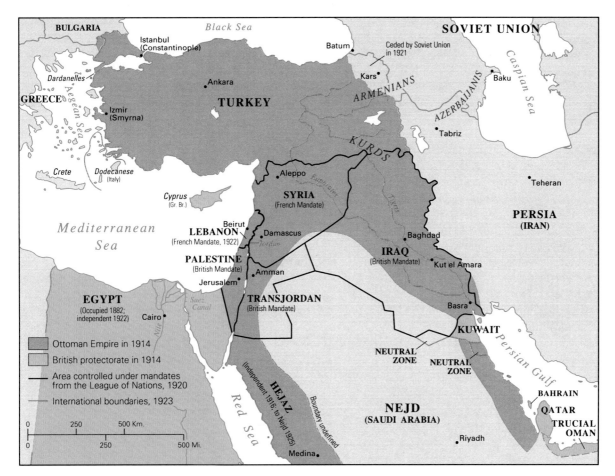

MAP 27.5 The Partition of the Ottoman Empire, 1914–1923 By 1914 the Ottoman Turks had been pushed out of the Balkans, and their Arab provinces were on the edge of revolt. That revolt, in alliance with the British, erupted in the First World War and contributed greatly to the Ottomans' defeat. Refusing to grant independence to the Arabs, the Allies established League of Nations mandates and replaced Ottoman rulers in Syria, Iraq, Transjordan, and Palestine.

Western reaction to events in Syria and Iraq was swift and decisive. A French army stationed in Lebanon attacked Syria, taking Damascus in July 1920. Faisal fled, and the French took over. Meanwhile, the British put down an uprising in Iraq with bloody fighting and established effective control there. Western imperialism, in the form of League of Nations mandates, appeared to have replaced Ottoman rule in the Arab Middle East (see Map 27.5).

The Allies sought to impose even harsher terms on the defeated Turks than on the "liberated" Arabs. A treaty forced on the helpless Ottoman sultan dismembered the Turkish heartland. Great Britain and France occupied parts of modern-day Turkey, and Italy and Greece also claimed shares. There was a sizable Greek minority in western Turkey, and Greek nationalists wanted to build a modern Greek empire modeled on long-dead Christian Byzantium. In 1919 Greek armies carried by British ships landed on the Turkish coast at Smyrna and advanced unopposed into the interior. Turkey seemed finished.

But Turkey produced a great leader and revived to become an inspiration for many modernizing reformers. Mustafa Kemal (1881–1938), later known as **Atatürk,** which means "father of the Turks," was a military man who had directed the successful defense of the Dardanelles against British attack. Watching the Allies' aggression and the sultan's cowardice after the armistice, in early 1919 he moved to central Turkey and gradually unified the Turkish resistance. Refusing to acknowledge the Allied dismemberment of their country, the Turks battled on through 1920 despite staggering defeats. The

Mustafa Kemal Surnamed Atatürk, meaning "father of the Turks," Mustafa Kemal and his supporters imposed revolutionary changes aimed at modernizing and westernizing Turkish society and the new Turkish government. Dancing here with his adopted daughter at her high-society wedding, Atatürk often appeared in public in elegant European dress—a vivid symbol for the Turkish people of his radical break with traditional Islamic teaching and custom. *(Hulton Archive/Getty Images)*

next year they won a great victory in central Turkey, and the Greeks and their British allies sued for peace. After long negotiations, the resulting Treaty of Lausanne (1923) solemnly abolished the hated Capitulations, which the European powers had imposed over the centuries to give their citizens special privileges in the Ottoman Empire, and recognized the territorial integrity of a truly independent Turkey. Turkey lost only its former Arab provinces.

Mustafa Kemal, a nationalist without religious faith, believed that Turkey should modernize and secularize along Western lines. He established a republic, had him-

self elected president, and created a one-party system—partly inspired by the Bolshevik example—in order to transform his country. The most radical reforms pertained to religion and culture. For centuries most of the intellectual and social activities of believers had been regulated by Islamic religious authorities. Profoundly influenced by the example of western Europe, Mustafa Kemal set out to limit the place of religion and religious leaders in daily affairs. He decreed a revolutionary separation of church and state, promulgated law codes inspired by European models, and established a secular public school system. Women received rights that they never had before. By the time of his death in 1938, Mustafa Kemal had implemented successfully much of his revolutionary program. He had moved Turkey much closer to Europe, foretelling current efforts by Turkey to join the European Union as full-fledged member.

American Rejection of the Versailles Treaty

The rapidly concluded Versailles treaty of early 1919 was not perfect, but within the context of war-shattered Europe it was an acceptable beginning. The principle of national self-determination, which had played such a large role in starting the war, was accepted for Europe and served as an organizing framework. Germany had been punished but not dismembered. A new world organization complemented a traditional defensive alliance of satisfied powers. The serious remaining problems could be worked out in the future. Moreover, Allied leaders had seen speed as essential for another reason: they detested Lenin and feared that his Bolshevik Revolution might spread. They realized that their best answer to Lenin's unending calls for worldwide upheaval was peace and tranquillity for war-weary peoples.

There were, however, two great interrelated obstacles to such peace: Germany and the United States. Plagued by communist uprisings, reactionary plots, and popular disillusionment with losing the war at the last minute, Germany's moderate socialists and their liberal and Catholic supporters faced an enormous challenge. Like French republicans after 1871, they needed time (and luck) if they were to establish firmly a peaceful and democratic republic. Progress in this direction required understanding but firm treatment of Germany by the victorious Western Allies, particularly by the United States.

However, the U.S. Senate and, to a lesser extent, the American people rejected Wilson's handiwork. Republican senators led by Henry Cabot Lodge refused to ratify the

Treaty of Versailles without changes in the articles creating the League of Nations. The key issue was the League's power—more apparent than real—to require member states to take collective action against aggression. Lodge and others believed that this requirement gave away Congress's constitutional right to declare war. In failing health, Wilson, with narrow-minded self-righteousness, rejected all attempts at compromise. In doing so, he ensured that the treaty would never be ratified by the United States in any form and that the United States would never join the League of Nations. Moreover, the Senate refused to ratify Wilson's treaties forming a defensive alliance with France and Great Britain. America turned its back on Europe.

The Wilson-Lodge fiasco and the newfound gospel of isolationism represented a tragic and cowardly renunciation of America's responsibility. Using America's action as an excuse, Great Britain, too, refused to ratify its defensive alliance with France. Bitterly betrayed by its allies, France stood alone. Very shortly France was to take actions against Germany that would feed the fires of German resentment and seriously undermine democratic forces in the new republic. The great hopes of early 1919 had turned to ashes by the end of the year. The Western alliance had collapsed, and a grandiose plan for permanent peace had given way to a fragile truce. For this and for what came later, the United States must share a large part of the guilt.

Chapter Summary

Book Companion Site
To assess your mastery of this chapter,
visit **bedfordstmartins.com/mckaywest**

- **What caused the Great War, and why did it have such revolutionary consequences?**
- **What was the impact of total war on civilian populations?**
- **Why did World War I bring socialist revolution in Russia?**
- **How did the Allies fashion a peace settlement, and why was it unsuccessful?**

World War I had truly revolutionary consequences because, first and foremost, it was a war of committed peoples. In France, Britain, and Germany in particular, governments drew on genuine popular support. This support reflected in part the diplomatic origins of the war, which citizens saw as growing out of an unwanted crisis in the Balkans and an inflexible alliance system of opposing blocs. More importantly, popular support reflected the way western European society had been unified under the nationalist banner in the later nineteenth century, despite the fears that the growing socialist movement aroused in conservatives.

The relentlessness of total war helps explain why so many died, why so many were crippled physically and psychologically, and why Western civilization would in so many ways never be the same again. More concretely, the war swept away monarchs and multinational empires. National self-determination apparently triumphed across Europe, not only in Austria-Hungary but also in many of Russia's west-

ern borderlands. Except in Ireland and parts of Soviet Russia (and the Arab Middle East), the revolutionary dream of national unity, born of the French Revolution, had finally come true.

Two other revolutions were products of the war. In Russia the Bolsheviks established a radical regime, smashed existing capitalist institutions, and stayed in power with a new kind of authoritarian rule. Whether the new Russian regime was truly Marxian or socialist was questionable, but it indisputably posed a powerful, ongoing revolutionary challenge to Europe and its colonial empires.

More subtle but quite universal in its impact was an administrative revolution. This revolution, born of the need to mobilize entire societies and economies for total war, greatly increased the power of government. Freewheeling market capitalism and a well-integrated world economy were among the many casualties of the administrative revolution, and greater social equality was everywhere one of its results. Thus even in European countries where a communist takeover never came close to occurring, society still experienced a great revolution.

Finally, the "war to end war" did not bring peace—only a fragile truce. In the West, the Allies failed to maintain their wartime solidarity. Germany remained unrepentant and would soon have more grievances to nurse. Moreover, the victory of national self-determination in eastern Europe created small, weak states and thus a power vacuum between a still-powerful Germany and a potentially mighty communist Russia. A vast area lay open to military aggression from two sides.

Key Terms

Three Emperors' League
Triple Entente
trench warfare
Lusitania
total war
War Raw Materials Board
Petrograd Soviet
Army Order No. 1
Bolsheviks
Constituent Assembly
war communism
Cheka
League of Nations
Treaty of Versailles
Balfour Declaration
Atatürk

Suggested Reading

Davis, Belinda J. *Home Fires Burning: Food, Politics, and Everyday Life in Berlin in World War I.* 2000. A moving account of women struggling to feed their families.

Eksteins, Modris. *Rites of Spring: The Great War and the Birth of the Modern Age.* 1989. An imaginative cultural investigation that has won critical acclaim.

Fromkin, David. *A Peace to End All Peace.* 2001. A brilliant reconsideration of the collapse of the Ottoman Empire and its division by the Allies.

Gatrell, Peter. *Russia's First World War: A Social and Economic History.* 2005. An excellent resource for students and specialists.

Herwig, Holger H. *The First World War: Germany and Austria, 1914–1918.* 1997. Ably follows the hard road to defeat and collapse.

Higonnet, Margaret R., Jane Jenson, Sonya Michel, and Margaret Collins Weitz, eds. *Behind the Lines: Gender and the Two World Wars.* 1989. Examines the changes that the war brought for women and for relations between the sexes.

Hobsbawm, Eric. *The Age of Extremes: A History of the World, 1914–1991.* 1996. A provocative interpretation by a famous historian, with a good discussion of war and revolution.

Howard, Michael. *The First World War: A Very Short Introduction.* 2007. A fine brief introduction.

Macmillan, Margaret. *Paris, 1919: Six Months That Changed the World.* 2001. A comprehensive, exciting account of all aspects of the peace conference.

Neiberg, Michael S. *Fighting the Great War: A Global History.* 2006. A lively and up-to-date account.

Read, Christopher. *From Tsar to Soviets: The Russian People and Their Revolution, 1917–1921.* 1996. A highly recommended account of the Russian Revolution.

Remarque, Erich Maria. *All Quiet on the Western Front.* Originally published in 1928, this novel remains one of the most moving fictional treatments of World War I.

Tucker, Jonathan. *War of Nerves: Chemical Warfare from World War I to Al-Qaeda.* 2007. A comprehensive and informative survey of chemical warfare.

Winter, J. M. *The Experience of World War I.* 1988. A striking illustrated history of the war.

Zuckerman, Larry. *The Rape of Belgium: The Untold Story of World War I.* 2004. A poignant examination of German atrocities.

Notes

1. M. Beloff, quoted in *U.S. News & World Report,* March 8, 1976, p. 53.
2. Quoted in J. Remak, *The Origins of World War I* (New York: Holt, Rinehart & Winston, 1967), p. 84.
3. Quoted in F. P. Chambers, *The War Behind the War, 1914–1918* (London: Faber & Faber, 1939), p. 168.
4. Quoted in R. O. Paxton, *Europe in the Twentieth Century* (New York: Harcourt Brace Jovanovich, 1975), p. 109.
5. A. B. Ulam, *The Bolsheviks* (New York: Collier Books, 1968), p. 349.
6. Ibid., p. 405.
7. H. Nicolson, *Peacemaking 1919* (New York: Grosset & Dunlap Universal Library, 1965), pp. 8, 31–32.
8. Quoted ibid., p. 24.

Arab Political Aspirations in 1919

Great Britain and France had agreed to divide up the Arab lands, and the British also had made conflicting promises to Arab and Jewish nationalists. However, President Wilson insisted at Versailles that the right of self-determination should be applied to the conquered Ottoman territories, and he sent an American commission of inquiry to Syria, even though the British and French refused to participate. The commission canvassed political views throughout greater Syria, and its long report with many documents reflected public opinion in the region in 1919.

To present their view to the Americans, Arab nationalists from present-day Syria, Lebanon, Israel, and Jordan came together in Damascus as the General Syrian Congress, and they passed the following resolution on July 2, 1919. In addition to the Arab call for political independence, the delegates addressed the possibility of French rule under a League of Nations mandate and the establishment of a Jewish national home.

We the undersigned members of the General Syrian Congress, meeting in Damascus on Wednesday, July 2nd, 1919, . . . provided with credentials and authorizations by the inhabitants of our various districts, Moslems, Christians, and Jews, have agreed upon the following statement of the desires of the people of the country who have elected us to present them to the American Section of the International Commission; the fifth article was passed by a very large majority; all the other articles were accepted unanimously.

1. We ask absolutely complete political independence for Syria within these boundaries. [Describes the area including the present-day states of Syria, Lebanon, Israel, and Jordan.]

2. We ask that the Government of this Syrian country should be a democratic civil constitutional Monarchy on broad decentralization principles, safeguarding the rights of minorities, and that the King be the Emir Faisal, who carried on a glorious struggle in the cause of our liberation and merited our full confidence and entire reliance.

3. Considering the fact that the Arabs inhabiting the Syrian area are not naturally less gifted than other more advanced races and that they are by no means less developed than the Bulgarians, Serbians, Greeks, and Roumanians at the beginning of their independence, we protest against Article 22 of the Covenant of the League of Nations, placing us among the nations in their middle stage of development which stand in need of a mandatory power.

4. In the event of the rejection by the Peace Conference of this just protest for certain considerations that we may not understand, we, relying on the declarations of President Wilson that his object in waging war was to put an end to the ambition of conquest and colonization, can only regard the mandate mentioned in the Covenant of the League of Nations as equivalent to the rendering of economical and technical assistance that does not prejudice our complete independence. And desiring that our country should not fall a prey to colonization and believing that the American Nation is farthest from any thought of colonization and has no political ambition in our country, we will seek the technical and economical assistance from the United States of America, provided that such assistance does not exceed 20 years.

5. In the event of America not finding herself in a position to accept our desire for assistance, we will seek this assistance from Great Britain, also provided that such assistance does not infringe the complete independence and unity of our country and that the duration of such assistance does not exceed that mentioned in the previous article.

Palestinian Arabs protest against large-scale Jewish migration into Palestine. *(Roger-Viollet/ Getty Images)*

6. We do not acknowledge any right claimed by the French Government in any part whatever of our Syrian country and refuse that she should assist us or have a hand in our country under any circumstances and in any place.

7. We oppose the pretensions of the Zionists to create a Jewish commonwealth in the southern part of Syria, known as Palestine, and oppose Zionist migration to any part of our country; for we do not acknowledge their title but consider them a grave peril to our people from the national, economical, and political points of view. Our Jewish compatriots shall enjoy our common rights and assume the common responsibilities.

8. We ask that there should be no separation of the southern part of Syria, known as Palestine, nor of the littoral western zone, which includes Lebanon, from the Syrian country. We desire that the unity of the country should be guaranteed against partition under whatever circumstances.

9. We ask complete independence for emancipated Mesopotamia [today's Iraq] and that there should be no economical barriers between the two countries.

10. The fundamental principles laid down by President Wilson in condemnation of secret treaties impel us to protest most emphatically against any treaty that stipulates the partition of our Syria country and against any private engagement aiming at the establishment of Zionism in the southern part of Syria; therefore we ask the complete annulment of these conventions and agreements.

The noble principles enunciated by President Wilson strengthen our confidence that our desires emanating from the depths of our hearts, shall be the decisive factor in determining our future; and that President Wilson and the free American people will be our supporters for the realization of our hopes, thereby proving their sincerity and noble sympathy with the aspiration of the weaker nations in general and our Arab people in particular.

We also have the fullest confidence that the Peace Conference will realize that we would not have risen against the Turks, with whom we had participated in all civil, political, and representative privileges, but for their violation of our national rights, and so will grant us our desires in full in order that our political rights may not be less after the war than they were before, since we have shed so much blood in the cause of our liberty and independence.

We request to be allowed to send a delegation to represent us at the Peace Conference to defend our rights and secure the realization of our aspirations.

Questions for Analysis

1. What kind of state did the delegates want?

2. How did the delegates want to modify an unwanted League of Nations mandate to make it less objectionable?

3. Did the delegates view their "Jewish compatriots" and the Zionists in different ways? Why?

Source: "Resolution of the General Syrian Congress at Damascus, 2 July 1919," from the King-Crane Commission Report, in *Foreign Relations of the United States: Paris Peace Conference,* 1919, 12: 780–781.

Victory at Smyrna. Turks celebrate victory over Greek forces at Smyrna in October 1922. This was one of the final battles in the Turkish War for Independence that led to establishing the Republic of Turkey in 1923.

(Price/Getty Images)

28 NATIONALISM IN ASIA, 1914–1939

Chapter Preview

The First World War and Western Imperialism
• How did modern nationalism—the dominant force in most of the world in the twentieth century—develop in Asia between the First and Second World Wars?

The Middle East
• How did the collapse of the Ottoman Empire in World War I shape the history of the Middle East for the rest of the century?

Toward Self-Rule in India
• What role did Gandhi and his campaign of militant nonviolence play in leading India to independence from the British?

Turmoil in East Asia
• Why did some of the Asian nationalist movements come into brutal conflict?

From Asia's perspective the First World War was largely a European civil war that shattered Western imperialism's united front and convulsed prewar relationships throughout Asia. Most crucially, the war speeded the development of modern nationalism in Asia. Before 1914 the nationalist gospel of anti-imperialist political freedom and racial equality had already won converts among Asia's westernized, educated elites. In the 1920s and 1930s it increasingly won the allegiance of the masses. As in nineteenth-century Europe, nationalism in Asia between 1914 and 1939 became a mass movement with potentially awesome power.

There were at least three reasons for the upsurge of nationalism in Asia. First and foremost, nationalism provided the most effective means of organizing the anti-imperialist resistance both to direct foreign rule and to indirect Western domination. Second, nationalism called for fundamental changes and challenged old political and social practices and beliefs. Thus modernizers used it to contest the influence and power of conservative traditionalists. Third, nationalism offered a vision of a free and prosperous future, and provided an ideology to ennoble the sacrifices the struggle would require.

Nationalism also had a dark side. As in Europe (see page 679), Asian nationalists developed a strong sense of "we" and "they." "They" were often the enemy—the oppressor. European imperialists were just such a "they," and nationalist feeling generated the power to destroy European empires and challenge foreign economic domination. But, as in Europe, Asian nationalism also stimulated bitter conflicts and wars between peoples, in two different ways.

First, it stimulated conflicts between relatively homogeneous peoples in large states, rallying, for example, Chinese against Japanese and vice versa. Second, nationalism often heightened tensions between ethnic (or religious) groups within states, especially states with diverse populations, like British India and the Ottoman Empire. Such states had been formed by authoritarian rulers and their armies and bureaucracies, very much like the Austro-Hungarian and Russian empires before 1914. When their rigid rule declined or snapped, the different nationalistic peoples might easily quarrel, seeking to divide the existing state or to dominate the enemy "they" within its borders.

The modern nationalism movement has never been monolithic. In Asia especially, where the new and often narrow ideology of nationalism was grafted onto old, rich, and complex civilizations, the range of historical experience has been enormous. Between the outbreak of the First and Second World Wars each Asian country developed a distinctive national movement rooted in its own unique culture and history. Each nation's people created their own national reawakening, which renovated thought and culture as well as politics and economics.

● ● ● ● ● ● ● ● ● ● ● ● ● ● ● ● ● ● ● ●

THE FIRST WORLD WAR AND WESTERN IMPERIALISM

How did modern nationalism—the dominant force in most of the world in the twentieth century—develop in Asia between the First and Second World Wars?

Every Asian national movement sought genuine freedom from foreign imperialism. The First World War profoundly affected these aspirations by altering relations between Asia and Europe. In the words of a distinguished Indian historian, "the Great War of 1914–1918 was from the Asian point of view a civil war within the European community of nations."[1] For four years Asians watched Kipling's haughty bearers of "the White Man's Burden" (see page 724) vilifying and destroying each other. Japan's defeat of imperial Russia in 1904 (see page 768) had shown that an Asian power could beat a European Great Power; now for the first time Asians saw the entire West as divided and vulnerable.

In China and Japan few people particularly cared who won the distant war in Europe. In British India and French Indochina enthusiasm was also limited, but the war's impact was unavoidably greater. Total war required that the British and the French draft their colonial subjects into the conflict, uprooting hundreds of thousands of Asians to fight the Germans and the Ottoman Turks. This too had major consequences. An Indian or Vietnamese soldier who fought in France and came in contact there with democratic and republican ideas was less likely to accept foreign rule when he returned home.

The British and the French also made rash promises to gain the support of colonial peoples during the war. British leaders promised Europe's Jewish nationalists a homeland in Palestine, while promising Arab nationalists independence from the Ottoman Empire. In India the British were forced in 1917 to announce a new policy of self-governing institutions in order to counteract Indian popular unrest fanned by wartime inflation and heavy taxation. After the war the nationalist genie the colonial powers had called on refused to slip meekly back into the bottle.

President Wilson's war aims also raised the hopes of peoples under imperial rule. In January 1918 Wilson proposed his Fourteen Points (see page 836), whose key idea was national self-determination for the peoples of Europe and the Ottoman Empire. Wilson also recommended that in all colonial questions "the interests of native populations be given equal weight with the desires of European governments," and he seemed to call for national self-rule. This subversive message had enormous appeal for educated Asians, fueling their hopes of freedom.

Military service and Wilsonian self-determination also fired the hopes of some Africans and some visionary African American supporters of African freedom. The First World War, however, had less impact on European imperialism in sub-Saharan Africa than in Asia and the Arab world. For sub-Saharan Africa, the Great Depression and the Second World War were much more influential in the growth of nationalist movements (see pages 1000–1004).

After winning the war, the Allies tried to re-establish or increase their political and economic domination in Asia and Africa. Although fatally weakened, Western imperialism remained very much alive in 1918, partly because President Wilson was no revolutionary. At the Versailles Peace Conference he compromised on colonial questions in order to achieve some of his European goals and the creation of the League of Nations. Also, Allied statesmen and ordinary French and British citizens quite rightly believed their colonial empires had contributed to their ultimate victory over the Central Powers. They would not give up such valuable possessions voluntarily. If pressed, Europeans said their administration was preparing colonial subjects for eventual self-rule, but only in the distant future.

The compromise at Versailles between Wilson's vague, moralistic idealism and the European preoccupation with "good administration" was a system of League of Nations mandates over Germany's former colonies and the old Ottoman Empire. Article 22 of the League of Nations Covenant, which was part of the Treaty of Versailles, assigned territories "inhabited by peoples incapable of governing themselves" to various "developed nations." "The well-being and development of such peoples" was declared "a sacred trust of civilization." The **Permanent Mandates Commission,** whose members came from European countries with colonies, was created to oversee the developed nations' fulfillment of their international responsibility. Thus the League elaborated a new principle—development toward the eventual goal of self-government—but left its implementation to the colonial powers themselves.

The mandates system demonstrated that Europe was determined to maintain its imperial power and influence, leaving patriots throughout Asia bitterly disappointed after the First World War. They saw France, Great Britain, and other nations—industrialized Japan was the only Asian state to obtain mandates—grabbing Germany's colonies as spoils of war and extending the existing system of colonial rule in Muslim North Africa into the territories of the old Ottoman Empire. Yet Asian patriots did not give up. They preached national self-determination and struggled to build mass movements capable of achieving freedom and independence.

In this struggle Asian nationalists were encouraged by Soviet communism. After seizing power in 1917, Lenin declared that the Asian inhabitants of the new Soviet Union were complete equals of the Russians with a right to their own development. (In actuality this equality hardly existed, but the propaganda was effective nonetheless.) The Communists also denounced European and American imperialism and

Chronology

1914–1918 World War I

1915 Japan seizes German holdings in China and expands into southern Manchuria

1916 Sykes-Picot Agreement divides Ottoman Empire between Britain and France

1916–1917 Arab revolt against Turkish rule grows

1917 Balfour Declaration establishes Jewish homeland in Palestine

1919 Amritsar Massacre in India; May Fourth Movement in China; Treaty of Versailles

1920 Faisal proclaimed king of Syria but quickly deposed by French, who establish their mandate in Syria

1920s New Culture Movement challenges traditional Chinese values

1920s–1930s Large numbers of Jews immigrate to Palestine; Hebrew becomes common language there

1923 Sun Yatsen allies Nationalist Party with Chinese Communists; Kita Ikki advocates ultranationalism in Japan

1923–1938 Mustafa Kemal imposes Western reforms to modernize and secularize Turkey

1925–1941 Reign of Reza Shah Pahlavi in Iran

1927 Jiang Jieshi, leader of Nationalist Party, purges his Communist allies

1930 Gandhi leads Indians on march to the sea to protest the British salt tax

1931 Japan occupies Manchuria

1932 Iraq gains independence in return for military alliance with Great Britain

1934 Mao leads Chinese Communists on Long March; Philippines gain self-governing commonwealth status from United States

1935 Turkish National Assembly introduces family names on European model; Mustafa Kemal granted the surname Atatürk

1937 Japanese militarists launch general attack on China; Rape of Nanjing

Permanent Mandates Commission *A commission created by the League of Nations to oversee the developed nations' fulfillment of their international responsibility.*

pledged to support revolutionary movements in all colonial countries, even when they were primarily movements of national independence led by "middle-class" intellectuals instead of by revolutionary workers. Foreign political and economic exploitation was the immediate enemy, they said, and socialist revolution could wait until Western imperialism had been defeated. The example, ideology, and support of Soviet communism exerted a powerful influence in the 1920s and 1930s, particularly in China and French Indochina.

Nationalism's appeal in Asia was not confined to territories under direct European rule. The extraordinary growth of international trade after 1850 had drawn millions of Asian peasants and shopkeepers into the Western-dominated world economy, disrupting local markets and often creating hostility toward European businessmen. Moreover, Europe and the United States had forced even the most solid Asian states, China and Japan, to accept unequal treaties and humiliating limitations on their sovereignty. Thus the nationalist promise of genuine economic independence and true political equality with the West appealed as powerfully in old but weak states like China as in colonial territories like British India.

Finally, as in Russia after the Crimean War or in Japan after the Meiji Restoration, the nationalist creed after World War I went hand in hand with acceptance of modernization by the educated elites. Modernization promised changes that would enable old societies to compete effectively with the world's leading nations.

THE MIDDLE EAST

How did the collapse of the Ottoman Empire in World War I shape the history of the Middle East for the rest of the century?

The most flagrant attempt to expand Western imperialism occurred in the Middle East, or, more accurately, Southwest Asia—the vast expanse that stretches eastward from the Suez Canal and Turkey's Mediterranean shores across the Tigris-Euphrates Valley and the Iranian Plateau to the Arabian Sea and the Indus Valley. There the

● **Prince Faisal and His British Allies** On board a British warship on route to the Versailles Peace Conference in 1919, Prince Faisal is flanked on his right by the British officer T. E. Lawrence—popularly known as Lawrence of Arabia because of his daring campaign against the Turks. Faisal failed to win political independence for the Arabs, as the British backed away from the vague pro-Arab promises they had made during the war. *(Rowley Atterbury)*

British and the French successfully encouraged an Arab revolt in 1916 and destroyed the Ottoman Empire. Europeans then sought to replace Turks as principal rulers throughout the region, even in Turkey itself. Turkish, Arab, and Iranian nationalists, as well as Jewish nationalists arriving from Europe, reacted violently. They struggled to win dignity and nationhood, and as the Europeans were forced to make concessions, they sometimes came into sharp conflict with each other, most notably in Palestine.

The First World War and the Arab Revolt

Long subject to European pressure, the Ottoman Empire failed to reform and modernize in the late nineteenth century (see pages 726–729). Declining international stature and domestic tyranny led to revolutionary activity among idealistic exiles and young army officers who wanted to seize power and save the Ottoman state. These patriots, the so-called **Young Turks,** succeeded in the 1908 revolution, and subsequently they were determined to hold together the remnants of the vast multiethnic empire. Defeated by Bulgaria, Serbia, and Greece in the Balkan War of 1912, and stripped of practically all territory in Europe, the Young Turks redoubled their efforts in Southwest Asia. The most important of their possessions were Syria—consisting of modern-day Lebanon, Syria, Israel, and Jordan—and Iraq. The Ottoman Turks also claimed the Arabian peninsula but exercised only loose control there.

Young Turks *Idealistic Turkish exiles in Europe and young army officers in Istanbul who seized power in the revolution of 1908 and helped pave the way for the birth of modern secular Turkey.*

For centuries the largely Arabic populations of Syria and Iraq had been tied to their Ottoman rulers by their common faith in Islam (though there were Christian Arabs as well). Yet beneath the surface, ethnic and linguistic tensions simmered between Turks and Arabs, who were as different as Chinese and Japanese.

Young Turk actions after 1908 made the embryonic "Arab movement" a reality. The majority of Young Turks promoted a narrow Turkish nationalism. They further centralized the Ottoman Empire and extended the sway of the Turkish language, culture, and race. In 1909 the Turkish government brutally slaughtered thousands of Armenian Christians, a prelude to the wholesale massacre of more than a million Armenians during the First World War. Meanwhile, Arab discontent grew.

Primary Source: Letter from Turkey, Summer 1915 *Read an eyewitness account of the Armenian genocide, by a U.S. missionary from Massachusetts.*

In late 1914 the Turks willingly joined forces with Germany and Austria-Hungary. The Young Turks were pro-German because the Germans had helped reform the Ottoman armies before the war and had built important railroads, like the one to Baghdad. Alliance with Germany permitted the Turks to renounce the limitations on Ottoman sovereignty that the Europeans had imposed in the nineteenth century and also to settle old scores with Russia, the Turks' historic enemy.

The Young Turks' fatal alliance with the Central Powers pulled the entire Middle East into the European civil war and made it truly a global conflict. While Russia attacked the Ottomans in the Caucasus, the British protected their rule in Egypt and the Suez Canal, the lifeline to India. Thus Arab leaders opposed to Ottoman rule suddenly found an unexpected ally in Great Britain. The foremost Arab leader was Hussein ibn-Ali (1856–1931), a direct descendant of the prophet Muhammad. As the **sharif,** or chief magistrate, of Mecca, the Muslim world's holiest city, Hussein governed much of the Ottoman Empire's territory along the Red Sea, an area known as the Hejaz (see Map 28.1). Basically anti-Turkish, Hussein refused the Turkish sultan's call for a holy war against the Triple Entente. His refusal pleased the British, who feared a Muslim revolt in India.

sharif *A term for the chief magistrate of Mecca.*

In 1915 Hussein won vague British commitments for an independent Arab kingdom. When the British attempt to take the Dardanelles and capture Constantinople in 1915 failed miserably, Britain (and Russia) badly needed a new ally on the Ottoman front. In 1916 Hussein revolted against the Turks, proclaiming himself king of the Arabs. Hussein joined forces with the British under T. E. Lawrence, who in 1917 led Arab tribesmen and Indian soldiers in a highly successful guerrilla war against the Turks on the Arabian peninsula. In September 1918 British armies and their Arab allies rolled into Syria and occupied Damascus.

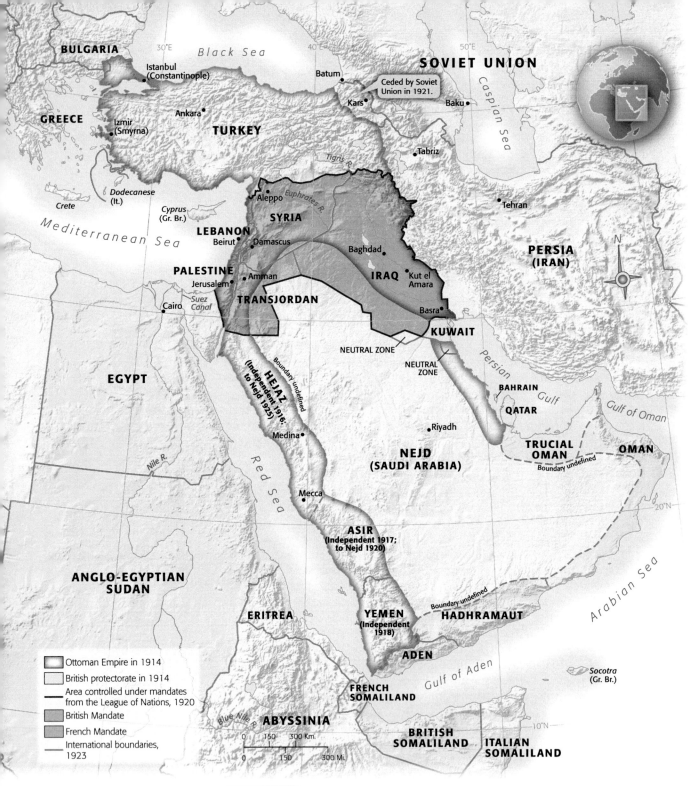

MAP 28.1 **The Partition of the Ottoman Empire, 1914–1923** The decline of the mighty Ottoman Empire began in 1699, when the Habsburgs conquered Hungary, and it accelerated after 1805, when Egypt became virtually independent. By 1914 the Ottoman Turks had been pushed out of the Balkans, and their Arab provinces were on the edge of revolt. That revolt erupted in the First World War and contributed greatly to the Ottomans' defeat. When the Allies then attempted to implement their plans, including independence for the Armenian people, Mustafa Kemal arose to forge in battle the modern Turkish state.

In the Ottoman province of Iraq, Britain occupied Basra in 1914 and captured Baghdad in 1917. Arabs rejoiced, and many patriots expected a large, unified Arab state to rise from the dust of the Ottoman collapse. Within two years, however, Arab nationalists felt bitterly betrayed by Great Britain and its allies, and this bitterness left a legacy of distrust and hatred toward the West.

Arab bitterness was partly directed at secret wartime treaties between Britain and France to divide and rule the old Ottoman Empire. In the 1916 **Sykes-Picot Agreement,** Britain and France secretly agreed that France would receive modern-day Lebanon, Syria, and much of southern Turkey, and Britain would receive Palestine, Jordan, and Iraq. The Sykes-Picot Agreement contradicted British (and later Wilsonian) promises concerning Arab independence after the war, and left Arab nationalists feeling cheated and betrayed.

Sykes-Picot Agreement   *The 1916 secret agreement between Britain and France that divided up the Arab lands of Lebanon, Syria, southern Turkey, Palestine, Jordan, and Iraq.*

A related source of Arab bitterness was Britain's wartime commitment to a Jewish homeland in Palestine. The **Balfour Declaration** of November 1917, made by the British foreign secretary Arthur Balfour, declared that

His Majesty's Government views with favor the establishment in Palestine of a National Home for the Jewish People, and will use their best endeavors to facilitate the achievement

Balfour Declaration   *A 1917 statement by British foreign secretary Arthur Balfour that supported the idea of a Jewish homeland in Palestine.*

● **The Armenian Atrocities**   When in 1915 some Armenians welcomed Russian armies as liberators after years of persecution, the Ottoman government ordered a genocidal mass deportation of its Armenian citizens from their homeland in the empire's eastern provinces. This photo, taken in Kharpert in 1915 by a German businessman from his hotel window, shows Turkish guards marching Armenian men off to a prison, where they will be tortured to death. A million Armenians died from murder, starvation, and disease during World War I. *(Armenian Library and Museum of America Archives)*

Primary Source:

The Balfour Declaration, Stating the British Government's Support for a Jewish Homeland in Palestine

Learn which questions were considered—and which were ignored—as Britain prepared to support the Zionist movement.

of this object, it being clearly understood that nothing shall be done which may prejudice the civil and religious rights of existing non-Jewish communities in Palestine, or the rights and political status enjoyed by Jews in any other country.

As careful reading reveals, the Balfour Declaration made contradictory promises to European Jews and Middle Eastern Arabs.

Some British Cabinet members apparently believed the Balfour Declaration would appeal to German, Austrian, and American Jews and thus help the British war effort. Others sincerely supported the Zionist vision of a Jewish homeland, but also believed that this homeland would then be grateful to Britain and help maintain British control of the Suez Canal.

In 1914 Jews were about 11 percent of the predominantly Arab population in the Ottoman territory that became, under British control, Palestine. The "National Home for the Jewish People" mentioned in the Balfour Declaration implied to the Arabs— and to the Zionist Jews as well—some kind of Jewish state that would be incompatible with majority rule. Moreover, a state founded on religious and ethnic exclusivity was out of keeping with both Islamic and Ottoman tradition, which had historically been more tolerant of religious diversity and minorities than had the Christian monarchs or nation-states in Europe.

Despite strong French objections, Hussein's son Faisal (1885–1933) attended the Versailles Peace Conference, but his efforts to secure Arab independence came to nothing. President Wilson wanted to give the Arab case serious consideration, but the British and the French were determined to rule Syria, Iraq, and Palestine as League of Nations mandates, and accept only the independence of Hussein's kingdom of Hejaz. In response, Arab nationalists met in Damascus as the General Syrian Congress in 1919 and unsuccessfully called again for political independence. (See the feature "Listening to the Past: Arab Political Aspirations in 1919" on pages 874–875.) Brushing aside Arab opposition, the British mandate in Palestine formally incorporated the Balfour Declaration and its commitment to a Jewish national home. In March 1920 Faisal's followers met as the Syrian National Congress and proclaimed Syria independent, with Faisal as king. A similar congress declared Iraq an independent kingdom.

Western reaction to events in Syria and Iraq was swift and decisive. A French army stationed in Lebanon attacked Syria, taking Damascus in July 1920. Faisal fled, and the French took over. Meanwhile, the British put down an uprising in Iraq with bloody fighting and established effective control there. Western imperialism appeared to have replaced Turkish rule in the Middle East (see Map 28.1).

The Turkish Revolution

In November 1918 the Allied fleet entered Constantinople, the Ottoman capital. A young English official wrote that he found the Ottoman Empire "utterly smashed." The Turks were "worn out," and without bitterness they awaited the construction of a "new system."[2] The Allies' new system was blatant imperialism, which proved harsher for the defeated Turks than for the "liberated" Arabs. A treaty forced on the helpless sultan dismembered Turkey and reduced it to a puppet state. Great Britain and France occupied parts of Turkey, and Italy and Greece claimed shares as well. There was a sizable Greek minority in western Turkey, and Greek nationalists cherished the "Great Idea" of a modern Greek empire modeled on long-dead Christian Byzantium. In 1919 Greek armies carried by British ships landed on the Turkish coast at Smyrna, met little resistance from the exhausted Turkish troops, and advanced into the interior. Turkey seemed finished.

But Turkey produced a great leader and revived to become an inspiration to the entire Middle East. Mustafa Kemal (1881–1938), the father of modern Turkey, was a military man, and sympathetic to the Young Turk movement. Kemal had distinguished himself in the Great War by directing the successful defense of the Dardanelles against

British attack. After the armistice, Mustafa Kemal watched with anguish the Allies' aggression and the sultan's cowardice. In early 1919 he began working to unify Turkish resistance.

The sultan, bowing to Allied pressure, initially denounced Kemal, but the cause of national liberation proved more powerful. The catalyst was the Greek invasion and attempted annexation of much of western Turkey. A young Turkish woman described feelings she shared with countless others:

After I learned about the details of the Smyrna occupation by Greek armies, I hardly opened my mouth on any subject except when it concerned the sacred struggle. . . . I suddenly ceased to exist as an individual. I worked, wrote and lived as a unit of that magnificent national madness.[3]

Treaty of Lausanne *The 1923 treaty that ended the Turkish war and recognized the territorial integrity of a truly independent Turkey.*

Refusing to acknowledge the Allied dismemberment of their country, the Turks battled on through 1920 despite staggering defeats. The next year the Greeks advanced almost to Ankara, the nationalist stronghold in central Turkey. There Mustafa Kemal's forces took the offensive and won a great victory. The Greeks and their British allies sued for peace. The resulting **Treaty of Lausanne** (1923) solemnly abolished the hated capitulations, which gave Europeans special privileges in the Ottoman Empire (see page 563), and recognized a truly independent Turkey. Turkey lost only its former Arab provinces.

Mustafa Kemal believed Turkey should modernize and secularize along Western lines. His first moves were political. Drawing on his prestige as a war hero, Kemal called on the National Assembly to depose the sultan and establish a republic. He had himself elected president and moved the capital from cosmopolitan Constantinople (now Istanbul) to Ankara in the Turkish heartland. Kemal savagely crushed the demands for independence of ethnic minorities like the Armenians and the Kurds, but he realistically abandoned all thought of winning back lost Arab territories. He then created a one-party system—partly inspired by the Bolshevik example—in order to work his will.

Kemal's most radical changes pertained to religion and culture. For centuries most believers' intellectual and social activities had been regulated by Islamic religious authorities. Profoundly influenced by the example of western Europe, Mustafa Kemal set out, like the philosophes of the Enlightenment, to limit religious influence in daily affairs. But, like Russia's Peter the Great, he employed dictatorial measures rather than reason to reach his goal. Kemal simply decreed a revolutionary separation of church and state. Secular law codes inspired by European models replaced religious courts. State schools replaced religious schools and taught such secular subjects as science, mathematics, and social sciences.

Mustafa Kemal also struck down many entrenched patterns of behavior. Women, traditionally secluded and inferior to males in Islamic society, received the right to vote. Civil law on a European model, rather than the Islamic code, now governed marriage. Women could seek divorces, and no man could have more than one wife at a time. Men were forbidden to wear the tall red fez of the Ottoman era as headgear; government employees were ordered to wear business suits and felt hats, erasing the visible differences between Muslims and "infidel"

● **Mustafa Kemal** Surnamed Atatürk, meaning "father of the Turks," Mustafa Kemal and his supporters imposed revolutionary changes aimed at modernizing and westernizing Turkish society and the new Turkish government. Dancing here with his adopted daughter at her high-society wedding, Atatürk often appeared in public in elegant European dress—a vivid symbol for the Turkish people of his radical break with traditional Islamic teaching and custom. *(Hulton Archive/Getty Images)*

Europeans. The old Arabic script was replaced with a new Turkish alphabet based on Roman letters, which facilitated massive government efforts to spread literacy after 1928. Finally, in 1935, family names on the European model were introduced. The National Assembly granted Mustafa Kemal the surname **Atatürk,** which means "father of the Turks."

By his death in 1938, Atatürk and his supporters had consolidated their revolution. Government-sponsored industrialization was fostering urban growth and new attitudes, encouraging Turks to embrace business and science. Poverty persisted in rural areas, as did some religious discontent among devout Muslims. But like the Japanese after the Meiji Restoration, the Turkish people had rallied around the nationalist banner to repulse European imperialism and were building a modern secular nation-state.

Iran and Afghanistan

In Persia (renamed Iran in 1935), strong-arm efforts to build a unified modern nation ultimately proved less successful than in Turkey. In the late nineteenth century Iran had also been subject to extreme foreign pressure, which stimulated efforts to reform the government as a means of reviving Islamic civilization. In 1906 a nationalistic coalition of merchants, religious leaders, and intellectuals revolted. The despotic shah was forced to grant a constitution and establish a national assembly, the **Majlis.** Nationalist hopes ran high.

Yet the 1906 Iranian revolution was doomed to failure, largely because of European imperialism. Without consulting Iran, Britain and Russia in 1907 simply divided the country into spheres of influence. Britain's sphere ran along the Persian Gulf; the Russian sphere encompassed the whole northern half of Iran (see Map 28.1). Thereafter Russia intervened constantly. It blocked reforms, occupied cities, and completely dominated the country by 1912. When Russian power collapsed in the Bolshevik Revolution, British armies rushed into the power vacuum. By bribing corrupt Iranians, Great Britain in 1919 negotiated a treaty allowing the installation of British "advisers" in every government department.

The Majlis refused to ratify the treaty, and the blatant attempt to make Iran a British satellite aroused the national spirit. In 1921 reaction against the British brought to power a military dictator, Reza Shah Pahlavi (1877–1944), who proclaimed himself shah in 1925 and ruled until 1941.

Inspired by Turkey's Mustafa Kemal, the patriotic, religiously indifferent Reza Shah had three basic goals: to build a modern nation, to free Iran from foreign domination, and to rule with an iron fist. The challenge was enormous. Iran was a vast, undeveloped country of deserts, mountain barriers, and rudimentary communications. The rural population was mostly poor and illiterate, and among the Persian majority were sizable ethnic minorities with their own aspirations. Furthermore, Iran's powerful religious leaders hated Western (Christian) domination but were no less opposed to a more secular, less Islamic society.

To realize his vision of a strong Iran, the energetic shah created a modern army, built railroads, and encouraged commerce. He won control over ethnic minorities such as the Kurds in the north and Arab tribesmen on the Iraqi border. He reduced the privileges granted to foreigners and raised taxes on the powerful Anglo-Persian Oil Company, which had been founded in 1909 to exploit the first great oil strike in the Middle East. Yet Reza Shah was less successful than Atatürk.

Because the European-educated elite in Iran was smaller than the comparable group in Turkey, the idea of re-creating Persian greatness on the basis of a secularized society attracted relatively few determined supporters. Many powerful religious leaders turned against Reza Shah, and he became increasingly brutal, greedy, and tyrannical, murdering his enemies and lining his pockets. His support of Hitler's Nazi Germany also exposed Iran's tenuous and fragile independence to the impact of European conflicts.

Atatürk *The name bestowed on the Turkish president Mustafa Kemal; it means "father of the Turks."*

Majlis *The national assembly established by the despotic shah of Iran in 1906.*

Primary Source:
The Link Between the Education of Girls and the Advancement of Iranian Society, 1907, 1909
Two articles argue that, if Iran is to become truly "civilized," it must recognize the virtues of educating women.

Afghanistan, meanwhile, was nominally independent in the nineteenth century, but the British imposed political restrictions and constantly meddled in the country's affairs. In 1919 the violently anti-British amir Amanullah (1892–1960) declared a holy war on the British government in India and won complete independence for the first time. Amanullah then decreed revolutionary reforms designed to hurl his primitive country into the twentieth century. The result was tribal and religious revolt, civil war, and retreat from reform. Islam remained both religion and law. A powerful but primitive patriotism enabled Afghanistan to win political independence from the West, but not to build a modern society.

The Arab States and Palestine

French and British mandates established at gunpoint forced Arab nationalists to seek independence by gradual means after 1920. Arab nationalists were indirectly aided by Western taxpayers, who wanted cheap—that is, peaceful—empires. As a result, Arabs won considerable control over local affairs in the mandated states, except Palestine, though the mandates remained European satellites in international and economic affairs.

In Iraq, the wily British chose Faisal, whom the French had deposed in Syria, as king. Faisal obligingly gave British advisers broad behind-the-scenes control. The king also accepted British ownership of Iraq's oil fields, consequently giving the West a stranglehold on the Iraqi economy. Given the severe limitations imposed on him, Faisal (r. 1921–1933) proved to be an able ruler, gaining the support of his people and encouraging moderate reforms. In 1932 he secured Iraqi independence at the price of a restrictive long-term military alliance with Great Britain.

Egypt had been occupied by Great Britain since 1882 (see page 732) and a British protectorate since 1914. Following intense nationalist agitation after the Great War, Great Britain in 1922 proclaimed Egypt formally independent but continued to occupy the country militarily and control its politics. In 1936, the British agreed to restrict their troops to their bases in the Suez Canal Zone.

The French were less compromising in Syria. They practiced a policy of divide-and-rule, carving out a second mandate in Lebanon and generally playing off ethnic and religious minorities against each other. Lebanon eventually became a republic, dominated by a very slender Christian majority and under French protection. Arab nationalists in Syria finally won promises of Syrian independence in 1936 in return for a treaty of friendship with France.

In short, the Arab states gradually freed themselves from Western political mandates but not from the Western military threat or from pervasive Western influence. Of great importance, large Arab landowners and urban merchants increased their wealth and political power after 1918, and they often supported the Western hegemony, from which they benefited greatly. Western control of the newly discovered Arab oil fields helped to convince radical nationalists that economic independence and genuine freedom had not yet been achieved.

Relations between the Arabs and the West were complicated by the tense situation in the British mandate of Palestine, and that situation deteriorated in the interwar years. Both Arabs and Jews denounced the British, who tried unsuccessfully to compromise with both sides. Arab nationalist anger, however, was aimed primarily at Jewish settlers. The key issue was Jewish migration from Europe to Palestine.

Zionism *The movement toward Jewish political nationhood started by Theodor Herzl.*

A small Jewish community had survived in Palestine ever since the dispersal of the Jews in Roman times. But Jewish nationalism, known as **Zionism,** took shape in Europe in the late nineteenth century under the leadership of Theodor Herzl (see page 707). Herzl believed that only a Jewish state could guarantee Jews dignity and security. The Zionist movement encouraged the world's Jews to settle in Palestine, but until 1921 the great majority of Jewish emigrants preferred the United States.

After 1921 the situation changed radically. An isolationist United States drastically limited immigration from eastern Europe, where war and revolution had kindled anti-Semitism. Moreover, the British began honoring the Balfour Declaration despite Arab protests. Thus Jewish immigration to Palestine from turbulent Europe grew rapidly. In the 1930s German and Polish persecution created a mass of Jewish refugees. By 1939 the Jewish population of Palestine had increased almost fivefold since 1914 and accounted for about 30 percent of all inhabitants.

Jewish settlers in Palestine faced formidable difficulties. Although much of the land purchased by the Jewish National Fund was productive, the sellers of such land were often wealthy absentee Arab landowners who cared little for their Arab tenants' welfare. When the new Jewish owners subsequently replaced those age-old Arab tenants with Jewish settlers, Arab farmers and intellectuals burned with a sense of injustice. Moreover, most Jewish immigrants came from urban backgrounds and preferred to establish new cities like Tel Aviv or to live in existing towns, where they competed with the Arabs. The land issue combined with economic and cultural friction to harden Arab protest into hatred. Anti-Jewish riots and even massacres ensued.

The British gradually responded to Arab pressure and tried to slow Jewish immigration. This effort satisfied neither Jews nor Arabs, and by 1938 the two communities were engaged in an undeclared civil war. On the eve of the Second World War, the frustrated British proposed an independent Palestine with the number of Jews permanently limited to only about one-third of the total population. Zionists felt themselves in grave danger.

kibbutz *A Jewish collective farm on which each member shared equally in the work, rewards, and defense of the farm.*

In the face of adversity Jewish settlers from many different countries gradually succeeded in forging a cohesive community. Hebrew, for centuries used only in religious worship, was revived as a living language to bind the Jews in Palestine together. Despite its slow beginnings, rural development achieved often remarkable results. The key unit of agricultural organization was the **kibbutz,** a collective farm on which each member shared equally in the work, rewards, and defense of the farm. An egalitarian socialist ideology also characterized industry, which grew rapidly. By 1939 a new but old nation was emerging in the Middle East.

Reuven Rubin: First Fruits (or First Pioneers) (1923) Whereas Jerusalem was the center of Jewish religious culture and conservative art in the 1920s, the new coastal city of Tel Aviv sprang up secular, and it gloried in avant-garde modern art (see pages 884–886). In this painting Rubin, a leader of Tel Aviv's modernist school, depicts Jewish pioneers in a stark, two-dimensional landscape and conveys an exotic "Garden of Eden" flavor. Arriving from Romania, Rubin was bowled over by Palestine. "The world about me became clear and pure: life was formless, blurred, primitive." *(Reuven Rubin,* First Fruits, *1922, Coll. Rubin Museum, Tel-Aviv, Israel)*

TOWARD SELF-RULE IN INDIA

What role did Gandhi and his campaign of militant nonviolence play in leading India to independence from the British?

The national movement in British India grew out of two interconnected cultures, Hindu and Muslim, which came to see themselves as fundamentally different in rising to challenge British rule. Nowhere has modern nationalism's power both to unify and to divide been more strikingly demonstrated than in India.

Promises and Repression (1914–1919)

Indian nationalism had emerged in the late nineteenth century (see page 753), and when the First World War began, the British feared revolt. Instead, Indians supported the war effort. About 1.2 million Indian soldiers and laborers voluntarily served in Europe, Africa, and the Middle East. The British government in India and the native Indian princes sent large supplies of food, money, and ammunition. In return, the British opened more good government jobs to Indians and made other minor concessions.

As the war in distant Europe ground on, however, inflation, high taxes, food shortages, and a terrible influenza epidemic created widespread suffering and discontent. The prewar nationalist movement revived, stronger than ever, and moderates and radicals in the Indian National Congress joined forces. Moreover, in 1916 Hindu leaders in the Congress Party hammered out an alliance—the **Lucknow Pact**—with India's Muslim League. The League was founded in 1906 to uphold Muslim

Lucknow Pact *A 1916 alliance between Hindus leading the Indian National Congress and the Muslim League.*

Jallianwala Bagh Massacre This is a highly dramatized painting of the massacre in the Jallian-wala Bagh (Garden) in Amritsar on April 13, 1919. Having banned gatherings of five persons or more, General Dyer ordered the fifty British Indian Army troops under his command to open fire on unarmed men, women, and children who had gathered on a Sunday to celebrate the Sikh festival of *Baisakhi*. The soldiers fired 1,650 rounds of ammunition (until they ran out of bullets), killing nearly 400 and wounding some 1,100 others. The terror-stricken people had no means of escape for the Indian troops blocked the only exit from the Bagh. *(Courtesy, Indialog Publications Pvt. Ltd., Delhi. Photo: Amrit and Rabindra Dingh, Fine Arts, U.K.)*

> **Primary Source:**
> **An Indian Nationalist Condemns the British Empire**
> *In this excerpt from a speech, an Indian nationalist and feminist accuses the British Empire of betraying its ideals and losing its soul.*

interests, as, under British rule, the once-dominant Muslim minority had fallen behind the Hindu majority. The Lucknow Pact forged a powerful united front of Hindus and Muslims and called for putting India on equal footing with self-governing British dominions like Canada, Australia, and New Zealand.

The British response was contradictory. On the one hand, the secretary of state for India made the unprecedented announcement in August 1917 that British policy in India called for the "gradual development of self-governing institutions and the progressive realization of responsible government." In late 1919 the British established a dual administration: part Indian and elected, part British and authoritarian. Such uncontroversial activities as agriculture and health were transferred from British to Indian officials who were accountable to elected provincial assemblies. More sensitive matters like taxes, police, and the courts remained solely in British hands.

Old-fashioned authoritarian rule seriously undermined the positive impact of this reform. Despite the unanimous opposition of the elected Indian members, the British in 1919 rammed the repressive Rowlatt Acts through India's Imperial Legislative Council. These acts indefinitely extended wartime "emergency measures" designed to curb unrest and root out "conspiracy." The result was a wave of rioting across India.

Under these tense conditions a crowd of some ten thousand gathered to celebrate a Sikh religious festival in an enclosed square in the Sikh holy city of Amritsar in the northern Punjab province. Unknown to the crowd, the local English commander, General Reginald Dyer, had banned all public meetings that very day. Dyer marched his native Gurkha troops into the square and, without warning, ordered them to fire into the unarmed mass at point-blank range until the ammunition ran out. Offical British records of the Amritsar Massacre list 379 killed and 1,137 wounded, but these figures remain hotly contested for being too low. India stood on the verge of more violence and repression and, sooner or later, terrorism and guerrilla war. That India took a different path to national liberation was due largely to Mohandas "Mahatma" Gandhi (1869–1948), the most influential Indian of modern times.

The Roots of Militant Nonviolence

By the time of Gandhi's birth in 1869, the Indian subcontinent was firmly controlled by the British. Part of the country was ruled directly by British (and subordinate Indian) officials, answerable to the British Parliament in London. In each of the so-called protected states, the native prince—usually known as the *maharaja*—remained the titular ruler, although he was bound to the British by unequal treaties and had to accept the "advice" of the British resident assigned to his court.

Gandhi grew up in one of the small protected states north of Bombay. Gandhi's father was the well-to-do head of a large extended family. Gandhi's mother was devoted but undogmatic in religious matters, and she exercised a strong influence on her son.

After his father's death, Gandhi went to study law in England. After passing the English bar and returning to India, he decided in 1893 to try a case for some wealthy Indian merchants in South Africa. It was a momentous decision.

In South Africa, Gandhi took up the plight of the expatriate Indian community. White plantation owners there imported poor Indians as indentured laborers on five-year renewable contracts. When some Indians completed their terms and remained in South Africa as free persons and economic competitors, the Dutch and British settlers passed brutally discriminatory laws. Poor Indians had to work on plantations or return to India; rich Indians lost the vote. Gandhi undertook his countrymen's legal defense, and in 1896 a white mob almost lynched the "coolie lawyer."

Meanwhile, Gandhi was searching for a spiritual theory of social action. He studied Hindu and Christian teachings, and gradually developed a weapon for the weak that he called **Satyagraha.** Gandhi conceived of Satyagraha, loosely translated as "Soul Force," as a means of striving for truth and social justice through love, suffering, and conversion of the oppressor. Its tactic is active nonviolent resistance.

As the undisputed leader of South Africa's Indians before the First World War, Gandhi put his philosophy into action. When South Africa's white government severely restricted Asian immigration and internal freedom of movement, Gandhi organized a nonviolent mass resistance campaign. Thousands of Indian men and women marched in peaceful protest and withstood beatings, arrest, and imprisonment.

In 1914, South Africa's exasperated whites agreed to many of the Indians' demands. They passed a law abolishing discriminatory taxes on Indian traders, recognizing the legality of non-Christian marriages, and permitting the continued immigration of free Indians. Satyagraha—militant nonviolence in pursuit of social justice—proved itself a powerful force in Gandhi's hands.

Satyagraha *Loosely translated as "Soul Force," which Gandhi believed was the means of striving for truth and social justice through love, suffering, and conversion of the oppressor.*

Gandhi Leads the Way

In 1915 Gandhi returned to India. His reputation had preceded him: the masses hailed him as a *Mahatma,* or "Great Soul"—a Hindu title of veneration for a man of great knowledge and humanity. Drawing on his South African experience, Gandhi in 1920 launched a national campaign of nonviolent resistance to British rule. Denouncing British injustice, he urged his countrymen to boycott British goods, jobs, and honors. He told peasants not to pay taxes or buy English cloth or the heavily taxed liquor. Gandhi electrified the people, initiating a revolution in Indian politics.

The nationalist movement had previously touched only the tiny, prosperous, Western-educated elite. Now both the illiterate masses of village India and the educated classes

● **Gandhi Arrives in Delhi, October 1939** A small frail man, Gandhi possessed enormous courage and determination. His campaign of nonviolent resistance to British rule inspired the Indian masses and mobilized a nation. Here he arrives for talks with the British viceroy after the outbreak of World War II. *(Corbis)*

heard Gandhi's call for militant nonviolent resistance. It particularly appealed to the masses of Hindus who were not members of the warrior caste or the so-called military races and who were traditionally passive and nonviolent. The British had regarded ordinary Hindus as cowards. Gandhi told them that they could be courageous and even morally superior:

What do you think? Wherein is courage required—in blowing others to pieces from behind a cannon, or with a smiling face to approach a cannon and be blown to pieces? Who is the true warrior—he who keeps death always as a bosom-friend, or he who controls the death of others? Believe me that a man devoid of courage and manhood can never be a passive resister.[4]

Gandhi made Congress into a mass political party, welcoming members from every ethnic group and cooperating closely with the Muslim minority.

In 1922 some Indian resisters turned to violence, murdering twenty-two policemen. Savage riots broke out, and Gandhi abruptly called off his campaign. Arrested for fomenting rebellion, Gandhi told the British judge that he had committed "a Himalayan blunder to believe that India had accepted nonviolence." Released from prison after two years, Gandhi set up a commune, established a national newspaper, and set out to reform Indian society and improve the lot of the poor. He welcomed the outcaste untouchables, worked to help child widows, and promoted native cottage industry production. For Gandhi moral improvement, social progress, and the national movement went hand in hand. Above all, Gandhi nurtured national identity, self-respect, and courage in India's people.

The 1920–1922 resistance campaign left the British severely shaken, but the commission formed in 1927 to consider further steps toward self-rule included no Indian members. Indian resentment was intense. In 1929 the radical nationalists, led by the able and aristocratic Jawaharlal Nehru (1889–1964), pushed through the National Congress a resolution calling for virtual independence within a year. The British stiffened, and Indian radicals talked of a bloody showdown.

Into this tense situation Gandhi masterfully reasserted his leadership, taking a hard line toward the British, but insisting on nonviolent methods. He organized a massive resistance campaign against the hated salt tax, which affected every Indian family. Gandhi himself led fifty thousand people in a spectacular march to the sea where he made salt in defiance of the law. A later demonstration at the British-run Dhrasana salt works resulted in many of the 2,500 nonviolent marchers being beaten senseless by policemen in a brutal and well-publicized encounter. Over the next months the British arrested Gandhi and sixty thousand other protesters for making and distributing salt. In 1931 the frustrated and unnerved British released Gandhi from jail and sat down to negotiate with him, as an equal, over Indian self-rule. Negotiations resulted in a new constitution in 1935, which greatly strengthened India's parliamentary representative institutions. It was practically a blueprint for independence, which came quickly after World War II.

Despite his best efforts, Gandhi failed to heal a widening split between Hindus and Muslims. Indian nationalism, based largely on Hindu symbols and customs, increasingly disturbed the Muslim minority. Tempers mounted and both sides committed atrocities. By the late 1930s Muslim League leaders were calling for the creation of a Muslim nation in British India, a "Pakistan" or "land of the pure." As in Palestine, the rise of conflicting nationalisms in India would lead to tragedy (see pages 990–994).

• • • • • • • • • • • • • •

TURMOIL IN EAST ASIA

Why did some of the Asian nationalist movements come into brutal conflict?

Because of the efforts of the Meiji reformers, nationalism and modernization were well developed in Japan by 1914. Japan competed politically and economically with the world's leading nations, building its own empire and proclaiming its special mission in Asia. China lagged far behind, but after 1912 the pace of nationalist development there began to quicken.

In the 1920s the Chinese nationalist movement managed to win a large measure of political independence from the imperialist West and promoted extensive modernization. These achievements were soon undermined, however, by internal conflict and war with an expanding Japan. Nationalism also flourished elsewhere in Asia, scoring a major victory in the Philippine Islands.

The Rise of Nationalist China

The 1911 Revolution, which overthrew the Qing Dynasty (see page 763), opened an era of unprecedented change for Chinese society. Before the revolution many progressive Chinese realized that fundamental technological and political reforms were necessary to save the Chinese state, but most hoped to preserve the traditional core of Chinese civilization and culture. The fall of the ancient dynastic system shattered such hopes. If the emperor himself was no longer sacred, what was?

The central figure in the revolution was a crafty old military man, Yuan Shigai (Yüan Shih-k'ai). Called out of retirement to save the dynasty, Yuan (1859–1916) betrayed the Manchus and convinced the revolutionaries that he could unite the country peacefully and prevent foreign intervention. Once elected president of the republic, however, Yuan concentrated on building his own power. In 1913 he used military force to dissolve China's parliament and ruled as a dictator. China's first modern revolution had failed.

The extent of the failure became apparent only after Yuan's death in 1916. The central government in Beijing almost disintegrated. For more than a decade power resided in a multitude of local military leaders, the so-called warlords. Their wars, taxes, and corruption created terrible suffering.

● **Students Demonstrating in Tiananmen Square, Beijing, Summer 1919** The news that the Versailles Peace Conference left China's Shandong Peninsula in Japanese hands brought an explosion of student protest on May 4, 1919. Student demonstrations in the capital's historic Tiananmen Square continued through June, as the May Fourth Movement against foreign domination took root and grew. *(Photo from Kautz Family YMCA Archives. Reproduced with permission.)*

May Fourth Movement *A nationalist movement against foreign imperialists; it began as a student protest against the decision of the Versailles Peace Conference to leave the Shandong Peninsula in the hands of Japan.*

Foreign imperialism intensified the agony of warlordism. Although China declared its neutrality in 1914, Japan used the Great War as an opportunity to seize Germany's holdings on the Shandong (Shantung) Peninsula and in 1915 forced China to accept Japanese control of Shandong and southern Manchuria (see Map 28.2). Japan's expansion angered China's growing middle class and enraged China's young patriots. On May 4, 1919, five thousand students in Beijing exploded against the decision of the Versailles Peace Conference to leave the Shandong Peninsula in Japanese hands. This famous incident launched the **May Fourth Movement,** which opposed both foreign domination and warlord government.

The May Fourth Movement and the anti-imperialism of Bolshevik Russia renewed Chinese nationalist hopes. In 1923 Sun Yatsen (1866–1925) decided to ally his Nationalist Party, or Guomindang (Kuomintang), with the Communist Third International and the newly formed Chinese Communist Party. The result was the first of many so-called national liberation fronts, in keeping with Lenin's blueprint for temporarily uniting all anticonservative, anti-imperialist forces in a common revolutionary struggle.

Sun, however, was no Communist. In his *Three Principles of the People,* elaborating on the official Nationalist Party ideology—nationalism, democracy, and people's livelihood—nationalism remained of prime importance:

Compared to the other peoples of the world we have the greatest population and our civilization is four thousand years old; we should be advancing in the front rank with the nations of Europe and America. But the Chinese people have only family and clan solidarity, they do not have national spirit. . . . If we do not earnestly espouse nationalism and weld together our four hundred million people into a strong nation, there is a danger of China's

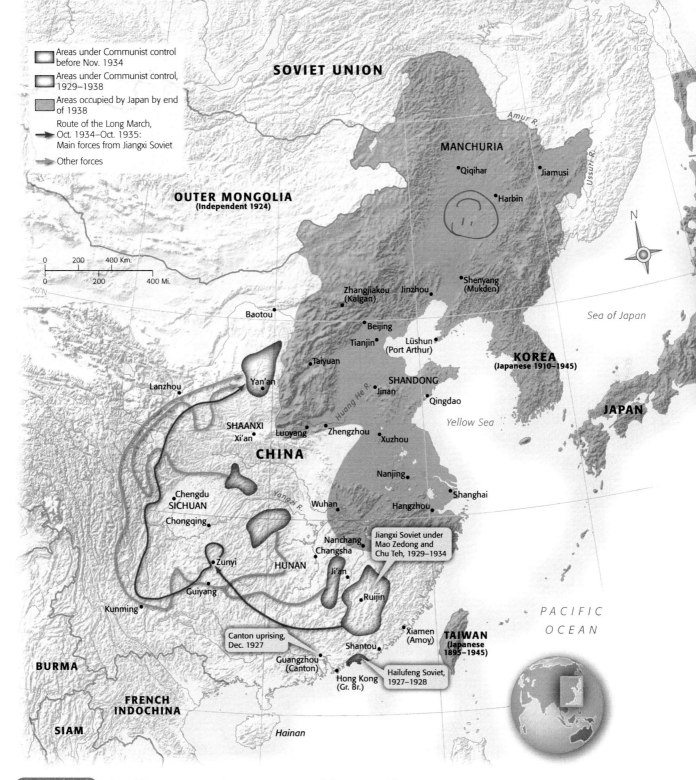

Legend:
- Areas under Communist control before Nov. 1934
- Areas under Communist control, 1929–1938
- Areas occupied by Japan by end of 1938
- Route of the Long March, Oct. 1934–Oct. 1935: Main forces from Jiangxi Soviet
- Other forces

SOVIET UNION

MANCHURIA

- Qiqihar
- Jiamusi
- Harbin

OUTER MONGOLIA
(Independent 1924)

- Shenyang (Mukden)
- Zhangjiakou (Kalgan)
- Jinzhou
- Baotou
- Beijing
- Tianjin
- Lüshun (Port Arthur)
- Taiyuan

KOREA
(Japanese 1910–1945)

- Lanzhou
- Yan'an
- SHAANXI
- Xi'an
- Luoyang
- Zhengzhou
- SHANDONG
- Jinan
- Qingdao

CHINA

Sea of Japan

JAPAN

- Xuzhou
- Nanjing
- Shanghai
- Hangzhou

Yellow Sea

- Chengdu
- SICHUAN
- Chongqing
- Wuhan

0   200   400 Km.
0   200   400 Mi.

- Nanchang
- Changsha
- Zunyi
- HUNAN
- Ji'an

Jiangxi Soviet under Mao Zedong and Chu Teh, 1929–1934

- Guiyang
- Ruijin
- Kunming

PACIFIC OCEAN

Canton uprising, Dec. 1927

- Xiamen (Amoy)
- Shantou
- Guangzhou (Canton)
- Hong Kong (Gr. Br.)

TAIWAN
(Japanese 1895–1945)

Hailufeng Soviet, 1927–1928

BURMA

FRENCH INDOCHINA

SIAM

Hainan

MAP 28.2 **The Chinese Communist Movement and the War with Japan, 1927–1938** After urban uprisings ordered by Stalin failed in 1927, Mao Zedong succeeded in forming a self-governing Communist soviet in mountainous southern China. Relentless Nationalist attacks between 1930 and 1934 finally forced the Long March to Yenan, where the Communists were well positioned for guerrilla war against the Japanese.

being lost and our people being destroyed. If we wish to avert this catastrophe, we must espouse nationalism and bring this national spirit to the salvation of the country.[5]

Democracy, in contrast, had a less exalted meaning. Sun equated it with firm rule by the Nationalists, who would improve people's lives through land reform and welfare measures.

Sun planned to use the Nationalist Party's revolutionary army to crush the warlords and reunite China under a strong central government. When Sun unexpectedly died in 1925, Jiang Jieshi (Chiang Kai-shek), the young Japanese-educated director of the party's army training school, took his place. In 1926 and 1927 Jiang (1887–1975) led Nationalist armies in a successful attack on warlord governments in central and northern China. In 1928 the Nationalists established a new capital at Nanjing (Nanking). Foreign states recognized the Nanjing government, and superficial observers believed China to be truly reunified.

In fact, national unification was only skin-deep. China remained a vast agricultural country plagued by foreign concessions, regional differences, and a lack of modern communications. Moreover, the uneasy alliance between the Nationalist Party and the Chinese Communist Party had turned into a bitter, deadly rivalry. Justifiably fearful of Communist subversion of the Nationalist government, Jiang decided in April 1927 to liquidate his left-wing "allies" in a bloody purge. Chinese Communists went into hiding and vowed revenge.

China's Intellectual Revolution

New Culture Movement *An intellectual revolution, sometimes called the Chinese Renaissance, that attacked traditional Chinese, particularly Confucian, culture and promoted Western ideas of science, democracy, and individualism, from around 1916 to 1923.*

Nationalism was the most powerful idea in China between 1911 and 1929, but it was only one aspect of a complex intellectual revolution, generally known as the **New Culture Movement,** that hammered at traditional Chinese thought and custom, advocated cultural renaissance, and pushed China into the modern world.

The New Culture Movement was founded by young Western-oriented intellectuals in Beijing during the May Fourth era. These intellectuals fiercely attacked China's ancient Confucian ethics, which subordinated subjects to rulers, sons to fathers, and wives to husbands. As modernists, they provocatively advocated new and anti-Confucian virtues: individualism, democratic equality, and the critical scientific method. They also promoted the use of simple, understandable written language as a means to clear thinking and mass education. China, they said, needed a whole new culture, a radically different worldview.

**Primary Source:
Our Attitude Toward Modern Civilization of the West**
A Chinese professor rejects the idea that Eastern civilization is more "spiritual" than the "materialistic" West.

Many intellectuals thought the radical worldview China needed was Marxian socialism. It too was Western in origin, "scientific" in approach, and materialist in its denial of religious belief and Confucian family ethics. But while liberalism and individualism reflected the bewildering range of Western thought since the Enlightenment, Marxian socialism offered the certainty of a single all-encompassing creed. As one young Communist intellectual exclaimed, "I am now able to impose order on all the ideas which I could not reconcile; I have found the key to all the problems which appeared to me self-contradictory and insoluble."[6]

Though undeniably Western, Marxism provided a means of criticizing Western dominance, thereby salving Chinese pride. Chinese Communists could blame China's pitiful weakness on rapacious foreign capitalistic imperialism. Thus Marxism, as modified by Lenin and applied by the Bolsheviks in the Soviet Union, appeared as a means of catching up with the hated but envied West. For Chinese believers, it promised salvation soon.

Chinese Communists could and did interpret Marxism-Leninism to appeal to the masses—the peasants. Mao Zedong (Mao Tse-tung) in particular quickly recognized the impoverished Chinese peasantry's enormous revolutionary potential. A member of a prosperous, hard-working peasant family, Mao (1893–1976) converted to Marx-

● **Mao Zedong** Adapting Marxian theory to Chinese reality, Mao concentrated on the revolutionary potential of the peasantry. In this propagandistic painting, typical of Chinese art after the Communist takeover in 1949, the young Mao speaks to a group of worshipful peasant soldiers on the Long March, while Lenin and Marx look down with approval. *(Library of Congress)*

ian socialism in 1918. He began his revolutionary career as an urban labor organizer. In 1925 protest strikes by Chinese textile workers against their Japanese employers unexpectedly spread from the big coastal cities to rural China, prompting Mao to reconsider the peasants. Investigating the rapid growth of radical peasant associations in Hunan province, Mao argued passionately in a 1927 report that

the force of the peasantry is like that of the raging winds and driving rain. It is rapidly increasing in violence. No force can stand in its way. The peasantry will tear apart all nets which bind it and hasten along the road to liberation. They will bury beneath them all forces of imperialism, militarism, corrupt officialdom, village bosses and evil gentry.[7]

Mao's first experiment in peasant revolt—the Autumn Harvest Uprising of September 1927—was not successful, but Mao learned quickly. He advocated equal distribution of land and broke up his forces into small guerrilla groups. After 1928 he and his supporters built up a self-governing Communist soviet, centered at Ruijin (Juichin) in southeastern China, and dug in against Nationalist attacks.

China's intellectual revolution also stimulated profound changes in popular culture and family life. After the 1911 Revolution Chinese women enjoyed increasingly greater freedom and equality. Foot binding was outlawed and attacked as cruel and uncivilized. Arranged marriages and polygamy declined. Women gradually gained unprecedented educational and economic opportunities. Thus rising nationalism and the intellectual revolution interacted with monumental changes in Chinese family life. (See the feature "Individuals in Society: Ning Lao, a Chinese Working Woman.")

From Liberalism to Ultranationalism in Japan

The efforts of the Meiji reformers (see page 764) to build a powerful nationalistic state and resist Western imperialism were spectacularly successful and deeply impressed Japan's fellow Asians. The Japanese, alone among Asia's peoples, had mastered modern industrial technology by 1910 and fought victorious wars against both China and Russia. The First World War brought more triumphs. In 1915 Japan easily seized Germany's Asian holdings and held on to most of them as League of Nations mandates. The Japanese economy expanded enormously. Profits soared as Japan won new markets that wartime Europe could no longer supply.

In the early 1920s Japan seemed to make further progress on all fronts. Most Japanese nationalists believed that Japan had a semidivine mission to enlighten and protect Asia, but some were convinced that they could achieve their goal peacefully. In 1922 Japan signed a naval arms limitation treaty with the Western powers and returned some of its control over the Shandong Peninsula to China. These conciliatory moves reduced tensions in East Asia. At home Japan seemed headed toward genuine democracy. The electorate expanded twelvefold between 1918 and 1925 as all males over

● **Japanese Suffragists** In the 1920s Japanese women pressed for political emancipation in demonstrations like this one, but they did not receive the right to vote until 1946. Like these suffragists, some young women adopted Western fashions. Most workers in modern Japanese textile factories were also women. *(Time Life Pictures/Getty Images)*

Ning Lao, a Chinese Working Woman

The voice of the poor and uneducated is often muffled in history. Thus *A Daughter of Han,* a rare autobiography of an illiterate working woman as told to an American friend, offers unforgettable insights into the evolution of ordinary Chinese life and family relations.

Ning Lao was born in 1867 to poor parents in the northern city of Penglai on the Shandong Peninsula. Her foot binding was delayed to age nine, "since I loved so much to run and play." When the bandages were finally drawn tight, "my feet hurt so much that for two years I had to crawl on my knees."* Her arranged marriage at age fourteen was a disaster. She found that her husband was a drug addict ("in those days everyone took opium to some extent") who sold everything to pay for his habit. Yet "there was no freedom then for women," and "it was no light thing for a woman to leave her house" and husband. Thus Ning Lao endured her situation until her husband sold their four-year-old daughter to buy opium. Taking her remaining baby daughter, she fled.

Taking off her foot bandages, Ning Lao became a beggar. Her feet began to spread, quite improperly, but she walked without pain. And the beggar's life was "not the hardest one," she thought, for a beggar woman could go where she pleased. To care better for her child, Ning Lao became a servant and a cook in prosperous households. Some of her mistresses were concubines (secondary wives taken by rich men in middle age), and she concluded that concubinage resulted in nothing but quarrels and heartache. Hot tempered and quick to take offense and leave an employer, the hard-working woman always found a new job quickly. In time she became a peddler of luxury goods to wealthy women confined to their homes.

The two unshakable values that buoyed Ning Lao were a tough, fatalistic acceptance of life—"Only fortune that comes of itself will come. There is no use to seek for it"—and devotion to her family. She eventually returned to her husband, who had mellowed, seldom took opium, and was "good" in those years. "But I did not miss him when he died. I had

The tough and resilient Ning Lao (right) with Ida Pruitt. (Reproduced with permission of Eileen Hsu-Belzer)

my newborn son and I was happy. My house was established. . . . Truly all my life I spent thinking of my family." Her lifelong devotion was reciprocated by her son and granddaughter, who cared for her well in her old age.

Ning Lao's remarkable life story encompasses both old and new Chinese attitudes toward family life. Her son moved to the capital city of Beijing, worked in an office, and had only one wife. Her granddaughter, Su Teh, studied in missionary schools and became a college teacher and a determined foe of arranged marriages. She personified the trend toward greater freedom for Chinese women.

Generational differences also highlighted changing political attitudes. When the Japanese invaded China and occupied Beijing in 1937, Ning Lao thought that "perhaps the Mandate of Heaven had passed to the Japanese . . . and we should listen to them as our new masters." Her nationalistic granddaughter disagreed. She urged resistance and the creation of a new China, where the people governed themselves. Leaving to join the guerrillas in 1938, Su Teh gave her savings to her family and promised to continue to help them. One must be good to one's family, she said, but one must also work for the country.

Questions for Analysis

1. Compare the lives of Ning Lao and her granddaughter. In what ways were they different and similar?

2. In a broader historical perspective, what do you find most significant about Ning Lao's account of her life? Why?

*Ida Pruitt, *A Daughter of Han: The Autobiography of a Chinese Working Woman* (New Haven, Conn.: Yale University Press, 1945), p. 22. Other quotations are from pages 83, 62, 71, 182, 166, 235, and 246.

twenty-five won the vote. Two-party competition was intense. Japanese living standards were the highest in Asia. Literacy was universal.

Japan's remarkable rise, however, was accompanied by serious problems. Japan had a rapidly growing population, but scarce natural resources. As early as the 1920s Japan was exporting manufactured goods in order to pay for imports of food and essential raw materials. Deeply enmeshed in world trade, Japan was vulnerable to every boom and bust. These economic realities broadened support for Japan's colonial empire. Before World War I, Japanese leaders saw colonial expansion primarily in terms of international prestige and national defense. They believed that control of Taiwan, Korea, and Manchuria provided an essential "outer ring of defense" to protect the home islands from Russian attack and Anglo-American imperialism. Now, in the 1920s, Japan's colonies also seemed essential for markets, raw materials, and economic growth.

Japan's rapid industrial development also created an imbalanced "dualistic" economy. The modern sector consisted of a handful of giant conglomerate firms, the **zaibatsu,** or "financial combines." Zaibatsu firms like Mitsubishi employed thousands of workers and owned banks, mines, steel mills, cotton factories, shipyards, and trading companies, all of them closely interrelated. Zaibatsu firms wielded enormous economic power and dominated the other sector of the economy, an unorganized multitude of peasant farmers and craftsmen. The result was financial oligarchy, corruption of government officials, and a weak middle class.

Behind the façade of party politics, the old and new elites—the emperor, high government officials, big businessmen, and military leaders—were jockeying savagely for the real power. Cohesive leadership, which had played such an important role in Japan's modernization by the Meiji reformers, had ceased to exist. By far the most serious challenge to peaceful progress, however, was fanatical nationalism. As in Europe, ultranationalism first emerged in Japan in the late nineteenth century but did not flower fully until the First World War and the 1930s.

Though often vague, Japan's ultranationalists shared several fundamental beliefs. They were violently anti-Western. They rejected democracy, big business, and Marxian socialism, which they blamed for destroying the older, superior Japanese practices they wanted to restore. Reviving old myths, they stressed the emperor's godlike qualities and the samurai warrior's code of honor and obedience. Despising party politics, they assassinated moderate leaders and plotted armed uprisings to achieve their goals. Above all else, the ultranationalists preached foreign expansion. Like Western imperialists shouldering "the White Man's Burden," Japanese ultranationalists thought their mission was a noble one. "Asia for the Asians" was their anti-Western rallying cry. As the famous ultranationalist Kita Ikki wrote in 1923, "Our seven hundred million brothers in China and India have no other path to independence than that offered by our guidance and protection."[8]

The ultranationalists were noisy and violent in the 1920s, but it took the Great Depression of the 1930s to tip the scales decisively in their favor. The worldwide depression, which had dire consequences for many countries (see Chapter 29), hit Japan like a tidal wave in 1930. Exports and wages collapsed; unemployment and raw suffering soared. Starving peasants ate the bark off trees and sold their daughters to brothels. The ultranationalists blamed the system, and people listened.

Japan Against China

Among those who listened with particular care were young Japanese army officers in Manchuria, the underpopulated, resource-rich province of northeastern China controlled by the Japanese army since its victory over Russia in 1905. Many junior Japanese officers in Manchuria came from the peasantry and were distressed by the stories

zaibatsu *Giant conglomerate firms in Japan.*

● **Japanese Atrocities in China** In December 1937, after the fall of the Chinese capital Nanjing, Japanese soldiers went on a horrifying rampage. These Japanese recruits are using Chinese prisoners of war as live targets in a murderous bayonet drill. Other Chinese prisoners were buried alive by their Japanese captors. *(Hulton Archive/Getty Images)*

of rural suffering they heard from home. They also knew the Japanese army's budget and prestige had declined in the prosperous 1920s.

The rise of Chinese nationalism worried the young officers most. This new political force, embodied in the Guomindang unification of China, challenged Japanese control over Manchuria. In response, junior Japanese officers in Manchuria, in cooperation with top generals in Tokyo, secretly manufactured an excuse for aggression in late 1931. They blew up some Japanese-owned railroad tracks near the city of Shenyang (Mukden) and then with reinforcements rushed in from Korea quickly occupied all of Manchuria in "self-defense."

In 1932 Japan proclaimed Manchuria an independent state and installed a member of the old Qing Dynasty as puppet emperor. When the League of Nations condemned its aggression in Manchuria, Japan resigned in protest. Japanese aggression in Manchuria showed that the army, though reporting directly to the Japanese emperor, was clearly an independent force subject to no outside control.

The Japanese puppet state named Manchukuo in northeast China became the model for the subsequent conquest and occupation of China and then Southeast Asia. Throughout the 1930s, the Japanese worked to integrate Manchuria (and Korea and

Taiwan) into a large, self-sufficient economic bloc that provided resources, markets, and investment opportunities safe from Western power in East Asia. While exporting raw materials, state-sponsored Japanese companies in Manchuria also built steel mills and heavy industry to supply vital military goods. At home, newspapers and newsreels glorified Japan's efforts and mobilized public support for colonial empire.

For China the Japanese conquest of Manchuria was disastrous. Japanese aggression in Manchuria drew attention away from modernizing efforts. The Nationalist government promoted a massive boycott of Japanese goods but lost interest in social reform. Above all, the Nationalist government after 1931 completely neglected land reform and the Chinese peasants' grinding poverty.

As in many poor agricultural societies throughout history, Chinese peasants paid roughly half of their crops to their landlords as rent. Land ownership was very unequal. One study estimated that a mere 4 percent of families, usually absentee landlords living in cities, owned fully half the land. Poor peasants and farm laborers—70 percent of the rural population—owned only one-sixth of the land. As a result, peasants were heavily in debt and chronically underfed. A contemporaneous Chinese economist spelled out the revolutionary implications: "It seems clear that the land problem in China today is as acute as that of eighteenth-century France or nineteenth-century Russia." Mao Zedong certainly agreed.

Having abandoned land reform, partly because they themselves were often landowners, the Nationalists under Jiang Jieshi devoted their energies between 1930 and 1934 to great campaigns of encirclement and extermination against the Communists' rural power base in southeastern China. In 1934 they closed in for the kill, but, in one of the most incredible sagas of modern times, the main Communist army broke out, beat off attacks, and retreated 6,000 miles in twelve months to a remote region on the northwestern border (see Map 28.2). Of the estimated 100,000 men and women who began the **Long March,** only 8,000 to 10,000 reached the final destination. There Mao built up his forces once again, established a new territorial base, and won local peasant support by undertaking land reform.

Long March *The 6,000-mile retreat of the Communist army to a remote region on the northwestern border of China, during which tens of thousands lost their lives.*

In Japan politics became increasingly chaotic. In 1937 the Japanese military and the ultranationalists were in command. Unable to force China to cede more territory in northern China, they used a minor incident near Beijing as a pretext for a general attack. This marked the beginning of World War II in Asia, although Japan issued no declaration of war. The Nationalist government, which had just formed a united front with the Communists, fought hard, but Japanese troops quickly took Beijing and northern China. Taking the great port of Shanghai after ferocious combat, the Japanese launched an immediate attack up the Yangzi River (see Map 28.2).

Foretelling the horrors of World War II, the Japanese air force bombed Chinese cities and civilian populations with unrelenting fury. Nanjing, the capital, fell in December 1937. Entering the city, Japanese soldiers went berserk and committed dreadful atrocities over seven weeks. Tens of thousands of Chinese were killed, and many thousands of women were raped. The "Rape of Nanjing" combined with other Japanese atrocities to outrage world opinion. The Western Powers denounced Japanese aggression but, with tensions rising in Europe, took no action.

By late 1938 Japanese armies occupied sizable portions of coastal China (see Map 28.2). But the Nationalists and the Communists had retreated to the interior, and both refused to accept defeat. In 1939, as Europe edged toward another great war, the undeclared war between China and Japan bogged down in a savage stalemate. The bloody undeclared war provided a spectacular example of conflicting nationalisms.

Southeast Asia

The tide of nationalism was also rising in Southeast Asia. Like their counterparts in India, China, and Japan, nationalists in French Indochina, the Dutch East Indies, and the Philippines urgently wanted genuine political independence and freedom from foreign rule. In both French Indochina and the Dutch East Indies, they ran up against an imperialist stone wall. The obstacle to Filipino independence came from America and Japan.

In the words of one historian, "Indochina was governed by Frenchmen for Frenchmen, and the great liberal slogans of liberty, equality, and fraternity were not considered to be export goods for overseas dominions."[9] This uncompromising attitude stimulated the growth of an equally stubborn communist opposition under Ho Chi Minh, which despite ruthless repression emerged as the dominant anti-French force.

In the East Indies—modern Indonesia—the Dutch made some concessions after the First World War, establishing a people's council with very limited lawmaking power. But in the 1930s the Dutch cracked down hard, jailing all the important nationalist leaders. Like the French, the Dutch were determined to hold on.

In the Philippines, however, a well-established nationalist movement achieved greater success. As in colonial Latin America, the Spanish in the Philippines had been indefatigable missionaries. By the late nineteenth century the Filipino population was 80 percent Catholic. Filipinos shared a common cultural heritage and a common racial origin. Education, especially for girls, was quite advanced for Southeast Asia, and already in 1843 a higher percentage of people could read in the Philippines than in Spain itself. Economic development helped to create a westernized elite, which turned first to reform and then to revolution in the 1890s. As in Egypt and Turkey, long-standing intimate contact with Western civilization created a strong nationalist movement at an early date.

Filipino nationalists were bitterly disillusioned when the United States, having taken the Philippines from Spain in the Spanish-American War of 1898, ruthlessly beat down a patriotic revolt and denied the universal Filipino desire for independence. The Americans claimed the Philippines were not ready and might be seized by Germany or Britain. As the imperialist power in the Philippines, the United States encouraged education and promoted capitalistic economic development. As in British India, an elected legislature was given some real powers. In 1919 President Wilson even promised eventual independence, though subsequent Republican administrations saw it as a distant goal.

As in India and French Indochina, demands for independence grew. One important contributing factor was American racial attitudes. Americans treated Filipinos as inferiors and introduced segregationist practices borrowed from the American South. American racism made passionate nationalists of many Filipinos. However, it was the Great Depression that had the most radical impact on the Philippines.

As the United States collapsed economically, the Philippines suddenly appeared to be a liability rather than an asset. American farm groups lobbied for protection from cheap Filipino sugar. To protect American jobs, labor unions demanded an end to Filipino immigration. In 1934 Congress made the Philippines a self-governing commonwealth and scheduled independence for 1944. Sugar imports were reduced, and immigration limited to only fifty Filipinos per year.

Like Britain and France in the Middle East, the United States was determined to hold on to its big military bases in the Philippines as it permitted increased local self-government and promised eventual political independence. Some Filipino nationalists denounced the continued presence of U.S. fleets and armies. Others were less certain that the American presence was the immediate problem. Japan was fighting in China and expanding economically into the Philippines and throughout Southeast Asia. By 1939 a new threat to Filipino independence appeared to come from Asia itself.

Chapter Summary

To assess your mastery of this chapter, go to
bedfordstmartins.com/mckayworld

Key Terms

Permanent Mandates
  Commission
Young Turks
sharif
Sykes-Picot Agreement
Balfour Declaration
Treaty of Lausanne
Atatürk
Majlis
Zionism
kibbutz
Lucknow Pact
Satyagraha
May Fourth Movement
New Culture Movement
zaibatsu
Long March

• *How did modern nationalism—the dominant force in most of the world in the twentieth century—develop in Asia between the First and Second World Wars?*

The Asian nationalist revolt against the West began before the First World War. But only after 1914 did Asian nationalist movements broaden their bases sufficiently to challenge Western domination effectively. These mass movements sought human dignity as well as political freedom. Generally speaking, Asian nationalists favored modernization and adopted Western techniques and ideas even as they rejected Western rule. Everywhere Asian nationalists had to fight long and hard, though their struggle gained momentum from growing popular support and the encouragement of the Soviet Union.

• *How did the collapse of the Ottoman Empire in World War I shape the history of the Middle East for the rest of the century?*

The collapse of the Ottoman Empire in World War I left a power vacuum that both Western imperialists and Turkish, Arab, Persian, and Jewish and other nationalists sought to fill. The Turks, who had ruled the old Ottoman Empire, created the modern secular state of Turkey under the leadership of Mustafa Kemal. He brutally crushed the budding nationalism of the Kurds and Armenians. A nationalist movement in Iran, led by the military dictator Reza Shah Pahlavi, gained independence from British control, as did Afghanistan under the anti-British amir Amanullah. The British made promises to both the Palestinians and Jewish Zionists regarding independent homelands in Palestine, creating an impasse that has yet to be settled. France and England had divided areas of the Middle East between them during the war, and then claimed jurisdiction over them as League of Nations mandates. The British and French maintained various degrees of control over the Arab states of Iraq, Syria, Lebanon, Egypt, and Arabia after the war but lost much of their influence over the next two decades as Arab nationalists pushed for complete independence.

• *What role did Gandhi and his campaign of militant nonviolence play in leading India to independence from the British?*

In facing the might of the British Empire Gandhi knew that the Indian people were not capable of fighting a military campaign against the British without suffering hundreds of thousands, perhaps millions, of deaths. But he realized that a few thousand British could do nothing if 350 million Indians refused to cooperate or obey British laws. By employing active, nonviolent resistance, which he called Satyagraha, Gandhi and his millions of Hindu and Muslim followers were able to bring British colonial rule in India to a standstill, leading to Indian independence in 1947. Regrettably, however, Gandhi was not able to control the extreme religious nationalism of the Muslims and Hindus following independence. After bloody massacres on both sides, Muslim Pakistan and Bangladesh split off from predominantly Hindu India (see Chapter 32).

• *Why did some of the Asian nationalist movements come into brutal conflict?*

Asia's nationalist movements arose out of separate historical experiences and distinct cultures. Variations on the common theme of nationalism were evident in China, Japan, and the Philippines. This diversity helps explain why Asian peoples became defensive in their relations with one another while rising against Western rule. Like earlier nationalists in Europe, Asian nationalists developed a strong sense of "we" and "they"; "they" included other Asians as well as Europeans. Nationalism meant freedom, modernization, and cultural renaissance, but it nonetheless proved to be a mixed blessing.

Suggested Reading

Chang, Jung, and Jon Halliday. *Mao: The Unknown Story.* 2006. New, and very controversial, biography of the Chinese leader.

Chow, Tse-tung. *The May Fourth Movement: Intellectual Revolution in Modern China.* 1960. The classic study of the Chinese intellectual revolution that began in 1919.

Erikson, Eric. *Gandhi's Truth: On the Origins of Militant Nonviolence.* 1969. A classic study of Gandhi's life and the origins of Satyagraha.

Fromkin, David. *A Peace to End All Peace: The Fall of the Ottoman Empire and the Creation of the Modern Middle East.* 2001. A very thorough but very readable introduction to the Middle East in the early twentieth century.

Hourani, Albert, and Malise Ruthven. *History of the Arab Peoples.* 2003. One of the best single volume histories of the Arab peoples.

Hsü, Immanuel C.Y. *The Rise of Modern China,* 6th ed. 1999. Sixth edition of a classic history of modern China.

Irokawa, Daikichi. *The Age of Hirohito: In Search of Modern Japan.* 1995. An excellent brief account by a leading Japanese historian.

Lacqueur, Walter. *A History of Zionism. From the French Revolution to the Establishment of the State of Israel.* 1972. Good general history of Zionism and the founding of Israel.

Mango, Andrew. *Atatürk.* 2000. Rich, well-researched biography of this complex Turkish leader.

Myers, Ramon H., and M. Peattie, eds. *The Japanese Colonial Expansion, 1895–1945.* 1984. Broad collection of essays covering all of Japan's colonial empire, both formal and informal.

Osborne, Milton. *Southeast Asia: An Introductory History,* 9th ed. 2005. Ninth edition of the classic introduction to the region's history.

Owen, Norman, David Chandler, and William R. Roff. *The Emergence of Southeast Asia: A New History.* 2004. New history looking at both individual countries and social and economic themes, including gender and ecology.

Reischauer, Edwin O. *Japan: The Story of Nation,* 4th ed. 1991. The classic history in its fourth edition by America's leading historian on Japan.

Spence, Jonathan. *The Search for Modern China.* 1990. Important study of modern China by a leading Chinese scholar.

Wolpert, Stanley. *India.* 2005. An excellent introduction to India's history.

Young, Louise. *Japan's Total Empire: Manchuria and the Culture of Wartime Imperialism.* 1998. A fascinating pioneering work on Japanese imperialism.

Notes

1. K. M. Panikkar, *Asia and Western Dominance: A Survey of the Vasco da Gama Epoch of Asian History* (London: George Allen & Unwin, 1959), p. 197.

2. H. Armstrong, *Turkey in Travail: The Birth of a New Nation* (London: John Lane, 1925), p. 75.

3. Quoted in Lord Kinross, *Atatürk: A Biography of Mustafa Kemal, Father of Modern Turkey* (New York: Morrow, 1965), p. 181.

4. Quoted in E. Erikson, *Gandhi's Truth: On the Origins of Militant Nonviolence* (New York: W. W. Norton, 1969), p. 225.

5. Quoted in W. T. deBary, W. Chan, and B. Watson, *Sources of Chinese Tradition* (New York: Columbia University Press, 1964), pp. 768–769.

6. Quoted in J. F. Fairbank, E. O. Reischauer, and A. M. Craig, *East Asia: Tradition and Transformation* (Boston: Houghton Mifflin, 1973), p. 774.

7. Quoted in B. I. Schwartz, *Chinese Communism and the Rise of Mao* (Cambridge, Mass.: Harvard University Press, 1951), p. 74.

8. Quoted in W. T. deBary, R. Tsunoda, and D. Keene, *Sources of Japanese Tradition,* vol. 2 (New York: Columbia University Press, 1958), p. 269.

9. Quoted in W. Bingham, H. Conroy, and F. Iklé, *A History of Asia,* vol. 2, 2d ed. (Boston: Allyn and Bacon, 1974), p. 480.

Listening to the PAST

Arab Political Aspirations in 1919

Great Britain and France had agreed to divide up the Arab lands, and the British also had made conflicting promises to Arab and Jewish nationalists. However, President Wilson insisted at Versailles that the right of self-determination should be applied to the conquered Ottoman territories, and he sent an American commission of inquiry to Syria, even though the British and French refused to participate. The commission canvassed political views throughout greater Syria, and its long report with many documents reflected public opinion in the region in 1919.

To present their view to the Americans, Arab nationalists from present-day Syria, Lebanon, Israel, and Jordan came together in Damascus as the General Syrian Congress, and they passed the following resolution on July 2, 1919. In addition to the Arab call for political independence, the delegates addressed the possibility of French rule under a League of Nations mandate and the establishment of a Jewish national home.

We the undersigned members of the General Syrian Congress, meeting in Damascus on Wednesday, July 2nd, 1919, . . . provided with credentials and authorizations by the inhabitants of our various districts, Moslems, Christians, and Jews, have agreed upon the following statement of the desires of the people of the country who have elected us to present them to the American Section of the International Commission; the fifth article was passed by a very large majority; all the other articles were accepted unanimously.

1. We ask absolutely complete political independence for Syria within these boundaries. [Describes the area including the present-day states of Syria, Lebanon, Israel, and Jordan.]

2. We ask that the Government of this Syrian country should be a democratic civil constitutional Monarchy on broad decentralization principles, safeguarding the rights of minorities, and that the King be the Emir Faisal, who carried on a glorious struggle in the cause of our liberation and merited our full confidence and entire reliance.

3. Considering the fact that the Arabs inhabiting the Syrian area are not naturally less gifted than other more advanced races and that they are by no means less developed than the Bulgarians, Serbians, Greeks, and Roumanians at the beginning of their independence, we protest against Article 22 of the Covenant of the League of Nations, placing us among the nations in their middle stage of development which stand in need of a mandatory power.

4. In the event of the rejection by the Peace Conference of this just protest for certain considerations that we may not understand, we, relying on the declarations of President Wilson that his object in waging war was to put an end to the ambition of conquest and colonization, can only regard the mandate mentioned in the Covenant of the League of Nations as equivalent to the rendering of economical and technical assistance that does not prejudice our complete independence. And desiring that our country should not fall a prey to colonization and believing that the American Nation is farthest from any thought of colonization and has no political ambition in our country, we will seek the technical and economical assistance from the United States of America, provided that such assistance does not exceed 20 years.

5. In the event of America not finding herself in a position to accept our desire for assistance, we will seek this assistance from Great Britain, also provided that such assistance does not infringe the complete independence and unity of our country and that the duration of such assistance does not exceed that mentioned in the previous article.

6. We do not acknowledge any right claimed by the French Government in any part whatever of our Syrian country and refuse that she should assist us or have a hand in our country under any circumstances and in any place.

7. We oppose the pretensions of the Zionists to create a Jewish commonwealth in the southern part of Syria, known as Palestine, and oppose Zionist migration to any part of our country; for we do not acknowledge their title but consider them a grave peril to our people from the national, economical, and political points of view. Our Jewish compatriots shall enjoy our common rights and assume the common responsibilities.

Palestinian Arabs protest against large-scale Jewish migration into Palestine. *(Roger-Viollet/Getty Images)*

8. We ask that there should be no separation of the southern part of Syria, known as Palestine, nor of the littoral western zone, which includes Lebanon, from the Syrian country. We desire that the unity of the country should be guaranteed against partition under whatever circumstances.

9. We ask complete independence for emancipated Mesopotamia [today's Iraq] and that there should be no economical barriers between the two countries.

10. The fundamental principles laid down by President Wilson in condemnation of secret treaties impel us to protest most emphatically against any treaty that stipulates the partition of our Syria country and against any private engagement aiming at the establishment of Zionism in the southern part of Syria; therefore we ask the complete annulment of these conventions and agreements.

The noble principles enunciated by President Wilson strengthen our confidence that our desires emanating from the depths of our hearts, shall be the decisive factor in determining our future; and that President Wilson and the free American people will be our supporters for the realization of our hopes, thereby proving their sincerity and noble sympathy with the aspiration of the weaker nations in general and our Arab people in particular.

We also have the fullest confidence that the Peace Conference will realize that we would not have risen against the Turks, with whom we had participated in all civil, political, and representative privileges, but for their violation of our national rights, and so will grant us our desires in full in order that our political rights may not be less after the war than they were before, since we have shed so much blood in the cause of our liberty and independence.

We request to be allowed to send a delegation to represent us at the Peace Conference to defend our rights and secure the realization of our aspirations.

Questions for Analysis

1. What kind of state did the delegates want?

2. How did the delegates want to modify an unwanted League of Nations mandate to make it less objectionable?

3. Did the delegates view their "Jewish compatriots" and the Zionists in different ways? Why?

Source: "Resolution of the General Syrian Congress at Damascus, 2 July 1919," from the *King-Crane Commission Report, in Foreign Relations of the United States: Paris Peace Conference, 1919*, 12: 780–781.

A Crowd of Enthusiastic Hitler Supporters, in a photograph by Hugo Jaeger. *(Time Life Pictures/Getty Images)*

30 DICTATORSHIPS AND THE SECOND WORLD WAR

Chapter Preview

Authoritarian States
• *What was the nature of twentieth-century dictatorships and authoritarian rule?*

Stalin's Soviet Union
• *How were the five-year plans part of the totalitarian order in the Soviet Union?*

Mussolini and Fascism in Italy
• *How was Italian fascism a halfway house between conservative authoritarianism and modern totalitarianism?*

Hitler and Nazism in Germany
• *Why were Hitler and his Nazi regime initially so popular?*

The Second World War
• *How did Hitler's actions lead to another world war?*

The era of anxiety and economic depression was also a time of growing strength for political dictatorship. Popularly elected governments and basic civil liberties declined drastically. In Europe on the eve of the Second World War, liberal democratic governments were surviving only in Great Britain, France, the Low Countries, the Scandinavian nations, and neutral Switzerland. Dictatorship seemed the wave of the future worldwide. Thus the intellectual and economic crisis discussed in Chapter 29 and the decline in liberal political institutions and the rise of dictatorships discussed in this chapter were interrelated elements of a global crisis.

The mid-twentieth-century era of dictatorship is a highly disturbing chapter in the history of civilization. The key development was not only the resurgence of authoritarian rule but also the rise of a particularly ruthless and dynamic tyranny that reached its full realization in the Soviet Union and Nazi Germany in the 1930s. Stalin and Hitler mobilized their peoples for enormous undertakings and ruled with unprecedented severity. Hitler's mobilization was ultimately directed toward racial aggression and territorial expansion, and his sudden attack on Poland in 1939 started World War II. Hitler's successes then encouraged the Japanese to expand their stalemated Chinese campaign into a vast Pacific war by attacking Pearl Harbor and advancing into South Asia.

Nazi and Japanese armies were defeated by a great coalition, and today we want to believe that the era of totalitarian dictatorship was a terrible accident, that Stalin's slave labor camps and Hitler's gas chambers "can't happen again." But the cruel truth is that horrible atrocities continue to plague the world in our time. The Khmer Rouge inflicted genocide on its people in Kampuchea, and civil war led to ethnically motivated atrocities in Bosnia, Rwanda, Burundi, and Sudan, recalling the horrors of the Second World War. And there are other examples. A deeper understanding of these brutal dictatorships will help us guard against their recurrence.

AUTHORITARIAN STATES

What was the nature of twentieth-century dictatorships and authoritarian rule?

Both conservative and radical dictatorships arose in the 1920s and the 1930s. Although they sometimes overlapped in character and practice, they were in essence profoundly different. Conservative authoritarian regimes were an old story in world history. Radical, totalitarian dictatorships were a new and frightening development.

Conservative Authoritarianism

The traditional form of antidemocratic government in world history was conservative authoritarianism. Like Russia's tsars and China's emperors, the leaders of such governments tried to prevent major changes that would undermine the existing social order. To do so, they relied on obedient bureaucracies, vigilant police departments, and trustworthy armies. They forbade popular participation in government or else severely limited it to natural allies such as landlords, bureaucrats, and high church officials. They persecuted liberals, democrats, and socialists as subversive radicals, often consigning them to jail, exile, or death.

Yet old-fashioned authoritarian governments were limited in their power and in their objectives. They had neither the ability nor the desire to control many aspects of their subjects' lives. Preoccupied with the goal of mere survival, these governments largely limited their demands to taxes, army recruits, and passive acceptance. As long as the people did not try to change the system, they often had considerable personal independence.

After the First World War, this kind of authoritarian government revived, especially in Latin America and in the less-developed eastern part of Europe. In eastern Europe parliamentary regimes founded on the wreckage of empires in 1918 fell one by one. By early 1938 only Czechoslovakia remained true to liberal political ideals. Conservative dictators also took over in Spain and Portugal.

There were several reasons for this development. These lands lacked strong traditions of self-government, with its necessary restraint and compromise. Moreover, many of these new states, such as Yugoslavia, were torn by ethnic conflicts that threatened their very existence. Dictatorship appealed to nationalists and military leaders as a way to repress such tensions and preserve national unity. Large landowners and the church were still powerful forces in these predominantly agrarian areas, and they often looked to dictators to save them from progressive land reform or communist agrarian upheaval. Finally, the Great Depression delivered the final blow to fragile democracies in Austria, Bulgaria, Romania, Greece, Estonia, and Latvia.

Although some of the conservative authoritarian regimes adopted certain Hitlerian and fascist characteristics in the 1930s, their general aims were limited. They were concerned more with maintaining the status quo than with mobilizing the masses or forcing society into rapid change or war. This tradition continued into the late twentieth century, especially in some of the Latin American military dictatorships.

Radical Totalitarian Dictatorships

By the mid-1930s a new kind of radical dictatorship had emerged in the Soviet Union, Germany, and, to a lesser extent, Italy. Scholars generally agree that these radical dictatorships violently rejected liberal values and exercised unprecedented control over the masses. Further interpretation of these regimes, however, has caused heated controversy and debate.

One extremely useful approach relates the radical dictatorships to the rise of modern totalitarianism. The concept of **totalitarianism** emerged in the 1920s and 1930s.

totalitarianism *A dictatorship that exercises unprecedented control over the masses and seeks to mobilize them for action.*

In 1924 Benito Mussolini spoke of the "fierce totalitarian will" of his movement in Italy. In the 1930s observers linked Italian and especially German fascism with Soviet communism in "a 'new kind of state' that could be called totalitarian." "All doubts" about the totalitarian nature of both dictatorships "were swept away for most Americans,"[1] following the Hitler-Stalin alliance in 1939.

Some scholars argue that modern totalitarian dictatorship burst on the scene with the revolutionary total war effort of 1914–1918. The war called forth a tendency to subordinate all institutions and all classes to the state in order to achieve one supreme objective: victory. As the French thinker Elie Halévy put it in 1936 in his influential *The Era of Tyrannies,* the varieties of modern totalitarian tyranny—fascism, Nazism, and communism—could be thought of as "feuding brothers" with a common father: the nature of modern war.[2]

Halévy and others believed Lenin and the Bolsheviks carried the crucial experience of World War I further during the Russian civil war. Lenin showed how a dedicated minority could achieve victory over a less determined majority and subordinate institutions and human rights to the needs of a single group—the Communist Party—and its leader. Lenin's model of single-party dictatorship inspired imitators, including Adolf Hitler. The modern totalitarian state reached maturity in the 1930s in the Stalinist U.S.S.R. and Nazi Germany.

Scholars have also argued that the totalitarian state used modern technology and communications to exercise complete political power, and then complete control over the economic, social, intellectual, and cultural aspects of people's lives as well. Deviation from the norm, even in art or family behavior, could become a crime.

This vision of total state represented a radical revolt against liberalism. Classical liberalism (see page 679) sought to limit state power and protect individual rights. Moreover, liberals stood for rationality, peaceful progress, economic freedom, and a strong middle class. All of that disgusted totalitarians. They believed in willpower, preached conflict, and worshiped violence. The individual was infinitely less valuable than the state.

Unlike old-fashioned authoritarianism, modern totalitarianism was based not on an elite but on people who had already become engaged in the political process, most notably through commitment to nationalism and socialism. Thus totalitarian societies were fully mobilized societies moving toward some goal and possessing boundless dynamism. As soon as one goal was achieved, another arose at the leader's command. As a result totalitarianism was a *permanent* revolution, an *unfinished* revolution, in which rapid, profound change imposed from on high went on forever.

There were major differences between Stalin's communist U.S.S.R. and Hitler's Nazi Germany. Soviet communism, growing out of Marxian socialism, seized all private property (except personal property) for the state and crushed the middle classes.

Chronology

1921   New Economic Policy in Soviet Union

1922   Mussolini seizes power in Italy

1924–1929   Buildup of Nazi Party in Germany

1927   Stalin comes to power in Soviet Union

1928   Stalin's first five-year plan

1929   Start of collectivization in Soviet Union; Lateran Agreement

1929–1939   Great Depression

1932–1933   Famine in Ukraine

1933   Hitler appointed chancellor in Germany; Nazis begin to control intellectual life and blacklist authors

1934   Sergei Kirov, Stalin's number-two man, is murdered

1935   Mussolini invades Ethiopia

1936   Start of great purges under Stalin

1939   Germany occupies Czech lands; Germany invades Poland; Britain and France declare war on Germany

1940   Japan signs formal alliance with Germany and Italy

1941   SS stops Jewish emigration from Europe; Germany invades Soviet Union; bombing of Pearl Harbor; United States enters war

1941–1945   Six million Jews killed in death camps

1944   Allied invasion at Normandy

1945   Atomic bombs dropped on Japan; end of war

● **Nazi Mass Rally, 1936** This picture captures the essence of the totalitarian interpretation of dynamic modern dictatorship. The uniformed members of the Nazi Party have willingly merged themselves into a single force and await the command of the godlike leader. *(AP/Wide World Photos)*

fascism *A movement characterized by extreme, often expansionist nationalism, an antisocialism aimed at destroying working-class movements, alliances with powerful capitalists and landowners, a dynamic and violent leader, and glorification of war and the military.*

Nazi Germany, growing out of extreme nationalism and racism, criticized big landowners and industrialists, but both private property and the middle classes survived. This difference in property and class relations led some scholars to speak of "totalitarianism of the left"—Stalinist Russia—and "totalitarianism of the right"—Nazi Germany.

A second group of observers in the 1930s approached radical dictatorships outside the Soviet Union through the concept of **fascism.** These writers severely criticized fascism, linking it to decaying capitalism and domestic class conflict. Mussolini and Hitler, however, proudly used the term to describe their movements' supposedly "total" and revolutionary character. Orthodox Marxists argued that powerful capitalists used fascist ideology to create a mass movement capable of destroying the revolutionary working class and thus protect their enormous profits.

Comparative studies of European fascist movements show that they shared many characteristics, including extreme nationalism, an antisocialism aimed at destroying working-class movements, alliances with powerful capitalists and landowners, a dynamic and violent leader, and glorification of war and the military. These studies also highlight how fascist movements generally failed to gain political power.

In recent years, many historians have tended to adopt a third approach, emphasizing the uniqueness of developments in each country. This is especially true for Hitler's Germany, where some elements of the totalitarian interpretation have been nuanced and revised. A similar revaluation of Stalin's U.S.S.R. is in progress now that communism's collapse has opened the former Soviet Union's archives to new research.

In summary, despite conflicting interpretations the concept of totalitarianism remains a valuable tool for historical understanding. It correctly highlights that both Hitler's Germany and Stalin's Soviet Union made an unprecedented "total claim" on the beliefs and behaviors of their respective citizens.[3] As for fascism, antidemocratic, antisocialist fascist movements sprang up all over Europe, but only in Italy and Germany (and some would say Spain) were they able to take power. Finally, it is important to remember that the problem of Europe's radical dictatorships is complex, with few easy answers.

STALIN'S SOVIET UNION

How were the five-year plans part of the totalitarian order in the Soviet Union?

Lenin's harshest critics claim that he established the basic outlines of a modern totalitarian dictatorship after the Bolshevik Revolution and during the Russian civil war. If this is so, then Joseph Stalin (1879–1953) certainly finished the job. A master of political infighting, Stalin cautiously consolidated his power and eliminated his enemies in the mid-1920s. Then in 1928, as the ruling Communist Party's undisputed leader, he launched the first **five-year plan**—the "revolution from above," as he so aptly termed it.

Extremely ambitious, the five-year plans marked the beginning of a renewed attempt to mobilize and transform Soviet society along socialist lines. The means Stalin and the small Communist Party elite chose in order to do so were constant propaganda, enormous sacrifice, and unlimited violence and state control. Thus many historians argue that the Soviet Union in the 1930s became a dynamic, modern totalitarian state.

five-year plan *Launched by Stalin and termed "revolution from above," its ultimate goal was to generate new attitudes, new loyalties, and a new socialist humanity.*

From Lenin to Stalin

By spring 1921 Lenin and the Bolsheviks had won the civil war, but they ruled a shattered and devastated land. Many farms were in ruins, and food supplies were exhausted. Drought and war in southern Russia combined to produce the worst famine in generations. Industrial production also broke down completely. The Bolsheviks had destroyed the economy as well as their foes.

In the face of economic disintegration, riots by peasants and workers, and an open rebellion by previously pro-Bolshevik sailors at Kronstadt, Lenin changed course. In March 1921 he announced the **New Economic Policy (NEP),** which re-established limited economic freedom in an attempt to rebuild agriculture and industry. Peasant producers could sell their surpluses in free markets, as could private traders and small handicraft manufacturers. Heavy industry, railroads, and banks, however, remained wholly nationalized.

The NEP was shrewd and successful both politically and economically. Politically, it was a necessary but temporary compromise with the Soviet Union's overwhelming peasant majority, which Lenin realized was the only force capable of overturning his government. Economically, the NEP brought rapid recovery. In 1926 industrial output surpassed the level of 1913, and Soviet peasants were producing almost as much grain as before the war.

New Economic Policy (NEP) *Lenin's policy of re-establishing limited economic freedom in an attempt to rebuild agriculture and industry in the face of economic disintegration.*

As the economy recovered, an intense power struggle began in the Communist Party's inner circles, for Lenin left no chosen successor when he died in 1924. The principal contenders were the stolid Stalin and the flamboyant Trotsky.

Joseph Dzhugashvili—later known as Stalin—was a shoemaker's son. He studied for the priesthood but was expelled from his theological seminary. By 1903 he was a Bolshevik revolutionary in southern Russia. Stalin was a good organizer but had no experience outside Russia. Trotsky, an inspiring leader who had planned the 1917 takeover (see page 832) and created the victorious Red Army, appeared to have all the advantages. Yet it was Stalin who succeeded Lenin, because he gained the all-important support of the party, the only genuine source of power in the one-party state. Rising to general secretary of the party's Central Committee just before Lenin's first stroke in 1922, Stalin used his office to win friends and allies with jobs and promises.

With cunning skill Stalin gradually achieved absolute power between 1922 and 1927. Stalin used the moderates to crush Trotsky, then he turned against the moderates and destroyed them as well. Stalin's final triumph came at the party congress of December 1927, which condemned all "deviation from the general party line"

● **Kazimir Malevich: Suprematism, ca. 1917**
Russian artists occupied a prominent position in the international avant-garde in the early twentieth century, and the Ukrainian-born Malevich is widely recognized as a leading figure in the development of modern abstract art. Malevich originated the theory of suprematism, whereby he abandoned images from nature and painted pure forms that were beautiful in themselves, as in this outstanding example. When the Bolsheviks condemned abstraction and demanded "socialist realism," Malevich returned to more recognizable forms and taught design. *(Erich Lessing/Art Resource, NY)*

formulated by Stalin. He then launched his revolution from above—the real revolution for millions of ordinary citizens.

The Five-Year Plans

The 1927 party congress marked the end of the NEP and the beginning of the era of socialist five-year plans. The first five-year plan had staggering economic objectives. In just five years, total industrial output was to increase by 250 percent and agricultural production by 150 percent, and one-fifth of the peasants were to give up their private plots and join socialist collective farms. By 1930 economic and social change was sweeping the country.

Stalin unleashed his "second revolution" for a variety of interrelated reasons. First, like Lenin, Stalin and his militant supporters were deeply committed to socialism as they understood it. Second, there was the old problem of catching up with the advanced and presumably hostile Western capitalist nations. "We are fifty or a hundred years behind the advanced countries," Stalin said in 1931, "We must make good this distance in ten years. Either we do it, or we shall go under."[4]

Domestically, there was the peasant problem. For centuries peasants had wanted to own the land, and finally they had it. Sooner or later, the communists reasoned, the peasants would become conservative little capitalists and threaten the regime. Therefore, Stalin decided on a preventive war against the peasantry in order to bring it under the state's absolute control.

That war was **collectivization**—the forcible consolidation of individual peasant farms into large, state-controlled enterprises. Beginning in 1929 peasants were ordered to give up their land and animals and become members of collective farms. As for the **kulaks,** the better-off peasants, Stalin instructed party workers to "liquidate them as a class." Stripped of land and livestock, the kulaks were generally not even permitted to join the collective farms. Many starved or were deported to forced-labor camps for "re-education."

Since almost all peasants were in fact poor, the term *kulak* soon meant any peasant who opposed the new system. Whole villages were often attacked. One conscience-stricken colonel in the secret police confessed to a foreign journalist,

I am an old Bolshevik. I worked in the underground against the Tsar and then I fought in the Civil War. Did I do all that in order that I should now surround villages with machine guns and order my men to fire indiscriminately into crowds of peasants? Oh, no, no![5]

Forced collectivization led to disaster. Many peasants slaughtered their animals and burned their crops in sullen, hopeless protest. Between 1929 and 1933 the number of horses, cattle, sheep, and goats in the Soviet Union fell by at least half. Nor were the state-controlled collective farms more productive. Grain output barely increased between 1928 and 1938. Collectivized agriculture made no substantial financial contribution to Soviet industrial development during the first five-year plan.

The disaster's human dimension was absolutely staggering. Stalin himself confided to Winston Churchill at Yalta in 1945 that 10 million people had died in the course of collectivization. In Ukraine the drive against peasants snowballed into a general assault on Ukrainians as reactionary nationalists and enemies of socialism. The result was a terrible man-made famine in Ukraine in 1932 and 1933, which probably claimed 6 million lives.

Collectivization was a cruel but real victory for communist ideologues. By 1938, 93 percent of peasant families had been herded onto collective farms. Regimented as state employees and dependent on the state-owned tractor stations, the collectivized peasants were no longer even a potential political threat to the regime.

The industrial side of the five-year plans was more successful—indeed, quite spectacular. Soviet industry produced about four times as much in 1937 as in 1928. No other major country had ever achieved such rapid industrial growth. Heavy industry led the way; consumer industry grew quite slowly. Urban development accelerated, and more than 25 million people migrated to cities during the 1930s.

The sudden creation of dozens of new factories (and the increasingly voracious military) demanded tremendous resources purchased at enormous sacrifice. The money was collected from the people by means of heavy, hidden sales taxes. Firm labor discipline and foreign engineers also made important contributions to rapid industrialization. Trade unions lost most of their power, and individuals could not move without police permission. When factory managers needed more hands they were sent millions of "unneeded" peasants from collective farms over the years.

Foreign engineers were hired to plan and construct many of the new factories. Highly skilled American engineers, hungry for work in the depression years, were particularly important until newly trained Soviet experts began to replace them after 1932. Siberia's new gigantic steel mills were modeled on America's best. Thus Stalin's planners harnessed even the skill and technology of capitalist countries to promote the surge of socialist industry.

Life and Culture in Soviet Society

Stalin's five-year plans aimed also to create a new kind of society and human personality. The utopian vision of a new humanity floundered, but Stalin did build a new society whose broad outlines existed into the mid-1980s.

collectivization *The forcible consolidation of individual peasant farms into large, state-controlled enterprises.*

kulaks *Better-off peasants who were stripped of land and livestock under Stalin. They generally were not permitted to join the collective farms, and many of them starved or were deported to forced-labor camps for "re-education."*

РОССИЙСКАЯ СОЦИАЛИСТИЧЕСКАЯ ФЕДЕРАТИВНАЯ   СОВЕТСКАЯ РЕСПУБЛИКА

Р.Ф.С.Р.

**ОРУЖИЕМ МЫ ДОБИЛИ ВРАГА
ТРУДОМ МЫ ДОБУДЕМ ХЛЕБ
ВСЕ ЗА РАБОТУ, ТОВАРИЩИ!**

● **"Let's All Get to Work, Comrades!"** Art in the Stalinist era generally followed the official doctrine of socialist realism, representing objects in a literal style and celebrating Soviet achievements. Characteristically, this poster glorifies the working class, women's equality (in hard labor at least), mammoth factories, and the Communist Party (represented by the hammer and sickle by the woman's foot). Assailed by propaganda, Soviet citizens often found refuge in personal relations and deep friendships. *(From Art of the October Revolution, Mikhail Guerman [Aurora Publishers, Leningrad]. Reproduced by permission)*

> **Primary Source:**
> **Letters to Izvestiya on the Abortion Issue, May–June 1936**
> *Find out what some citizens of the Soviet Union thought about a proposed ban on abortion.*

Life was hard in Stalin's Soviet Union. Because consumption was reduced to pay for investment, there was no improvement in the average standard of living. The masses lived primarily on black bread and wore old, shabby clothing. Stores experienced constant shortages, although very heavily taxed vodka was always readily available. Housing shortages were a particularly serious problem. A relatively lucky family received one room for all its members and shared both a kitchen and a toilet with others on the floor. Less fortunate people built scrap-lumber shacks in shantytowns.

Despite the hardships, idealism and ideology had real appeal for many communists, who saw themselves heroically building the world's first socialist society while capitalism crumbled and fascism rose in the West. This optimistic belief in the Soviet Union's future also attracted many disillusioned Westerners to communism in the 1930s.

On a more practical level Soviet workers did receive some important social benefits, such as old-age pensions, free medical services, free education, and child day-care centers. Unemployment was almost unknown. Finally, there was the possibility of personal advancement.

The keys to improving one's position were specialized skills and technical education. Rapid industrialization required massive numbers of trained experts, such as skilled workers, engineers, and plant managers. Thus the Stalinist state broke with the egalitarian policies of the 1920s and provided tremendous incentives to those who could serve its needs. A growing technical and managerial elite joined with the political and artistic elites in a new upper class, whose members were rich, powerful, and insecure. Thus millions struggled for an education.

Soviet society's radical transformation profoundly affected women's lives. Marxists traditionally believed that both capitalism and middle-class husbands exploited women. The Russian Revolution of 1917 immediately proclaimed complete equality of rights for women. In the 1920s divorce and abortion were made easily available, and women were urged to work outside the home and liberate themselves sexually. After Stalin came to power, sexual and familial liberation was played down, and the most lasting changes for women involved work and education.

While many peasant women continued to work on farms, millions of women now toiled in factories and heavy construction. The more determined women entered the ranks of the better-paid specialists in industry and science. Medicine practically became a woman's profession. By 1950, 75 percent of all doctors in the Soviet Union were women. The massive mobilization of women was a striking characteristic of the Soviet state.

Culture lost its autonomy in the 1930s and became thoroughly politicized through constant propaganda and indoctrination. Party activists lectured workers in factories and peasants on collective farms, while newspapers, films, and radio broadcasts endlessly recounted socialist achievements and capitalist plots. Writers and artists who could effectively combine genuine creativity and political propaganda became the darlings of the regime.

Stalinist Terror and the Great Purges

In the mid-1930s the great offensive to build socialism and a new socialist personality culminated in ruthless police terror and a massive purging of the Communist Party. In late 1934 Stalin's number-two man, Sergei Kirov, was suddenly and mysteriously murdered. Although Stalin himself probably ordered Kirov's murder, he used the incident to launch a reign of terror.

In August 1936 sixteen prominent Old Bolsheviks confessed to all manner of plots against Stalin in spectacular public show trials in Moscow. Then in 1937 the secret police arrested a mass of lesser party officials and newer members, also torturing them and extracting more confessions for more show trials. In addition to the party faithful, union officials, managers, intellectuals, army officers, and countless ordinary citizens were struck down. In all at least 8 million people were probably arrested, and millions of these were executed or never returned from prisons and forced-labor camps.

Stalin recruited 1.5 million new members to take the place of those purged. Thus more than half of all Communist Party members in 1941 had joined since the purges. "These new men were 'thirty-something' products of the Second Revolution of the 1930s, Stalin's upwardly mobile yuppies, so to speak."[6] This new generation of Stalin-formed Communists served the leader effectively until his death in 1953, and then governed the Soviet Union until the early 1980s.

Stalin's mass purges remain baffling, for almost all historians believe that those purged posed no threat and confessed to crimes they had not committed. Revisionist historians have challenged the long-standing interpretation that blames the great purges on Stalin's cruelty or madness. They argue that Stalin's fears were exaggerated but genuine and were shared by many in the party and in the general population who were bombarded daily with ideology and political slogans. Investigations and trials snowballed into a mass hysteria, a new witch-hunt.[7] In short, a popular but deluded Stalin found large numbers of willing collaborators for crime as well as for achievement.

• • • • • • • • • • • • • • • • •

MUSSOLINI AND FASCISM IN ITALY

How was Italian fascism a halfway house between conservative authoritarianism and modern totalitarianism?

Mussolini's movement and his seizure of power in 1922 were important steps in the rise of dictatorships between the two world wars. Like all the future dictators, the young Mussolini hated liberalism and wanted to destroy it in Italy. He and his supporters were the first to call themselves "fascists"—revolutionaries determined to create a certain kind of totalitarian state. Few scholars today would argue that Mussolini succeeded. His dictatorship was brutal and theatrical, but it remained a halfway house between conservative authoritarianism and modern totalitarianism.

The Seizure of Power

In the early twentieth century Italy was a liberal state with civil rights and a constitutional monarchy. On the eve of the First World War the parliamentary regime finally granted universal male suffrage. But there were serious problems. Poverty was widespread, and many peasants were more attached to their villages and local interests than to the national state. Moreover, the papacy, many devout Catholics, conservatives, and landowners remained strongly opposed to the middle-class lawyers and politicians who ran the country largely for their own benefit. Church-state relations were often tense. Class differences were also extreme, and by 1912 the Socialist Party's radical wing led the powerful revolutionary socialist movement.[8]

● **Hitler and Mussolini in Italy, May 1938** At first Mussolini distrusted Hitler, but Mussolini's conquest of Ethiopia in 1936 and Hitler's occupation of the Rhineland brought the two dictators together in a close alliance. State visits by Mussolini to Berlin in 1937 and by Hitler to Rome in 1938 included gigantic military reviews, which were filmed to impress the whole world. Uniformed Italian fascists accompany this motorcade. *(Time Life Pictures/Getty Images)*

Black Shirts *A private army under Mussolini that destroyed Socialist newspapers, union halls, and Socialist Party headquarters, eventually pushing Socialists out of the city governments of northern Italy.*

The war worsened the political situation. Having fought on the Allied side almost exclusively for purposes of territorial expansion, the parliamentary government bitterly disappointed Italian nationalists with Italy's modest gains at Versailles. Workers and peasants also felt cheated: to win their support during the war, the government had promised social and land reform, which it did not deliver after the war.

The Russian Revolution inspired and energized Italy's revolutionary socialist movement, and radical workers and peasants began occupying factories and seizing land in 1920. These actions scared and mobilized the property-owning classes. Thus by 1921 revolutionary socialists, antiliberal conservatives, and frightened property owners were all opposed—though for different reasons—to the liberal parliamentary government.

Into these crosscurrents of unrest and fear stepped the blustering, bullying Benito Mussolini (1883–1945). Son of a village schoolteacher and a poor blacksmith, Mussolini began his political career as a Socialist Party leader and radical newspaper editor before World War I. Expelled from the Italian Socialist Party for supporting the war and wounded in 1917, Mussolini returned home and began organizing bitter war veterans into a band of fascists— from the Italian word for "a union of forces."

At first Mussolini's program was a radical combination of nationalist and socialist demands, including territorial expansion, workers' benefits, and land reform for peasants. It competed directly with the well-organized Socialist Party and failed to get off the ground. When Mussolini saw that his violent verbal assaults on rival Socialists won him growing support from conservatives and the frightened middle classes, he shifted gears in 1920. In thought and action Mussolini was a striking example of the turbulent uncertainty of the age of anxiety.

Mussolini and his private army of **Black Shirts** began to grow violent, attacking Socialist organizers and meetings. Few people were killed, but Socialist newspapers, union halls, and local Socialist Party headquarters were destroyed. A skillful politician, Mussolini allowed his followers to convince themselves that they were not just opposing the "Reds" but were also making a real revolution of their own, helping the little people against the established interests.

With the government breaking down in 1922, largely because of the chaos created by his direct-action bands, Mussolini stepped forward as the savior of order and property, demanding the existing government's resignation and his own appointment by the king. In October 1922 a large group of fascists marched on Rome to threaten the king and force him to call on Mussolini. The threat worked. Victor Emmanuel III (r. 1900–1946), who had no love for the old liberal politicians, asked Mussolini to form a new cabinet. Thus, after widespread violence and a threat of armed uprising, Mussolini seized power "legally." The king and parliament immediately granted Mussolini dictatorial authority for one year.

The Regime in Action

Mussolini became dictator on the strength of Italians' rejection of parliamentary government coupled with fears of Soviet-style revolution. In 1924 he declared his desire to "make the nation Fascist," and imposed a series of repressive measures. Press freedom was abolished, elections were fixed, and the government ruled by decree. Mussolini arrested his political opponents, disbanded all independent labor unions, and put dedicated Fascists in control of Italy's schools. He created a fascist youth movement, fascist labor unions, and many other fascist organizations. He trumpeted his goal in a famous slogan of 1926: "Everything in the state, nothing outside the state, nothing against the state." By year's end Italy was a one-party dictatorship under Mussolini's unquestioned leadership.

Mussolini, however, did not complete the establishment of a modern totalitarian state. His Fascist Party never destroyed the old power structure. Interested primarily in personal power, Mussolini was content to compromise with the old conservative classes that controlled the army, the economy, and the state. He never tried to purge these classes or even move very vigorously against them. He controlled labor but left big business to regulate itself, profitably and securely. There was no land reform.

Mussolini also drew increasing support from the Catholic Church. In the **Lateran Agreement** of 1929, he recognized the Vatican as a tiny independent state and agreed to give the church heavy financial support. The pope urged Italians to support Mussolini's government.

Nothing better illustrates Mussolini's unwillingness to harness everyone and everything for dynamic action than his treatment of women. He abolished divorce and told women to stay at home and produce children. In 1938 women were limited by law to a maximum of 10 percent of the better-paying jobs in industry and government. Italian women appear not to have changed their attitudes or behavior in any important way under fascist rule.

Mussolini's government passed no racial laws until 1938 and did not persecute Jews savagely until late in the Second World War, when Italy was under Nazi control. Nor did Mussolini establish a truly ruthless police state. Only twenty-three political prisoners were condemned to death between 1926 and 1944. In spite of much pompous posing by the chauvinist leader, Mussolini's fascist Italy, though repressive and undemocratic, was never really totalitarian.

Lateran Agreement *A 1929 agreement that recognized the Vatican as a tiny independent state, with Mussolini agreeing to give the church heavy financial support. In turn, the pope expressed his satisfaction and urged Italians to support Mussolini's government.*

• • • • • • • • • • • •

HITLER AND NAZISM IN GERMANY

Why were Hitler and his Nazi regime initially so popular?

The most frightening dictatorship developed in Nazi Germany. A product of Hitler's evil genius, as well as of Germany's social and political situation and the general attack on liberalism and rationality in the age of anxiety, the Nazi movement shared some of the characteristics of Mussolini's Italian model and fascism. But Nazism asserted an unlimited claim over German society and proclaimed the ultimate power of its endlessly aggressive leader—Adolf Hitler. Nazism's aspirations were truly totalitarian.

The Roots of Nazism

Nazism grew out of many complex developments, of which the most influential were extreme nationalism and racism. These two ideas captured the mind of the young Hitler, and it was he who dominated Nazism for as long as it lasted.

Nazism *A movement born of extreme nationalism and racism and dominated by Adolf Hitler for as long as it lasted.*

Born the fourth child of a successful Austrian customs official and an indulgent mother, Adolf Hitler (1889–1945) spent his childhood in small towns in Austria. He did poorly in high school and dropped out at age sixteen. He then headed to Vienna, where he found most of the perverted beliefs that guided his life.

In Vienna Hitler soaked up extreme German nationalism, which was particularly strong there. Austro-German nationalists believed Germans to be a superior people and central Europe's natural rulers. They often advocated union with Germany and violent expulsion of "inferior" peoples as the means of maintaining German domination of the Austro-Hungarian Empire. Hitler was deeply impressed by Vienna's mayor, Karl Lueger (1844–1910). With the help of the Catholic trade unions, Lueger had won the support of Vienna's lower classes, and he showed Hitler the enormous potential of anticapitalist and antiliberal propaganda.

From Lueger and others Hitler eagerly absorbed virulent anti-Semitism, racism, and hatred of Slavs. He developed an unshakable belief in the crudest, most exaggerated distortions of the Darwinian theory of survival, the superiority of Germanic races, and the inevitability of racial conflict. Anti-Semitism and racism became Hitler's most passionate convictions, his explanation for everything. The Jews, he claimed, directed an international conspiracy of finance capitalism and Marxian socialism against German culture, German unity, and the German race. Hitler's belief was totally irrational, but he never doubted it.

Hitler greeted the outbreak of the Great War as a salvation. The struggle and discipline of war gave his life meaning, and when Germany was suddenly defeated in 1918, Hitler's world was shattered. Convinced that Jews and Marxists had "stabbed Germany in the back," he vowed to fight on.

In late 1919 Hitler joined a tiny extremist group in Munich called the German Workers' Party, which promised a uniquely German "national socialism" that would abolish the injustices of capitalism and create a mighty "people's community." By 1921 Hitler had gained absolute control of this small but growing party. Already a master of mass propaganda and political showmanship, his most effective tool was the mass rally, where he often worked his audience into a frenzy with wild attacks on the Versailles treaty, the Jews, war profiteers, and Germany's Weimar Republic.

In late 1923 the Weimar Republic seemed on the verge of collapse, and Hitler, inspired by Mussolini's recent easy victory, attempted an armed uprising in Munich. Despite the failure of the poorly organized plot and Hitler's arrest, Nazism had been born.

Hitler's Road to Power

At his trial Hitler violently denounced the Weimar Republic, and he gained enormous publicity and attention. Moreover, he learned from his unsuccessful revolt. Hitler concluded that he had to undermine, rather than overthrow, the government and come to power legally through electoral competition. He also used his brief prison term to dictate *Mein Kampf.* There he expounded on his basic themes: "race," with a stress on anti-Semitism; "living space," with a sweeping vision of war and conquered territory; and the leader-dictator, called the **Führer,** with unlimited, arbitrary power.

Führer *"Leader-dictator" with unlimited, arbitrary power; this title was bestowed upon Adolf Hitler.*

In the years of prosperity and relative stability between 1924 and 1929, Hitler concentrated on building his National Socialist German Workers' Party, or Nazi Party. The Nazis remained a small splinter group, however, until the 1929 Great Depression shattered economic prosperity and presented Hitler with a fabulous opportunity. By the end of 1932 an incredible 43 percent of the labor force was unemployed. Industrial production fell by one-half between 1929 and 1932. No factor contributed more to Hitler's success than the economic crisis. Hitler began promising German voters economic as well as political and international salvation.

Hitler rejected free-market capitalism and advocated government programs to bring recovery. He pitched his speeches especially to middle- and lower-middle-class groups and to skilled workers striving for middle-class status. As the economy collapsed, great numbers of these people "voted their pocketbooks"[9] and deserted the conservative and moderate parties for the Nazis. In the 1930 election the Nazis won 6.5 million votes and 107 seats, and in July 1932 the Nazis gained 14.5 million votes—38 percent of the total—and became the largest party in the Reichstag.

Hitler and the Nazis also appealed strongly to German youth. Indeed, in some ways the Nazi movement was a mass movement of young Germans. Hitler himself was only forty in 1929, and he and most of his top aides were much younger than other leading German politicians. "National Socialism is the organized will of the youth," proclaimed the official Nazi slogan. In 1931 almost 40 percent of Nazi Party members were under thirty, compared with 20 percent of Social Democrats. National recovery, exciting and rapid change, and personal advancement made Nazism appealing to millions of German youths.

Hitler also came to power because normal democratic government broke down. Germany's economic collapse in the Great Depression convinced many voters that the country's republican leaders were stupid and corrupt, thereby adding to Hitler's appeal. Disunity on the left was another nail in the republic's coffin. The Communists refused to cooperate with the Social Democrats, even though the two parties together outnumbered the Nazis in the Reichstag, even after the 1932 elections. German Communists (and the still complacent Stalin) believed that Hitler's fascism represented the last agonies of monopoly capitalism and that a communist revolution would soon follow his taking power.

Finally, Hitler excelled in dirty backroom politics. In 1932 he succeeded in gaining support from key people in the army and big business who thought they could use him to their own advantage. Many conservative and nationalistic politicians thought similarly. Thus in January 1933 Hindenburg legally appointed Hitler, leader of Germany's largest party, chancellor of Germany.

The Nazi State and Society

Hitler quickly and skillfully established an unshakable dictatorship. When the Reichstag building was partly destroyed by fire, Hitler blamed the Communist Party, and he convinced President Hindenburg to sign dictatorial emergency acts that practically abolished freedom of speech and assembly and most personal liberties. He also called for new elections.

When the Nazis won only 44 percent of the votes, Hitler immediately outlawed the Communist Party and arrested its parliamentary representatives. Then on March 23, 1933, the Nazis forced through the Reichstag the so-called **Enabling Act,** which gave Hitler absolute dictatorial power for four years. Hitler and the Nazis took over the government bureaucracy intact, installing many Nazis in top positions.

Enabling Act *The act pushed through the Reichstag by the Nazis that gave Hitler absolute dictatorial power for four years.*

Hitler next outlawed strikes and abolished independent labor unions, which were replaced by the Nazi Labor Front. Professional people—doctors and lawyers, teachers and engineers—also saw their previously independent organizations swallowed up in Nazi associations. Publishing houses and universities were put under Nazi control, and passionate students and pitiful professors burned forbidden books in public squares. Modern art and architecture were ruthlessly prohibited. Life became violently anti-intellectual. As the cynical Joseph Goebbels, later Nazi minister of propaganda, put it, "When I hear the word 'culture' I reach for my gun."[10] By 1934 a brutal dictatorship characterized by frightening dynamism and total obedience to Hitler was already largely in place.

In June 1934 Hitler ordered his elite personal guard—the SS—to arrest and shoot without trial roughly a thousand long-time Nazi storm troops. Shortly thereafter army leaders surrendered their independence and swore a binding oath of "unquestioning obedience . . . to the Leader of the German State and People, Adolf Hitler." The SS grew rapidly. Under its methodical, inhuman leader, Heinrich Himmler

Ganz Deutschland hört den Führer mit dem Volksempfänger

● **Reaching a National Audience** This poster ad promotes the VE-301 receiver, "the world's cheapest radio," and claims that "All Germany listens to the Führer on the people's receiver." Constantly broadcasting official views and attitudes, the state-controlled media also put the Nazis' favorite entertainment—gigantic mass meetings that climaxed with Hitler's violent theatrical speeches—on an invisible stage for millions. *(Bundesarchiv Koblenz Plak 003-022-025)*

Primary Source:
Speech to the National Socialist Women's Association, September 1935
Learn what the Nazis believed were the proper roles for women in society—from the woman appointed to disseminate their beliefs.

(1900–1945), the SS joined with the political police, the Gestapo, to expand its network of special courts and concentration camps. Nobody was safe.

From the beginning Jews were a special object of Nazi persecution. By late 1934 most Jewish lawyers, doctors, professors, civil servants, and musicians had lost their jobs and the right to practice their professions. In 1935 the infamous Nuremberg Laws classified as Jewish anyone having one or more Jewish grandparents and deprived Jews of all rights of citizenship. By 1938 roughly one-quarter of Germany's half million Jews had emigrated, sacrificing almost all their property in order to leave Germany.

In late 1938 the attack on the Jews accelerated. A well-organized wave of violence destroyed homes, synagogues, and businesses, after which German Jews were rounded up and made to pay for the damage. It became very difficult for Jews to leave Germany. Some Germans privately opposed these outrages, but most went along or looked the other way. Although this lack of response reflected the individual's helplessness in a totalitarian state, it was more certainly a sign of the strong popular support Hitler's government enjoyed.

Hitler's Popularity

Hitler had promised the masses economic recovery—"work and bread"—and he delivered, launching a large public works program to pull Germany out of the depression. Work began on superhighways, offices, gigantic sports stadiums, and public housing. In 1935 Germany turned decisively toward rearmament. Unemployment dropped steadily, and by 1938 everyone had work. The average standard of living increased moderately. Business profits rose sharply. For millions of people economic recovery was tangible evidence that Nazi promises were more than show and propaganda.

For the masses of ordinary German citizens who were not Jews, Slavs, Gypsies, Jehovah's Witnesses, communists, or homosexuals, Hitler's government meant greater equality and more opportunities. In 1933 class barriers in Germany were generally high. Hitler's rule introduced changes that lowered these barriers. For example, stiff educational requirements favoring the well-to-do were relaxed. The new Nazi elite included many young and poorly educated dropouts, rootless lower-middle-class people like Hitler who rose to the top with breathtaking speed. More generally, the Nazis tolerated privilege and wealth only as long as they served party needs.

Yet few historians today believe that Hitler and the Nazis brought about a real social revolution, as an earlier generation of scholars often argued. The well-educated classes held on to most of their advantages, and only a modest social leveling occurred in the Nazi years. Significantly, the Nazis shared with the Italian fascists the stereotypical view of women as housewives and mothers. Only under the relentless pressure of war did they reluctantly mobilize large numbers of German women for office and factory work.

Not all Germans supported Hitler, however, and a number of German groups actively resisted him after 1933. Tens of thousands of political enemies were imprisoned, and thousands were executed. In the first years of Hitler's rule, the principal resisters were trade union communists and socialists. The expansion of the SS system of terror after 1935 smashed most of these leftists. Catholic and Protestant churches produced a second group of opponents. Their efforts were directed primarily at preserving genuine religious life, however, not at overthrowing Hitler. Finally in 1938 (and again from 1942 to 1944) some high-ranking army officers, who feared the consequences of Hitler's reckless aggression, plotted, unsuccessfully, against him.

Aggression and Appeasement (1933–1939)

Although economic recovery and somewhat greater opportunity for social advancement won Hitler support, the guiding and unique concepts of Nazism remained space and race—the territorial expansion of the superior German race. As we shall see, German expansion was facilitated by the uncertain, divided, pacific Western democracies, which tried to buy off Hitler to avoid war.

Hitler realized that his aggressive policies had to be carefully camouflaged at first, for the Treaty of Versailles limited Germany's army to only a hundred thousand men. As Hitler told some army commanders in February 1933, the early stages of his policy of "conquest of new living space in the East and its ruthless Germanization" had serious dangers. If France had real leaders, Hitler said, it would "not give us time but attack us, presumably with its eastern satellites."[11] Thus while Hitler loudly proclaimed his peaceful intentions, Germany's withdrawal from the League of Nations in October 1933 indicated its determination to rearm. When in March 1935 Hitler established a general military draft and declared the "unequal" Versailles treaty disarmament clauses null and void, some European leaders appeared to understand the danger and warned him against future aggressive actions.

But the emerging united front against Hitler quickly collapsed. Britain adopted a policy of appeasement, granting Hitler everything he could reasonably want (and more) in order to avoid war. The last chance to stop the Nazis came in March 1936 when Hitler suddenly marched his armies into the demilitarized Rhineland, brazenly violating the Treaties of Versailles and Locarno. An uncertain France would not move without British support, however, and Britain refused to act (see Map 30.1).

British appeasement, which practically dictated French policy, lasted far into 1939. It was motivated by British feelings of guilt toward Germany and the pacifism of a population still horrified by the memory of the Great War. As in Germany, many powerful British conservatives underestimated Hitler. They also believed that Soviet communism was the real danger and that Hitler could be used to stop it. Such strong anticommunist feelings made an alliance between the Western Powers and Stalin unlikely.

As Britain and France opted for appeasement and the Soviet Union watched all developments suspiciously, Hitler found powerful allies. In 1935 the bombastic Mussolini attacked the independent African kingdom of Ethiopia. The Western Powers and the League of Nations piously condemned Italian aggression, but Hitler supported Italy energetically. In 1936 Italy and Germany signed an agreement on close cooperation, the so-called Rome-Berlin Axis. Japan, which wanted support for its occupation of Manchuria, soon joined the Axis alliance.

At the same time, Germany and Italy intervened in the Spanish civil war (1936–1939). Their support eventually

> **Primary Source:**
> **The Centerpiece of Nazi Racial Legislation: The Nuremberg Laws**
> *These laws defined who was a Jew, forbade marriage between Germans and Jews, and paved the way for the Holocaust.*

● **Hitler's Success with Aggression** This biting criticism of appeasing leaders by the cartoonist David Low appeared shortly after Hitler remilitarized the Rhineland. Appeasement also appealed to millions of ordinary citizens in Britain and France who wanted to avoid another great war at any cost. *(Solo Syndication/Associated Newspapers)*

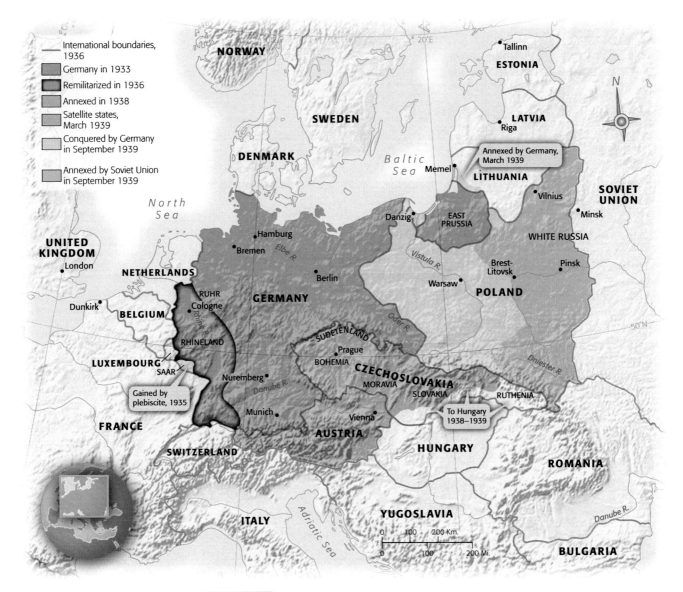

MAP 30.1 **The Growth of Nazi Germany, 1933–1939** Until March 1939, Hitler brought ethnic Germans into the Nazi state; then he turned on the Slavic peoples, whom he had always hated. He stripped Czechoslovakia of its independence and prepared for an attack on Poland in September 1939.

helped General Francisco Franco's fascist movement defeat republican Spain. Spain's only official aid came from the Soviet Union, for public opinion in Britain and especially in France was hopelessly divided on the Spanish question.

In late 1937 Hitler moved forward with his plans to crush Austria and Czechoslovakia as the first step in his long-contemplated drive to the east for living space. By threatening Austria with invasion, Hitler forced the Austrian chancellor in March 1938 to put local Nazis in control of the government. The next day German armies moved in unopposed, and Austria became two provinces of Greater Germany (see Map 30.1).

Simultaneously, Hitler began demanding that the pro-Nazi, German-speaking minority of western Czechoslovakia—the Sudetenland—be turned over to Germany. Democratic Czechoslovakia, however, was prepared to defend itself. Moreover, France had been Czechoslovakia's ally since 1924, and if France fought, the Soviet Union was pledged to help. War appeared inevitable, but appeasement triumphed again. In September 1938 Prime Minister Chamberlain flew to Germany three times in four-teen days. In these negotiations, to which the Soviet Union was deliberately not in-vited, Chamberlain and the French agreed with Hitler that the Sudetenland should be ceded to Germany immediately. Returning to London from the Munich Conference, Chamberlain told cheering crowds that he had secured "peace with honor . . . peace for our time." Sold out by the Western Powers, Czechoslovakia gave in.

Hitler's armies occupied the remainder of Czechoslovakia in March 1939. The ef-fect on Western public opinion was electrifying. For the first time, there was no pos-sible rationale of self-determination for Nazi aggression, because Hitler was treating the Czechs and Slovaks as captive peoples. When Hitler used the question of German minorities in Danzig as a pretext to confront Poland, a suddenly militant Chamberlain declared that Britain and France would fight if Hitler attacked his eastern neighbor. Hitler did not take these warnings seriously and decided to press on.

In an about-face that stunned the world, Hitler offered and Stalin signed a ten-year Nazi-Soviet nonaggression pact in August 1939. Each dictator promised to remain neutral if the other became involved in war. An attached secret protocol ruthlessly divided eastern Europe into German and Soviet zones "in the event of a political ter-ritorial reorganization." The British and French felt betrayed for they, too, had been negotiating with Stalin. But Stalin had remained distrustful of Western intentions, and Hitler had offered territorial gain.

For Hitler, everything was set. He told his generals on the day of the nonaggression pact, "My only fear is that at the last moment some dirty dog will come up with a mediation plan." On September 1, 1939, German armies and warplanes smashed into Poland from three sides. Two days later Britain and France, finally true to their word, declared war on Germany. The Second World War had begun.

• • • • • • • • • • • • •

THE SECOND WORLD WAR

How did Hitler's actions lead to another world war?

War broke out in both western and eastern Europe because Hitler's ambitions were essentially unlimited. On both war fronts Nazi soldiers scored enormous successes until late 1942, establishing a horrifyingly vast empire of death and destruction. Hit-ler's victories increased tensions in Asia between Japan and the United States and prompted Japan to attack the United States and overrun much of Southeast Asia. Yet reckless German and Japanese aggression also raised a mighty coalition determined to smash the aggressors. Led by Britain, the United States, and the Soviet Union, the Grand Alliance—to use Winston Churchill's favorite term—functioned quite effec-tively in military terms. Thus the Nazi and Japanese empires proved short-lived.

Hitler's Empire in Europe (1939–1942)

Using planes, tanks, and trucks in the first example of a **blitzkrieg,** or "lightning war," Hitler's armies crushed Poland in four weeks. The Soviet Union quickly took its part of the booty—the eastern half of Poland and the Baltic states of Lithuania, Estonia, and Latvia. In the west French and British armies dug in; they expected another war of attrition and economic blockade. But in spring 1940 the lightning war struck again. After occupying Denmark, Norway, and Holland, German motorized columns broke through southern Belgium and into France.

blitzkrieg *"Lightning war" us-ing planes, tanks, and trucks, the first example of which Hitler used to crush Poland in four weeks.*

Events Leading to World War II

1919	Treaty of Versailles is signed; J. M. Keynes publishes *Economic Consequences of the Peace.*
1919–1920	U.S. Senate rejects the Treaty of Versailles.
1921	Germany is billed $33 billion in reparations.
1922	Mussolini seizes power in Italy; Germany proposes a moratorium on reparations.
January 1923	France and Belgium occupy the Ruhr; Germany orders passive resistance to the occupation.
October 1923	Stresemann agrees to reparations based on Germany's ability to pay.
1924	Dawes Plan: German reparations are reduced and put on a sliding scale; large U.S. loans to Germany are recommended to promote German recovery; Adolf Hitler dictates *Mein Kampf.*
1924–1929	Spectacular German economic recovery occurs; circular flow of international funds enables sizable reparations payments.
1925	Treaties of Locarno promote European security and stability.
1926	Germany joins the League of Nations.
1928	Kellogg-Briand Pact renounces war as an instrument of international affairs.
1929	U.S. stock market crashes.
1929–1939	Great Depression rages.
1931	Japan invades Manchuria.
1932	Nazis become the largest party in the Reichstag.
January 1933	Hitler is appointed chancellor of Germany.
March 1933	Reichstag passes the Enabling Act, granting Hitler absolute dictatorial power.
October 1933	Germany withdraws from the League of Nations.
1935	Nuremberg Laws deprive Jews of all rights of citizenship.
March 1935	Hitler announces German rearmament.
June 1935	Anglo-German naval agreement is signed.
October 1935	Mussolini invades Ethiopia and receives Hitler's support.
March 1936	German armies move unopposed into the demilitarized Rhineland.
July 1936	Civil war breaks out in Spain.
1937	Japan invades China; Rome-Berlin Axis in effect.
March 1938	Germany annexes Austria.
September 1938	Munich Conference: Britain and France agree to German seizure of the Sudetenland from Czechoslovakia.
March 1939	Germany occupies the rest of Czechoslovakia; appeasement ends in Britain.
August 1939	Nazi-Soviet nonaggression pact is signed.
September 1, 1939	Germany invades Poland.
September 3, 1939	Britain and France declare war on Germany.

As Hitler's armies poured into France, aging marshal Henri-Philippe Pétain formed a new French government—the so-called Vichy government—and accepted defeat. By July 1940 Hitler ruled practically all of western continental Europe; Italy was an ally, the Soviet Union a friendly neutral (see Map 30.2). Only Britain, led by the uncompromising Winston Churchill (1874–1965), remained unconquered.

To mount an amphibious invasion of Britain, Germany first needed to gain control of the air. In the Battle of Britain, up to a thousand German planes attacked British airfields and key factories in a single day, dueling with British defenders high in the skies. In September Hitler angrily began indiscriminately bombing British cities in an attempt to break British morale. British aircraft factories increased production, and the heavily bombed people of London defiantly dug in. In September and October 1940 Britain was beating Germany three to one in the air war. There was no possibility of an immediate German invasion of Britain.

Hitler now allowed his lifetime obsession with a vast eastern European empire for the "master race" to dictate policy. In June 1941 German armies suddenly attacked the Soviet Union along a vast front. By October Leningrad was practically surrounded, Moscow was besieged, and most of Ukraine had been conquered. But the Soviets did not collapse, and when a severe winter struck German armies outfitted in summer uniforms, the invaders were stopped.

Stalled in Russia, Hitler had come to rule an enormous European empire stretching from the outskirts of Moscow to the English Channel. He and the top Nazi leadership began building their **New Order.** In doing so, they showed what Nazi victory would have meant.

Hitler's New Order was based firmly on the guiding principle of Nazi totalitarianism: racial imperialism. Within this New Order the Nordic peoples—the Dutch, Norwegians, and Danes—received preferential treatment, for they were racially related to the Germans. The French, an "inferior" Latin people, occupied the middle position.

New Order *Hitler's program, based on the guiding principle of racial imperialism that gave preferential treatment to the Nordic peoples.*

● **London, 1940** Hitler believed that his relentless terror bombing of London—the "blitz"—could break the will of the British people. He was wrong. The blitz caused enormous destruction, but Londoners went about their business with courage and calm determination, as this unforgettable image of a milkman in the rubble suggests. *(Hulton-Deutsch Collection/Corbis)*

Slavs in the conquered eastern territories were treated with harsh hatred as "subhumans." Hitler envisioned a vast eastern colonial empire where Poles, Ukrainians, and Russians would be enslaved and forced to die out, while Germanic peasants resettled the resulting abandoned lands. Hitler needed countless helpers, however, and these accomplices came forth. Himmler and the elite SS corps shared Hitler's ideology of barbarous racial imperialism. Supported (or condoned) by military commanders and German policemen in the occupied territories, the SS corps pressed relentlessly to implement the program of destruction and to create a "mass settlement space" for Germans. Many Poles, captured communists, Gypsies, and Jehovah's Witnesses were murdered in cold blood.

MAP 30.2 **World War II in Europe** The map shows the extent of Hitler's empire at its height, before the Battle of Stalingrad in late 1942 and the subsequent advances of the Allies until Germany surrendered on May 7, 1945.

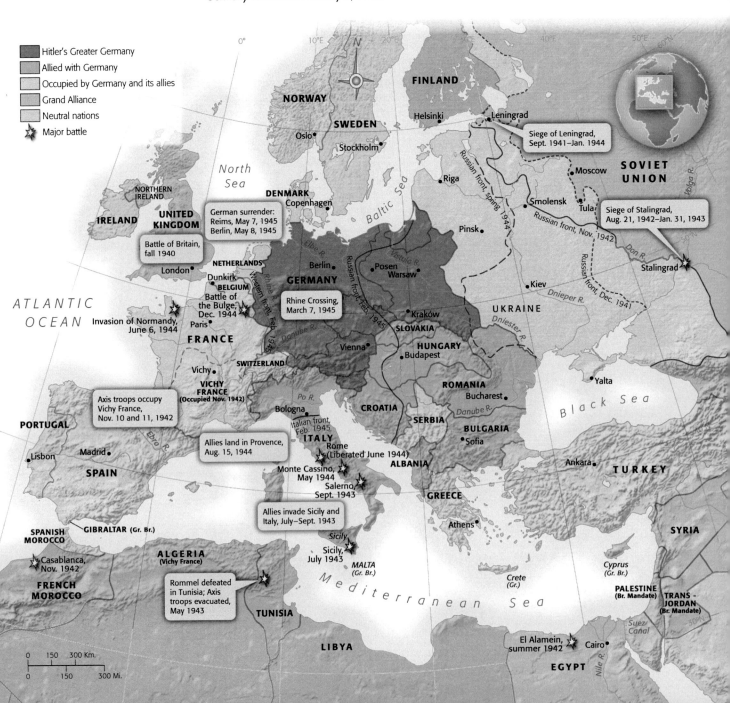

Finally, the Nazi state condemned all European Jews to extermination in the **Holocaust.** After the fall of Warsaw the Nazis began deporting all German Jews to occupied Poland, and in 1941 expulsion spiraled into extermination on the Russian front. Himmler's SS killing squads and regular army units forced Soviet Jews to dig giant pits, which became mass graves as the victims were lined up on the edge and cut down by machine guns. Then in late 1941 Hitler and the Nazi leadership, in some still-debated combination, ordered the SS to stop all Jewish emigration from Europe and speeded up planning for mass murder. All over the Nazi empire Jews were systematically arrested, packed like cattle onto freight trains, and dispatched to extermination camps.

Arriving at their destination, small numbers of Jews were sent to nearby slave labor camps, where they were starved and systematically worked to death. (See the feature "Individuals in Society: Primo Levi.") But most victims were taken by force or deception to "shower rooms," which were actually gas chambers. For fifteen to twenty minutes came the terrible screams and gasping sobs of men, women, and children choking to death on poison gas. Then, only silence. Special camp workers quickly yanked the victims' gold teeth from their jaws, and the bodies were then cremated, or sometimes boiled for oil to make soap. The extermination of European Jews was the ultimate monstrosity of Nazi racism and racial imperialism. By 1945, 6 million Jews had been murdered.

Who was responsible for this terrible crime? An older generation of historians usually laid most of the guilt on Hitler and the Nazi leadership. Ordinary Germans had little knowledge of the extermination camps, it was argued, and those who cooperated had no alternative given the brutality of Nazi terror and totalitarian control. But in recent years many studies have revealed a much broader participation of German people in the Holocaust and popular indifference (or worse) to the Jews' fate.

In most occupied countries, local non-German officials also cooperated in the arrest and deportation of Jews. As in Germany, only a few exceptional bystanders did not turn a blind eye. Thus some scholars have concluded that the key for most Germans (and most people in occupied countries) was that they felt no personal responsibility for Jews and therefore were not prepared to help them. This meant that many individuals, conditioned by Nazi racist propaganda but also influenced by peer pressure and brutalizing wartime violence, were psychologically prepared to perpetrate ever-greater crimes, from mistreatment to arrest to mass murder.

Holocaust *The attempted extermination of all European Jews by the Nazi state.*

> **Primary Source:**
> **Memoirs**
> *Read what the man responsible for administering and overseeing the Holocaust thought and felt about his "work."*

● **Prelude to Murder** This photo captures the terrible inhumanity of Nazi racism. Frightened and bewildered families from the soon-to-be-destroyed Warsaw Ghetto are being forced out of their homes by German soldiers for deportation to concentration camps. There they face murder in the gas chambers. *(Hulton Archive/Getty Images)*

Japan's Asian Empire

By late 1938, 1.5 million Japanese troops were bogged down in China, holding a great swath of territory but unable to defeat the Nationalists and the Communists (see pages 868–870). Nor had Japan succeeded in building a large, self-sufficient Asian economic zone, for it still depended on oil and scrap metal from the Netherlands East Indies and the United States. Thus Japanese leaders followed events in Europe closely, looking for alliances and actions that might improve their position in Asia. At home they gave free rein to the anti-Western ultranationalism that had risen in the 1920s and 1930s (see pages 866, 868): proclaiming Japan's liberating mission in Asia; glorifying the warrior virtues of honor and sacrifice; and demanding absolute devotion to the semidivine emperor. (See the feature "Listening to the Past: Radical Nationalism for Japanese Students" on pages 934–935).

The outbreak of war in Europe in 1939 and Hitler's early victories opened up opportunities for the Japanese in Asia. In China the Japanese redoubled their brutal efforts to crush peasant support for the Nationalists and the Communists. Implementing a brutal "three-alls" policy—"kill all, burn all, destroy all"—Japanese troops massacred whole villages, torched buildings, slaughtered farm animals, and committed shocking atrocities. In March 1940 the Japanese set up a Chinese puppet government in Nanjing, but the fighting—and the atrocities—continued until the war ended.

In Southeast Asia European empires appeared vulnerable. In September 1940 Japan signed a formal alliance with Germany and Italy and forced the French to accept Japanese domination of northern French Indochina. The United States had repeatedly condemned Japanese aggression in China. Now the United States also opposed Japanese expansion, because it feared that embattled Britain would collapse if it lost the support of its Asian colonies. Applying economic sanctions in October 1940, the United States stopped scrap iron sales to Japan and later froze all Japanese assets in the United States.

Japan's invasion of southern Indochina in July 1941 further worsened relations with the United States. President Franklin Roosevelt demanded that Japan withdraw from China, keeping only Manchuria. Japan refused. The United States responded by cutting off U.S. oil sales to Japan and thereby reducing Japan's oil supplies by 90 percent. Japanese leaders now increasingly believed that war with the United States was inevitable, for Japan's battle fleet would run out of fuel in eighteen months and its industry would be crippled. After much debate Japanese leaders decided to launch a surprise attack on the United States. They hoped to cripple their Pacific rival, gain time to build a defensible Asian empire, and eventually win an ill-defined compromise peace.

The Japanese attack on the U.S. naval base at Pearl Harbor in the Hawaiian Islands was a complete surprise but a limited success. On December 7, 1941, the Japanese sank or crippled every American battleship, but by chance all the American aircraft carriers were at sea and escaped unharmed. This enabled rapid American recovery, because aircraft carriers dominated the Pacific war. More important, most Americans felt superior to the Japanese, and they were humiliated by this unexpected defeat. Pearl Harbor overwhelmed American isolationism and brought Americans together in a spirit of anger and revenge.

Hitler immediately declared war on the United States. Simultaneously, Japanese armies successfully attacked European and American colonies in Southeast Asia. Japanese armies were small (because most soldiers remained in China), but they were well trained, well led, and highly motivated. They defeated larger Dutch and British armies to seize the Netherlands East Indies and its rich oil fields, and the British colonies of Hong Kong, Malaya, and Singapore. After American forces surrendered the Philippines in May 1942, Japan held a vast empire in Southeast Asia and the western Pacific (see Map 30.3).

Individuals IN SOCIETY

Primo Levi

Primo Levi, who never stopped thinking, writing, and speaking about the Holocaust. *(Giansanti/ Corbis Sygma)*

Most Jews deported to Auschwitz were murdered as soon as they arrived, but the Nazis made some prisoners into slave laborers and a few of these survived. Primo Levi (1919–1987), an Italian Jew, became one of the most influential witnesses to the Holocaust and its death camps.

Like much of Italy's small Jewish community, Levi's family belonged to the urban professional classes. The young Primo graduated in 1941 from the University of Turin with highest honors in chemistry. But since 1938, when Italy introduced racial laws, he had faced growing discrimination, and two years after graduation he joined the antifascist resistance movement. Quickly captured, he was deported to Auschwitz with 650 Italian Jews in February 1944. Stone-faced SS men picked only ninety-six men and twenty-nine women to work in their respective labor camps. Primo was one of them.

Nothing prepared Levi for what he encountered. The Jewish prisoners were kicked, punched, stripped, branded with tattoos, crammed into huts, and worked unmercifully. Hoping for some sign of prisoner solidarity in this terrible environment, Levi found only a desperate struggle of each against all and enormous status differences among prisoners. Many stunned and bewildered newcomers, beaten and demoralized by their bosses—the most privileged prisoners—simply collapsed and died. Others struggled to secure their own privileges, however small, because food rations and working conditions were so abominable that ordinary Jewish prisoners perished in two to three months.

Sensitive and noncombative, Levi found himself sinking into oblivion. But instead of joining the mass of the "drowned," he became one of the "saved"—a complicated surprise with moral implications that he would ponder all his life. As Levi explained in *Survival in Auschwitz* (1947), the usual road to salvation in the camps was some kind of collaboration with German power.* Savage German criminals were released from prison to become brutal camp guards; non-Jewish political prisoners competed for jobs entitling them to better conditions; and, especially troubling for Levi, a small number of Jewish men plotted and struggled

for the power of life and death over other Jewish prisoners. Though not one of these Jewish bosses, Levi believed that he himself, like almost all survivors, had entered the "gray zone" of moral compromise. Only a very few superior individuals, "the stuff of saints and martyrs," survived the death camps without shifting their moral stance.

For Levi, compromise and salvation came from his profession. Interviewed by a German technocrat for the camp's synthetic rubber program, Levi performed brilliantly in scientific German and savored his triumph as a Jew over Nazi racism. Work in the warm camp laboratory offered Levi opportunities to pilfer equipment that could then be traded for food and necessities with other prisoners. Levi also gained critical support from three saintly prisoners who refused to do wicked and hateful acts. And he counted "luck" as essential for his survival: in the camp infirmary with scarlet fever in February 1945 as advancing Russian armies prepared to liberate the camp, Levi was not evacuated by the Nazis and shot to death like most Jewish prisoners.

After the war Primo Levi was forever haunted by the nightmare that the Holocaust would be ignored or forgotten. Always ashamed that so many people whom he considered better than himself had perished, he wrote and lectured tirelessly to preserve the memory of Jewish victims and guilty Nazis. Wanting the world to understand the Jewish genocide in all its complexity so that never again would people tolerate such atrocities, he grappled tirelessly with his vision of individual choice and moral compromise in a hell designed to make the victims collaborate and persecute each other.

*Primo Levi, *Survival in Auschwitz: The Nazi Assault on Humanity*, rev. ed. 1958 (London: Collier Books, 1961), pp. 79–84, and *The Drowned and the Saved* (New York: Summit Books, 1988). These powerful testimonies are highly recommended.

Questions for Analysis

1. Describe Levi's experience at Auschwitz. How did camp prisoners treat each other? Why?

2. What does Levi mean by the "gray zone"? How is this concept central to his thinking?

3. Will a vivid historical memory of the Holocaust help prevent future genocide?

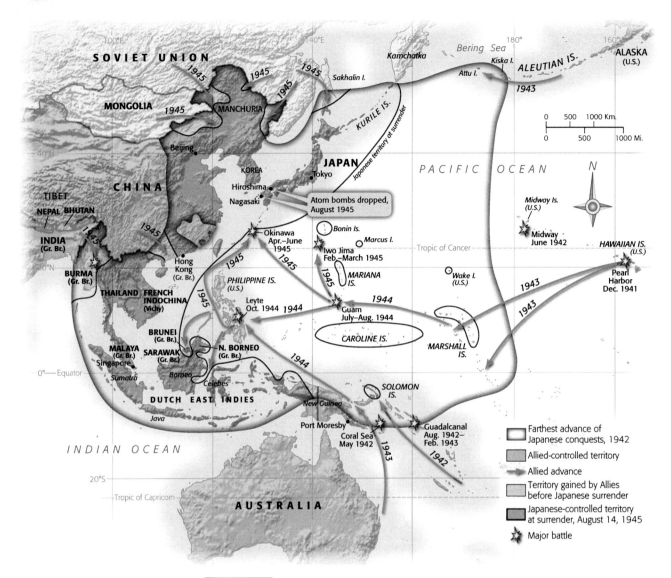

MAP 30.3 **World War II in the Pacific** Japanese forces overran an enormous amount of territory in 1942, which the Allies slowly recaptured in a long, bitter struggle. As this map shows, Japan still held a large Asian empire in August 1945, when the unprecedented devastation of atomic warfare suddenly forced it to surrender.

The Japanese claimed they were freeing Asians from Western imperialism, and they called their empire the Greater East Asian Co-prosperity Sphere. Some, perhaps many, Japanese army officers and officials sincerely believed that they were creating a mutually advantageous union for Asia's long-term development. Initially they tapped currents of nationalist sentiment, and most local populations were glad to see the Western Powers go. But Asian faith in "co-prosperity" and support for Japan steadily declined as the war went on. Why was this so?

A key factor was that although the Japanese set up anticolonial governments and promised genuine independence, real power always rested with Japanese military commanders and their superiors in Tokyo. The "independent" governments established in the Philippines, French Indochina, Burma, and the Netherlands East Indies were basically shams. Moreover, the Japanese never treated local populations as equals.

● **The War in the Philippines** U.S. and Philippine forces held out on the Bataan peninsula until April 1942, when seventy-six thousand soldiers surrendered to the Japanese military. Most of the prisoners were sick, wounded, or suffering from malnutrition, and the Japanese systematically executed many of them. Other prisoners, such as those pictured here, were marched to exhaustion without water in the blazing sun on the infamous Bataan Death March, and many were bayoneted or beaten to death. (Bettmann/Corbis)

As Japanese living standards plummeted and heavy industry sputtered, the Japanese occupiers exploited local peoples for Japan's wartime needs. They cut wages, imposed supply quotas on raw materials, and drafted local people for military and labor service. Ships left for Japan laden with rice, oil, and raw materials, but they returned empty, if they returned at all.

The Japanese often exhibited great cruelty toward prisoners of war and civilians, as they had toward the Chinese since 1937. After the fall of Hong Kong in December 1941, for example, wounded prisoners there were murdered and burned, and there was a mass rape of nurses. Elsewhere Korean, Dutch, and Indonesian women were forced into sexual bondage, providing sex for Japanese soldiers as "comfort women." Recurring cruel behavior also aroused local populations against the invaders.

The Grand Alliance

While the Nazis and the Japanese built their savage empires, the Allies faced the hard fact that chance, rather than choice, had brought them together. Stalin had been co-operating fully with Hitler between August 1939 and June 1941, and only the Japanese attack on Pearl Harbor in December 1941 had overwhelmed powerful isolationism in the United States.

As a first step toward building an unshakable alliance, U.S. president Franklin D. Roosevelt accepted the policy of **"Europe first"** as proposed by Winston Churchill (Chamberlain's successor as British prime minister). Only after Hitler was defeated would the United States turn toward the Pacific for an all-out attack on Japan, the lesser threat. The Americans and the British also put immediate military needs first, consistently postponing tough political questions relating to the eventual peace settlement that might have split the alliance.

To further encourage mutual trust, the Allies adopted the principle of the "unconditional surrender" of Germany and Japan. This policy cemented the Grand Alliance because it denied Germany and Japan any hope of dividing their foes.

"Europe first" *The military strategy, set forth by Churchill and adopted by Roosevelt, that called for the defeat of Hitler in Europe before the United States launched an all-out strike against Japan in the Pacific.*

The Grand Alliance's military resources were awesome. The United States possessed a unique capacity to wage global war with its mighty industry, large population, and national unity. These were all harnessed in 1942 to gear up rapidly for all-out war. In 1943 America out produced not only Germany, Italy, and Japan but also all of the rest of the world combined.[12]

Britain continued to make a great contribution as well. The British economy was totally and effectively mobilized, and the sharing of burdens through rationing and heavy taxes on war profits maintained social harmony. Britain, the impregnable floating fortress, became a gigantic frontline staging area for the decisive blow to the heart of Germany.

As for the Soviet Union, so great was its strength that it might well have defeated Germany without Western help. In the face of the German advance, whole factories and populations were successfully evacuated to eastern Russia and Siberia. There war production was reorganized and expanded, and the Red Army was increasingly well supplied and well led. Above all, Stalin drew on the massive support and heroic determination of the Soviet people, especially those in the central Russian heartland. Broad-based Russian nationalism, as opposed to narrow communist ideology, became the powerful unifying force in what the Soviet people appropriately called the "Great Patriotic War of the Fatherland."

Finally, the United States, Britain, and the Soviet Union had the resources of much of the world at their command. They were also aided by a growing resistance movement against the Nazis throughout Europe, even in Germany. After the Soviet Union was invaded in June 1941, communists throughout Europe took the lead in the underground resistance, joined by a growing number of patriots, Christians, and agents sent by governments-in-exile in London.

The War in Europe (1942–1945)

Barely halted at the gates of Moscow and Leningrad in 1941, the Germans renewed their offensive against the Soviet Union in 1942 and attacked the southern city of Stalingrad in July. In November 1942 Soviet armies counterattacked, quickly surrounding the entire German Sixth Army of 300,000 men. By late January 1943 only 123,000 soldiers were left to surrender. Hitler, who had refused to allow a retreat, suffered a catastrophic defeat. In summer 1943 the larger, better-equipped Soviet armies took the offensive and began moving forward (see Map 30.2).

Not yet prepared to attack Germany directly through France, the Western Allies saw heavy fighting in North Africa (see Map 30.2). In summer 1942 British forces finally defeated combined German and Italian armies at the Battle of El Alamein, only seventy miles from Alexandria. Almost immediately thereafter an Anglo-American force landed in Morocco and Algeria. These French possessions, which were under the control of Pétain's Vichy French government, quickly went over to the Allied side.

Having driven the Axis powers from North Africa by spring 1943, Allied forces invaded Italy. War-weary Italians deposed Mussolini, and the new Italian government publicly accepted unconditional surrender in September 1943. Italy, it seemed, was liberated. But then German commandos in a daring raid rescued Mussolini and put him at the head of a puppet government. German armies seized Rome and all of northern Italy. Fighting continued in Italy.

Indeed, bitter fighting continued in Europe for almost two years. Germany, less fully mobilized for war than Britain in 1941, applied itself to total war in 1942 and enlisted millions of German women and millions of prisoners of war and slave laborers from all across occupied Europe in that effort. Between early 1942 and July 1944 German war production actually tripled in spite of heavy bombing by the British and American air forces. Terrorized at home and frightened by the prospect of unconditional surrender, the Germans fought on with suicidal stoicism.

On June 6, 1944, American and British forces under General Dwight Eisenhower landed on the beaches of Normandy, France, in history's greatest naval invasion. In a hundred dramatic days more than 2 million men and almost a half million vehicles pushed inland and broke through German lines. Rejecting proposals to strike straight at Berlin in a massive attack, Eisenhower moved forward cautiously on a broad front. Not until March 1945 did American troops cross the Rhine and enter Germany.

The Soviets, who had been advancing steadily since July 1943, reached the outskirts of Warsaw by August 1944. On April 26, 1945 the Red Army met American forces on the Elbe River. The Allies had closed their vise on Nazi Germany and overrun Europe. As Soviet forces fought their way into Berlin, Hitler committed suicide in his bunker, and on May 7 the remaining German commanders capitulated.

● **The Normandy Invasion, Omaha Beach, June 6, 1944** Airborne paratroopers landed behind German coastal fortifications around midnight, and U.S. and British forces hit several beaches at daybreak as Allied ships and bombers provided cover. U.S. troops secured full control of Omaha Beach by nightfall, but at a price of three thousand casualties. Allied air power prevented the Germans from bringing up reserves and counterattacking. *(Naval Historical Foundation, Washington, D.C.)*

The War in the Pacific (1942–1945)

While gigantic armies clashed on land in Europe, the greatest naval battles in history decided the fate of warring nations in Asia. In April 1942 the Japanese devised a complicated battle plan to take Port Moresby in New Guinea and also destroy U.S. aircraft carriers in an attack on Midway Island (see Map 30.3). Having broken the secret Japanese code, the Americans skillfully deployed the small number of ships at their disposal and won decisive naval victories. First, in the Battle of the Coral Sea in May 1942, an American carrier force halted the Japanese advance on Port Moresby and relieved Australia from the threat of invasion. Then, in the Battle of Midway in June 1942, American carrier-based pilots sank all four of the attacking Japanese aircraft carriers and established overall naval equality with Japan in the Pacific.

● **"Follow Me!"** This painting by Charles McBarron, Jr., shows the action at Red Beach on October 20, 1944, in the Battle of Leyte Gulf in the Philippine Islands. It captures the danger and courage of U.S. troops, which had to storm well-fortified Japanese positions again and again in their long island-hopping campaign. The officer exhorts his men, and death is all around. *(The Granger Collection, New York)*

Badly hampered in the ground war by the Europe first policy, the United States gradually won control of the sea and air as it geared up massive production of aircraft carriers, submarines, and fighter planes. By 1943 the United States was producing one hundred thousand aircraft a year, almost twice as many as Japan produced in the entire war. By 1944 hundreds of American submarines were hunting in "wolf packs," decimating shipping and destroying economic links in Japan's far-flung, overextended empire. In July 1943 the Americans and their Australian allies opened an "island-hopping" campaign toward Japan. Pounding Japanese forces on a given island with saturation bombing, American army and marine units would then hit the beaches with rifles and flamethrowers and secure victory in hand-to-hand combat.

The Pacific war was brutal—a "war without mercy," in the words of a leading American scholar—and atrocities were committed on both sides.[13] Aware of Japanese atrocities in China and the Philippines, the U.S. Marines and Army troops seldom took Japanese prisoners after the Battle of Guadalcanal in August 1942, killing even those rare Japanese soldiers who offered to surrender. American forces moving across the central and western Pacific in 1943 and 1944 faced unyielding resistance and this resistance hardened American hearts as American casualties kept rising. A product of spiraling violence, mutual hatred, and dehumanizing racial stereotypes, the war without mercy intensified as it moved toward Japan.

In June 1944 giant U.S. bombers began a relentless bombing campaign of the Japanese home islands. In October 1944 American forces under General Douglas MacArthur landed on Leyte Island in the Philippines. The Japanese believed they could destroy MacArthur's troops and transport ships before the main American fleet arrived. The result was the four-day Battle of Leyte Gulf, the greatest battle in naval history, with 282 ships involved. The Japanese lost 13 large warships, including

Primary Source:
The Decision to Use the Atomic Bomb
Learn why President Truman was advised to drop atomic bombs on Japan—from the chairman of the committee that gave him that advice.

4 aircraft carriers, while the Americans lost only 3 small ships in their great triumph. The Japanese navy was practically finished.

In spite of massive defeats, Japanese troops continued to fight with enormous courage and determination. Indeed, the bloodiest battles of the Pacific war took place on Iwo Jima in February 1945 and on Okinawa in June 1945. MacArthur and his commanders believed the conquest of Japan might cost a million American casualties and possibly 10 million to 20 million Japanese lives. In fact, Japan was almost helpless, its industry and dense, fragile wooden cities largely destroyed by incendiary bombing and uncontrollable hurricanes of fire. Yet the Japanese seemed determined to fight on, if only with bamboo spears, ever ready to die for a hopeless cause.

On August 6 and 9, 1945, the United States dropped atomic bombs on Hiroshima and Nagasaki in Japan. Mass bombing of cities and civilians, one of the terrible new practices of World War II, had led to the final nightmare—unprecedented human destruction in a single blinding flash. On August 14, 1945, the Japanese announced their surrender. The Second World War, which had claimed the lives of more than 50 million soldiers and civilians, was over.

● **A Hiroshima Survivor Remembers** Yasuko Yamagata was seventeen when she saw the brilliant blue-white "lightning flash" that became a fiery orange ball consuming everything that would burn. Thirty years later Yamagata painted this scene, her most unforgettable memory of the atomic attack. An incinerated woman, poised as if running with her baby clutched to her breast, lies near a water tank piled high with charred corpses. *(Courtsey, Hiroshima Peace Memorial Museum)*

Chapter Summary

To assess your mastery of this chapter, go to
bedfordstmartins.com/mckayworld

• What was the nature of twentieth-century dictatorships and authoritarian rule?

The Second World War marked the climax of the tremendous practical and spiritual maladies of the age of anxiety, which led in many lands to the rise of dictatorships. Many of these dictatorships were variations on conservative authoritarianism, but there was also a fateful innovation—a new kind of radical dictatorship that was exceptionally dynamic and theoretically unlimited in its actions. The totalitarian regimes formed in the 1920s and 1930s—specifically in Hitler's Germany and Stalin's Russia, and to a lesser extent in Mussolini's Italy, Franco's Spain, Hirohito's Japan, and Salazar's Portugal—were violent, dynamic, and profoundly antiliberal. They all, to a greater or lesser extent, asserted a total claim on the lives of their citizens, posed ambitious goals, and demanded popular support. Stalin's Russia and Hitler's Germany in particular

Key Terms

totalitarianism
fascism
five-year plan
New Economic Policy (NEP)
collectivization
kulaks
Black Shirts
Lateran Agreement
Nazism
Führer
Enabling Act
blitzkrieg
New Order
Holocaust
"Europe first"

exuded tremendous dynamism and awesome power. That dynamism, however, was channeled in quite different directions. Stalin and the Communist Party aimed at building their kind of socialism and the new socialist personality at home. Hitler and the Nazi elite aimed at unlimited territorial and racial aggression on behalf of a "master race"; domestic recovery was only a means to that end.

• *How were the five-year plans part of the totalitarian order in the Soviet Union?*

The five-year plans initiated in the Soviet Union in 1928 were a critical part of Stalin's efforts to totally control the Russian economy and society. Meant to introduce a "revolution from above," the plans were extremely ambitious efforts to modernize and industrialize the U.S.S.R. along socialist lines and to create a new socialist humanity. They set staggering industrial and agricultural objectives and replaced private lands with (often forced) collectivization. Labor unions were severely weakened, and foreign experts from Europe and America were brought in to lend their skill and expertise to the building of new factories and machinery in order to catch up with the more advanced capitalist nations of the West.

• *How was Italian fascism a halfway house between conservative authoritarianism and modern totalitarianism?*

In Italy Mussolini's hatred of liberalism led him to set up the first fascist government. Although brutal in its methods, it was never truly a totalitarian state on the order of Hitler's Germany or Stalin's Soviet Union. Mussolini did create a one-party dictatorship by abolishing press freedoms, disbanding independent trade unions, rigging elections, and ruling by decree. Mussolini allowed the old conservative classes to retain control of the economy, army, and the state bureaucracy. He gained the support of the Roman Catholic Church by recognizing the Vatican as a tiny independent state in 1929. Racial laws were never a very significant aspect of Mussolini's rule, as they were for Hitler, and Jews were not severely persecuted until Italy came under Nazi control toward the end of World War II. Thus, though repressive and undemocratic, fascist Italy was never really a totalitarian state.

• *Why were Hitler and his Nazi regime initially so popular?*

Hitler created a model totalitarian state in Germany, initially with the support of most of the German people. Hitler began by drawing on the anger and sense of betrayal many Germans felt after losing the Great War, and the humiliation of the terms of the Versailles Treaty. The war was followed by a period of astronomical inflation and unemployment. He added to the economic and patriotic discontent by drawing on the racist sentiments about "inferior" peoples, such as the Jews and the Slavs, which had deep roots in German history and culture. He convinced many Germans that Jews and Marxists had caused Germany to lose the war, and that a worldwide Jewish conspiracy continued to harm German culture, German unity, and the German race. Hitler was also a master of mass propaganda and political showmanship and effectively used the new propaganda tools of the movies and the radio to reach mass audiences. When the Great Depression struck, Hitler appealed to people's economic welfare, and made great promises that caused voters to desert the old leaders and turn to this dynamic new voice. Finally, Hitler was successful in gaining the support of Germany's young people by directly answering their needs and concerns, by appointing young party members to positions of power, and by emphasizing rapid change, national recovery, and personal advancement.

• How did Hitler's actions lead to another world war?

Hitler and his Nazi followers' genocidal racism and unlimited aggression made war inevitable, first with the western European democracies, then with hated eastern neighbors, and finally with the United States. Plunging Europe into the ultimate nightmare, unlimited aggression unwittingly forged a mighty coalition that smashed the racist Nazi empire and its leader. In the words of the ancient Greeks, he whom the gods would destroy, they first make mad.

Suggested Reading

Applebaum, Anne. *Gulag.* 2004. An excellent survey of Stalin's labor-death camps.

Arendt, Hannah. *The Origins of Totalitarianism.* 1951. Controversial, classic philosophical-historical study.

Brendon, Piers. *The Dark Valley. A Panorama of the 1930s.* Masterful, sweeping account of this tumultuous decade.

Brooker, Paul. *Twentieth Century Dictatorships: The Ideological One-Party State.* 1995. Comparative analysis.

Fitzpatrick, Sheila. *Everyday Stalinism: Ordinary Life in Extraordinary Times.* 1999. Social and cultural history.

Gilbert, Martin. *The Second World War: A Complete History,* rev. ed. 2004. Massively detailed global survey.

Glantz, David M. *When Titans Clashed: How the Red Army Stopped Hitler.* 1995. Authoritative account of the Eastern Front in World War II.

Hasegawa, Tsuyoshi. *Racing the Enemy: Stalin, Truman and the Surrender of Japan.* 2005. Masterful diplomatic history with controversial new account of the end of the war.

Hillberg, Raul. *The Destruction of the European Jews, 1933–1945,* rev. ed. 3 vols. 1985. A monumental classic.

Hsiung, James C., and Seven Levine, eds. *China's Bitter Victory: The War with Japan, 1937–1945.* 1992. Investigates various aspects of the long struggle.

Keegan, John. *The Second World War.* 1990. Broad survey by a distinguished military historian.

Kershaw, Ian. *The Nazi Dictatorship, Problems and Perspectives of Interpretation,* 2nd ed. 1989. Interpretive, historiographical.

Levi, Primo. *Survival at Auschwitz.* 1947. First published in English as *If This Is a Man;* memoir and meditation on the meaning of survival.

Lewin, Moshe. *The Making of the Soviet System.* 1985. Social history, especially agrarian.

Marrus, Michael. *The Holocaust in History.* 1987. Classic interpretive survey.

Weinberg, Gerhard. *World at Arms: A Global History of World War II.* 1994. Global survey with political-diplomatic emphasis.

Wright, Gordon. *The Ordeal of Total War,* rev. ed. 1997. Explores scientific, psychological, and economic dimensions of the war.

Notes

1. A. Gleason, *Totalitarianism: The Inner History of the Cold War* (New York: Oxford University Press, 1995), p. 50.
2. E. Halévy, *The Era of Tyrannies* (Garden City, N.Y.: Doubleday, 1965), pp. 265–316, esp. p. 300.
3. I. Kershaw, *The Nazi Dictatorship: Problems and Perspectives of Interpretation,* 2d ed. (London: Edward Arnold, 1989), p. 34.
4. Quoted in A. G. Mazour, *Soviet Economic Development: Operation Outstrip, 1921–1965* (Princeton, N.J.: Van Nostrand, 1967), p. 130.
5. Quoted in I. Deutscher, *Stalin: A Political Biography,* 2d ed. (New York: Oxford University Press, 1967), p. 325.
6. M. Malia, *The Soviet Tragedy: A History of Socialism in Russia* (New York: Free Press, 1994), p. 248.
7. R. Thurston, *Life and Terror in Stalin's Russia, 1934–1941* (New Haven, Conn.: Yale University Press, 1996), esp. pp. 16–106; and Malia, *The Soviet Tragedy,* pp. 227–270.
8. R. Vivarelli, "Interpretations on the Origins of Fascism," *Journal of Modern History* 63 (March 1991): 41.
9. W. Brustein, *The Logic of Evil: The Social Origins of the Nazi Party, 1925–1933* (New Haven, Conn.: Yale University Press, 1996), pp. 52, 182.
10. Quoted in R. Stromberg, *An Intellectual History of Modern Europe* (New York: Appleton-Century-Crofts, 1966), p. 393.
11. Quoted in K. D. Bracher, *The German Dictatorship: The Origins, Structure and Effects of National Socialism* (New York: Praeger, 1970), p. 289.
12. H. Willmott, *The Great Crusade: A New Complete History of the Second World War* (New York: Free Press, 1989), p. 255.
13. J. Dower, *War Without Mercy: Race and Power in the Pacific War* (New York: Pantheon, 1986).

Listening to the
PAST

Radical Nationalism for Japanese Students

*I*n August 1941, only four months before Japan's coordinated attack on Pearl Harbor and colonial empires
in Southeast Asia, Japan's Ministry of Education
*issued "The Way of Subjects." Required reading for high
school and university students, this twenty-page pamphlet
summed up the basic tenets of Japanese ultranationalism,
which had become dominant in the 1930s.*

*As this selection suggests, ultranationalism in Japan
combined a sense of mission with intense group solidarity
and unquestioning devotion to a semidivine emperor. Thus
Japanese expansion into Manchuria and the war in China
were part of Japan's sacred calling to protect the throne
and to free Asia from Western exploitation and misrule. Of
course, an unknown percentage of students (and adults)
did not believe that the myths of Japan's state religion
were literally true. Nevertheless, they were profoundly
influenced by extremist nationalism: Japanese soldiers'
determination to fight to the death was a prime indicator
of that influence.*

The way of the subjects of the Emperor issues from
the policy of the Emperor and is to guard and maintain the Imperial Throne coexistent with the Heavens
and the Earth. This is not an abstract principle but a
way of daily practices based on history. The life and
activities of the nation are all attuned to the task of
strengthening the foundation of the Empire. . . .

Modern history, in a nutshell, has been marked
by the formation of unified nations in Europe and
their contests for supremacy in the acquisition of
colonies. . . . Their march into all parts of the world
paved the way for their subsequent world domination
politically, economically, and culturally and led them
to believe that they alone were justified in their outra-
geous behavior. . . .

The thoughts that have formed the foundation of
Western civilization since the early modern period
are individualism, liberalism, materialism, and so on.
These thoughts regard the strong preying on the
weak as reasonable, unstintedly promote the pursuit
of luxury and pleasure, encourage materialism, and
stimulate competition for acquiring colonies and

securing trade, thereby leading the world to a veritable
hell of fighting and bloodshed [in the First World
War]. . . . [Thereafter] a vigorous movement was
started by Britain, France, and the United States to
maintain the status quo by any means. Simultaneously,
a movement aiming at social revolution through class
conflict on the basis of thoroughgoing materialism like
Communism also vigorously developed. On the other
hand, Nazism and Fascism arose with great force.
The basic principles of the totalitarianism in Germany
and Italy are to remove the evils of individualism and
liberalism.

That these [totalitarian] principles show great
similarity to Eastern culture and spirit is a noteworthy
fact that suggests the future of Western civilization
and the creation of a new culture. Thus, the orientation of world history has made the collapse of the old
world order a certainty. Japan has hereby initiated the
construction of a new world order based on moral
principles.

The Manchurian Affair [the Japanese invasion of
Manchuria in 1931] was a violent outburst of Japanese
national life long suppressed. Taking advantage of this,
Japan in the glare of all the Powers made a step toward
the creation of a world based on moral principles and
the construction of a new order. This was a manifestation of the spirit, profound and lofty, embodied in the
founding of Empire, and an unavoidable action for its
national life and world mission. . . .

The general tendency of world domination by Europe and America has begun to show signs of a change
since the Russo-Japanese War of 1904–05. Japan's
victory attracted the attention of the entire world, and
this caused a reawakening of Asiatic countries, which
had been forced to lie prostrate under British and
American influence, with the result that an independence movement was started.

Hopes to be free of the shackles and bondage of
Europe and America were ablaze among the nations of
India, Turkey, Arabia, Thailand, Vietnam, and others.
This also inspired a new national movement in China.
Amid this stormy atmosphere of Asia's reawakening,

Japan has come to be keenly conscious of the fact that the stabilization of East Asia is her mission, and that the emancipation of East Asian nations rests solely on her efforts. . . .

Japan has a political mission to help various regions in the Greater East Asian Co-prosperity Sphere [the Japanese term for Japan's Asian empire], which are reduced to a state of quasi-colony by Europe and America, and rescue them from their control. Economically, this country will have to eradicate the evils of their exploitation and then set up an economic structure for coexistence and co-prosperity. Culturally, Japan must strive to fashion East Asian nations to abandon their following of European and American culture and to develop Eastern culture for the purpose of contributing to the creation of a just world. The East has been left to destruction for the past several hundred years. Its rehabilitation is not an easy task. It is natural that unusual difficulties attend the establishment of a new order and the creation of a new culture. Overcoming these difficulties will do much to help in establishing a world dominated by morality, in which all nations can co-operate and all people can secure their proper positions. . . .

In Japan, the Emperors of a line unbroken for ages eternal govern and reign over it, as the Heavens and the Earth endure, since the Imperial Foundress, Amaterasu-o-Mikami, . . . caused Her grandson Ninigi-no-Mikoto to descend on the eight great countries and She commanded him, saying: "This country, fruitful and abounding in rice, is the land over which Our descendants shall rule. Go you, therefore, down and reign over it. Under you and your offspring it shall prosper as long as the Heavens and the Earth endure." . . .

The Imperial Family is [therefore] the fountain source of the Japanese nation, and national and private lives issue from this. In the past, foreign nationals came to this country only to enjoy the benevolent rule of the Imperial Family, and became Japanese subjects spiritually and by blood. The Imperial virtues are so great and boundless that all are assimilated into one.

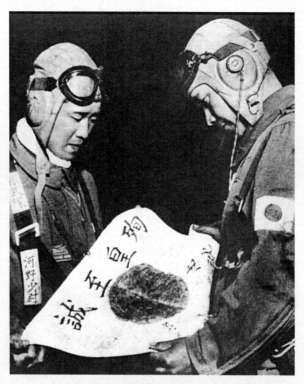

Kamikaze pilots ponder the message on the flag that they will take on their suicide mission: "All for the Emperor, we are happy to die for him." *(Archives Mondadori, Milan)*

Here is the reason for the present glorious state, in which the Emperor and his subjects are harmonized into one great unit. That the myriad subjects with one mind are glad to be unified in their devotion to the Throne is the substance of the Imperial subjects.

The way of the subjects is to be loyal to the Emperor in disregard of self. . . . To serve the Emperor is its key point. Our lives will become sincere and true when they are offered to the Emperor and the state. . . . All must be unified under the Emperor. Herein lies the significance of national life in Japan.

Questions for Analysis

1. How does "The Way of Subjects" interpret modern history? In what ways do Western thought and action threaten Japan?

2. What is Japan's mission in Asia?

3. What is the basis of Japanese sovereignty? What is the individual's proper role in society?

Source: "The Way of Subjects," in *Tokyo Record,* copyright 1943 by Otto D. Tolischus and renewed 1970 by Naya G. Tolischus. Reprinted by permission of Houghton Mifflin Harcourt Publishing Company.

African Market. This bustling market in Monrovia, Liberia, reflects the vibrant diversity of modern Africa. *(Tim Hetherington/ Panos Pictures)*

32 LATIN AMERICA, ASIA, AND AFRICA IN THE CONTEMPORARY WORLD

Chapter Preview

Latin America: Moving Toward Democracy
• How was Latin America similar to, and different from, the other Third World nations?

The Resurgence of East Asia
• How did the defeat of Japan lead to East Asian resurgence after World War II?

New Nations and Old Rivalries in South Asia
• How did Hindus and Muslims adjust to the end of British colonial rule?

The Islamic Heartland
• What was the dual nature of nationalism in the Islamic heartland?

Imperialism and Nationalism in Sub-Saharan Africa
• How did Kwame Nkrumah represent the new leaders of independent Africa?

Sub-Saharan Africa Since 1960
• What are some of the common features of independent Africa since 1960?

Interpreting the Experiences of the Emerging World
• How do the writings of Chinua Achebe represent the common experiences of peoples in the emerging world?

Historians often describe the cold war era as "bipolar," consisting of (1) the United States and its allies in the West and East and (2) the Soviet Union and its allies in the West and East. Of course, the world was not truly bipolar. Two-thirds of the world's people were certainly influenced by the two superpowers' actions and were often willing or unwilling participants in their global power struggle. Just as often, they simply watched anxiously from the sidelines, hoping the two giants would not destroy them and the planet with nuclear weapons. While the United States and the Soviet Union faced each other in a deadly confrontation, people in the so-called Third World went about their daily lives.

The term *Third World* has its origins in the 1950s, when many thinkers, journalists, and politicians viewed Africa, Asia, and Latin America as a single entity, different from both the capitalist, industrialized "First World" and the communist, industrialized "Second World." Or, in contemporary scholarly jargon, they imagined and "constructed" Africa, Asia, and Latin America as a unit for effective analysis and action. Despite differences in history and culture, African, Asian, and Latin American countries—for a generation—did share many characteristics linking them together that encouraged a common consciousness and ideology.

First, nearly all African, Asian, and Latin American countries had experienced political or economic domination, nationalist reaction, and a struggle for genuine independence. Precisely because of their shared sense of past injustice and continued exploitation, many influential Latin Americans identified with the Third World, despite their countries' greater affluence.

Second, Asian, African, and most Latin American countries had—many still do—predominately agricultural economies, earning the majority of their revenues from one or two cash crops whose production was frequently controlled and exploited by First World countries or by multinational agribusinesses. In the second half of the twentieth century they became united by their growing awareness of their common poverty and dependency on First World markets to set prices and buy their raw materials.

Third, in the 1950s and 1960s a majority of people in most poor countries lived in the countryside and depended on agriculture for a living. By contrast, most First World people lived in cities and depended mainly on industry and urban services for employment. Not everyone in the Third World was poor; a small elite were quite wealthy. But the average standard of living was low, and massive poverty was ever present.

Finally, Third World peoples were united in their opposition to political and economic oppression in all its forms, particularly colonialism, neocolonialism, and racism. Their leaders believed genuine independence and social justice were the real challenges before them, and they worked in the United Nations for a restructuring of the world economic system (see page 1023).

LATIN AMERICA: MOVING TOWARD DEMOCRACY

How was Latin America similar to, and different from, the other Third World nations?

After the Second World War Latin America experienced a many-faceted recovery, somewhat similar to that of Europe, though beginning earlier. After a generation, Latin America also experienced its own period of turbulence and crisis. Many Latin American countries responded by establishing authoritarian military regimes until, in the late 1980s, Latin America copied eastern Europe by electing civilian governments and embracing economic liberalism for the first time since the 1920s.

Economic Nationalism in Latin America

The growth of economic nationalism was a common development throughout Latin America in much of the twentieth century. Just as Spanish and Portuguese colonies won political independence in the early nineteenth century, much of recent history has witnessed a quest for genuine economic independence. To understand the rise of economic nationalism, one must remember that Latin American countries developed as producers of foodstuffs and raw materials exported to Europe and the United States in return for manufactured goods and capital investment. This exchange brought considerable economic development but exacted a heavy price: neocolonialism (see pages 786–787). Latin America became dependent on foreign markets, products, and investments. Industry did not develop, and large landowners profited the most from economic development, using their advantage to enhance their social and political power.

The Great Depression made matters worse. Prices and exports of Latin American commodities collapsed as Europe and the United States drastically reduced their purchases and raised tariffs to protect domestic products. With their foreign sales plummeting, Latin American countries could not buy the industrial goods they needed from abroad. The global depression provoked a profound shift toward economic nationalism after 1930, as popularly based governments worked to reduce foreign influence and gain control of their own economies and natural resources. These efforts were fairly successful. By the late 1940s factories in Argentina, Brazil, and Chile could generally satisfy domestic consumer demand for the products of light industry. In the 1950s some countries began moving into heavy industry. Economic nationalism and the rise of industry are particularly striking in the two largest and most influential countries, Mexico and Brazil, which account for half of Latin America's population.

Primary Source:
Speech to the Nation
In this excerpt from a radio address given in 1938, President Lázaro Cárdenas announces his decision to nationalize the Mexican oil industry.

The Mexican Revolution of 1910 overthrew the elitist, upper-class rule of the tyrant Porfirio Díaz, culminating in 1917 in a new constitution. This radical nationalistic document called for universal suffrage, massive land reform, benefits for labor, and strict control of foreign capital. Progress was modest until 1934, when a charismatic young Indian from a poor family, Lázaro Cárdenas, became president and dramatically revived the languishing revolution. Under Cárdenas many large estates were divided among small farmers or were returned undivided to Indian communities. Meanwhile, state-supported Mexican businessmen built many small factories to meet domestic needs. In 1938 Cárdenas nationalized the petroleum industry. Also, the 1930s saw the flowering of a distinctive Mexican culture that proudly embraced the long-despised Indian past.

In the 1940s and 1950s more moderate Mexican presidents used the state's power to promote industrialization, and the Mexican economy grew rapidly until the late 1960s. The upper and middle classes reaped the lion's share of the benefits.

Brazilian politics was dominated by the coffee barons and by regional rivalries after the fall of Brazil's monarchy in 1889. Regional rivalries and deteriorating economic conditions allowed a military revolt led by Getúlio Vargas to seize control of the federal government in 1930. Vargas established a mild dictatorship that lasted until 1945. His rule was generally popular, combining effective economic nationalism and moderate social reform.

Modernization continued for the next fifteen years, and Brazil's economy boomed. Economic nationalism was especially vigorous under the flamboyant President Juscelino Kubitschek. Between 1956 and 1960 the government borrowed heavily from international bankers to promote industry and build the new capital of Brasília in the midst of a wilderness. Kubitschek's slogan was "Fifty Years' Progress in Five." By the late 1950s economic and social progress seemed to be bringing less violent, more democratic politics to Latin America. These expectations were shaken by the Cuban Revolution.

Authoritarianism and Democracy in Latin America

Achieving nominal independence in 1898 as a result of the Spanish-American War, Cuba was practically an American protectorate until the 1930s. Cuba's political institutions were weak and its politicians corrupt. Yet Cuba was one of Latin America's most prosperous countries by the 1950s, although enormous differences remained between rich and poor.

Fidel Castro (b. 1927) and his guerrilla forces overthrew the Cuban government in late 1958. Castro had promised a "real" revolution, and it soon became clear that

Chronology

1946–1964 Decolonization in Africa and Asia

1947 Separation of India and Pakistan

1948 End of British mandate in Palestine; Jews proclaim state of Israel

1949–1954 Mass arrests, forced-labor camps, and Communist propaganda in China

1949–present Harsh restrictions against religion and speech in China

1956 Nasser nationalizes Suez Canal Company

1964–1973 Vietnam War

1965 Cultural Revolution in China; intellectuals are exiled and art is destroyed

1967 Six-Day War in Israel

1975–present Slower population growth in Asia and Latin America

Late 1970s–present Revival of Islamic fundamentalism

1978 Islamic revolution in Iran

1980–1988 Iran-Iraq War

1989 Chinese military puts down student revolt in Tiananmen Square

1991 Congress Party in India embraces Western capitalist reforms; Gulf War

1994 Nelson Mandela becomes president of South Africa

1995 Assassination of Israeli prime minister Yitzhak Rabin

2004 Death of PLO leader Yasir Arafat

2008 Retirement of Cuban president Fidel Castro after 49 years as ruler

● **Brasília: Metropolitan Cathedral** The Metropolitan Cathedral at night in Brazil's capital city, Brasília. The cathedral was inaugurated in 1970, ten years after the inauguration of the planned city that replaced Rio de Janeiro as Brazil's capital. *(Augusto C. B. Real)*

"real" meant "communist." Middle-class Cubans began fleeing to Miami. Cuban relations with the Eisenhower administration deteriorated rapidly. In April 1961 the U.S. president, John Kennedy, tried to use Cuban exiles to topple Castro, but Kennedy abandoned the exiles as soon as they landed ashore at the Bay of Pigs.

After routing the Bay of Pigs forces, Castro moved to build an authoritarian communist society: an alliance with the Soviet bloc; a Communist Party dictatorship; state ownership; a Castro cult; prisons and emigration to silence opposition; and the exportation of communist revolutions throughout Latin America. Fearing Castro would succeed, the United States in 1961 funded the new hemispheric Alliance for Progress, intended to promote long-term economic development and social reform.

U.S. aid contributed modestly to continued Latin American economic development in the 1960s, but democratic social reforms—the other half of the Alliance for Progress formula—stalled. Conflict between leftist movements and ruling elites grew, won most often by the elites and their military allies, but at the cost of imposing a new kind of conservative authoritarianism. By the late 1970s only Costa Rica, Venezuela, Colombia, and Mexico retained some measure of democratic government. Brazil, Argentina, and Chile represented the general trend.

In Brazil, intense political competition in the early 1960s prompted President João Goulart to swing to the left to gain fresh support. When Goulart appeared ready to use force to break up landed estates and extend the vote to Brazil's many illiterates, army leaders staged a coup in 1964. Industrialization and urbanization went forward under right-wing military rule, but social inequalities increased.

In Argentina the military ousted the dictatorial populist and economic nationalist Juan Perón in 1955 and restored elected democratic government. Then, worried by a Peronist revival and following the Brazilian example, the army took control in 1966 and again in 1976 after a brief civilian interlude. Repression escalated following each military takeover. Though culturally and economically advanced, Argentina became a brutal military dictatorship.

Events in Chile were truly tragic, given its long tradition of democracy and moderate reform. When Salvador Allende, a doctor and the Marxist head of a coalition of communists, socialists, and radicals, won a plurality in 1970, he was duly elected president by the Chilean Congress. Allende completed the nationalization of the American-owned copper companies and proceeded to socialize private industry, accelerate the breakup of landed estates, and radicalize the poor. Marxism in action evoked a powerful backlash. In 1973, with widespread conservative support and U.S. backing, the traditionally impartial army struck in a well-organized coup. Allende died, probably murdered, and thousands of his supporters were arrested, or worse. As in Argentina, the military imposed a harsh despotism.

The military governments that revived antidemocratic authoritarianism in Latin America blocked not only Marxist and socialist programs but most liberal and moderate reforms as well. The new authoritarians were, however, determined modernizers, deeply committed to nationalism, industrialization, technology, and some modest social progress. They even promised free elections in the future.

That time came in the 1980s, when another democratic wave gained momentum throughout Latin America. In Argentina the military government of General Leopoldo Galtieri gradually lost almost all popular support because of its "dirty war" against its own citizens, in which thousands arbitrarily accused of opposing the regime were imprisoned, tortured, and murdered. In 1982, in a desperate gamble to rally the people, Argentina's military rulers seized the Falkland (or Malvinas) Islands (see Map 26.2 on page 783) from Great Britain. The British rout of Argentina's poorly led

● **Justice for the Victims of Chile's General Pinochet** With their faces covered with death masks, demonstrators outside Britain's High Court in 2000 hold up crosses carrying pictures of the "Disappeared"—the thousands kidnapped and allegedly murdered between 1973 and 1988 under the military dictatorship of General Pinochet. The High Court ruled against extraditing Pinochet to Spain to stand trial, but he was finally charged with torture and murder when he returned to Chile. *(Dan Chung/Reuters New-Media Inc./Corbis)*

troops forced the humiliated generals to schedule national elections. The democratically elected government prosecuted the former military rulers for their crimes and laid solid foundations for liberty and political democracy.

The Brazilian military was relatively successful in its industrialization effort, but proved unable (or unwilling) to improve the social and economic position of the masses. In 1985, after twenty-one years of rule, the military leaders allowed civilian politicians to have a try. Chile also turned from right-wing military dictatorship to elected government. Thus by the late 1980s, 94 percent of Latin Americans lived under regimes that guaranteed elections and civil liberties.

The most dramatic developments in Central America occurred in Nicaragua. In 1979 the Sandinistas, a broad coalition of liberals, socialists, and Marxist revolutionaries, drove long-time dictator Anastasio Somoza from power. The new leaders wanted genuine political and economic independence from the United States, as well as thoroughgoing land reform, some nationalized industry, and friendly ties with communist countries. These policies infuriated the Reagan administration, which sought to overthrow the Sandinista government by creating a counterrevolutionary mercenary army, the Contras, and supplying it with military aid funded illegally through military weapons sales to Iran. After years of civil war, the Nicaraguan economy collapsed, and the Sandinista government's popularity eventually declined. The Sandinistas surrendered power when they were defeated in free elections by a coalition of opposition parties.

The Reagan administration also helped engineer a 1986 coup in Haiti, where "Papa Doc" Duvalier, followed by his son, "Baby Doc," had for decades ruled in one of the most repressive dictatorships in the Americas, with U.S. support. Although "Baby Doc" was forced into exile, the country experienced a period of violence and disorder until semi-fair elections were held in 1994 with the help of U.S. military intervention. More than thirteen years later, however, Haiti remained not only the Western Hemisphere's poorest country but also in political turmoil with no improvement in sight.

Latin America in the 1990s

In the 1990s Latin America's popularly elected governments relaxed economic relations with other countries, moving decisively from tariff protection and economic nationalism toward free markets and international trade. In so doing, they revitalized their economies and registered solid gains. In 1994 Mexico joined with the United States and Canada in the North American Free Trade Agreement (NAFTA). Hoping to copy the success of the European Union, twelve South American countries (Brazil, Argentina, Paraguay, Uruguay, Venezuela, Bolivia, Colombia, Ecuador, Peru, Guyana, Suriname, and Chile) met in Cuzco, Peru, in December 2004 and signed the Cuzco Declaration, announcing the formation of the Union of South American Nations. The Constitutive Treaty formally establishing the union was signed on May 23, 2008, in Brasília, Brazil. The union will provide a free-trade zone for its members and compete economically with the United States and the European Community.

• • • • • • • • • • • • • • •

THE RESURGENCE OF EAST ASIA

How did the defeat of Japan lead to East Asian resurgence after World War II?

Except for Japan, most Asian countries recovered slowly after World War II. In the early 1950s the two Koreas and China were at war in the Korean peninsula, and the Vietnamese were fighting among themselves and against the French. The Nationalist Chinese in Taiwan were adjusting to life in exile from the mainland. Hong Kong, Singapore, Indonesia, South Korea, and the Philippines were recovering from years of colonial rule and Japanese occupation. Over the next forty years, China and the "Asian Tigers" developed some of the largest and fastest-growing economies in the world, but liberal democracy remained elusive.

The Communist Victory in China

Communism triumphed in China for many reasons. As a noted historian forcefully argued, however, "Japanese aggression was . . . the most important single factor in Mao's rise to power."[1] Half of Japan's overseas armies were pinned down in China in 1945, in a long war that exhausted the established government and its supporters. Jiang Jieshi's Nationalists had mobilized 14 million men, and a staggering 3 million Chinese soldiers had been killed or wounded. The war created massive Chinese deficits and runaway inflation, hurting morale and ruining lives. Mao and the Communists had avoided pitched battles and concentrated on winning peasant support and forming a broad anti-Japanese coalition. By reducing rents, promising land redistribution, enticing intellectuals, and spreading propaganda, Mao and the Communists emerged in peasant eyes as the true patriots, the genuine nationalists.

When Japan suddenly collapsed in August 1945, Communists and Nationalists both rushed to seize evacuated territory. Heavy fighting broke out in Manchuria, and civil war began in earnest in April 1946. By 1948 the demoralized Nationalist forces were disintegrating before the better-led, more determined Communists. The following year Jiang Jieshi and 2 million mainland Chinese fled to Taiwan, and in October 1949 Mao Zedong proclaimed the People's Republic of China.

Within three years the Communists consolidated their rule. The Communist government seized the holdings of landlords and rich peasants—10 percent of the farm population had owned between 70 and 80 percent of the land—and distributed it to 300 million poor peasants and landless laborers. This revolutionary land reform was extremely popular. Meanwhile, as Mao admitted in 1957, eight hundred thousand "class enemies" were summarily liquidated between 1949 and 1954; the true figure is probably much higher. All visible opposition from the old ruling groups was destroyed.

Finally, Mao and the Communists reunited China's 550 million inhabitants in a strong centralized state. Claiming a new Mandate of Heaven, they set out to prove that China was once again a great power. This was the real significance of China's participation in the Korean War. From 1950 to 1953, the Chinese army's ability to fight the American "imperialists" to a bloody standstill on the Korean peninsula mobilized the masses and increased Chinese self-confidence.

Mao's China

Wanting to assert Chinese power and prestige in world affairs, Mao and the party looked to the Soviet Union for inspiration in the early 1950s. Along with the gradual collectivization of agriculture, China adopted a typical Soviet-style five-year plan to develop large factories and heavy industry rapidly. Russian specialists built many Chinese plants. Soviet economic aid was also considerable. The first five-year plan was successful, as undeniable economic growth followed the Communists' social revolution.

In the cultural and intellectual realms, too, the Chinese followed the Soviet example. Basic civil and political rights, which the Nationalists had seriously curtailed, were now simply abolished. Temples and churches were closed, and press freedom died. Soviet-style puritanism took hold, as the Communists quickly eradicated prostitution and drug abuse, which they had long regarded as humiliating marks of exploitation and national decline. They enthusiastically promoted Soviet-Marxian ideas concerning women and the family. Full equality, work outside the home, and state-supported child care became primary goals.

Great Leap Forward *Mao Zedong's acceleration of development in which industrial growth was to be based on small-scale backyard workshops run by peasants living in gigantic self-contained communes.*

By the mid-1950s China seemed to be firmly set on the Marxist-Leninist course of development, but in 1958 it began to go its own way. Mao proclaimed a spectacular acceleration of development, a **Great Leap Forward** in which soaring industrial growth would be based on small-scale backyard workshops run by peasants living in gigantic self-contained communes. The creation of a new socialist personality that rejected individualism and traditional Confucian family values, such as filial piety and acceptance of parental authority, was a second goal.

The intended great leap produced an economic disaster, for frantic efforts with primitive technology often resulted only in chaos. In the countryside land went untilled as peasants turned to industrial production. As many as 20 million to 30 million people died in famines that swept the country in 1960–1961, one of the greatest human disasters in world history. When Soviet premier Nikita Khrushchev criticized Chinese policy in 1960, Mao condemned him and his Russian colleagues as detestable "modern revisionists." The Russians abruptly cut off economic and military aid, splitting the communist world apart.

Mao lost influence in the party after the Great Leap Forward fiasco and the Sino-Soviet split, but in 1965 the old revolutionary staged a dramatic comeback. Fearing that China was becoming bureaucratic, capitalistic, and "revisionist" like the Soviet Union, Mao launched the **Great Proletarian Cultural Revolution.** He sought to purge the party and to recapture the revolutionary fervor of his guerrilla struggle (see pages 864–865). The army and the nation's young people, especially students, responded enthusiastically, organizing themselves into radical cadres called **Red Guards.** The young people denounced their teachers and practiced rebellion in the name of revolution. One Red Guard manifesto exulted that "Revolution is rebellion, and rebellion is the soul of Mao Tse-tung's thought."[2]

Great Proletarian Cultural Revolution *A movement launched by Mao Zedong that attempted to purge the party of time-serving bureaucrats and recapture the revolutionary fervor of his guerrilla struggle.*

Red Guards *Radical cadres formed by young people who would attack anyone identified as an enemy of either the Communist Party or Chairman Mao.*

The Red Guards sought to erase all traces of "feudal" and "bourgeois" culture and thought. Ancient monuments and countless works of art, antiques, and books were destroyed. Party officials, professors, and intellectuals were exiled to remote villages to purify themselves with heavy labor. Universities were shut down for years. Thousands of people died, many of them executed, and millions more were sent to rural forced-labor camps. The Red Guards attracted enormous worldwide attention and served as an extreme model for the student rebellions in the West in the late 1960s (see page 959).

The Limits of Reform

Mao and the Red Guards succeeded in mobilizing the masses, shaking up the party, and creating greater social equality. But the Cultural Revolution also created growing chaos and a general crisis of confidence, especially in the cities. Persecuted intellectuals, technicians, and purged party officials launched a counterattack on the radicals and regained much of their influence by 1969. Thus China shifted to the right at the same time that Europe and the United States did. This shift in China opened the door to a limited but lasting reconciliation between China and the United States in 1972.

The moderates were led by Deng Xiaoping (1904–1997), a long-time member of the Communist elite who had been branded a dangerous capitalist agent during the Cultural Revolution. After Mao's death in 1976, Deng and his supporters initiated a series of new policies, embodied in the ongoing campaign of the "Four Modernizations"—agriculture, industry, science and technology, and national defense.

China's 800 million peasants experienced the greatest and most beneficial change from this modernization campaign, what Deng proudly called China's "second revolution." At first glance this may seem surprising. Peasant support had played a major role in the 1949 Communist victory. After 1949 land reform and rationing undoubtedly improved the diet of poor peasants. Subsequently, literacy campaigns taught rural people how to read, and "barefoot doctors"—local peasants trained to do simple

● **Shaming of Enemies During the Cultural Revolution**   During the Chinese Cultural Revolution in the 1960s, young Chinese militants and Red Guards attacked people identified as enemies of the Communist Party and Chairman Mao. Many of these "enemies" were intellectuals such as teachers and artists, but they could be neighbors and even parents who were considered bourgeoisie. Here a victim is paraded through the streets wearing a dunce cap with his crimes written on it. *(Wide World Photos)*

diagnosis and treatment—brought modern medicine to the countryside. But rigid collectivized agriculture failed to provide either the peasants or the country with adequate food. Levels of agricultural production and per capita food consumption were only slightly higher in the mid-1970s than in 1937, before the war with Japan.

Determined to modernize the economy, Deng looked to the peasants as natural allies. China's peasants were allowed to farm the land in small family units rather than in large collectives and to produce what they could produce best and "dare to be rich." Peasants responded enthusiastically, increasing food production by more than 50 percent between 1978 and 1984.

The successful use of free markets and family responsibility in agriculture encouraged further economic experimentation. Foreign capitalists were allowed to open factories in southern China, and they successfully exported Chinese products around the world. Chinese private enterprise was also permitted in cities, where snack shops, beauty parlors, and a host of small businesses sprang up. China's Communist Party leaders also drew on the business talent of wealthy "overseas" Chinese in Hong Kong and Taiwan who knew the world market, needed new sources of cheap labor, and played a key role in the emerging Greater China. The Chinese economy grew rapidly between 1978 and 1987, and per capita income doubled in these years.

Change, however, was also circumscribed. Most large-scale industry remained state owned, and cultural change proceeded slowly. Above all, the Communist Party zealously preserved its monopoly of political power. When the worldwide movement for greater democracy and political freedom in the late 1980s also took root in China, the government responded by banning all demonstrations and slowing the trend toward a freer economy. Inflation then soared to more than 30 percent a year. The economic

● **Chinese Students in 1989** These exuberant demonstrators in Tiananmen Square personify the idealism and optimism of China's prodemocracy movement. After some hesitation the Communist government crushed the student leaders and their supporters with tanks and executions, reaffirming its harsh, authoritarian character. *(Erika Lansner/stockphoto.com)*

Tiananmen Square *The site of a Chinese student revolt in 1989 at which Communists imposed martial law and arrested, injured, or killed hundreds of students.*

reversal, the continued lack of political freedom, and the conviction that Chinese society was becoming more corrupt led China's idealistic university students to spearhead demonstrations in April 1989.

The students evoked tremendous popular support, and more than a million people streamed into Beijing's central **Tiananmen Square** on May 17 supporting their demands. The government then declared martial law and ordered the army to clear the students. Masses of courageous Chinese citizens blocked the soldiers' entry into the city for two weeks, but in the early hours of June 4, 1989, tanks rolled into Tiananmen Square. At least 700 students died as a wave of repression, arrests, and executions descended on China. China's Communist leaders claimed they had saved the country from plots to destroy socialism and national unity.

In the months after Tiananmen Square communism fell in eastern Europe, the Soviet Union broke apart, and China's rulers felt vindicated. They believed their strong action had preserved Communist power, prevented chaos, and demonstrated the limits of permissible reform. After some hesitation Deng, and his successor Jiang Zemin, reaffirmed economic liberalization. Private enterprise and foreign investment boomed in the 1990s. Consumerism was encouraged, and the living standard rose. But critics of Communist rule were jailed, and every effort was made to ensure the People's Army would again crush the people if ordered. Thus China coupled growing economic freedom with continued political repression, embracing only one half of the trend toward global liberalization and rejecting the other.

These policies continued into the twenty-first century. In 2001, after long negotiations, China joined the World Trade Organization, giving it all the privileges and obligations of participation in the liberal global economy. Politically communist, China now has a full-blown capitalist economy. From 1978, when Deng Xiaoping took over and launched economic reforms, through 2008, the Chinese economy has grown at an average annual rate of over 9 percent; foreign trade at an average of 16 percent. Average per capita income in China has doubled every ten years.

But China continues to have a miserable human rights record. In 2002 Hu Jintao succeeded the aging Jiang Zemin, and introduced modest legal reforms. He remains clearly committed, however, to maintaining a strong authoritarian state. As China prepared to host the 2008 Summer Olympic Games, there was some hope that, as promised, China's Communist leaders would make significant human rights, labor rights, and press freedom reforms before the games began. In spring 2008, however, the Chinese harshly crushed demonstrations in Tibet (see the feature "Individuals in Society: The Dalai Lama" on page 1061), which sparked worldwide protest, including disruption of the Olympic torch global relay. As the Olympic Games opened in August 2008, the Chinese, with only perfunctory pressure from world leaders, had made no effort to institute democratic reforms.

The Asian "Economic Tigers"

China's exploding economy has replicated the rapid industrial progress that characterized first Japan and then Asia's "Economic Tigers" (or "Four Dragons")—Taiwan, Hong Kong, Singapore, and South Korea.

Both South Korea and Taiwan were typical underdeveloped countries in the early postwar years—poor, small, agricultural, densely populated, and lacking in natural resources. They also had suffered from Japanese imperialism and from destructive civil wars with communist foes. Yet they managed to make good. How was this possible?

First, economic development became a national mission in South Korea and Taiwan. Radical land reform expropriated large landowners and drew the mass of small farmers into a competitive market economy. Probusiness governments cooperated with capitalists, opposed strikes, and did nothing to improve the long hours and low wages of self-sacrificing workers. These governments protected their own farmers and industrialists from foreign competition while also securing almost free access to the large American market. Second, both countries succeeded in preserving many cultural fundamentals even as they accepted and mastered Western technology. Third, tough nationalist leaders—Park Chung Hee in South Korea and Jiang Jieshi in Taiwan—maintained political stability at the expense of genuine political democracy.

After a military coup overthrew Park in 1980, South Korea suffered under an even more authoritarian regime through the 1980s until democracy was restored at the end of the decade. South Korea's economy, however, continued to grow and expand. By the late 1990s South Korea had one of the largest economies in the world and is a world leader in shipbuilding and high-technology products. Its GDP is about twenty times larger than North Korea's.

In 1949 after Jiang Jieshi had fled to Taiwan with his Nationalist (Kuomintang) troops and around 2 million refugees, he re-established the Republic of China (ROC) in exile. Over the next fifty years, Taiwan created one of the world's most highly industrialized capitalist economies, becoming a world leader in high-technology and electronic manufacturing and design.

● **Lights in the Night in the Eastern Hemisphere** This NASA photo uniquely illustrates differences in wealth between the North and South. Human-made lights shine brightly from developed countries and heavily populated cities. Africa's continent-wide economic poverty is clearly evident, while North Korea sits in stark dark contrast to the blaze of light from South Korea and the other "Asian Tigers." *(Image by Craig Mayhew and Robert Simmons, NASA GSFC)*

A large threatening cloud hangs over the island, however. As one of the United Nations' founding members in 1945, Jiang's ROC government held one of the Security Council's five permanent seats. In 1971 the United Nations expelled the ROC, and its Security Council seat was given to the People's Republic of (mainland) China. This action left Taiwan in political limbo: should it remain the ROC or become an independent Republic of Taiwan? Meanwhile, mainland China claims authority over Taiwan, considers it part of "One China," and has threatened to attack if Taiwan declares its formal independence. Pro-independence candidate Chen Shui-bian defeated the Kuomintang candidate in 2000 to become the first non-Kuomintang president in Taiwan's postwar history. Though he adopted a somewhat more moderate stance, he still supported independence and remained defiant toward the mainland. On January 12, 2008, however, the Taiwanese people gave the Kuomintang Party (KMT) a landslide victory in parliamentary elections, and Chen immediately resigned as chairperson of his Democratic Progressive Party. The KMT won 81 of 113 seats in parliament. In March 2008 the KMT leader, Ma Ying-jeou, won the presidential elections with 58 percent of the vote. He has dropped talk of Taiwanese independence and is seeking closer relations with the mainland. Thus, the tension surrounding the standoff between China and Taiwan, potentially one of most explosive situations in the world, may have eased.

In 1965 the largely Chinese city of Singapore was pushed out of the Malayan-dominated Federation of Malaysia. The independent city-state of Singapore prospered on the hard work and inventiveness of its largely Chinese population. Singapore's government promoted education, private enterprise, high technology, and affordable housing for all citizens. Since the mid-1990s Singapore has enjoyed one of the highest per capita incomes in the world. The government, dominated by the People's Action Party since independence, forcefully promotes conservative family values and strict social discipline.

The British first occupied Hong Kong in 1841. Primarily a center of oceanic trade in the nineteenth century, Hong Kong turned to finance, such as banking and insurance, and to manufacturing in the twentieth. On July 1, 1997, the United Kingdom returned Hong Kong to Chinese control. Under the agreement Hong Kong became the Hong Kong Special Administrative Region (SAR) of China, and China promised that, under its "one country, two systems" formula, China's socialist economic system would not be imposed on Hong Kong. Hong Kong remains one of the most vibrant global economies. It is the world's tenth-largest trading entity and eleventh-largest banking center, and it continues to have one of the world's highest per capita GDPs.

Since recovering from a series of economic crises in the late 1990s, a vibrant, independent East Asia has emerged as an economic powerhouse, an event of enormous significance in long-term historical perspective.

Political and Economic Progress in Southeast Asia

While the Philippines and Indonesia gained independence quickly after 1945, the attainment of stable political democracy proved a more difficult goal. As ethnic conflicts and cold war battles divided their countries, Filipino and Indonesian leaders frequently turned to authoritarian rule and military power in an effort to impose order and unity. By the early twentieth-first century both the Philippines and Indonesia were moving toward more stable governments and growing economies.

During the Second World War the Philippine Islands suffered greatly under Japanese occupation. After the war the United States retained its large military bases (they were finally closed in 1992) but granted the Philippines independence in 1946. The Philippines pursued American-style two-party competition until 1965 when President Ferdinand Marcos (1917–1989) subverted the constitution and ruled as dictator. In 1986 a widespread popular rebellion forced him into exile and Corazón Aquino became president. Aquino and the presidents who have followed her have made some progress in improving the economy. Many Filipinos work abroad. Their remittances back home, plus rapid growth in exports to China and strong sales of semiconductor electronics, helped the Philippine economy grow at over 7 percent in 2007. Despite the growing economy, communist insurgents and Muslim separatists continue to threaten the Philippines' political stability.

The Netherlands East Indies emerged in 1949 as independent Indonesia under the nationalist leader Achmed Sukarno (1901–1970). Like the Philippines, the populous new nation encompassed a variety of peoples, islands, and religions (85 percent of the population practices Islam; see Map 32.2 on page 995). A military coup led by General Suharto forced Sukarno out in 1965. Suharto's authoritarian rule concentrated mainly on economic development. Blessed with large oil revenues, Indonesia achieved solid economic growth for a generation. Increasingly tied to the world economy, Indonesia in 1997 was suddenly devastated by financial crisis. Suharto was forced to resign in 1998.

After Suharto's fall, freely elected governments attacked corruption and reversed the economic decline. In 2000 Indonesia gave East Timor political independence. In 2004 in the first direct presidential elections ever held, the Indonesians elected Susilo Bambang Yudhoyono as president. Despite years of natural disasters—a 2004 Indian Ocean tsunami, earthquakes, severe floods, and outbreaks of the bird flu (avian influenza)—and militant Islamic terrorist acts, the economy grew at over 6 percent in 2007, its fastest pace in eleven years.

The Reunification of Vietnam

French Indochina experienced the bitterest struggle for independence in Southeast Asia. The French tried to reimpose imperial rule there after the communist and nationalist guerrilla leader Ho Chi Minh (1890–1969) declared an independent republic in 1945, but they were decisively defeated in the 1954 Battle of Dien Bien Phu. At the subsequent international peace conference, French Indochina gained independence. Laos and Cambodia became separate states, and Vietnam was "temporarily" divided into two hostile sections at the seventeenth parallel pending elections to select a single unified government within two years.

● **Capitalism in Today's Vietnam** Swarms of "angry bees" in the street of Hanoi, Vietnam, where there are an estimated four million people and two million bikes. Motorbikes make up 90 percent of all the vehicles on the road in this rapidly modernizing country, and their numbers will only increase as Vietnam adopts market capitalism and its citizens have more disposable income. An accident death rate of over one thousand per month caused the government to mandate safety helmets as of 2008. (Maxim Marmur/Getty Images)

The elections were never held, and a civil war soon broke out between the two Vietnamese governments, one communist and the other anticommunist. The United States invested tremendous military effort but fought its Vietnam War (1964–1973) as a deeply divided country (see pages 959–961). The tough, dedicated communists eventually proved victorious in 1975 and created a unified Marxist nation. In 1986 Vietnamese communists began to turn from central planning toward freer markets and private initiative with mixed results. The Vietnamese economy has grown 7 to 8 percent per year since 1990, but these numbers are deceiving because inflation and unemployment are also very high. Vietnam remains one of the poorest countries in the region. Still, Communist officials are committed to a market economy, and Vietnam became the World Trade Organization's 150th member on January 11, 2007. Vietnam's Communist leaders, however, continue to zealously guard their monopoly of political power.

• • • • • • • • • • • • • • • • •

NEW NATIONS AND OLD RIVALRIES IN SOUTH ASIA

How did Hindus and Muslims adjust to the end of British colonial rule?

The South Asian subcontinent has transformed itself no less spectacularly than China, Japan, and the "Asian Tigers." India's national independence movements triumphed decisively over weakened and demoralized British imperialism after the Second World War. The newly independent nations of India, Pakistan, and Bangladesh exhibited many variations on the dominant themes of national renaissance and modernization, especially as the struggle for political independence receded into the past. Ethnic and religious rivalries greatly complicated the process of renewal and development.

The End of British India

After the First World War, Mahatma Gandhi and the Indian Congress Party developed the philosophy of Satyagraha (militant nonviolence) to oppose British rule of India and to lessen oppression of the Indian poor by the Indian rich (see pages 857–861). Gradually and grudgingly, Britain's rulers introduced reforms culminating in limited self-government in 1937.

The Second World War accelerated the drive toward independence. In 1942 Gandhi called on the British to "Quit India" and threatened another civil disobedience campaign. He and the other Congress leaders were quickly arrested and jailed for most of the war. Thus, India's wartime support for hard-pressed Britain was substantial but not always enthusiastic. Meanwhile, the Congress Party's prime political rival skillfully seized the opportunity to increase its influence.

Muslim League *The rival to the Indian Congress, it argued for separate homelands for Muslims and Indians.*

That rival was the **Muslim League,** led by the English-educated lawyer Muhammad Ali Jinnah (1876–1948). Jinnah feared Hindu domination of an independent Indian state led by the Congress Party. Asserting in nationalist terms the right of Muslim areas to separate from the Hindu majority, Jinnah described the Muslims of India as "a nation with our distinct culture and civilization, . . . our own distinctive outlook on life and of life."[3] In March 1940 Jinnah called on the British government to grant the Muslim and Hindu peoples separate homelands by dividing India into autonomous national states. Gandhi regarded Jinnah's two-nation theory as simply untrue and as promising the victory of hate over love.

Britain's Labour government agreed to speedy independence for India after 1945, but conflicting Hindu and Muslim nationalisms and religious hatred led to murderous clashes between the two communities in 1946. When it became clear that Jinnah

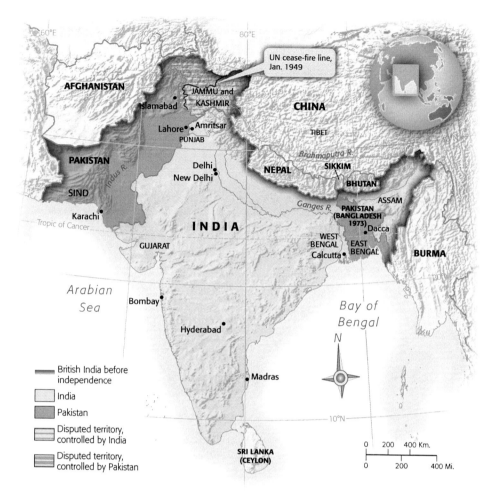

MAP 32.1 **The Partition of British India, 1947** Violence and fighting were most intense where there were large Hindu and Muslim minorities—in Kashmir, the Punjab, and Bengal. The tragic result of partition, which occurred repeatedly throughout the world in the twentieth century, was a forced exchange of populations and greater homogeneity on both sides of the border.

and the Muslim League would accept nothing less than an independent Pakistan, India's last viceroy—war hero Lord Louis Mountbatten (1900–1979)—proposed partition. Both sides accepted. At midnight on August 14, 1947, one-fifth of humanity gained political independence (see Map 32.1).

Yet independence through partition brought tragedy. In the weeks following independence communal strife exploded into an orgy of massacres and mass expulsions. Perhaps a hundred thousand Hindus and Muslims were slaughtered, and an estimated 5 million made refugees. Congress Party leaders were completely powerless to stop the wave of violence. "What is there to celebrate?" exclaimed Gandhi in reference to independence, "I see nothing but rivers of blood."[4] In January 1948, Gandhi himself was gunned down by a Hindu fanatic.

After the ordeal of independence, relations between India and Pakistan—both members of the British Commonwealth—remained tense. Fighting over the disputed area of Kashmir continued until 1949 and broke out again in 1965–1966, 1971, and 1999 (see Map 32.1).

Pakistan and Bangladesh

Pakistan's western and eastern provinces were separated by more than a thousand miles of Indian territory, as well as by language, ethnic background, and social custom. They shared only the Muslim faith. The Bengalis of East Pakistan constituted a

● **Bhutto's Assassination** Pakistani presidential candidate Benazir Bhutto stands up in her campaign van just moments before she was assassinated on December 27, 2007. In the initial confusion it was reported that an assassin fired at her with a pistol and then threw a bomb. Scotland Yard investigators later determined that she died when the force of the bomb explosion slammed her head into part of the open hatch. *(AP Images)*

majority of Pakistan's population as a whole but were neglected by the central government, which remained in the hands of West Pakistan's elite after Jinnah's death. In essence, East Pakistan remained a colony of West Pakistan.

Tensions came to a head in the late 1960s. Bengali leaders calling for virtual independence were charged with treason, and martial law was proclaimed in East Pakistan. In 1971 the Bengalis revolted. Despite savage repression the Bengalis won their independence as the new nation of Bangladesh in 1973. Bangladesh is the world's eighth most populous country, and also one of its poorest.

Emerging as completely separate states after 1973, Pakistan and Bangladesh both moved erratically from semi-authoritarian one-party rule toward competitive parliamentary systems with open elections. In the process each also experienced a series of military takeovers, restorations of civilian authority, political assassinations, and charges of official corruption. Each achieved some economic improvement but little social progress, especially for women.

India Since Independence

Jawaharlal Nehru (1889–1964) and the Congress Party ruled India for a generation after independence and introduced major social reforms. Hindu women and even young girls were granted legal equality, including the right to vote, to seek divorce, and to marry outside their castes. The constitution abolished the untouchable caste. In practice less discriminatory attitudes toward women and untouchables evolved slowly—especially in the villages, where 85 percent of the people lived.

The Congress Party leadership tried with modest success to develop the country economically by means of democratic socialism. But population growth of about 2.4 percent per year ate up much of the increase in output. Intense poverty remained the lot of most people and encouraged widespread corruption within the bureaucracy. The Congress Party maintained a moralizing neutrality in the cold war and sought to group India and other newly independent states in Asia and Africa into a "third force" of "nonaligned" nations. This effort culminated in the Afro-Asian Conference in Bandung, Indonesia, in 1955.

Nehru's daughter, Indira Gandhi (1917–1984), became prime minister in 1966. Mrs. Gandhi (whose deceased husband was no relation to Mahatma Gandhi) dominated Indian political life for a generation. In 1975 Mrs. Gandhi subverted parliamentary democracy and proclaimed a state of emergency. Attacking dishonest officials, black-marketeers, and tax evaders, she also threw the weight of the government behind a heavy-handed campaign of mass sterilization to reduce population growth. More than 7 million men were sterilized in 1976.

Many believed that Mrs. Gandhi's emergency measures marked the end of the parliamentary democracy and Western liberties introduced in the last phase of British rule. But Mrs. Gandhi—true to the British tradition—called for free elections. She suffered a spectacular electoral defeat, largely because of the vastly unpopular sterilization campaign and her subversion of democracy. Her successors, however, fell to fighting among themselves, and in 1980 Mrs. Gandhi won an equally stunning electoral victory. Her defeat and re-election undoubtedly strengthened India's democratic tradition.

Separatist ethnic nationalism plagued Mrs. Gandhi's last years in office. Democratic India remained a patchwork of religions, languages, and peoples, always threatening to further divide the country along ethnic or religious lines. Most notable among these were the 15 million Sikhs of the Punjab in northern India (see Map 32.1), who have their own religion—a blend of Islam and Hinduism—and a distinctive culture. Most Sikhs wanted greater autonomy for the Punjab, and by 1984 some Sikh radicals were fighting for independence. Mrs. Gandhi cracked down hard, and she was assassinated by Sikhs in retaliation. Violence followed as Hindu mobs slaughtered over a thousand Sikhs throughout India.

Elected prime minister in 1984 by a landslide sympathy vote, one of Mrs. Gandhi's sons, Rajiv Gandhi (1944–1991), showed considerable skill at effecting a limited reconciliation with a majority of the Sikh population. Under his leadership the Congress Party also moved away from the socialism of his mother and grandfather. In 1991 the Congress Party wholeheartedly embraced market reforms, capitalist development, and Western technology and investment. These reforms were successful, and since the 1990s India's economy has experienced explosive growth.

Holding power almost continuously from 1947, the Congress Party was challenged increasingly by Hindu nationalists in the 1990s. These nationalists argued forcefully that India was based, above all, on Hindu culture and religious tradition and that these values had been badly compromised by the Western secularism of Congress Party leaders and by the historical influence of India's Muslims. Campaigning also for a strong Indian military, the Hindu nationalist party finally gained power in 1998. The new government immediately exploded nuclear devices, asserting its vision of a militant Hindu nationalism. In 2004 a center-left coalition, the United Progressive Alliance (UPA), dominated by the Congress Party, regained control of the government.

Pakistan also exploded a nuclear weapon in 1998, and relations between Pakistan and India continued to worsen. In December 2001, the two nuclear powers had massive armies facing each other, poised for war, until intense diplomatic pressure forced them to step back from the abyss. In April 2005 both sides agreed to open business and trade relations and to work to negotiate a peaceful solution to the Kashmir dispute. Since then, although Islamic and Hindu chauvinism remain strong, this agreement has reduced the immense hostility that existed between the two countries.

● **Indira Gandhi's Funeral** Covered with beautiful flower wreaths and carried to her funeral pyre by devoted friends, the body of the assassinated leader was then cremated in a solemn public ceremony according to Hindu religion and custom. Although the strong-willed Gandhi flirted with dictatorship, she nurtured and strengthened modern India's vibrant democratic tradition. *(David Turnley/Corbis)*

THE ISLAMIC HEARTLAND

What was the dual nature of nationalism in the Islamic heartland?

Throughout the vast *Ummah* ("world of Islam"; see Map 32.2), nationalism remained the primary political force after 1945. Anti-Western and anticommunist in most instances, Muslim nationalism generally combined a strong secular state with deep devotion to Islam. Cold war conflicts and enormous oil resources enhanced the region's global standing.

Nationalism in the Arab countries of North Africa and Southwest Asia wore two faces. The idealistic side focused on the Pan-Arab dream of uniting all Arabs in a single nation that would be strong enough to resist the West, defeat the new state of Israel, and achieve genuine independence. Despite political and economic alliances like the Arab League, this vision floundered on intense regional, ideological, and personal rivalries. Thus a more practical Arab nationalism focused largely on nation building within former League of Nations mandates and European colonies.

Subsequent one-party dictatorships, corruption, and continued daily hardship, however, caused some Islamic preachers and devoted laypeople in the late 1970s to charge that the model of modernizing, Western-inspired nationalism, had failed. These critics, labeled fundamentalists in the West, urged a return to strict Islamic principles and traditional morality. They evoked a sympathetic response among many educated Muslims as well as among villagers and city dwellers, and in Iran they gained power.

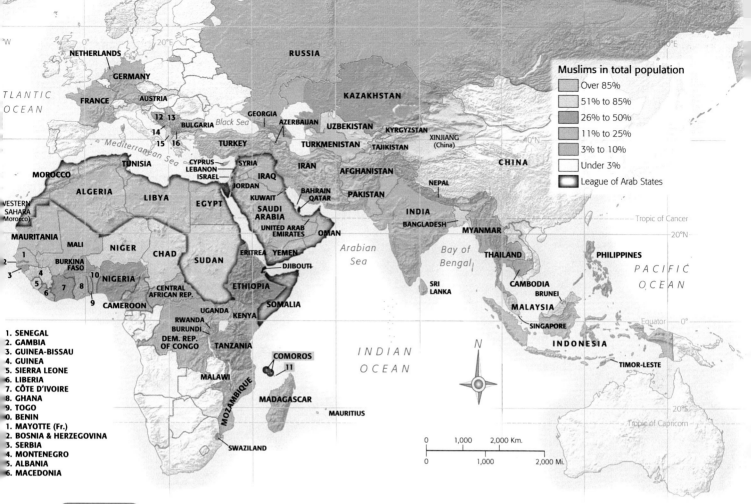

MAP 32.2 **Modern Islam, 2007** Although the Islamic heartland remains the Middle East and North Africa, Islam is growing steadily in Africa south of the Sahara and is the faith of heavily populated Indonesia. *(Source: Data from CIA World Factbook, 2007)*

Muslims in total population
- Over 85%
- 51% to 85%
- 26% to 50%
- 11% to 25%
- 3% to 10%
- Under 3%
- League of Arab States

1. SENEGAL
2. GAMBIA
3. GUINEA-BISSAU
4. GUINEA
5. SIERRA LEONE
6. LIBERIA
7. CÔTE D'IVOIRE
8. GHANA
9. TOGO
10. BENIN
11. MAYOTTE (Fr.)
12. BOSNIA & HERZEGOVINA
13. SERBIA
14. MONTENEGRO
15. ALBANIA
16. MACEDONIA

The Arab-Israeli Conflict

Before the Second World War, Arab nationalists were loosely united in their opposition to the colonial powers and to Jewish migration to Palestine. The British had granted independence to Egypt and Iraq before the war, and the French followed suit with Syria and Lebanon in 1945. Attention then focused even more sharply on British-mandated Palestine. The situation was volatile. Jewish settlement in Palestine was strenuously opposed by the Palestinian Arabs and the seven independent states of the newly founded Arab League (Egypt, Iraq, Jordan, Lebanon, Saudi Arabia, Syria, and Yemen). Murder and terrorism flourished, nurtured by bitterly conflicting Arab and Jewish nationalisms.

The British announced in 1947 their intention to withdraw from Palestine in 1948. The insoluble problem was dumped in the United Nations' lap. In November 1947 the United Nations General Assembly passed a plan to partition Palestine into two separate states—one Arab and one Jewish (see Map 32.3). The Jews accepted, but the Arabs rejected, partition of Palestine.

By early 1948 an undeclared civil war was raging in Palestine. When the British mandate officially ended on May 14, 1948, the Jews proclaimed the state of Israel. Arab countries immediately attacked the new Jewish state, but the Israelis drove off the invaders and conquered more territory. Roughly nine hundred thousand Arab refugees fled or were expelled from old Palestine. This war left an enormous legacy of Arab bitterness toward Israel and its political allies, Great Britain and the United

Primary Source:
Arab and Israeli Soccer Players Discuss Ethnic Relations in Israel, 2000
Learn how Arabs and Jews get along in the world of professional soccer in Israel.

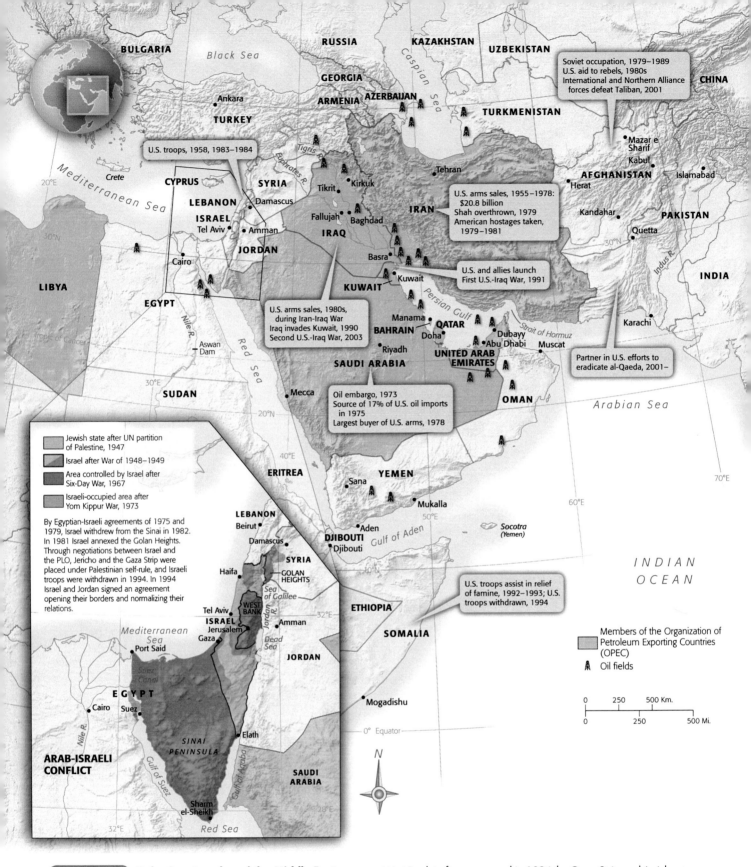

MAP 32.3 Palestine, Israel, and the Middle East

Since the British mandate expired on May 14, 1948, there have been five major wars and innumerable armed clashes in what was formerly Palestine. After winning the War of Independence in 1948, Israel achieved spectacular victories in 1967 in the Six-Day War, occupying the Sinai Peninsula, the Golan Heights, and the West Bank. The Yom Kippur War of 1973 eventually led to the Israeli evacuation of the Sinai and peace with Egypt. In 1993 Israel and the Palestine Liberation Organization agreed in principle to self-rule for Palestinian Arabs in the West Bank in five years, and in 1994 the Gaza Strip and Jericho were placed under the administration of the Palestinian Authority. Negotiations in Washington in 2000 failed to reach a final peace agreement, and armed conflict began again. The Israeli army reoccupied much of the West Bank, and the peace process collapsed. The election of Mahmoud Abbas as PLO leader following the death of Yasir Arafat in 2004 resulted in resumed negotiations and some concessions by both sides. These included, in July and August 2005, the removal of all Jewish settlers from the Gaza Strip.

States. It also led in 1964 to the creation of the **Palestine Liberation Organization (PLO)**, a loose union of Palestinian refugee groups opposed to Israel.

The Development of Egypt

In Egypt the humiliation of Arab defeat triggered a nationalist revolution. A young army colonel named Gamal Abdel Nasser (1918–1970) drove out the corrupt and pro-Western king Farouk in 1952. Nasser enjoyed powerful influence in the Middle East and throughout Asia and Africa.

Nasser preached the gospel of neutralism in the Cold War, but accepted Soviet aid to demonstrate Egypt's independence of the West. Relations with Israel and the West worsened, and in 1956 Nasser nationalized the European-owned Suez Canal Company, Europe's last vestige of power in the Middle East. Outraged, the British and French joined forces with the Israelis and successfully invaded Egypt. The Americans, however, unexpectedly sided with the Soviets and forced the British, French, and Israelis to withdraw from Egypt. Nasser's great victory encouraged anti-Western radicalism, hopes of Pan-Arab political unity, and a vague "Arab socialism." Yet the Arab world remained deeply divided except in their bitter opposition to Israel and support for the right of Palestinian refugees to return to their homeland.

In late 1977 Egypt's president Anwar Sadat made a pathbreaking official visit to Israel, which led to direct negotiations between Israel and Egypt, effectively mediated by U.S. president Jimmy Carter, and a historic though limited peace settlement. Each country gained: Egypt got back the Sinai Peninsula, which Israel had taken in the 1967 Six-Day War (see Map 32.3), and Israel obtained peace and normal relations with Egypt. Israel also kept the Gaza Strip, taken from Egypt in 1967 and home to about 1 million Palestinians. Some Arab leaders denounced Sadat's initiative as treason.

After Sadat's assassination by Islamic radicals in 1981, Egypt's relations with Israel deteriorated badly. Yet Egypt and Israel maintained their fragile peace, and Sadat's successor as president, Hosni Mubarak (r. 1981 to present), concentrated on curbing fundamentalism and promoting economic development.

Israel and the Palestinians

In 1988 young Palestinians in the occupied territories began a prolonged campaign of rock throwing and civil disobedience against Israeli soldiers. Inspired increasingly by Islamic fundamentalists, the Palestinian uprising eventually posed a serious challenge not only to Israel but also to the secular Palestinian liberation movement, long led from abroad by Yasir Arafat (1929–2004). The result was an unexpected and mutually beneficial agreement in 1993 between Israel and the PLO. Israel agreed to recognize Arafat's organization and start a "peace process" that granted Palestinian self-rule in Gaza and Jericho and called for self-rule throughout the West Bank in five years. In return, Arafat renounced terrorism and abandoned the long-standing demand that Israel must withdraw from all land occupied in the 1967 war.

The 1993 agreement and the peace process were hotly debated in an increasingly divided Israel. In 1995 a right-wing Jewish extremist assassinated Prime Minister Yitzhak Rabin (r. 1992–1995). In 1996 a coalition of opposition parties won a slender majority, charging the Palestinian leadership with condoning anti-Jewish terrorism. The new Israeli government limited Palestinian self-rule where it existed and expanded Jewish settlements in the West Bank. On the Palestinian side, dissatisfaction with the peace process grew. Between 1993 and 2000 the number of Jewish settlers in the West Bank doubled to two hundred thousand and Palestinian per capita income declined by 20 to 25 percent. In addition, many Palestinians viewed Arafat's administration as corrupt and self-serving.

Palestine Liberation Organization (PLO) *Created in 1964, a loose union of Palestinian refugee groups opposed to Israel and working toward Palestinian home rule.*

● **Israel's Wall of Separation** A Palestinian man waves as he walks across the hills near Jerusalem, where Israel's wall of separation divides Israeli and Palestinian territory. Israelis argue that the wall, made of concrete and covered with razor wire, protects them from Palestinian militants and suicide bombers. Increasingly it is described by Palestinians and others as a Berlin Wall–like structure, a symbol of Israelis forcing a separation, an Israeli version of apartheid, between the two peoples. *(AP Photo/ Wide World Photos)*

Nevertheless, in early 2000 Arafat, Israeli prime minister Ehud Barak, and U.S. president Bill Clinton met in Washington to negotiate a final peace agreement. The key Israeli proposal, however, did not offer what the Palestinians wanted—a sovereign and independent state—and they rejected it. The failed negotiations unleashed an explosion of tit-for-tat violence beginning in September 2000 in Israel and in the West Bank and Gaza Strip. In 2003 the Israelis began building a "fence" around the West Bank, which has met opposition from Israelis and Palestinians alike.

The death of Yasir Arafat, the PLO's long-time leader, in November 2004 marked a major turning point in the Israeli-Palestinian dispute. Mahmoud Abbas, Arafat's successor, is viewed as moderate and pragmatic. After taking office in January 2005, he immediately called for a peaceful solution to the conflict. Peace talks between the two sides have made very little progress, however, and in some ways matters have become worse. In January 2006 the militant Palestinian Islamist political party Hamas won elections in the Gaza Strip, seizing control from Abbas and the PLO. (See the Epilogue.) While Hamas remains isolated in Gaza, Abbas and the Israelis have been negotiating over the West Bank, with some renewed U.S. involvement by President George W. Bush and Secretary of State Condoleezza Rice in 2007–2008.

Nationalism, Fundamentalism, and Competition

The recent history of the non-Arab states of Turkey and Iran and of the Arab state of Iraq (see Map 32.2) testifies to the diversity of national development in the Muslim world. It also dramatically illustrates the intense competition between rival states and the growing strength of Islamic revival.

Turkey remained basically true to Atatürk's vision of a thoroughly modernized, secularized, Europeanized state (see pages 852–854). Islam continued to exert less influence in daily life and thought as Turkey joined NATO in 1952 and eventually sought full membership in the European Union (EU). Turkey, however, was not one of the ten eastern European countries admitted to the EU in 2004. Many Europeans questioned Turkey's dedication to the protection of human rights and feared that Turkish membership in the EU would result in a large inflow of unwanted Muslim immigrants. Turkey's long-running dispute with the Cyprian Greeks over Cyprus (which became an EU member in 2004) and continued refusal to take responsibility for its role in the Armenian genocide during World War I have further clouded its chances for membership.

After 1945 Iran tried again to follow Turkey's example, as it had before 1939 (see page 854). Once again its success was limited. The new shah—Muhammad Reza Pahlavi (r. 1941–1979), the son of Reza Shah Pahlavi—angered Iranian nationalists by courting Western powers and Western oil companies. In 1953, the freely elected prime minister Muhammad Mossaddeq tried to nationalize the British-owned Anglo-Iranian Oil Company, and the shah was forced to flee to Europe. But Mossaddeq's victory was short-lived. Loyal army officers, with the help of the American CIA, quickly restored the shah to his throne.

The shah set out to build a powerful modern nation to ensure his rule. Iran's gigantic oil revenues provided the necessary cash. The shah undermined the power bases of the traditional politicians—large landowners and religious leaders—by means of land reform, secular education, and increased power for the central government. Modernization surged forward, but at the price of ancient values, widespread corruption, and harsh dictatorship. The result was a violent reaction against modernization and secular values: an Islamic revolution in 1979 aimed at infusing strict Islamic principles into all aspects of personal and public life. Led by the Islamic cleric Ayatollah Ruholla Khomeini, the fundamentalists deposed the shah and tried to build their vision of a true Islamic state.

Iran's Islamic republic frightened its neighbors. Iraq, especially, feared that Iran—a nation of Shi'ite Muslims—would succeed in getting Iraq's Shi'ite majority to revolt against its Sunni leaders. Thus in September 1980 Iraq's strongman, Saddam Hussein (1937–2006), launched a surprise attack. With their enormous oil revenues and military machines, Iranians and Iraqis—Persians and Arabs—clashed in a savage eight-year conflict that killed hundreds of thousands of soldiers before finally grinding to a halt in 1988.

Emerging from the eight-year war with a big, tough army equipped by Western countries and the Soviet bloc, Hussein now eyed Kuwait's great oil wealth. In August 1990 he ordered his forces to overrun his tiny southern neighbor and proclaimed its annexation to Iraq. To Saddam's surprise, his aggression brought a vigorous international response and touched off the Gulf War. In early 1991 his troops were chased out of Kuwait by an American-led, United Nations–sanctioned military coalition, which included some Arab forces from Egypt, Syria, and Saudi Arabia.

Iraq and Iran went in different directions in the 1990s. The United Nations Security Council imposed stringent economic sanctions on Iraq as soon as it invaded Kuwait, and these sanctions remained after the Gulf War to force Iraq to destroy its weapons of mass destruction. United Nations inspectors destroyed many such weapons, but the United States charged Iraq with deceit and ongoing weapons development. An American-led invasion of Iraq in 2003 overthrew Saddam Hussein's regime (see pages 1025–1026).

As secular Iraq spiraled downward toward collapse and foreign occupation, Iran appeared to back away from fundamentalism. Following the constitution established by the Ayatollah Khomeini, executive power in Iran was divided between a Supreme Leader and twelve-member Guardian Council selected by high Islamic clerics, and a president and parliament elected by universal male and female suffrage. After 1990 the Supreme Leader remained a very conservative religious leader, but a growing reform movement pressed for a relaxation of strict Islamic decrees and elected a moderate, Mohammad Khatami, as president in 1997 and again in 2001. The Supreme

● **Iranian Elections, June 2005** This Iranian woman displays her support for the relatively moderate former Iranian president, Akbar Hashemi Rafsanjani, during an election rally in June 2005. To the surprise, shock, and dismay of Iranian moderates and many in the West, the ultraconservative mayor of Teheran, Mahmoud Ahmadinejad, won a landslide victory. With his election all the governing organs of the Iranian government were in the hands of ultraconservative Islamic hardliners. *(AP Photo/Wide World Photos)*

Leader, controlling the army and the courts, vetoed many of Khatami's reform measures and jailed some of the religious leadership's most vocal opponents.

Khatami had to step down in 2005, and elections were held in June. Dubious election returns gave the presidency to an ultraconservative Islamic hardliner, Mahmoud Ahmadinejad. His populist speeches and actions have made him quite popular among some elements of Iranian society. His calls for Israel's destruction; support of extremist groups in Iraq, Gaza, and Lebanon; and refusal to suspend Iran's nuclear program, however, have caused much anxiety and anger in the West. Despite this setback, many Iranians believe moderate, secular reform is inevitable, for, as one Iranian journalist observed, "Fundamentalism is good for protest, good for revolution, and good for war, but not so good for development. No country can organize its society on fundamentalism."[5]

Algeria and Civil War

The important North African country of Algeria also illustrated the development of nationalism and then fundamentalism. Nationalism in the French colony of Algeria was emboldened by Nasser's great triumph in Egypt and by France's defeat in Indochina. But Algeria's large European population—known as the *pieds noirs* ("black feet") because its members wore black shoes instead of sandals—was determined to keep Algeria part of France, and the Algerian war for independence was long, bitter, and bloody. Finally, in 1962, Algeria became an independent Arab state. The European population quickly fled.

The victorious anticolonial movement, known as the **National Liberation Front** (FLN), used revenues from Algeria's nationalized oil fields to promote state-owned industries, urban growth, and technical education. But the FLN also imposed a one-party state, crushing dissent. In the 1980s many dissatisfied Algerians looked to Islam for moral and social revival, and in the early 1990s the Islamic opposition swept municipal and national elections. The FLN called out the army, claiming the fundamentalists would "hijack" democracy and create an Islamic dictatorship. Military rule then led to growing violence and armed struggle between the government and the fundamentalist opposition that has lasted into the 2000s. Algeria's ruthless civil war placed in bold relief the cultural and ideological divisions simmering just below the surface in the Muslim world.

IMPERIALISM AND NATIONALISM IN SUB-SAHARAN AFRICA

How did Kwame Nkrumah represent the new leaders of independent Africa?

National Liberation Front *The name of the victorious anticolonial movement in Algeria.*

Most of sub-Saharan Africa won political independence fairly rapidly after World War II. Only Portugal's colonies and white-dominated southern Africa remained beyond the reach of African nationalists by 1964. The rise of independent states in sub-Saharan Africa resulted directly from both a reaction against Western imperialism and the growth of African nationalism.

The Growth of African Nationalism

Western intrusion was the critical factor in the development of African nationalism, as it had been in Asia and the Middle East. But two things were different about Africa. First, because the imperial system and Western education did not solidify in Africa until after 1900 (see pages 741–743), national movements began to come of age only in the 1920s and reached maturity after 1945. Second, Africa's multiplicity of ethnic groups, coupled with imperial boundaries that often bore no resemblance to existing ethnic boundaries, greatly complicated the development of political—as distinct from cultural—nationalism. Was a modern national state to be based on ethnic or clan loyalties (as it had been in France and Germany)? Was it to be a continent-wide union of all African peoples? Or would the multiethnic territories arbitrarily carved out by competing European empires become the new African nations? Only after 1945 did a tentative answer emerge.

A few educated West Africans in British colonies had articulated a kind of black nationalism before 1914. But the first real impetus came from the United States and the British West Indies. The most renowned participant in this "black nationalism" was W. E. B. Du Bois (1868–1963). The first black to receive a Ph.D. from Harvard, this brilliant writer and historian organized Pan-African congresses in Paris during the Versailles Peace Conference and in Brussels in 1921. **Pan-Africanists** sought black solidarity and, eventually, a vast self-governing union of all African peoples. The flamboyant Jamaican-born Marcus Garvey (1887–1940) was the most influential Pan-Africanist voice in Africa. Young, educated Africans rallied to his call of "Africa for the Africans" and European expulsion from Africa.

Pan-Africanists *People, such as Marcus Garvey, who promoted solidarity among all blacks and the eventual self-governing union of all African peoples.*

In the 1920s many educated French and British Africans experienced a strong surge of pride and cultural nationalism. African intellectuals in Europe formulated and articulated the rich idea of *négritude,* or blackness: racial pride, self-confidence, and joy in black creativity and the black spirit. This westernized African elite pressed for more equal access to government jobs, modest steps toward self-government, and an end to humiliating discrimination. They claimed the right to speak for ordinary Africans and denounced the government-supported chiefs as "Uncle Toms," yet their demands remained moderate.

The Great Depression was the decisive turning point in the development of African nationalism. For the first time unemployment was widespread among educated Africans. African peasants and small business people who had been drawn into world trade, and who sometimes profited from booms, also felt the agony of the decade-long bust, as did urban workers. In some areas the result was unprecedented mass protest. The Gold Coast **cocoa holdups** of 1930–1931 and 1937–1938 are the most famous examples.

Cocoa completely dominated the Gold Coast's economy. As prices plummeted after 1929, cocoa farmers refused to sell their beans to the large British firms that fixed prices and monopolized the export trade. Instead, the farmers organized cooperatives to cut back production and sell their crops directly to European and American chocolate manufacturers. The cocoa holdups succeeded in mobilizing much of the population against the foreign companies and demonstrated the power of mass organization and mass protest. Mass movements for national independence would not be far behind.

cocoa holdups *A mass protest in the 1930s by Gold Coast producers of cocoa, who refused to sell their beans to British firms and instead sold them directly to European and American chocolate manufacturers.*

Achieving Independence with New Leaders

The repercussions of the Second World War in black Africa greatly accelerated the changes begun in the 1930s. Many African soldiers who served in India were powerfully impressed by Indian nationalism. As mines and plantations strained to meet wartime demands, towns mushroomed into cities where tin-can housing, inflation, and shortages of consumer goods created discontent and hardship.

Nationalism in Black Africa

1919	Du Bois organizes first Pan-African congress.
1920s	Cultural nationalism grows among Africa's educated elites.
1929	Great Depression brings economic hardship and discontent.
1930–1931	Farmers in the Gold Coast organize first cocoa holdups.
1939–1945	World War II accelerates political and economic change.
1951	Nkrumah and Convention People's Party win national elections in Ghana.
1957	Nkrumah leads Ghana—former Gold Coast—to independence.
1958	De Gaulle offers commonwealth status to France's African territories; Guinea alone chooses independence.
1960	Nigeria becomes an independent state.
1966	Ghana's Nkrumah deposed in military coup.
1967	Ibos secede from Nigeria to form state of Biafra.
1979	Nigeria's military rulers permit elected civilian government.
1980	Blacks rule Zimbabwe—formerly Southern Rhodesia—after long civil war with white settlers.
1984	South Africa's whites maintain racial segregation and discrimination.
1989–1990	South African government begins process of reform; black leader Nelson Mandela freed from prison.
1994	Mandela elected president of South Africa.

Western imperialist attitudes also changed. Both the British and the French acknowledged the need for rapid social and economic improvement in their colonies; both began sending money and aid on a large scale for the first time. The principle of self-government was written into the United Nations charter and was supported by Great Britain's postwar Labour government. Thus the key question for African colonies became their rate of progress toward self-government. The British and the French were in no rush. But a new breed of African leader was emerging. Impatient and insistent, these modern African nationalists were remarkably successful: by 1964 almost all of western, eastern, and central Africa had achieved statehood, usually without much bloodshed.

These new postwar African leaders formed an elite by virtue of advanced European or American education, and they were profoundly influenced by Western thought. But compared with the interwar generation of educated Africans, they were more radical and humbler in social origin. Among them were former schoolteachers, union leaders, government clerks, and unemployed students, as well as lawyers and prize-winning poets.

Postwar African leaders accepted prevailing colonial boundaries to avoid border disputes and achieve freedom as soon as possible. Sensing a loss of power, traditional rulers sometimes became the new leaders' worst political enemies. Skillfully, the new leaders channeled postwar hope and discontent into support for mass political organizations. Eventually they came to power by winning the general elections that the colonial governments belatedly called to choose their successors.

Ghana Shows the Way

Perhaps the most charismatic of this generation of African leaders was Kwame Nkrumah (1909–1972). Nkrumah spent ten years studying in the United States, where he was deeply influenced by European socialists and Marcus Garvey. Nkrumah returned to the Gold Coast immediately after the Second World War and entered politics. Under his leadership the Gold Coast—which he rechristened "Ghana"— became the first independent African state to emerge from colonialism.

Nkrumah came to power by building a radical mass party appealing particularly to modern elements—former servicemen, market women, union members, urban toughs, and cocoa farmers. He and his party injected the joy and enthusiasm of religious revivals into their rallies and propaganda: "Self-Government Now" was their credo, secular salvation the promise.

Rejecting halfway measures—"We prefer self-government with danger to servitude in tranquility"—Nkrumah and his Convention People's Party staged strikes and riots. Arrested, the "Deliverer of Ghana" campaigned from jail and saw his party win a smashing victory in the 1951 national elections. Called from prison to head the transitional government, Nkrumah and his nationalist party defeated both westernized moderates and more traditional political rivals in free elections. By 1957 Nkrumah had achieved worldwide fame and influence as Ghana became independent.

> **Primary Source:**
> **Parable of the Eagle, Limbo, Prayer for Peace, Vultures**
> *The literature of four African writers expresses the traumatic effects of colonialism.*

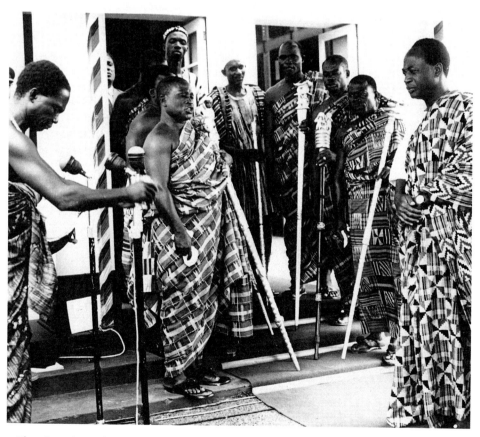

● **The Opening of Parliament in Ghana**   As part of an ancient ritual, two medicine men pour out sacred oil and call on the gods to bless the work of the Second Parliament and President Kwame Nkrumah, standing on the right. The combination of time-honored customs and modern political institutions was characteristic of African states after they secured independence. *(Wide World Photos)*

After Ghana's breakthrough, independence for other African colonies followed rapidly. As in Algeria, the main problem in some colonies was the permanent white settlers, as distinguished from the colonial officials. Wherever white settlers were numerous, as in Kenya, they sought to preserve their privileged position. But only in Southern Rhodesia and South Africa were whites numerous enough to prevail for long. Southern Rhodesian whites declared independence illegally in 1965 and held out until 1980, when black nationalists won a long liberation struggle and renamed the country Zimbabwe. Majority rule in South Africa took even longer.

French-Speaking Regions

Primary Source:
Comments on Algeria, April 11, 1961
Read excerpts of a press conference held by Charles de Gaulle, in which he declares France's willingness to accept Algerian independence.

Decolonization took a somewhat different course in French-speaking Africa. France tried hard to hold on to Indochina and Algeria after 1945. Thus although France upped its aid to its African colonies, independence remained a dirty word until Charles de Gaulle came to power in 1958. Seeking to head off radical nationalists and receiving the crucial support of moderate black leaders, de Gaulle chose a divide-and-rule strategy. He divided the French West Africa and French Equatorial Africa federations into thirteen separate governments, thus creating a "French commonwealth." Plebiscites were called in each territory to ratify the new arrangement. An affirmative vote meant continued ties with France; a negative vote signified immediate independence and a complete break with France.

De Gaulle's gamble was shrewd. The educated black elite—as personified by the influential poet-politician Léopold Sédar Senghor, who now led Senegal's government—loved France and dreaded a sudden divorce. (See the feature "Individuals in Society: Léopold Sédar Senghor, Poet and Statesman.") They also wanted French aid to continue. France, in keeping with its ideology of assimilation, had given the vote to its educated colonial elite after the Second World War, and about forty Africans held French parliamentary seats after 1946. For both cultural and practical reasons, therefore, French Africa's leaders tended to be moderate and in no rush for independence.

In Guinea, however, a young nationalist named Sekou Touré (1922–1984) led his people in overwhelming rejection of the new constitution in 1958. Inspired by Ghana's Nkrumah, Touré laid it out to de Gaulle face-to-face: "We have to tell you bluntly, Mr. President, what the demands of the people are. . . . We have one prime and essential need: our dignity. But there is no dignity without freedom. . . . We prefer freedom in poverty to opulence in slavery."[6]

The Belgians, long-time practitioners of paternalism coupled with harsh, selfish rule in their enormous Congo colony, had always discouraged the development of an educated elite. In 1959, therefore, when after wild riots they suddenly decided to grant independence, the fabric of government simply broke down. Independence was soon followed by violent ethnic conflict, civil war, and foreign intervention. The Belgian Congo was the great exception to black Africa's generally peaceful and successful transition to independence between 1957 and 1964.

SUB-SAHARAN AFRICA SINCE 1960

What are some of the common features of independent Africa since 1960?

The facility with which most of black Africa achieved independence stimulated buoyant optimism in the early 1960s. But within a generation democratic government and civil liberties gave way to one-party rule or military dictatorship and widespread corruption.

The rise of authoritarian government in Africa after independence must be viewed in historical perspective. Representative institutions on the eve of independence were

Léopold Sédar Senghor, Poet and Statesman

President Léopold Sédar Senghor in 1965. *(Hulton Archive/Getty Images)*

Of all the modern leaders in French-speaking Africa, Léopold Sédar Senghor (1906–2001) was the most famous and the most intriguing. His early years in a dusty village in southern Senegal were happy and varied. Later, in cold and lonely Paris, he would feast on memories of this "kingdom of childhood." Senghor's father, a successful peanut merchant, lived in the port city of Joal and had two dozen children and several wives. His last wife, Senghor's mother, remained in her village, where her extended family taught the boy the legends and mysteries of his people. In a famous poem, Senghor later wrote that his mother's brother, Uncle Waly the shepherd, could hear "what is beyond hearing," and that he lovingly explained to the wondering child "the signs that the Ancestors give in the calm seas of the constellations."*

Islam is Senegal's majority religion and the Wolof its dominant ethnic group. But Senghor's family was staunchly Christian and of the Serer people, and when he was seven, his practical father sent him to a French mission school near Joal. Learning French and Wolof, Senghor made rapid progress. When he was seventeen, his teachers sent him on to the colonial capital of Dakar, where he became the top student in the predominately white lycée. In 1928 he received a rare scholarship for advanced study in Paris. Working hard in elite schools and settling on a university career, Senghor became the first African to win the equivalent of a Ph.D. He then took a position as a classics teacher in a lycée near Paris. It was an extraordinary achievement.

Senghor's chance to pursue advanced education reflected French colonial policy in Africa. The French believed that most Africans deserved only a little practical schooling, but they also wanted to create a tiny elite of "black Frenchmen." This elite would link the French rulers and the African masses, who would need permanent French guidance. In the 1930s the brilliant Senghor seemed a model of elitist assimilation.

In fact, however, Senghor was experiencing a severe identity crisis. Who was he? How could he reconcile his complex African heritage with his French education and culture? Making close friends with other black intellectuals in Paris and strongly influenced by African

American music and literature, Senghor concluded that he would never be a "black Frenchman," for in European eyes the most accomplished African always remained exotic and inferior. He then found a new identity in racial pride and the idea of *négritude,* or blackness (see page 1001).

Yet Senghor did not repudiate Europe. Instead, he reconciled his identity crisis—his being torn "between the call of the Ancestors and the call of Europe"—by striving to hold his "two sides" in equilibrium and "peaceful accord." He advocated "cross-fertilization" for Africa and Europe, which, he believed, would benefit both continents.†

Serving in the French army in World War II and turning to politics after 1945, Senghor was elected Senegal's deputy to the French National Assembly. Idolized in Senegal, he joined with other African deputies to press for greater autonomy, as well as for harmony between France and Africa. He led Senegal into Charles de Gaulle's "French commonwealth" in 1958 and then on to independence in 1960. All the major political parties in Senegal were merged to form a one-party government, with Senghor as president. Wisely avoiding dictatorship, ethnic conflict, and military rule, he led Senegal until 1980, when he retired voluntarily. Lionized in France as a great poet and statesman, Senghor was increasingly criticized by some young Senegalese, who grumbled that the aging leader had become too cooperative with France—a real "black Frenchman."

Questions for Analysis

1. What cultural and intellectual forces influenced Senghor's development? Why did he have difficulty reconciling these influences?

2. How did Senghor fit into the whole process of decolonization and African independence?

*Quoted in J. Vaillant, *Black, French, and African: A Life of Léopold Sédar Senghor* (Cambridge, Mass.: Harvard University Press, 1990), p. 18.

†Ibid., p. 146.

an imperial afterthought, and the new African countries faced tremendous challenges. Above all, ethnic divisions threatened civil conflicts that could tear the fragile states apart. Yet this did not happen. Strong leaders used nationalism, first harnessed to throw off foreign rule, to build one-party regimes and promote unity. Unfortunately, nation building by idealistic authoritarians often deteriorated into brutal dictatorships, frequent military coups, and civil strife. Then, in the early 1990s, a powerful reaction to this decline, inspired by the eastern European revolutions, resulted in a surge of democratic protest, which achieved major political gains and rekindled in part the optimism of the independence era.

Striving for National Unity

Africa's imperial legacy is more negative than positive. Although some countries left generally better legacies than others—Britain's was better than Belgium's or Portugal's, for example—overall the "civilizing mission" did more harm than good. On something of a positive note, the forty or so states (see Map 32.4 on page 1008) inherited varying degrees of functioning bureaucracies, some elected political leaders, and some modern infrastructure—transportation, schools, hospitals, and the like. And every country inherited the cornerstone of imperial power—a tough, well-equipped army to maintain order. But other features of the imperialist legacy served to torment independent Africa.

The disruption of traditional life had caused real suffering and resulted in unobtainable post-independence expectations. The prevailing export economies were weak, lopsided, and concentrated in foreign hands. Technical, managerial, and medical skills were in acutely short supply. Above all, the legacy of political boundaries imposed by foreigners without regard to ethnic and cultural groupings weighed heavily on post-independence Africa. Nearly every new state encompassed a variety of peoples who might easily develop conflicting national aspirations.

Great Britain and France had granted their African colonies democratic government as they prepared to depart. Yet belated Western-style democracy served the new multiethnic states poorly. After freedom from imperialism no longer provided a unifying common objective, political parties often coalesced along regional and ethnic lines. Many African leaders concluded that democracy threatened to destroy the existing states and prevent social and economic progress. Thus these leaders maintained the authoritarian tradition they inherited from the imperialists, and free elections often gave way to dictators and one-party rule.

After Ghana won its independence, for instance, Nkrumah jailed without trial his main opponents—chiefs, lawyers, and intellectuals—and outlawed opposition parties. Nkrumah worked to build a "revolutionary" one-party state and a socialist economy. By the mid-1960s his grandiose economic projects had almost bankrupted Ghana, and in 1966 the army suddenly seized power while he was visiting China.

The French-speaking countries also shifted toward one-party government to promote state unity and develop distinctive characteristics that could serve as the basis for statewide nationalism. Mali followed Guinea into Marxist radicalism. Senegal and the Ivory Coast stressed moderation and close economic and cultural ties with France.

Like Nkrumah, many of the initial leaders at the helm of one-party states were eventually overthrown by military leaders. The rise of would-be Napoleons was lamented by many Western liberals and African intellectuals, who often failed to note that military rule was also widespread in Latin America, Asia, and the Near East in the 1970s and 1980s.

As elsewhere, military rule in Africa was authoritarian and undemocratic. In Uganda, for instance, the brutal Idi Amin (1925?–2003) seized power in 1971, packed the army with his ethnic supporters, and terrorized the population for a decade. Yet military regimes generally did manage to hold their countries together, and many, like their Latin American counterparts (see pages 979–982), were committed to social and economic modernization. Drawing on an educated and motivated elite, they sometimes accomplished much. As economic and social conditions stagnated and often declined in African countries from the mid-1970s to the early 1990s, however, army leaders and dictators became more and more greedy and dishonest. By the late 1980s military rulers and one-party authoritarian regimes were coming under increasing pressure to hand over power to more democratic forces.

Nigeria, Africa's Giant

Nigeria's history illustrates just how difficult genuine nation building could be after independence was achieved. "Nigeria" was a name coined by the British to designate their nineteenth-century conquests in the Niger River basin, which encompassed many ancient kingdoms and hundreds of ethnic groups. Also, for administrative convenience, the British consolidated the northern Muslim territories and the southern Christian or animist areas. Despite this diverse population, by 1945 Nigeria had spawned a powerful independence movement, and independence was achieved in 1960 (see Map 32.4).

The key constitutional question was the relationship between the central government and the various regions. Ultimately Nigeria adopted a federal system, whereby the national government at Lagos shared power with three regional or state governments in

● **Nigerian Presidential and Parliamentary Elections, April 2003** In April 2003, Nigeria held its first presidential and parliamentary elections since the end of military rule in 1999. Over 60 million voters turned out across the country to choose for candidates from thirty political parties. Here federal police watch as election officials begin counting the ballots after sorting them by party. *(Corbis)*

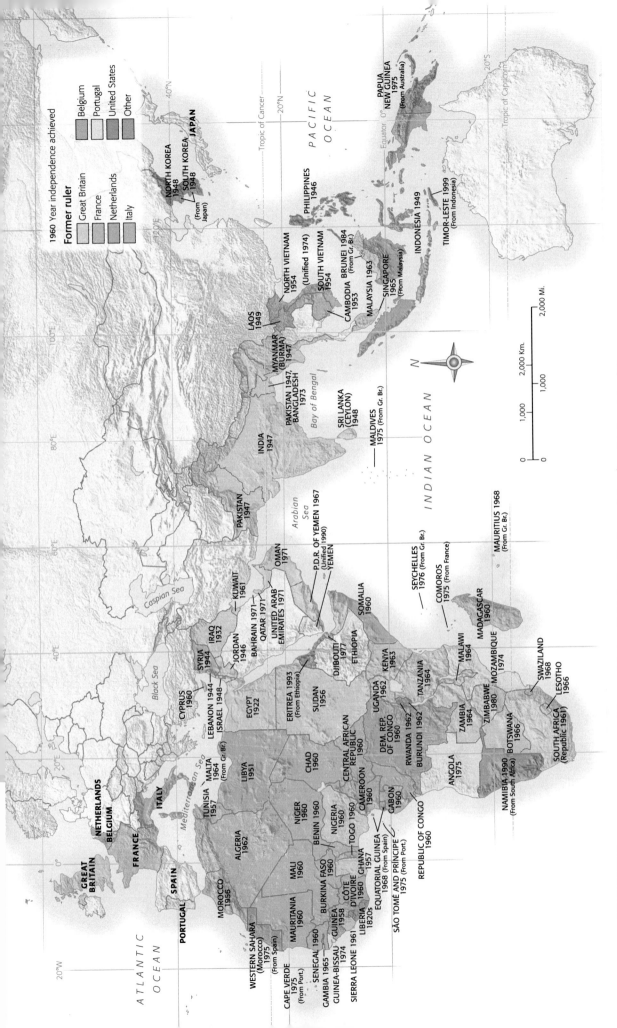

MAP 32.4 The New States in Africa and Asia Divided primarily along religious lines into two states, British India led the way to political independence in 1947. Most African territories achieved statehood by the mid-1960s, as European empires passed away, unlamented.

Former ruler
- Great Britain
- France
- Netherlands
- Italy

1960 Year independence achieved
- Belgium
- Portugal
- United States
- Other

ATLANTIC OCEAN

GREAT BRITAIN
FRANCE
PORTUGAL
SPAIN
BELGIUM
NETHERLANDS
ITALY

WESTERN SAHARA 1975 (Morocco) (From Spain)
CAPE VERDE 1975 (From Port.)
SENEGAL 1960
GAMBIA 1965
GUINEA-BISSAU 1974
GUINEA 1958
SIERRA LEONE 1961
LIBERIA 1820s
CÔTE D'IVOIRE 1960
GHANA 1957
EQUATORIAL GUINEA 1968 (From Spain)
SÃO TOMÉ AND PRÍNCIPE 1975 (From Port.)
REPUBLIC OF CONGO 1960
GABON 1960
TOGO 1960
BENIN 1960
NIGERIA 1960
NIGER 1960
BURKINA FASO 1960
MALI 1960
MAURITANIA 1960
ALGERIA 1962
MOROCCO 1956
TUNISIA 1957
LIBYA 1951
CHAD 1960
CAMEROON 1960
CENTRAL AFRICAN REPUBLIC 1960
ANGOLA 1975
NAMIBIA 1990 (From South Africa)
BOTSWANA 1966
SOUTH AFRICA (Republic 1961)
LESOTHO 1966
SWAZILAND 1968
ZIMBABWE 1980
ZAMBIA 1964
DEM. REP. OF CONGO 1960
MOZAMBIQUE 1974
MALAWI 1964
TANZANIA 1964
BURUNDI 1962
RWANDA 1962
UGANDA 1962
KENYA 1963
SOMALIA 1960
ETHIOPIA
DJIBOUTI 1977
ERITREA 1993 (From Ethiopia)
SUDAN 1956
EGYPT 1922
MALTA 1964 (From Gr. Br.)
CYPRUS 1960
LEBANON 1944
ISRAEL 1948
SYRIA 1944
JORDAN 1946
IRAQ 1932
KUWAIT 1961
BAHRAIN 1971
QATAR 1971
UNITED ARAB EMIRATES 1971
OMAN 1971
P.D.R. OF YEMEN 1967 YEMEN (Unified 1990)
MADAGASCAR 1960
COMOROS 1975 (From France)
SEYCHELLES 1976 (From Gr. Br.)
MAURITIUS 1968 (From Gr. Br.)

PAKISTAN 1947
INDIA 1947
PAKISTAN 1947, BANGLADESH 1973
SRI LANKA (CEYLON) 1948
MALDIVES 1975 (From Gr. Br.)
MYANMAR (BURMA) 1947
LAOS 1949
NORTH VIETNAM 1954 (Unified 1974)
SOUTH VIETNAM 1954
CAMBODIA 1953
BRUNEI 1984 (From Gr. Br.)
MALAYSIA 1963
SINGAPORE 1965 (From Malaysia)
INDONESIA 1949
TIMOR-LESTE 1999 (From Indonesia)
PHILIPPINES 1946
NORTH KOREA 1948
SOUTH KOREA 1948 (From Japan)
JAPAN
PAPUA NEW GUINEA 1975 (From Australia)

ATLANTIC OCEAN
PACIFIC OCEAN
INDIAN OCEAN
Caspian Sea
Black Sea
Mediterranean Sea
Arabian Sea
Bay of Bengal

Tropic of Cancer
Tropic of Capricorn
Equator

20°W 0° 20°E 40°E 60°E 80°E 100°E 120°E
40°N 20°N 0° 20°S

0 1,000 2,000 Mi.
0 1,000 2,000 Km.

N

the north, west, and east. Each region had a dominant ethnic group and a corresponding political party. The parties were expected to cooperate in the national parliament, and the rights of minorities were protected by law.

After independence Nigerians' bright hopes gradually dimmed because of growing ethnic rivalries. In 1967 these intense rivalries erupted into a civil war. The crisis began in 1964 when some young military officers, many of whom were Ibos from the southeast, seized the government and executed its leaders.

At first the young officers were popular, but the Muslim northerners had long distrusted the hard-working, clannish, non-Muslim Ibos. When the Ibo-led military council proclaimed a centralized dictatorship, wild mobs in northern cities massacred thousands of Ibos. When a group of northern officers then seized the national government in a countercoup, the traumatized Ibos revolted and proclaimed the independent state of Biafra in 1967.

The Biafran war lasted three years. The Ibos fought with heroic determination, believing that political independence was their only refuge from genocide. Heavily outnumbered, the Ibos were gradually surrounded. Perhaps millions starved to death as Biafra became a symbol of monumental human tragedy.

Having preserved the state in the 1960s, Nigeria's military rulers focused on building a nation in the 1970s. Although the federal government held the real power, the country was divided into nineteen small, manageable units to handle local and cultural matters. The defeated Ibos were pardoned, and Iboland was rebuilt with federal oil revenues.

Except for a couple of brief periods of civilian rule, combinations of Hausa-Fulani Muslim army officers ruled until 1998, when the brutal military dictator General Sani Abacha suddenly died and gave Nigeria renewed hope for unity and democracy. In 1999 Nigerians voted in free elections and re-established civilian rule; the April 2003 elections marked the first civilian transfer of power in Nigeria's history.

Nigeria is the world's eleventh-largest oil producer and a member of OPEC. Oil provides about 20 percent of Nigeria's GDP, 95 percent of its foreign exchange earnings, and about 65 percent of its budgetary revenues. Nigeria still needs to diversify its economy, however, if it is to overcome massive poverty and become economically stable. Nigeria's leaders must also calm the religious strife that continues to divide the country. Since 2000, riots between Muslims and non-Muslims have left thousands dead in the predominately Muslim northern Nigerian states, where there is a movement to implement shari'a (Islamic law) as the law of the state.

The Struggle in Southern Africa

After the great rush toward political independence in the early 1960s, decolonization stalled. Southern Africa remained under white minority rule, largely because of the numerical strength and determination of its white settlers.

In Portuguese Angola and Mozambique, the white population actually increased from 70,000 to 380,000 between 1940 and the mid-1960s, as white settlers using forced native labor established large coffee farms. As economic exploitation grew, so did resentment. Nationalist liberation movements arose to wage unrelenting guerrilla warfare. After a coup overturned the long-established dictatorship in Portugal, African liberation forces seized control in Angola and Mozambique in 1975. Shortly thereafter a coalition of nationalist groups also won in Zimbabwe after a long struggle.

The battle in South Africa threatened to be still worse. The racial conflict in the white-ruled Republic of South Africa could be traced back in part to the outcome of the South African War (see page 816). After the British finally conquered the inland Afrikaner republics, they agreed to grant all of South Africa self-government—South

Africa became basically a self-governing British dominion, like Canada and Australia—as soon as possible. English and moderate Afrikaners ruled jointly and could also decide which nonwhites, if any, should vote.

In 1913 the new South African legislature passed the **Native Land Act,** which limited black ownership of land to native reserves encompassing a mere one-seventh of the country. Poor, overpopulated, and too small to feed themselves, the rural native reserves served as a pool of cheap, temporary black labor for white farms, gold mines, and urban factories. Legally, the black worker was only a temporary migrant who could be returned at will by the employer or the government. The native reserves system, combining racial segregation and indirect forced labor, formed the foundation of white supremacy in South Africa.

Some extreme Afrikaner nationalists, however, refused to accept defeat and any British political presence. They elaborated an even more potently racist Afrikaner nationalist platform of white supremacy and racial segregation that between 1910 and 1948 gradually won them political power from their English-speaking settler rivals. After their decisive 1948 electoral victory, Afrikaner nationalists spoke increasingly for a large majority of South African whites.

Once in control, successive Afrikaner governments wove the somewhat haphazard early racist measures into an authoritarian fabric of racial discrimination and inequality. This system was officially known as **apartheid,** meaning "apartness" or "separation." The population was divided into four legally unequal racial groups: whites, blacks, Asians, and racially mixed "coloureds." Although Afrikaner propagandists claimed that apartheid served the interests of all racial groups by preserving separate cultures and racial purity, most observers saw it as a way of maintaining the lavish privileges of the white minority, which accounted for only one-sixth of the total population.

After 1940, South Africa became the most highly industrialized country in Africa. Rapid urbanization followed, changing the face of the country, but good jobs in the cities were reserved for whites. Whites lived in luxurious modern central cities. Blacks, as temporary migrants, were restricted to outlying black townships plagued by poverty, crime, and white policemen.

South Africa's harsh white supremacy elicited many black nationalist protests from the 1920s onward. By the 1950s blacks—and their coloured, white, and Asian allies—were staging large-scale peaceful protests. A turning point came in 1960, when police at Sharpeville fired into a crowd of demonstrators and killed sixty-nine blacks. The main black nationalist organization—the **African National Congress (ANC)**—was then outlawed but sent some of its leaders abroad to establish new headquarters. Other members, led by a young black lawyer named Nelson Mandela (b. 1918), stayed in South Africa to set up an underground army to oppose the government. Captured after seventeen months, Mandela was tried for treason and sentenced to life imprisonment. (See the feature "Listening to the Past: The Struggle for Freedom in South Africa" on pages 1018–1019.)

By the late 1970s the white government had apparently destroyed the moderate black opposition within South Africa. Operating out of the sympathetic black states of Zimbabwe and Mozambique to the north, the militant ANC turned increasingly to armed struggle. South Africa struck back hard and forced its neighbors to curtail the ANC's guerrilla activities. Fortified by these successes, South Africa's white leaders launched in 1984 a program of cosmetic "reforms." For the first time, the 3 million coloureds and the 1 million South Africans of Asian descent were granted limited parliamentary representation. But no provision was made for any representation of the country's 22 million blacks, and laws controlling black movement and settlement were maintained.

The government's self-serving reforms provoked black indignation and triggered a massive reaction. In the segregated townships young black militants took to the

Native Land Act *A 1913 South African law that limited black ownership of land to native reserves encompassing only one-seventh of the country.*

apartheid *The system of racial segregation and discrimination that was supported by the Afrikaner government.*

African National Congress (ANC) *The main black nationalist organization in South Africa; it was led by Nelson Mandela.*

> **Primary Source:**
> **The Rivonia Trial Speech to the Court**
> *Read how Nelson Mandela defended himself against charges of treason before an all-white South African court in 1964.*

● **Men of Destiny** Nelson Mandela shakes hands with Frederik de Klerk following a televised presidential debate in the 1994 electoral campaign. Mandela won and replaced de Klerk as president of South Africa after 350 years of white supremacy. De Klerk became vice president. Both leaders vowed to build a multiracial democratic society. *(Mark Peters/Sipa Press)*

streets, attacking in particular black civil servants and policemen as agents of white oppression. Heavily armed white security forces clashed repeatedly with black protesters, who turned funerals for fallen comrades into mass demonstrations. Between 1985 and 1989 five thousand died and fifty thousand were jailed without charges because of the political unrest.

By 1989 the white government and the black opposition had reached an impasse. Black protesters had been bloodied but not beaten, and their freedom movement had gathered worldwide support. The U.S. Congress had applied strong sanctions against South Africa in October 1986, and the Common Market had followed. The white government still held power, but harsh repression of black resistance had failed.

The political stalemate ended in September 1989 with the election of a new state president, Frederik W. de Klerk, an Afrikaner lawyer and politician. A late-blooming reformer, de Klerk cautiously opened a dialogue with ANC leaders. Negotiating with Nelson Mandela, whose reputation had soared during his long years in prison, de Klerk lifted the state of emergency, legalized the ANC, and freed Mandela in February 1990. Mandela then courageously suspended the ANC's armed struggle and met with de Klerk for serious talks on South Africa's political future. They reached an agreement calling for universal suffrage, which meant black majority rule. They also guaranteed the civil and economic rights of minorities, including job security for white government workers.

Elected South Africa's first black president by an overwhelming majority in May 1994, Mandela told his jubilant supporters of his "deep pride and joy—pride in the ordinary, humble people of this country. . . . And joy that we can loudly proclaim from the roof tops—free at last!"[7] Heading the new "government of national unity," which included de Klerk as vice president, Mandela and the South African people set about building a democratic, multiracial nation. The new constitution guaranteed all political parties some legislative seats until 1998.

In an imaginative attempt to heal the wounds of apartheid, the new black majority government established the Truth and Reconciliation Commission. This commission let black victims speak out and share their suffering, and it also offered white perpetrators amnesty from prosecution in return for fully confessing their crimes. Mandela's ministers repudiated their earlier socialist beliefs and accepted global capitalism as the only way to develop the economy and reduce widespread black poverty.

In 1999 Thabo Mbeki succeeded Mandela as South Africa's president. The magnitude of the problems facing Mandela and Mbeki in availability of health care, housing, electricity, water, and the other amenities necessary for a decent standard of living in the twenty-first century were truly daunting, but significant progress has been made. Much still needs to be done, and all under the heavy burden of the worst AIDS crisis in the world (see pages 1055–1056). Still, South Africa at independence had a better education system, a more viable infrastructure, and a more diversified economy than any other African country. Many people across southern Africa, and even farther north, are looking to South Africa to be the economic engine that drives the continent.

Political Reform in Africa Since 1990

Democracy's triumph in South Africa was part of a broad trend toward elected civilian government that swept through sub-Saharan Africa after 1990. Political protesters rose up and forced one-party authoritarian regimes to grant liberalizing reforms and call national conferences, which often led to competitive elections and new constitutions. These changes occurred in almost all African countries; in the words of two leading scholars, "they amounted to the most far-reaching shifts in African political life since the political independence of thirty years earlier."[8]

Many factors contributed to this historic watershed. The anticommunist revolutions of 1989 in eastern Europe were extremely important. They showed Africans that even the most well-entrenched one-party regimes could be opposed, punished for prolonged misrule, and replaced with electoral competition and even democracy. The decline of military rule in Latin America and the emerging global trend toward political and economic liberalism worked in the same direction.

The end of the cold war also transformed Africa's relations with Russia and the United States. Both superpowers had viewed Africa as an important cold war battleground, and both had given large-scale military and financial aid to their allies, as well as to "uncommitted" African leaders who often played one side against the other. Communism's collapse in Europe brought an abrupt end to communist aid to Russia's African clients, leaving them weakened and much more willing to compromise with opposition movements.

American involvement in Africa also declined. During the cold war U.S. leaders had generally supported "pro-Western" African dictators, no matter how corrupt or repressive. This interventionist policy gave way to a less intense (and much cheaper) interest in free elections and civil rights in the 1990s. A striking example of this evolution was steadfast U.S. support for the "anticommunist" General Mobutu Sese Seko after he seized power in 1965 in Zaire (the former Belgian Congo, renamed the Democratic Republic of the Congo in 1997). Mobutu looted and impoverished his country for decades before the United States cut off aid in the early 1990s, thereby helping an opposition group topple the dying tyrant in 1997.

If events outside Africa established conditions favoring political reform, Africans themselves were the principal actors in the shift toward democracy. They demanded reform because long years of mismanagement and repression had delegitimized one-party rule.

Above all, the strength of the democratic opposition rested on a growing class of educated urban Africans, for post-independence governments had enthusiastically expanded opportunities in education, especially higher education. In the typical West African state of Cameroon, the number of students graduating from the French-speaking national university jumped from a minuscule 213 in 1961 to 10,000 in 1982 and 41,000 in 1992.[9] The growing middle class of educated professionals—generally pragmatic, moderate, and open to new ideas—chafed at the ostentatious privilege of tiny closed elites and pressed for political reforms that would democratize social and economic opportunities. Thus after 1990 sub-Saharan Africa participated fully in the global trend toward greater democracy and human rights.

The world's media have generally focused on the African governments and economies that failed in the years since 1990. Eight years into the twenty-first century, however, many African countries continue to make significant progress in the consolidation of democracy and human rights. Even some of the countries that experienced horrible civil war and nearly complete disintegration in the 1990s and early 2000s—such as Sierra Leone, Liberia, Angola, the Central African Republic, and Guinea-Bissau—have begun to pull back from the abyss. Ivory Coast experienced years of civil war after its first-ever military coup in 1999. Rebels continue to control the country's northern half, but they and the government met and signed the Ouagadougou Agreement in March 2007, committing themselves to disarmament and reunification and the holding of elections sometime in 2008.

Democracy, however, is still a long struggle away in many African countries. All of North Africa remains under the control of one-party, authoritarian rulers, and Eritrea, Ethiopia, Equatorial Guinea, Zimbabwe, Swaziland, Cameroon, and Gambia have increasingly brutal dictatorships. Sudan's authoritarian Islamic rulers ended their long civil war with the Christians and animists in the south, only to have pro-government Arab militias attack Muslim ethnic Africans in the western Darfur region. The genocidal attacks have caused tens of thousands of deaths and an estimated 2 million refugees. Congo-Kinshasa, Rwanda, Burundi, and Somalia remain perilously close to the abyss of unimaginable violence they experienced in the 1990s. In Kenya, riots following the bitterly contested and questionable re-election of Mwai Kibaki as president on December 27, 2007, resulted in over 250 deaths in the first week after the election. Often considered one of Africa's most stable nations, Kenya unexpectedly erupted into chaos, with interethnic violence forcing hundreds of thousands to flee their homes.

Many of the most stable, democratic countries are in southern Africa: Botswana, South Africa, Zambia, and Namibia have all made the transition from colonialism to democracy. With a few stops and starts, Malawi, Nigeria, Niger, and Madagascar are also making good progress. Much of the political progress is closely linked to economic progress. As Zimbabwe's authoritarian regime under Robert Mugabe has created a corrupt, immoral, human rights nightmare, it has also suffered total economic collapse. More politically stable countries such as Ghana have seen their economies grow and foreign investments increase. Countries in western and central Africa may soon undergo revolutionary political and economic change as a result of the oil and natural gas boom in those regions. Chad, Mauritania, Angola, Nigeria, Gabon, São Tomé and Príncipe, Congo Brazzaville, and Equatorial Guinea could all benefit from complete economic turnarounds, and others will follow.

● ● ● ● ● ● ● ● ● ● ● ● ● ● ● ● ● ● ●

INTERPRETING THE EXPERIENCES OF THE EMERGING WORLD

How do the writings of Chinua Achebe represent the common experiences of peoples in the emerging world?

Having come of age during and after the struggle for political emancipation, numerous intellectuals embraced the vision of Third World solidarity, and some argued that genuine independence and freedom from outside control required a total break with the former colonial powers and a total rejection of Western values. This was the mes-

● **Nigeria's Conscience** Chinua Achebe's powerful novels focus on complex and believable individuals caught up in the unfolding drama of colonialism, independence, and nation building in Africa. Achebe is an intensely serious writer, a man who speaks for his people and believes in the high moral calling of literature and art. *(Photo, Chido Nangwu)*

sage of Frantz Fanon (1925–1961) in his powerful study of colonial peoples, *The Wretched of the Earth* (1961).

According to Fanon, a French-trained black psychiatrist from the Caribbean island of Martinique, decolonization is always a violent and totally consuming process whereby one "species" of men, the colonizers, is completely replaced by an absolutely different species—the colonized, the wretched of the earth. During decolonization the colonized masses mock colonial values, "insult them, and vomit them up" in a psychic purge.

Fanon believed that throughout Africa and Asia the former imperialists and their local collaborators—the "white men with black faces"—remained the enemy:

During the colonial period the people are called upon to fight against oppression; after national liberation, they are called upon to fight against poverty, illiteracy, and underdevelopment. The struggle, they say, goes on.

. . . We are not blinded by the moral reparation of national independence; nor are we fed by it. The wealth of the imperial countries is our wealth too. . . . Europe is literally the creation of the Third World. The wealth which smothers her is that which was stolen from the underdeveloped peoples.[10]

Fanon's passionate, angry work became a sacred text for radicals attacking imperialism and struggling for liberation.

As countries gained independence and self-rule, some writers looked beyond wholesale rejection of the industrialized powers. They too were "anti-imperialist," but often also activists and cultural nationalists who applied their talents to celebrating the rich histories and cultures of their peoples. Many did not hesitate to criticize their own leaders or fight against oppression and corruption.

The Nigerian writer Chinua Achebe (b. 1930) rendered these themes with acute insight and vivid specificity in his short, moving novels. Achebe sought to restore his people's self-confidence by reinterpreting the past. For Achebe the "writer in a new nation" had first to embrace the "fundamental theme":

This theme—quite simply—is that the African people did not hear of culture for the first time from Europeans; that their societies were not mindless but frequently had a philosophy of great depth and volume and beauty; that they had poetry and above all, they had dignity. It is this dignity that many African peoples all but lost in the colonial period, and it is this that they must now regain. The worst thing that can happen to any people is the loss of their dignity and self-respect. The writer's duty is to help them regain it by showing what happened to them, what they lost.[11]

In *Things Fall Apart* (1958) Achebe achieved his goal by vividly bringing to life the men and women of an Ibo village at the beginning of the twentieth century, with all their virtues and frailties. Woven into the story are the proverbs and wisdom of a sophisticated people and the beauty of a vanishing world. In later novels Achebe portrays the post-independence disillusionment of many writers and intellectuals, which reflected trends in many developing nations in the 1960s and 1970s: the rulers seemed increasingly corrupted by Western luxury and estranged from the rural masses.

From the 1970s onward Achebe was active in the struggle for democratic government in Nigeria. In his novel *Anthills of the Savannah* (1989), he calls upon Africa to stand on its own two feet, take responsibility, and realize that widespread corruption is frustrating hopes of progress and genuine independence. Yet in his recent essays and speeches he also returns to his earlier theme of the West's enduring low opinion of Africa—ever the "dark continent," the savage, non-Western "other world."

The Nobel Prize–winning novelist V. S. Naipaul, born in Trinidad in 1932 of Indian parents, also castigated governments in the developing countries for corruption, ineptitude, and self-deception. Another of Naipaul's recurring themes is the poignant loneliness and homelessness of people uprooted by colonialism and Western expansion.

Chapter Summary

To assess your mastery of this chapter, go to
bedfordstmartins.com/mckayworld

Key Terms

Great Leap Forward
Great Proletarian Cultural
 Revolution
Red Guards
Tiananmen Square
Muslim League
Palestine Liberation
 Organization (PLO)
National Liberation Front
Pan-Africanists
cocoa holdups
Native Land Act
apartheid
African National Congress
 (ANC)

• How was Latin America similar to, and different from, the other Third World nations?

Nearly all the countries of Central and South America had gained their independence by the mid-1800s. This was just the time when Europe initiated a second great period of colonization that resulted in the colonization of much of Africa, Asia, and the Middle East. Despite their independence, many Latin Americans still believed the West was economically exploiting their countries through a form of neocolonialism. Politically throughout most of the twentieth century, Latin American countries were ruled by conservative, authoritarian leaders, some of them harsh and cruel dictators supported by the West. Thus many Latin Americans felt closer ties to the colonized peoples of Asia and Africa than they did to Western colonizers. In the 1980s much of Latin America turned toward free elections, civil liberties, and freer markets, abandoning the long-standing commitment to economic nationalism.

• How did the defeat of Japan lead to East Asian resurgence after World War II?

When World War II ended with the Japanese defeat, long suppressed nationalist movements pushed for political independence across East Asia. Mao Zedong's Communist forces took over in China, and the pro-Western Nationalist leader Jiang Jieshi was defeated. Meanwhile, thirty-five years of Japanese occupation of the Korean peninsula ended only to have the country divided, with the northern half controlled by a communist government installed by Stalin. The North became one of the harshest dictatorships and poorest countries in the world, while the South became one of the "Asian tigers," a modern, industrial powerhouse with one of the highest standards of living in the world. The other Asian tigers—Taiwan, Hong Kong, and Singapore—also left the war and colonial rule behind them to develop vibrant global economies. Vietnam had to fight a long war of independence against the French and then the Americans before beginning an economic recovery.

• How did Hindus and Muslims adjust to the end of British colonial rule?

The Hindu and Muslim populations of India threw off British colonial rule only to go to war among themselves. Mahatma Gandhi was unable to convince the two groups to remain united in an independent India, and the Muslims broke away to create two new countries, Bangladesh and Pakistan. Pakistan and India have remained at odds ever since, often violently, because of religious hatred and territorial disputes in the Kashmir region of northwest India.

• What was the dual nature of nationalism in the Islamic heartland?

The Muslim world was also rejuvenated after 1945, most notably under Nasser in Egypt. Nasser was respected throughout the Arab world for having stood up to the West and was a symbol of the pan-Arab, anti-Western movement. Pan-Arabism, the uniting of all Arabs into a single nation, was a dream of many Arabs, but regional, ideological, and personal rivalries made such unification impossible. Nationalism thus took a more traditional turn as individual states developed out of territories that had been League of Nations mandates and European colonies. Common to all these states was a deep devotion to Islam.

• How did Kwame Nkrumah represent the new leaders of independent Africa?

In black Africa a generation of nationalist leaders successfully guided colonial territories to self-rule by the middle of the 1960s. The father of independent Africa was Kwame Nkrumah, a Ghanaian who, like many African nationalists, had spent many years studying in the West. He returned to Ghana after World War II and led an independence movement against British rule. Again, like many other nationalist leaders, Nkrumah was arrested by the British after leading mass strikes and demonstrations and was elected while in jail to lead a transitional government. In 1957 Ghana became the first sub-Saharan country to gain independence from colonial rule.

• What are some of the common features of independent Africa since 1960?

By the mid-1960s nearly all African countries had won independence. The two largest colonial powers, Britain and France, had tried, although belatedly, to set up democratic governments in their former colonies. The new leaders of these countries, however, soon turned their backs on democracy and resorted to authoritarian, one-party rule. Opposition parties were outlawed, and political opponents were jailed, sent into exile, or killed. Many of these early dictators were overthrown by military juntas, as happened, for example, in Ghana and Nigeria. Despite the high expectations all Africans held after throwing off colonial rule, most have lived, and continue to live, under harsh and corrupt authoritarian governments.

• How do the writings of Chinua Achebe represent the common experiences of peoples in the emerging world?

There are many artists in the emerging world who have eloquently described the common experiences of peoples living under colonial rule and then in newly independent nations. One of the most famous of these artists is Chinua Achebe, a Nigerian writer whose novels have been translated into many languages because of their universal appeal. One of Achebe's primary themes is that Africans had their own cultures, philosophies, poetry, and dignity before the Europeans arrived and tried to force their own values on the peoples they colonized. This theme he fully developed in his first and most widely read novel, *Things Fall Apart.* In later novels Achebe described the disillusionment felt by many Africans (and peoples of Asia and Latin America as well) with the corruption and authoritarian rule of post-independence governments.

Suggested Reading

Beck, Roger B. *The History of South Africa.* 2000. Introduction to South African history with emphasis on the twentieth century.

Chang, Jung, and Jon Halliday. *Mao: The Unknown Story.* 2005. Controversial new biography of the Chinese communist leader.

Church, Peter. *A Short History of South-East Asia.* 4th ed. 2005. A concise but comprehensive survey of the region's history.

Collins, Robert O., and James M. Burns. *A History of Sub-Saharan Africa.* 2007. Clearly written introduction to the continent's history.

Davidson, Basil. *The Black Man's Burden: Africa and the Curse of the Nation State.* 1993. A thought-provoking reconsideration by a noted historian.

Du Bois, W. E. B. *The World and Africa.* 1947. A classic text by the distinguished American black thinker.

Jayakar, Pupul. *Indira Gandhi: An Intimate Biography.* 1993. Very readable narrative of the powerful and controversial Indian prime minister.

Guha, Ramachandra. *India After Gandhi: The History of the World's Largest Democracy.* 2007. In-depth study of the last sixty years of Indian history and development.

Kenyatta, Jomo. *Facing Mount Kenya.* 1953. Powerful commentary and autobiography by one of Africa's foremost revolutionary and political leaders.

Lowenthal, Abraham F., and Gregory F. Treverton, eds. *Latin America in a New World.* 1994. Analyzes the move toward regional cooperation and market economies.

Meredith, Robyn. *The Elephant and the Dragon: The Rise of India and China and What It Means for All of Us.* 2005. Useful and accessible introduction to these two economic giants.

Mahbubani, Kishore. *The New Asian Hemisphere: The Irresistible Shift of Global Power to the East.* 2008. A history and analysis of the rise of Asia in world politics and economics by one of Asia's leading intellectuals.

Nehru, Jawaharlal. *An Autobiography.* 1962. Classic personal account of India's history in the first half of twentieth century by its first president.

Osborne, Milton. *Southeast Asia: An Introductory History.* 9th rev. ed. 2005. Classic introduction to the region.

Wasserstrom, Jeffrey N., ed. *Twentieth Century China: New Approaches.* 2002. Collection of essays on cultural and national developments using recently released archives.

Notes

1. S. Schram, *Mao Tse-tung* (New York: Simon and Schuster, 1966), p. 151.
2. Quoted in P. B. Ebrey, ed., *Chinese Civilization and Society: A Source Book* (New York: Free Press, 1981), p. 393.
3. Quoted in W. Bingham, H. Conroy, and F. Iklé, *A History of Asia,* vol. 2, 2d ed. (Boston: Allyn and Bacon, 1974), p. 459.
4. Quoted in K. Bhata, *The Ordeal of Nationhood: A Social Study of India Since Independence, 1947–1970* (New York: Atheneum, 1971), p. 9.
5. Quoted in B. Baktiari and H. Vaziri, "Iran's Liberal Revolution?" *Current History,* January 2002, p. 21.
6. Quoted in R. Hallett, *Africa Since 1875: A Modern History* (Ann Arbor: University of Michigan Press, 1974), pp. 378–379.
7. *Chicago Tribune,* May 3, 1994, section 1, p. 5.
8. M. Bratton and N. van de Walle, *Democratic Experiments in Africa: Regime Transitions in Comparative Perspectives* (Cambridge: Cambridge University Press, 1997), p. 3.
9. D. Birmingham and P. Martin, eds., *History of Central Africa: The Contemporary Years Since 1960* (London: Routledge, 1998), p. 59.
10. F. Fanon, *The Wretched of the Earth* (New York: Grove Press, 1968), pp. 43, 93–94, 97, 102.
11. C. Achebe, *Morning Yet on Creation Day* (London: Heinemann, 1975), p. 81.

Listening to the PAST

The Struggle for Freedom in South Africa

Many African territories won political freedom in the mid-1960s, but in South Africa the struggle was long and extremely difficult. Only in 1990 did the white government release Nelson Mandela from prison and begin negotiations with the famous black leader and the African National Congress (ANC). Only in 1994 did Mandela and the ANC finally come to power and establish a new system based on majority rule and racial equality.

Born in 1918 into the royal family of the Transkei, Nelson Mandela received an education befitting the son of a chief. But he ran away to escape an arranged marriage, experienced the harsh realities of black life in Johannesburg, studied law, and became an attorney. A born leader with a natural air of authority, Mandela was drawn to politics and the ANC. In the 1950s the white government responded to the growing popularity of Mandela and the ANC with tear gas and repression.

In 1960 the ANC called a general strike to protest the shooting of peaceful protesters at Sharpeville. Acts of sabotage then shook South Africa, and Mandela led the underground opposition. Betrayed by an informer, he was convicted of treason in 1964 and sentenced to life imprisonment. Mandela defended all of the accused in the 1964 treason trial. The following selection is taken from Mandela's opening statement.

At the outset, I want to say that the suggestion made by the State in its opening that the struggle in South Africa is under the influence of foreigners or communists is wholly incorrect. I have done whatever I did, both as an individual and as a leader of my people, because of my experience in South Africa and my own proudly felt African background, and not because of what any outsider might have said.

In my youth in the Transkei I listened to the elders of my tribe telling stories of the old days. Amongst the tales they related to me were those of wars fought by our ancestors in defence of the fatherland. . . . I hoped then that life might offer me the opportunity to serve my people and make my own humble contribution to their freedom struggle. . . .

It is true that there has often been close cooperation between the ANC [African National Congress] and the Communist Party. But cooperation is merely proof of a common goal—in this case the removal of White supremacy—and is not proof of a complete community of interests. . . . What is more, for many decades communists were the only political group in South Africa who were prepared to treat Africans as human beings and their equals; who were prepared to eat with us, talk with us, live with us, and work with us. . . . Because of this, there are many Africans who today tend to equate freedom with communism. . . .

I turn now to my own position. I have denied that I am a communist. . . . [But] I am attracted by the idea of a classless society, an attraction which springs in part from Marxist reading and, in part, from my admiration of the structure and organization of early African societies in this country. The land, then the main means of production, belonged to the tribe. There were no rich or poor and there was no exploitation. . . .

[Unlike communists] I am an admirer of the parliamentary system of the West. . . . [Thus] I have been influenced in my thinking by both West and East. . . . [I believe] I should be absolutely impartial and objective. I should tie myself to no particular system of society other than of socialism. I must leave myself free to borrow the best from the West and from the East. . . .

Our fight is against real, and not imaginary, hardships or, to use the language of the State Prosecutor, "so-called hardships." . . . Basically, we fight against two features which are the hallmarks of African life in South Africa and which are entrenched by legislation which we seek to have repealed. These features are poverty and lack of human dignity, and we do not need communists or so-called "agitators" to teach us about these things.

South Africa is the richest country in Africa, and could be one of the richest countries in the world. But it is a land of extremes and remarkable contrasts. The Whites enjoy what may well be the highest standard of living in the world, while Africans live in poverty and

Nelson Mandela at the time of his imprisonment in 1964. (Mohamed Lounes/Gamma)

misery. . . . Poverty goes hand in hand with malnutrition and disease. . . .

The lack of human dignity experienced by Africans is the direct result of the policy of White supremacy. White supremacy implies Black inferiority. Legislation designed to preserve White supremacy entrenches this notion. . . . Because of this sort of attitude, Whites tend to regard Africans as a separate breed. They do not look upon them as people with families of their own; they do not realize that they have emotions. . . .

Africans want to be paid a living wage. Africans want to perform work which they are capable of doing, and not work which the Government declares them to be capable of. . . . Africans want a just share in the whole of South Africa; they want security and a stake in society.

Above all, we want equal political rights, because without them our disabilities will be permanent. I know this sounds revolutionary to the Whites in this country, because the majority of voters will be Africans. This makes the White man fear democracy.

But this fear cannot be allowed to stand in the way of the only solution which will guarantee racial harmony and freedom for all. It is not true that the enfranchisement of all will result in racial domination. Political division, based on color, is entirely artificial and, when it disappears, so will the domination of one color group by another. The ANC has spent half a century fighting against racialism. When it triumphs it will not change that policy.

This then is what the ANC is fighting. Their struggle is a truly national one. It is a struggle of the African people, inspired by their own suffering and their own experience. It is a struggle for the right to live.

During my lifetime I have dedicated myself to this struggle of the African people. I have fought against White domination, and I have fought against Black domination. I have cherished the ideal of a democratic and free society in which all persons live together in harmony and with equal opportunities. It is an ideal which I hope to live for and to achieve. But if need be, it is an ideal for which I am prepared to die.

Questions for Analysis

1. How does Nelson Mandela respond to the charge that he and the ANC are controlled by communists?

2. What factors influenced Mandela's thinking? In what ways has he been influenced by "both East and West" and by his African background?

3. According to Mandela, what is wrong with South Africa? What needs to be done?

4. What are Mandela's goals for South Africa? Are his goals realistic, idealistic, or both?

Source: Slightly adapted from Nelson Mandela, *No Easy Walk to Freedom: Articles, Speeches and Trial Addresses* (London: Heinemann, 1973), pp. 163, 179–185, 187–189. Reprinted by permission of Heinemann Publishers (Oxford) Ltd.

Italians protesting government economic policies gather in front of the Roman Coliseum during a nationwide strike in October 2003. *(Philippe Desmazes/AFP/Getty Images)*

The Decline of Communism in Eastern Europe
• *In what ways did Solidarity confront the communist system in Poland, and how did Mikhail Gorbachev try to reverse the decline of communism in the Soviet Union?*

The Revolutions of 1989
• *How did anticommunist revolutions sweep through eastern Europe in 1989, and what were the immediate consequences?*

Building a New Europe in the 1990s
• *How, in the 1990s, did the different parts of a reunifying Europe meet the challenges of postcommunist reconstruction, resurgent nationalism, and economic union?*

New Challenges in the Twenty-first Century
• *Why did the prospect of population decline, the reality of large-scale immigration, and concern for human rights emerge as critical issues in contemporary Europe?*

The West and the Islamic World
• *How and why did relations between the West and the Islamic world deteriorate dramatically in the early twenty-first century?*

The Future in Perspective
• *What does the study of history have to tell us about the future?*

REVOLUTION, REBUILDING, AND NEW CHALLENGES: 1985 TO THE PRESENT

In the late twentieth century, massive changes swept through eastern Europe and opened a new era in human history. In the 1980s a broad movement to transform the communist system took root in Poland, and efforts to reform and revitalize the communist system in the Soviet Union snowballed out of control. In 1989 revolutions swept away communist rule throughout the entire Soviet bloc. The cold war came to a spectacular end, West Germany absorbed East Germany, and the Soviet Union broke into fifteen independent countries. Thus after forty years of cold war division, Europe regained an underlying unity, as faith in democratic government and some kind of market economy became the common European creed. In 1991 hopes for peaceful democratic progress throughout Europe were almost universal.

The post–cold war years saw the realization of some of these hopes, but the new era brought its own problems and tragedies. The cold war division of Europe had kept a lid on ethnic conflicts and nationalism, which suddenly burst into the open and led to a disastrous civil war in the former Yugoslavia. Moreover, most western European economies were plagued by high unemployment and struggling to adapt to the wide-open global economy, which undermined cherished social benefits and complicated the task of working together with the former communist states. Thus in eastern Europe, the process of rebuilding shattered societies was more difficult than optimists had envisioned in 1991, and in western Europe, the road toward greater unity and eastward expansion proved bumpy. Nevertheless, the will to undo the cold war division prevailed, and in 2004 eight former communist countries as well as the islands of Cyprus and Malta joined the European Union—a historic achievement.

Book Companion Site
This icon will direct you to primary sources and study materials available at **bedfordstmartins.com/mckaywest**

The new century brought a growing awareness of a new set of fundamental challenges, which were related to the prospect of population decline, the reality of large-scale immigration, and the promotion of human rights. These challenges promised to preoccupy Western society for years to come.

More dramatically, the old, often contentious question of relations with the Islamic world suddenly re-emerged as a critical issue after the attack on New York's World Trade Center and the Pentagon in 2001. After the West united in a quick response against the Taliban in Afghanistan, the subsequent war in Iraq divided western Europe and threatened the future of Western cooperation in world affairs. The war in Iraq also complicated the ongoing integration of Europe's rapidly growing Muslim population.

The Decline of Communism in Eastern Europe

Following the 1968 invasion of Czechoslovakia, the crucial event of the Brezhnev era (pages 997–999), the Soviet Union repeatedly demonstrated that it remained a harsh and aggressive dictatorship. It paid only lip service to egalitarian ideology at home and was determined to uphold its rule throughout eastern Europe. Thus the Soviet Union eventually crushed the Solidarity movement in Poland, the powerful, peaceful challenge to Communist rule in Poland in the early 1980s. Periodic efforts to achieve fundamental political change were doomed to failure sooner or later—or so it seemed to most Western experts into the mid-1980s.

And then Mikhail Gorbachev burst on the scene. The new Soviet leader opened an era of reform that was as sweeping as it was unexpected. Although many believed that Gorbachev would soon fall from power, his reforms rapidly transformed Soviet culture and politics, and they drastically reduced cold war tensions. But communism, which Gorbachev wanted so desperately to revitalize in order to save it, continued to decline as a functioning system throughout the Soviet bloc.

● *In what ways did Solidarity confront the communist system in Poland, and how did Mikhail Gorbachev try to reverse the decline of communism in the Soviet Union?*

Solidarity in Poland

Gorbachev's reforms interacted with a resurgence of popular protest in the Soviet Union's satellite empire. Developments in Poland were most striking and significant.

Poland had been an unruly satellite from the beginning. Stalin said that introducing communism to Poland was like putting a saddle on a cow. Efforts to saddle the cow—really a spirited stallion—led to widespread riots in 1956 (see page 997). As a result, Polish Communists dropped their efforts to impose Soviet-style collectivization on the peasants and to break the Roman Catholic Church. Most agricultural land remained in private hands, and the Catholic Church thrived. Thus the Communists failed to monopolize society.

They also failed to manage the economy effectively. Even the booming 1960s saw little economic improvement. In 1970 Poland's working class rose again in angry protest. A new Communist leader came to power, and he wagered that massive inflows of Western capital and technology, especially from rich and now-friendly West Germany (see page 1008), could produce a Polish "economic miracle." Instead, bureaucratic incompetence and the first oil shock in 1973 put the economy into a nosedive. Workers, intellectuals, and the church became increasingly restive. Then the real Polish miracle occurred: Cardinal Karol Wojtyla, archbishop of Cracow, was elected pope in 1978. In June 1979, he returned from Rome, preaching love of Christ and country and the "inalienable rights of man." Pope John Paul II drew enormous crowds and electrified the Polish nation. The economic crisis became a moral and spiritual crisis as well.

In August 1980, the sixteen thousand workers at the gigantic Lenin Shipyards in Gdansk (formerly known as Danzig) laid down their tools and occupied the plant. As other workers joined "in solidarity," the strikers advanced revolutionary demands, including the right to form free-trade unions, freedom of speech, release of political prisoners, and economic reforms. After eighteen days of shipyard occupation, the government gave in and accepted the workers' demands in the **Gdansk Agreement.** In a state where the Communist Party claimed to rule on behalf of the proletariat, a working-class revolt had won an unprecedented victory.

Book Companion Site
Primary Source: The "Twenty-one Demands": A Call for Workers' Rights and Freedom in a Socialist State

Led by feisty Lenin Shipyards electrician and devout Catholic Lech Walesa (b. 1943), the workers proceeded to organize their free and democratic trade union. They called it **Solidarity.** Joined by intellectuals and supported by the Catholic Church, Solidarity became the union of a nation. By March 1981, a full-time staff of 40,000 linked 9.5 million union members together as Solidarity published its own newspapers and cultural and intellectual freedom blossomed in Poland. Solidarity's leaders had tremendous support, and the ever-present threat of calling a nationwide strike gave them real power in ongoing negotiations with the Communist bosses.

But if Solidarity had power, it did not try to take the reins of government in 1981. History, the Brezhnev Doctrine, and virulent attacks from communist neighbors all seemed to guarantee the intervention of the Red Army and a terrible bloodbath if Polish Communists "lost control." Thus the Solidarity revolution remained a "self-limiting revolution" aimed at defending the cultural and trade-union freedoms won in the Gdansk Agreement, and it refused to use force to challenge directly the Communist monopoly of political power.

Solidarity's combination of strength and moderation postponed a showdown, as the Soviet Union played a waiting game of threats and pressure. After a confrontation in March 1981, Walesa settled for minor government concessions, and Solidarity dropped plans for a massive general strike. Criticism of Walesa's moderate leadership grew, and Solidarity lost its cohesiveness. The worsening economic crisis also encouraged grassroots radicalism, as the Polish Communist leadership shrewdly denounced Solidarity for promoting economic collapse and provoking Soviet invasion. In December 1981, Communist leader General Wojciech Jaruzelski suddenly struck, proclaiming martial law, arresting Solidarity's leaders, and "saving" the nation.

Outlawed and driven underground, Solidarity fought successfully to maintain its organization and to voice the aspirations of the Polish masses after 1981. Part of the reason for the union's survival was the government's unwillingness (and probably its inability) to impose full-scale terror. Moreover, millions of Poles decided to continue acting as if they were free, even though they were not. Cultural and intellectual life remained extremely vigorous as the faltering Polish economy continued to deteriorate. Thus popular support for outlawed Solidarity remained strong under martial law in the 1980s, preparing the way for the union's political rebirth toward the end of the decade.

The rise and survival of Solidarity showed the desire of millions of eastern Europeans for greater political liberty and the enduring appeal of cultural freedom, trade-union rights, patriotic nationalism, and religious feeling. Not least, Solidarity's challenge encouraged fresh thinking in the Soviet Union, ever the key to lasting change in the Eastern bloc.

Chronology

1985   Glasnost leads to greater freedom of speech and expression in the Soviet Union

1985–   Decline in birthrate in industrialized nations continues

1986   Single European Act lays groundwork for single currency

August 1989   Solidarity gains power in Poland

November 1989   Collapse of the Berlin Wall

November–December 1989   Velvet Revolution ends communism in Czechoslovakia

October 1990   Reunification of Germany

1990–1991   First war with Iraq

July 1991   Failed coup against Gorbachev in Russia

December 1991   Dissolution of the Soviet Union

1991   Maastricht treaty sets financial criteria for European monetary union

1991–2000   Resurgence of nationalism and ethnic conflict in eastern Europe

1991–2001   Civil war in Yugoslavia

1992–1997   "Shock therapy" in Russia causes decline of the economy

1993   Creation of the European Union; growth of illegal immigration in Europe

1996   Cronin, *The World the Cold War Made*

1998–   Growing support for global human rights in Europe

1999   Russian economy booms

September 2001   Terrorist attack on the United States

2001   War in Afghanistan

January 2002   New euro currency goes into effect in the European Union

2003   Second war in Iraq begins

2004   Ten new states join European Union

November 2005   Young Muslims riot in France

2006   Murderous sectarian conflict in Iraq increases

Lech Walesa and Solidarity   An inspiration for fellow workers at the Lenin Shipyards in the dramatic and successful strike against the Communist bosses in August 1980, Walesa played a key role in Solidarity before and after it was outlawed. Speaking here to old comrades at the Lenin Shipyards after Solidarity was again legalized in 1988, Walesa personified an enduring opposition to Communist rule in eastern Europe. *(G. Merrillon/Gamma Presse/EYEDEA)*

Gorbachev's Reforms in the Soviet Union

Fundamental change in Russian history has often come in short, intensive spurts, which contrast vividly with long periods of immobility. The era of reform launched by Mikhail Gorbachev in 1985 was one such decisive transformation. Gorbachev's initiatives brought political and cultural liberalization to the Soviet Union, and they then permitted democracy and national self-determination to triumph spectacularly in the old satellite empire and eventually in the Soviet Union itself, although this was certainly not Gorbachev's original intention.

As we have seen (page 998), the Soviet Union's Communist Party elite seemed secure in the early 1980s as far as any challenge from below was concerned. The long-established system of administrative controls continued to stretch downward from the central ministries and state committees to provincial cities, and from there to facto-

ries, neighborhoods, and villages. At each level of this massive state bureaucracy, the overlapping hierarchy of the Communist Party, with its 17.5 million members, continued to watch over all decisions and manipulate every aspect of national life. Organized opposition was impossible, and average people simply left politics to the bosses.

Yet the massive state and party bureaucracy was a mixed blessing. It safeguarded the elite, but it promoted apathy in the masses. Therefore, when the ailing Brezhnev finally died in 1982, his successor, the long-time chief of the secret police, Yuri Andropov (1914–1984), tried to invigorate the system. Relatively little came of these efforts, but they combined with a sharply worsening economic situation to set the stage for the emergence in 1985 of Mikhail Gorbachev (b. 1931), the most vigorous Soviet leader in a generation.

Trained as a lawyer and working his way up as a Communist Party official in the northern Caucasus, Gorbachev was smart, charming, and tough. Gorbachev believed in communism, but he realized it was failing to keep up with Western capitalism and technology. This was eroding the Soviet Union's status as a superpower. Thus Gorbachev (and his intelligent, influential wife, Raisa, a dedicated professor of Marxist-Leninist thought) wanted to save the Soviet system by revitalizing it with fundamental reforms. Gorbachev was also an idealist. He wanted to improve conditions for ordinary citizens. Understanding that the endless waste and expense of the cold war arms race had had a disastrous impact on living conditions in the Soviet Union, he realized that improvement at home required better relations with the West.

In his first year in office, Gorbachev attacked corruption and incompetence in the bureaucracy, and he consolidated his power. He attacked alcoholism and drunkenness, which were deadly scourges of Soviet society, and elaborated his ambitious reform program.

The first set of reform policies was designed to transform and restructure the economy, in order to provide for the real needs of the Soviet population. To accomplish this economic "restructuring," or **perestroika,** Gorbachev and his supporters permitted an easing of government price controls on some goods, more independence for state enterprises, and the setting up of profit-seeking private cooperatives to provide personal services for consumers. These timid economic reforms initially produced a few improvements, but shortages then grew as the economy stalled at an intermediate point between central planning and free-market mechanisms. By late 1988, widespread consumer dissatisfaction posed a serious threat to Gorbachev's leadership and the entire reform program.

Book Companion Site
Primary Source: The Last Heir of Lenin Explains His Reform Plans: Perestroika and Glasnost

Gorbachev's bold and far-reaching campaign "to tell it like it is" was much more successful. Very popular in a country where censorship, dull uniformity, and outright lies had long characterized public discourse, the new-found "openness," or **glasnost,** of the government and the media marked an astonishing break with the past. Long-banned and vilified émigré writers sold millions of copies of their works in new editions, while denunciations of Stalin and his terror became standard fare in plays and movies. Thus initial openness in government pronouncements quickly went much further than Gorbachev intended and led to something approaching free speech and free expression, a veritable cultural revolution.

Democratization was the third element of reform. Beginning as an attack on corruption in the Communist Party, it led to the first free elections in the Soviet Union

Mikhail Gorbachev   In his acceptance speech before the Supreme Soviet (the U.S.S.R.'s parliament), newly elected president Mikhail Gorbachev vowed to assume "all responsibility" for the success or failure of perestroika. Previous parliaments were no more than tools of the Communist Party, but this one actively debated and even opposed government programs. *(Vlastimir Shone/Gamma Presse/EYEDEA)*

since 1917. Gorbachev and the party remained in control, but a minority of critical independents was elected in April 1989 to a revitalized Congress of People's Deputies. Millions of Soviets then watched the new congress for hours on television as Gorbachev and his ministers saw their proposals debated and even rejected. Thus

MAP 31.1 Democratic Movements in Eastern Europe, 1989 With Gorbachev's repudiation of the Brezhnev Doctrine, the revolutionary drive for freedom and democracy spread throughout eastern Europe. Countries that had been satellites in the orbit of the Soviet Union began to set themselves free to establish their own place in the universe of free nations.

sion. Thus nationalist demands continued to grow in the non-Russian Soviet republics.

Finally, the Soviet leader brought "new political thinking" to the field of foreign affairs and acted on it. He withdrew Soviet troops from Afghanistan and sought to reduce East-West tensions. Of enormous importance, he sought to halt the arms race with the United States and convinced President Ronald Reagan of his sincerity. In December 1987, the two leaders agreed in a Washington summit to eliminate all land-based intermediate-range missiles in Europe, setting the stage for more arms reductions. Gorbachev also encouraged reform movements in Poland and Hungary and pledged to respect the political choices of the peoples of eastern Europe, repudiating the Brezhnev Doctrine. By early 1989, it seemed that if Gorbachev held to his word, the tragic Soviet occupation of eastern Europe might well wither away, taking the long cold war with it once and for all.

The Revolutions of 1989

Instead, history accelerated. In 1989 Gorbachev's plan to reform communism in order to save it snowballed out of control. A series of largely peaceful revolutions swept across eastern Europe (see Map 31.1), overturning existing communist regimes and ending the communists' monopoly of power. Watched on television in the Soviet Union and around the world, these stirring events marked the triumph and the transformation of long-standing opposition to communist rule and foreign domination in eastern Europe.

The revolutions of 1989 had momentous consequences. First, the peoples of eastern Europe joyfully re-entered the mainstream of contemporary European life and culture, after having been conquered and brutalized by Nazis and communists for almost sixty years. Second, Gorbachev's reforms boomeranged, and a complicated anticommunist revolution swept through the Soviet Union, as the multinational empire broke into a large Russia and

millions of Soviet citizens took practical lessons in open discussion, critical thinking, and representative government. The result was a new political culture at odds with the Communist Party's monopoly of power and control.

Democratization ignited demands for greater autonomy and even for national independence by non-Russian minorities, especially in the Baltic region and in the Caucasus. In April 1989, troops with sharpened shovels charged into a rally of Georgian separatists in Tbilisi and left twenty dead. But whereas China's Communist leaders brutally massacred similar prodemocracy demonstrators in Beijing in June 1989 and reimposed rigid authoritarian rule, Gorbachev drew back from repres-

fourteen other independent states. Third, West Germany quickly absorbed its East German rival and emerged as the most influential country in Europe. Finally, the long cold war came to an abrupt end, and the United States suddenly stood as the world's only superpower.

• *How did anticommunist revolutions sweep through eastern Europe in 1989, and what were the immediate consequences?*

The Collapse of Communism in Eastern Europe

Solidarity and the Polish people led the way to revolution in eastern Europe. In 1988 widespread labor unrest, raging inflation, and the outlawed Solidarity's refusal to cooperate with the military government had brought Poland to the brink of economic collapse. Thus Solidarity skillfully pressured Poland's frustrated Communist leaders into another round of negotiations that might work out a sharing of power to resolve the political stalemate and the economic crisis. The subsequent agreement in early 1989 legalized Solidarity and declared that a large minority of representatives to the Polish parliament would be chosen by free elections in June 1989. Still guaranteed a parliamentary majority and expecting to win many of the contested seats, the Communists believed that their rule was guaranteed for four years and that Solidarity would keep the workers in line.

Lacking access to the state-run media, Solidarity succeeded nonetheless in mobilizing the country and winning most of the contested seats in an overwhelming victory. Moreover, many angry voters crossed off the names of unopposed party candidates, so that the Communist Party failed to win the majority its leaders had anticipated. Solidarity members jubilantly entered the Polish parliament, and a dangerous stalemate quickly developed. But Solidarity leader Lech Walesa, a gifted politician who always repudiated violence, adroitly obtained a majority by securing the allegiance of two minor procommunist parties that had been part of the coalition government after World War II. In August 1989, the editor of Solidarity's weekly newspaper was sworn in as Poland's new noncommunist leader.

In its first year and a half, the new Solidarity government cautiously introduced revolutionary political changes. It eliminated the hated secret police, the Communist ministers in the government, and finally Jaruzelski himself, but it did so step by step in order to avoid confrontation with the army or the Soviet Union. However, in economic affairs, the Solidarity-led government was radical from the beginning. It applied **shock therapy** designed to make a clean break with state planning and move quickly to market mechanisms and private property. Thus the Solidarity government abolished controls on many prices on January 1, 1990, and reformed the monetary system with a "big bang."

Hungary followed Poland. Hungary's Communist Party boss, János Kádár, had permitted liberalization of the rigid planned economy after the 1956 uprising in exchange for political obedience and continued Communist control. In May 1988, in an effort to retain power by granting modest political concessions, the party replaced Kádár with a reform communist. But opposition groups rejected piecemeal progress, and in the summer of 1989 the Hungarian Communist Party agreed to hold free elections in early 1990. Welcoming Western investment and moving rapidly toward multiparty democracy, Hungary's Communists now enjoyed considerable popular support, and they believed, quite mistakenly it turned out, that they could defeat the opposition in the upcoming elections. In an effort to strengthen their support at home and also put pressure on East Germany's hard-line Communist regime, the Hungarians opened their border to East Germans and tore down the barbed-wire "iron curtain" with Austria. Thus tens of thousands of dissatisfied East German "vacationers" began pouring into Hungary, crossed into Austria as refugees, and continued on to immediate resettlement in thriving West Germany.

The flight of East Germans led to the rapid growth of a homegrown protest movement in East Germany. Intellectuals, environmentalists, and Protestant ministers took the lead, organizing huge candlelight demonstrations and arguing that a democratic but still socialist East Germany was both possible and desirable. These "stayers" failed to convince the "leavers," however, who continued to flee the country en masse. In a desperate attempt to stabilize the situation, the East German government opened the Berlin Wall in November 1989, and people danced for joy atop that grim symbol of the prison state. East Germany's aging Communist leaders were swept aside, and a reform government took power and scheduled free elections.

In Czechoslovakia, communism died quickly in November–December 1989 in an almost good-humored ousting of Communist bosses. This so-called **Velvet Revolution** grew out of popular demonstrations led by students, intellectuals, and a dissident playwright turned moral revolutionary named Václav Havel. The protesters practically took control of the streets and forced the Communists into a power-sharing arrangement, which quickly resulted in the resignation of the Communist

Demonstrators During the Velvet Revolution   Hundreds of thousands of Czechoslovakian citizens flooded the streets of Prague in peaceful, daily protests after the police savagely beat student demonstrators in mid-November 1989. On the night of November 24, three hundred thousand people roared "Dubček-Havel" when Alexander Dubček, the aging reformer ousted in 1968 by the Soviets, stood on a balcony with Václav Havel, the leading opponent of communism. That night the communists agreed to share power, and a few days later they resigned from the government. *(Corbis)*

government. As 1989 ended, the Czechoslovakian assembly elected Havel president.

Only in Romania was revolution violent and bloody. There ironfisted Communist dictator Nicolae Ceauşescu (1918–1989) had long combined Stalinist brutality with stubborn independence from Moscow. Faced with mass protests in December, Ceauşescu, alone among eastern European bosses, ordered his ruthless security forces to slaughter thousands, thereby sparking a classic armed uprising. After Ceauşescu's forces were defeated, the tyrant and his wife were captured and executed by a military court. A coalition government emerged from the fighting, although the legacy of Ceauşescu's oppression left a very troubled country.

The Disintegration of the Soviet Union

As 1990 began, revolutionary changes had triumphed in all but two eastern European states—tiny Albania and the vast Soviet Union. The great question now became whether the Soviet Union would follow its former satellites and whether reform communism would give way to a popular anticommunist revolution.

In February 1990, as competing Russian politicians noisily presented their programs, and nationalists in the non-Russian republics demanded autonomy or independence from the Soviet Union, the Communist Party suffered a stunning defeat in local elections throughout the country. As in the eastern European satellites, democrats and anticommunists won clear majorities in the leading cities of the Russian Federation. Moreover, in Lithuania the people elected an uncompromising nationalist as president, and the newly chosen parliament declared Lithuania an independent state. Gorbachev responded by placing an economic embargo on Lithuania, but he refused to use the army to crush the separatist government. The result was a tense political stalemate, which undermined popular support for Gorbachev. Separating himself further from Communist hardliners, Gorbachev asked Soviet citizens to ratify a new constitution, which formally abolished the Communist Party's monopoly of political power and expanded the power of the Congress of People's Deputies. Retaining his post as party secretary, Gorbachev convinced a majority of deputies to elect him president of the Soviet Union.

Gorbachev's eroding power and his unwillingness to risk a universal suffrage election for the presidency strengthened his great rival, Boris Yeltsin (1931–2007). A radical reform communist who had been purged by party conservatives in 1987, Yeltsin embraced the democratic movement, and in May 1990 he was elected leader of the Russian Federation's parliament. He boldly announced that Russia would put its interests first and declare its independence from the Soviet Union, thereby broadening the base of the anticommunist movement as he joined the patriotism of ordinary Russians with the democratic aspirations of big-city intellectuals. Gorbachev tried to save the Soviet Union with a new treaty that would link the member republics in a looser, freely accepted confederation, but six of the fifteen Soviet republics rejected Gorbachev's pleas.

The Fall of the Berlin Wall   The sudden opening of the Berlin Wall in November 1989 dramatized the spectacular collapse of communism throughout eastern Europe. Built by the Soviet leader Nikita Khrushchev in 1961, the hated barrier had stopped the flow of refugees from East Germany to West Germany. *(Patrick Piel/Gamma Presse/EYEDEA)*

Celebrating Victory, August 1991 A Russian soldier flashes the victory sign in front of the Russian parliament, as the last-gasp coup attempt of Communist hardliners is defeated by Boris Yeltsin and an enthusiastic public. The soldier has cut the hammer and sickle out of the Soviet flag, consigning those famous symbols of proletarian revolution to what Trotsky once called the "garbage can of history." *(Filip Horvat/Corbis Saba)*

Opposed by democrats and nationalists, Gorbachev was also challenged again by the Communist old guard. Defeated at the Communist Party congress in July 1990, a gang of hardliners kidnapped a vacationing Gorbachev and his family in the Caucasus and tried to seize the Soviet government in August 1991. But the attempted coup collapsed in the face of massive popular resistance, which rallied around Yeltsin, recently elected president of the Russian Federation by universal suffrage. As the world watched spellbound on television, Yeltsin defiantly denounced the rebels from atop a stalled tank in central Moscow and declared the "rebirth of Russia." The army supported Yeltsin, and Gorbachev was rescued and returned to power as head of the Soviet Union.

The leaders of the coup wanted to preserve Communist power, state ownership, and the multinational Soviet Union, but they succeeded only in destroying all three. An anticommunist revolution swept the Russian Federation as Yeltsin and his supporters outlawed the Communist Party and confiscated its property. Locked in a personal and political duel with Gorbachev, Yeltsin and his democratic allies declared Russia independent and withdrew from the Soviet Union. All the other Soviet republics also left. The Soviet Union—and Gorbachev's job—ceased to exist on December 25, 1991 (see Map 31.2). The independent republics of the old Soviet Union then established a loose confederation, the Commonwealth of Independent States, which played only a minor role in the 1990s.

German Unification and the End of the Cold War

The sudden death of communism in East Germany in 1989 reopened the "German question" and raised the

MAP 31.2 Russia and the Successor States After the attempt in August 1991 to depose Gorbachev failed, an anticommunist revolution swept the Soviet Union. Led by Russia and Boris Yeltsin, the republics that formed the Soviet Union declared their sovereignty and independence. Eleven of the fifteen republics then formed a loose confederation called the Commonwealth of Independent States, but the integrated economy of the Soviet Union dissolved into separate national economies, each with its own goals and policies.

threat of renewed cold war conflict over Germany. Taking power in October 1989, East German reform communists, enthusiastically supported by leading East German intellectuals and former dissidents, wanted to preserve socialism by making it genuinely democratic and responsive to the needs of the people. They argued for a **third way,** which would go beyond the failed Stalinism they had experienced and the ruthless capitalism they saw in the West. These reformers supported closer ties with West Germany, but they feared unification and wanted to preserve a distinct East German identity.

These efforts failed, and within a few months East Germany was absorbed into an enlarged West Germany, much like a faltering company is merged into a stronger rival and ceases to exist. Three factors were particularly important in this sudden absorption. First, in the first week after the Berlin Wall was opened, almost 9 million East Germans—roughly one-half of the total population—

poured across the border into West Germany. Almost all returned to their homes in the East, but the joy of warm welcomes from long-lost friends and loved ones and the exhilarating experience of shopping in the well-stocked stores of the much wealthier West aroused long-dormant hopes of unity among ordinary citizens.

Second, West German chancellor Helmut Kohl and his closest advisers skillfully exploited the historic opportunity on their doorstep. Sure of support from the United States, whose leadership he had steadfastly followed, in November 1989 Kohl presented a ten-point plan for a step-by-step unification in cooperation with both East Germany and the international community. Kohl then promised the struggling citizens of East Germany an immediate economic bonanza—a one-for-one exchange of all East German marks in savings accounts and pensions into much more valuable West German marks. This generous offer helped a well-financed conservative-liberal **Alliance for**

Germany, which was set up in East Germany and was closely tied to Kohl's West German Christian Democrats, to overwhelm those who argued for the preservation of some kind of independent socialist society in East Germany. In March 1990, the Alliance outdistanced the Socialist Party and won almost 50 percent of the votes in an East German parliamentary election. (The Communists ignominiously fell to fringe-party status.) The Alliance for Germany quickly negotiated an economic union on favorable terms with Chancellor Kohl.

Finally, in the summer of 1990, the crucial international aspect of German unification was successfully resolved. Unification would once again make Germany the strongest state in central Europe and would directly affect the security of the Soviet Union. But Gorbachev swallowed hard—Western cartoonists showed Stalin turning over in his grave—and negotiated the best deal he could. In a historic agreement signed by Gorbachev and Kohl in July 1990, a uniting Germany solemnly affirmed its peaceful intentions and pledged never to develop nuclear, biological, or chemical weapons. Germany also sweetened the deal by promising to make enormous loans to the hard-pressed Soviet Union. In October 1990, East Germany merged into West Germany, forming henceforth a single nation under the West German laws and constitution.

The peaceful reunification of Germany accelerated the pace of agreements to liquidate the cold war. In November 1990, delegates from twenty-two European countries joined those from the United States and the Soviet Union in Paris and agreed to a scaling down of all their armed forces. The delegates also solemnly affirmed that all existing borders in Europe—from unified Germany to the newly independent Baltic republics—were legal and valid. The **Paris Accord** was for all practical purposes a general peace treaty, bringing an end to World War II and the cold war that followed.

Peace in Europe encouraged the United States and the Soviet Union to scrap a significant portion of their nuclear weapons in a series of agreements. In September 1991, a confident President George H. W. Bush also canceled the around-the-clock alert status for American bombers outfitted with atomic bombs, and a floundering Gorbachev quickly followed suit. For the first time in four decades, Soviet and American nuclear weapons were no longer standing ready to destroy capitalism, communism, and life itself.

The Gulf War of 1991

As anticommunist revolutions swept eastern Europe and East-West tensions rapidly disappeared, the Soviet Union lost both the will and the means to be a global superpower. Yet the United States retained the strength and the desire to influence political and economic developments on a global scale. Thus the United States, still flanked by many allies, emerged rather suddenly as the world's only surviving superpower.

In 1991 the United States used its military superiority on a grand scale in a quick war with Iraq in western Asia. Emerging in 1988 from an eight-year war with neighboring Iran with a big, tough army equipped by the Soviet bloc, western Europe, and the United States, Iraq's strongman Saddam Hussein (1937–2006) set out to make himself the leader of the entire Arab world. Eyeing the great oil wealth of his tiny southern neighbor, Saddam Hussein's forces suddenly invaded Kuwait in August 1990 and proclaimed the annexation of Kuwait.

Reacting vigorously to free Kuwait, the United States mobilized the U.N. Security Council, which in August 1990 imposed a strict naval blockade on Iraq. Receiving the support of some Arab states, as well as of Great Britain and France, the United States also landed 500,000 American soldiers in Saudi Arabia near the border of Kuwait. When a defiant Saddam Hussein refused to withdraw from Kuwait, the Security Council authorized the U.S.-led military coalition to attack Iraq. The American army and air force then smashed Iraqi forces in a lightning-quick desert campaign, although the United States stopped short of toppling Saddam because it feared a sudden disintegration of Iraq more than Saddam's hanging on to power.

The defeat of Iraqi armies in the Gulf War demonstrated the awesome power of the U.S. military, rebuilt and revitalized by the spending and patriotism of the 1980s. Little wonder that in the flush of yet another victory, the first President Bush spoke of a **"new world order,"** an order that would apparently feature the United States and a cooperative United Nations working together to impose stability throughout the world.

Building a New Europe in the 1990s

The fall of communism, the end of the cold war, and the collapse of the Soviet Union opened a new era in European and world history. The dimensions and significance of this new era, opening suddenly and unexpectedly, are subject to debate. We are so close to what is going on that we lack vital perspective. Yet the historian must take a stand.

First, it seems clear that Europe took giant strides toward a loose unification of fundamental institutions and beliefs and that many broad economic, social, and political trends operated all across the continent in the 1990s. We shall focus on three of the most important trends: the pressure on national economies increasingly caught up in global capitalism; the defense of social achievements under attack; and a resurgence of nationalism and ethnic conflict. Second, with these common themes providing an organizational framework, we shall examine the course of development in the three overlapping but still distinct regions of contemporary Europe. These are Russia and the western states of the old Soviet Union, previously communist eastern Europe, and western Europe.

• *How, in the 1990s, did the different parts of a reunifying Europe meet the challenges of postcommunist reconstruction, resurgent nationalism, and economic union?*

Common Patterns and Problems

The end of the cold war and the disintegration of the Soviet Union ended the division of Europe into two opposing camps with two different political and economic systems. Thus, although Europe in the 1990s was a collage of diverse peoples with their own politics, cultures, and histories, the entire continent shared an underlying network of common developments and challenges.

Of critical importance, in economic affairs European leaders embraced, or at least accepted, a large part of the neoliberal, free-market vision of capitalist development. This was most strikingly the case in eastern Europe, where states such as Poland and Hungary implemented market reforms and sought to create vibrant capitalist economies. Thus postcommunist governments in eastern Europe freed prices, turned state enterprises over to private owners, and sought to move toward strong currencies and balanced budgets. Milder doses of this same free-market medicine were administered by politicians and big business to the lackluster economies of western Europe. These initiatives and proposals for further changes marked a considerable modification in western Europe's still-dominant welfare capitalism, which featured government intervention, high taxes, and high levels of social benefits.

Two factors were particularly important in accounting for this ongoing shift from welfare state activism to tough-minded capitalism. First, Europeans were only following practices and ideologies revived and enshrined in the 1980s in the United States and Great Britain (see page 1012). Western Europeans especially took American prescriptions more seriously because U.S. prestige and power were so high after the United States "won the cold war" and because the U.S. economy continued to

outperform its western European counterparts in the Clinton years. Second, the deregulation of markets and the privatization of state-controlled enterprises were an integral part of the powerful trend toward a wide-open, wheeler-dealer global economy. The rules of the global economy, which were laid down by Western governments, multinational corporations, and international financial organizations such as the International Monetary Fund (IMF), called for the free movement of capital and goods and services, as well as low inflation and limited government deficits. Accepting these rules and attempting to follow them was the price of full participation in the global economy.

The ongoing computer and electronics revolution strengthened the move toward a global economy. That revolution thrived on the diffusion of ever-cheaper computational and informational capacity to small research groups and private businesses, which were both cause and effect of the revolution itself. By the 1990s, an inexpensive personal computer had the power of a 1950s mainframe that filled a room and cost hundreds of thousands of dollars. The computer revolution reduced the costs of distance, speeding up communications and helping businesses tap cheaper labor overseas. Reducing the friction of distance made threats of moving factories abroad ring true and helped hold down wages at home.

Globalization, the emergence of a freer global economy, probably did speed up world economic growth as enthusiasts invariably claimed, but it also had powerful and quite negative social consequences. Millions of ordinary citizens in western Europe believed that global capitalism and freer markets were undermining hard-won social achievements. As in the United States and Great Britain in the 1980s, the public in other countries generally associated globalization with the increased unemployment that accompanied corporate downsizing, the efforts to reduce the power of labor unions, and, above all, government plans to reduce social benefits. The reaction was particularly intense in France and Germany, where unions remained strong and socialists championed a minimum of change in social policies.

Indeed, the broad movement toward neoliberal global development sparked a powerful counterattack as the 1990s ended. Financial crises, which devastated many of Asia's smaller economies and threatened to spread, triggered this reaction. Many critics and protesters argued increasingly that globalization damaged poor countries as much as wealthy ones. Above all, critics insisted that globalization hurt the world's poor, because multinational corporations destroyed local industries and paid pitiful wages, and because international financial organizations

Santiago Calatrava: Tenerife Concert Hall, 2003 One of the most celebrated of the "postmodern" architects, who go beyond the modernism that dominated from the 1920s to the 1970s, Calatrava is known for swooping shapes and unusual spaces that convey a sense of motion to his buildings. The enormous, free-standing "roof" of this concert hall rises on a waterfront property like a cresting, crashing wave, linking the ocean with the city and beckoning tourists to Tenerife and Portugal's Canary Islands. Postmodern architects rely heavily on three-dimensional computer modeling to fashion complex forms and translate them into construction blueprints. (*Barbara Burg and Oliver Schuh/Palladium Photodesign, Cologne, Germany*)

demanded harsh balanced budgets and deep cuts in government social programs. These attacks shook global neoliberalism, but it remained dominant.

Political developments across Europe also were loosely unified by common patterns and problems. The demise of European communism brought the apparent triumph of liberal democracy everywhere. All countries embraced genuine electoral competition, with elected presidents and legislatures and the outward manifestations of representative liberal governments. With some notable exceptions, such as discrimination against Gypsies, countries also guaranteed basic civil liberties. Thus, for the first time since before the French Revolution, almost all of

Europe followed the same general political model, although the variations were endless.

The triumph of the liberal democratic program led the American scholar Francis Fukuyama to discern in 1992 the "end of history" in his influential book by that title. According to Fukuyama, first fascism and Nazism and then communism had been definitively bested by liberal democratic politics and market economics. Conversely, as James Cronin perceptively noted in 1996 in *The World the Cold War Made*, the fall of communism also marked the return of nationalism and national history.[1] The cold war and the superpowers generally kept their allies and clients in line, either by force or by granting them conditional aid. As soon as the cold war was over, nationalism and ethnic conflict re-emerged, and history, as the story of different peoples, began again.

The resurgence of nationalism in the 1990s led to terrible tragedy and bloodshed in parts of eastern Europe, as it did in several hot spots in Africa and Asia. During the civil wars in Yugoslavia, many observers feared that national and ethnic hatreds would spread throughout eastern Europe and infect western Europe in the form of racial hostility toward minorities and immigrants. Yet if nationalist and racist incidents were a recurring European theme, they remained limited in the extent of their damage. Of critical importance in this regard was the fact that all European states wished to become or remain full-fledged members of the European society of nations and to join eventually an ever-expanding European Community, renamed the **European Union** in 1993. States that embraced national hatred and ethnic warfare, most notably Serbia, were branded as outlaws and boycotted and isolated by the European Union and the international community. The process of limiting resurgent nationalism in Europe was almost as significant as the resurgence itself.

Recasting Russia

Politics and economics were closely intertwined in Russia after the attempted Communist coup in 1991 and the dissolution of the Soviet Union. President Boris Yeltsin, his democratic supporters, and his economic ministers wanted to create conditions that would prevent forever a return to communism and would also right the faltering economy. Following the example of some postcommunist governments in eastern Europe and agreeing with those Western advisers who argued that private economies were always best, the Russian reformers opted in January 1992 for breakneck liberalization. Their "shock therapy" freed prices on 90 percent of all Russian goods, with the exception of bread, vodka, oil, and public transportation. The government also launched a rapid privatization of industry and turned thousands of factories and mines over to new private companies. Each citizen received a voucher worth 10,000 rubles (about $22) to buy stock in private companies, but control of the privatized companies usually remained in the hands of the old bosses, the managers and government officials from the communist era.

President Yeltsin and his economic reformers believed that shock therapy would revive production and bring prosperity after a brief period of hardship. The results of the reforms were in fact quite different. Prices increased 250 percent on the very first day, and they kept on soaring, increasing twenty-six times in the course of 1992. At the same time, Russian production fell a staggering 20 percent. Nor did the situation stabilize quickly. Throughout 1995 rapid but gradually slowing inflation raged, and output continued to fall. According to most estimates, in 1996 the Russian economy produced at least one-third and possibly as much as one-half less than in 1991. Only in 1997 did the economy stop declining, before crashing yet again in 1998 in the wake of Asia's financial crisis.

Rapid economic liberalization worked poorly in Russia for several reasons. Soviet industry had been highly monopolized and strongly tilted toward military goods. Production of many items had been concentrated in one or two gigantic factories or in interconnected combines that supplied the entire economy. With privatization these powerful state monopolies became powerful private monopolies, which cut production and raised prices in order to maximize their financial returns. Moreover, powerful managers and bureaucrats forced Yeltsin's government to hand out enormous subsidies and credits to reinforce the positions of big firms and to avoid bankruptcies and the discipline of a free market. The managerial elite also combined with criminal elements to intimidate would-be rivals and prevent the formation of new businesses. Not that most ordinary Soviet citizens were eager to start businesses. In the end, enterprise directors and politicians succeeded in eliminating worker ownership and converted large portions of previously state-owned industry into their own private property.

Runaway inflation and poorly executed privatization brought a profound social revolution to Russia. A new capitalist elite acquired great wealth and power, while large numbers of people fell into abject poverty, and the majority struggled in the midst of decline to make ends meet.

Managers, former officials, and financiers who came out of the privatization process with large shares of the old state monopolies stood at the top of the reorganized elite. The richest plums were found in Russia's enormous oil and natural resources industries, where unscrupulous enterprise directors pocketed enormous dishonest gains. The new elite was more highly concentrated than ever before. By 1996 Moscow, with 5 percent of Russia's population, accounted for 35 percent of the country's national income and controlled 80 percent of its capital resources.

At the other extreme, the vast majority saw their savings become practically worthless. Pensions lost much of their value, and whole markets were devoted to people selling off their personal goods to survive. Perhaps the most telling statistic, summing up millions of hardships and tragedies, was the truly catastrophic decline in the life expectancy of the average Russian male from sixty-nine years in 1991 to only fifty-eight years in 1996.

Rapid economic decline in 1992 and 1993 and rising popular dissatisfaction encouraged a majority of communists, nationalists, and populists in the Russian parliament to oppose Yeltsin and his coalition of democratic reformers and big-business interests. The erratic, increasingly hard-drinking Yeltsin would accept no compromise and insisted on a strong presidential system. Winning in April 1993 the support of 58 percent of the population in a referendum on his proposed constitution, Yeltsin then brought in tanks to crush a parliamentary mutiny in October 1993 and literally blew away the opposition. Subsequently, Yeltsin consolidated his power, and in 1996 he used his big-business cronies in the media to win an impressive come-from-behind victory. But effective representative government failed to develop, and many Russians came to equate "democracy" with the corruption, poverty, and national decline they experienced throughout the 1990s.

This widespread disillusionment set the stage for the "managed democracy" of Vladimir Putin, first elected president as Yeltsin's chosen successor in 2000 and re-elected in a landslide in March 2004. An officer in the secret police in the communist era, Putin maintained relatively free markets in the economic sphere but re-established semi-authoritarian political rule. Aided greatly by high oil prices for Russia's most important export, this combination worked well and seemed to suit most Russians. In 2007, the Russian economy had been growing rapidly for eight years, the Russian middle class was expanding, and the elected parliament supported Putin overwhelmingly. Proponents of liberal democracy were in retreat, while conservative Russian intellectuals were on the offensive, arguing

Russia's Leading Capitalist on Trial, 2004 Mikhail Khodorkovsky emerged from the privatization of Russian industry as the progressive chief and largest shareholder of Yukos, Russia's most successful oil company. But after he supported liberal opposition parties in 2002, an increasingly authoritarian President Putin jailed the billionaire, charged him with tax fraud, and confiscated his wealth before the trial even began. Putin's behavior was widely criticized in the West, but most ordinary Russians applauded because they believed the super rich had plundered the Russian state. *(Alexander Natruskin/Reuters/Corbis)*

that free markets and capitalism required strong political rule to control corruption and prevent chaos. Historians saw a reassertion of Russia's long authoritarian tradition.

Putin's forceful, competent image in world affairs also soothed the country's injured pride and symbolized its national resurgence. Nor did the government permit any negative television reports on the civil war in Chechnya, the tiny republic of 1 million Muslims on Russia's southern border, which in 1991 had declared its independence from the Russian Federation (see Map 31.2). The savage conflict in Chechnya continued, largely unreported, with numerous atrocities on both sides.

Progress in Eastern Europe

Developments in eastern Europe shared important similarities with those in Russia, as many of the problems were the same. Thus the postcommunist states of the former satellite empire worked to replace state planning and socialism with market mechanisms and private property. Western-style electoral politics also took hold, and as in Russia, these politics were marked by intense battles between presidents and parliaments and by weak political parties. The social consequences of these revolutionary changes were similar to those in Russia. Ordinary citizens and the elderly were once again the big losers, while the young and the ex-Communists were the big winners. Inequalities between richer and poorer regions also increased. Capital cities such as Warsaw, Prague, and Budapest concentrated wealth, power, and opportunity as never before, while provincial centers stagnated and old industrial areas declined. Crime and gangsterism increased in the streets and in the executive suites.

Yet the 1990s saw more than a difficult transition, with high social costs, to market economies and freely elected governments in eastern Europe. Many citizens had never fully accepted communism, which they equated with Russian imperialism and the loss of national independence. The joyous crowds that toppled communist regimes in 1989 believed that they were liberating the nation as well as the individual. Thus communism died and nationalism was reborn.

The surge of nationalism in eastern Europe recalled a similar surge of state creation after World War I. Then, too, authoritarian multinational empires had come crashing down in defeat and revolution. Then, too, nationalities with long histories and rich cultures had drawn upon ideologies of popular sovereignty and national self-determination to throw off foreign rule and found new democratic states.

The response to this opportunity in the former communist countries was quite varied in the 1990s, but most observers agreed that Poland, the Czech Republic, and Hungary were the most successful (see Map 31.3). Each of these three countries met the critical challenge of economic reconstruction more successfully than Russia, and each could claim to be the economic leader in eastern Europe, depending on the criteria selected. The reasons for these successes included considerable experience with limited market reforms before 1989, flexibility and lack of dogmatism in government policy, and an enthusiastic embrace of capitalism by a new entrepreneurial class. In the first five years of reform, Poland created twice as many new businesses as Russia, with a total population only one-fourth as large.

The three northern countries in the former Soviet bloc also did far better than Russia in creating new civic institutions, legal systems, and independent broadcasting networks that reinforced political freedom and national revival. Lech Walesa in Poland and Václav Havel in Czechoslovakia were elected presidents of their countries and proved as remarkable in power as in opposition. After Czechoslovakia's "Velvet Revolution" in 1989, Havel and the Czech parliament accepted a "velvet divorce" in 1993 when Slovakian nationalists wanted to break off and form their own state. All three northern countries managed to control national and ethnic tensions that might have destroyed their postcommunist reconstruction.

Above all, and in sharp contrast to Russia, the popular goal of "rejoining the West" reinforced political moderation and compromise. Seeing themselves as heirs to medieval Christendom and liberal democratic values in the 1920s, Poles, Hungarians, and Czechs hoped to find security in NATO membership and economic prosperity in western Europe's ever-tighter union. Membership required many proofs of character and stability, however. Providing these proofs and endorsed by the Clinton administration, Poland, Hungary, and the Czech Republic were accepted into the NATO alliance in 1997. Gaining admission to the European Union (EU) proved more difficult, because candidates also had to accept and be ready to apply all the rules and regulations that the EU had developed since 1956—an awesome task.

Romania and Bulgaria were the eastern European laggards in the postcommunist transition. Western traditions were much weaker there, and both countries were much poorer than neighbors to the north. In 1993 Bulgaria and Romania had per capita national incomes of $1,140, in contrast to Hungary ($3,830) and the Czech Republic ($2,710). Although Romania and Bulgaria eventually made progress in the late 1990s, full membership for both countries in either NATO or the EU still lay far in the future.

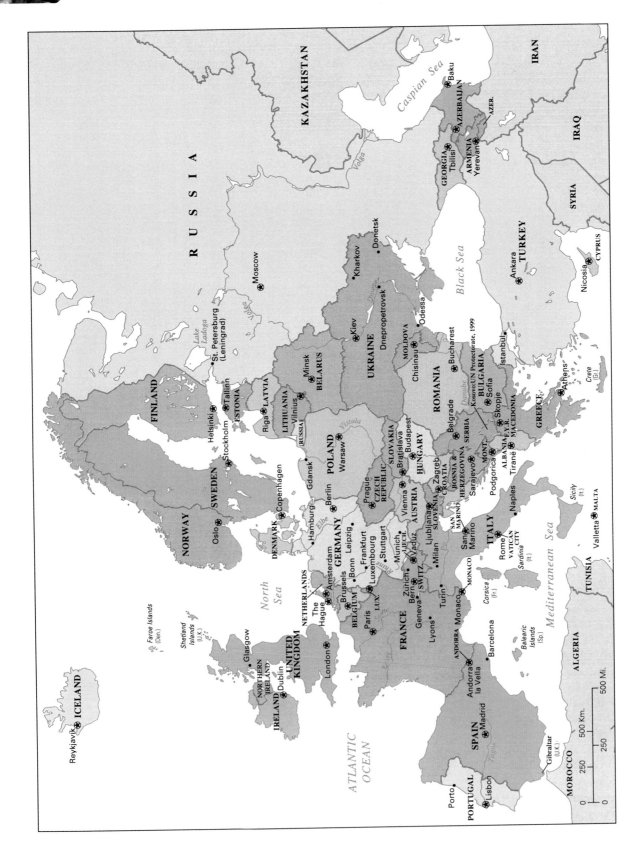

Escape from Srebrenica   A Bosnian Muslim refugee arrives at the United Nations base in Tuzla and with her anguished screams tells the world of the Serbian atrocities. Several thousand civilians were murdered at Srebrenica, and Western public opinion finally demanded decisive action. Efforts continue to arrest those Serbs believed responsible and to try them for crimes against humanity. *(J. Jones/Corbis Sygma)*

Tragedy in Yugoslavia

The great postcommunist tragedy was Yugoslavia, which under Josip Tito had been a federation of republics and regions under strict communist rule (see page 996). After Tito's death in 1980, power passed increasingly to the sister republics, which encouraged a revival of regional and ethnic conflicts that were exacerbated by charges of ethnically inspired massacres during World War II and a dramatic economic decline in the mid-1980s.

The revolutions of 1989 accelerated the breakup of Yugoslavia. Serbian president Slobodan Milosevic intended to grab land from other republics and unite all Serbs, regardless of where they lived, in a "greater Serbia." In 1989 Milosevic arbitrarily abolished self-rule in the Serbian province of Kosovo, where Albanian-speaking people

---

Mapping the Past

MAP 31.3 Contemporary Europe   No longer divided by ideological competition and the cold war, today's Europe features a large number of independent states. Several of these states were previously part of the Soviet Union and Yugoslavia, both of which broke into many different countries. Czechoslovakia also divided on ethnic lines, while a reunited Germany emerged, once again, as the dominant nation in central Europe. ❶ Which countries shown here were previously part of the Soviet Union? ❷ Which countries were part of Yugoslavia? ❸ Where did the old "iron curtain" run? (See Map 30.2, page 988, if necessary.)

MAP 31.4 The Ethnic Composition of Yugoslavia, 1991
Yugoslavia had the most ethnically diverse population in eastern Europe. The Republic of Croatia had substantial Serbian and Muslim minorities. Bosnia-Herzegovina had large Muslim, Serbian, and Croatian populations, none of which had a majority. In June 1991, Serbia's brutal effort to seize territory and unite all Serbs in a single state brought a tragic civil war.

constituted the overwhelming majority. Milosevic's moves strengthened the cause of separatism, and in June 1991 Slovenia and Croatia declared their independence. Slovenia repulsed a Serbian attack, but Milosevic's armies managed to take about 30 percent of Croatia. In 1992 the civil war spread to Bosnia-Herzegovina, which had declared its independence. Serbs—about 30 percent of that region's population—refused to live under the more numerous Bosnian Muslims (see Map 31.4). Yugoslavia had once been a tolerant and largely successful multiethnic state, with different groups living side by side and often intermarrying. The Bosnian civil war unleashed ruthless brutality, with murder, rape, destruction, and the herding of refugees into concentration camps.

While scenes of horror shocked the world, the Western nations had difficulty formulating an effective response. The turning point came in July 1995, when Bosnian Serbs overran Srebrenica—a Muslim city previously declared a United Nations "safe area"—and killed several thousand civilians. World outrage prompted NATO to bomb Bosnian Serb military targets intensively, and the Croatian army drove all the Serbs from Croatia. In November 1995, President Bill Clinton helped the warring sides hammer out a complicated accord that gave the Bosnian Serbs about 49 percent of Bosnia and the Muslim-Croatian peoples the rest. Troops from NATO countries patrolled Bosnia to try to keep the peace.

The Albanian Muslims of Kosovo had been hoping for a restoration of self-rule, but they gained nothing from the Bosnian agreement. In early 1998, frustrated Kosovar militants formed the **Kosovo Liberation Army (KLA)** and began to fight for independence. Serbian repression of the Kosovars increased, and in 1998 Serbian forces attacked both KLA guerrillas and unarmed villagers, displacing 250,000 people within Kosovo. By January 1999, the Western Powers, led by the United States, were threatening Milosevic with heavy air raids if he did not withdraw Serbian armies from Kosovo and accept self-government (but not independence) for Kosovo. Milosevic refused, and in March 1999 NATO began bombing Yugoslavia. Serbian paramilitary forces responded by driving about 780,000 Kosovars into exile. NATO redoubled its highly destructive bombing campaign, which eventually forced Milosevic to withdraw and allowed the joyous Kosovars to regain their homeland. The impoverished Serbs eventually voted the still-defiant Milosevic out of office, and in July 2001 a new pro-Western Serbian government turned him over to the war crimes tribunal in the Netherlands, to stand trial for crimes against humanity. The civil wars in the former Yugoslavia were a monument to human cruelty and evil in the worst tradition of the twentieth century. But ongoing efforts to preserve peace, repatriate refugees, and try war criminals also testified to the regenerative power of liberal values and human rights as the twenty-first century unfolded.

Unity and Identity in Western Europe

The movement toward western European unity, which since the late 1940s had inspired practical politicians seeking economic recovery and idealistic visionaries imagining a European identity that transcended destructive national rivalries, received a powerful second wind in the mid-1980s. The Single European Act of 1986 laid down a detailed legal framework for establishing a single market, which would add the free movement of labor, capital, and services to the existing free trade in goods. With work proceeding vigorously toward the single market, which went into effect in 1993 as the European Community proudly rechristened itself the European Union (EU), French president François Mitterrand and German chancellor Helmut Kohl took the lead in pushing for a monetary union of EU members. After long negotiations and compromises, designed especially to overcome Britain's long-standing reluctance to cede aspects of sovereignty, in December 1991 the member states reached an agreement in the Dutch town of Maastricht. The **Maastricht treaty** set strict financial criteria for joining the proposed monetary union, with its single currency, and set 1999 as the target date for its establishment. The treaty also anticipated the development of common policies on defense and foreign affairs after achieving monetary union.

Western European elites and opinion makers generally supported the decisive step toward economic integration embodied in the Maastricht treaty. They saw monetary union as a means of coping with Europe's ongoing economic problems, imposing financial discipline, cutting costs, and reducing high unemployment. European elites also viewed monetary union as a historic, irreversible step toward a basic political unity. This unity would allow western Europe as a whole to regain its rightful place in world politics and to deal with the United States as an equal.

The Maastricht plan for monetary union encountered widespread skepticism and considerable opposition from ordinary people, leftist political parties, and patriotic nationalists. Ratification votes were close, especially when the public rather than the politicians could vote yes or no on the question.

There were several interrelated reasons for this widespread popular opposition. Many people resented the unending flow of rules handed down by the EU's ever-growing bureaucracy in Brussels, which sought to impose common standards on everything from cheese to day care and undermined national practices and local traditions. Moreover, increased unity meant yielding still more power to distant "Eureaucrats" and political insiders, thereby undermining popular sovereignty and democratic control through national politics and electoral competition. Above all, many ordinary citizens feared that the new Europe was being made at their expense. Joining the monetary union required national governments to meet stringent fiscal standards and impose budget cuts. The resulting reductions in health care and social benefits hit ordinary citizens and did nothing to reduce western Europe's high unemployment rate.

Events in France dramatically illustrated these developments. Mitterrand's Socialist government had been forced to adopt conservative financial policies in the 1980s (see page 1012), and in early 1993 a coalition of conservatives and moderates won an overwhelming victory by promising a vigorous attack on unemployment. However, the Maastricht criteria soon forced the new government to resume deficit-reducing cuts in health benefits and transportation services. France's powerful unions and railroad workers responded with a crippling national strike that shut down rail traffic throughout France for almost a month. Yet despite the enormous inconvenience and economic damage, many people felt that the transport workers were also fighting for them. The government had to back down, and soon the Socialists returned to power. The Socialists quickly passed a controversial new law to reduce the legal workweek to thirty-five hours in an attempt to reduce France's stubborn 12 percent unemployment rate without budget-busting spending. More generally, much of the western European public increasingly saw laws to cut the workweek and share the work as a way to reconcile desires for social welfare and a humane market economy with financial discipline and global competition.

Battles over budgets and high unemployment throughout the European Union in the 1990s raised profound questions about the meaning of European unity and identity. Would the European Union expand as promised to include the postcommunist nations of eastern Europe, and if it did, how could Muslim Turkey's longstanding application be ignored? How could a European Union of twenty-five to thirty countries have any real cohesion and common identity? Conversely, would a large, cohesive Europe remain closely linked with the United States in the NATO alliance and with an evolving Western tradition?

The merging of East Germany into the German Federal Republic suggested the enormous difficulties of full East-West integration under the best conditions. After 1991 Helmut Kohl's Germany pumped massive investments into its new eastern provinces, but Germans in the east still saw factories closed and social dislocation. Unemployment in Germany reached a postwar high of 12.8 percent in late 1997, and it soared to 20 percent in the eastern region. Germany's generous social benefits cushioned the economic difficulties, but many ordinary citizens felt hurt and humiliated.

Eastern German women suffered in particular. Before unification, the overwhelming majority had worked outside the home, effectively supported by cheap child care, flexible hours, and the prevailing socialist ideology. Now they faced expensive child care and a variety of pressures to stay at home and let men take the hard-to-find jobs. Many of these women, who had found autonomy and self-esteem in paid work, felt a keen sense of loss. They helped vote Kohl out of office in 1998.

Instructed by the serious difficulties of unification in Germany, western Europeans proceeded cautiously in considering new requests for EU membership. Sweden, Finland, and Austria were admitted because they had strong capitalist economies and because they no longer needed to maintain the legal neutrality that the Soviet Union had required during the cold war.

Turkey's Struggle for EU Membership Turkish elites and the general population want to "join Europe," but the road to EU membership is proving long and difficult. The EU has required Turkey to make many constitutional reforms and give greater autonomy to Turkish Kurds. Yet the Turks face ever more demands, and many now believe that the real roadblock is Europe's anti-Muslim feeling. *(CartoonStock Limited)*

At the same time the former communist states pressed toward meeting the EU's detailed criteria for membership. In December 2000, the EU's fifteen members agreed to begin final negotiations with the eight leading eastern candidates in the near future. The very smooth establishment of the euro on January 1, 2002, when brand-new euros entered the billfolds of all euro-zone citizens as their unified common currency, built confidence and brought an acceleration of arduous but triumphant negotiations. Thus on May 1, 2004, the European Union added 70 million people and expanded to include 455 million citizens in twenty-five different countries. The largest newcomer by far was Poland, followed in descending size by the Czech Republic, Hungary, Slovenia, Slovakia, Estonia, Lithuania, Latvia, Malta, and Cyprus.

In June 2004, more than two years after charging a special commission to write "a new constitution for European citizens," the leaders of the European Union reached agreement on the final document. Above all, the new constitution, with almost 350 articles, established a single rulebook to replace the complex network of treaties concluded by the member states since the 1957 creation of the European Economic Community. The EU constitution created a president, a foreign minister, and a voting system weighted to reflect the number of people in the different states. The result of intense debate and many compromises, the constitution moved toward a more centralized federal system in several fields, but each state retained veto power in the most sensitive areas, such as taxation, social policy, and foreign affairs. In order for the constitution to take effect, each and every EU country needed to ratify it.

Nine countries, led by Germany, Italy, and seven eastern European members, soon ratified the constitution by parliamentary action, while seven states planned to go beyond the political elites and let the voters decide. The referendum campaigns were noisy and contentious, as generally well-informed citizens debated whether the new constitution surrendered too much national sovereignty to an emerging central European government in Brussels. British voters were considered most likely to vote no, but both the French and the Dutch beat them to it, rejecting the new constitution by clear majorities. Nationalist fears about losing sovereignty were matched by fears that an unwieldy European Union would grow to include Ukraine, Georgia, and Muslim Turkey—countries with cultures and histories that were very different from those in western Europe. Thus the long postwar march toward ever greater European unity stopped, or at least stalled, and the European Union concentrated on fully integrating the new eastern European members.

New Challenges in the Twenty-first Century

As the twenty-first century opened and the historic movement toward European unity began to include postcommunist eastern Europe, European society faced new uncertainties. Of great significance, Europe continued to experience a remarkable **baby bust,** as birthrates fell to levels that seemed to promise a shrinking and aging population in the future. At the same time, the peaceful, wealthy European Union attracted rapidly growing numbers of refugees and illegal immigrants from the former Soviet Union, the Middle East, Africa, and Asia. The unexpected arrival of so many newcomers raised many perplexing questions and prompted serious thinking about European identity, Europe's humanitarian mission, and Europe's place in the world.

- *Why did the prospect of population decline, the reality of large-scale immigration, and concern for human rights emerge as critical issues in contemporary Europe?*

The Prospect of Population Decline

Population is still growing rapidly in many poor countries, but this is not the case in the world's industrialized nations. In 2000, women in developed countries had only 1.6 children on average; only in the United States did women have, almost exactly, the 2.1 children necessary to maintain a stable population. In European countries, where women have been steadily having fewer babies since the 1950s, national fertility rates ranged from 1.2 to 1.8 children per woman. Italy, once renowned for big Catholic families, had achieved the world's lowest birthrate—a mere 1.2 babies per woman. In 2006, the European fertility rate was little changed at about 1.4 children per woman.

If the current baby bust continues, the long-term consequences could be dramatic, though hardly predictable. At the least, Europe's population would decline and age. Projections for Germany are illustrative. Total German population, barring much greater immigration, would gradually decline from 82 million in 2001 to only 62 million around 2050. The number of people of working age would drop by a third, and almost half of the population would be over sixty. Social security taxes paid by the shrinking labor force would need to soar for the skyrocketing costs of pensions and health care for seniors to be met—a recipe for generational tension and conflict. As the premier of Bavaria, Germany's biggest state, has warned, the prospect of demographic decline was a "ticking time bomb under our social welfare system and entire economy."[2]

Why, in times of peace, were Europeans failing to reproduce themselves? Certainly the uneven, uninspiring European economic conditions of the 1980s and much of the 1990s played some role. High unemployment fell heavily on young people and often frustrated their plans to settle down and have children. Some observers also argued that a partial rejection of motherhood and parenting was critical. They noted that many women chose to have no children or only one child. By 2000, 30 percent of German women born in 1965 were childless, whereas 90 percent would have had children in earlier generations. In the Catholic countries of southern Europe, where strong pressures to have children still exist, a quarter of the couples were fulfilling their "social duty" with a single child.

In our view, the ongoing impact of careers for married women and the related drive for gender equality remained the decisive factors in the long-term decline of postwar birthrates. After World War II, Western women married early, had their children early, and then turned increasingly to full-time employment, where they suffered from the discrimination that drove the women's movement (see pages 1009–1010). As the twenty-first century opened, women had attained many (but not all) of their objectives. They did as well as or better than men in school, and educated young women earned almost as much as their male counterparts.

Research showed that European women (and men) in their twenties, thirties, and early forties still wanted to have two or even three children—about the same number as their parents had wanted. But unlike their parents, young couples did not realize their ideal family size. Many women postponed the birth of their first child into their thirties in order to finish their education and establish themselves in their careers. Then, finding that raising even one child was more difficult and time-consuming than anticipated, new mothers tended to postpone and eventually forgo a second child. This was especially true of professional women. The better educated and the more economically successful a woman was, the more likely she was to stop with a single child or to have no children at all.

By 2005 some population experts believed that European women were no longer postponing having children. At the least, birthrates appeared to have stabilized. Moreover, the frightening implications of dramatic population decline had emerged as a major public issue. Opinion leaders, politicians, and the media started to press the case for more babies and more support for families with children. Europeans may respond with enough vigor to limit the extent of their population decline and avoid societal disaster.

The Growth of Immigration

As European demographic vitality waned in the 1990s, a surge of migrants from Africa, Asia, and eastern Europe headed for western Europe. Some migrants entered the European Union legally, but increasing numbers were smuggled in past beefed-up border patrols. Large-scale immigration emerged as a contentious and critical challenge.

Historically a source rather than a destination of immigrants, booming western Europe drew heavily on North Africa and Turkey for manual laborers from about 1960 until about 1973, when unemployment started to rise and governments abruptly stopped the inflow. Many foreign workers stayed on, however, eventually bringing their families to western Europe and establishing permanent immigrant communities there.

A new and different surge of migration into western Europe began in the 1990s. The collapse of communism in the East and savage civil wars in Yugoslavia sent hundreds of thousands of refugees fleeing westward. Equally brutal conflicts in Afghanistan, Iraq, Somalia, and Rwanda—to name only four countries—brought thousands more from Asia and Africa. Illegal immigration into the European Union also exploded, rising from an estimated 50,000 people in 1993 to perhaps 500,000 a decade later. This movement exceeded the estimated 300,000 unauthorized foreigners entering the United States each year.

In the early twenty-first century, many migrants still applied for political asylum and refugee status, but most were eventually rejected and classified as illegal job seekers. Certainly, greater economic opportunities exerted a powerful pull. Germans earned on average five times more than neighboring Poles, who in turn earned much more than people farther east and in North Africa.

Illegal immigration also soared because powerful criminal gangs turned to "people smuggling" for big, low-risk profits. Ruthless Russian-speaking gangs played an important role in the trade, passing their human cargo across Russia and through the Balkans to western Europe. A favorite final leg involved Albanian smugglers with speedy motorboats, who slipped across the narrow Adriatic Sea past Italian coastal patrols and landed their high-paying passengers on the beaches of southern Italy. From there new arrivals could head off unimpeded in al-

Illegal Immigrants from Eritrea   Italian police have just rescued these young immigrants from an overloaded boat off the coast of Italy. Fleeing civil war and desperate for work, the immigrants are weary because of the long and dangerous voyage from Libya. Every year thousands of illegal immigrants try to reach Italy and Spain from North Africa. Many are found dead on the shoreline. *(Mimi Mollica/Corbis)*

most any direction, because in 1998 the European Union abolished all border controls between member states. After 2000, growing numbers from Africa and the Middle East tried similar entries across the Strait of Gibraltar into southern Spain.

A large portion of the illegal immigrants were young women from eastern Europe, especially Russia and Ukraine. Often lured by criminals promising jobs as maids or waitresses and sometimes simply kidnapped and sold like slaves from hand to hand for a few thousand dollars, these women were smuggled into the most prosperous parts of central Europe and into the European Union and forced into prostitution or worse.

Illegal immigration generated intense discussion and controversy in western Europe. A majority opposed the newcomers, who were accused of taking jobs from the unemployed and somehow undermining national unity. The idea that cultural and ethnic diversity could be a force for vitality and creativity ran counter to deep-seated be-

liefs. Concern about illegal migration in general often fused with fears of Muslim immigrants and Muslim residents who had grown up in Europe. As busy mosques came to outnumber dying churches in parts of some European cities, rightist politicians especially tried to exploit widespread doubts that immigrant populations from Muslim countries would ever assimilate to the different national cultures. These doubts increased after the attack on New York's World Trade Center, as we shall see later in the chapter.

An articulate minority challenged the anti-immigrant campaign and its racist overtones. They argued that Europe badly needed newcomers—preferably talented newcomers—to limit the impending population decline and provide valuable technical skills. European leaders also focused on improved policing of EU borders and tougher common procedures to combat people smuggling and punish international crime. Above all, growing illegal immigration pushed Europeans to examine the whys of this dramatic human movement and to consider how it related to Europe's proper role in world affairs.

Promoting Human Rights

The tide of refugees and illegal job seekers made thinking people in western Europe acutely aware of their current good fortune, the sweet fruit of more than fifty years of peace, security, and rising standards of living. The nearby agonies of barbarism and war in the former Yugoslavia vividly recalled the horrors of World War II, and they cast in bold relief the ever-present reality of collective violence in today's world. At the same time, western European countries were generally doing their best to limit or expel the foreigners arriving at their gates, as we have seen. This ongoing rejection gave some Europeans a guilty conscience and a feeling that they needed to do more when they had so much and so many others had so little. As a result, European intellectuals and opinion makers began to envision a new historic mission for Europe—the promotion of domestic peace and human rights in those lands plagued by instability, violence, and oppression.

European leaders and humanitarians believed that Europe's mission required more global agreements and new international institutions to set moral standards and to regulate countries, political leaders, armies, corporations, and individuals. In practice, this meant more curbs on the sovereign rights of the world's states, just as the states of the European Union had imposed increasingly strict standards of behavior on themselves in order to secure the rights and welfare of EU citizens. As Nicole Gnesotto, the director of the European Union's institute, concluded, the EU has a "historical responsibility" to make morality "a basis of policy," because "human rights are more important than states' rights."[3] In general, the United States reacted coolly to the idea of preferring human rights to states' rights. American leaders stressed the preservation of U.S. freedom of action in world affairs, particularly after George W. Bush was elected president in 2000.

In practical terms, western Europe's evolving human rights mission meant, first of all, humanitarian interventions to stop civil wars and to prevent tyrannical governments from slaughtering their own people. Thus the European Union joined with the United States to inter-

Fighting the AIDS Epidemic These women, financed in part by the European Union, are treating an AIDS patient at his home in Mozambique. In 2004 the United Nations estimated that about 42 million persons were infected with HIV, the virus that causes AIDS. AIDS is the fourth-leading cause of death in the world. *(Black Star/stockphoto.com)*

vene militarily to stop the killing in Bosnia, Kosovo, and Macedonia and to protect the rights of embattled minorities (see pages 1037–1039). The states of the EU also vigorously supported UN-sponsored conferences and treaties that sought to verify the compliance of anti–germ warfare conventions, outlawed the use of hideously destructive land mines, and established a new international court to prosecute war criminals.

Europeans also pushed for broader definitions of individual rights. Abolishing the death penalty in the European Union, for example, they condemned its continued use in China, the United States, Saudi Arabia, and some other countries as inhumane and uncivilized. Rights for Europeans in their personal relations also continued to expand. In the pacesetting Netherlands, for example, a growing network of laws gave prostitutes (legally recognized since 1917) pensions and full workers' rights and legalized gay and lesbian marriages, the smoking of pot in licensed coffee shops, and assisted suicide (euthanasia) for the terminally ill.

As the twenty-first century opened, western Europeans also pushed as best they could to extend their broad-based concept of social and economic rights to the world's poor countries. These efforts were related to sharp criticism of globalization and unrestrained capitalism (see pages 1031–1032), criticism that helped socialists regain power in several countries in the European Union. Quite typically, Europe's moderate social democrats combined with human rights campaigners in 2001 to help African governments secure drastic price cuts from the big international drug companies on the drug cocktails needed to combat Africa's AIDS crisis. Strong advocates of greater social equality and state-funded health care, European socialists embraced morality as a basis for action and the global expansion of human rights as a primary goal.

The West and the Islamic World

A hundred years from now, when historians assess developments in the early twenty-first century, they will almost certainly highlight the dramatic deterioration in the long, rich, up-and-down relationship between the West and the Islamic world. They will examine the reasons that the peaceful conclusion of the cold war and the joyful reunification of a divided continent gave way to spectacular terrorist attacks, Western invasions of Muslim countries, and new concern about Muslims living in the West. Unfortunately, we lack the perspective and the full range of source materials that future historians will have at their disposal.

Yet we are deeply involved in this momentous historical drama, and we must try to find insight and understanding.

● *How and why did relations between the West and the Islamic world deteriorate dramatically in the early twenty-first century?*

The al-Qaeda Attack of September 11, 2001

On the morning of September 11, 2001, two hijacked passenger planes from Boston crashed into and destroyed the World Trade Center towers in New York City. Shortly thereafter a third plane crashed into the Pentagon, and a fourth, believed to be headed for the White House or the U.S. Capitol, crashed into a field in rural Pennsylvania. These terrorist attacks took the lives of more than three thousand people from many countries and put the personal safety of ordinary citizens at the top of the West's agenda. Stunned and horrified, the peoples and governments of the world joined Americans in heartfelt solidarity.

The United States, led by President George W. Bush, launched a military campaign to destroy the perpetrators of the crime—Saudi-born millionaire Osama bin Laden's al-Qaeda network of terrorists and Afghanistan's reactionary Muslim government, the Taliban. Drawing on the world's sympathy and building a broad international coalition that included western Europe, Russia, and Pakistan, the United States joined its tremendous airpower with the faltering Northern Alliance in Afghanistan, which had been fighting the Taliban for years. By mid-October 2001 American special forces on the ground were directing precision air strikes that devastated Taliban and al-Qaeda troops, and a rejuvenated Northern Alliance took the offensive. In mid-November the Taliban collapsed, and jubilant crowds in the capital of Kabul welcomed Northern Alliance soldiers as liberators. Afghan opposition leaders and United Nations mediators worked out plans for a new broad-based government, while American planes, ground troops, and tribal fighters searched for bin Laden and his die-hard supporters in their mountain hideaways. In 2002 foreign governments, aid organizations, and the United Nations turned to the arduous task of helping the Afghans get themselves back on their feet after a generation of conflict and civil war following the 1979 Soviet invasion of their country.

In trying to make some sense out of the heinous attack of September 11, 2001, and the current wave of terrorist action in general, it is helpful to realize that civil war and terrorism often went hand in hand in the twentieth century. Beginning in the 1920s and peaking in the 1960s, many nationalist movements used terrorism in their battles to achieve political independence and decolonization. This was the case in several new states, including Algeria, Cyprus, Ireland, Israel, and Yemen.[4] Those fighting for independence and political power often targeted police forces for assassination campaigns, thereby breaking down confidence in the colonial government and provoking counter-atrocities that generated increased support for the independence movement.

In the Vietnam War era, a second wave of terrorism saw some far-left supporters of the communist Vietcong, such as the American Weathermen, the German Red Army Faction, and the Italian Red Brigade, practicing "revolutionary terror" in an effort to cripple the Western heartland. These groups engineered a series of deadly bombings, assassinations, and kidnappings. These terrorists also hijacked airplanes—more than one hundred each year in the 1970s—in order to take hostages and blackmail governments into meeting some demand, such as the release of convicted fellow terrorists. Some terrorists trained in the facilities of the PLO (the Palestine Liberation Organization) operated international networks and targeted Israel and U.S. installations abroad. This second wave receded in the 1980s as painstaking police work and international cooperation defeated these "revolutionaries" in country after country.

In recent years a third wave has been building, leading toward al-Qaeda's attack on the World Trade Center and the Pentagon on September 11, 2001. In analyzing this third wave, many commentators were quick to stress the role of extreme Islamic fundamentalism as a motivating factor. But the most perceptive scholars noted that recent deadly attacks had been committed by terrorists inspired by several religious faiths and religious sects and were by no means limited to Islamic extremists.[5] These scholars noted that the different terrorist movements in today's

New York, September 11, 2001 Pedestrians race for safety as the World Trade Center towers collapse after being hit by jet airliners. Al-Qaeda terrorists with box cutters hijacked four aircraft and used three of them as suicide missiles to perpetrate their unthinkable crime. Heroic passengers on the fourth plane realized what was happening and forced their hijackers to crash in a field. *(AP Images/Suzanne Plunkett)*

world need to be linked to underlying political conflicts and civil wars for meaningful understanding.

When this perspective is applied to Osama bin Laden and al-Qaeda members, two stages stand out. First, in the long bitter fighting against the Soviet Union and the local communists in Afghanistan, bin Laden and like-minded "holy warriors" developed terrorist skills and a narrow-minded, fanatical Islamic puritanism. They also developed a hatred of most existing Arab governments, which they viewed as corrupt, un-Islamic, and unresponsive to the needs of ordinary Muslims. The objects of their hostility included the absolute monarchy of oil-rich Saudi Arabia (bin Laden's own country), pro-Western but undemocratic Egypt, and the secular, one-party dictatorship of Saddam Hussein.

Second, when these Islamic extremists returned home from Afghanistan and began to organize, they usually met the fate of many earlier Islamic extremists and were jailed or forced into exile, often in tolerant Europe. There they blamed the United States for being the supporter and corrupter of existing Arab governments, and they organized murderous plots against the United States—a despised proxy for the Arab rulers they could not reach. This development set the stage for the 1998 bombing of the U.S. embassy in Nairobi, Kenya, which claimed nearly 200 lives, the World Trade Center atrocity, and the U.S.-led counterattack on al-Qaeda in Afghanistan.

The War in Iraq

Unfortunately, Western unity in Afghanistan soon turned into bitter quarreling and international crisis over the prospect of war with Iraq. As soon as he was elected in 2000, President Bush and his most influential advisers, led by Vice President Dick Cheney and Secretary of Defense Donald Rumsfeld, began to consider how to overthrow Iraq's Saddam Hussein and remake the Middle East. Paul O'Neill, Bush's secretary of the treasury, summed up discussions on Iraq by the president and his cabinet this way: "From the start, they were building the case against Hussein and looking at how we could take him out and change Iraq into a new country. And, if we did that, it would solve everything."[6] And indeed, many in the administration believed that the United States could create a democratic, pro-American Iraq, an Iraq that would transform the Middle East, make peace with Israel, provide easy access to the world's second-largest oil reserves, and show small states the folly of opposing the United States. The most effective prowar argument, however, played on American fears of renewed terrorism and charged that Saddam Hussein was

still developing weapons of mass destruction in flagrant disregard of his promise to end all such programs following the first war with Iraq, in 1991 (see page 1030). Saddam had used chemical weapons in his war with Iran in the 1980s and against the Kurdish population of northern Iraq, and the Bush administration argued that sooner or later he would probably use these terrible weapons against the United States and its allies or would give them to anti-American fanatics like those who struck New York on September 11, 2001.

In August 2002, Vice President Cheney promised Iraqi exiles that the United States would depose Saddam, although according to the United Nations charter, the Security Council has the sole authority to use armed force, except in self-defense, and Iraq, impoverished by a decade of tough United Nations sanctions, gave no indication of attacking any of its neighbors, much less the United States. Moreover, large numbers of Americans shared widespread doubts in Europe about the legality—and wisdom—of an American attack on Iraq and argued for a peaceful settlement of the Iraqi weapons crisis. So the Bush administration reluctantly agreed to new Security Council resolutions requiring Iraq to accept the return of United Nations weapons inspectors and destroy any remaining prohibited weapons. Iraq accepted the inspectors, declaring it had destroyed all prohibited weapons.

As 2003 opened, the inspectors operated freely in Iraq and found no weapons of mass destruction. However, the United States and Britain said Iraq was hiding prohibited weapons, moved armies to the Middle East, and lobbied for a new United Nations resolution authorizing immediate military action against Iraq. The world followed the debates in the Security Council with unprecedented interest and generally opposed an attack on Iraq. France, Russia, China, Germany, and a majority of the smaller states argued for continued weapons inspections. Western governments became bitterly divided, and the Security Council deadlocked and failed to act.

In March 2003 the United States and Britain invaded Iraq from bases in Kuwait and quickly overwhelmed the Iraqi army. Yet even as Saddam's dictatorship collapsed, the confident expectation of a long and peaceful occupation in a pro-American Iraq was impaired by serious errors of American judgment. As chaos spread and looters stripped government buildings and hospitals of everything from computers to faucets, American and British troops simply turned a blind eye and took no action. Disbanding the Iraqi army also alienated the population, worsened security, and created mass unemployment, while the failure to seize huge stocks of weapons left Iraqi

The Golden Mosque of Samarra: Before and After   Built to commemorate two of Shi'ite Islam's most revered saints, the Golden Mosque drew countless Shi'ite pilgrims. Then, on June 13, 2006, insurgents dressed as Iraqi policemen entered the mosque, overwhelmed the guards, and detonated two bombs that collapsed the golden dome and destroyed the mosque. Sectarian conflict exploded. (A second terrorist bombing in June 2007 levelled the two minarets seen on the right.) *(AP Images/Khalid Mohammed, Hameed Rasheed)*

insurgents with guns and explosives for subsequent counterattacks. The allies found no weapons of mass destruction, which raised many questions about a prewar manipulation of intelligence data.

American efforts to establish a stable, pro-American Iraq proved difficult if not impossible. Poor postwar planning and management by President Bush and his top aides was one factor, but there were others. Modern Iraq, a creation of Western imperialism after World War I (see page 906), is a fragile state with three distinct groups: non-Arab Kurds, and Sunnis and Shi'ites—Arab Muslims who were forever divided by a great schism in the seventh century. Saddam's dictatorship preached Arab and Iraqi nationalism, but it relied heavily on the Sunni minority—20 percent of the population—and repressed the Shi'ites, who made up 60 percent of the population. Jailed or ousted from their positions by American forces, top Sunnis quickly turned against the occupation, rallied their supporters, and launched an armed insurgency. By late 2004, radical Sunnis and al-Qaeda converts were slipping into Iraq, where they directed horrendous suicide bombings at American soldiers, Iraqi security forces, and defenseless Shi'ite civilians.

Believing in democracy and representative institutions, the Americans restored Iraqi sovereignty in July 2004, formed a provisional government, and held relatively free national elections in January 2005. Boycotted by the Sunnis, these elections brought the Shi'ite majority to power and marked the high point of Iraqi and American hopes for security and a gradual reconciliation with the Sunni population. Instead, Sunni fighters and jihadist extremists stepped up their deadly campaign. Then, in February 2005 in a carefully planned operation, they blew up the beautiful Golden Mosque of Samarra, one of the most sacred shrines of Shi'ite Islam. This outrage touched off violent retaliation. Shi'ite militias became death squads, killing Sunnis and driving them from their homes. By 2006 a deadly sectarian conflict had taken hold of Baghdad. American soldiers, continuing loyally to do their duty, were increasingly caught in the crossfire. In 2007, as President Bush faced widespread opposition at home, it seemed unlikely that yet another intensification of American efforts to create stability in Iraq would succeed.

The West and Its Muslim Citizens

The attack on the World Trade Center and the long war in Iraq, signaling a dramatic worsening of relations between the West and the Islamic world, had major repercussions in Western countries. In the United States there were great fears of more terrorist attacks, but to almost everyone's surprise Europe received the extremists' next blows. In May 2004 Moroccan Muslims living in Spain exploded bombs planted on morning trains bound for Madrid and killed 252 commuters. A year later a similar attack was carried out in London by British citizens of Pakistani descent, young men who had grown up in Britain and seemed to be ordinary fellows.

Even more traumatic for the tolerant Dutch and many other Europeans was the repeated stabbing and brutal murder of Theo van Gogh by a young Dutch Muslim. Van Gogh, a provocative filmmaker, had joined an anti-Islamic feminist and refugee from East Africa in making a vulgar ten-minute film that mocked the prophet Muhammad and denounced Islam's treatment of women. For his "blasphemy," van Gogh was "executed" by the son of Moroccan immigrants, who proudly explained his action to the court in colloquial Dutch.

These spectacular attacks and lesser actions by Islamic militants sharpened the European debate on immigration (see pages 1042–1044). A shrill chorus warned that, in addition to the security danger, Europe's rapidly growing Muslim population posed a dire threat to the West's entire Enlightenment tradition, which embraced freedom of thought, representative government, toleration, separation of church and state, and, more recently, equal rights for women and gays. Islamic extremists and radical clerics settled in Europe were, the critics claimed, rejecting these fundamental Western values and preaching instead the supremacy of Islamic laws for Muslims living in Europe, and even for non-Muslim Europeans on some issues. Moreover, the critics claimed, many "moderate" Islamic teachers were really anti-Western radicals playing for time. (See the feature "Individuals in Society: Tariq Ramadan.") And time was on the side of Euro-Islam. Europe's Muslim population, estimated at 15 million in 2006, appeared likely to double to 30 million by 2025, and it would increase rapidly thereafter as the number of non-Europeans plummeted (see pages 1041–1042).

Admitting that Islamic extremism could pose a serious challenge, many mainstream observers focused instead on the problem of immigrant integration. Whereas the first generation of Muslim immigrants—predominately Turks in Germany, Algerians in France, Pakistanis in Britain, and Moroccans in the Netherlands—had found jobs as unskilled workers in Europe's great postwar boom, they and their children had been hard hit after 1973 by the general economic downturn. Immigrants also suffered from the ongoing decline of European manufacturing due to globalization. Provided for modestly by the welfare state and housed minimally in ugly housing projects, many Muslims of the second and third generations were finding themselves locked out in their adopted countries. In short, economics, inadequate job training, and discrimination trumped religion and extremist teachings.

This argument was strengthened by widespread rioting in France in November 2005 that saw hundreds of young second- and third-generation Muslim immigrants go on a rampage. Almost always French by birth, language, and education, marauding groups of "Arabs" torched hundreds of automobiles night after night in Paris suburbs and large cities. (See the feature "Listening to the Past: The French Riots: Will They Change Anything?" on pages 1054–1055.) The rioters complained bitterly of very high unemployment, systematic discrimination, and exclusion. Religious ideology appeared almost nonexistent in their thinking. Studies sparked by the rioting in France found poor, alienated Muslims in unwholesome ghettos throughout western Europe.

Although Muslim immigrants in the United States certainly experienced increased hostility after the September 11 attack, it was generally recognized that they were integrating more successfully with their adopted homeland than were their European counterparts. This is partly because the United States believes that it has always been a nation of immigrants, whereas the European ideal remains the homogeneous national state. Equally important, Muslim immigrants to the United States have often been well educated, have come from several countries speaking different languages, and have spread out within cities and across the country. Muslim immigrants to western Europe, usually a larger percentage of the host country's population than in America, have generally been poor rural people with limited education who came to do manual labor. In each of the leading host countries, they came mainly from a single Muslim country and then lived together on the fringes of the largest cities. Muslim immigrants to the United States brought more "human capital," and this facilitated more successful integration.

Finally, the fact that Americans and western Europeans have gone their separate ways on religion probably impacts their relations with their Muslim citizens. A large though declining number of Americans still take religion seriously, whereas western Europeans have largely abandoned Christianity, with less than 5 percent of the population attending church on most Sundays. Thus many Americans still can—or should—understand and even appreciate the power of Islam for devout Muslims, whereas western Europeans tend to find all traditional religious belief irrational and out-of-date. This is why, in addition to determined efforts to root out anti-Muslim discrimination, the renowned French scholar Olivier Roy argues, Europe must recognize that Islam is now a European religion and a vital part of European life. This recognition, he argues, will open the way to eventual full acceptance of European Muslims in both political and cultural terms. It will head off the resentment that can drive Europe's Muslim believers to separatism and acts of terror.

The Future in Perspective

● *What does the study of history have to tell us about the future?*

For centuries astrologers and scientists, experts and ordinary people, have sought to peek into the future. And although it may seem that the study of the past has little to say about the future, the study of history over a long period is actually very useful in this regard. It helps put the future in perspective.

Certainly, history is full of erroneous predictions, a few of which we have mentioned in this book. Yet lack of success has not diminished the age-old desire to look into the future. Self-proclaimed experts even pretend that they have created a new science of futurology. With great pomposity, they often act as if their hunches and guesses about future human development are inescapable realities. Yet the study of history teaches healthy skepticism regarding such predictions, however scientific and learned they may appear. Past results suggest that most such predictions will simply not come true, or at least not in the anticipated ways. Thus history provides some psychological protection from the visions of modern prognosticators.

This protection is particularly valuable when we realize that views of the future tend to swing between pessimistic and optimistic extremes from one generation, or even from one decade, to the next. These swings back and forth between optimism and pessimism, which one historian has aptly called "the great seesaw" in the development of the Western world, reflect above all the current situation of the observers.[7] Thus in the economic stagnation and revived cold war of the 1970s and 1980s, many projections into the future were quite pessimistic, just as they were very optimistic in the 1950s and 1960s. Many people in the Western world feared that conditions were going to get worse rather than better. For example, there were fears that pollution would destroy the environment and that the traditional family would disappear. Some gloomy experts predicted that twenty to thirty states might well have nuclear weapons by the end of the twentieth century. Many forecasters and politicians predicted

that the energy crisis—in the form of skyrocketing oil prices—meant disaster in the form of lower standards of living at best and the collapse of civilization at worst. In fact, oil prices collapsed in the early 1980s and generally stayed low until the second Iraq war in 2003. It was heartening in that time of pessimism to know that most dire predictions do not prove true, just as the same knowledge of likely error is sobering in times of optimistic expectations.

Optimistic visions of the future were certainly in the air after the end of the cold war. The pendulum had definitely swung, most notably in the United States. Untroubled in the late 1990s by the high unemployment and the early stages of corporate downsizing that soured the mood in western Europe, the United States celebrated its dynamic economy and its booming stock market. U.S. military power, leadership in world affairs, and excellence in advanced technologies also encouraged optimism and rosy projections.

In 2000 the American mood shifted. The dot-com bubble burst, and in 2001 the U.S. economy slid into a recession. The al-Qaeda attack on New York and the tragic war in Iraq, with its endless carnage and suicide bombings, led to many pessimistic forecasts of a long uphill struggle against global extremism, especially Islamic extremism. Most frightening of all were grim warnings by some self-described experts who predicted that terrorist groups were likely to succeed in developing or buying biological and nuclear weapons of mass destruction, which they would then turn on millions of innocent people with unspeakable cruelty. Such nightmare scenarios are not impossible, but we should remember that modern governments possess tremendous resources that they can mobilize to control individuals and opposition groups, especially when the leading states decide to work together, as they did immediately after September 11, 2001. Once again, just as it is sobering to know that the rosiest predictions in optimistic times usually do not prove true, so is it heartening to know that the direst projections in pessimistic times normally do not come to pass.

Whatever does or does not happen, the study of history puts the future in perspective in other ways. We have seen that every age has its problems and challenges. Others before us have trodden the paths of uncertainty and crisis. This knowledge helps save us from exaggerated self-pity in the face of our own predicaments.

Perhaps our Western heritage may rightly inspire us with pride and measured self-confidence. We stand, momentarily, at the head of the long procession of Western civilization. Sometimes the procession has wandered, or backtracked, or done terrible things. But it has also

Individuals in Society

Tariq Ramadan

Religious teacher, activist professor, and media star, Tariq Ramadan (b. 1962) is Europe's most famous Muslim intellectual. He is also a controversial figure, praised by many as a moderate bridge-builder and denounced by others as an Islamic militant in clever disguise.

Born in Switzerland of Egyptian ancestry, Ramadan is the grandson of Hassan al-Banna, the charismatic founder of the powerful Muslim Brotherhood. Al-Banna fought to reshape Arab nationalism within a framework of Islamic religious orthodoxy and anti-British terrorism until he himself was assassinated in 1949. Growing up in Geneva, where his father sought refuge in 1954 after Nasser's anti-Islamic crackdown in Egypt, the young Tariq attended mainstream public schools, played soccer, and absorbed a wide-ranging Islamic heritage. For example, growing up fluent in French and Arabic, he learned English mainly from listening to Pakistani Muslims discuss issues with his father, who represented the Muslim Brotherhood and its ideology in Europe.

Ramadan studied philosophy and French literature as an undergraduate at the University of Geneva, and he then earned a doctorate in Arabic and Islamic studies. Marrying a Swiss woman who converted to Islam, Ramadan moved his family to Cairo in 1991 to study Islamic law and philosophy. It proved to be a pivotal experience. Eagerly anticipating the return to his Muslim roots, Ramadan gradually realized that only in Europe did he feel truly "at home." In his personal experience he found his message: that Western Muslims should feel equally "at home" and that they should participate fully as active citizens in their adopted countries.

In developing his message, Ramadan left the classroom and focused on creating non-scholarly books, audio cassettes that sell in the tens of thousands, and media events. Slim and elegant in well-tailored suits and open collars, Ramadan is a brilliant speaker. His public lectures in French and English draw hundreds of Muslims (and curious non-Muslims).

Ramadan argues that Western Muslims basically live in security, have fundamental legal rights, and can freely practice their religion. He notes that Muslims in the West are often more secure than are believers in the Muslim world, where governments are frequently repressive and arbitrary. According to Ramadan, Islamic teaching requires Western Muslims to obey Western laws, although in rare cases they may need to plead "conscientious objection" and disobey on religious grounds. Becoming full citizens and refusing to live in parallel as the foreign Other, Muslims should work with non-Muslims on matters of common concern, such as mutual respect, better schools, and economic justice.* Ramadan is most effective with second- or third-generation college

Tariq Ramadan.
(AP Images/Keystone/Salvatore Di Nolfi)

graduates. He urges them to think for themselves and distinguish the sacred revelation of Islam from the nonessential cultural aspects that their parents brought from African and Asian villages.

With growing fame has come growing controversy. In 2004, preparing to take up a professorship in the United States, he was denied an entry visa on the grounds that he had contributed to a Palestinian charity with ties to terrorists. Defenders disputed the facts and charged that his criticism of Israeli policies and the invasion of Iraq were the real reasons. Ramadan's critics also claim that he says different things to different groups: hard-edged criticism of the West found on tapes for Muslims belies the reasoned moderation of his books. Some critics also argue that his recent condemnation of Western capitalism and globalization is an opportunistic attempt to win favor with European leftists and does not reflect a self-proclaimed Islamic passion for justice. Yet, on balance, Ramadan's reputation remains intact.† An innovative bridge-builder, he symbolizes the growing importance of Europe's Muslim citizens.

Questions for Analysis

1. What is Ramadan's message to Western Muslims? How did he reach his conclusions?
2. Do you think Ramadan's ideas are realistic? Why?

*See, especially, Tariq Ramadan, *Western Muslims and the Future of Islam* (Oxford: Oxford University Press, 2004).

†See Ian Buruma, *The New York Times Magazine*, February 4, 2007.

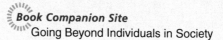

Book Companion Site
Going Beyond Individuals in Society

carried the efforts and sacrifices of generations of toiling, struggling ancestors. Through no effort of our own, we are the beneficiaries of those sacrifices and achievements. Now that it is our turn to carry the torch onward, we may remember these ties with our forebears.

To change the metaphor, we in the West are like a card player who has been dealt many good cards. Some of them are obvious, such as our technical and scientific heritage or our commitment to human rights, religious freedom, and the individual. Others are not so obvious, sometimes half-forgotten or even hidden up the sleeve. Think, for example, of the Christian Democrats, the moderate Catholic party that emerged after World War II to play such an important role in the western European renaissance. And in the almost miraculous victory of peaceful revolution in eastern Europe in 1989—in what Czech playwright-turned-president Václav Havel called "the power of the powerless"—we see again the regenerative strength of the Western ideals of individual rights, representative government, and nationhood in the European homeland. We hold a good hand.

Our study of history, of mighty struggles and fearsome challenges, of shining achievements and tragic failures, gives a sense of the essence of life itself: the process of change over time. Again and again we have seen how peoples and societies evolve, influenced by ideas, human passions, and material conditions. As surely as anything is sure, this process of change over time will continue as the future becomes the present and then the past. And students of history are better prepared to make sense of this unfolding process because they have already observed it. They know how change is rooted in existing historical forces, and their projections will probably be better than many of the trendy speculations of futurologists. Students of history are also prepared for the new and unexpected in human development, for they have already seen great breakthroughs and revolutions. They have an understanding of how things really happen.

Demonstrating for Peace   Millions long for peace, but history and current events suggest that bloody conflicts will continue. Yet there is cause for some cautious optimism: since 1945 wars have been localized and cataclysmic catastrophes like World Wars I and II have been averted. Holding torches, some 3,500 people form the sign of peace in an antiwar, antiviolence rally in Heroes Square in central Budapest. The rally marked the third anniversary of the U.S.-led invasion of Iraq. *(Peter Kollanyi/epa/Corbis)*

Chapter Summary

- *In what ways did Solidarity confront the communist system in Poland, and how did Mikhail Gorbachev try to reverse the decline of communism in the Soviet Union?*

- *How did anticommunist revolutions sweep through eastern Europe in 1989, and what were the immediate consequences?*

- *How, in the 1990s, did the different parts of a reunifying Europe meet the challenges of postcommunist reconstruction, resurgent nationalism, and economic union?*

- *Why did the prospect of population decline, the reality of large-scale immigration, and concern for human rights emerge as critical issues in contemporary Europe?*

- *How and why did relations between the West and the Islamic world deteriorate dramatically in the early twenty-first century?*

- *What does the study of history have to tell us about the future?*

The rise of Solidarity in Poland showed again that the communist system in eastern Europe depended ultimately on Soviet armies. Therefore, when the Russian leader Mikhail Gorbachev refused to use force abroad and his ambitious reforms at home spiraled out of control, the peoples of eastern Europe rose and overturned communist rule in the spectacular, peaceful revolutions of 1989. In a dramatic finale, the democratic movement triumphed in the Soviet Union, the two Germanies joined in a single state, the cold war ended, and the United States remained the only superpower.

In the 1990s, post–cold war Europe grappled with neoliberal market economies, welfare systems under continuing attack, and globalization. Social and economic reconstruction in Russia was less successful than it was in eastern Europe, with the glaring exception of the former Yugoslavia, which was destroyed by resurgent ethnic nationalism. Eastern Europe's rebuilding and its determination to "rejoin Europe" stimulated the long postwar movement toward European unity, and the newly named European Union expanded to include almost all of Europe west of Russia, Ukraine, and the Caucasus. This triumph was the shining achievement of the post–cold war era.

The twenty-first century highlighted critical issues, and we have seen how the European baby bust, the growth of illegal immigration, and the increased commitment to human rights were all interrelated. The most disturbed development was the renewed hostility between the West and the Islamic world, which was marked indelibly by the al-Qaeda attack of 2001, the campaign to punish Afghanistan, and the American and British invasion of Iraq. Essentially an effort to remake Iraq (and the Arab world) along Western lines, the war in Iraq saw American soldiers run up against a potent combination of Arab nationalism, Islamic extremism, and sectarian conflict. War in the Middle East encouraged shrill cries about an ominous Muslim threat from immigrants living in western Europe, but a study of history would suggest that these fears were greatly exaggerated.

Book Companion Site
To assess your mastery of this chapter, visit **bedfordstmartins.com/mckaywest**

Key Terms

Gdansk Agreement	Paris Accord
Solidarity	"new world order"
perestroika	globalization
glasnost	European Union
shock therapy	Kosovo Liberation
Velvet Revolution	Army (KLA)
third way	Maastricht treaty
Alliance for	baby bust
Germany	

Suggested Reading

Bernstein, Richard B. *Out of the Blue: A Narrative of September 11, 2001.* 2003. A gripping account by a talented journalist.

Brubaker, Rogers. *Nationalism Reframed: Nationhood and the National Question.* 1996. An excellent analysis of the contemporary resurgence of nationalism.

(continued on page 1056)

The French Riots: Will They Change Anything?

In late November 2005, young Muslim males rioted
for several nights in the suburbs of Paris and other
French cities. Receiving saturation coverage from the
media, this explosion of car-burning and arson
ignited controversy and debate throughout France
and across Europe. What caused the riots? What
could and should be done? How did the conditions of
second- and third-generation Muslims in France
compare with conditions of Muslims in other Western
countries?

One penetrating commentary, aimed at an
American audience and reprinted here, came from
William Pfaff, a noted author and political columnist
with many years of European experience. As you
read Pfaff's analysis, note in particular the contrast
he draws between the French government's policy
toward Muslims and the policy pursued in Britain
and the Netherlands.

The rioting in France's ghetto suburbs is a
phenomenon of futility—but a revelation
nonetheless. It has no ideology and no purpose
other than to make a statement of distress and
anger. It is beyond politics. It broke out
spontaneously and spread in the same way,
communicated by televised example, ratified by
the huge attention it won from the press and
television and the politicians, none of whom had
any idea what to do.

It has been an immensely pathetic spectacle,
whose primary meaning has been that it
happened. It has been the most important
popular social phenomenon in France since the
student uprisings of 1968. But those uprisings . . .
had consequences for power. The new riots have
nothing to do with power.

They started with the accidental electrocutions
of two boys hiding from the police, who they
thought were after them. The police say there was
no pursuit and they had no interest in the boys.
However, under the policies of the minister of

interior—the presidential candidate Nicolas
Sarkozy—there had been a general police crackdown in these ugly suburban clusters of
deteriorating high-rise apartments built years ago
to house immigrant workers. They were meant to
be machines for living. The police attention meant
random identity checks, police suspicion, and
harassment of young men hanging about—maybe
dealing in drugs, maybe simply doing nothing
because there is nothing for them to do. (In the
past, they at least had to do national military
service, which was a strong integrative force, but
now France has a professional army.)

Their grandfathers came to France, mostly from
North Africa, to do the hard labor in France's
industrial reconstruction after the Second World
War. Their fathers saw the work gradually dry up
as Europe's economies slowed, following the first
oil shock in the early 1970s. After that came
unemployment. The unemployment rate in the
zones where there has been the most violence is
nearly 40 percent and among young people it is
higher. Many of the young men in these places
have never been offered a job. When they applied,
their names often excluded them.

Their grandfathers were hard-working men.
Their fathers saw their manhood undermined by
unemployment. These young men are doomed to
be boys. They often take their frustration out on
their sisters and girlfriends, who are more likely to
have done well in school and found jobs—and
frequently a new life—outside the ghetto. . . .

The Muslim mothers and wives of the French
ghetto are often confined in the home. Drugs are
big business in the American ghetto; they are not
that big in France. The crimes of the French
ghetto are robbery and shoplifting, stealing
mobile phones, stealing cars for joyrides, burning
them afterward to eliminate fingerprints, or
burning cars just for the hell of it, as well as
robbing middle-class students in the city and

1054

making trouble on suburban trains, looking for excitement.

Religion is important . . . in the French ghetto, it provides the [shell] that protects against the France that excludes Muslims. To the European Muslim, it seems that all of the powerful in the world are in collusion to exclude Muslims—or are at war with them. The war in Iraq, on television, is the constant backdrop to Muslim life in Europe. There are itinerant imams who can put the young ghetto Muslim on the road to danger and adventure in Afghanistan, Pakistan, Iraq—or elsewhere. There are plenty more who preach a still deeper ghettoization: a retreat inside Islamic fundamentalism, totally shutting out a diabolized secular world.

One would think there would be a revolutionary potential in these ghettos, vulnerability to a mobilizing ideology. This seems not to be so. We may be living in a religious age, but it is not one of political ideology. In any case, it is difficult to imagine how the marginalized, thirteen- to twenty-three-year-old children of the Muslim immigration could change France other than by what they are doing, which is to demonstrate that the French model of assimilating immigrants as citizens, and not as members of religious or ethnic groups, has failed for them. It has failed because it has not seriously been tried.

The ghettoization of immigrant youth in France is the consequence of negligence. It has been as bad as the ghettoization through political correctness of Muslims in Britain and the Netherlands, where many people who thought of themselves as enlightened said that assimilation efforts were acts of cultural aggression. The immigrant in France is told that he or she is a citizen just like everyone else, with all the rights and privileges of citizenship—including the right to be unemployed.

Nicolas Sarkozy's zero tolerance of crime and of the petty mafias in the ghetto contributed to touching off these riots, but until recently he was the only French politician to say there has to be affirmative action to get an immigrant elite out of the ghettos and into important roles in French life, where they can pull their communities after them. Some affirmative action has been attempted in recruiting candidates for the elite *grandes écoles* [state schools] that train the French administrative and political class, where the cultural hurdles are

French police face off with young rioters, silhouetted against the flames of burning automobiles. *(Reuters/Corbis)*

immense for candidates. Virtually no children of the Muslim immigration are prominent in mainstream electoral politics; the political parties have yet to make a serious effort to include them. The present government has one junior minister of Algerian origin. I am not aware of any Muslims of immigrant origin in French diplomacy or the top ranks of police and military.

President Jacques Chirac has announced a civilian national service agency to give training and employment to 50,000 young people from the troubled zones by 2007. The age of apprenticeship has been lowered to fourteen, with a corresponding drop in the age of compulsory academic schooling and new measures to support apprenticeships. There will be more money for schools, local associations, and housing construction and renovation. This is change. Whether it is enough, and in time, is another matter.

Questions for Analysis

1. Describe the situation of young Muslims in France. What elements of their situation strike you most forcefully? Why?

2. France has maintained that, since all citizens are equal, they should all be treated the same way. Why has this policy failed for French Muslims? What alternatives would you suggest? Why?

Source: William Pfaff, "The French Riots: Will They Change Anything?" *The New York Review of Books,* December 15, 2005, pp. 88–89. Reprinted with permission from The New York Review of Books. Copyright © 2005 NYREV, Inc.

Buruma, Ian. *Murder in Amsterdam: The Death of Theo van Gogh and the Limits of Toleration.* 2006. A masterful, very readable investigation of the crime that electrified Europe.

Dobbs, Michael. *Down with Big Brother: The Fall of the Soviet Empire.* 1998. A superb firsthand study by an inspired journalist.

Johnson, Lonnie R. *Central Europe: Enemies, Neighbors, Friends.* 2001. A book that ably interprets developments in eastern Europe before and after the revolutions of 1989.

Lampe, John R. *Yugoslavia as History: Twice There Was a Country,* 2d ed. 2003. An excellent, judicious work on the tragedy in Yugoslavia.

Lucassen, Leo. *The Immigrant Threat: The Integration of Old and New Immigrants in Western Europe Since 1850.* 2005. Argues effectively that Muslims are assimilating as rapidly as previous immigrants.

Reid, T. R. *The United States of Europe: The New Superpower and the End of American Supremacy.* 2005. A lively, informative examination by a perceptive American.

Ross, George. *Jacques Delors and European Integration.* 1995. Analyzes the controversies surrounding the European Union in the 1990s.

Sakwa, Richard. *Putin: Russia's Choice.* 2003. Puts the Russian leader in social and historical context.

Shore, Zachary. *Breeding Bin Ladens: America, Islam, and the Future of Europe.* 2006. A comprehensive overview of the Muslim question in Europe.

Stiglitz, Joseph E. *Making Globalization Work.* 2006. An excellent overview of the successes and failures of globalization by a distinguished economist.

Suny, Ronald Grigor. *The Soviet Experiment: Russia, the USSR, and the Successor States.* 1998. An outstanding history of Russia in the 1990s.

Viorst, Milton. *Storm from the East: The Struggle Between the Arab World and the Christian West.* 2007. Recommended short study of twentieth-century developments within a broad historical perspective.

Woodward, Bob. *State of Denial: Bush at War, Part III.* 2006. Best-selling account based on extensive interviews.

Notes

1. F. Fukuyama, *The End of History and the Last Man* (New York: Free Press, 1992); and J. Cronin, *The World the Cold War Made: Order, Chaos, and Return of History* (New York: Routledge, 1996), pp. 267–281.
2. Quoted in *The Economist,* January 6, 2001, p. 6.
3. Quoted by Flora Lewis, *International Herald Tribune,* June 15, 2001, p. 6.
4. D. Rappaport, "The Fourth Wave: September 11 in the History of Terrorism," *Current History,* December 2001, pp. 419–424.
5. Ibid.
6. R. Suskind, *The Price of Loyalty: George W. Bush, the White House, and the Education of Paul O'Neill* (New York: Simon and Schuster, 2004), p. 86.
7. G. Blainey, *The Great Seesaw: A New View of the Western World* (London: Macmillan, 1988).